THE SOCIAL AND
ECONOMIC HISTORY
OF THE
ROMAN EMPIRE

THE SOCIAL AND ECONOMIC HISTORY OF THE ROMAN EMPIRE

BY

M. ROSTOVTZEFF

SECOND EDITION
Revised by
P. M. FRASER

VOLUME II

DOMI
NVS
ILLV
MINA
TIO
MEA

OXFORD
AT THE CLARENDON PRESS

Oxford University Press, Great Clarendon Street, Oxford OX2 6DP

Oxford New York

Athens Auckland Bangkok Bogotá Buenos Aires Calcutta
Cape Town Chennai Dar es Salaam Delhi Florence Hong Kong Istanbul
Karachi Kuala Lumpur Madrid Melbourne Mexico City Mumbai
Nairobi Paris São Paulo Singapore Taipei Tokyo Toronto Warsaw
and associated companies in
Berlin Ibadan

Oxford is a registered trade mark of Oxford University Press

Published in the United States by
Oxford University Press Inc., New York

© Oxford University Press 1957

Special edition for Sandpiper Books Ltd., 1998

ISBN 0-19-814231-5

1 3 5 7 9 10 8 6 4 2

Printed in Great Britain
on acid-free paper by
Bookcraft (Bath) Ltd.,
Midsomer Norton

CONTENTS

VOLUME II

ABBREVIATIONS
OF TITLES OF PERIODICALS, ETC., USED IN THE DESCRIPTION OF THE PLATES AND IN THE NOTES

(For abbreviations employed in citing publications of inscriptions and papyri, see Index III)

Abh. Berl. Akad.	*Abhandlungen der preußischen Akademie der Wissenschaften.*
Abh. d. sächs. Ges.	*Abhandlungen der k. sächsischen Gesellschaft der Wissenschaften.*
AJP	*American Journal of Philology.*
Amer. Hist. Rev.	*American Historical Review.*
Amer. Journ. Arch.	*American Journal of Archaeology.*
Anal. Acad. Rom.	*Analele Academiei Române.*
Annali d. Ist.	*Annali dell' Istituto di corrispondenza archeologica di Roma.*
Ann. d. R. Sc. arch. di Atene	*Annali della Reale Scuola archeologica di Atene.*
Ann. ép.	R. Cagnat et M. Besnier, *Année épigraphique,* in *Revue archéologique* and separately.
Arch. Anz.	*Archäologischer Anzeiger,* in *Jahrbuch des deutschen archäologischen Instituts.*
Arch. d. miss. scient.	*Archives des missions scientifiques.*
Arch.-ep. Mitth. aus Oest.	*Archäologisch-epigraphische Mittheilungen aus Oesterreich.*
Arch. Értesítő	*Archeologiai Értesítő* (in Hungarian).
Arch. f. Papyr.	*Archiv für Papyrusforschung.*
Arch. f. Rel.	*Archiv für Religionswissenschaft.*
Arch. Journ.	*Archäological Journal.*
Arch. Zeit.	*Archäologische Zeitung.*
Ath. Mitth.	*Mittheilungen des deutschen archäologischen Instituts, Athenische Abtheilung.*
Atti e Mem. della Soc. Istriana	*Atti e Memorie della Società Istriana di archeologia e storia patria.*
BCH	*Bulletin de correspondance hellénique.*
Berl. phil. Woch.	*Berliner philologische Wochenschrift.*
Bibl. des Ec.	*Bibliothèque des Écoles françaises d'Athènes et de Rome.*
Boll. di fil. cl.	*Bollettino di filologia classica.*
Bonn. Jahrb.	*Jahrbücher des Vereins der Altertumsfreunde im Rheinlande.*
BSA	*Annual of the British School of Archaeology at Athens.*
Bull. arch. du Com. des trav. hist.	*Bulletin archéologique du Comité des travaux historiques.*
Bull. Comm. arch. com.	*Bullettino della Commissione archeologica comunale di Roma.*
Bull. de la Comm. arch. de Russie	*Bulletin de la Commission archéologique de Russie* (in Russian, with French sub-title).

Bull. d. Ist. di dir. rom.	*Bullettino dell' Istituto di diritto Romano.*
Bull. Soc. arch. Alex.	*Bulletin de la Société archéologique d'Alexandrie.*
Bull. Soc. Ant. de France	*Bulletin de la Société nationale des Antiquaires de France.*
Byz.-Griech. Jahrb.	*Byzantinisch-griechische Jahrbücher.*
Byzant. Zeitschr.	*Byzantinische Zeitschrift.*
Class. Phil.	*Classical Philology.*
Class. Rev.	*Classical Review.*
Class. Weekly	*Classical Weekly.*
C. R. Acad. Inscr.	*Comptes-rendus de l'Académie des Inscriptions et Belles-Lettres.*
Denkschr. Wien. Akad.	*Denkschriften der österreichischen Akademie der Wissenschaften.*
E. Espérandieu, *Rec. gén.*	E. Espérandieu, *Recueil général des bas-reliefs de la Gaule romaine,* i–ix, 1907–1925.
Gaz. arch.	*Gazette archéologique.*
Gött. gel. Anz.	*Göttingische gelehrte Anzeigen.*
Gött. gel. Nachr.	*Nachrichten der Gesellschaft der Wissenschaften zu Göttingen.*
Hist. Zeitschr.	*Historische Zeitschrift.*
Jahrb. f. Altertumsk.	*Jahrbuch für Altertumskunde.*
JDAI	*Jahrbuch des deutschen archäologischen Instituts.*
JEA	*Journal of Egyptian Archaeology.*
JHS	*Journal of Hellenic Studies.*
Journ. Sav.	*Journal des Savants.*
JRAS	*Journal of the Royal Asiatic Society.*
JRS	*Journal of Roman Studies.*
Korr.-Blatt der westd. Zeitschr.	*Korrespondenzblatt der westdeutschen Zeitschrift für Geschichte und Kunst.*
Lit. Zentralbl.	*Literarisches Zentralblatt.*
Mél. de l'Éc. fr. de Rome	*Mélanges de l'École française de Rome.*
Mém. de l'Ac. d. Inscr.	*Mémoires de l'Académie des Inscriptions et Belles-Lettres.*
Mém. prés. à l'Acad.	*Mémoires présentés par divers savants à l'Académie des Inscriptions et Belles-Lettres.*
Mem. d. Acc. di Napoli	*Memorie della Reale Accademia di archeologia di Napoli.*
Mon. Ant. *or* Mon. dei Lincei	*Monumenti antichi pubblicati per cura della R. Accademia dei Lincei.*
Mon. Piot	*Monuments et Mémoires E. Piot.*
Mus. belge	*Musée belge.*
Nachr. d. gött. Ges.	See *Gött. gel. Nachr.*
Neue Heid. Jahrb.	*Neue Heidelberger Jahrbücher.*
Neue Jahrb. (kl. Alt.)	*Neue Jahrbücher für das klassische Altertum.*
Not. d. Scavi	*Notizie degli Scavi di Antichità.*
Nouv. Arch. d. miss. scient.	*Nouvelles Archives des missions scientifiques.*
Nouv. Rev. hist. du droit fr. et étr.	*Nouvelle Revue historique du droit français et étranger.*
Num. Chr.	*Numismatic Chronicle.*

Numism. Zeitschr.	*Numismatische Zeitschrift.*
Oest. Jahresh.	*Jahreshefte des österreichischen archäologischen Instituts.*
Pauly-Wissowa	Pauly-Wissowa-Kroll, *Realencyclopädie der klassischen Altertumswissenschaft.*
Philol.	*Philologus.*
Phil. Woch.	See *Berl. phil. Woch.*
Preuß. Jahrb.	*Preußische Jahrbücher.*
S. Reinach, *Rép. d. peint.*	S. Reinach, *Répertoire des peintures grecques et romaines* (1922).
S. Reinach, *Rép. d. rel.*	S. Reinach, *Répertoire des reliefs grecs et romains,* i–iii (1909–1912).
Rend. (Acc.) Lincei	*Rendiconti della Reale Accademia dei Lincei.*
Rev. arch.	*Revue archéologique.*
Rev. bibl(ique)	*Revue biblique internationale.*
Rev. ét. anc.	*Revue des études anciennes.*
Rev. de phil.	*Revue de philologie.*
Rev. ét. gr.	*Revue des études grecques.*
Rev. d. quest. hist.	*Revue des questions historiques.*
Rev. hist.	*Revue historique.*
Rev. num.	*Revue numismatique.*
Rh. Mus.	*Rheinisches Museum für Philologie.*
Riv. fil.	*Rivista di filologia.*
Riv. di st. ant.	*Rivista di storia antica.*
Röm. Mitth.	*Mittheilungen des deutschen archäologischen Instituts, römische Abtheilung.*
Schmollers Jahrb.	*Schmollers Jahrbuch für Gesetzgebung, Verwaltung und Volkswirtschaft im deutschen Reich.*
Sitzb. Bayr. (*or* Münch.) Akad.	*Sitzungsberichte der bayrischen Akademie der Wissenschaften.*
Sitzb. Berl. Akad.	*Sitzungsberichte der preußischen Akademie der Wissenschaften.*
Sitzb. Heid. Akad.	*Sitzungsberichte der Heidelberger Akademie der Wissenschaften.*
Sitzb. Wien. Akad.	*Sitzungsberichte der Akademie der Wissenschaften in Wien.*
Sonderschr. d. öst. Inst.	*Sonderschriften des österreichischen archäologischen Instituts.*
Studien Gesch. Kol. *or* Studien	*Studien zur Geschichte des römischen Kolonates,* von M. Rostowzew, 1910 (*Arch. f. Papyr.*, Beiheft I).
TAPA	*Transactions of the American Philological Association.*
Westd. Zeitschr.	*Westdeutsche Zeitschrift für Geschichte und Kunst.*
Wiss. Mitt. (aus Bosnien)	*Wissenschaftliche Mittheilungen aus Bosnien und Herzegowina.*
Woch. kl. Phil.	*Wochenschrift für klassische Philologie.*
Zeitschr. d. Sav.-St.	*Zeitschrift der Savigny-Stiftung für Rechtsgeschichte.*
Zeitschr. f. äg. Spr.	*Zeitschrift für ägyptische Sprache und Altertumskunde.*
Zeitschr. f. ges. Staatsw.	*Zeitschrift für gesammte Staatswissenschaften.*
Zeitschr. f. Neutest. Wissenschaft	*Zeitschrift für die Neutestamentliche Wissenschaft.*

Abbreviations

Zeitschr. f. Num.	*Zeitschrift für Numismatik.*
Zeitschr. f. öst. Gymn.	*Zeitschrift für österreichische Gymnasien.*
Zeitschr. f. vergl. Rechts- wiss.	*Zeitschrift für vergleichende Rechtswissenschaft.*

NOTES

1. *Italy and the Civil Wars*

1 On the economic conditions of Greece in the 5th and 4th cent. B.C., and especially of Athens, see G. Glotz, *Le Travail dans la Grèce ancienne* (1920); J. Beloch, *Griechische Geschichte*, 2nd ed., iii (1922), pp. 313 ff. (IX. Abschnitt, 'Die wirtschaftliche Entwickelung seit dem Peloponnesischen Kriege'); F. Oertel, in R. von Pöhlmann, *Geschichte der sozialen Frage und des Sozialismus in der antiken Welt*, ii³ (1925), pp. 511 ff.; cf. H. Knorringa, *Emporos* (1926); J. Hasebroek, *Staat und Handel im alten Griechenland*, (1928) [Eng. trans., *Trade and Politics in Ancient Greece* (1933)]; G. M. Calhoun, *The Business Life of Ancient Athens* (1926); A. M. Andreades, Σύστημα Ἑλληνικῆς Δημοσίας Οἰκονομίας I. i (1928) [revised ed. in Eng. trans., *A History of Greek Public Finance*, vol. i, transl. by Carroll N. Brown (Harvard Univ. Press, 1933)]; E. Ziebarth, *Beiträge zur Gesch. des Seeraubes u. Seehandels im alten Griechenland* (1929); J. Hasebroek, *Griechische Wirtschafts- und Gesellschaftsgeschichte* (1931). I must point out that I use the expression 'capitalism' in its wider meaning, of the economic form which aims at profit, not at consumption. Naturally, modern capitalism is of a wholly different kind, and in the typical forms it manifests today unknown to the ancient world. See the relevant literature in Chap. VII, note 104.

2 This important topic will be dealt with at length in my forthcoming book: *The Hellenistic Period. Social and Economic Development* [*The Social and Economic History of the Hellenistic World*, 3 vols. (Oxford, Clarendon Press, 1941), corr. impr. 1953]. Polybius' description of the wars of the end of the 3rd and the beginning of the 2nd cent., waged in Greece Proper, on the islands, and in Asia Minor, is a mine of information on this subject. I have observed with pleasure the arguments adduced by U. Kahrstedt, *Gött. gel. Anz.* 1928, p. 85, to show that war became more and more humane in the Hellenistic age. Even if grounds existed for admitting such humanization in the first part of the Hellenistic age, they would not be valid for the age of Philip II and his contemporaries.

3 Demosth. Κατὰ Τιμοκρ. 149 (p. 746): οὐδὲ τῶν χρεῶν τῶν ἰδίων ἀποκοπὰς οὐδὲ γῆς ἀναδασμὸν τῆς Ἀθηναίων οὐδ' οἰκιῶν, cf. Dittenberger, *Syll.*³ 526, 22 ff.: οὐ/[δὲ γᾶς] ἀναδασμὸν οὐδὲ οἰκιᾶ[ν] οὐδὲ | [ο]ἰκοπέδων οὐδὲ χρεῶν ἀ[[ποκοπ]ὰν ποιήσω, and Isocr. *Panath.* (12), 259 (p. 287 b). In the person of Cercidas (fr. 1, see J. U. Powell and E. A. Barber, *New Chapters in the History of Greek Literature* (1921); cf. A. D. Knox, *The First Greek Anthologist* (1923)) we have now one of the political and social preachers and reformers of the 3rd cent. who, though belonging to the bourgeois class, were forced to accept γῆς ἀναδασμόν and χρεῶν ἀποκοπήν as a preventive measure against social revolution. Cf. R. von Pöhlmann, *Geschichte der sozialen Frage und des Sozialismus in der antiken Welt*, i³ (1925), pp. 332 ff. and W. W. Tarn, 'The Social Question in the Third Century', in *The Hellenistic Age* (1923), pp. 108 ff.; id. *Hellenistic Civilization*³ (1952), pp. 108 ff.

4 W. S. Ferguson, *Hellenistic Athens* (1911).

5 The problem of Hellenistic economic and social life will be treated in the book quoted in note 2 [see op. cit. ibid.]. A summary of the conditions has been given by J. Beloch, *Griech. Gesch.*, iv (1925); P. Jouguet, *L'Impérialisme macédonien et l'hellénisation de l'Orient* (1926) [Eng. trans. 1928]; J. Kaerst, *Gesch. d. Hellenismus*², ii (1926); W. W. Tarn, *Hellenistic Civilization* [3rd ed. with G. T. Griffith, 1952]; F. Heichelheim, *Wirtschaftliche Schwankungen der Zeit von Alexander bis Augustus* (1930). On Ptolemaic

Egypt see M. Rostovtzeff, 'Ptolemaic Egypt', *CAH* vii (1928), pp. 533 ff. (with bibliography), cf. W. W. Tarn, 'Ptolemy II', *JEA* 14, 1928, pp. 246 ff. On Syria see M. Rostovtzeff, 'Syria and the East', *CAH* vii, pp. 587 ff. (with bibliography), cf. W. Otto, 'Beiträge zur Seleukidengeschichte des III Jahrh. v. Chr.', *Abhl. Munch. Akad.* xxxiv. 1 (1928). On the Pergamene kingdom, see my article in *Anatolian Studies presented to Sir W. M. Ramsay* (Manchester, 1923), which discusses the evidence we possess on scientific and capitalistic agriculture in the Hellenistic period; cf. my chapter 'Pergamum', *CAH* viii, pp. 590 ff., and my chapters 'Rhodes and Delos', and 'The Bosporan Kingdom', ibid., pp. 619 ff., 561 ff. An abundant source of information is furnished by the papyri containing the correspondence of Zenon, the manager of a large estate of Apollonius, the *dioiketes* of Ptolemy Philadelphus, for which see M. Rostovtzeff, *A Large Estate*, p. 49 (corn-growing), pp. 93 ff. (viticulture), pp. 107 ff. (stock-breeding), pp. 117 ff. (horses); C. C. Edgar, *Zenon Papyri in the University of Michigan Collection* (1931), introd., pp. 1 ff. (bibliography of Apollonius and Zeno); Rolf Johannesen, 'Ptolemy Philadelphus and Scientific Agriculture', *Class. Phil.* 18, 1923, pp. 156 ff.; H. A. Thompson, 'Syrian Wheat in Hellenistic Egypt', *Arch. f. Papyr.* 9, pp. 207 ff. Interesting evidence has been published by Edgar, 'Miscellanea', *Bull. Soc. arch. Alex.* 19, 1923, pp. 6 (117) ff., concerning an effort of Zenon to acclimatize Sicilian swine in Egypt; cf. P. Viereck, *Philadelpheia* (1928, *Morgenland*, Heft 16), pp. 40 ff.; id. *Gnomon*, 6, 1930, pp. 115 ff. The fact that Theophrastus was read in Hellenistic Egypt is attested by the discovery of a fragment of περὶ ζῴων (P.Lit. Lond. 164). Cf. the remarkable book of M. Schnebel, *Die Landwirtschaft im hellenist. Ägypten* (Münchener Beiträge zur Papyr. 7, 1925); W. L. Westermann, 'Egyptian Agricultural Labour', *Agricultural History*, 1, 1927, pp. 34 ff., and my remarks on *P. Teb.* 703.

[6] A fine characterization of the Hellenistic monarchies (though exaggerated as regards the negative side) is given by Aelius Aristides in his wonderful speech Εἰς Ῥώμην (xxiv κ, xiv D), 27: Μακεδόνες οὐκ ἐν Μακεδονίᾳ, ἀλλ᾽ οὗ δύναιντο βασιλεύοντες ἕκαστοι ὥσπερ φρουροὶ μᾶλλον τῶν πόλεων καὶ τῶν χωρίων ὄντες ἢ ἄρχοντες, ἀνάστατοί τινες βασιλεῖς οὐχ ὑπὸ τοῦ μεγάλου βασιλέως, ἀλλ᾽ ὑφ᾽ ἑαυτῶν αὐτοὶ γεγενημένοι, εἰ δὲ οἷόν τε εἰπεῖν, σατράπαι ἔρημοι βασιλέως. καίτοι τὴν τοιαύτην κατάστασιν πότερον λῃστείᾳ μᾶλλον ἢ βασιλείᾳ προσεοικέναι φήσομεν;

[7] The best treatment of the important problem of Rome's first attempts to create a world state, an *Imperium Romanum*, is to be found in Tenney Frank, *Roman Imperialism* (1913) (cf. id. *A History of Rome* (1923), pp. 136 ff.), and especially M. Holleaux, *Rome, la Grèce et les monarchies hellénistiques au IIIme siècle avant J.-C.* (*273–205*), (*Bibl. des Éc.* 124, 1921), and G. de Sanctis, *Storia dei Romani*, iv, 1, 'La fondazione dell'impero' (1922), pp. 1 ff. Cf. F. B. Marsh, *The Founding of the Roman Empire*[2] (1927), chs. i. and ii; L. Homo, *L'Italie primitive et les débuts de l'impérialisme romain* (1926). On the economic revival of Greece in the second half of the 2nd cent. B.C., A. Wilhelm, 'Urkunden aus Messene', *Oest. Jahresh.* 17, 1914, pp. 84 ff. On the exactions of the Roman revolutionary leaders, especially Sulla in the East, the same article, pp. 97 ff., cf. R. O. Jollife, *Phases of Corruption in Roman Administration in the last Century of the Roman Republic* (Chicago, 1919). New evidence on the robberies of the pirates in the Mediterranean is supplied by the inscription of Delphi—a translation into Greek of one of the laws which gave extraordinary powers to a general for operations against them (*SEG* i. 161 [= ‡*Fouilles de Delphes*, iii. 4. 37 = Riccobono, *FIRA*[2] 9]). The date of the inscription is still a subject of controversy, see Pomtow, *Klio*, 17, 1917, pp. 171 ff.; E. Cuq, *C.R. Acad. Inscr.* 1923, pp. 129 ff.; M. A. Levi, *Riv. fil.* 52, 1924, pp. 80 ff.; G. Colin, *BCH* 48, 1924, pp. 58 ff.; J. Colin, *Rev. arch.* 1923 (2), pp. 289 ff.; E. Cuq, ibid. 1924 (1), pp. 208 ff.; H. Stuart Jones, 'A Roman law concerning Piracy', *JRS*, 16, 1926, pp. 155 ff.; A. Radin, *Class. Journ.* 23, 1927, pp. 678 ff. The dates assigned to the law

are 101 B.C. (G. Colin, M. Levi, H. Stuart Jones), 74 B.C. (J. Colin), and 67 B.C. (E. Cuq). Cf. also H. A. Ormerod, *Piracy in the Ancient World* (1924), and E. Ziebarth, *Beitr. z. Gesch. d. Seeraubes u. Seehandels im alten Griechenland* (1929), p. 33. A remarkable metrical inscription found at Corinth speaks of the transport of M. Antonius' fleet (102 B.C.) across the Isthmus: L. Ross Taylor and Allen B. West, *Corinth*, viii. 2 (1931), pp. 1 ff., no. 1.

⁸ Tenney Frank, *An Economic History of Rome to the End of the Republic* (1920, 2nd ed. 1927), gives a very good survey of the chief phenomena of the economic life of Rome and Italy in the Republican period. In the last five chapters the author includes in his treatment the economic evolution of the Empire. My views coincide with his in the most important points; in the following notes I shall indicate the points in which we disagree. Cf. *CAH* vii and viii (chapters by various authors on the internal history of Rome); T. Rice Holmes, *The Roman Republic and the Founder of the Empire* (1923), i, pp. 65 ff., and the good survey given by H. Nissen, *Italische Landeskunde*, ii (1902), pp. 80 ff. For the conditions of Southern Italy, Etruria, and Sicily in the pre-Roman period, see E. Pais, *Storia dell'Italia antica* i, ii (1925); cf. E. Ciaceri, *Storia della Magna Grecia*, i–iii (1924–32). For Etruria see P. Ducati, *Etruria antica*, i, ii (1925); David Randall MacIver, *The Etruscans* (1927). For the early period of the economic history of Rome see, besides the works quoted above, I. Greaves, *Essays on the History of Roman Land-tenure* (in Russian, 1899), pp. 496 ff.; cf. E. Kornemann in Pauly–Wissowa, Suppl. iv, cols. 84 ff. and cols. 238 ff. (art. 'Bauernstand' and 'Domänen'), and Orth, ibid. xii, cols. 624 ff. (art. 'Landwirtschaft'). I am not as confident as Frank seems to be, and as W. Soltau (in his articles in *Philologus* [72, 1913], pp. 358 ff.; 75, 1919, pp. 233 ff.; cf. id. *BPW*, 1913, cols. 891–5]) is, about the trustworthiness of our sources in regard to the constitutional and the economic evolution of the early Roman Republic. The annals were obviously a splendid field for many politicians of the 2nd and 1st cent. B.C. to fight out a political battle on the basis of economic issues, using as weapons supposed historical facts of the remote past. Even such facts as the dates of the foundation of the early colonies (e.g. Ostia) appear in the light of new discoveries to be mere inventions. In dealing with the economic evolution of early Republican Rome, we must therefore content ourselves with very general conclusions, based not on alleged historical facts, especially those of a legislative character, but on survivals of certain institutions and on general considerations. On the present state of the problem of the sources see E. Kornemann, 'Niebuhr und die Aufgaben der altrömischen Geschichte', *Hist. Zeitschr.* 145, 1931, pp. 277 ff.

⁹ In my book quoted in note 2 it will be shown that the war booty taken by the Romans in Greece and in Asia Minor consisted mainly of men and cattle (one of the most important texts which illuminates this subject is Plut. *Luc.* 14. 25, which speaks of Asia Minor). Greece at that time was a very poor country, already ruined by the barbarous warfare of the end of the 3rd and the beginning of the 2nd cent. B.C. On the poverty of Greece at that time see Polyb. ii. 62, and the masterly article of A. Wilhelm, 'Urkunden aus Messene', *Oest. Jahresh.* 17, 1914, pp. 90 f. and 107 ff., cf. H. Lipsius, *Rh. Mus.* 71, 1916, pp. 161 ff. Asia Minor was richer, but still her wealth consisted mostly of cattle and men, which were much easier to capture and to sell than the coined money and the valuables of the households.

¹⁰ There is no good treatment in modern literature of the important question of the sources of the income of the senatorial class in general. The most recent books on the Roman senatorial class, those of M. Gelzer, *Die Nobilität der römischen Republik* (1912), and F. Münzer, *Römische Adelsparteien und Adelsfamilien* (1920) (cf. M. Gelzer, 'Die römische Gesellschaft zur Zeit Ciceros', *Neue Jahrb. kl. Abt.* 45, 1920, pp. 1 ff.; W. Kroll, 'Die röm. Gesellschaft in der Zeit Ciceros', *Neue Jahrb. f. Wiss. u. Jug.* 4,

1928, pp. 308 ff., and 'Die Privatwirtschaft der Zeit Ciceros', ibid. 5, 1929, pp. 417 ff.), deal exclusively with the political and social aspect of the subject. There is not even a good monograph on such a typical representative of the new *nobilitas* (J. Vogt, *Homo Novus, Ein Typus d. röm. Republik* (1926)) as Cicero, whose economic life we know fairly well; see the biography of Cicero by T. Petersson, *Cicero. A Biography* (Berkeley (California), 1920), pp. 212 ff., and his very incomplete bibliography (he ignores, for instance, the monograph of A. Lichtenberger, *De Ciceronis re privata* (Paris, 1895); cf. A. Früchtl, *Die Geldgeschäfte bei Cicero* (1912). I am certain that a close study of our sources for the Republican period would supply abundant and instructive material on this question.

11 The remark made in note 10 holds for the equestrian class as a whole, see my *Geschichte der Staatspacht in der römischen Kaiserzeit* (1902) (*Philol.* Suppl. ix. 3), pp. 367 ff. Two good monographs, however, have been published on the most representative member of this class, T. Pomponius Atticus: I. Greaves, *Essays on the History of Roman Land-Tenure* (in Russian), i (St. Petersburg, 1899), pp. 246 ff., and A. H. Byrne, *Titus Pomponius Atticus* (Bryn Mawr, 1920). It is a pity that Miss Byrne has not used for her first chapter ('Atticus as a Man of Business') the essay of Greaves, which she might have found quoted in the well-known volume of G. Salvioli, *Le Capitalisme dans le monde antique* (1906) [Germ. trans., 2nd ed., 1922, Ital. trans. 1929]. Salvioli has some fine remarks on Atticus (pp. 46 ff.), which are ignored by Miss Byrne. The remarkable book of A. Stein, *Der röm. Ritterstand* (1927), gives only a short chapter on the earlier history of the equestrian order before the Empire. Cf. B. Kübler, *Zeitschr. d. Sav.-St.* 48, 1928, pp. 657 ff.

12 On the large numbers of Italians in the Orient see the excellent book of J. Hatzfeld, *Les Trafiquants italiens dans l'Orient hellénique* (*Bibl. des Éc.* 115, 1919), cf. T. Frank, *An Economic History*², p. 290; P. Roussel, *Délos, colonie athénienne* (*Bibl. des Éc.* 111, 1916), pp. 72 ff.; Ch. Picard, in *BCH* 44, 1920, pp. 263 ff.; M. Besnier, in *Journ. Sav.* 1920, pp. 263 ff.; P. Roussel, *Délos* (1925), pp. 15 ff., and the notes of Durrbach, *Choix d'inscriptions de Délos* (1921–2), on nos. 64, 65, and, in particular, 66; cf. 132, 138, and 141. Cf. M. Bulard, *La Religion domestique dans la colonie italienne de Délos* (*Bibl. des Éc.* 131, 1926); cf. my chapter 'Rhodes and Delos', *CAH* viii (with bibliography). From South Italy also come the Roman citizens mentioned in the third Augustan edict of Cyrene (see Chap. II, notes 6 and 8); A. von Premerstein, *Zeitschr. d. Sav.-St.* 48, 1928, pp. 458 ff., and ibid. 51, 1931, pp. 431 ff.; J. Stroux and L. Wenger, 'Die Augustusinschrift auf dem Marktplatze von Kyrene', *Abhl. Bayr. Akad.* 34, 1928, 2. The powerful corporation of Roman citizens in Laconia, mentioned in an inscription of Gythion of the age of Tiberius, was undoubtedly of more ancient origin (see below). On the family of the Apustii of Abdera, see A. Wilhelm, *Sitzb. Wien. Akad.* 183, 1921, pp. 21 ff., and M. Holleaux, *BCH* 38, 1914, pp. 63 ff., cf. G. Seure, ibid. 36, 1912, p. 614. Most of the Italian *negotiatores* were, of course, half-Greeks from South Italy, but some certainly came from other parts of Italy, if not from Rome itself: see J. Hatzfeld, op. cit., pp. 238 ff., S. B. Kougeas, ' Ἐπιγραφικαὶ ἐκ Γυθείου συμβολαί ', Ἑλληνικά, 1, 1928, pp. 7 ff., 152 ff., and M. Rostovtzeff, 'L'Empereur Tibère et le culte impérial', *Rev. hist.* 1930, pp. 1 ff., with bibliography on the inscription of Gythion.

13 I need not insist on these points, which are carefully treated by T. Frank, *Economic History*², pp. 90 ff. (agriculture) and pp. 108 ff., 219 ff. (industry); cf. H. Gummerus, 'Handel und Industrie,' Pauly–Wissowa, ix. 2, cols. 1444 ff. W. Heitland, *Agricola, a Study of Agriculture and Rustic Life in the Greco-Roman World from the Point of View of Labour* (Cambridge, 1921), gives a good collection of quotations from Greek and Roman authors in chronological order; and R. Scalais, 'La Production agricole dans l'État romain et les importations de blés provinciaux jusqu'à la 2ᵐᵉ guerre

punique', *Mus. Belge*, 1925, pp. 143 ff. Cf. G. Curcio, *La primitiva civiltà latina agricola e il libro dell'agricoltura di M. Porcio Catone* (1929).

[14] S. Gsell, *Histoire de l'Afrique du Nord*, iv (1918), pp. 1 ff., esp. pp. 18 ff. The exploitation of the soil of the Carthaginian territory was certainly intensified after the Second Punic War, as it remained the only safe source of income both for the state and for the Carthaginian aristocracy. Notice that immediately after the Second Punic War Carthage, together with Numidia, Sicily, and Sardinia, was able to provide large quantities of cereals for the provisioning of the city of Rome and of the Roman army: Liv. xxxi. 19 (200 B.C.)—200,000 *modium tritici* for Rome and the same quantity for the Macedonian army: id. xxxvi. 3, 1; 4, 5 ff. (191 B.C.)—Carthage offers a large quantity of wheat as a gift; the senate will accept it, if Rome was allowed to pay for it.

[15] The leading part taken by the big landowners in the decision to destroy Carthage is well illustrated by the familiar story of the return of Cato from an embassy to Carthage and his appearance in the senate with his lap full of fresh figs. We must not forget that Cato was one of the progressive landowners of this period, and that he strongly advocated in his manual on agriculture the planting of vineyards, olive-trees, and orchards: see H. Gummerus, 'Der römische Gutsbetrieb,' &c., *Klio*, Beiheft 5, 1906, pp. 19 ff., cf. E. Cavaignac, *Population et capital dans le monde méditerranéen antique* (Fac. des lettres de l'Univ. de Strasbourg) (1923), pp. 95 ff. (bold generalizations based on scanty evidence). Carthage, with her flourishing gardens and olive groves, was a dangerous rival of the Italian landowners, especially because of her old commercial relations with the Western markets. I cannot agree with Frank, *Economic History*[2], p. 115, n. 15, who maintains that Italy had no importance in the economic life of the world in the 2nd cent. B.C. The material collected in note 12 shows the importance which the bankers and great Italian merchants had for the economic life of Greece in the early 2nd cent. B.C. (Durrbach, *Choix*, 64 and 66), and also the importance of the export of wine and oil from Italy in the early 1st cent. B.C. (Durrbach, *Choix*, 141 and 142). The export of wine and oil undoubtedly began at a date earlier than that of the two preserved inscriptions (note the large number of amphorae with Italian marks found at Delos). Frank maintains that after the Second Punic War the territory of Carthage was no longer sufficient to feed the population of the city. I doubt this very much (see note 14). But if it were true, it would be the reason why Carthage multiplied her orchards and olive groves. Thus cultivated, the soil was able to produce fruit and oil in sufficient quantity to cover the cost of the import of corn. Naturally, after the Third Punic War Rome did not also destroy the other cities which, like Carthage, produced oil. Does Frank believe that Roman senators were without any sense of honour? Trade in wine and oil were the main sources of the growing prosperity of Italy; compare the inscriptions testifying to the export of Campanian wines even to Africa (166–157 B.C.), *CIL* viii. 22637. 62; x. 8051. 20; S. Gsell, *Histoire de l'Afrique du Nord*, iv, p. 150; and Plin. *NH* xv. 1 (in the third consulate of Pompey (52 B.C.) Italy supplied the provinces with oil; Pliny probably has especially in mind the Oriental provinces). Cf. note 16.

[16] On the conditions which prevailed in Gaul before the Roman conquest see the excellent work of C. Jullian, *Histoire de la Gaule*, ii (1908), p. 330. Notice that at that time Italy exported many industrial products (metallurgical and textile) to Gaul; the export of horses was probably prohibited (Liv. xliii. 5, 8 ff.).The main commodity imported from Italy was wine, as is shown by the numerous amphorae of Italian types and with Italian stamps which have been found in the Celtic cities of central Gaul; see O. Bohn, 'Die ältesten römischen Amphoren in Gallien', *Germania*, 7, 1923, pp. 8 ff.; 9, 1925, pp. 78 ff. Bohn has shown that already by the middle of the 2nd cent. B.C. a lively trade in Italian wine had begun, and that the amphorae (of the same

type as those found at Delos and Carthage) came from South Italy and Sicily. The stamps of these amphorae are collected in *CIL* xiii. 3. Italian wine also undoubtedly found its way to the Rhine region. One of the stamps which prove this (from Coblenz) is most interesting: it bears the name of Postumus Curius, the same person who subsequently changed his name to C. Rabirius Postumus, the noted client of Cicero, *cuius res in pluribus provinciis versata est* (Cic. *Pro Rab.* 4). The same stamp (Dessau, *ILS* 9445=*CIL* i². 2340) has been found on amphorae of South Italy and Sicily. Cf. H. Dessau, *Hermes*, 46, 1911, p. 613; 47, 1912, p. 320; O. Bohn, op. cit., p. 15. Cf. A. Oxé, *Germania*, 8, 1924, pp. 80 ff. Oxé has proved that the majority of the names which are written in full on these stamps belong to persons of senatorial and equestrian rank of the age of Cicero and Caesar. These people were undoubtedly owners of vineyards in Southern Italy and in Sicily. The importance of the Danube market is emphasized by the rapid development of Aquileia, the centre of the Italian trade with the Danube lands. The export of wine and oil to these lands gradually transformed Northern Italy from a land of pigs, sheep, and corn into a land of vineyards; see the picture given by Herodian for the late 2nd and the early 3rd cent. A.D. (viii. 2. 3): ἡ δὲ Ἀκυληία . . . ὥσπερ τι ἐμπόριον Ἰταλίας ἐπὶ θαλάττῃ προκειμένη καὶ πρὸ τῶν Ἰλλυρικῶν ἐθνῶν πάντων ἰδρυμένη . . . πρὸς οἶνόν τε μάλιστα πολύγονον χώραν γεωργοῦντες ἀφθονίαν ποτοῦ παρεῖχον τοῖς ἄμπελον μὴ γεωργοῦσιν. Cf. viii. 4. 5: description of the territory of Aquileia entirely planted with vines; and Strabo, iv. 207; v. 214; vii. 314. On Aquileia and her commercial importance, E. Maionica, *Aquileia zur Römerzeit* (Görz, 1881); H. Nissen, *Italische Landeskunde*, ii (1902), pp. 229 ff.; Ch. Hülsen in Pauly–Wissowa, ii, cols. 318 ff., cf. H. Willers, *Neue Untersuchungen über die römische Bronzeindustrie* (1907), pp. 27 ff.; A. Gnirs, *Oest. Jahresh.* 18, 1915, p. 143 (commerce in ivory objects); H. Gummerus, in Pauly–Wissowa, ix. 2, cols. 1469; L. Friedländer–G. Wissowa, *Sittengeschichte Roms*, i, 9th–10th ed., p. 375; K. Herfurth, *De Aquileiae commercio* (Halle, 1889); A. Calderini, *Aquileia Romana* (1929); G. Brusin, *Aquileia. Guida storica e artistica* (1929). I give the bibliography here to avoid repeating the references when I come to speak of Aquileia again. Cf. Chap. II, note 35.

[17] I cannot see why Frank persists in believing that the measure of the Roman senate, which dates somewhere about 154 (or 125) B.C., was intended to protect the viticulture of Massilia, and not that of Italy, and was therefore limited to a very restricted region in the neighbourhood of Massilia (*Roman Imperialism*, p. 280; *Economic History*², p. 116, note 19). Cic. *De rep.* iii. 6. 9 is positive in affirming that the measure was intended to protect the interests of Italy and not those of Massilia. Wine was imported into Gaul in large quantities in 69 B.C. (Cic. *Pro Font.* 9. 9, cf. Diod. v. 26. 3: O. Bohn, *Germania*, 7, 1923, p. 9). The prohibition was probably dropped later in the 1st cent. B.C., when Southern Gaul became a land of intensive Italian colonization, practically a part of Italy; see S. Reinach, *Rev. arch.* 1901 (2), pp. 350–74; M. Besnier, ibid. 1919 (2), p. 34; C. Jullian, *Histoire de la Gaule*, iii, p. 99; iv, pp. 183 ff. There was nothing new and nothing peculiar in this treatment of Gaul by Rome. Rome in this respect was the heir of Carthage, which always endeavoured to prevent her provinces (Sicily, Sardinia, and Spain) from growing vines and olive-trees. The provinces were for Carthage both a market for the wine and oil produced in the territories of the Punic cities in Africa, and granaries which allowed her to develop her culture of vines and olives. Hence her measures for the promotion of corn-growing and the prohibition of viticulture in her provinces. Competition in the trade in wine and olive-oil (partly imported, partly produced on the spot) was the main reason for the constant wars of Carthage against the Greek cities of Sicily and South Italy. As Etruria did not produce wine and olive-oil, it was a natural customer, friend, and ally of the Carthaginians. The policy of Carthage in regard at least to Sicily and Sardinia, and later Africa her-

self, was inherited and carried on by Rome in the same spirit and for the same reasons. Hence Cicero's picture of Sicily as chiefly a corn-growing province; hence the absence of vineyards and olive-groves in Sardinia until late in the imperial period; hence also the late development of olive-growing and viticulture in Africa. Gaul naturally had been subject to the same policy, and so was Spain in the 2nd cent. B.C. (Frank, l.c., quotes against my views Polyb. xxxiv. 8, which speaks of pre-Roman Lusitania, and the well-known descriptions of Varro and Strabo, which refer to the latter part of the 1st. cent. B.C.). The action of Domitian in respect of vine-planting in the provinces was a revival of this policy: see Chap. VI. On the policy of Carthage as regards Sardinia see E. Pais, *Storia della Sardegna e della Corsica durante il dominio romano*, ii (1923), pp. 505 ff.; S. Gsell, *Histoire ancienne de l'Afrique du Nord*, iv (1918), pp. 20 ff., and on viticulture, pp. 18 ff. Part of the wine exported by the Carthaginians came probably from Greece, Gsell, ibid., pp. 152 f. On the policy of the Romans, Pais, ibid., i, pp. 329 ff.

[18] J. Hatzfeld, *Les Trafiquants italiens*, pp. 212 ff.; F. Durrbach, *Choix*, no. 141. For the Italian bankers at Delos see the inscriptions mentioned in note 12 of this chapter.

[19] W. Heitland, in *JRS* 8, 1918, p. 38, finds that the picture given by me in my *Studien zur Geschichte des römischen Kolonates*, p. 313, where I speak of armies recruited by Pompey and Domitius Ahenobarbus from the large numbers of their slaves and *coloni*, 'is greatly overdrawn'. But the texts, especially those of Caesar, are explicit, and the information they provide cannot be either eliminated or 'overdrawn'; cf. J. Kromayer, in *Neue Jahrb. kl. Alt.* 23/24, 1914, p. 162; Frank, *Economic History*², pp. 355 ff.; T. Rice Holmes, *The Roman Republic*, i (1923), pp. 106 and 56. Cf. E. Wiehn, *Die illegalen Heereskommanden in Rom bis auf Caesar* (1926), pp. 27 ff. (on the recruitment of Pompey's army in Picenum among the clients of his family).

[20] On the Gracchi see the excellent articles of F. Münzer, 'Ti.' and 'C. Sempronius Gracchus', in Pauly–Wissowa; cf. Frank, *Economic History*², pp. 126 ff.; G. de Sanctis, 'Rivoluzione e reazione nell'età dei Gracchi', *Atene e Roma*, N.S. 2, 1921, pp. 209 ff.; W. Ensslin, 'Die Demokratie u. Rom', *Philol.* 82, 1927, pp. 313 ff.; D. Kontchalovsky, 'Recherches sur l'hist. du mouvement agraire des Gracques', *Rev. hist.* 153, 1926, pp. 161–86; F. B. Marsh, 'In defense of the Corn-dole', *Class. Journ.* 22, 1926–7, pp. 10–25; P. Teruzzi, 'La Legislaz. agraria in Italia all'epocha dei Gracchi', *Riv. d'Italia*, 5, 1926, pp. 26 ff., and 'Studi sulla legislaz. agraria di Roma', *Arch. Giurid.* 47, 1927, pp. 1 ff.; E. Fabricius, *Zeitschr. d. Sav.-St.* 47, 1927, p. 488; U. Kahrstedt, 'Die Grundlagen u. Voraussetzungen der röm. Revolution', *Neue Wege zur Antike*, 4, 1927, pp. 97 ff.; J. Carcopino, *Autour des Gracques, Études critiques* (1928); id. 'Les Lois agraires des Gracques et la guerre sociale', *Bull. de l'Assoc. G. Budé*, 1929, pp. 3–23; id. 'La République romaine de 123 avant J. C. à la mort de César, *Histoire Ancienne*, ed. G. Glotz, vol. iii, *Hist. romaine*, ii (1929 f.); M. Gelzer, *Gnomon*, 5, 1929, pp. 648 ff. For older works see the valuable bibliography of Münzer, locc. citt. On the law of 111 B.C. Ch. Saumagne, *Rev. phil.* 1927, pp. 50 ff.; cf. M. A. Levi, 'Intorno alla legge agraria del 111 A.C.', *Riv. fil.* 1929, pp. 231 ff. On the *lex Mamilia Roscia Peducaea Alliena Fabia*, probably the last of the laws which liquidated the legislation of the Gracchi, see E. Fabricius, 'Ueber die Lex M. R. P. A. F.', *Sitzb. Heid. Akad.* 1924–5, 1; cf. M. Gelzer, *Gnomon*, 1, 1925, p. 103; Hardy, *Class. Quart.* 19, 1925, p. 185. On the agrarian laws in general, cf. the (antiquated and superficial) article of Vançura in Pauly–Wissowa, xii, cols. 1150 ff. On the later agrarian laws, especially the law of Servilius Rullus, E. G. Hardy, *Some Problems in Roman History* (1924), pp. 43 ff., 68 ff.; M. A. Levi, *Atene e Roma*, N.S. 3, 1922, pp. 239 ff. (history of the *ager Campanus*); W. Ensslin in *Neue Jahrb.* 54, 1924, pp. 15 ff.; and S. Gsell, *Hist. de l'Afr.* vii (1928), pp. 74 ff. The rapid growth of slave labour in the

2nd cent. B.C. is attested by the frequent revolts of slaves in Latium (Liv. xxxii. 26. 4), in Etruria (id. xxxiii. 36. 1), and in Apulia (id. xxxix. 29. 8 ff.; 41. 6).

21 The new evidence on the 'Social' war supplied by the well-known inscription of Pompeius Strabo (*CIL* i². 709 = Dessau, *ILS* 8888) has given rise to many valuable discussions on that war in general and on the spread of Roman citizenship in particular. I quote only the two last articles on this subject; in both of them the reader will find a good bibliography: C. Cichorius, *Römische Studien* (1922), pp. 130 ff. (revised text of the inscription), and G. H. Stevenson, *JRS* 9, 1919, pp. 95 ff.; cf. T. Rice Holmes, op. cit. i, p. 46; E. Wiehn, *Die illegalen Heereskommanden in Rom bis auf Caesar* (1926), pp. 62 ff.

22 On the extraordinary military commands see the valuable article of A. E. R. Boak, *Amer. Hist. Rev.* 24, 1918–19, pp. 1 ff. Sulla endeavoured to make the extraordinary command as little dangerous as possible to the rule of the senatorial class, but it was only natural that it was the first thing to revive after his death and that it gradually became the mainstay of the Roman state; cf. J. Carcopino, *Sylla ou la monarchie manquée* (1931).

23 On Pompey and Caesar see E. Meyer's *Caesars Monarchie und das Principat des Pompeius: innere Geschichte Roms von 66 bis 44 v. Chr.* (Stuttgart und Berlin, 1919, 2nd ed.); cf. T. Rice Holmes, *The Roman Republic*, iii (1923), p. 335. Add to the bibliography quoted by Meyer and Holmes: Frank B. Marsh, *The Founding of the Roman Empire* (Oxford, 1927); the article on Caesar by P. Groebe in Pauly–Wissowa, x. 1, cols. 186 ff.; M. Gelzer, 'Caesar der Politiker und Staatsmann', *Meister der Politik* (Stuttgart und Berlin, 1921), and id. 'Caesars Monarchie und das Prinzipat des Pompeius', *Vierteljahresschrift f. Soz. u. Wirtschaftsg.* 15, 1919, pp. 522 ff.

24 On Augustus see Chap. II, note 1.

25 Varro, *RR* i. 2. 3: 'cum consedissemus, Agrasius: Vos, qui multas perambulastis terras, ecquam cultiorem Italia vidistis? inquit. Ego vero, Agrius, nullam arbitror esse quae tam tota sit culta.' Cf. 6 f.: 'contra quid in Italia utensile non modo non nascitur, sed etiam non egregium fit? quod far conferam Campano? quod triticum Apulo? quod vinum Falerno? quod oleum Venafro? non arboribus consita Italia, ut tota pomarium videatur? ... in qua terra iugerum unum denos et quinos denos culleos fert vini, quot quaedam in Italia regiones?' &c. I have quoted this well-known text to show that there is no doubt whatever about the fertility of Italy and its high state of cultivation in the second half of the 1st cent. B.C. I cannot see any patriotic exaggeration in the words of Varro, and I see no contradiction between this picture and the words of Gracchus describing the 'solitudo Italiae' (see J. Kromayer, in *Neue Jahrb. kl. Alt.* 17, 1914, pp. 145 ff.). The picture of Gracchus must be limited to some parts of Etruria. Moreover, what Gracchus had in mind was not the economic conditions in general but the situation of the peasants throughout Italy and especially in Etruria. I cannot see where Frank, *History of Rome*, p. 329, has found in Varro's words quoted above that 'Varro mentions that Italy *was again acquiring* the appearance of a garden'. 'Was again acquiring' is not what Varro says. Nor do I see any contradiction between the statement of Varro cited above and his complaints about the necessity of Italy's importing corn and even wine from abroad (*RR* ii, pr.). Varro wanted Italy to be self-supporting and was a fervent preacher of agriculture as against pasturage. Hence his invectives against the Roman capitalists, who expected better returns from pasturage than from corn and vine-growing. I see not the slightest indication of any exhaustion of the soil in Italy in the time of Varro. Complaints about exhaustion are one of the most common topics in landowners' discussions of their economic situation. They do not mean anything real, and are based on some accidental phenomena like the conditions of the *tribus Papinia* in Latium (Varro, *RR* i. 9); cf. T. Frank, *AJP* 51, 1930,

pp. 70 ff. I shall return to the theory of the exhaustion of the soil and shall quote the numerous articles and books on this subject in Chap. VIII. An illuminating example of the development of Italy in the 2nd and 1st cent. B.C. may be found in the history of Pompeii, as revealed by the excavations and by the historical studies of H. Nissen, G. Fiorelli, and A. Mau. The somewhat small and poor Italian city of the early Samnitic period, with modest, rather small houses without wall-painting and with a kitchen garden behind a rustic *atrium*, was gradually transformed in the late Samnitic period (in the 2nd cent. B.C.), under the influence of growing wealth and as a result of refined tastes, into a splendid city of large and beautiful buildings, both public and private, of the so-called 'Tufa' period, with elaborate columns, spacious *atria*, large peristyles with gardens and fountains and with elegant wall-painting of the so-called first Pompeian, i.e. the common Hellenistic, style. We may realize how rapidly the wealth of the city grew in the period after the Second Punic War, and especially in the second half of the 2nd cent. To the same period belongs the first industrialization of life in Pompeii, the first shops connected with large houses (e.g. the so-called house of Pansa). There is no break between this period and the time after the establishment of Sulla's colony. The houses and some *villae rusticae* (e.g. the villa Item and villas of Boscoreale) remain as large and as beautiful as they were before. A new manner of construction and a new style of decoration were introduced, but these new styles were as beautiful and as expensive as the earlier ones. There was no such thing as a lasting economic decay of Pompeii at this time. And so it was also in the Augustan period, with its refined third style of painting, which certainly shows strong Alexandrine influence, while the second style testifies rather to a local art influenced by Asia Minor. The change reflects the altered orientation of economic relations. Instead of Asia Minor, the Pompeian port in the Augustan period entered into close relations with Alexandria, and Campania in general began to compete with Alexandria in some branches of industrial production. The last post-Augustan period, the period of the fourth style, was the period of the intensive industrialization of the city and of the rise of new rich families of *parvenus*, some of them former slaves like the Trimalchio of Petronius. Of this period I shall speak in my next two chapters. Thus the Sullan and post-Sullan period, the period of the civil wars, was in no way a period of decay either from the economic or from the cultural point of view. We must bear in mind that it was the time of Cicero, Catullus, Caesar, and Varro. Pompeii and Campania do not seem to have been exceptional. The economic history of the rest of Italy shows the same general lines of evolution. As the wealth of Pompeii in the Republican period and in the time of Augustus was based mainly on agriculture, especially on the production of wine (see Chap. II, note 23), there is not the slightest reason for assuming any exhaustion of the fertile Campanian soil either in the 1st cent. B.C. or in the 1st cent. A.D.

[26] On the *villae rusticae* in general see G. Fiorelli, 'Ville Stabiane', in an Appendix to the Italian translation of the Dictionary of Rich (*Dizionario alle antichità greche e romane* (Firenze, 1864–5), ii, pp. 423 ff.), and A. Mau, *Pompeji in Leben und Kunst* (2nd ed. 1908), pp. 382 ff. Some villas were enumerated by H. F. de Cou, *Antiquities from Boscoreale in Field Museum of Natural History* (1912)(*Field Museum of N.H. Public.*, 152, Anthropological Series, vii. 4), cf. Pernice in *JDAI*, 15, *Arch. Anz.*, p. 177; cf. R. C. Carrington, 'Studies in the Campanian "villae rusticae" ', *JRS* 21, 1931, pp. 110 ff.; J. Day, 'Agriculture in the Life of Pompeii', *Yale Class. Stud.* 3, 1932, pp. 167 ff. Both these authors give list of villas. I owe to Day the completion of my list by the addition of seven items (12a, 13a, 37–41). I give the list here for the reader's convenience.

The following villas have been excavated (the enumeration is in chronological order):

1–12. The villas which were excavated in the 17th cent., of which four were carefully described by Fiorelli in his article on the villas of Stabiae and the rest were published by M. Ruggiero (with plans and the diary of the excavations). The descriptions of Fiorelli were repeated by Ruggiero; as for the four villas which had been described by Fiorelli there were no diaries of Vega in the archives. M. Ruggiero, *Degli scavi di Stabia dal 1749 al 1782* (Napoli, 1881), pls. IX–XIX.

12a. Contrada Moregine, east of Pompeii, *Not. d. Scavi*, 1880, pp. 495 ff.; 1881, pp. 25 ff. The owner was M. Ampius; *Neapolis*, 2, 1914, p. 169.

13. The villa of Boscoreale, where the famous treasure of silver plate, now partly in the Louvre, partly in the collection of Baron E. Rothschild, was found. A. Héron de Villefosse, in *Mon. Piot*, 5, 1899, pp. 7 ff.; Mau–Kelsey, *Pompeii*, chap. 45; Pasqui, *Mon. Ant.*, 7, 1897, pp. 397–554.

13a. Boscoreale, *Not. d. Scavi*, 1895, pp. 207 ff.

14. Boscoreale, Giuliana (F. Zurlo). *Not. d. Scavi*, 1895, p. 214; 1897, pp. 391 ff.

15. Boscoreale. *Not. d. Scavi*, 1898, pp. 419 ff.

16. Boscoreale, Grotta Franchini (F. Vona). Owner of the villa P. Fannius Synistor or more probably L. Herennius Florus (M. della Corte, *Neapolis*, 2, 1915, p. 172). Beautiful decorations of the early second style. Frescoes in the Metropolitan Museum and the Museum of Naples. Agricultural implements reproduced on our pl. XI. F. Barnabei, *La Villa Pompeiana di P. Fannio Sinistore* (1901).

17. Scafati, Muregine (Maria Liguori). *Not. d. Scavi*, 1898, pp. 33 ff.

18. Scafati, Muregine (Pasquale Malerba). *Not. d. Scavi*, 1900, pp. 203 ff.

19. Scafati, Spinelli (M. Acanfora). *Not. d. Scavi*, 1899, pp. 392 ff. The owner probably was Cn. Domitius Auctus.

20. Torre Annunziata near the Porta Vesuvio of Pompei (D'Aquino-Masucci). The owner probably was T. Siminius Stepanus. *Not. d. Scavi*, 1897, pp. 337 ff.; 1898, pp. 494 ff.; 1899, p. 236, cf. 1900, pp. 69 ff.

21. Fondo Barbatelli, near the Porta Vesuvio. *Not. d. Scavi*, 1899, pp. 439, 493; 1900, pp. 30, 70, 500, 599; cf. 584.

22. Boscoreale, contrada Centopiedi al Tirone (P. Vitiello). *Not. d. Scavi*, 1903, pp. 64 ff. Mural decorations in the first and the second style.

23. Boscotrecase, contrada Setari (N. Vitelli). Owner L. Arellius Successus. Room N decorated in the first style. *Not. d. Scavi*, 1899, p. 297; M. Della Corte, *Mem. d. Acc. di Napoli*, 2, 1911, p. 191.

24. The well-known villa Item with splendid decorations of the early second style. *Not. d. Scavi*, 1910, pp. 139 ff. and 1922, pp. 480 ff.; A. Maiuri, *La Villa dei misteri* (1931), pp. 89 ff.

25–30. Six villas illustrated by M. Della Corte in *Not. d. Scavi*, 1921, pp. 415 ff. One of these villas (no. III) belonged to a certain Asellius, whose procurator was Thallus, another (no. V) to a member of the well-known Pompeian aristocratic family of the Popidii (N. Popidius Florus); cf. M. Della Corte, *Neapolis*, 2, 1914, p. 173.

31. The villa in the contrada Rota (comune di Boscotrecase), excavated by E. Santini in 1903–5 (now covered by the lava stream of 1906); see M. Della Corte, *Not. d. Scavi*, 1922, pp. 459 ff. The villa was certainly the property of the last son of Agrippa, Agrippa Postumus (see A. Mau, *CIL* iv. 6499 note). After his death it passed into the possession of the successors of Augustus and became probably an imperial estate. This fact, which was not recognized by Della Corte, is shown by the following documents. On four amphorae found in the villa were written in ink Greek names of slaves or freedmen of Agrippa. One of these men has the title of *actor*: *CIL* iv. 6499, Νεικασίου Ἀγρ(ίππου) [ac]toris; cf. 6995–6997 where the same Greek name is connected with the name of Agrippa and in 6997 with the title διο(πενσάτωρ?). In the same villa was found a tile bearing the following stamp: Pupil(li) Agrip(pae) Tub(erone) (et) Fabio

co(n)s(ulibus)—11 b.c. (On the praenomen Pupillus of Agrippa Postumus see *CIL* vi. 18548.) In *CIL* x. 924 are enumerated four slaves, the first *ministri* of the Pagus Augustus Felix Suburbanus (7 b.c.). The first is Dama pup(i) Agrippae (cf. *CIL* ii. 1528). Finally, in a *graffito* of the same villa we read the following sarcastic pentameter (*CIL* iv. 6893): 'Caesaris Augusti femina mater erat', which certainly refers to Julia, the daughter of Augustus, mother of Agrippa Postumus. There is no doubt that the villa belonged originally to Agrippa Postumus and was probably built by his father (see the beautiful wall decoration partly of the second and partly of an early third style). The two seals of Ti. Claudius Eutychus Caesaris l(ibertus), which were found in a cupboard of the villa (*Not. d. Scavi*, 1922, p. 460), belonged, therefore, not to the owner (as Della Corte suggests), but to the manager of the villa, an agent of the emperor.

32. Some remains of a villa in the contrada S. Abbondio (comune di Scafati), excavated in 1908, see M. Della Corte, *Not. d. Scavi*, 1922, p. 479.

33–36. Four villas, two near Stabiae and two near Scafati (contrada Spinelli and contrada Crapolla). M. Della Corte, *Not. d. Scavi*, 1923, p. 271 ff.

Some of the villas belong, as is shown by the style of the wall-paintings, to the late-Republican or early-Augustan time, some may be still earlier.

[27] On Sicily, R. Scalais, 'La Propriété agricole et pastorale de la Sicile depuis la conquête romaine jusqu'aux guerres serviles', *Mus. Belge*, 1925, pp. 77 ff.; J. Carcopino, 'La Sicile agricole au dernier siècle de la république romaine', *Vierteljahresschrift f. Soz.- u. Wirtschaftsg.* 4, 1906, pp. 128 ff.; my *Studien z. Gesch. röm. Kol.* (1910), pp. 229 ff., and article 'Frumentum', Pauly–Wissowa, vii. 1, cols. 129 ff.; F. H. Cowles, *Caius Verres* (Cornell Studies in Class. Phil., 1917); E. S. Jenison, *The History of the Province of Sicily* (Boston, 1919); J. Carcopino, *La Loi d'Hiéron et les Romains* (1919); K. Ziegler, *RE* ii, A, cols. 2502 ff.; M. A. Levi, 'La Sicilia e il dominium in solo provinciali', *Athenaeum*, n.s. vii, 1929, pp. 514 ff. We are well informed about the economic life of Sicily in the time of Cicero and Verres. Thereafter almost complete darkness reigns. Sicily may have suffered heavily during the later stages of the civil wars when it was the main source of income of Sex. Pompey. But this temporary calamity cannot account for the supposed disappearance of Sicily from the corn-producing and exporting countries. The mountainous parts remained, as before, grazing-lands. But what happened to the valleys? I am inclined to think that they gradually underwent the same transformation as Italy, especially South Italy, and that the lowlands and hills became centres of viticulture and gardening. At the same time they still produced large quantities of corn (see my article 'Frumentum', col. 131; add to the sources quoted in that article Ael. Aristides, Εἰς Ῥώμην (*Or.* xxvi, ed. Keil), § 13; the mosaic of Ostia with the personifications of the four corn-producing provinces, Spain, Sicily, Africa, Egypt; see G. Calza, *Bull. Com.* 1912, pp. 103 ff. (according to the competent judgement of M. Blake, the mosaic belongs to the early 1st cent. A.D.); and for a still later period Cassiod. *Var.* 4. 7). I cannot believe in the theory of the complete exhaustion of the fertile Sicilian soil. As regards labour employed in Sicily, I cannot help thinking that the γεωργοί of Cicero (about 12,000–13,000) were well-to-do landowners who worked their estates and farms in just the same way as the landowners in Italy, i.e. partly by means of slaves, partly through tenants and serfs of the ancient γεωμόροι. On the Κιλλύριοι, serfs of the γεωμόροι in the 5th cent. B.C., J. Beloch, *Griech. Gesch.*, i². 1, p. 305, note 3. On Sardinia and Corsica see E. Pais, *Storia della Sardegna*, &c., i and ii (1923).

[28] See note 19.

[29] T. Frank, *Economic History*², pp. 324 ff.

[30] J. Kromayer, in *Neue Jahrb. kl. Alt.* 17, 1914, pp. 157 ff.

³¹ E. Kornemann, 'Colonia', Pauly–Wissowa, iv, col. 575; E. Pais, 'Serie cronologica delle colonie romane e latine dall'età regia fino all'impero', *Mem. Acc. Lincei*, Ser. v, vol. 17, fasc. 8 (1924); Th. Mommsen, 'Zum römischen Bodenrecht', *Hist. Schr.* ii, p. 87; H. Nissen, *Ital. Landeskunde*, ii, pp. 27 ff. and 32 ff. On the military colonies of the Roman emperors from Augustus to Trajan, see Ritterling in Pauly–Wissowa, xii, cols. 1213 ff. As early as 189 B.C. and 181 B.C., when the colonies of Bononia and Aquileia were created, the lots assigned to the colonists ran from 50 *iugera* to 140, almost a *centuria* (H. Nissen, op. cit., ii, pp. 230 and 264). It is hard to suppose that plots of this size could have been cultivated by one family. Probably, therefore, the Roman colonists were landowners, who resided in the cities and cultivated the land either through slaves or through tenants. Under these conditions it is easy to understand how Aquileia became from the very beginning a rich town of well-to-do landowners before she developed into a commercial city.

³² W. Heitland (see note 19) does not believe in a large emigration of Italian peasants to the provinces. His reason is that there were no peasants in Italy in the 1st cent. B.C. But there is no doubt that many parts of Italy in the 1st cent. B.C. and later were still lands of peasants and some of them very poor peasants, tenants of large landed proprietors. I have already quoted the evidence on the large numbers of *coloni* in Central Italy who lived on the estates of the Roman magnates of the 1st cent. B.C. In Northern Italy the peasantry consisted of the remnants of the Celtic population and of the inhabitants of the 'attributed' territories (see Chap. VI). We have, of course, no evidence to show that this class of Italians emigrated to the provinces as well as the well-to-do class of city *bourgeoisie*. I cannot but think, however, that the violent convulsions of Italy in the 1st cent. and the repeated redistributions of land (the territories of whole cities were given to the veterans by Augustus after Philippi) affected not only the city *bourgeoisie* but also the small landowners, both independent peasants and tenants. Without such an assumption we could not explain the complete romanization of Southern Gaul, Southern Spain, and some parts of Africa. And who were the colonists that were settled in Macedonia by Augustus (Cass. Dio, 51. 4)? All of them well-to-do landowners? It is true that, like so many other points in ancient history, the existence of such an emigration cannot be strictly proved. But Heitland himself, in combating my hypothesis, has collected good evidence in its support; cf. his *Agricola*, p. 274 (with an inadequate note by Reid on the cities of Africa). I regret that even Kubitschek, in dealing with the double communities of Africa (Roman citizens and natives) in his valuable article on the cities of Palestine, did not take into consideration the whole of the available material ('Zur Geschichte von Städten des römischen Kaiserreiches', *Sitzb. Wien. Akad.* 177, 1916, 4, pp. 97 ff.). Cf. R. Cagnat, 'L'Annone d'Afrique', *Mém. de l'Ac. d. Inscr.* 40, 1916, p. 258; cf. Chap. VII, note 71. On the Gracchan colony in Carthage, C. Cichorius, *Römische Studien* (1922), pp. 113 ff. It seems, judging from the examples adduced by Kubitschek, as if the system of double communities was applied by the Romans exclusively to some ancient Phoenician cities both in Africa and in Phoenicia (the double community of Ascalon).

³³ I may confine myself to these brief remarks on the commerce, banking, and industry of the ancient world in the 1st cent. B.C., since this topic forms the main subject of Frank's book, *Economic History*², pp. 219 ff. (Industry at the end of the Republic), pp. 275 ff. (Capital), pp. 298 ff. (Commerce), and has also been treated with competence and learning by H. Gummerus, 'Industrie und Handel', Pauly–Wissowa, ix. 2, cols. 1444 ff.; cf. R. Scalais, 'Le Développement du commerce de l'Italie rom. entre la première guerre punique et la deuxième', *Mus. Belge*, 32, 1928, pp. 187 ff. On the labour employed in the Arretine potteries cf. M. E. Park, *The Plebs in Cicero's Days* (Bryn Mawr College, 1918). Interesting evidence testifying to a large use of free

labour in public works is furnished by the important inscriptions dealing with the organization of labour for the regulation of the river Athesis (Adige) after the battle of Actium. The men employed may have been some of the veterans of Augustus' army and the measure one of the ways of occupying this unruly element while Augustus was looking for lands to be given them (*CIL* v. 2603, and F. Barnabei in *Not. d. Scavi*, 1915, p. 139=*L'An. ép.* 1916, 60). Attention may be drawn to an important inscription of Delos, studied by E. Cuq, *BCH* 46, 1922, pp. 198 ff.; cf. Durrbach, *Choix*, 163, cf. 165, which shows how some Roman leaders (Gabinius and probably behind him Pompey) tried to restore the prosperity of Delos after Pompey's war against the pirates (58 B.C.) [=*SEG* i. 335=*Inscr. Délos*, 1511]. It is well known that the growing prosperity of Italy, especially South Italy, and the corresponding growth of the beautiful harbour of Puteoli prevented Delos from regaining even a small part of her former importance and concentrated world commerce to a large extent (in competition with Alexandria) in Puteoli: see Ch. Dubois, *Pouzzoles antique* (1907); R. Cagnat, 'Le Commerce et la propagation des religions dans le monde romain', *Conférences faites au Musée Guimet*, 31, 1909, pp. 131 ff. (on Delos, Puteoli, and Rome); cf. K. Lehmann-Hartleben, 'Die antiken Hafenanlagen des Mittelmeers', *Klio*, Beiheft 14, 1923, pp. 152 ff. (Delos), pp. 163 ff. (Puteoli). It is also interesting to follow the development of Roman banking on Hellenistic, especially Athenian, Rhodian, and Delian models: see R. Herzog, *Aus der Geschichte des Bankwesens im Altertum. Tesserae nummulariae* (1919) (cf. M. Cary, *JRS* 13, 1923, pp. 110 ff.; J. Babelon, *Aréthuse* 5, 1928, pp. 6 ff.); F. Pringsheim, 'Zum römischen Bankwesen', *Vierteljahresschrift f. Soz.- u. Wirtschaftsg.* 15, 1919, pp. 513 ff.; B. Laum, Pauly–Wissowa, Suppl. iv, cols. 72 ff.; cf. B. Salin, *Schmollers Jahrb.* 45, 1921, pp. 196 ff.; E. Ziebarth, *Beiträge zur Gesch. d. Seeraubes*, &c. (1929), pp. 85 f.

11. *Augustus and the Policy of Restoration and Reconstruction*

1 The best summary of the state of the controversy and a good bibliography are given by E. Kornemann, 'Die römische Kaiserzeit', in Gercke and Norden, *Einleitung in die Altertumswissenschaft*, iii (1912, 2nd ed. 1914) [3rd ed. 1933], pp. 266 ff. ('Republik und Monarchie'); and by E. Schönbauer, 'Untersuchungen zur röm. Staats- und Wirtschaftsrecht, I, Wesen u. Ursprung d. röm. Prinzipats', *Zeitschr. d. Sav.-Stif.* 47, 1927, pp. 264 ff. In the article of K. Fitzler and O. Seeck on Augustus, Pauly–Wissowa, x, cols. 275 ff., the controversy is not even mentioned and the bibliography is utterly antiquated. In the article of Schönbauer the reader will find a good exposition (cf. also O. Plasberg, *Cicero in seinen Werke u. Briefen* (1926), pp. 135 ff.) of the state of the question concerning the influence exercised on Augustus by the theories developed by Cicero regarding the *princeps* (or *rector*) in the *De Republica*, and also a good analysis (with bibliography) of the concept of *auctoritas* employed by Augustus himself to define his position in the Roman state (*Res. Gest.* chap. 34); cf. W. M. Ramsay and A. von Premerstein, 'Monumentum Ancyranum', *Klio*, Beiheft 19, 1927. I am glad to notice that the views of Schönbauer regarding the juridical character of the principate of Augustus agree with those set out by me in the text of this chapter. I believe, like him, that the Augustan principate was a new form of government accepted with tacit consent by the great mass of the population of the Empire and, in particular, by Roman citizens. On Augustus and his government see, apart from the writings of Schönbauer, and E. Kornemann's *Mausoleum und Tatenbericht des Augustus* (1921): H. Dessau, *Gesch. der röm. Kaiserzeit*, i (1924); T. Rice Holmes, *The Architect of the Roman Empire* (1928); D. McFayden, *The History of the Title Imperator* (1920); id. *The Rise of the Princeps' Jurisdiction within the City of Rome* (Washington Univ. 86, 10), pp. 181 ff.; id. 'The Princeps and the Senatorial Provinces', *Class. Phil.* 16, 1921, pp. 34 ff.; H. Willrich, 'Augustus bei

Tacitus', *Hermes*, 42, 1927, pp. 54 ff.; M. Gottschald, *Augustus und seine Zeit* (1927). It should be pointed out that the old controversy about the *maius imperium* of Augustus in senatorial provinces, through which the theory of the 'diarchy' was definitely put on one side, has been resolved by one of the edicts found at Cyrene (cf. notes 4, 6, and 8 of the present chapter: A. von Premerstein, *Zeitschr. d. Sav.-St.* 48, 1928, p. 435). It may be added that new and important information, useful for a better comprehension of Augustus, has been brought to light by the complete excavation of his mausoleum. The important group of inscriptions found there have not yet been published: an interesting preliminary notice is given by A. Munzo and A. M. Colini, *Il Mausoleo di Augusto* (1930) [cf. *L'An. ép.* 1928, 88; G. Lugli, *I monumenti antichi*, iii (1938), pp. 206 ff., fig. 45].

² All the statements on the army of the Augustan period are conjectural. We are fairly familiar with its organization, but we are ill informed on the social aspect of the imperial guard, the legions, the auxiliary troops, the fleet, and the police force. What we need to know is not only the system of recruitment of the Roman army but also the social standing of the soldiers of Augustus. The masterly treatment of the problem of recruitment by Th. Mommsen ('Die Conscriptionsordnung der römischen Kaiserzeit', *Hermes*, 19, 1884, pp. 1–79; 210–34; *Ges. Schr.* vi, pp. 20 ff.) became classical, and his results are accepted by all the scholars who have recently dealt with the same subject (a good bibliography in W. Liebenam's article, Pauly–Wissowa, v, cols. 615 ff.; cf. R. Cagnat in Daremberg–Saglio, *Dict. d. ant.* ii. 1, pp. 217 ff.; A. von Domaszewski, *Gesch. d. röm. Kaiser*, i, pp. 170 ff.; id. 'Die Rangordnung des römischen Heeres', *Bonn. Jahrb.* 117, 1908, pp. 192 ff.; Ritterling, Pauly–Wissowa, xii, cols. 1213 f., s.v. 'Legio'; H. M. D. Parker, *The Roman Legions* (1928), pp. 169 ff.). New material is contributed by R. Cagnat, *L'Armée romaine d'Afrique²* (1912–13), pp. 287 ff.; J. Lesquier, *L'Armée romaine d'Égypte* (1918), pp. 203 ff. The only scholar who has expressed views differing from those of Mommsen is O. Seeck, *Rh. Mus.* 48, 1893, pp. 616 ff. His article, however, is very rarely quoted and has never been used. For the time of Augustus our information is unfortunately very scanty; but it is probable that before 43 B.C. the legions of the Western armies were recruited almost exclusively among the Roman citizens of Italy, Narbonese Gaul, and Baetica, while the eastern armies included, alongside Roman citizens of the western provinces, numerous Galatians, and a certain number of Cappadocians. The place occupied by the Galatians is explained undoubtedly partly by the tradition which originated with Antony, and partly by their good quality as troops. We may also suppose that Augustus and his successors wished to romanize those parts of Asia Minor, the population of which was of Western origin, and therefore more susceptible to romanizing influences than the hellenized parts of that region. We must not forget that Galatia and Cappadocia were very important provinces from the military point of view, and that it was therefore desirable to have there a number of romanized veterans of local extraction. Compare the creation of military colonies in Asia Minor by Augustus (e.g. Pisidian Antioch). On the soldiers of oriental origin in the armies of Antony and Augustus see now the collection of the evidence in O. Cuntz, 'Legionäre des Antonius u. Augustus aus dem Orient', *Oest. Jahresh.* 25, 1929, pp. 20 ff. Cuntz has collected the names of the oriental veterans which appear in the oldest inscriptions of Illyricum, Macedonia, Asia Minor, and Egypt, and reaches the conclusion that Augustus largely used recruits raised in Asia Minor, Egypt, and Macedonia for the eastern legions. Still more difficult is the question of the social *milieu* to which the recruits belonged. The systematic organization by Augustus of the young generation of Roman freeborn citizens both in Rome and in the Italian cities, of which I shall speak later (see note 5), and the fact that it seems to have been confined in the time of Augustus to Italy and perhaps to the provincial

cities of *cives Romani* only, show how important Augustus deemed it to educate the youth of Italy in a military, religious, and loyal spirit. His object certainly was to fill up with these wholly reliable elements his reformed permanent army, including both the corps of officers and the mass of common soldiers. It must be pointed out that the majority of soldiers recruited in Italy come from the Roman colonies of Western Italy, and the same may be said of Narbonese Gaul and Spain (see the sketch drawn from the material collected by Ritterling, op. cit., in H. M. D. Parker, *The Roman Legions* (1928), pp. 169 ff.). I am therefore disposed to believe that the ideal of Augustus was not an army of proletarians but an army based on the propertied classes of the cities of *cives Romani*. It is hardly credible, too, that the soldiers of the *auxilia* were recruited from the lower classes of the population of the Roman provinces, the *peregrini*. Here, however, all is darkness.

³ I have explained my views on this subject in a short article 'Augustus' in the *University of Wisconsin Studies in Language and Literature*, no. 15, 1922, pp. 134 ff.; cf. *Röm. Mitt.* 38–39, 1923–4, pp. 281 ff., and my book *Mystic Italy* (1928), from which I here reproduce one passage. It is useless to quote the immense bibliography on the subject of the attitude of the poets of the Augustan age towards the policy of Augustus, which may be easily consulted in the newest editions of the Histories of Roman Literature by Teuffel and by Schanz. Cf. T. Frank, *Vergil. A biography* (1922), pp. 174 ff.; K. Allen, 'The Fasti of Ovid and the Augustan Propaganda', *AJP* 43, 1922, pp. 250 ff. On the religious conditions of the time of Augustus see now the excellent remarks of W. Weber, 'Der Prophet und sein Gott', *Beihefte zum alten Orient*, no. 3, 1925, pp. 28 ff.; cf. Ed. Norden, *Die Geburt des Kindes* (1924), and F. Boll, 'Sulla quarta ecloga di Virgilio', *Memorie d. R. Acc. di Bologna*, Sc. Mor., ser. ii, vols. 5–7, 1923, pp. 1 ff.; J. Carcopino, *Virgile et le mystère de la IVᵉ églogue* (1930). On the name Augustus see the works on the concept of *auctoritas* in *Res Gestae*, chap. 34 (cf. note 1); cf. G. Hirst, 'The significance of Augustior as applied to Hercules and to Romulus', *AJP* 47, 1926, pp. 347 ff.; K. Scott, 'The identification of Augustus with Romulus-Quirinus', *TAPA* 46, 1925, pp. 86 ff. On the Imperial cult in the time of Augustus see the well-documented book of Lily Ross Taylor, *The Divinity of the Roman Emperors* (1931) (Philol. Monogr. published by Amer. Philol. Assoc., no. 1). On the monuments of art of the Augustan age, see Mrs. A. Strong, *La Scultura romana*, i (1923)–ii (1926); and *Apotheosis and After-Life* (1915); cf. L. R. Taylor, 'The Worship of Augustus in Italy during his Lifetime', *TAPA* 51, 1920, pp. 116 ff., and 'The Altar of Manlius in the Lateran', *Amer. Journ. Arch.* 25, 1921, pp. 387 ff.; Helen Cox Bowerman, *Roman Sacrificial Altars* (Bryn Mawr, 1913), and my article 'Le Gobelet d'argent du trésor de Boscoreale dans la collection de M. le baron E. Rothschild', *Mém. de l'Ac. des Inscr.* 13, 1925; cf. K. Scott, 'Mercur-Augustus u. Horaz C. i, 2', *Hermes*, 63, 1928, pp. 15 ff.; K. Lehmann-Hartleben, 'Der Altar von Bologna', *Röm. Mitt.* 42, 1927, pp. 163 ff.; E. Loewy, 'Zum Augustus von Prima Porta', ibid., pp. 204 ff. (with bibliography of the various interpretations of reliefs on the cuirass on this statue). It would be an attractive and important study to collect and investigate all the monuments of art and of art-industry bearing on the cult of Augustus and his family. Taken together, these monuments represent another unwritten 'Res Gestae Divi Augusti'.

⁴ See the second edict of Cyrene (cf. notes 6 and 8) and the commentary of A. von Premerstein, *Zeitschr. d. Sav.-St.* 48, 1928, pp. 458 ff.; cf. Arangio-Ruiz, *Riv. fil.* 56, 1928, pp. 334 ff. At Cyrene the situation was that some Roman citizens who stated that they knew something 'which concerned the security of the *princeps* and public interest' (line 45: ὁ πρὸς τὴν ἐμὴν σωτηρίαν τά τε δημόσια πράγματα ἀνῆκεν) were imprisoned by the governor and sent to Rome in chains. At Rome the trial was conducted by the emperor in person, who concluded that the men 'knew absolutely nothing and every-

thing they said in the provinces was complete invention, and lies'. They were all sent back to their country, except one who had been accused by a Cyrenaean embassy of having removed a statue of the emperor from a public place. This is all recounted by the emperor in a special edict sent to the city with the purpose of clearing the governor's name. In my opinion this incident must be explained as follows. There was continual disagreement between the Roman citizens and the Greeks of Cyrene; in their anger against the Greeks the Roman citizens went to the governor and accused some of their opponents of conspiracy (apparently in ambiguous terms). Since they thus meddled with matters within the governor's competence, and there was, in addition, a suspicion that they were not themselves wholly innocent of complicity in the affair the governor, in a fit of rage, considered the *delatores* as criminals and sent them to Rome for trial. At the same time, there set out from Cyrene, undoubtedly with the governor's permission, an embassy which laid precise charges against the *delatores*, in Rome. In his judgement the emperor tried to please all parties: the governor, the Roman citizens (who were very dissatisfied with the treatment inflicted on their fellow-citizens), and the Greeks. The event, though of little importance and quite local in its significance, shows how widespread the idea of conspiracies and murder was, and how anxious the government was to be informed in this respect of all such occurrences in the provinces. In addition, it throws considerable light on imperial jurisdiction (see A. von Premerstein, l.c.) and on the history of *crimina maiestatis*; cf. J. Stroux and L. Wenger, 'Die Augustus-Inschrift auf d. Marktpl. von Kyrene', *Bayer. Abh.* xxxiv. 2, 1928, p. 72, n. 2, and W. von Uxkull-Gyllenband, *Gnomon*, 6, 1930, p. 127, cf. p. 125.

5 On the policy of Augustus in regard to the different classes of the population of Italy, see in general L. Friedländer–G. Wissowa, *Darstellungen aus der Sittengeschichte Roms*, 9th ed., i (1919), pp. 114 ff. On the senatorial class, the nobility, see especially M. Gelzer, *Hermes*, 50, 1915, pp. 395 ff.; E. Stein, ibid. 52, 1917, pp. 564 ff.; W. Otto, ibid. 51, 1916, pp. 73 ff.; L. Friedländer, op. cit., p. 115; A. Stein, *Der römische Ritterstand*, pp. 30 and 103; E. Groag, *Strena Buličiana* (1924), pp. 254 ff. Th. A. Abele, *Der Senat unter Augustus* (1907) (*Stud. z. Gesch. u. Kult. d. Alt.* i. 2), deals with the political functions of the senate only. On the political behaviour of the senatorial class under Augustus, G. Boissier, *L'Opposition sous les Césars*; E. Grimm, *Investigations into the History of the Development of the Imperial Power*. Vol. i, *The Roman Imperial Power from Augustus to Nero* (St. Petersburg, 1900) (in Russian). On the equestrian class, L. Friedländer–G. Wissowa, op. cit. i, pp. 145 ff.; A. Stein, *Der römische Ritterstand* (1927). On the 'third' class, ibid., pp. 158 ff. On the organization of the younger generation in Rome and in the Italian cities see my article 'Römische Bleitesserae', *Klio*, Beiheft 3, 1905; cf. the article of C. Jullian, 'Juvenes', in Daremberg and Saglio, iii. 1, pp. 782 ff., and of Ziebarth in Pauly–Wissowa, x. 2, cols. 1357 f. Fresh evidence for Pompeii has been collected by M. Della Corte, *Iuventus* (Arpino, 1924), cf. A. Rosenberg, *Der Staat der alten Italiker* (1913), pp. 93 ff., and *Hermes*, 49, 1914, pp. 267 ff.; L. Cesano, *Rassegna Numismatica* (1911), pp. 51 ff.; L. R. Taylor, 'Severi', *JRS* 14, 1924, pp. 158 ff.; A. Stein, *Der römische Ritterstand*, pp. 82 ff. On the *Iuvenes* in Africa, S. Gsell, *Inscriptions latines d'Algérie*, i. 3079 (note). On the *Iuventus Manliensium* at Virunum (Noricum), R. Egger, *Führer durch die Antikensammlung des Landesmuseum in Klagenfurt* (1921), p. 24, and in *Oest. Jahresh.* 18, 1915, p. 115. We may also note a passage in Philo, *Leg. ad G.* 30, where the author evidently has in mind the military preparation of the noble Roman youth: οὐδὲ ἤσκητό πω ταῖς ὁπλομαχίαις, αἱ μελέται καὶ προγυμνάσματα παίδων ἐφ' ἡγεμονίᾳ τρεφομένων εἰσὶ διὰ τοὺς ἐνισταμένους πολέμους.

6 E. Kornemann in Pauly–Wissowa, Suppl. i, col. 315, ll. 50 ff.; cf. A. von Premerstein, 'Ius Italicum', ibid. x. 1, col. 1239. In the third edict of Cyrene (see the bibliography in note 8) Augustus emphasizes the duty of Roman citizens of Greek origin in

Cyrene to submit, in the interests of the Greek communities (cf. p. 310/11), to the burden of the municipal 'liturgies' (by this he meant both the *munera personalia* and the *munera patrimonii*, including the municipal taxes). This distinction among the Roman citizens of Cyrene, according to whether they are of Italian or Greek extraction, is very significant for the policy of Augustus. It seems that in the time of Augustus there were in many, if not all, Greek communities of the East, numerous Roman citizens of Greek origin. No doubt they had mostly obtained the citizenship during the civil wars between Pompey, Caesar, Antony, and Augustus himself (A. von Premerstein, *Zeitschr. d. Sav.-St.* 48, 1928, p. 472, and my article 'Caesar and the south of Russia', *JRS* 7, 1917, pp. 27 ff.). As these new citizens were undoubtedly the most conspicuous and wealthy members of their communities, the question of their *immunitas* was of great importance for the Greek cities. This is the reason why both Caesar (*IG* xii. 2. 35, cf. Rostovtzeff, l.c., p. 32), and also Augustus in this edict, instruct the Roman citizens of Mytilene and Cyrene respectively, to undertake their share of the municipal liturgies. While Caesar, however, evidently extends his provision to all Roman citizens, Augustus, following his general policy, distinguishes between Italians and Greeks, and thus creates a class of Roman citizen in the east possessing minor rights. Naturally the rule did not apply to those who had received the *immunitas* as a personal privilege (l. 59: οἷς ἀνεισφορία ὁμοῦ σὺν τῆι πολιτήιαι δέδοται). Cf. Chap. III, note 8, and J. Stroux and L. Wenger, op. cit., pp. 58 f.

⁷ In the reign of Augustus began the development which led towards the suppression of the system of tax-farming. It is true that the *publicani* continued to exist under Augustus in almost every branch of tax-collection. But there is some evidence which indicates that the way towards the gradual transformation of the tax-farming system was first shown by Augustus: see my *Gesch. d. Staatspacht* (1902) (*Philol.*, Suppl. ix. 3), pp. 378 ff.

⁸ New evidence on the way in which Augustus (through the senate) set about the difficult problem of the administration of justice in the mismanaged provinces has been unexpectedly provided by the last of the five edicts of the emperor (with attached *senatusconsultum*) [*SEG* ix. 8 = Riccobono, *FIRA*² 68], which were published by the city of Cyrene and found there. The *S.C.*, dated 4 B.C., contains in essentials the provisions proposed to the senate by Augustus and by his council (Συμβούλιον, *consilium*). It consists of a new and more effective regulation of the *de repetundis* procedure. I cannot examine this document in detail here (see the excellent studies—with translation and commentary—by A. von Premerstein, *Zeitschr. d. Sav.-St.* 48, 1928, pp. 478 ff., and J. Stroux and L. Wenger, 'Die Augustus-Inschr. auf d. Marktpl. von Kyrene', *Bayer. Abh.* xxxiv. 2,1928, pp. 94 ff.; cf. J. G. C. Anderson, *JRS* 17, 1927, pp. 33 ff.; G. Klaffenbach, *Hermes*, 63, 1928, pp. 368 ff., E. Malcovati, *Caesaris Augusti operum fragmenta³* (1948), pp. 59 ff.; V. Arangio-Ruiz, 'L'Editto di Augusto a Cirene', *Riv. fil.* 56, 1928, pp. 321 ff.; W. von Uxkull-Gyllenband, *Gnomon*, 6, 1930, pp. 121 ff. (Uxkull-Gyllenband tries to show that by the fourth edict Augustus intended to abolish the autonomous jurisdiction of the cities and to introduce Roman law into the provinces in the greatest possible degree); A. von Premerstein, *Zeitschr. d. Sav.-St.* 51, 1931, pp. 431 ff.). I must content myself with quoting the last sentences of the imperial edict, lines 79 ff.: ἐξ οὗ δῆλον ἔσται πᾶσιν | τοῖς τὰς ἐπαρχήας κατοικοῦσιν ὅσην φροντίδα ποιούμε|θα ἐγώ τε καὶ ἡ σύνκλητος τοῦ μηδένα τῶν ἡμῖν ὑποτασ⟨σ⟩ο|μένων παρὰ τὸ προσῆκόν τι πάσχιν ἢ εἰσπράτ⟨τ⟩εσθαι.

⁹ On the procurators of Augustus, O. Hirschfeld, *Die kaiserlichen Verwaltungsbeamten* (2nd ed. 1905); H. Mattingly, *The Imperial Civil Service of Rome* (1910); W. T. Arnold, *Roman Provincial Administration* (3rd ed. 1914).

¹⁰ See my *Studien z. Gesch. röm. Kol.* (1910), p. 289, note 1. Unfortunately the full evidence on this point has never been collected. The book of F. F. Abbott and A. C. Johnson, *Municipal Administration in the Roman Empire* (1926), does not contain a chapter on the urbanization of the empire. A good sketch of the Roman provinces under Augustus and of the progress made in urbanization under his government is to be found in T. Frank, *Economic History²*, ch. xviii, pp. 347 ff. I believe, however, that Frank attributes too much importance to Caesar's 'paternalistic' tendencies in regard to the economic and social problems of the empire, and too little, on the other hand, to the policy of *laissez-faire* pursued by Augustus. Even without offering rewards to those who took up residence in a city, urban life could be made more comfortable and lucrative. That is what Augustus did throughout the Empire, and it is this which led the population of the provinces to create new centres of urban life. See also Dessau, *Gesch. d. röm. Kaiserzeit*, ii. 2 (1930).

¹¹ It is unnecessary to cite the well-known works on the reorganization of Egypt by Augustus. It may suffice to mention L. Mitteis and U. Wilcken, *Grundzüge und Chrestomathie der Papyruskunde* (1912); W. Schubart, *Einführung in die Papyruskunde* (1918); id. *Ägypten von Alexander dem Großen bis Mohammed* (1922), and especially A. Stein, *Untersuchungen zur Geschichte und Verwaltung Aegyptens unter römischer Herrschaft* (1915); J. Grafton Milne, *History of Egypt under Roman Rule³* (1924); B. A. van Groningen, 'L'Égypte et l'empire', *Aegyptus*, 7, 1926, pp. 189 ff.; J. G. Milne, 'The Ruin of Egypt by Roman Mismanagement', *JRS* 17, 1927, pp. 1 ff.; M. A. Levi, 'L'Esclusione dei senatori dall'Egitto augusteo', *Aegyptus*, 5, 1924, pp. 231 ff.; M. Rostovtzeff, 'Roman Exploitation of Egypt in the First Century A.D.', *Journ. of Econ. and Business Hist.* 1, 1929, pp. 337 ff.; Dessau, *Gesch. d. röm. Kaiserzeit*, ii. 2 (1930), pp. 635 ff. Interesting fresh evidence on the question of the history of the βουλή of Alexandria is contained in the papyrus published by M. Norsa and G. Vitelli, 'Da papiri greci d. Società Italiana', *Bull. Soc. arch. Alex.* 25, 1930, pp. 9 ff., and restudied by Wilcken, *Arch. f. Papyr.* 9, pp. 523 ff.: republished as *PSI* 1160 [=*SB* 7748 = Musurillo, *Acts of the Pagan Martyrs*, no. 1]. The fragment raises many problems which cannot be discussed here. According to the editors, with whom Wilcken agrees, the fragment is the last part of a treaty between Augustus and an Alexandrian embassy, shortly before 30 B.C., that is, immediately after the capture of Alexandria. The embassy had come to request the preservation or restoration of the βουλή. The question is: have we here a fragment of a genuine document? In favour of this interpretation is the double numeration of the pages, which would suggest that we have a τόμος συγκολλήσιμος, and the form of the document, which is that of a ὑπομνηματισμός. Against it is the language of the fragment, which contains phrases inappropriate in official speech, but unobjectionable in common language (ἐπίτροπος, instead of ἔπαρχος, which, as Wilcken has emphasized, occurs also in Philo; also δεσπότα). One might therefore think of a literary product akin to the so-called *Acts of the Alexandrian Martyrs*, that is, a political pamphlet on the βουλή. I must confess my uncertainty between these two alternatives. One thing, however, seems to me unlikely, namely, that the document (if it be a document) belongs to 30 B.C. The arguments of the orator would hardly have been comprehensible to Augustus in 30 B.C. The main problems of Alexandrian life here discussed only became burning questions under Roman rule: the questions of maintaining the purity of the citizenship, of the violence of officials—the Ἴδιος λόγος and the πράκτορες—and of the composition of embassies. I think it very doubtful whether all these problems were already acute in the late Ptolemaic period, but we know that they were very acute under Roman rule (in particular the question of the violence of officials became very serious after the confiscations ordered by Augustus). If the fragment is really an official document, granted that the writing does not permit a later date, I should be

inclined to assign the document to the last years of the government of Augustus. The fact that the emperor is called Καῖσαρ is an argument in favour of the reign of Augustus, but not of a date earlier than 27 B.C., since Augustus always bore that title in Egypt. It is true that the Alexandrians had recourse to Augustus on numerous occasions on account of the βουλή, and the audiences must have been held in Rome. Unfortunately I cannot enter into all the details of the problem here; cf. G. de Sanctis, 'La Bule degli Alessandrini', *Atti d. r. Accad. d. Scienze di Torino,* 61, 1930, pp. 513 ff.; J. H. Oliver, 'The βουλή Papyrus', *Aegyptus,* 11, 1931, pp. 161 ff.; W. Schubart, 'Die βουλή von Alexandria', *Bull. Inst. franç. d'arch. or.* 30, 1930, pp. 407 ff.; E. Breccia, *Bull. Soc. arch. Alex.* 26, 1931, pp. 352 ff., and the reply of M. Norsa and G. Vitelli to these articles, 'Sul papiro delle βουλή d'Alessandria', ibid. 27, 1932, pp. 1 ff.

¹² On the reorganization of Gaul by Augustus, O. Hirschfeld, 'Die Organisation der drei Gallien durch Augustus', *Klio,* 8, 1908, pp. 464 ff. (*Kl. Schr.* pp. 112 ff.). According to Hirschfeld, the reform of Augustus legalized the ancient city-less condition of the Gallic tribes. This statement of Hirschfeld led Kornemann to an unconvincing parallel between Gaul and Egypt (*Klio,* 11, 1911, p. 390, and *Die röm. Kaiserzeit,* pp. 275 f.). There is no doubt that Hirschfeld exaggerated the rural character of the Gallic *civitates*: the cities began to grow rapidly in Gaul immediately after the reorganization of the country by Augustus, see C. Jullian, *Hist. de la Gaule,* iv (1914), pp. 67 ff. and 316 ff. Cf. H. Dessau, *Gesch. d. röm. Kaiserzeit,* i, pp. 480 ff.; On Spain, A. Schulten in Pauly–Wissowa, viii, cols. 2037 f.; J. J. Nostrand, *The Reorganization of Spain by Augustus* (1916); R. Knox McElderry, *JRS* 8, 1918, pp. 53 ff.; E. Albertini, *Les Divisions administratives de l'Espagne romaine* (1923). On Africa, A. Schulten, *Das römische Afrika* (1899). Cf. Chaps. VI and VII. It seems to me that Frank (*Econ. Hist.²,* especially pp. 368 ff.) follows Hirschfeld a little too closely, at least as far as Gaul is concerned, and does not pay sufficient attention to the new and ever-increasing material accumulating in the French museums. I do not know of any basis for his contention that 'on the whole Celtic Gaul remained under Augustus, and long after, a region of drinking, hunting, and jousting barbarian lords, and their hard-working farm folk' (p. 370). I know of no gravestone on which such a barbaric magnate is represented, while, on the other hand, funerary monuments (partly of the 1st cent. A.D.) which show us the townsfolk working hard and enjoying prosperity form a substantial part of the contents of French museums. Is this pure chance?

¹³ As regards foreign policy, the article of K. Fitzler and O. Seeck in Pauly–Wissowa gives a good and careful survey of all the events of Augustus' rule. Cf. H. Dessau, *Gesch. d. röm. Kaiserzeit,* i, pp. 360 ff.; Ritterling in Pauly–Wissowa, xii, cols. 1213 ff.

¹⁴ On the wars in Africa see R. Cagnat, *L'Armée romaine d'Afrique²,* pp. 4 ff.; id. 'Comment les Romains se rendirent maîtres de toute l'Afrique du Nord', *Ann. du Musée Guimet,* 38, 1912, pp. 155 ff. On the results of the Arabian war see my article in *Arch. f. Papyr.* 4, pp. 306 ff. Cf. the articles of Kornemann and Schur quoted in Chap. III, notes 16 and 17; and O. Cuntz, *Oest. Jahresh.* 25, 1929, pp. 80 ff.

¹⁵ On the private estates in Egypt see Chap. VII, note 44. On the veterans as farmers, W. Westermann, 'An Egyptian Farmer', *Wisconsin Studies in Language and Literature,* no. 3, pp. 171 ff.; cf. *A Large Estate in Egypt,* p. 13, note 27; Bror Olsson, *Papyrusbriefe aus der frühesten Kaiserzeit* (1925).

¹⁶ See my articles 'Fiscus' in De Ruggiero, *Dizionario epigrafico,* and in Pauly–Wissowa. For the Hellenistic parallels see my article on Pergamon in *Anatolian Studies presented to Sir William Ramsay* (Manchester, 1923). Cf. A. von Premerstein, *Oest. Jahresh.* 15, 1912, pp. 200 f.; F. F. Abbott and A. C. Johnson, *Municipal Administration,*

pp. 117 ff. The question of the Roman tax-system in the provinces must be made the object of a particular study. I fear that it is a simplification to emphasize the contrast between Egypt and the other provinces in respect of assessment and collection of the land-tax. Hyginus (Lachmann, *Grom. veteres*, p. 205), in his general description of the several forms of land-tax on country estates, describes a very complicated and individual assessment. On the municipal taxes see Chap. V, note 7. The expenditure of Augustus for state purposes from his private purse is emphasized as the main point in his 'economic' policy by M. P. Nilsson, 'Den ekonomiska Grundvalen för Augustus principat', *Eranos*, 12, 1912, pp. 95 ff.; cf. F. Petri, 'Die Wohlfartspflege des Augustus', *Neue Jahrb. f. Wiss. u. Jug.* 3, 1927, pp. 286 ff. U. Wilcken, 'Zu den Impensae der Res gestae divi Augusti', *Sitzb. Berl. Akad.* 27, 1931, believes that all the 'impensae' mentioned in the *Res Gestae* were made from the *privatum* and the *patrimonium* of Augustus, without touching the funds of the *fiscus*.

[17] The evidence on the fortunes of the members of the family of Augustus and of his friends and associates has never been collected and investigated. Some hints may be found in O. Hirschfeld, 'Der Grundbesitz der römischen Kaiser', *Klio*, 2, 1902, pp. 45–72, 284–315 (*Kl. Schr.*, pp. 576 ff.), and in L. Friedländer–G. Wissowa, *Sitteng. Roms* (9th ed. 1920), i, pp. 121 ff. On the fortune of Maecenas, P. S. Frandsen, *C. Cilnius Maecenas* (Altona, 1842), p. 97; cf. on his Egyptian estates the works quoted in Chap. VII, note 45. On the large estates of Agrippa see Dio, liv, 29; Hor. *Epist.* i. 12 (extensive cattle-breeding in Sicily); I. Greaves, *Essays on the History of Roman Land-tenure*, i, pp. 143 ff. (in Russian). On C. Iulius Eurycles, one of the minor partisans of Augustus, and the uncrowned king of Laconia, see E. Kjellberg, 'C. Iulius Eurykles', *Klio*, 17, 1920, pp. 441 ff.; L. R. Taylor and A. B. West, *Corinth*, viii. 2, nos. 67, 68, pp. 42 ff.; cf. the inscriptions of Gythion mentioned above, Chap. I, note 12. When Horace speaks of large fortunes, he mentions almost exclusively the big estates in Italy and in the provinces (Sardinia, Sicily, Africa, Gaul), specifying the types of crops which were characteristic of each: *Carm.* i. 31. 3 ff.; iii. 16. 25 ff.; i. 1. 9; ii. 16. 33; *Epod.* 1. 25; 4. 13 ff.

[18] On Trimalchio, his fortune and his economic life, see the excellent article of I. Greaves, 'Essays on the History of Roman Land-tenure. The Large House-economy in the Time of the Highest Economic Bloom of the Roman World. The Data of Petronius on the Agrarian History of the 1st cent. A.D.', *Journ. of the Min. of Publ. Educ.*, 361, 1905, pp. 42 ff. (in Russian); S. Dill, *Roman Society from Nero to Marcus Aurelius* (1921), pp. 128 ff., and the notes of P. Friedländer to the text of Petronius in his edition of the *Cena Trimalchionis*. Trimalchio certainly began his career in the Augustan period. Another man of the same type is the freedman owner of 1,000 *iugera* of land in the ager Falernus, Hor. *Epod.* 4. 13 ff. Combination of sea commerce and land-tenure as the two main sources of wealth in Hor. *Carm.* i. 31. 3 ff.: 'non opimae | Sardiniae segetes feraces, | non aestuosae grata Calabriae | armenta, non aurum aut ebur Indicum, | non rura quae Liris quieta | mordet aqua taciturnus amnis. | premant Calenam falce quibus dedit | fortuna vitem, dives ut aureis | mercator exsiccet culullis | vina Syra reparata merce. |' The emphasis laid on these two chief sources of wealth is typical of the poets of the Augustan age (see E. H. Brewster, *Roman Craftsmen and Tradesmen of the Early Roman Empire* (1917), pp. 30 ff.). In regard to the character of commerce in the Augustan age, it is important to emphasize the great part which Italy and Italian merchants played at this time in the commercial life of the East: see the inscription of Puteoli set up in honour of two Calpurnii by the 'mercatores qui Alexandr[iai] Asiai Syriai negotiantu(r)' (*CIL* x. 1797). The Calpurnii were certainly rich merchants whose influence predominated in the Oriental markets. One of them was the first to build a temple to Augustus in Puteoli (*CIL* x. 1613). The same relations with the East

(under Tiberius) are indicated by the erection by the Augustales (i.e. wealthy freedmen) of Puteoli of a copy or imitation of the great monument which was set up at Rome to Tiberius by the fourteen cities of Asia Minor after the terrible earthquakes of A.D. 17, 23, and 29 (*CIL* x. 1624). There is no doubt that the action of the Augustales was due partly to the fact that they were of Asiatic origin, and still more to their interest in the prosperity of the Asiatic cities, i.e. in the development of their commerce with Asia Minor: see Ch. Dubois, *Pouzzoles antique* (*Bibl. des Éc.* 98, 1907), p. 77 and p. 104; V. Pârvan, *Die Nationalität der römischen Kaufleute im römischen Kaiserreiche* (1909), p. 12; U. E. Paoli, 'Grossi e piccoli commercianti nelle liriche di Orazio', *Riv. fil.* 52, 1924, pp. 45 ff. Compare the Roman *negotiatores* of Gythion in Laconia in the time of Tiberius, referred to in the inscription mentioned in Chap. I, note 12, and the influential *conventus c. R. qui in Asia negotiantur*, under Claudius (A.D. 43–44), J. Keil, *Forsch. Eph.* iii, p. 110, 19 [=*L'An. ép.* 1924, 69].

19 On Puteoli see note 18. On Pompeii, the material collected by M. Della Corte, 'Le Case ed i abitanti di Pompei' in *Neapolis* and in the *Riv. Indo-Greco-Italica* (Napoli), vols. 1–7, 1917–23; cf. Zottoli, 'Publio Paquio Proculo panettiere', *Rend. Lincei*, 17, 1908, pp. 555 ff. (see, however, M. Della Corte, *JRS* 16, 1926, pp. 145 ff., who has shown that P. Paquius Proculus was in fact not a baker); M. Della Corte, 'Fullones', *Volume in onore di Mons. G. A. Galante* (Napoli, 1920).

20 Some evidence on this point will be found in my article 'Caesar and the South of Russia', *JRS* 7, 1917, p. 36. Cf. the role played in the life of their cities by Aristagoras of Istros, Dittenberger, *Syll.*³ 708, Niceratus of Olbia, ibid. 730 [=*IOSPE* i², 34], and Acornion of Dionysopolis, ibid. 762. To the same time belongs Chaeremon of Nysa, who was able to give to C. Cassius in 88 B.C. a gift of 60,000 *modii* of barley (ibid. 741 [= (ll. 16 ff. only) Welles, *Roy. Cor.* 73/4]) and that of Stratonax of Apollonia, who helped the city of Callatis when it was harried by the barbarians (Kalinka, *Antike Denkmäler.* 94; cf. Crönert, *Oest. Jahresh.* 11, 1908, Beibl., p. 105), and the well-known families of Asia Minor, e.g. those of Pythodorus, Polemon, and Mithradates of Pergamon, and C. Julius Eurycles of Sparta (note 17). More modest was the rich merchant of Leros (Michel, *Recueil*, 372). It would be worth while to collect the evidence on these local magnates of the East of the 1st cent. B.C. and 1st cent. A.D.; cf. my chapter 'Rhodes and Delos', *CAH* viii, pp. 649 ff. [and *Soc. and Econ. Hist. Hell. World*, p. 1527, n. 98].

21 See the general descriptions of Italy in Strabo (book v, cf. iv and vi) and in Pliny (*NH* iii. 5 ff.), and cf. the short description in Pomponius Mela. A careful reading of these sources and especially of the second volume of H. Nissen, *Ital. Landeskunde* (1902), as well as the delightful little book of A. L. Frothingham, *Roman Cities in Italy and Dalmatia* (1910), will enable the reader to realize the accuracy of my statement. By his careful investigation of the existing Roman remains from the architectural point of view, Frothingham has shown how fundamental was the work done in the cities in the Augustan age; cf. T. Ashby, *The Roman Campagna in Classical Times* (1927), p. 44.

22 I. Greaves, *Essays on the History of Roman Land-tenure*, i, pp. 94 ff. On the new excavations on the supposed site of the villa of Horace conducted by the Italian government see G. Lugli, 'La villa sabina di Orazio', *Mon. dei Lincei*, 1927, pp. 457 ff., and his delightful *Guida* (1931). Cf. G. Lafaye's article 'Villa' in Daremberg–Saglio, v, p. 883, note 23; J. Hammer, *Class. Weekly*, 17, 1924, pp. 201 ff.; G. H. Hallam, *Horace at Tibur, and the Sabine Farm*² (1927); and H. Philipp's article 'Sabinum' in Pauly-Wissowa, Zw. R. i, cols. 1590 ff., with the map on col. 2554. On Italian agriculture see R. Billiard, *L'Agriculture dans l'antiquité d'après les Géorgiques de Virgile* (1928), cf. P. d'Hérouville, 'Virgile apiculteur', *Mus. Belge*, 30, 1926, p. 161; 31, 1927, pp. 37 ff.; id. 'Zootechnie virgilienne; Les bovidés', *Rev. de phil.* 1925, pp. 143 ff.

²³ A list of the excavated Campanian *villae rusticae* is given in Chap. I, note 26. Some of these villas certainly belong to the late Republican or the early Augustan age. It is notable that many of them, and particularly the most beautiful ones, were built in the time of Augustus, as is shown by their decoration in the second or third Pompeian style of wall-painting. I would remind the reader of the villa of Agrippa Postumus as one of the best examples. An economic analysis of one of these villas has been given by Frank, *Economic History*², pp. 265 ff.; cf. id., *History of Rome*, pp. 404 ff. Not all the excavated villas, however, belong to the same economic type. Thus far I have noticed three different types of Campanian villas: (1) a combination of a fair, sometimes even luxurious, summer residence and of a real *villa rustica* with rooms appropriated for the agricultural exploitation of a rather large estate. Such are the two best preserved villas of Boscoreale, probably the villa Item, and nos. III, V, and VI of the villas published by Della Corte, as well as the villa of Agrippa Postumus. Some Stabian examples belong to the same type. It must be assumed that the owners of these villas did not live in them but resided in cities, and came to stay in the villas from time to time. The owner of one of them at least (no. V of Della Corte), N. Popidius Florus, was certainly a resident of Pompeii. (2) A real farm-house, modest, spacious, and clean, built for the use of a well-to-do farmer who probably lived in his villa all the year round. To this type belong nos. I and IV of Della Corte and no. XVI of Stabiae. Two of these sold their own wine to the travellers who went to and from Pompeii and Stabiae and to neighbours. In no. I of Della Corte and in no. XVI of Stabiae a large wine-shop (*trattoria*) is connected with the house. (3) A third type is represented by no. II of Della Corte. I agree with him that such a house, with no wall decorations whatever, with small and bare living-rooms, and with large cellars and wine-presses can be explained only as an agricultural factory run by slaves and visited from time to time by the owner. On pl. x of this volume will be found an illustration of one of the modest villas, almost a peasant's house, on pl. viii views of villas which were pure summer resorts, and on pl. xi some agricultural implements which were found in the villas of Boscoreale.

It is worth noting that almost all the villas of which the owners are known, apart from that of Agrippa Postumus, belonged to rich or well-to-do citizens of Pompeii. It seems that the largest part of the territories of Pompeii and Stabiae was owned by citizens of these cities, who resided there and derived their regular income mostly from their wine estates. Another important fact which has been already emphasized by Frank is that all the excavated villas, without exception, were like American farms, i.e. they were not houses of peasants but real agricultural factories, producing wine and oil in bulk for sale. There is no trace of the famous 'house-economy' in them. The volume of their production is illustrated by the large size of the wine-presses and the huge capacity of the court-cellars of most of the Pompeian and Stabian villas. Important testimony is furnished by the *graffiti* discovered in villa no. I of Della Corte (the villa of the rich farmer), *CIL* iv. 6886: 'palos acutos DCCCXL qui non acuti CDLX summa MCCC', and in the villa of Agrippa Postumus, ibid. 6887: 'in acervo magno pali sunt MXXIII', and 6888: 'in ba . . . pali quadri nov(i)' (over this *graffito* is a number, apparently 500); cf. the large mass of *pali* discovered in the villa no. VII of Della Corte, *Not. d. Scavi*, 1923, pp. 271 ff. Such large quantities of stakes testify to quite a large vineyard; cf. H. Gummerus in Pauly–Wissowa, ix. 2, col. 1455, 48.

For a study of the economic life of these villas we have some data which have not been used by my predecessors. (See now the articles by Carrington and Day quoted in Chap. I, note 26, which contain an economic analysis of the Pompeian villas.) In an electoral programme (*CIL* iv. 6672) Casellius is recommended by the *vindemitores*, probably hired helpers at the time of vintage. The kind of labour used by the owners is admirably shown by the plan of the villa of Agrippa Postumus. The back yard was the slave-barrack and the stables. The slaves lived in eighteen small rooms, almost identical with those in the gladiatorial barrack of Pompeii. Near by was the *ergastulum*, the prison-house for the slaves. The iron stocks were found in this room, not in use at the time of the catastrophe. The large stables for horses were placed between the living-quarters of the slaves and the prison. We have seen that the managers of the villas were themselves either slaves or freedmen. The beautiful residential part of the villa was occupied probably by these managers, but was built for occasional visits of the masters. An interesting account written on one of the walls of the slave-yard mentions horse-fodder (*CIL* iv. 6897: 'pabu(li) spo(rtae) xx' and perhaps 'medica', clover). The same general features and the same accommodation for the slaves are shown by the plan of, and the finds in, the large villa near Stabiae (no. VIII of Della Corte), *Not. d. Scavi*, 1923, pp. 275 ff. Peculiar features of this villa are the cows kept in the *stabulum* and the large cheese-factory. Thus in every detail the excavations of the villas near Pompeii confirm and illustrate the pictures given in the treatises of Varro and Columella.

The importance of the wine-production of Pompeii is illustrated also by the inscriptions on the wine amphorae found there. Almost all of them mention names of well-known Pompeian citizens, owners of large houses in the city and of wine estates in its territory. The inscriptions may be easily consulted in the Supplement of *CIL* iv (A. Mau). See the collection of material by P. Remark, *De amphorarum inscriptionibus latinis* (1912), pp. 11 ff., especially pp. 17 and 22, and the remarks of M. Della Corte in his articles 'Case ed abitanti di Pompei' in *Neapolis* and in *Riv. Indo-Greco-Italica*, vols. 1–7; and the analysis given by J. Day in the article cited in Chap. I, note 26.

[24] I. Greaves, op. cit., pp. 133 ff. Horace often alludes to such large estates, e.g. *Epod.* 1. 25 ff.: 'non ut iuvencis illigata pluribus aratra nitantur mea, pecusve Calabris ante sidus fervidum Lucana mutet pascuis. . . .' Cf. *Carm.* i. 1. 9. He frequently quotes estates of historical persons sometimes without naming them (*Epod.* 4. 13: 'arat Falerni mille fundi iugera'), sometimes named and addressed as his personal friends and acquaintances, *Sat.* i. 5. 50 (the villa of Cocceius Nerva); *Epist.* ii. 2. 160 (estate of a certain Orbius); *Carm.* ii. 16, cf. *Epist.* i. 12. 22 (estates of Pompeius Grosphus), and that *Epistle* itself, a letter to his friend Iccius who was the manager of the *lati-fundium* of Agrippa in Sicily (see the instructive analysis of this letter by I. Greaves, op. cit., pp. 143 ff.). The most characteristic description of the same sort by Tibullus is iii. 3. 11: 'nam grave quid prodest pondus mihi divitis auri arvaque si findant pinguia mille boves?'

[25] I. Greaves, op. cit., pp. 178 ff. and 164 ff.; Hor. *Carm.* ii. 18. In *Sat.* ii. 2 (Greaves, op. cit., p. 173) Horace portrays an old tenant-farmer, formerly the owner of the plot on which he now works as a tenant of a veteran.

[26] On the commercial relations of the Roman Empire, especially of Egypt, with the East see the careful study of the late M. Chwostow, *History of the Oriental Commerce of Greco-Roman Egypt (332 B.C.–A.D. 284)* (Kazan, 1907) (in Russian); cf. my review of this book in *Arch. f. Papyr.* 4, p. 298. Cf. Chap. III, notes 16 and 17.

[27] There are no special works on Roman trade within the Empire. The best, though in each case very short, treatment is given by L. Friedländer–G. Wissowa, *Sitteng. Roms*, i, pp. 363 ff., and R. Cagnat–M. Besnier, article 'Mercatura' in Daremberg–Saglio, iii. 2, pp. 1772 ff.: see especially the register on p. 1778 and the enumeration of the principal markets in the provinces on pp. 1777 ff. The article 'Industrie und Handel' by H. Gummerus in Pauly–Wissowa, ix. 2, cols. 1454 ff., pays more attention to industry than to commerce. A special point is excellently treated by V. Pârvan, *Die*

Nationalität der Kaufleute im römischen Kaiserreiche (1909). The most recent book on the subject, M. P. Charlesworth's *Trade Routes and Commerce of the Roman Empire*[2] (1926), contains a good survey of the trade routes and of the articles which were exchanged, but fails to give an adequate account of the organization of commerce and of its economic importance, cf. my review in *JRS* 14, 1924, pp. 268–70. Very useful and exhaustive is the treatment by M. Besnier of the commerce in lead, 'Le Commerce du plomb à l'époque romaine', *Rev. arch.* 1920 (2), p. 211; 1921 (1), pp. 36 ff., and 1921 (2), pp. 98 ff.; cf. H. Brewster, *Roman Craftsmen and Tradesmen of the Early Empire* (1917) (a very useful collection of texts from poets of the Augustan and Flavian age). In the following notes I quote some facts which remained unknown to Cagnat, Besnier, and Gummerus. There are good descriptions of the various aspects of ancient commerce in the work of H. Schaal, *Vom Tauschhandel zum Welthandel* (1931), pt. ii, 'Hellenismus und römische Kaiserzeit'.

28 See Chap. I, note 27, and note 17 to this chapter. Sicilian wine is mentioned as the fourth best by Pliny (*NH* xiv. 6. 66). The main centres of production were Messana and Tauromenium; cf. the amphorae of Tauromenian wine at Pompeii, *CIL* iv. 2618, 5563–8; *Not. d. Scavi*, 1914, p. 199, and 1915, p. 335, no. 5. It must, however, be emphasized that Sicily in the time of Augustus and during the whole of the 1st cent. A.D. was still a fertile corn-land.

29 Petronius, *Cena Trim.* 76: 'nemini tamen nihil satis est. concupivi negotiari. ne multis vos morer, quinque naves aedificavi, oneravi vinum—et tunc erat contra aurum—misi Romam. putares me hoc iussisse: omnes naves naufragarunt, factum, non fabula. uno die Neptunus trecenties sestertium devoravit. putatis me defecisse? non mehercules mi haec iactura gusti fuit, tamquam nihil facti. alteras feci maiores et meliores et feliciores... oneravi rursus vinum, lardum, fabam, seplasium, mancipia.' Cf. *CIL* iv. 5894, with *Add.*; A. Sogliano, *Not. d. Scavi*, 1905, p. 257 [*L'An. ép.* 1905, 77]: 'M. Terenti Artritaci in nave Cn. Senti Omeri Ti. Claudi Orpei vect(a)'—wine or *garum* imported to Pompeii by a company of shipowners (?). Cf. note 22.

30 Large quantities of Capuan bronze plate, along with bronze plate probably made in Alexandria and in Asia Minor, are characteristic of the big cemeteries of the Augustan age in the Caucasus. See, e.g., the necropolis of Bori published by E. Pridik in *Materials for the Arch. of South Russia*, 34 (1914) (in Russian). Some Capuan bronze vessels have been found as far away as the province of Viatka, *C.R. de la Comm. arch.* 1913–15, p. 213, fig. 261 (in Russian): the type of one of the bronze pans is similar to the typical pans of the 1st cent. A.D. See H. Willers, *Neue Untersuchungen über die römische Bronzeindustrie*, pp. 77 ff. Another set of the same period was found in the government of Podolia, *C.R. de la Comm. arch.* 1913–15, p. 201, fig. 255 (in Russian). In general, Capuan bronze plate is exceedingly common in South Russia, especially in the 1st cent. A.D. It is, however, difficult to determine whether the trade of East Russia with Italy already began under Augustus or was only inaugurated under his successors. We find Italian articles (glass and bronzes) in large quantities at Panticapaeum in the 1st cent. A.D. (see note 32), and some of the tombs there containing glass and bronzes from South Italy may be of the Augustan age, though the majority are slightly later. It is clear that the bronze objects found in North Russia came through Panticapaeum and not through the Baltic: the beginnings of this trade probably therefore belong to the 1st cent. A.D. On the development of the trade of Eastern Germany and Scandinavia with Italy in the 1st cent. A.D., see Chap. III, note 19; cf. J. Kostrzewski, *Reall. d. Vorgeschichte*, iii, pp. 280 ff.

31 Some Aucissa pins from the river Don were published by me in *Bull. de la*

Comm. arch. de Russie, 65, 1917, pp. 22 ff. (in Russian); cf. C. Jullian, *Histoire de la Gaule*, v, p. 304, note 6; F. Haverfield, in *Arch. Journ.* 60, 1903, p. 236, and 62, 1905, p. 265.

32 See, e.g., my *Ancient Decorative Painting in South Russia* (1914), pp. 206 ff. (in Russian).

33 See Chap. I, note 13.

34 See Chap. III, note 20.

35 On Aquileia see the works quoted in Chap I, note 16. No investigation has been made of the special articles produced by Aquileia. The wonderful assemblage of amber articles in the Museum of the city and in a private collection in Udine has never been published. These articles were exported as far as Rome, Pompeii, the Dalmatian coast, Africa, and Belgium: see, e.g. F. Cumont, *Comment la Belgique fut romanisée* (2nd ed. 1919), p. 51, fig. 20; G. Smirich, *Führer durch das K.K. Staatsmuseum zu Zara* (1912), p. 103. There is a large collection of Aquileian amber articles found in South Italy in the British Museum and another in the Museo delle Terme at Rome. Reference may also be made here to an amber bead with a ram's head, found at Butzke in Pommern; see E. Jungklaus, *Röm. Funde in Pommern* (1924), p. 89. Does this come from Aquileia? A very good survey of the objects stored in the picturesque and well-arranged Museum of Aquileia was given by E. Maionica, *Guida dell'I.R. Museo dello Stato in Aquileia* (Vienna, 1911); cf. G. Brusin, *Aquileia, Guida stor. ed artist.* (1929). The chapters on glass (Maionica, pp. 87 f., Brusin, pp. 221 ff.) and amber (Maionica, pp. 88 f., Brusin, pp. 162 ff.) are particularly interesting. The inscriptions on two glass bottles found at Linz on the Danube (*Sentia Secunda facit Aquileiae vit(ra)*) show that Aquileia exported glass of her own production (Brusin, pp. 10 and 222). Among the iron objects the most conspicuous and the most interesting are the various agricultural implements, of which large quantities were used by the Aquileians themselves (Maionica, pp. 97 ff.; Brusin, pp. 200 ff.). An investigation of the same implements found in Dalmatia and in the Danube provinces would be worth while. They may have come from the factories of Aquileia: see the bas-relief on a funeral monument of a *faber ferrarius*, above, Pl. xxx, 4. Naturally we cannot expect to find in Aquileia the arms which were fabricated there for the Danubian army. A *faber aciarius* named L. Herennius was buried beneath a beautiful sepulchral altar with a long inscription, Brusin, p. 48, fig. 25 [=*L'An. ép.* 1932, 1]. On the discovery of gold, Polybius, xxxiv. 10, 10.

36 See Chap. I, note 13; cf. T. Frank, *A History of Rome*, pp. 375 ff. I cannot, however, agree with the author that the organization of industry and trade in Rome and in the larger cities was identical with that of Pompeii. The many tombstones of artisans found in Rome attest the existence of small shops in Rome, but they do not tell us anything about the organization of the larger ones. Moreover, there was a special style of tombstones, a conventional language, so to speak, used in such monuments. They may be used for studying the technical side of a given craft, but they are hardly specific enough to warrant conclusions on the standing and the economic status of the buried man. The systematic excavations of Ostia have shown us how utterly different were the houses of Ostia and of Rome from those of Pompeii: see G. Calza, 'La Preminenza dell'insula nella edifizia romana', *Mon. dei Lincei*, 23, 1913, pp. 541 ff.; E. Cuq, 'Une statistique de locaux affectés à l'habitation dans la Rome impériale', *Mém. de l'Ac. Inscr.* 11, 1915, pp. 279 ff.; G. Calza, 'La Statistica delle abitazioni e il calcolo della popolazione in Roma imperiale', *Rend. Lincei*, 26, 1917, pp. 3 ff., and his reports in the *Not. d. Scavi*; cf. a summary of these reports by the same author in *Atene e Roma*, 3, 1922, pp. 229 ff. and his excellent article 'Le Origine latine dell'abitazione moderna', *Architettura e arti decorative*, 3, 1923, and also J. Stutten, 'Wohnhäuser der

römischen Kaiserzeit', *Bauamt und Gemeindeleben*, 15, 1924, pp. 146 ff. We have learnt also from the same excavations what large and beautiful buildings were used not only by the state but also by some private dealers for storing goods and carrying out the operations connected with storage (see the articles 'Horrea' in Pauly–Wissowa and Daremberg–Saglio; cf. P. Romanelli, *Diz. epigr.* iii, pp. 967 ff.), and we cannot ignore the very great danger of speaking of large commercial and industrial cities on the basis of a study confined to some small and provincial centres of city life. I have no doubt that Rome was much more like Alexandria than Pompeii, and that Ostia was a Rome in miniature. Characteristic of the early imperial age (perhaps of the time of Augustus) is the block near the forum recently excavated by G. Calza (*Not. d. Scavi*, 1923, pp. 177 ff., and pls. iv ff.). Three large commercial and industrial buildings (near the *curia*) present each of them a new type unknown at Pompeii. The most interesting is the big 'bazaar' (numbered C on Calza's map, pl. iv), a court (or kind of private square) accessible from two streets and surrounded by large and high shops very unlike the small and dark shops of Pompeii. Some of these shops open on the street, some into the court. Cf. G. Calza, *Ostia, Guida storico-monumentale*[2], (1928) [cf. id. *Scavi di Ostia*, i, *Topografia Generale* (1953)], and J. Carcopino, *Ostie* (Les Visites d'Art) (1929). The wonderful excavations of the 'Palazzo del mercato' of Trajan, near the emperor's Forum, show how 'modern' Roman trade was in Trajan's time. I examined this 'sala di mercato', which was used for the sale of the latest literary productions, and could see that its layout satisfied all the requirements of modern trade. See C. Ricci, *Il mercato di Traiano* (1929); id. *Il Foro di Augusto e la Casa dei Cavalieri di Rodi* (1930) (Capitolium).

[37] On Alexandrian industry, W. Schubart, *Ägypten von Alexander dem Großen bis Mohammed* (1922), pp. 51 ff.; E. Breccia, *Alexandrea ad Aegyptum* (Eng. ed. 1922), p. 41 (with bibliography). The organization of industry in the villages and the small towns of Egypt is fairly well known to us since the publication of the volumes of Reil, *Beiträge zur Kenntnis des Gewerbes im hellenistischen Ägypten* (1913), and M. Chwostow, *Studies in the organization of industry and commerce in greco-roman Egypt*, vol. i, *The textile industry* (1914) (in Russian); cf. my review of the latter in the *Journ. of the Min. of Publ. Educ.* 1914 (in Russian), and U. Wilcken, *Grundzüge*, pp. 239 ff.; W. Schubart, *Einführung*, pp. 414 ff. and 428 ff., with an enumeration of the various trades. It is, however, very dangerous to apply this picture to Alexandria, the relation being the same as that between Rome and Pompeii. Pompeii and the cities of Egypt worked chiefly for the local market; Alexandria and, to a certain extent, Rome, for world export.

[38] On the textile industry of Asia Minor see my article on the economic development of the Pergamene kingdom, in *Anatolian Studies presented to Sir William Ramsay* (Manchester, 1924). Cf. Orth in Pauly–Wissowa, xii, cols. 606 ff. (art. 'Lana'); cf. below Chap. V, note 42.

III. *The Military Tyranny of the Julii and Claudii*

[1] The history of the Roman emperors has been repeatedly written by many eminent modern scholars. I need not enumerate the long list of titles. It will be enough to name the best of the most recent works: A. von Domaszewski, *Gesch. der römischen Kaiser* (3rd ed. 1922); H. Stuart Jones, *The Roman Empire* (1908); J. B. Bury, *History of the Roman Empire* (1893); E. Kornemann, 'Die römische Kaiserzeit' in Gercke–Norden, *Einleitung in die Altertumswissenschaft*, vol. iii (2nd ed. 1914) [3rd ed. 1933]; G. Bloch, *L'Empire romain. Évolution et décadence* (1922); L. Homo, *L'Empire romain* (1925); M. P. Nilsson, *Imperial Rome* (1925); H. Dessau, *Gesch. d. röm. Kaiserzeit*, i–ii (1924–30); V. Chapot, *Le Monde romain* (1927). On the constitutional evolution see E. Grimm, *Studies in the History of the Development of the Roman Imperial Power*, vols. i–ii (1900–1) (in

Russian); O. Th. Schulz, *Das Wesen des römischen Kaisertums der ersten zwei Jahrhunderte* (1916); id. *Die Rechtstitel u. Regierungsprogramme auf röm. Kaisermünzen* (1925); E. Täubler, 'Römisches Staatsrecht und römische Verfassungsgeschichte', *Hist. Zeitschr.* 120, 1919, pp. 189 ff.; cf. chap. II, note 1. The standard works on this subject are still, of course, the second part of the second volume of Th. Mommsen's *Staatsrecht* and E. Herzog, *Geschichte und System des römischen Staatsrechts*, ii (pp. 233 ff. and 332 ff. on the Roman principate as a tyranny). An interesting study on the constitutional history of the Roman Empire is Kornemann's, *Doppelprinzipat u. Reichsteilung im Imperium Romanum* (1930). The dependence of the emperors (after Tiberius) on the praetorian guard is emphasized by coins of Caligula, Claudius, and Nero. Caligula minted some copper with the legend 'adlocut(io) coh(ortium)' without the usual 'S.C.', showing four 'aquilae' which symbolized the praetorian cohorts (Mattingly, *Coins of the R.E.* (1923), p. cxlv). Still more explicit are the coins of Claudius with the legend 'imper(ator) recept(us)' and a picture of the praetorian camp, alluding to his proclamation by the praetorians. To this type corresponds another with the legend 'praetor(iani) recept(i)', showing the figures of the emperor and a praetorian soldier clasping hands (Mattingly, op. cit., pp. clii f.). The type of Caligula was repeated by Nero (Mattingly, op. cit., p. clxxvi). On the sources the most recent work is the sketch of A. Rosenberg, *Einleitung und Quellenkunde zur römischen Geschichte* (1921), which cannot replace the fundamental work of H. Peter, *Die geschichtliche Literatur über die römische Kaiserzeit* (1897). On the imperial cult, E. Beurlier, *Le Culte impérial* (Paris, 1891); E. Kornemann, 'Zur Geschichte der ant. Herrscherkulte', *Klio*, 1, 1901/2, pp. 51–146; J. Toutain, *Les Cultes païens dans l'Empire romain*, i (1907), pp. 42 ff.; F. Blumenthal, 'Der ägyptische Kaiserkult', *Arch. f. Papyr.* 5, pp. 317 ff.; A. Deissmann, *Licht vom Osten* (4th ed. 1923), pp. 287 ff.; H. Heinen, *Klio*, 11, 1911, pp. 129 ff.; L. R. Taylor, *TAPA* 51, 1920, pp. 116 ff.; W. Otto, *Hermes* 45, 1910, pp. 448 ff.; G. Herzog-Hauser in Pauly–Wissowa, Suppl. iv, cols. 820 ff. (art. 'Kaiserkult'); E. Bickermann, 'Die römische Kaiserapotheose', *Arch. f. Rel.* 27, 1929, pp. 1 ff.; L. R. Taylor, *The Divinity of the Roman Emperor* (1931). For Tiberius see the inscription of Gython (cf. Chap. I, note 12), and L. R. Taylor's 'Tiberius' Refusals of Divine Honours', *TAPA* 60, 1929, pp. 87 ff.; cf. K. Scott, *Class. Phil.* 27, 1932, pp. 435 ff., and J. Gagé, 'La Victoria Augusta et les Auspices de Tibère', *Rev. arch.* 1930 (2), pp. 15 ff. On Claudius in this respect see H. I. Bell, *Jews and Christians in Egypt* (1924), pp. 5 ff., and *Juden u. Griechen im römischen Alexandreia* (Beiheft zum *Alten Orient*, 9, 1926). On the identification of emperors with gods, especially with Hercules, see P. Riewald, 'De imperatorum Romanorum cum ceteris dis et comparatione et aequatione', *Diss. Phil. Halenses*, 20. 3, 1912, and my own article 'Commodus-Hercules in Britain', *JRS* 13, 1923; cf. Chap. II, note 3. Other books and articles will be quoted in the following notes. The part which was played in the history of the imperial cult in and after the time of Augustus by attempts to identify the emperors with the great gods who promoted civilization and prosperity—Hercules, Mercury, Apollo, and Bacchus—and the empresses with the corresponding goddesses—Venus, Juno, and Minerva—is explained by the importance of these gods and goddesses in the domestic cult of Italy, the cult of the Genius, the Lares, and the Penates. Excellent illustrations may be found in the domestic shrines of Pompeii, e.g. in the house Reg. I, ins. IX, no. 1 (*Not. d. Scavi*, 1913, pp. 34 f.), where we have representations of Hercules, Mercury, Apollo, perhaps Bacchus and (Venus), Juno, and Minerva. Cf. *Not. d. Scavi*, 1899, p. 340, fig. 2 (the same series of gods), and scores of other examples. So also at Ostia and Delos. The subject needs fresh treatment. There is no mention of these correlations in Boehm's article, 'Lares' in Pauly–Wissowa, xii, cols. 806 ff.

² O. Hirschfeld, *Die kaiserlichen Verwaltungsbeamten bis auf Diocletian*² (1905); id. *Kl.*

Schr. (1913); my articles 'Fiscus' in Pauly–Wissowa, vi, and in Ruggiero, *Diz. epigr.*; M. Bang in L. Friedländer–G. Wissowa, *Sitteng. Roms*, iv, 10th ed., pp. 26 ff. (chaps. v and vi). On the *ager publicus* and its gradual incorporation in the imperial domains (from the administrative point of view), see my *Studien z. Gesch. röm. Kol.*, p. 326. Claudius' edict on the *cursus publicus*, *CIL* iii. 7251 = Dessau, *ILS* 214 = *IG* v. 2, p. 5 = F. F. Abbott and A. C. Johnson, *Municipal Administration in the Rom. Empire*, p. 354, no. 51: 'T[i]. Claudius Caesar Aug. G[erm]anicus pontif. max. trib. pot. VIIII imp. XVI p. p. [A.D. 49–50] dicit: cu[m] et colonias et municipia non solum Ita[lia]e verum etiam provinciarum item civita[ti]um (*lege* civitates) cuiusque provinciae lebare oneribu[s] veh[iculor]um praebendorum saepe tem[ptaviss]em [e]t c[um sati]s multa remedia invenisse m[ihi viderer, p]otu[it ta]men nequitiae hominum [non satis per ea occurri]....' On the letter to the Alexandrians see H. I. Bell, *Jews and Christians in Egypt* (1924), pp. 1 ff.; id. *Juden u. Griechen im römischen Alexandreia* (1926); H. Stuart Jones, 'Claudius and the Jewish Question at Alexandria', *JRS* 16, 1926, pp. 17 ff., and the bibliographies in the German work of Bell and the article of Jones. Cf. E. Grupe, *Zeitschr. d. Sav.-St.* 48, 1928, p. 573 (on the style of the edict as compared with that of the edict for the Anauni and of the speech in the Senate concerning the *ius honorum* of the Gauls (cf. also, S. Lösch, *Epistula Claudiana: Der neuentdeckte Brief des Kaisers Claudius v. J. 41 n. Chr., und das Urchristentum* (1930)). On the speech in the senate see Ph. Fabia, *La Table claudienne de Lyon* (1929); cf. De Sanctis, *Riv. fil.* 57, 1929, p. 575. New evidence on the definitive organization of the *fiscus* as the imperial financial administration by the Emperor Claudius is given by two inscriptions: one of Lycosura in Arcadia mentioning the *fiscus* as receiving payments from the provincial cities in A.D. 42 (*IG* v. 2. 516 = Dittenberger, *Syll.*³ 800; cf. A. von Premerstein, *Oest. Jahresh.* 15, 1912, pp. 200ff.) and one of Volubilis in Mauretania, for which see below, note 5. The edict of Paulus Fabius Persicus (A.D. 44), proconsul of Asia (Ephesus; R. Heberdey, *Forschungen in Ephesos*, ii, pp. 112 ff., nos. 21–22; J. Keil, *Oest. Jahresh.* 23, 1926, Beibl., pp. 282 ff. [= ‡F. K. Dörner, *Der Erlass d. Statthalters v. Asia Paullus Fabius Persicus* (Greifswald, 1935), cf. *L'An. ép.* 1936, 141]), provides valuable evidence as to the spirit which animated the government of Claudius. The leading thought of the edict is affectionate solicitude for the province and a deep sense of duty: in this respect the edict of Fabius is the forerunner of some other documents of the period of the enlightened monarchy. Notice also the allusion of Fabius (Keil, l.c., p. 283, ll. 11 ff.), to the leading principles of Claudius' policy: ἥδειον ὅμως ὁμολογῶι πρὸς ταύτην ἐπιτετάσθα[ι τὴν] γνώμην τῶι ὑποδείγματι τοῦ κρατίστου καὶ ἀλ[η]θῶς δικαιοτάτου ἡγεμόνος, ὃς πᾶν τὸ τῶν ἀνθρώπων γένος εἰς τὴν ἰδίαν ἀνα⟨δε⟩δε{ι}γμένος κηδεμονίαν ἐν τοῖς πρώτοις καὶ πᾶσιν ἡδίστοις φιλανθρώποις καὶ τοῦτο κεχάρισ⟨τ⟩αι τὸ τὰ ἴδια ἑκάστωι ἀποκατασταθῆναι. Still more important is the discourse of Claudius, *BGU* 611 [= *M. Chrest.* 370], as we have it after the excellent revision of the text by J. Stroux, 'Eine Gerichtsreform des Kaisers Claudius', *Sitzb. Münch. Akad.* 1929 (8): note his excellent remarks on the character of the emperor, pp. 80 ff. I have not seen A. Momigliano, *L'Opera dell'imperatore Claudio* (1932) [Eng. trans. *Claudius: The Emperor and his Achievement* (Oxford, 1934)].

³ On the distributions of corn and money see M. Rostovtzeff, 'Die römischen Bleitesserae', *Klio*, Beiheft 3, 1905, pp. 10 ff.; O. Hirschfeld, *Die k. Verwaltungsb.*, pp. 230 ff.; G. Cardinali, 'Frumentatio' in Ruggiero, *Diz. epigr.* iii, pp. 224 ff.; and also my articles 'Frumentum' in Pauly–Wissowa, vii, cols. 172 ff., and 'Congiarium', ibid. iv, cols. 875 ff. The difficult problems of the character of the *professiones* in the so-called *lex Iulia municipalis* [*FIRA*² 13] and of the character of the law itself are now solved by the ingenious article of A. von Premerstein, 'Die Tafel von Heraclea und die Acta Caesaris', *Zeitschr. d. Sav.-St.*, 43, 1923, pp. 45 ff. (on the *professiones* see ibid., pp. 58 ff.). There is no doubt that the *professiones* were intended to regulate the corn-

distributions of Caesar. Cf. T. Rice Holmes, *The Roman Republic*, iii, pp. 553 ff., and E. G. Hardy, *Some Problems in Roman History* (1924), pp. 239 ff. On the shows, L. Friedländer–G. Wissowa, *Sitteng. Roms*, ii, 10th ed., pp. 205 ff. (Drexel, Chaps. XVI–XVIII); O. Hirschfeld, loc. cit., pp. 285 ff.

⁴ On the procurators of the provinces, O. Hirschfeld, *Die kais. Verwaltungsb.*, pp. 343 ff. and 410 ff.; my article 'Fiscus' in Pauly–Wissowa, vi, cols. 2865 ff.; R. Cagnat in Daremberg–Saglio, iv, pp. 662 ff.; H. Mattingly, *The Imperial Civil Service of Rome* (1910), pp. 102 ff.

⁵ The best survey of the general development of city life in the Roman Empire is given by Th. Mommsen in the fifth volume of his *History of Rome* [Eng. trans. *The Provinces of the Roman Empire*² (1909)]. A mass of material is collected in the *Corpus Inscriptionum Latinarum*. The general introductions to the separate volumes which deal with the history of Italy and of the provinces and the special introductions to the inscriptions of the various cities are all of them so many preparatory chapters for a history of the urbanization of the Empire. Unfortunately we have nothing similar for the Greek East, except for Greece itself and some of the Greek islands, which were of little importance for the Empire. Despite the fact that a large stock of material is there collected and well prepared for use, there are no works describing the general development of the urbanization of the Empire. The most recent books on the subject, by J. S. Reid, *The Municipalities of the Roman Empire* (Cambridge, 1913), and F. F. Abbott and A. C. Johnson, *Municipal Administration in the Roman Empire* (1926) (with a collection of documents concerning municipal administration; Part II. 1. Municipal Documents in Greek and Latin from Italy and the Provinces; 2, Documents from Egypt) cannot replace the old but still indispensable volumes of E. Kuhn, *Die städtische und bürgerliche Verfassung des römischen Reiches*, vols. i and ii (1864, 1865), especially vol. ii, cf. id. *Die Entstehung der Städte der Alten* (1878). Cf. W. E. Heitland, *Last Words on the Roman Municipalities* (1928). The attitude of Claudius to urbanization is illustrated by his activity in North Italy where the important problem of the latinization and urbanization of the various tribes conquered and pacified by Augustus, living in the sub-alpine valleys, was still unsettled. The whole question has been studied by E. Pais, *Dalle guerre puniche a Cesare Augusto*, ii. (1918), pp. 375 ff., *Sulla romanizzazione della Valle d'Aosta*; pp. 427 ff., *Intorno alla gente degli Euganei*; pp. 477 ff., *Intorno alla conquista ed alla romanizzazione della Liguria e della Transpadana occidentale*. An important inscription of Augusta Pretoria (*Not. d. Scavi*, 1894, p. 369 [= *L'An. Ep.* 1895, 22]; Pais, l.c., p. 375 and pl. VIII), dedicated by the *Salassi incol(ae) qui initio se in colon(iam) con(tulerunt)*, in honour of their patron Augustus (23–22 B.C.), shows that Augustus himself began to incorporate the Romanized parts of the Alpine peoples in the colonies to which the tribes themselves had been assigned. The considerable use of Alpine people in the praetorian guard and in the legions (E. Ritterling, *Klio*, 21, 1926, pp. 82 ff.) resulted in a large diffusion of Roman civilization and the concession of the Latin right to those tribes, and encouraged the transformation of their rural settlements into cities. This transformation was slow, but it is no chance that we find the name of Claudius connected both with the extension of the Latin citizenship to Alpine peoples and their urban centres, and with the incorporation of the *incolae* of a Roman colony, who were members of an Alpine stock, in the colony itself. For the former of these two classes compare the history of the Euganean tribes, the Octodurenses and the Centroxes (Pais, l.c., pp. 460 ff., cf. ibid., pp. 468 ff. on the Euganeans of Val Trompia and Val Camonica); for the second compare the grant of Roman citizenship to the Anauni in the city of Tridentum in A.D. 46 (cf. the edict of Claudius, *CIL* v. 5050 = Dessau, *ILS* 206 = Bruns⁷, 79 = Abbott and Johnson, op. cit., p. 347, no. 49 [= Riccobono, *FIRA*² 71]; cf. Reid, op. cit., pp. 166 ff.; Pais, op. cit., pp. 469 ff. and *passim*). This transformation of much of North Italy was

completed by the Flavians (Pais, l.c., p. 468), but cf. Tergeste, *CIL* v. 532 (Antoninus Pius). On Claudius' grant of citizenship to the *incolae* of the city of Volubilis in Mauretania, L. Chatelain, *C. R. Acad. Inscr.* 1915, p. 396 [= *L'An. ép.* 1916, 42 = *FIRA²* 70]; E. Cuq, *Journ. Sav.* 1917, pp. 480 and 538, and *C. R. Acad. Inscr.* 1918, p. 227, and 1920, p. 339; G. de Sanctis, *Atti d. R. Acc. di Torino*, 53, 1918, pp. 451 ff.; E. Weiss, *Zeitschr. d. Sav.-St.* 42, 1921, p. 639; R. Cagnat and L. Chatelain, *Inscriptions latines de l'Afrique* (1923), no. 634 = Abbott and Johnson, op. cit., p. 356, no. 53 [= Riccobono, *FIRA²* 70]. Another inscription of Volubilis mentions the same grant of Claudius, L. Chatelain, *C. R. Acad. Inscr.* 1924, pp. 77 ff. [= *L'An. ép.* 1924, 66; cf. Riccobono, op. cit., p. 416, lemma to 70]: 'muni(cipium) Volub(ilitanum) impetrata c(ivitate) R(omana) et conubio, et oneribus remissis' (A.D. 44). Cf. L. A. Constans in *Mus. Belge*, 28, 1924, pp. 103 ff.; P. Wuilleumier, *Rev. ét. anc.* 28, 1926, pp. 323 ff. On the colonies of Claudius see E. Kornemann, 'Colonia', in Pauly–Wissowa, iv, cols. 535 ff., and Ritterling, ibid. xii, cols. 1251 ff.; cf. on Mauretania, E. Cuq, *Journ. Sav.* 1917, p. 542. On the tendency of Claudius to extend the Roman citizenship to large numbers of provincials see (Sen.) *Apocoloc.* 13; J. S. Reid, op. cit., p. 191; H. Dessau, *Gesch. d. röm. Kaiserzeit*, ii, p. 152. But the statement of the *Apocolocyntosis* is an exaggeration in the spirit of the senatorial opposition. In granting the franchise Claudius acted with a circumspection which reminds us of Augustus rather than of Caesar (cf. Chap. II, note 5); cf. also his attitude towards the Alexandrians and their request to receive a city council and some other privileges, H. I. Bell, op. cit. The first emperor really to break with the tradition of Augustus was Vespasian (on his military colonies see Ritterling, op. cit., col. 1273).

⁶ On the civil war of 69–70 see B. W. Henderson, *Civil War and Rebellion in the Roman Empire* (1908); cf. N. Feliciani, 'L'anno dei quattro imperatori', *Riv. di stor. ant.* 11, 1906, pp. 3 ff. and 378 ff., and the general works quoted in note 1. That many Senators contemplated the possibility of doing away with the principate and restoring the ancient régime of the senate is not a just inference from the acts of Vindex and of Verginius Rufus, from the oath taken to the 'Senate and People of Rome' by two legions of the Upper Rhine after their revolt against Galba, and from the free use in 69 and afterwards of the term *libertas*, a term which had been used by Augustus himself, and after his time both by the party loyal to the emperors and by the opposition. For the great majority of the population of the Empire *libertas* meant the constitutional principate established by Augustus. To fight for *libertas* against individual *principes* was to fight against tyranny. The definition of tyranny was ready to hand in the writings of the Greek philosophers, especially in those of the Middle Stoa (Panaitios) popularized by Cicero in his *De Republica* (see R. Reitzenstein, *Gött. gel. Nachr.* 1917, pp. 399 ff. and 481 ff., and cf. R. Heinze, *Hermes*, 59, 1924, pp. 73 ff., and Reitzenstein, ibid., pp. 356 ff.; cf. Schönbauer's paper quoted in Chap. II, note 1). We must, however, avoid exaggeration. After Caligula's death a large portion of the senate wished to put an end to the principate: see Dio, 60. 1. 1 f.; Suet. *Cal.* 60, and *Claud.* 11. 1: 'imperio stabilito nihil antiquius duxit quam id biduum, quo de mutando rei publicae statu haesitatum erat, memoriae eximere'. The idea was certainly still alive in 69, but it was not strong enough to lead to action. On *libertas* in the early Empire, Ph. Fabia, *Klio*, 4, 1904, pp. 42 ff.; E. Kornemann in Gercke and Norden, *Einleitung in die Altertumsw.* iii, 2nd ed., pp. 274 ff.; O. Th. Schulz, *Das Wesen des röm. Kaisertums*, p. 39. The discontent in the provinces in the time of Nero was increased by the heavy burden of Neronian taxation and especially by the dishonesty of the emperor's procurators. It is worthy of note that one of the first measures of Galba in Spain, after being proclaimed emperor, was the abolition of a tax of 2½ per cent., probably the well-known *quadragesima Galliarum et Hispaniarum* (*CIL* xiv. 4708). 'Quadragensuma remissa' is the legend on some coins minted by Galba in Spain. The type of these coins shows three prisoners,

marshalled by an officer, being led under some sort of arch. I think that Mattingly is right in recognizing in the prisoners the procurators of Nero and in referring to the execution of Obultronius Sabinus and Cornelius Marcellus by Galba (Tac. *Hist.* i. 37); cf. the general attitude of Galba towards the procurators of Nero (Plut. *Galba*, 4). Mattingly, *Coins of the R.E.*, p. ccix; cf. H. Dessau, *Gesch. d. röm. Kaiserzeit*, ii, p. 305, who tacitly rejects Mattingly's explanation.

⁷ Tac. *Hist.* i. 85: 'non tamen quies urbi redierat: strepitus telorum et facies belli, militibus ut nihil in commune turbantibus, ita sparsis per domos occulto habitu et maligna cura in omnes quos nobilitas aut opes aut aliqua insignis claritudo rumoribus obiecerat.' *Hist.* ii. 56: 'ceterum Italia gravius atque atrocius quam bello adflictabatur. dispersi per municipia et colonias Vitelliani spoliare, rapere, vi et stupris polluere . . . ipsique milites *regionum gnari* refertos agros, dites dominos in praedam aut, si repugnatum foret, ad exitium destinabant. . . .' Cf. 62: 'exhausti conviviorum apparatibus principes civitatum; vastabantur ipsae civitates,' and iv. 1: 'nec deerat egentissimus quisque e plebe et pessimi servitiorum prodere ultro *dites dominos*, alii ab amicis monstrabantur.' Cf. Th. Mommsen, *Ges. Schr.* vi, p. 38.

⁸ It is well known that the exclusion of Italians under Vespasian from military service in the legions was deduced by Mommsen from the lists of legionary soldiers, especially those of the *leg. I Adiutrix* (*Ges. Schr.* vi, pp. 36 ff.). This theory goes far beyond the evidence. Ritterling, *RE* xii. col. 1386 (cf. also *Westd. Zeitschr.* 12, 1893, pp. 105 ff.) has shown that the prevalence of Illyrians among the soldiers of *I. Adiutrix* who died at Mainz is probably due to the fact that these men had at one time been marines; this legion is known to have been constituted in A.D. 68 of levies taken from the crews. On the other hand, the lists of soldiers with indication of birth-place compiled by Ritterling show clearly that the number of soldiers recruited in Italy (including North Italy) gradually declined. Consequently the army of Domitian, and, still more, that of Trajan, was composed primarily of soldiers born in the provinces, together with a small number of North Italians. This process is admirably illustrated by the history of *legio XV Apollinaris*. At the beginning of the 1st cent., until the middle of Nero's reign, this legion had its headquarters at Carnuntum. We have many inscriptions of its soldiers for this period, and not one of them is a provincial. The same legion was stationed again at Carnuntum after 69, under the Flavians and Trajan, and we have another group of inscriptions: some of the soldiers are still Italian, but the majority are of provincial birth, and, more precisely, born in the cities of the provinces (see Ritterling, l.c., cols. 1752 and 1758). Cf. H. Dessau, *Gesch. d. röm. Kaiserzeit*, i, p. 288; H. M. D. Parker, *The Roman Legions* (1928), pp. 178 ff.; R. Paribeni, *Optimus Princeps*, i (1928), pp. 59 ff. How ample the opportunities for recruitment in Italy were is shown by the fact that in 66 or 67 Nero had no difficulty in creating a new legion (*I Italica*) of purely Italian recruits. The social *milieu* to which these new recruits belonged is clear from Nero's promise to the sailors to enrol them in a new legion (*I Adiutrix*), a promise which Galba was compelled to fulfil. The same thing was done by Vespasian in the case of the *II Adiut.ix* under the pressure of circumstances (Ritterling in Pauly–Wissowa, xii, cols. 1260 and 1267). Ritterling (l.c.) suggests that even the two new legions of Vespasian were recruited mostly in Italy, which of course is purely conjectural. In the 2nd cent. the conditions remained the same. It is known that M. Aurelius was able to raise in Italy two new legions, the *II Pia* and *III Concors*, both surnamed *Italica* (Ritterling, op. cit., cols. 1300 f.; J. Schwendemann, *Der historische Wert der Vita Marci bei den S.H.A.* (1923), pp. 43 ff.; *CIL* vi. 1377 = Dessau, *ILS* 1098). If, then, the Italians were willing to enter the ranks of the army, the fact that they disappear almost completely from the legions after Vespasian is significant and implies a special policy on the part of the emperors. It should be mentioned in this connexion that,

according to *Scr. Hist. Aug.*, M. Aur. 11. 7, and Hadr. 12. 4, in the time of Nerva, Trajan, Hadrian, and M. Aurelius the burden of recruitment pressed most heavily, not on Italy (apart from the *regio Transpadana*), but on those Spaniards who already enjoyed or had received from Vespasian the rights of Roman or Italian citizenship, i.e. on the Romanized provincials. Clearly, therefore, the Flavians and the Antonines, though they urgently needed Romanized soldiers, refrained from using Italy in general as a recruiting-ground, and preferred to overburden the northern region of the peninsula and the Romanized parts of the Western provinces. Cf. Chap. IV, note 35.

9 On Petronius see the work of I. Greaves quoted in Chap. II, note 18. On Columella, H. Gummerus, 'Der römische Gutsbetrieb', *Klio*, Beiheft 5, 1906; Gertrud Carl, 'Die Agrarlehre Columellas', *Vierteljahresschrift. f. Soz.- u. Wirtschafts.* 19, 1926, pp. 1 ff.

10 It is impossible to cite all the evidence on the rapid development of the prosperity of the Eastern provinces, but one example may be quoted, that of Prusa in Bithynia, the native city of Dio Chrysostom. From Dio's Bithynian speeches, especially *Or. 36*, we know more or less the economic history of the city as reflected in the story of Dio's family (cf. H. von Arnim, *Leben und Werke des Dio von Prusa* (1898), pp. 116 ff.). The rapid development of Prusa did not begin before the period of the Empire. The fortune of Dio's family, both on the mother's and the father's side, was formed in the early 1st cent. A.D. It went on decreasing from the time of Dio's grandfather to that of his father, and then increased under his father's and his own management. It is a typical fortune of a bourgeois of the early Empire (*Or.* 46. 6 ff.). The basis of it was land, which in older times was mostly corn-land. Under Dio's management (the change may have dated from the time of his father) the corn-land was almost entirely planted with vineyards. Along with viticulture, grazing was an important source of Dio's income. Corn-production was reduced to a minimum. One sees the influence of the treatises on scientific agriculture. As a subsidiary source of income, Dio engaged in money-lending and in building and organizing shops (ἐργαστήρια), which certainly formed part of his city houses. There is no difference, therefore, between Italy and Asia Minor in the 1st cent. A.D. as regards the typical husbandry of the city *bourgeoisie*.

11 The progress of urbanization in the kingdoms of Numidia and Mauretania from the time they became vassals of Rome is described by St. Gsell, *Hist. de l'Afrique*, v (1927), pp. 223 ff., vii (1928), pp. 123 ff., viii (1928), pp. 206 ff. It is a great mistake to speak of city life in the Western provinces as an artificial creation of the Roman emperors. The sending out of a colony, the grant of the rights of a Roman or Latin colony or of a Roman *municipium*, were not acts by which urban life was created; they presupposed the existence of it before the colony was founded or municipal privileges were granted. Of such a kind, without doubt, was the urbanization of Spain (J. S. Reid, l.c., p. 243); cf. Chap. VI. The greatest achievement of the Roman emperors was to create economic and political conditions which made it possible to promote urban life in countries where it had existed in germ only. In doing so, they certainly had some practical purposes in mind (easier administration, recruiting, better returns from taxes, &c.). Even in Britain the Romans found germs of urban life already existing, and did their best to help the native population and the emigrants from Italy and the provinces to develop those germs.

12 The development of vine-growing in Gaul in the 1st cent. A.D. is attested by the fact that Gallic wine was exported to Ireland after that. This island was known to Gallic merchants from the time of Augustus, and direct relations existed between it and the western ports of Gaul. See H. Zimmer, *Sitzb. Berl. Akad.* 1909, pp. 370 ff.,

cf. pp. 430 ff.; E. Norden, *Die germanische Urgeschichte in Tacitus' Germania* (third reprint) (1923), p. 439; id. 'Philemon der Geograph', *Janus*, 1, 1921, pp. 182 ff. Cf., however, F. Haverfield, *Eng. Hist. Rev.* 1913, p. 1 ff., and J. G. C. Anderson, *Cornelii Taciti de Vita Agricolae*, ed. H. Furneaux² (1922), introd., p. xlix and note to ch. xxiv, § 2.

¹³ The history of the South-Italian 'terra sigillata' in the 1st cent. has often been described and need not be repeated here. It is amazing to find how this Gallic pottery practically killed the Italian import in Gaul, Britain, Germany, and the Danube provinces, see H. Gummerus in Pauly–Wissowa, ix. 2, cols. 1475 ff., cf. R. Knorr, *Töpfer und Fabriken der verzierter Terra-Sigillata des I. Jahrhunderts* (1919). On the lamps, S. Loeschke, *Lampen aus Vindonissa. Ein Beitrag zur Geschichte von Vindonissa und des antiken Beleuchtungswesen* (1919). A brilliant general sketch may be found in K. Schumacher, *Siedelungs- und Kulturgeschichte der Rheinlande*, ii (1923), pp. 262 ff. The most striking instance of the rapid spread of Gallic pottery is the discovery at Pompeii of probably two boxes of the best products of La Graufesenque in South Gaul and a find of identical pottery with the same ornaments and the same factory stamps at Rottweil on the Neckar (R. Knorr, l.c., p. 8).

¹⁴ On Petra and the cities east of the Jordan see the bibliography quoted in Chap. V, note 4. On trade, in particular, see H. Guthe, 'Die griechischrömische Städte des Ostjordanlandes', *Das Land der Bibel*, ii. 5 (1918), and A. Kammerer, *Pétra et la Nabatène* (1930). The excavations at Jerash by the government of Transjordan and Yale University have shown that the oldest Roman monuments there date from the age of Tiberius; under the Flavians we observe intense building activity: thus its great prosperity was not wholly due to Trajan. See the inscriptions found at Jerash, A. H. M. Jones, *JRS* 18, 1928, pp. 144 ff.; 20, 1930, pp. 43 ff. [C. B. Welles in *Gerasa*, pp. 355–494]. With regard to the development of the trade of Petra in Hellenistic times, I may refer to the honorific decree of Priene for Moschion (cf. *Arch. f. Papyr.* 4, p. 306, note 1). This man journeyed, probably on business, to Alexandria and Petra (*Inschr. Priene*, 108, ll. 163 ff.). Another trip of the same sort to Syria is mentioned ibid., no. 121, l. 49. On the trade of the late Ptolemaic period with Somaliland see U. Wilcken, *Zeitschr. f. äg. Spr.* 60, 1925, pp. 90 ff.

¹⁵ On the trade of Palmyra in general see L. Friedländer–G. Wissowa, *Sitteng. Roms*, i, 9th ed., p. 375; cf. M. P. Charlesworth, *Trade-routes and Commerce of the R.E.*, pp. 48 ff.; H. Schaal, *Vom Tauschhandel zum Welthandel* (1931), pp. 131 ff.; Rostovtzeff, 'Les inscriptions caravanières de Palmyre', *Mélanges Glotz*, ii (1932), pp. 793 ff.; id. 'The caravan gods of Palmyra', *JRS* 22, 1932, pp. 107 ff.; id. *The Caravan Cities: Petra and Jerash, Palmyra and Dura* (1932). New light has been thrown on the development of Palmyra and the adjacent region by the important discoveries of H. Breasted and F. Cumont in the Hellenistic and Roman city and fort of Dura on the Euphrates, see F. Cumont, *Fouilles de Doura-Europos*, 1922–3 (1926), Introd., esp. pp. xxxi ff. (on the trade of Palmyra). Dura had been, in the course of centuries, first a Macedonian, then a Parthian, then a Roman, and finally a Palmyrene fortress, controlling the point at which the caravans which came from the lower Euphrates abandoned the route along the river to reach Palmyra across the desert. The excavations at Dura were continued by Yale University: see *The Excavations at Dura-Europos*, &c., *Preliminary Reports*, i–ix (3) (1929–52) [*Final Report*, iv (pts. i (1–2)–iv (1)) (1943), vi (1949)]. On the history of Palmyra see the bibliography in Chap. V, note 4. A lively commerce between the Phoenician cities, Egypt and Meroë on the one side and Palmyra, i.e. the Parthian kingdom, on the other, is attested by some peculiar articles of jewellery (circular brooches inlaid with coloured stones), which were a speciality of the Partho-Sarmatian art and of which some examples have been found in Phoenician cities and in Meroë: see my *Iranians and Greeks in South Russia* (1922), pp. 133 and 233, and my

article in the *Mon. Piot*, 26, 1923, p. 157; cf. G. A. Reisner, 'The Meroitic king-dom of Ethiopia,' *JEA* 9, 1923, pls. VIII and X, 2, and id. *Museum of Fine Arts Bulletin*, Boston, 21, 1923, p. 27 (figure). (I am convinced that the products of jewel-lery found at Meroë were mostly imported.) A similar circular brooch was found at Byblos in the temple of Egyptian gods in a jar which contained objects of various dates, see P. Montet, *C. R. Acad. Inscr.* 1923, p. 91, fig. 3. Cf. Chap. V, note 20, and especially the words of Ael. Aristides quoted in that note. Aristides mentions Palmyrene, i.e. Parthian, jewels. Some typical Partho-Palmyrene examples were found at Dura in 1929: see *Dura, Preliminary Report*, ii (1931), pls. XLIV–XLVI.

[16] The latest study of the Periplus is that of E. Kornemann, 'Die historischen Nachrichten des Periplus Maris Erythraei über Arabien', *Janus*, 1, 1921, pp. 54 ff. Cf. W. Schur, 'Die Orientpolitik des Kaisers Nero', *Klio*, Beiheft 15, 1923; D. Leuze, *Or. Lit. Zeitg.*, 1924, pp. 543 ff.; W. Schur, *Klio*, 20, 1925, pp. 215 ff. A new edition of the Periplus is given by H. Frisk, *Le Périple de la Mer Erythrée suivi d'une étude sur la tradition et la langue, Göteborgs Högskolas Årskrift*, 33, 1921 (1).

[17] Sewell, *JRAS* 1904, pp. 591 ff.; cf. M. P. Charlesworth, l.c., p. 69 and note on p. 255. The development of a sound exchange is shown by the gradually decreasing numbers of Roman gold and silver coins found in India. The decrease is partly ex-plained also by a predilection which the Indians showed for the coins of Augustus and Tiberius; cf. the popularity of the coins of Philip in Gaul, of Lysimachus in South Russia, and of the *serrati* and *bigati* in Germany. Cf. W. Schur, 'Die Orientpolitik des Kaisers Nero,' *Klio*, Beiheft 15, 1923, pp. 52 ff., especially 54 ff.; K. Regling, *Zeitschr. f. Num.* 29, 1912, pp. 217 ff.; B. L. Ullman, *Philol. Quart.* 1, 1922, pp. 311 ff. It is possible that the coins of Tiberius, because of their popularity with the Indians, were struck as a real 'commercial money' (*Handelsmünze*) by his successors; compare on this type of coins B. Pick, *Die Münzkunde in der Altertumswissenschaft* (1922), pp. 30 ff. Alexandrian glass was imported to India and from there to China as early as the Hellenistic period. A beautiful Alexandrian glass vase was acquired by the Royal Ontario Museum at Toronto. It was found in China (in a tomb of the province of Honan) and belongs certainly to the Hellenistic period: see J. Pijoan, *Burlington Magazine*, 41, 1922, pp. 235 ff. The glass was cast, not blown, and is adorned with engraved medallions (one representing the head of Athena), which shows that it must be dated not later than the 2nd cent. B.C. The Freer gallery in Washington owns a beautiful bronze head of a dragon of the Han period: two glass pearls, certainly Alexandrian work, are inserted in the eyes of the dragon. On western influences on Chinese art of the Han period, see M. Rostovtzeff, *Inlaid Bronzes of the Han Dynasty in the Collection of C. T. Loo* (1927); see also A. Herrmann, *Lou-Lan* (1931), with excellent bibliography.

[18] On the development of the Arabian and Indian commerce in the 1st cent. A.D. see the books of M. Chwostow (quoted in Chap. II, note 26) and the articles of E. Kornemann (quoted in note 16) and of W. Schur (quoted in note 17); cf. H. G. Raw-linson, *Intercourse between India and the Western World from the Earliest Times to the Fall of Rome* (1916) [2nd ed. 1926] and M. P. Charlesworth, op. cit., pp. 58 ff.; E. H. Warming-ton, *The Commerce between the Roman Empire and India* (1928); H. Schaal, *Vom Tauschhandel zum Welthandel* (1931), pp. 149 ff. I do not think that the discovery of the direct route to India was due to the efforts of the Roman government. It was due to Alexandrian merchants. The Roman government helped these merchants because it was profitable for the *fiscus*. I see no necessity to concentrate all the measures taken by the Roman government in the time of Nero, who (or whose teachers and ministers, Seneca and Burrus), it is supposed, carried out a consistent mercantile policy. It is possible (we have no dates for these events) that an alliance between the Himyarites and the Romans was concluded as early as the time of Augustus, that Augustus first occupied

Leuke Kome and perhaps Adana (?), that the next step was taken by Claudius and Nero (the occupation of Syagros (?)), and some other by the Flavians. We must not exaggerate the importance of governmental measures, and we have not the slightest ground for supposing the existence of any economic policy on the part of the emperors of the 1st cent. The trade with India grew naturally in the atmosphere of a great Empire; of course, the Empire protected this trade which already existed and was growing. We shall see later that in the 2nd cent. A.D. there was probably a squadron of warships which maintained the security of the Red Sea (Chap. V, note 19). Had this existed without interruption from the Ptolemaic period, or did it disappear under Augustus, to be recreated later under the Flavians or later? The statement in Pliny that ships going to India carried archers for defence seems to be opposed to the existence of a fleet in the Red Sea, but it does not exclude the possibility. The numerous ostraka found at Coptos, referring to the trade between Coptos and Berenice and Myus Hormus, are very interesting for the history of the eastern and southern trade of Egypt in the early Empire. They are now in London in the collection of University College, London (Flinders Petrie Collection), and were published in a masterly edition by J. G. Tait, *Greek Ostraca in the Bodleian Library at Oxford and various other Collections*, i (1930), nos. 220–304. On this work see further my review, *Gnomon*, 7, 1931, pp. 21 ff. After Augustus very little was done to protect it. We see no serious attempts to occupy the Arabian coast or fight the growing kingdom of Axûm or even to maintain any military fleet in the Red Sea. The trade was carried on by the merchants at their own risk.

[19] On the first commercial relations of the Romans with the Germans see E. Norden, 'Die germanische Urgeschichte', *Tacitus' Germania* (1923), pp. 428 ff. Archaeological material from North-east Germany: E. Tungklaus, *Römische Funde in Pommern* (1924), particularly pp. 102 ff. Professor Rodenwaldt has called my attention to a recent discovery of early Roman antiquities at Lübsow (district of Greifenberg, near Stettin), now in the Museum für pommer'sche Altertümer in Stettin. I owe to the kindness of Dr. Kunkel a series of photographs of these discoveries from Lübsow and some other places. They attest a lively exchange of articles between North Germany and Italy. See W. Kunkel, *Mannus*, Ergänzungsbd. v (1927), pp. 119 ff. and J. Kostrzewski, 'Capuanisches Geschirr im Norden', *Reall. d. Vorgeschichte*, iii, pp. 280 ff., pl. 132. For Scandinavia see Montelius, 'Der Handel in der Vorzeit', *Praehist. Zeitschr.* 2, 1910, pp. 249–91; T. Arne, *Det stara Svitgod* (1917); id. 'Tenetid och romersk jarnålder i Russland med särskild hänsyn till de römerska denarfynden', *Oldtiden*, 7, 1918, pp. 207 ff.; for Norway, H. Shetelif, *Préhistoire de la Norvège* (1926), pp. 136 ff.; A. W. Brøgger, *Kulturgeschichte des norwegischen Altertums* (1926), pp. 232 ff. On the 'discovery' of the route through Carnuntum, Pliny, *NH* xxxvii. 3. 45: 'DC M p. fere a Carnunto Pannoniae abesse litus id Germaniae, ex quo invehitur, percognitum nuper, vivitque eques R. ad id comparandum missus ab Iuliano curante gladiatorium munus Neronis principis. Qui et commercia ea et litora peragravit, etc'. For the sea-route: F. Friis-Johansen, *Hobyfundet*; for that of the Dnieper, M. Rostovtzeff, *Iranians and Greeks in South Russia*, p. 234, no. 16; T. Arne, *Det stara Svitgod*, pp. 16 ff.; H. Schaal, *Vom Tauschhandel zum Welthandel*, pp. 165 ff. and 182 ff. On the discovery of Roman coins in independent Germany, see St. Bolin, *Fynden av romerska mynt i det fria Germanien* (1926), cf. *Bericht der röm.-germ. Kommission*, for 1929 (1930), pp. 86 ff. Cf. Chap. V, note 17.

[20] The aspect of a prosperous medium-sized city in Campania is revealed by the excavations in Pompeii. It is needless to repeat here the excellent sketch of Pompeii from the economic point of view which has been given by T. Frank ('The economic life of an ancient city,' *Class. Phil.* 13, 1918, pp. 225 ff.; repeated in an enlarged shape in *Econ. Hist.*², pp. 245 ff. and in *Hist. of Rome*, pp. 375 ff.). I regret, however, that he

has not used the splendid material furnished by the mural decorations of the Pompeian houses. Those in the shops give a true and realistic picture of what went on there (see, e.g. M. Della Corte, 'Fullones', quoted in Chap. II, note 19). Extraordinarily interesting are the shop advertisements recently uncovered in the Strada dell' Abbondanza, one of the most commercial and industrial streets of Pompeii (see one specimen on pl. XVI); these frescoes are partly published in the *Notizie degli Scavi* from 1911 to 1916. We are still waiting for the publication of the discoveries made under the direction of V. Spinazzola, and of the very interesting frescoes of the splendid tomb found near Porta Vesuvio, which illustrate the activity of a Pompeian aedile [V. Spinnazola, *Pompei alla luce degli scavi nuovi di via dell' Abbondanza (anni 1910–1923)* (Rome 1953: two vols. of text and one of plates)]. Still more important are the mural decorations in the large and rich houses of the town. Some of the owners of these houses liked to reproduce on their walls not only mythological scenes but also scenes of daily life, naturally replacing the actual workmen, who appear in the frescoes of the shops, by attractive figures of little Cupids, and thus giving the scenes an idyllic character which is very characteristic of the tendencies of the times (cf. Virgil's *Bucolica* and the so-called 'landscape bas-reliefs' of the idyllic, not the heroic, type). I have no doubt that under this disguise the owners of the houses portrayed on their walls the economic life of the city, and in part their own life. The most famous example, though not at all unique, is the well-known frieze of the 'black' room of the House of the Vettii (see pl. XIV and XV). The chief subject of this frieze is the production and sale of wine. I have no doubt that Vettius owned one or many villas of the above-described type in the territory of Pompeii. It is a pity that, owing to the disappearance of the frescoes on the left wall of the room, the series of representations of the owner's sources of income from the country is incomplete. What is left deals with wine-production; specially interesting is the fresco showing a wholesale wine-shop and a customer tasting a special brand of wine. The central wall is filled with other representations of the same type (vintaging, crushing of grapes (?), a Bacchic procession). The wall on the right hand is devoted to commercial and industrial concerns, characteristic of Pompeii. The Pompeian landowners brought roses and sold them in a shop in the form of garlands. Part of the oil produced in the same villas they transformed into perfumes and sold them in their perfume shops. Besides, there were at Pompeii, goldsmiths' shops and fulleries. All these branches of industry were well represented not only in Pompeii, but throughout Campania, having been mostly imported thither from Alexandria (cf. Chap. II, p. 70, and notes 30–32). On the frieze of the house of the Vettii see A. Mau, *Pompeji in Leben und Kunst*[2], p. 351 (plate), and pp. 354 f., figs. 186 and 187 [Eng. trans. by F. W. Kelsey, 1902]. Relations with Alexandria are attested not only by the many important articles which were imported thence to Pompeii but also by the pictures on the pillars which flanked the entrance to the house, Regio, ii, ins. 2, no. 4 (*Not. d. Scavi*, 1914, p. 180). They represent the divine protectors of the house and of the landlord, who are Minerva (protector of industry) and Alexandria or Egypt. Beneath the head of Alexandria is the figure of Mercury.

Another important point suggested by the study of the monuments of Pompeii is the gradual industrialization of life in the city. This has been shown very clearly by the excavations in the Strada dell' Abbondanza. In the earlier period (down to the end of the 1st cent. B.C.) Pompeii was mainly a city of landowners and of residential houses. With the establishment of the Empire industrialization sets in and reaches its climax in the period just before the destruction of the city. In the early part of the 1st cent. A.D. the Strada dell' Abbondanza was still a street of residential houses. At the time of the eruption most of the residential houses were owned by industrialists and shop-keepers, and the street became one of the busiest parts of Pompeii. The most important concerns were those connected with clothing. It is no accident that the only large exchange building was built by Eumachia for the *fullones* and that this building is connected with the Strada dell' Abbondanza. Next in importance to the production of woollen clothes (favoured by the neighbourhood of the large grazing region of Samnium and Apulia) was the making of perfumes (Campania was rich in flowers, especially roses) and of fish-sauce (*garum*), a natural product of a city by the sea. On Pompeii as a harbour, see M. Della Corte in *Ausonia*, 10, 1921, p. 83.

The process of the industrialization of Pompeii is wonderfully illustrated by the houses (Regio, i, ins. 7, n. 3 ff.) recently excavated by A. Maiuri, and admirably published by him (*Not. d. Scavi*, 1927, fasc. 1–3). It is interesting to observe that a small residential house, that of M. Fabius Amandius, was spared notwithstanding the industrialization, though enclosed between the house of a wealthy man and a number of shops. Such instances are not exceptional. A typical middle-class house of the late commercial period of Pompeian life is that of P. Cornelius Tages (or Teges), nos. 10–12, which was formed by joining two older houses (Maiuri, op. cit., pp. 32 ff.). It is the house of the 'bronze ephebe' (actually a Ganymede), a beautiful Greek statue converted into a torch bearer. The decoration of the house is just what might be expected of a *nouveau riche*: see Amelung, 'Bronzener Ephebe aus Pompeji', *JDAI* 42, 1927, pp. 127 ff. The owner of this house, like many other owners of houses formerly belonging to the aristocracy, was a libertus.

The industrialization of Pompeii is one of the most important features of its economic life in the 1st cent. A.D. The arts and crafts at Pompeii must be studied from this point of view. A careful investigation of the history of the Pompeian buildings would certainly furnish unexpected evidence on the history of trade and crafts in the city. The same result would follow from an historical examination of the thousands of industrial products found in the town. A collection of shop advertisements and other pictures of the same kind would certainly be of great use for such a study. The advertisements, however, must be studied not by themselves but in connexion with the shops to which they belong, with the electoral programmes of the various corporations which are mostly grouped around the shops of their members, with the *graffiti* in the shops and the houses, with the trade-marks and other inscriptions on the amphorae and on the various products of industry, and with the industrial products themselves.

The industrialization of life was in no way confined to Pompeii and to Campania. It was a general phenomenon: witness Aquileia, of which we have spoken above. With it is connected one of the most important problems of the economic history of the Empire. Why did industrialization not progress? Why did agriculture prevail over industry? We are able to follow the economic development of Pompeii step by step: we see how the landowners, while remaining landowners, invested larger and larger sums of money in industry, and how capitalistic industry gradually prevailed over the small artisans. Why did this process stop? To this crucial problem I shall endeavour to give an answer in the following chapters. For Italy the time of the Julio-Claudian emperors was still the period of progressive industrialization.

[21] Col. iii. 3. 1; Plin. *NH* xiv. 3. 36 ff. See the chapters on Columella and Pliny in W. Heitland, *Agricola*, pp. 250 ff. and 281 ff.; G. Carl, *Vierteljahresschrift f. Soz.- u. Wirtschaftsg.* 19, 1926, pp. 1 ff. I see no reason to assume a decline in viticulture in the time just before Columella and a revival through his influence, as conjectured by O. Seeck, *Gesch. d. Unterg. d. antiken Welt*, i, p. 371. On the development of viticulture in Northern Italy see Mart. iii. 56 and 57 (Ravenna). The low prices in Martial's time were probably due to the wars in the Danube provinces. It is unfortunate that we do not know the provenance and the date of the interesting bas-relief now in the Museum at Ince Blundell (see my article in *Röm. Mitt.* 26, 1911, pp. 281, fig. 3 [= B. Ashmole,

Ancient Marbles at Ince Blundell, p. 108, no. 298, and pl. 46]). The relief represents a large storehouse of wine, of the same type as the storehouses in the villas of Pompeii: in the right corner of it the manager is seated at a counter under a special projecting roof, transacting his business (see pl. xxxiii, 2).

²² On this point see W. Heitland, *Agricola*, pp. 250 ff., chapter on Columella, and *passim*, G. Carl, l.c.

²³ On slaves in industry, Sen. *Exc. controv.* ii. 7, p. 358 B; Plin. *NH* xxxvii. 13. 203; on large masses of slaves in general see, e.g. Liv. vi. 12. 5; Tac. *Ann.* xii. 65. On the tendency to increase the numbers of slaves by promoting family life among them, cf. the well-known advice of Columella, i. 8. 19, and Petr. *Cena Tr.* 53 (on the children born on the Cumaean estate of Trimalchio). There was nothing new in this system; cf. App. *BC* i. 7 (29). I cannot wholly accept the statement of Frank about Pompeii. He insists (*Econ. Hist.*², p. 268) on the fact that most of the shops of the city which were not connected with the living-rooms of the corresponding houses, and so were probably let to outsiders by the owners of the houses, were managed by free artisans. I cannot help thinking that the shops may have been rented to slaves (legally of course to their masters) working for their masters in individual shops. From the existence of associations of craftsmen we cannot decide whether the craftsmen were slaves, or freeborn men, or freedmen. The fact that many people bought wine and food at small counters does not show that they were free: slave-artisans had certainly pocket-money; how else could they acquire a *peculium*? On the other hand, the facts that prostitutes, mostly slaves, recommended candidates for election (see M. Della Corte, *Not. d. Scavi*, 1911, pp. 419 ff. and 455 ff.; cf. *CIL* iv. 1507. 6) and that the *vico-ministri* were, to a large extent, slaves, show that a certain freedom of action and even a certain political influence were enjoyed by other than freeborn people. The large number of slaves owned by some of the leading families of Pompeii is shown by the inscriptions of the cemetery of the *familia* (i.e. the establishment of slaves and freedmen) of the Epidii recently discovered near the town (M. Della Corte, *Not. d. Scavi*, 1916, pp. 302 ff.). The cemetery was probably used by the same *familia* from the Samnitic period. There is no doubt that the Epidii themselves were not buried in this cemetery but in rich tombs along the roads leading to Pompeii. The modest cemetery was reserved for the 'household', which kept together for more than a century. Further evidence is furnished by the villas of which I have spoken repeatedly. In the villa of Agrippa Postumus (*Not. d. Scavi*, 1922, pp. 459 ff.) eighteen rooms on one side of the back-yard of the villa were reserved for the slaves. This implies at least eighteen slaves and probably many more. The villa of Agrippa is not larger than many of the other excavated villas. The villa near Stabiae, similar to that of Agrippa (no. VIII of Della Corte), has at least nineteen slave *cubicula* and a large *ergastulum* (*Not. d. Scavi*, 1923, p. 277, fig. 4). We can see that the number of slaves who worked in the vineyards of Campania was very large in A.D. 79. There is no doubt that industry also was based on slave labour.

²⁴ See note 13.

²⁵ On the large estates of favourites of the emperors in Egypt, see Chap. II, note 15, and Chap. VII, note 43. Acte, the mistress of Nero, possessed large corn-growing estates in Sardinia which had a tile and jar factory connected with them; see E. Pais, *Storia della Sardegna e della Corsica durante il dominio Romano*, i (1923), pp. 342 ff.; cf. p. 338. To the same type of landowners belongs also Seneca, who possessed many estates in different parts of the Roman Empire, especially in Egypt (οὐσία Σενεκιανή is often mentioned along with the οὐσίαι of other imperial favourites, beginning with Maecenas). One of the large estates of Seneca is described by Columella, iii. 3. 3. It lay near Nomentum, and was famous for its vineyards and their model management. The

wonderful achievements of Seneca in viticulture remind us of Pliny's story of Remmius Palaemon (*NH* xiv. 4. 49–50). On Seneca's estate near Nomentum, cf. Suet. *De ill. gramm.* 23; Plin. *NH* xiv. 4. 49–52; Sen. *Epist.* 104. 110, and *Nat. Quaest.* iii. 7. 1. The large estates in general are depicted by Seneca in his famous eighty-ninth letter; cf. 90. 39: 'licet agros agris adiciat vicinum vel pretio pellens vel iniuria.' In *Epist.* 41. 7 Seneca gives a short description of a typical fortune of a rich man: 'familiam formosam habet et domum pulchram, multum serit, multum fenerat.' For him, however, the rich men *par excellence* are the freedmen, *Epist.* 27. 5. As a common topic of the Cynic διατριβαί (cf. J. Geffcken, *Kynika und Verwandtes* (1909), pp. 42 ff.), the existence of large properties and the moral perversity of the system are mentioned by Seneca, *Contr.* v. 5: 'arata quondam populis rura singulorum nunc ergastulorum sunt, latiusque vilici quam reges imperant'; Pers. iv. 26; Lucr. i. 158–82. It is evident that large estates remained the outstanding feature of the economic life of the Empire throughout the 1st cent. We must not forget, however, that the medium-sized property, especially in Campania, was not dead. The growth of large estates in the provinces at the expense of small landowners is depicted, e.g. by Dio Chrys. *Or.* 46. 7: ἔστι μὲν γὰρ χωρία μοι καὶ πάντα ταῦτα ἐν ὑμετέρᾳ γῇ· τῶν δὲ ἐμοὶ γειτνιώντων οὐδεὶς πώποτε οὐδεὶς οὔτε πλούσιος οὔτε πένης—πολλοὶ δὲ καὶ τοιούτων μοι γειτνιῶσιν—ᾐτιάσατο ἐμὲ ὡς ἀφαιρούμενός τινος ἢ ἐκβαλλόμενος, οὔτε δικαίως οὔτε ἀδίκως. A good parallel to the system of land-grabbing in Roman times by rich and influential men alike in Italy and in the provinces is afforded by the conditions which prevailed before 1914 throughout the Turkish Empire. The system is vividly depicted by C. L. Woolley, *Dead Towns and Living Men* (1920), pp. 222 ff. According to him, landlordism and the ownership of land by absentee and alien proprietors were steadily growing in Syria. A normal feature of a Syrian village was the existence, side by side with the peasants' houses, of a large stone villa belonging to a Turk who owned half the territory of the village, and to whom the peasants 'owe unpaid service for so many months of the year, and for that period are little better than his serfs'. The method of land-grabbing is the immemorial one. The peasant is forced, not by the amount of taxation in itself (which is more or less equivalent to the Roman *decuma*) but by the system of collection and the 'hand in glove' activity of the landlord and the government officers to take one loan after another and finally to mortgage his farm. Besides the taxes, the military levies help to enslave the peasant population and to transform the free peasant owner into a tenant serf. I do not know whether things are now changed.

[26] See M. Bang, 'Die Steuern dreier römischer Provinzen' in L. Friedländer–G. Wissowa, *Sitteng. Roms*, iv, 10th ed., pp. 297 ff., and my article 'Frumentum' in Pauly–Wissowa, vii, cols. 150 ff.

[27] See my article 'Frumentum' in Pauly–Wissowa, vii, cols. 184 ff. An excellent illustration of the difficulties of the corn-supply even in agricultural cities is afforded by the disturbances at Prusa, of which we possess a good account in the forty-sixth speech of Dio; cf. H. von Arnim, *Leben und Werke des Dio*, pp. 207 ff.; cf. Chap. V, note 9 and Chap. VIII, note 21.

[28] O. Hirschfeld, 'Der Grundbesitz der römischen Kaiser', *Kl. Schr.* pp. 516 ff.

[29] A series of documents of the age of Claudius and Nero (all from the Fayyûm) give valuable information regarding the rapid depopulation of the villages of that region. In *P.Corn.* 24 (A.D. 56) a collector of the poll-tax and of the ditches-tax writes that in the village of Philadelphia there were forty-four ἄποροι and ἀνεύρετοι, that is 'without estate liable to liturgies and taxes, and untraceable'. Certainly these people had escaped to some other village of Egypt, or to the marshes of the Delta in order to avoid taxes. The same situation occurs in an earlier papyrus (A.D. 45), *P.Graux* 1

(H. Henne, *Bull. Inst. franc. d'arch. or.* 21, 1923, pp. 189 ff.), also concerning Philadelphia. The collector of the poll-tax complains to the superintendent of the district because certain persons (ἄπορα ὀνόματα, that is people who have not paid their tax) were hiding, so it was reported, in the villages of another district. The superintendent of the Fayyûm therefore writes to his colleagues requesting them to put some police at the service of the tax-collector, finally, in *P.Graux* 2 (A.D. 54–59) six collectors of the poll-tax in six villages, including Philadelphia, write to the prefect, the famous Ti. Claudius Balbillus (H. Henne, l.c., pp. 211 ff.; M. Rostovtzeff, *JEA* 12, 1926, pp. 28 ff.; H. Stuart Jones, *JRS* 16, 1926, p. 18; C. Cichorius, *Rh. Mus.* 76, 1927, p. 102) as follows (ll. 7 ff.): 'In the past many rich people used to live in the villages mentioned, while now there are very few, because some have escaped because they were in arrears, and others died without leaving relatives. We therefore run the risk of having to stop our activity because of this exhaustion.' This agrees perfectly with the text of Philo (*de spec. leg.* iii. 153–63) where a well-known, probably more recent, case is discussed: a tax-collector contrived to obtain the payment of taxes by beating, torturing, and finally killing the heirs and relatives of some who had escaped (ἔφυγον), since they could not pay their quota as they were too poor (διὰ πενίαν or ἀπόρως ἔχοντες). The result of behaviour of this sort was exactly the same as in the papyri mentioned above. Philo says (l.c. 162): καὶ ὁπότε μηδεὶς λοιπὸς εἴη τῶν συγγενῶν, διέβαινε τὸ κακὸν καὶ ἐπὶ τοὺς γειτνιῶντας, ἔστι δ' ὅτε καὶ ἐπὶ κώμας καὶ πόλεις, αἳ ταχέως ἔρημοι καὶ κεναὶ τῶν οἰκητόρων ἐγένοντο, μετανισταμένων καὶ σκεδαννυμένων ἔνθα λήσεσθαι προσεδόκων. Evidently the worst evil was not so much the ruthless tax-collection as the fatal system of making whole groups responsible for single persons (cf. Wilcken, *Festschrift f. O. Hirschfeld*, pp. 125 ff.; G. Lumbroso, *Arch. f. Papyr.* 4, pp. 66 ff.; M. Rostovtzeff, *Studien z. Gesch. d. röm. Kol.*, p. 206). It cannot be a matter of chance to find so much material referring to a period from which otherwise we have so little evidence. No doubt the cruel exaction of taxes, and particularly of the new and oppressive poll-tax, was one cause of the impoverization of the peasants. But it was not the only cause. As long as land is productive—and it yields well, particularly in the Fayyûm, so long as it is cultivated—the peasants in the mass have enough to pay their taxes with. On the contrary; it seems probable that the irrigation of the Fayyûm was neglected in the second half of the 1st cent. A.D. We know that in this period the majority of the best land was owned by people living in Rome or Alexandria (Chap. VII, note 45), and can therefore suspect that the neglect was due to the fact that the interests of the peasants were sacrificed to those of the large landowners. In any case, one fact is certain: that in the second half of the 1st cent. A.D. conditions in Egypt were far from prosperous. Naturally some prefects tried to remedy the situation: for example, the above-mentioned prefects Balbillus and Vestinus, and Ti. Iulius Alexander who was so much at home in Alexandria and was a contemporary of Philo (see his edict: *OGIS* 669 [‡H. G. Evelyn White and J. H. Oliver, *The Temple of Hibis*, ii (1939), pp. 23 ff.]; cf. U. Wilcken, *Zeitschr. d. Sav.-St.* 42, 1921, pp. 124 ff.). Nobody was successful, however. Only when Vespasian had carried out his far-reaching reforms was a brief improvement noticeable. See M. Rostovtzeff, 'Exploitation of Egypt in the First Century A.D.', *Journ. of Econ. and Business Hist.* 1, 1929, pp. 337 ff.; cf. J. G. Milne, 'The Ruin of Egypt by Roman Mismanagement', *JRS* 17, 1927, pp. 15 ff.

30 On the important changes within the senatorial class, the disappearance of the old Republican aristocracy, both patrician and plebeian, and the rise of new families of Italian and provincial origin, see P. Willems, *Le Sénat de la république romaine* (2nd ed., 1885), i, pp. 308 ff. and 427 ff.; O. Ribbeck, *Senatores Romani qui fuerint idibus Martiis anni u. c. 710* (1899); F. Fischer, *Senatus Romanus qui fuerit Augusti temporibus* (1908); P. Willems and J. Willems, 'Le Sénat romain en l'an 63 après J. Chr.' *Mus. Belge*, 4–6,

1901–2 (and separately Louvain, 1902); B. Stech, 'Senatores Romani qui fuerint inde a Vespasiano usque ad Traiani exitum', *Klio*, Beiheft 10, 1912; G. Lully, *De senatorum Romanorum patria* (1918); E. Groag, *Strena Buličiana* (1924), pp. 254 ff. It is unnecessary to reproduce the statistics given by the authors cited above, especially those of B. Stech. On the Roman knights see A. Stein, *Der röm. Ritterstand* (1927). A thorough investigation into the most distinguished families of the various provinces is urgently needed.

[31] See the books quoted in Chap. II, note 4.

[32] On the slaves and freedmen of the imperial court, see L. Friedländer–G. Wissowa, *Sitteng. Roms*, i, 10th ed., pp. 34 ff.; cf. iv, 10th ed., pp. 26 ff. and 47 ff. (by M. Bang), and M. Bang, 'Caesaris servus', *Hermes*, 54, 1919, pp. 174 ff. On slaves and freedmen in general, M. Bang, 'Die Herkunft der römischen Sklaven', *Röm. Mitt.* 25, 1910, pp. 223–51 and 27, 1912, pp. 180–221; M. L. Strack, 'Die Freigelassenen in ihrer Bedeutung für die Gesellschaft der Alten', *Hist. Zeitschr.* 112, 1914, pp. 1 ff.; A. M. Duff, *Freedmen in the Early Roman Empire* (1928); R. H. Barrow, *Slavery in the Roman Empire* (1928), with good bibliographies of the institution of slavery in the ancient world: to the three last-mentioned works the reader may be referred for citations of the well-known books on slavery; cf. L. Friedländer–G. Wissowa, loc. cit., i, 10th ed., pp. 234 ff.; M. L. Gordon, 'The Freedman's son in Municipal Life', *JRS* 21, 1931, pp. 64 ff. An interesting case of an imperial slave with a large family of his own is attested by the inscription of a certain *Eleuther Tharsi Charitonis Aug.-Se.* dis(pensatoris) vic(arii) arc(arii) vicarius (P. Minga-zinni, *Bull. Com.* 53, 1925, p. 218, fig. 2, cf. H. Erman, *Servus Vicarius* (1896), p. 438). The Augustales as bearers of the expense of the imperial cult: M. Krasheninnikoff, *The Augustales and the sacral Magisterium* (St. Petersburg, 1895) (in Russian); cf. L. R. Taylor, 'Augustales, Seviri Augustales and Severi', *TAPA* 45, 1914, pp. 231 ff.; cf. *JRS* 14, 1924, pp. 158 ff. The importance in the life of a city of the *magistri* and *ministri* of various cults and especially the role played in municipal life by the 'associations of the cross-roads', which still play an important part in the modern life of Southern Italy under almost the same names, are illustrated by the chapels of these associations. Particularly characteristic are the newly discovered chapels in the Strada dell' Abbondanza at Pompeii: see M. Della Corte, *Not. d. Scavi*, 1911, pp. 417 ff. and 1913, p. 478. The four *ministri* of this *compitum* were slaves, like the *ministri* of the other *compita* of Pompeii, cf. Boehm in Pauly–Wissowa, xii, col. 810; and G. Grether, 'Pompeian Ministri', *Class. Phil.* 27, 1932, pp. 59 ff.

[33] T. Frank, 'Race Mixture in the Roman Empire', *Amer. Hist. Rev.* 21, 1915–16, pp. 689 ff.; V. Macchioro, *La biologia sociale e la storia* (Camerino, 1905), and in *Politisch-anthropolog. Revue*, 5, 1907, pp. 557 ff.; M. P. Nilsson, *Hereditas*, 2, 1921, pp. 370 ff.; M. L. Gordon, 'The Nationality of Slaves under the Early Roman Empire', *JRS* 14, 1924, pp. 93 ff.; G. La Piana, 'Foreign Groups in Rome during the First Two Centuries of the Empire', *Harv. Theol. Rev.* 20, 1927, pp. 183–403. We need an investigation not only of the racial composition of the proletariate of Rome and Italy and of the praetorians and other troops stationed in Rome, which is supplied by Frank and Macchioro, but also and above all an examination of the racial constitu-tion of the city *bourgeoisie*, the upper classes of the residents in the Italian cities. So far as my personal investigation of the problem goes, I am inclined to believe that the Italian-born residents, the native stock of ancient families and of the veterans of the civil wars, gradually decreased, even in the 1st cent. A.D. Their place was taken by freedmen. I believe that this process went on concomitantly with the industrialization of life in the cities and with the weakening of the class of proprietors of medium-sized estates. It was more rapid in Campania (e.g. at Pompeii), slower in Northern and Central Italy, especially in the agricultural regions. Compare, however, the large

numbers of freedmen or descendants of freedmen among the landowners in the territory of Veleia before and in the time of Trajan: F. G. de Pachtère, *La Table hypothécaire de Veleia* (1920), pp. 87 and 95. de Pachtère has shown also how shortlived were the landowning families in the territory of Veleia. Cf. M. L. Gordon, 'The Freedman's Son in Municipal Life', *JRS* 21, 1931, pp. 64 ff.

IV. *The Rule of the Flavians and the Enlightened Monarchy of the Antonines*

1 The material for the history of the Flavian emperors has been carefully collected by Weynand in Pauly–Wissowa, vi, cols. 2623 ff. (Vespasian); pp. 2695 ff. (Titus); pp. 2542 ff. (Domitian); B. W. Henderson, *Five Roman Emperors* (1927); H. Mattingly and E. Sydenham, *The Roman Imperial Coinage* ii (1926): *Vespasian to Hadrian*. I do not deal in this chapter with the constitutional reforms of Vespasian. It is well known that here also he appears, at least from the formal point of view, as a restorer of the principate of Augustus, see O. Hirschfeld, *Die kais. Verwaltungsb.²*, p. 475, against F. B. R. Hellems, *Lex de imperio Vespasiani* (Chicago, 1902); cf. the books quoted in Chap. II, note 1 and Chap. III, note 1.

2 On the recruitment of the Roman army under the Flavians see the books and articles quoted in Chap. III, note 8. It is obvious that my data on the social composition of the Roman army are purely hypothetical. There survive no statistics on the proportion of the recruitment in the towns as compared with the country. Certainly the barbarization was gradual and slow. The Italian peasant is naturally not the same as the peasant of Gaul or of the Danubian lands; and there were gradations among the peasants of the provinces. Egypt provides most interesting evidence (lists of soldiers): see the list of relevant documents in L. Amundsen 'A Latin Papyrus in the Oslo collection', *Symb. Osl.* 10, 1932, pp. 27 ff.

3 On this point see the articles quoted in Chap. II, note 10 and Chap. III, note 5.

4 See Chap. II, note 4.

5 H. von Arnim, *Leben und Werke des Dio von Prusa* (1898), pp. 304 ff.; L. François, *Essai sur Dion Chrysostome* (1921).

6 O. Hirschfeld, loc. cit., pp. 475 ff. and 83 f.; cf. my article 'Fiscus', in Pauly–Wissowa, vi, col. 2392.

7 See my *Studien z. Gesch. röm. Kol.*, pp. 379 ff.

8 Unfortunately we know very little of life in the large imperial and public estates of Italy and the provinces. The little we know is, however, enough to show that the conditions obtaining in the great imperial estates in Africa, as established especially by the Flavians, and in particular the relations between the *coloni* and the landowners, were on the 'normative' Hellenistic basis, not on the 'liberal' basis of Roman private law. I think I have shown this in my *Studien. z. Gesch. röm. Kol.* (1910). Gsell, *Hist. de l'Afr.* v, pp. 208 ff., makes the probable conjecture that the large imperial estates of Bagradas were first *ager publicus* of the Carthaginians, then royal land of the kings of Numidia, whence they passed into the hands of the Roman magnates, and ultimately, in the time of Nero and the Flavians, to the Roman emperors. It seems very likely to me that the kings of Numidia—if not indeed the Carthaginians—had regulated relations between tenants and landlords in a Hellenistic sense, and treated the peasant almost in the way in which βασιλικοὶ γεωργοί were treated in Egypt: whence came the so-called *operae*, or *corvées*. Hellenistic influences are evident, for instance, when we find reference in the Numidian kingdom to the ἐξέτασις (ἀναγραφή in the documents) of the foals (Strabo, 835 c, cf. Gsell, op. cit., i, pp. 153, 181, and 20, n. 4). This is the

same rule as we find in *P.Teb.* 703. These conditions were accepted by the Roman magnates and developed by the emperors. I have not been convinced by the arguments of T. Frank, *AJP* 47, 1926, pp. 55 ff., 153 ff., and *Economic History*², pp. 444 ff. The contrast between the 'normative' spirit of the imperial ordinances and the 'liberal' spirit of Roman civil law is too big, and cannot be explained away by emphatic statements. The same 'normative' spirit informs the regulations of the mines of Vipasca in Spain. The first regulations may be due to the Flavians; Hadrian followed in the same spirit. The monopolistic economy introduced and codified at Vipasca by an imperial law (*lex metallis dicta*) is almost identical with the monopolistic economy of Egypt in the Ptolemaic and Roman periods, as I have shown in my *Studien z. Gesch. röm. Kol.*, pp. 353 ff. E. Schönbauer, 'Zur Erklärung der lex metalli Vipascensis', *Zeitschr. d. Sav.-St.* 45, 1925, pp. 352 ff., and 46, 1926, pp. 181 ff., has developed this point of view.

⁹ See Chap. III, note 30.

¹⁰ On the very important problem of the admission of Greek-speaking men into the equestrian and senatorial aristocracy, see H. Dessau, 'Offiziere und Beamte des römischen Kaiserreiches', *Hermes*, 45, 1910, pp. 14 ff. and 615 ff.; Weynand in Pauly–Wissowa, vi, col. 2660; L. Friedländer–G. Wissowa, *Sitteng. Roms*, i, 9–10th ed., pp. 109 f.; B. Stech, *Senatores Romani*, &c., pp. 179 ff. Cf. C. S. Walton, 'Oriental Senators in the Service of Rome', *JRS* 19, 1929, pp. 38 ff. Walton's results are substantially the same as mine. Of the few senators of Greco-Oriental origin known to us under Vespasian, two had perhaps started their career already under Nero, one had been a partisan of Vespasian in the civil war, and at least one other was an ex-king. The same policy was pursued by Domitian. The first emperors to give the Greek aristocracy more or less equal rights with the Western in regard to military and civil service were Trajan and still more Hadrian. This was partly due to the greater competence of these oriental officials in eastern affairs, and in part was a concession of the emperors of the 2nd cent. to the state of feeling among the aristocracy of the Oriental cities, which is reflected in what Plutarch says about the ambitions of Greeks as regards the senate and the magistracies (*de Tranquill. An.*, 10, p. 470 c). The text shows that even under Trajan the Greeks were not fully satisfied with what they had got, and claimed much more. The same can be said of the equestrian order: see the relevant statistics of A. Stein, *Der röm. Ritterstand* (1927), pp. 412 ff. The East was not represented in the Equestrian order in any considerable proportion before the 2nd cent. A.D. The farther East we go, the later is the aristocracy of the region in question admitted to the privileged classes. Cf. L. Halin, 'Beamte griechischer und orientalischer Abstammung in der Kaiserzeit', *Festgabe des Gymnasiums Nürnberg*, 1926. The first consuls born in Asia Minor were Polemaenus of Sardis (A.D. 92) and Antius Quadratus (A.D. 93). The large estates of the latter in Asia Minor were inherited by the emperors, see W. M. Calder, *MAMA* i, p. 17. See also the important inscription of Miletus, published by A. M. Woodward, *BSA* 28, 1926/7 (publ. 1928), p. 120, where there is reference to a person (the name is missing, and the date is uncertain) of Miletus, who was the fifth senator of Asiatic birth and the first native of Miletus: αὐτὸς δὲ πλατύ[ση]μος δήμου ʽΡωμαίων πέμπ[τος] μὲν ἀπὸ τῆς Ἀσίας ὅλης ἐκ τ[οῦ αἱ]ῶνος, ἀπὸ δὲ Μιλήτου καὶ τῆς ἄλλη[ς ʼΙ]ωνίας μόνος καὶ [π]ρῶτος [= *L'An. ép.* 1930, 4].

¹¹ Cassius Dio, 65 (66). 12. 2 (p. 148 Boiss.): βασιλείας τε ἀεὶ κατηγόρει καὶ δημοκρα-τίαν ἐπήνει, cf., e.g., H. Stuart Jones, *The Roman Empire*, p. 117. The spirit of the sena-torial opposition was best expressed in the many books which dealt with the victims of the imperial persecutions, e.g. C. Fannius, *Exitus occisorum aut relegatorum a Nerone* (Plin. *Ep.* v. 5), or Titinius Capito, *Exitus illustrium virorum* (the victims of Domitian, Plin. *Ep.* viii. 12), which were probably freely used by Tacitus in his historical works.

See R. Reitzenstein, *Nachrichten Ges. d. Wiss. zu Göttingen*, phil.-hist. Kl., 1905, pp. 326 ff.; id. in *Sitzb. Heid. Akad.*, phil.-hist. Kl. 4, 1913 (14), pp. 52 f.; A. von Premerstein, 'Zu den sog. alexandrinischen Märtyrerakten', *Philol.*, Suppl. 16. 2, 1923, pp. 48 and 68. We must assume a strong influence of the Stoic and Cynic philosophers on these pamphlets.

12 An investigation of the ideas current in the Hellenistic age and in the first two centuries A.D. regarding the supreme power of one man in the state is urgently needed. E. R. Goodenough, 'The Political Philosophy of Hellenistic Kingship', *Yale Class. Stud.*, 1, 1928, pp. 55 ff., has shown, by an accurate analysis of some fragments of Pythagorean writings περὶ βασιλείας, how widespread were Pythagorean ideas on the king as νόμος ἔμψυχος, and how closely they were related to Persian and Indian concepts of royal power. Some references in Philo and Plutarch, and a fragment of Musonius, show that Pythagorean doctrines were widely diffused in the period of the early Empire, and that in intellectual circles of that period Stoic and Cynic theories on monarchy were not alone in the field. Many important problems concerning the development of political ideas in the Roman Empire are still unsolved. What is the origin and the philosophical justification of the idea of the Principate (see Chap. II, note 1)? When were Hellenistic ideas on the βασιλεύς applied to the principate? How many Pythagorean elements are to be found in the political philosophy of the Stoics and Cynics? An accurate collection of the fragments of Musonius and a study of his ideas would be very useful.

13 On Dio and his first stay at Rome see H. von Arnim, op. cit., pp. 142 ff.; W. Schmid in Pauly–Wissowa, v, cols. 848 ff.; Christ–Schmid–Stählin, *Gesch. d. gr. Lit.* ii. 1⁶, pp. 361 ff.

14 On the Cynics in general and on those of the second half of the 1st cent. A.D. in particular, see the excellent study of J. Bernays, *Lucian und die Kyniker* (1879), cf. P. Wendland, 'Die philosophische Propaganda und die Diatribe', *Die hellenistisch-römische Kultur* (2nd–3rd eds. 1912), pp. 75 ff. Wendland unfortunately disregards entirely the political character of the Cynic propaganda in the 1st and the earlier part of the 2nd cent. A.D.

15 The best evidence on the expulsion of the philosophers by Vespasian is given by Cassius Dio, 65 (66). 13 and 13, 1 a (vol. iii, pp. 146 f., Boiss.), cf. 15 (p. 149, Boiss.), and Suet. *Vesp.* 15. The death penalty imposed on Heras in the year 75 shows that he attacked the emperor personally.

16 Cassius Dio, 65 (66). 12 (after the speech of Helvidius Priscus): συνεχύθη τε ὁ Οὐεσπασιανὸς καὶ δακρύσας ἐκ τοῦ βουλευτηρίου ἐξῆλθε τοσοῦτον μόνον ὑπειπὼν ὅτι ‘ ἐμὲ μὲν υἱὸς διαδέξεται ἢ οὐδεὶς ἄλλος.’, cf. Suet. *Vesp.* 25. I cannot but think that Helvidius insisted in the senate that Vespasian should adopt the best man of the senatorial class, taking the Stoical and Cynical point of view. Vespasian refused even to listen to such suggestions. The sense of his words is: 'better the re-establishment of the Republic than the method suggested by Helvidius', cf. Weynand, op. cit., pp. 2676 f.

17 From the Alexandrian speech of Dio we know that, probably shortly before his visit to the city, there were serious riots in Alexandria which had been quelled by the Roman soldiers under the command of a certain Conon (*Or.* 32, 71–72). It is possible that these riots had been connected with a Jewish 'pogrom': see the so-called 'Acts of the Heathen Martyrs' of Hermaiscus, *P.Oxyr.* 1242 [=H. Musurillo, *Acts of the Pagan Martyrs* (1954), pp. 44 ff., no. VIII]; W. Weber in *Hermes*, 50, 1915, pp. 47 ff., cf. A. von Premerstein, 'Zu den sog. alexandrinischen Märtyrerakten', *Philol.*, Suppl. 16. 2, 1923.

18 There is a remarkable coincidence between the Πολιτικὰ Παραγγέλματα of Plutarch and the speeches delivered by Dio to some prominent Greek cities of the East, especially

the Alexandrians (32) and the Tarsians (33 and 34). The same leading themes appear
again in the Bithynian speeches of Dio, especially those addressed to his fellow citizens
of Prusa. Plutarch preaches to the politicians of the Greek cities a better understanding
of the real conditions of the Greek cities, which cannot be compared with those of the
glorious past (*Praecept. ger. reip.* 17, p. 814 A); an acquiescence in the measure of freedom
which is granted them by the Romans (ibid. 32, p. 824 c); an honest submission to, and
friendly relations with, the Roman governors (ibid. 17, p. 813 E and 18, p. 814 c);
and peace between the two classes of the population, the rich and the poor (ibid. 19,
p. 815 A and 32, p. 824 B). Almost identical is the advice given by Dio to the above-
named cities. In Tarsus a constant civil strife was going on both between the different
sections of the leading class (Dio, *Or.* 34. 16 f.) and between the leading class and the
proletariate (34. 21–23). There was also an unceasing strife with the governors and
the procurators (34. 9 and 15, cf. 42). It is well known that the conditions in the
Bithynian cities both under Vespasian (*Or.* 46) and after Dio's return from exile (see
the Bithynian speeches) were almost identical with those in Tarsus. Attempts
at a social revolution and a bitter struggle against the governors were the main
features in their life. It is unfortunate that J. Sölch in his study 'Bithynische
Städte im Altertum', *Klio*, 19, 1924, pp. 165 ff., makes no reference to the economic
and social problems that beset them. A similar political and social struggle between
the aristocracy and the proletariate was going on in the 'Herodian' cities of Palestine
in Nero's reign. We are well informed about Tiberias, where the proletariate consisted
of ναῦται ἄποροι, and some peasants: see Fl. Josephus, *Ant. Jud.* 18. 2, 3 (37–38) and
Vita, 9 (32–36) and 12 (66); cf. my *Studien*, p. 305 and Chap. VII, note 30.

[19] I am glad to see that the point of view which I was the first to emphasize (see my
article 'The Martyrs of Greek Civilization' in the Russian monthly *Mir Bozhij*, 1901),
viz. that the so-called 'Acts of the Heathen Martyrs' reflect the political opposition of
the Alexandrians to the Roman government and that they used the prosecutions of
the leaders of the Jewish 'pogroms' as a pretext for expressing their anti-Roman spirit,
seems to be nowadays generally accepted, though my article is almost never quoted
('Rossica sunt, non leguntur'). See Wilcken, 'Zum alexandrinischen Antisemitis-
mus', *Abh. d. sächs. Ges.* 27, 1909, pp. 825 (45) and 836 (56); id. *Grdzge.* pp. 44 ff. (with
a reference to my article); A. von Premerstein, 'Zu den sog. alexandrinischen
Märtyrerakten', *Philol.*, Suppl. 16. 2 (1923); H. I. Bell, *Juden und Griechen im römischen
Alexandria* (Beih. zum 'Alten Orient', 9, 1926); cf. W. Graf Uxkull-Gyllenband, 'Ein
neues Bruchstück aus den sog. Märtyrerakten', *Sitzb. Berl. Akad.* 1930 (28), pp. 664–679;
H. I. Bell, 'A New Fragment of the Acta Isidori', *Arch. f. Papyr.* 10, pp. 5 ff.; C. Hopkins,
'The Date of the Trial of Isidorus and Lampo before Claudius', *Yale Class. Stud.* 1,
1928, pp. 171 ff.; [H. Musurillo, *The Acts of the Pagan Martyrs* (1954)], see Chap. III,
note 2. I cannot enter here into the controversy on the character of the so-called
'Acts', which is debated by several modern scholars. It seems very likely that the
various pamphlets under the form of 'Acts', which were in circulation in Alexandria
and among the Greek population of Egypt, were codified somewhere about
the end of the 2nd cent., and that most of our fragments belong to this 'book' on the
Alexandrian martyrs of the emperors. I am convinced that some topics in the
'Acts' which remind one of the Cynic sermons (e.g. the emphasis laid by Isidorus
on the fact that he is not a slave and that the emperor is a παραφρονῶν βασιλεύς, the
insistence of the Alexandrians on their nobility and on their splendid education as
compared with the emperors' lack of education, &c.), and the tone of brusque
challenge to the imperial power which is the leading feature of almost all the 'Acts',
were first introduced into them, not at the end of the 2nd cent. (the time of the pre-
sumed codification), but much earlier and gradually. A good parallel to the 'Acts' is

furnished by Macc. II. 6 (ed. Swete) and IV. 5 (reports of the trial of prominent Jews before the τύραννος Antiochus Epiphanes). Note the ever-recurring theme of the τύραννος and the βασιλεύς in the long, bombastic, and impertinent speeches of the prosecuted Jews.

[20] A good illustration is given by the pictures drawn by Dio Chrysostom of Tarsus in Cilicia and of Kelainai in Phrygia; *Or.* 34. 8 (Tarsus): ὅθεν ταχὺ μείζων ἐγένετο ἡ πόλις καὶ διὰ τὸ μὴ πολὺν χρόνον διελθεῖν τὸν ἀπὸ τῆς ἁλώσεως, καθάπερ οἱ μεγάλῃ μὲν νόσῳ χρησάμενοι, ταχὺ δ' ἀνασφήλαντες, ἐπειδὰν τύχωσιν ἱκανῆς τῆς μετὰ ταῦτα ἐπιμελείας, πολλάκις μᾶλλον εὐέκτησαν and 35. 13 ff. (Kelainai).

[21] Cass. Dio, 65 (66). 15 (iii, p. 149, Boiss.).

[22] Cass. Dio, 66. 19. 3 b (iii, p. 154, Boiss.); *Orac. Sib.* iv. 119. 137; Weynand, loc. cit., col. 2721.

[23] Cass. Dio, 67. 16 and 18 (iii, pp. 184 and 185, Boiss.).

[24] On the measures taken by Domitian against the philosophers and on their chronology, see W. Otto, *Sitzb. Bayr. Akad.* 1919 (10), pp. 43 ff.; W. A. Baehrens, *Hermes*, 58, 1923, pp. 109 ff.; W. Otto, *Sitzb. Bayr. Akad.* 1923 (4), pp. 10 ff.

[25] See the speech of Dio, *Or.* 6, Περὶ τυραννίδος, cf. *Or.* 62, Περὶ βασιλείας καὶ τυραννίδος; cf. also Cass. Dio, 67. 12. 5 (iii, p. 179, Boiss.); Μάτερνον δὲ σοφιστήν, ὅτι κατὰ τυράννων εἶπέ τι ἀσκῶν, ἀπέκτεινε. Dio composed four speeches on βασιλεία, and allusions to his main ideas in the other speeches of the last period of his life are very frequent. The theme of the βασιλεία, having finally become current throughout the Empire, reappears in almost all Dio's speeches of this period. On his four speeches Περὶ βασιλείας (*Or.* 1–4) and the closely connected speeches 56 and 57, see H. von Arnim, op. cit., pp. 398 ff. A good study of the speeches of Dio from the political point of view was given by E. Grimm, *Studies in the History of the Development of the Roman Imperial Power*, ii (1901), pp. 160–256 (esp. pp. 224–7), cf. my review in the *Journ. of the Min. of Publ. Educ.* 341, 1902, pp. 148 ff., and the reply of Grimm, ibid., p. 172 (all in Russian).

[26] On the sources of Dio's speeches περὶ βασιλείας (to some extent Antisthenes but mostly the later Cynics and the Stoics), see E. Thomas, *Quaestiones Dioneae* (Leipzig, 1909).

[27] Especially the points concerning his relations with the soldiers and his imperialistic policy (the antithesis of πολεμικός and εἰρηνικός), *Or.* 1. 27 καὶ πολεμικὸς μὲν οὕτως ἐστὶν ὥστ' ἐπ' αὐτῷ εἶναι τὸ πολεμεῖν, εἰρηνικὸς δὲ οὕτως ὡς μηδὲν ἀξιόμαχον αὐτῷ λείπεσθαι. καὶ γὰρ δὴ καὶ τόδε οἶδεν, ὅτι τοῖς κάλλιστα πολεμεῖν παρεσκευασμένοις τούτοις μάλιστα ἔξεστιν εἰρήνην ἄγειν. Ibid. 28 ὅστις μὲν γὰρ ὑπερόπτης τῶν στρατευομένων καὶ οὐδεπώποτε ἢ σπανίως ἑώρακε τοὺς ὑπὲρ τῆς ἀρχῆς κινδυνεύοντας καὶ πονοῦντας, τὸν δὲ ἀνόνητον καὶ ἄνοπλον ὄχλον διατελεῖ θωπεύων is like a shepherd who does not care for his dogs, the result being that the flock is destroyed by both the wild beasts *and the dogs*. This passage is a splendid characterization of the rule of Nero and certainly alludes to him. As is well known, Nero is for Dio the perfect type of a tyrant. And finally ibid. 29 ὅστις δὲ τοὺς μὲν στρατιώτας διαθρύπτει μήτε γυμνάζων μήτε πονεῖν παρακελευόμενος is like a bad κυβερνήτης—an allusion both to Nero and to Domitian. Cf. the well-known utterance of Epictetus, *Diss.* 4. 5. 17 "τίνος ἔχει τὸν χαρακτῆρα τοῦτο τὸ τετρασσάριον"; "Τραιανοῦ." "Φέρε." "Νέρωνος." "ῥῖψον ἔξω, ἀδόκιμόν ἐστι, σαπρόν." When Plutarch speaks, in his Pythagorean treatise, *ad principem ineruditum*, 779 ff., of the stupidity of certain rulers who have themselves portrayed with the thunderbolt or the radiate crown, he has in mind not only some Hellenistic sovereigns, but also Caligula and Nero. Compare the scene on the arch of Beneventum, in which Trajan is greeted by Juppiter and other divinities (Chap. VIII, note 6), and a similar representation on

some gold coins of Trajan (F. S. Salisbury and E. Mattingly, 'The Reign of Trajan Decius', *JRS* 14, 1924, pp. 10 f.). The contrast is obvious: Trajan is protected by Juppiter: Caligula is himself Zeus Epiphanes. In *Or.* 3. 133 ff. there is another point which refers personally to Trajan. In speaking of the pleasures which are the true pleasures of a king, Dio rejects music and the theatre (a reference to Nero) and advocates hunting, which was the favourite pleasure of Trajan and Hadrian (see the circular medallions on the Arch of Constantine in Rome). It is worth noting that the ideas about the βασιλεία appear already in the Borysthenic speech, which certainly belongs to the period immediately after Dio's return from exile. In this matter I cannot share the ideas of H. von Arnim, loc. cit., pp. 483 ff. Gradually judgements on the emperors, from the point of view of the philosophy of the enlightened monarchy, crystallized in a type, which is found, for example, in Fronto, *ad Verum imp.* ii. 1, 8 (Naber, p. 119; Haines, ii, pp. 128 ff.[; van den Hout, i, p. 117]). According to this passage Caesar and Augustus are the founders of the Principate, Tiberius is put by himself with an *ille: imperatores autem deinceps ad Vespasianum usque eiusmodi omnes, ut non minus verborum puderet quam pigeret nomen et misereret facinorum.* This type, illuminated by a great artist, appears already in Tacitus.

²⁸ On the relations between Dio's first speech περὶ βασιλείας and the *Panegyricus* of Pliny (both delivered in A.D. 100), see H. von Arnim, loc. cit., p. 325; J. Morr, *Die Lobrede des jüngeren Plinius und die erste Königsrede des Dion von Prusa* (Progr. Troppau, 1915); K. Münscher, *Rh. Mus.* 73, 1920, p. 174.

²⁹ As we are dealing with a well-known period, it is unnecessary to enumerate and characterize all our literary sources and modern books, monographs, and articles (see Chap. III, note 1). The more important books and articles on subjects which are treated in this chapter will be found in the following notes. On the constitutional side, see the works quoted in Chap. III, note 1, and O. Th. Schulz, *Vom Prinzipat zum Dominat* (1919) (Preface and Introduction), cf. W. Weber, 'Trajan und Hadrian', *Meister der Politik* (1923).

³⁰ On the origin and the history of the family of Trajan see the excellent study of J. Rubel, 'Die Familie des Kaisers Traian', *Zeitschr. f. oest. Gymn.* 67, 1916, pp. 481 ff.; R. Paribeni, *Optimus Princeps*, i (1928), pp. 45 ff. On Hadrian, W. Gray, 'A Study of the Life of Hadrian prior to his Accession', *Smith College Studies in History*, iv. 2 (1919); B. W. Henderson, *The Life and Principate of the Emperor Hadrian* (1923). On Antoninus Pius and M. Aurelius, P. von Rohden in Pauly–Wissowa, ii, cols. 249 ff., and i, cols. 2279 ff. (cf. ii, col. 2434), and the articles in *Prosop. Imp. Rom.*; cf. the article of W. Weber quoted in note 29 and E. E. Bryant, *The Reign of Antoninus Pius* (1895). The picture of the family life of these emperors, as it can be gathered from the letters of Fronto, is, no doubt, characteristic for the nobility of the period, both Roman and provincial. It is the life of a landed aristocracy, clinging to the Roman tradition, and strict in outlook. Cf. M. Rostovtzeff, *Hadrian und M. Aurel* ('Menschen die Geschichte machen', i (1931), p. 184).

³¹ See note 10.

³² The same spirit of self-denying service to the country which is characteristic of the emperors and the officials of the 2nd cent. is shown also by the best citizens in the cities of the Empire. An excellent example is Dio of Prusa, who might have spent his life in the capital near his friend the emperor and yet remained most of the time in his native city; we must bear in mind that his life in Prusa was not a very pleasant one, as he was frequently attacked by his enemies and was in danger of losing his popularity with the masses of the people, see H. von Arnim, op. cit., *passim*. Another well-known instance is the great writer Plutarch. Nothing can be nobler than his words in the

Praecept. ger. reip. 15, p. 811 B, especially: ἐγὼ δ'ἀνάπαλιν πρὸς τοὺς ἐγκαλοῦντας, εἰ κεράμῳ παρέστηκα διαμετρουμένῳ καὶ φυράμασι καὶ λίθοις παρακομιζομένοις οὐκ ἐμαυτῷ | γέ φημι ταῦτ' οἰκονομεῖν ἀλλὰ τῇ πατρίδι; cf. Volkmann, *Leben, Schriften und Philosophie des Plutarch von Chaeronea* (1869), pp. 52 ff.; Christ–Schmid, *Gesch. d. gr. Lit.* ii. 1⁶, p. 488; in note 4 Schmid quotes a very interesting epigram which expresses the feelings of the Greeks of this period (J. Geffcken, *Gr. Ep.*, p. 82). On Plutarch as a Roman proconsul or procurator, see H. Dessau, *Hermes*, 45, 1910, p. 616. Another example is Sostratus of Boeotia, who lived on Parnassus, fought the robbers, and built roads (Luc. *Dem.* 1). It is doubtless tedious to read in thousands of inscriptions all over the Empire, recording decrees of the cities in honour of their distinguished citizens, the same praise of the liberality, the honesty, &c., of their magistrates, gymnasiarchs, priests, and so forth. But we must not forget that what the inscriptions say was perfectly true. Where shall we find in our own time thousands of rich men who would not only spend their time (without remuneration!) in managing the affairs of their city but also pay for it in the shape of a *summa honoraria* and voluntary gifts? It is usual to speak of ambition, petty desire for local celebrity, &c., but we should not overlook the facts that the ambition of an Opramoas was a noble one and that many people borrowed money to help their city and were ruined by doing so, see Plut., *de vitand. aer. al.*, pp. 827 ff. It is exceedingly instructive to read the excellent book of B. Laum, *Stiftungen in der griechischen und römischen Antike* (1914) (cf. J. C. Rockwell, *Private Baustiftungen für die Stadtgemeinde auf Inschriften der Kaiserzeit im Westen des römischen Reiches* (1909)), and to follow the story of these endless munificent gifts to the cities, which amounted sometimes to many millions. The public spirit which they displayed can be compared only with that shown by many rich Americans today. But relatively the Romans gave much more money for public purposes than modern Americans. On Aelius Aristides see A. Boulanger, *Aelius Aristide* (1923) (*Bibl. des Éc.* 126); on Lucian, Christ–Schmid, ii. 2⁵, pp. 550 ff. [6th ed., pp. 710 ff.]. A curious summary of the current opinion of the Eastern provincials on the Roman emperors of the 1st and particularly the 2nd cent. (the author was a Jew, but his judgement was not affected by his religion) is preserved in the 12th book of the *Oracula Sibyllina* (cf. book 5): see J. Geffcken, 'Römische Kaiser im Volksmunde der Provinz', *Gött. gel. Nachr.* 1901, pp. 183 ff., and cf. Rzach in Pauly–Wissowa, iv A, cols. 2155 ff. It is interesting to find that, along with the emperors of the 2nd cent., and especially M. Aurelius, Domitian is praised as a great benefactor of the Roman Empire. This may express the feelings of the Jews of this period, but it was certainly not the opinion of the leading classes in Asia Minor and Egypt.

³³ See the so-called 'Acts' of Appianus, U. Wilcken, 'Zum alex. Antisem.', pp. 822 ff. and *W. Chrest.* 20; Lietzmann, *Griechische Papyri*² (Kl. Texte), no. 21; A. von Premerstein, *Zu den sog. alex. Märtyrerakten* (1923), pp. 28 ff. Very striking is the enormous influence of the Cynic preaching discernible in this pamphlet: the opposition of τύραννος to βασιλεύς; the τυραννία, ἀφιλαγαθία, ἀπαιδευσία of Commodus, the tyrant, as opposed to M. Aurelius' qualities (φιλόσοφος, ἀφιλάργυρος, φιλάγαθος); the fierce challenge made to the emperor by the noble gymnasiarch, which reminds us of the behaviour of the Cynics in Rome under Vespasian and of Helvidius Priscus in the senate (Suet. *Vesp.* 15), &c. It is also noteworthy how purely political was the opposition of Appianus: it was directed against the 'robber' Commodus in the same sense as the opposition of the Roman senate against that emperor. Just as in the times of the Flavians, the Alexandrians were as bitter against the emperors as was the opposition in Rome. See *Acta App.* ii. 1 [Musurillo, *Acts*, &c., pp. 65 ff., no. XI] : στρ[α]φεὶς καὶ ἰδὼν Ἡλιόδωρον εἶπεν· "Ἡλιόδωρε, ἀπαγομένου μου οὐδὲν λαλεῖς;" Ἡλιόδωρος εἶπεν· "καὶ τίνι ἔχομεν λαλῆσαι μὴ ἔχον[τ]ες τὸν ἀκούοντα; τρέχε, τέκνον, τελεύτα· κλέος σοί ἐστιν ὑπὲρ τῆς γλυκυτάτης σου

πατρίδος τελευτῆσαι· μὴ ἀγωνία." (supplements partly of Premerstein); cf. iv. 3 ff. "τίς ἤδη τὸν δεύτερόν μου Ἀιδην προσκυνοῦντα . . . μετεκαλέσατο; ἆρα ἡ σύγκλητος ἢ σὺ ὁ λῄσταρχος;" ('Heliodorus, I am being carried off and you say nothing?' Heliodorus replied: 'To whom can I speak, there being no one to listen to me? Run, my child, die. It is a glory for you to die for your dearest fatherland. Don't be distressed'. . . . 'Who was it that called me up again, when I was already doing my second obeisance to Hades? *Was it the senate* or you the robber-chief?').

³⁴ The peace between the philosophers and the Roman emperors is attested by many facts. The attitude of Plotina towards the philosophers is well known, and so are the famous letters of Plotina to Hadrian, of Hadrian to Plotina, and of Plotina to the philosophers of the Epicurean school, *CIL* iii. 12283, cf. 14203. 15 = *Syll.*³ 834 = *IG* ii². 1099. Cf. A. Wilhelm, *Oest. Jahresh.* 2, 1899, pp. 270 ff.; J. Rubel, *Zeitschr. f. oest. Gymn.* 67, 1916, pp. 494 ff. See in general C. E. Boyd, *Public Libraries and Literary Culture in Ancient Rome* (1915); C. Barbagallo, *Lo stato e l'istruzione pubblica nell'impero romano* (1911), and especially L. Hahn, 'Ueber das Verhältnis von Staat und Schule in der römischen Kaiserzeit', *Philol.* 76, 1920, pp. 176 ff., and E. Ziebarth in Pauly–Wissowa, ii A, col. 766 (art. 'Schulen'); A. Gwynn, *Roman Education from Cicero to Quintilian* (1926); cf. Ch. H. Oldfather, 'The Greek Literary Texts from Greco-Roman Egypt' (*Univ. of Wisc. Studies in the Soc. Sciences and History*, 9, 1923). Unfortunately we know practically nothing of the great Museum of Ephesus with its associations of professors and doctors. The institution was already flourishing under Trajan, and the well-known C. Vibius Salutaris was much interested in it. See J. Keil, *Oest. Jahresh.* 8, 1905, pp. 128 ff., 135; *Forsch. Eph.*, ii, nos. 28g and 65; cf. ibid. iii, no. 68, and J. Keil, *Oest. Jahresh.* 23, 1926, p. 263. It is interesting that in the 2nd cent. A.D. some rhetoricians played an important part in the municipal life of Ephesus. How widely spread education was among men and women is shown by *P.Oxyr.* 1467, cf. Th. Reinach, *Rev. ét. anc.* 19, 1917, p. 32. Was not the changed policy of the emperors of the 2nd cent. towards education another victory of public opinion as represented by the philosophers? See Apollonius of Tyana, *Epist.* 54. i, p. 358 (Kays.): Ἀπολλώνιος δικαιωταῖς Ῥωμαίων· λιμένων καὶ οἰκοδομημάτων καὶ περιβόλων καὶ περιπάτων ἐνίοις ὑμῶν πρόνοια, παίδων δὲ τῶν ἐν ταῖς πόλεσιν ἢ νέων ἢ γυναικῶν οὔθ' ὑμῖν οὔτε τοῖς νόμοις φροντίς. The letter may be a forgery, but it reflects well the spirit of the period before the government interfered with the school-affairs of the cities.

³⁵ See, e.g., the interesting fragment of an inscription of Pergamon probably of the time of Hadrian, A. Conze, *Ath. Mitth.* 24, 1899, p. 197, no. 62 = *IGRR* iv. 444 [= Buckler, in *Anatolian Studies presented to Sir William Ramsay*, p. 33, no. 2], an edict of a proconsul taking measures against strikers who were engaged in the construction of a public building at Pergamon.

³⁶ Compulsory enlistment was used in critical times by all the emperors. But it did not become an institution, more or less a regular system, before Trajan, as is shown by the fact that there was a habit at that time of sending *vicarii* to the army in place of certain inhabitants of the province of Bithynia (Plin. *Ep. ad Tr.* 30; Th. Mommsen, *Ges. Schr.* vi, p. 36, note 2). It is to be noted that the Romanized population of Spain complained bitterly about repeated compulsory levies in the times of Trajan and Hadrian, *Scr. Hist. Aug.* M. Aur. 11. 7, and Hadr. 12. 4; J. Schwendemann, *Die historische Wert der Vita Marci bei den Scriptores Historiae Augustae* (1923), p. 43; Ritterling in Pauly–Wissowa, xii, col. 1300. I am glad to find that my interpretation of the words of the *SHA* agrees with that suggested by Domaszewski to Schwendemann. I must, however, insist that 'Italica adlectio' means compulsory enlistment of those who had the status of 'Italians' not only in North Italy but especially in Gaul and Spain, cf.

Chap. III, note 8. Cf. B. W. Henderson, *The Life and Principate of the Emperor Hadrian* (1923), pp. 171 ff. (on the military policy of Hadrian in general). On the compulsory levies of M. Aurelius see *Scr. Hist. Aug.* M. Aur. 21; *OGIS* 511; A. von Premerstein, *Klio*, 11, 1911, pp. 363 ff. (the Spartans; cf. L. Robert, *BCH* 52, 1928, p. 417 on *IG* v (1). 719), and 13, 1913, p. 84 (the *diogmitai*). The prevalence in the army of M. Aurelius of rural elements which did not even understand Latin or Greek is illustrated by the facts told by Cassius Dio, 72 (71). 5. 2 (iv, p. 256, Boiss.), about Bassaeus Rufus, the praetorian prefect of M. Aurelius: ἦν δὲ τῷ Μάρκῳ ὁ 'Ροῦφος ὁ Βασσαῖος ἔπαρχος, τὰ μὲν ἄλλα ἀγαθός, ἀπαίδευτος δὲ ὑπ' ἀγροικίας καὶ τὰ πρῶτά γε τοῦ βίου ἐν πενίᾳ τραφείς ... ὅτι ὁ Μάρκος ἐλάλει πρός τινα τῇ Λατίνων φωνῇ, καὶ οὐ μόνον ἐκεῖνος, ἀλλ' οὐδὲ ἄλλος τις τῶν παρόντων ἔγνω τὸ λαληθέν, ὥστε 'Ροῦφον τὸν ἔπαρχον εἰπεῖν· ' εἰκός ἐστι, Καῖσαρ, μὴ γνῶναι αὐτὸν τὰ παρ' ὑμῶν λαληθέντα· οὔτε γὰρ ἑλληνιστὶ ἐπίσταται ...' cf. *Exc. Val.* 302 f. ὅτι οὐδὲ ἑκὼν ἐστράτευτο, ἀλλ' ἀναδενδράδα εὑρεθεὶς κλῶν. The conscription of the 'latrones Dalmatiae atque Dardaniae' by M. Aurelius is brilliantly explained by C. Patsch, 'Arch-epigr. Untersuch. zur Geschichte der röm. Provinz Dalmatien', v (in *Wiss. Mitth. aus Bosnien*, &c., viii), 1902, pp. 123 ff., on the basis of some inscriptions in Dacia and Moesia Superior, as the liquidation of a rather dangerous revolt of native elements in Dalmatia at the time of the great wars on the Danube, cf. *Scr. Hist. Aug.*, Julianus, 1. 9. My assertion that in the 2nd cent. all the legionary soldiers were *de iure* Roman citizens must not be taken in the strictly juridical sense. As A. Segrè, *Aegyptus*, 9, 1928, pp. 303 ff., has shown, even in post-Hadrianic times in Egypt the Egyptians who served in the legions obtained citizenship only after the *honesta missio*. Was this treatment limited to oriental recruits? Cf. the *tirones Asiani* in *PSI* ix. 1063 (A.D. 117), and L. Amundsen, *Symb. Osl.* 10, 1932, pp. 22 ff.

v. *The Roman Empire under the Flavians and the Antonines. The Cities. Commerce and Industry*

[1] L. Boulanger, *Aelius Aristide et la sophistique dans la province d'Asie au IIme siècle de notre ère* (*Bibl. des Éc.* 126, 1923); cf. J. Mesk, 'Der Aufbau der xxvi Rede des Aelius Aristides', *Jahresb. über das K. K. Franz Joseph Realgymnasium* (Wien, 1909), pp. 5 ff.

[2] The best picture of the natural and gradual urbanization of a province is given by C. Jullian, in his admirable *Histoire de la Gaule*, v (1920), ch. ii, pp. 33 ff. ('Groupements humains et lieux bâtis'); cf. for the province of Africa, J. Toutain, *Les Cités romaines de la Tunisie* (*Bibl. des Éc.* 72, 1896). On the activity of Vespasian and his successors see Chap. VI, the sections concerning Spain and Dalmatia. On Spain our information is especially good: see *CIL* ii. 1610 = *ILS* 1981, and *CIL* ii. 1423 = *ILS* 6092 and *add.*; Weynand, *RE* vi. cols. 2659 ff.; McElderry, *JRS* 8, 1918, pp. 68 ff.; Abbott and Johnson, *Municipal Administration*, pp. 364 ff., nos. 60 and 61, and the well-known documents of Salpensa [Dessau, *ILS* 6088 = Riccobono, *FIRA*[2] 23] and Malaca [Dessau, *ILS* 6089 = Riccobono, *FIRA*[2] 24]. On the activity of Trajan in the Danubian countries see the valuable work of B. Filov, 'The Emperor Trajan and the Bulgarian Regions', *Bull. Soc. arch. bulg.* 5, 1915, pp. 171 ff. (in Bulgarian), and R. Paribeni, *Optimus Princeps*, i, pp. 309 ff. On the activity of the same emperor in Transjordan and in Arabia see Paribeni, op. cit., ii, pp. 1 ff. Epigraphical material from Gerasa shows that Trajan's work in Transjordan had already been largely prepared by the Flavians (A. H. M. Jones, *JRS* 18, 1928, p. 145, nos. 1 and 2; p. 147, no. 4, esp. pp. 152 ff., nos. 12–14 [= C. B. Welles, in C. Kraeling, *Gerasa, City of the Decapolis*, nos. 201, 200, 31, 51–52, 192]. On the urbanization of the provinces I shall speak more fully in the next two chapters, which will give a brief survey of the romanization of the various provinces.

[3] On ROME it is enough to quote O. Richter, *Topographie der Stadt Rom*, in

Müller's *Handbuch des kl. Alt.* iii. 2. 3, 2nd ed.; Jordan–Hülsen, *Topographie Roms*, vols. i–ii (1871–85), and vol. i³ (1907); Graffunder in Pauly–Wissowa, Zw. R. i, cols. 1008 ff.; S. B. Platner and Th. Ashby, *A Topographical Dictionary of Ancient Rome* (1929); G. Lugli, *I monumenti antichi di Roma*, i–iii (1931–8); cf. E. de Ruggiero, *Lo Stato e le opere pubbliche in Roma antica* (1925). On ALEXANDRIA see E. Breccia, *Alexandrea ad Aegyptum* (Eng. ed. 1922, with a bibliography); W. Schubert, *Ägypten vom Alexander dem Grossen bis auf Mohammed* (1922), pp. 1–136. On ANTIOCH, R. Förster, 'Antiochia am Orontes', *JDAI* 12, 1897, pp. 104 ff., cf. Pauly–Wissowa, *s.v.* Antiochia and Daphne; E. S. Bouchier, *A Short History of Antioch* (1921). On EPHESUS see the reports on the excavations in *Oest. Jahresh.*, Beibl., cf. *Forsch. Eph.* (1906 and foll.); J. Keil, *Ephesos. Ein Führer durch die Ruinenstätte* (1931); G. Lafaye, 'Éphèse romaine', *Conf. du Musée Guimet*, 32, 1909, pp. 1 ff.; Bürchner in Pauly–Wissowa, v, cols. 2773 ff.; P. Romanelli, *Diz. epigr.* ii, pp. 2110 ff.; Ch. Picard, *Éphèse et Claros* (*Bibl. des Éc.* 123, 1922), pp. 660 ff. On CARTHAGE, A. Audollent, *Carthage romaine* (*Bibl. des Éc.* 84, 1901); E. Babelon, *Guide à Carthage*; R. Cagnat, *Carthage, Timgad, Tébessa et les villes antiques de l'Afrique du Nord* (1909); on subsequent excavations in Carthage, see *Bull. arch. du Com. des trav. hist.* and *C. R. de la marche du Service des Antiquités de la Tunisie*. On LYONS, C. Jullian, *Histoire*, vols. iv–vi (*passim*), cf. A. Allmer et P. Dissard, *Musée de Lyon*, i–v (1888–93), esp. ii, pp. 138 ff.; P. Dissard, *Collection Récamier, Catalogue des plombs antiques* (1905).

⁴ It is impossible to enumerate here all the monographs on the various cities of Italy and the provinces. It will be sufficient to quote some general works where a good bibliography is to be found, and some monographs which are not quoted in these general works. The object of the appended bibliography is to give a selection of books, the study of which may serve to convey an idea of the different types of city in the Roman Empire. More monographs on the cities of the Empire are urgently wanted: they are the indispensable basis of a really satisfactory history of the Roman world. Brilliant pictures of city life in the provinces may be found in the classical fifth volume of Mommsen's *Römische Geschichte* [Eng. trans. *The Provinces of the Roman Empire*]; cf. V. Chapot, *Le Monde romain* (1927), and H. Dessau, *Gesch. der. röm. Kaiserzeit*, ii, 2 (1930). A survey of the provinces from the economic point of view is also given in the second edition of T. Frank's *Economic History*. I quote here these excellent works once and for all. Cf. from the point of view of the history of art H. Tiersch, *An den Rändern des römischen Reichs* (1911). On ITALY in general, see H. Nissen, *Ital. Landeskunde*, vols. i–ii (1883–1902); Lackeit, Philipp, and Scherling, in Pauly–Wissowa, Suppl. iii, cols. 1246 ff. On POMPEII, A. Mau, *Pompeji in Leben und Kunst*, 2nd ed. [Eng. trans. by Kelsey]; F. von Dulin, *Pompeji, eine hellenist. Stadt in Italien³* (1918). I cannot give here the complete titles of all the good guides to Pompeii (T. Warscher, M. Della Corte, A. Ippel, E. Pernice, N. Engelmann, A. Maiuri). Cf. L. Curtius, *Die Wandmalerei Pompejis* (1929); V. Spinazzola, *Le Arti decorative in Pompei* (1928); A. Maiuri, *Pompei. Visioni italiche* (no date); id. 'Aspetti e problemi dell'archeologia campana', *Historia*, 4, 1930, pp. 72 ff. On HERCULANEUM, A. Maiuri, *Ercolano. Visioni italiche* (1932), cf. *Nuova Antologia*, May 1929. On OSTIA, De Paschetto, *Ostia* (1912); J. Carcopino, *Virgile et les origines d'Ostie* (1919); cf. the important reports of G. Calza on his excavations in *Not. d. Scavi*, especially 1920–3, and his articles 'Gli scavi recenti nell'abitato di Ostia', *Mon. dei Lincei*, 26, 1920, pp. 322 ff., and 'L'importanza storico-archeologica della resurrezione di Ostia', *Atene e Roma*, 3, 1922, pp. 229 ff.; 'L'indagine storica di Ostia', *Bull. Com.* 53, 1925, pp. 232 ff.; and his brochure, *Ostia. Guida storica e monumentale*, 2nd ed.; J. Carcopino, 'Ostie', in *Les Visions d'Art*, 1929. Cf. Chap. II, note 36. On PUTEOLI, Ch. Dubois, *Pouzzoles antique* (*Bibl. des Éc.* 98, 1907); G. Spano, 'La "ripa Puteolana"', *Atti d. Acc. de Napoli*, ii (1928) (publ. 1931). On AQUILEIA, E. Majonica, *Führer durch das Staatsmuseum*

von Aquileia (K. K. Arch. Inst.) (1911); G. Brusin, *Aquileia* (1929); id. *Aquileia Nostra*, i (1930), pp. 22 ff.; cf. Chap. I, note 16 and Chap. II, note 34. On GAUL and GERMANY, C. Jullian, loc. cit.; F. Cumont, *Comment la Belgique fut romanisée* (2nd ed. 1919); H. Dragendorff, *Westdeutschland zur Römerzeit* (2nd ed. 1919); F. Koepp, *Die Römer in Deutschland*[3] (1926); F. Koepp and K. Bluemlein, *Bilder aus dem römisch-germanischen Kulturleben*[2] (1926); *Germania Romana. Ein Bilderatlas*[2] (1924–6); K. Schumacher, *Siedelungs- und Kulturgeschichte der Rheinlande*, vol. ii, *Die römische Periode* (1923); F. Hertlein, O. Paret, P. Goessler, Die Römer in Württemberg, i–iii (1928–32); J. Colin, *Les Antiquités romaines de la Rhénanie* (1927). Three model monographs on the ancient cities of Gaul are M. Clerc, *Aquae Sextiae. Histoire d'Aix en Provence dans l'antiquité* (1915); L. A. Constans, *Arles antique* (*Bibl. des Éc.* 119, 1921), and M. Clerc, *Massilia, Histoire de Marseille dans l'antiquité*, i–ii (1927–9). Some other monographs are less satisfactory, for example: B. A. Donnedieu, *La Pompéi de Provence* (Fréjus, 1927); J. Saintel, *Vaison dans l'antiquité*, i–iii (1926–7). On the interesting ruins of *Lugdunum Convenarum* (Saint-Bertrand de Comminges), in which excavations began in 1913, cf. J. Calmette, *Bull. Soc. Ant. de France*, 1928, pp. 253 ff.; P. Lavedan, R. Lizop, B. Sapène, *Les Fouilles de Saint-Bertrand de Comminges* (1929); id. *Rapport sur les fouilles*, &c. 1929–30 (1931). On the progress of excavation in France in 1915–30, see R. Lantier, *Ber. d. r. g. Komm.* 20, 1930, pp. 119 ff. For the cities of the Rhine see E. Sadée, *Das römische Bonn* (1925); A. Grenier, *Quatre villes romaines de Rhénanie* (*Trèves, Mayence, Bonn, Cologne*) (1925); D. Krencker, *Das römische Trier* (1926); R. Forrer, *Strasbourg-Argentorate préhistorique, gallo-romain et mérovingien* (1927); on Castra Vetera, see H. Lehner, *Römische-Germanisch Forschungen*, iv (1930), and *Das Römerlager Vetera bei Xanten* (1926). On Switzerland see F. Staehelin, *Die Schweiz in römischer Zeit*[3] (1948; herausgeg. durch die Stiftung von Schnyder v. Wartensee). On BRITAIN in general see F. Haverfield, *The Romanization of Roman Britain* (4th ed. 1923), and *Roman Occupation of Britain* (1924), and his monographs on various cities of Britain; R. G. Collingwood, *Roman Britain* (1932). Cf. the annual reports on Roman Britain by R. G. Collingwood and M. V. Taylor in *JRS* (since 1921). On London, F. Haverfield, *JRS* 1, 1911, pp. 141 ff.; *Royal Commission on Historical Monuments. An Inventory of the Historical Monuments in London*, vol. iii: *Roman London* (1928); Ziegler, *RE* xiii, cols. 1396 ff. On SPAIN, A. Schulten in Pauly–Wissowa, viii, cols. 2034 ff.; P. Paris, *Promenades archéologiques en Espagne* (1914 and 1921); E. S. Bouchier, *Spain under the Roman Empire* (1914); A. Schulten, *Hispania* (Barcelona, 1921). On AFRICA, S. Gsell, *Les Monuments antiques de l'Algérie* (1901); id. *Promenades archéologiques aux environs d'Alger* (1927); G. Boissier, *L'Afrique romaine*[5] (1912); A. Schulten, *Das römische Afrika* (1899); J. Toutain, *Les Cités romaines de la Tunisie* (1896); E. S. Bouchier, *Life and Letters in Roman Africa* (1913); R. Cagnat, 'Les Romains dans l'Afrique du Nord', *Riv. della Tripolitania*, 1, 1924–5, pp. 323 ff.; 2, 1925–6, pp. 75 ff. On some groups of ancient cities of Africa, see R. Cagnat, *Carthage, Timgad, Tébessa*, &c. (1909); id., *Visite à quelques villes africaines récemment fouillées* (*Ann. du Mus. Guimet, Bibl. de vulgarisation*, 39, 1912). On separate cities: Timgad, E. Boeswillwald, R. Cagnat, A. Ballu, *Timgad, une cité africaine sous l'Empire Romain* (1905); A. Ballu, *Guide illustré de Timgad*, 2nd ed.; Lambaesis, R. Cagnat, 'L'Asclepieium de Lambèse', *Atti d. Pontif. Acc. Rom. di Archeologia* (ser. iii), *Memorie*, i. 1 (1923); Khamissa and Announa, *Gouvernement général de l'Algérie. Khamissa, Mdaourouch, Announa. Fouilles exécutées par le Service des Monuments Historiques de l'Algérie*, vol. i (Khamissa), vol. iii (Announa) (1914–22); R. Johannessen, 'A Roman Town in Africa', *The History Quarterly*, 1, 1927, pp. 82 ff.; Djemila, R. Cagnat, *Mus. Belge*, 18, 1923, pp. 113 ff.; A. Ballu, *Guide illustré de Djemila* (1927); Volubilis, L. Chatelain, *C.R. Acad. Inscr.* 1922, pp. 28 ff.; Thugga, L. Poinssot, *Nouv. arch. d. miss. scient.* 13, 1906, pp. 103 ff.; 18, 1910, pp. 83 ff.; 21, 1916, pp. 1 ff.; 22, 1919, pp. 133 ff.; Bulla Regia, Uchi Majus, Siagu, Sufetula, Althiburos, Thuburbo Majus, A. Merlin and L. Poinssot, *Notes et Documents publiés par la Direction des Antiquités et Arts* (*Protectorat Français. Gouvernement Tunisien*), vols. i, ii, iv–vii(1908–22), cf. on Bulla Regia, L. Carton, *C.R. Acad. Inscr.* 1922, p. 326; Gigthis, L. A. Constans, *Gigthis. Études d'histoire et d'archéologie sur un emporium de la Petite Syrte* (1916). Cf. the illustrated catalogues of the Museums of Antiquities in Tunisia and Algeria—*Musées et collections archéologiques de l'Algérie et de la Tunisie*: Musée Alaoui (2nd ed.), d'Alger (with a supplement by P. Wuilleumier, 1928), de Cherchel (and supplement), de Lambèse, d'Oran, de Sfax, de Sousse, de Tébessa, de Timgad. On TRIPOLI and CYRENE, R. Paribeni, *Diz. epigr.* ii, pp. 1450 ff.; L. Homo, 'Les Romains en Tripolitaine et en Cyrénaique', *Rev. d. deux mondes*, 1914, Mars, pp. 389 ff.; S. Ferri, 'Tre anni di lavoro archeologico a Cirene', *Aegyptus*, 4, 1923, pp. 163 ff.; U. von Wilamowitz-Moellendorff, *Kyrene* (1928) [It. trans. Bergamo, 1930]; *Notiziario archeologico del ministero delle colonie*, esp. vol. 4 (1927); F. Noack, 'Archaeologische Entdeckungen in Tripolitanien', *Die Antike*, i, 1925, pp. 204 ff.; R. Cagnat, *Journ. Sav.* 1927, pp. 337 ff.; P. Romanelli, *Leptis Magna* (1925: *Africa Italiana*, i, 1926); S. Aurigemma, *I Mosaici di Zliten* (1926); R. Bartoccini, *Le terme di Lepcis Magna* (1930); *Africa Italiana*, 1–4, 1925–32; R. Bartoccini, *Guida di Leptis* (1927); id. *Guida di Sabratha* (1927); id. *Le antichità della Tripolitania* (1926). For subsequent discoveries see *Rivista della Tripolitania*, vol. 1, and *Africa Italiana* (8 vols. 1927–41). On DALMATIA, A. Venturi, E. Pais, A. Molmenti, *Dalmazia Monumentale* (1917); G. Kowalczyk, *Denkmäler der Kunst in Dalmatien* (1910). On Pola, A. Gnirs, *Pola. Ein Führer durch die antiken Baudenkmäler und Sammlungen* (1915), cf. *Not. d. Scavi*,1923, pp. 211 ff. On Salona and Spalato, E. Hébrard and J. Zeiller, *Spalato, le palais de Dioclétien* (1912); *Forschungen in Salona*, vols. i–iii (1917–39) (Oest. Arch. Inst.); *Recherches à Salone*, vols. i–ii (1928–33) (Fondation Rask-Ørsted); N. Vulič in Pauly–Wissowa, Zw. R. ii, col. 2003. PANNONIA. 'Emona, I. Theil', *Jahrb. f. Altertumsk.* 7, 1914, pp. 61 ff. ALBANIA. L. M. Ugolini, *Albania antica*, vols. i–3 (1927–42); id. *L'antica Albania* (1929), and the periodical *Albania*, vols. 1–6, 1925–39; C. Patsch, *Oest. Jahresh.*, 23, 1926, p. 210. MACEDONIA. On Thessalonica, O. Tafrali, *Topographie de Thessalonique* (1913), and *Thessalonique des origines au xiv s.* (1919); Ch. Diehl, *Salonique* (1920), cf. E. Hébrard, 'Les Travaux, &c., à l'arc de Galère et à l'église de St. Georges de Salonique', *BCH* 44, 1920, pp. 5 ff. (with bibliography). GREECE. On Athens, W. Judeich, *Topographie von Athen*² (1931), in Müller's *Handb. d. kl. Alt.* iii. 2. 2. On Corinth, *Corinth, Results of Excavations* [vols. i–xv (2) (1932–52) (in progress)] and Byvanck and Lenschau in Pauly–Wissowa, Suppl. iv, cols. 991 ff. On Rhodes, H. van Gelder, *Geschichte der alten Rhodier* (1900). (The Italian excavations yielded only very few objects of the Roman period: see *Clara Rhodos*, vols. 1 (1928) [–10, 1940].) On ASIA MINOR,W. M. Ramsay, *Historical Geography of Asia Minor* (1890); id. *The Cities of St.Paul* (1907). On the Roman province of Asia, V. Chapot, *La Province romaine d'Asie* (*Bibl. de l'École des Hautes Études*, 150, 1904), and J. Keil and A. von Premerstein, 'Bericht über eine Reise in Lydien', i, ii, iii, in *Denkschr. Wien. Akad.* 53, 1908; 54, 1911; and 57, 1914; W. H. Buckler, W. M. Calder, C. W. M. Cox, 'Asia Minor 1924', *JRS* 14, 1924, pp. 24 ff.; 15, 1925, pp. 141 ff.; 16, 1926, pp. 53 ff.; 17, 1927, pp. 49 ff.; W. M. Calder and others, *Monumenta Asiae Minoris Antiqua*, vol. i (1928) (in progress). On Miletus, *Milet. Ergebnisse der Ausgrabungen*, &c. (1906–28) (Königl. Mus. zu Berlin). Cf. Th. Wiegand, 'Gymnasien, Thermen u. Palaestren in Milet', *Sitzb. Berl. Akad.* 1928, pp. 22 ff. On Pergamon, *Altertümer von Pergamon*, vols. i (1885–1937) (K. Mus. zu Berlin), and the annual reports in *Ath. Mitth.* (The excavations were recommenced by the State Museums of Berlin: Th. Wiegand, 'Bericht über die Ausgrabungen in Pergamon', 1927, *Abh. Berl. Akad.* 1928 (3).) On Smyrna, the speeches of Aristides (*Or.* 17. 19 and 21, Keil); L. Boulanger, loc. cit., pp. 384 ff.; W. M. Calder, 'Smyrna as described by the Orator Aristides', *Studies in the History &c. of the Eastern Provinces of the Roman Empire*, ed. W. M. Ramsay (1906). On Sardis, Buerchner, *RE* ii A, cols. 2475 ff.; *Sardis, Publications of the*

American Society for the excavation of Sardis, vol. i, &c. (1916–32); cf. Th. L. Shear, *Amer. Journ. Arch.* 26, 1922, pp. 405 ff.; 31, 1927, pp. 19 ff. On Pamphylia and Pisidia, Ch. Lanckoroński, G. Niemann and E. Petersen, *Les Villes de la Pamphylie et de la Pisidie* (1890). On Antioch of Pisidia, W. M. Ramsay, 'Colonia Caesarea (Pisidian Antioch) in the Augustan Age', *JRS* 6, 1916, pp. 83 ff. and D. M. Robinson, *Amer. Journ. Arch.* 28, 1924, pp. 435 ff.; cf. W. M. Ramsay, 'Studies in the Roman province Galatia, VI' and 'IX', *JRS* 14, 1924, pp. 172 ff., and 16, 1926, pp. 102 ff.; D. M. Robinson, *JRS* 15, 1925, pp. 253 ff. and *Roman Sculptures from Colonia Caesarea* (Pisidian Antioch) (1926). On Lycia and Caria, O. Benndorf and G. Niemann, *Reisen in Lykien und Karien* (1884); E. Kalinka, *Tituli Asiae Minoris*, vol. ii: 'Tituli Lyciae linguis graeca et latina conscripti', [i–iii (1) (1920–41) (in progress)]; Bürchner in Pauly–Wissowa, x, cols. 1943 ff. (with bibliography), cf. G. Guidi and A. Maiuri, 'Viaggio di esplorazione in Caria', *Ann. d. R. Sc. arch. di Atene*, 4–5, 1924, pp. 345 ff. On Paphlagonia, R. Leonhardt, *Paphlagonia, Reisen und Forschungen* (1915). On Cilicia, Ruge in Pauly–Wissowa, xi, cols. 385 ff. (with bibliography). On Phrygia, W. M. Ramsay, *Cities and Bishoprics of Phrygia*, 2 vols. (1895–7); id. *The Letters to the Seven Churches of Asia* (1904). On Galatia, Brandis in Pauly–Wissowa, vii, cols. 519 ff. (with bibliography); W. M. Ramsay, 'Studies in the Roman province Galatia', *JRS* 16, 1926, pp. 201 ff. On Bithynia, Pontus, Armenia, Brandis in Pauly–Wissowa, iii, cols. 507 ff.; F. Cumont, J. G. C. Anderson, H. Grégoire, *Studia Pontica*, 3 vols. (1903–10); M. Rostovtzeff, 'Pontus, Bithynia and the Bosporus', *Ann. Brit. School Athens*, 32, 1918, pp 1 ff.; cf. *CAH* ix, pp. 211 ff. On Cyzicus, F. W. Hasluck, *Cyzicus* (1910). On Byzantium, H. Merle, *Die Geschichte der Städte Byzantion und Kalchedon* (1916). On Sinope, D. M. Robinson, *Ancient Sinope* (1906). Moesia Inferior. On Tomi and Istrus, V. Pârvan, 'Zidul Cetâtii Tomi', *Analele Academiei Romane*, 37, 1915, and id. 'Histria', ibid., 38, 1916. South Russia. On Panticapaeum and Olbia, E. H. Minns, *Scythians and Greeks* (1913); M. Rostovtzeff, *Iranians and Greeks in S. Russia* (1923). On Syria, C. Humann and O. Puchstein, *Reisen in Kleinasien und Nordsyrien* (1890) (Kommagene); H. C. Butler, *Publications of an American Arch. Expedition to Syria, 1899–1900*, 4 vols. (1904–5), and id. *Archaeological Expeditions to Syria in 1904–5 and 1909*, 3 div. (1907–16); E. Littmann, *Die Ruinenstätten und Schriftdenkmäler Syriens* (1917); E. S. Bouchier, *Syria as a Roman Province* (1916); R. Dussaud, *Topographie historique de la Syrie antique et médiévale* (1927); L. Jalabert and R. Mouterde, *Inscriptions grecques et latines de la Syrie*, vol. i–iii (1929–53) (in progress); R. Dussaud, P. Deschamps, H. Seyrig, *La Syrie antique et médiévale* (1931); M. Rostovtzeff, *The Caravan-Cities: Petra and Jerash, Palmyra and Dura* (1933). On Baalbek, Th. Wiegand, *Baalbek*, vols. i–iii. (Text und Tafeln, 1921–5), and Honigmann in Pauly–Wissowa, Suppl. iv, cols. 715 ff. On Palmyra, Prince P. Abamelek-Lazarew, *Palmyra* (Moscow, 1884, in Russian); J. B. Chabot, *Choix d'inscriptions de Palmyre* (1922); A. Gabriel, 'Recherches archéologiques à Palmyre', *Syria*, 7, 1927, pp. 71 ff. On Damascus, G. Watzinger and K. Wulzinger, *Wissenschaftliche Veröffentlichungen des deutsch-türkischen Denkmalschutzkommando herausg. von Th. Wiegand*, fasc. iv (1921). On Gerasa, Prince P. Abamelek-Lazarew, *Djerash* (Moscow, 1885, in Russian); H. Guthe, 'Gerasa', *Das Land der Bibel*, iii. 1–2, 1919. On Tyre, W. F. Fleming, *The History of Tyre* (1915), in Columbia University Oriental Studies, vol. x (superficial). On Berytus, L. Cheikho, *Beyrouth, Histoire et Monuments* (1927). On Seleuceia of Pieria (the port of Antioch and an important station of the Syrian fleet), Honigmann, Pauly–Wissowa, ii A, cols. 1184 ff.; V. Chapot, 'Séleucie de Piérie', *Mém. Soc. Ant. de France*, 1906, pp. 149 ff. Arabia. On Petra and Bostra, R. Brünnow and A. von Domaszewski, *Die Provincia Arabia*, 3 vols. (1904–5); A. Musil, *Arabia Petraea*, 3 vols. (1907); Libbey and Hoskins, *The Jordan Valley and Petra* (1905); G. Dalman, *Petra* (1908); H. Guthe, 'Die griechisch-römischen Städte des Ostjordanlandes', *Das Land der Bibel*, ii. 5, 1918; W. Bachmann, C. Watzinger, Th. Wiegand, *Petra* (1921); A.

Kennedy, *Petra, its History and Monuments* (1926); A. Kammerer, *Pétra et la Nabatène* (1929). MESOPOTAMIA. On Dura, F. Cumont, *Fouilles de Doura-Europos* (1926); P. V. C. Baur, A. Bellinger, M. Rostovtzeff, &c., *The Excavations at Dura-Europos*, Preliminary Report, i [–ix (3) (1952); Final Reports, iv (pt. 1 (1–2)–iv (1)) (1943); vi (1949).] For Seleuceia on Tigris see M. Streck, 'Seleucia und Ktesiphon', *Der Alte Orient*, 16. 3 and 4, 1917. For the University of Michigan's important excavations in the ruins of Seleuceia see *Preliminary Report upon the Excavations at Tel Umar* (1931). On PALESTINE, P. Thomsen, *Denkmäler Palästinas aus der Zeit Jesu* (1916); id. *Palästina und seine Kultur in fünf Jahrtausenden*[3] (1931); *Die Palästina-Literatur*, i–vi (for years 1895–1939).

⁵ On the minor African cities see the bibliography quoted in note 4. On Carnuntum and Aquincum, Pauly–Wissowa, articles 'Aquincum' and 'Carnuntum'; *Der römische Limes in Oesterreich*, vols. 1–12 (1900–14); W. Kubitschek and S. Frankfurter, *Führer durch Carnuntum*[6] (1923). On Virunum, R. Egger, *Führer durch die Antikensammlung des Landesmuseums in Klagenfurt* (1921). Poetovio, M. Abramič, *Poetovio: Führer durch die Denkmäler der römischen Stadt* (1925). Nicopolis ad Istrum, W. Dobrusky, *Sbornik za nar. Umotvorenija*, 18, 1906, pp. 704ff. (in Bulgarian); G. Seure, *Rev. arch.* 1907 (2), pp. 257 ff.; B. Filov, *Bull. Soc. Arch. Bulg.* 5, 1915, pp. 177–206 (in Bulgarian); S. Bobčev, *Bull. Inst. Arch. Bulg.* 5, 1928–9, pp. 50 ff. (in Bulgarian). On Doclea, P. Sticotti, *Die römische Stadt Doclea in Montenegro*, in *Schriften der Balkankommission*, vi (1913). On the cities in Britain see note 4. On Assos, J. T. Clarke, F. H. Bacon, R. Koldewey, *Investigations at Assos* (Boston, 1902–21). On the Egyptian 'metropoleis' in general see P. Jouguet, *La vie municipale dans l'Égypte romaine* (*Bibl. des Éc.* 104, 1911); id. 'Les métropoles égyptiennes à la fin du IIᵐᵉ siècle', *Rev. ét. gr.* 30, 1917, pp. 294 ff.; H. Schmitz, *Die hellenistisch-römischen Stadtanlagen in Ägypten* (1921). On Ptolemais, G. Plaumann, *Ptolemais in Oberägypten* (1910). On Hermupolis, G. Méautis, *Une métropole égyptienne sous l'empire romain, Hermoupolis la Grande* (1918). On Antinoupolis, E. Kühn, *Antinoopolis* (1913), and B. Kübler, *Antinoupolis* (1914). On Canopus and on the villages of the Fayyûm see E. Breccia, *Monum. de l'Égypte gréco-romaine*, i (1926); P. Viereck, *Philadelphia* (*Morgenland*, 16, 1928). On the excavation of Caranis, see pl. XLIV.

⁶ R. Cagnat and V. Chapot, *Manuel d'archéologie romaine*, vols. i, ii (1916–20); H. Stuart Jones, *Companion to Roman History* (1912); *The Legacy of Rome* (1923), especially the chapters on 'Architecture and Art' by G. McN. Rushforth and on 'Building and Engineering' by G. Giovannoni; it is a pity that the book does not contain a chapter on the Roman cities in general and on town-planning in the Roman Empire. Cf. F. Haverfield, *Ancient Town-planning* (1913); K. M. Swoboda, *Römische und romanische Paläste* (1919); T. H. Hughes and E. A. G. Lamborn, *Towns and Town-planning, Ancient and Modern* (1923); G. Calza, 'Teorie estetiche degli antichi sulla costruzione della città', *Bull. Comm. arch. com.* 1922, pp. 127 ff.; N. Cultrera, 'Architettura Ippodamea', *Mem. Acc. Lincei*, 27, 1924, pp. 357 ff.; A. von Gercken, *Griechische Stadtanlagen* (1924); P. Lavedan, *Histoire de l'architecture urbaine* (1926). The progress of archaeological investigation gradually corrects many erroneous ideas about the life of ancient cities. Thus, the idea that ancient streets had 'blind' fronts is now put out of court by the more careful excavations carried out both at Ostia and at Pompeii (see, e.g. *Not. d. Scavi*, 1912, pp. 31 ff, 64 ff., 102 ff.). Another false view concerning the darkness of the streets at night was already refuted by the evidence of Libanius and Ammianus Marcellinus, which shows that the streets of Antioch were brightly and abundantly lit. Cf. H. Lamer, 'Strassenbeleuchtung im späteren Altertum', *Phil. Woch.* 1927, p. 1472. Now we learn from some terracottas that Alexandria also had a well-organized system of street-lighting, see E. Breccia, 'Un tipo inedito della coroplastica antica "Il lampinaio" ', *Bull. Soc. arch. Alex.* 20, 1924, pp. 239 ff. The λυχνάπται are known to us from the service in the Egyptian temples, where the λυχναψία seems

to have been a religious festival. On the other hand, G. Spano, *Mem. d. Acc. di Napoli*, 1919, pp. 128 ff., has taught us that even in the case of Pompeii the theory of 'dark streets' was an exaggeration. With the evidence of the Alexandrian terracottas may be compared the well-known addition to one of the electoral posters of Pompeii: '*lanternari, tene scalam*'. It is, however, possible that the Alexandrian terracottas represent not the *lucernarii* of the streets of the city, but those of the great sanctuaries: see Wilcken, *UPZ* i, pp. 34 and 49.

7 On the income of a Greek city see H. Francotte, *Les Finances des cités grecques* (1909), cf. id. *Mus. Belge*, 11, 1907, pp. 53 ff. The sources of income remained in the Roman period the same as they had been in the Hellenistic epoch. A good survey is given in an inscription of Cos of the 1st cent. B.C., *SGDI* = *Syll.*³, 1000, 3632 [W. A. L. Vreeken, *De lege quadam Coorum* (Groningen, 1953)], cf. Dittenberger, *Syll.*³ 1262 (1st cent. A.D., Smyrna). For an earlier period compare the inscription of Telmessus, *OGIS* 55 [= *TAM* ii. 1]. Cf. also Cicero, *ad Att.* v. 16. 2, and my *Gesch. d. Staatspacht.* Cf. the fourth edict of Cyrene (Augustus: see Chap. II, note 6). For the period of the Roman Empire, see V. Chapot, *La province romaine d'Asie*, pp. 252 ff., and especially I. Levy, 'La vie municipale de l'Asie Mineure sous les Antonins', *Rev. ét. gr.* 8, 1895, pp. 203 ff.; 12, 1899, pp. 255 ff.; 14, 1901, pp. 350 ff. (for the East), and W. Liebenam, *Städteverwaltung im römischen Kaiserreiche* (1900), pp. 1 ff.; Abbott and Johnson, *Munic. Admin.*, pp. 138 ff. (both for the East and for the West). The question of the municipal tax-system under the Roman Empire should be made the object of an accurate special study. F. E. Abbott's thesis (op. cit., p. 138) that 'the residents of a civitas were practically exempt from the payment of municipal taxes' is undoubtedly wrong. We must distinguish carefully between East and West, between Italy and the Provinces, and in addition between the different types of cities. In the West the term *vectigalia* (lex Malac., *FIRA*² 24, ch. lxiii: cf. ep. Vespas. de Saborensibus, *FIRA*² 74) does not necessarily indicate the incomes of public lands only, and in the East we have evidence of many different kinds of taxes (including the land-tax). The payments made by the cleruchs of Aizani (Abbott and Johnson, op. cit., no. 82 [*OGIS* 502]) can hardly be considered a rent: at Stratonicea (ibid., no. 83 [*Syll.*³ 837]), τὰ τέλη τὰ ἐκ τῆς χώρας, are certainly some form of land-tax (cf. ibid., no. 104). These and similar taxes are levied as much on *civitates liberae* (for instance Athens: ibid., nos. 90–92 [*IG* ii.² 1100, 1103, 1104]), as on cities paying taxes to the fiscus. In some cases it is difficult to decide whether the city collected the tax for itself or for the state. Cf. the well-known inscription of Iotape (*CIG* 4411 = ‡Paribeni, *Mon. Ant.* 23, 1914, p. 175; cf. Hula, *Oest. Jahresh.* 5, 1902, p. 204) where the κυριακοὶ φόροι presuppose the existence of πολιτικοὶ φόροι. It is easier to register the cases in which the city gets an income deriving from its patrimony. For instance the rules for leasing or selling sacerdotal offices are interesting: see L. Robert, *BCH* 52, 1928, pp. 434 ff.

8 On the δημόσιοι in the Greek cities see Waszynski, *Hermes*, 34, 1899, pp. 553 ff.; A. Wilhelm, *Beiträge zur gr. Inschriftenkunde* (1909), pp. 229 ff.; G. Cardinali, *Rend. Lincei*, 1908, pp. 158 ff. On the *servi publici*, see L. Halkin, 'Les ésclaves publics chez les Romains', *Bibl. etc. de l'Univ. de Liége*, 1, 1897.

9 Cf. Chap. III, note 27. On the district roads in Italy and in the provinces, see O. Hirschfeld, *Die kais. Verwaltungsb.*, p. 208, note 1, and p. 209, note 3. Cf. the inscriptions in *Not. d. Scavi*, 1915, p. 26; ibid. 1918, p. 140 [= *L'An. ép.* 1919, 64]; 1921, p. 69 [= *L'An. ép.* 1922, 86]; and 1929, p. 220 [= *L'An. ép.* 1930, 122] (money paid by some *possessores agrorum* to whom the emperor had given a certain sum); cf. *CIL* ix. 6072, 6075. The inscription in *Not. d. Scavi*, 1918, p. 140, shows how heavy was the cost of land transport in Italy: the benefactor of the city of Velitrae is ready to bear the cost of repairing the road, provided that the city furnishes

him with money to pay the cost of the transportation of the stones, 'viam Mactorinam longa vetustate resciss(am) pecunia sua restituit acceptis ab r. p. in[ve]ctui silicis xiiii m. n.' Cf. L. Westermann, 'On inland transportation and communication in Antiquity', *Pol. Sc. Quart.* 43, 1928, pp. 364 ff. As regards the food-supply and famines, some examples will show how difficult was the problem of the corn-supply, not only for the large industrial and commercial cities. First it must be emphasized how anxious the cities were to provide cheap and good wheat and bread. In many lists of municipal magistrates of the Greek East we find this record: ἐπὶ (τοῦ δεῖνα) ὑγιεία, εὐετηρία, εἰρήνη, πλοῦτος ἐγένετο (usually only a part of these desirable things, not all together). This custom was introduced in the Hellenistic age (see the group of examples collected by A. Wilhelm, 'Επιτύμβιον H. Swoboda dargebracht (1927), pp. 343 ff.). We have a list of ἀγορανόμοι of Ephesus of the early 3rd cent. A.D.: under several names we find interesting information: Ἀγαθῆι [τύ]χ[ηι], Πό(πλιος) Στατῆνος Πετρωνιανὸς ὁ καὶ 'Ιουλιανὸς φιλοσέβ(αστος) πατὴρ ἱεροκήρυκος ἠγορανόμησε[ν ἀγν]ῶς καὶ εὐσταθῶς· ἐφ' οὗ ἐπράθη ὁ ἄρτος (fine white bread) οὐνκιῶν ιδ', ὀβ(ολῶν) δ', ὁ δὲ κιβάριος (coarse bread) οὐνκ(ιῶν) ι' ὀβ(ολῶν) β'· κόρος, ἀγνεία, εὐτυχῶς: *Forsch. Eph.* iii, pp. 101–2, no. 10, cf. 11, 12, 13, 15, 17, 18: cf. J. Keil, *Oest. Jahresh.* 23, 1926, Beibl., col. 282 (early 2nd cent. A.D.). Notice that not all the ἀγορανόμοι could boast of κόρος and ἀγνεία. Some of them (no. 16, cf. *Syll.*³ 839) record that they were so fortunate as to acquire corn from Egypt for their city (cf. Chap. VIII, note 21); in other documents we have evidence of wealthy citizens who helped their city by their money, especially in time of war (see *Forsch. Eph.* iii, pp. 153 ff., no. 71 and pp. 161 ff., no. 80). Compare also the inscription of Nonius Macrinus who helped the city in time of famine and pestilence (ibid., p. 117, no. 29). The rapid increase in the price of bread at Ephesus must also be noticed: comparison between the above-mentioned inscriptions and two other Ephesian inscriptions of the reign of Trajan (Heberdey, *Oest. Jahresh.* 3, 1900, Beibl., cols. 87 ff.; Keil, ibid. 23, 1926, Beibl., col. 282) shows that in the period between Trajan and Caracalla prices doubled without any good reason. At Magnesia-on-Maeander the well-known Moschion, son of Moschion, was elected σιτώνης by the city and lost 5,000 denarii in buying corn for it, καὶ σειτώνην γενόμενον καὶ ζημι(ω)θέντα δηνάρια πεντακισχίλια (*OGIS* 485, 9). At Stratonicea a σιτώνης gave 10,000 denarii of his own to buy corn, *BCH* 44, 1920, p. 93, no. 28; cf. ibid. 11, 1887, p. 32, no. 45 and *CIG* 2720 (the same rich family). At Thasos a rich man granted land and money to the city for the purchase of corn, *BCH* 45, 1921, p. 156, no. 9 [= *IG* xii, Suppl., p. 156, no. 364]. So at Mantinea, B. Laum, *Stiftungen*, ii. 5 [= *IG* v. 2. 268] (1st cent. A.D.). On the office of εὐποσιάρχης, cf. L. Robert, *BCH* 52, 1928, p. 414, no. iv. Incidental mentions of famines are frequent in our sources (σιτοδεῖαι, inopia, sterilitas annonae). Compare, for instance, Philostr. *Vita Apoll.* i. 15 (famines and riots at Aspendus in Pamphylia under Tiberius), the inscriptions of Corinth, *Corinth*, viii. 2, nos. 83 and 86, of the Claudian age, and the literary texts quoted by West in his commentary to these inscriptions, and some inscriptions of Panamara, J. Hatzfeld, *BCH* 51, 1927, p. 97, no. 64 (five years of famine) and p. 108, no. 83; cf. A. Wilhelm, *Beitr. zur gr. Inschriftenkunde*, p. 119; M. N. Tod, *BSA* 23, 1918–19, p. 72 (inscription of Lete). One of the most striking examples is the severe famine which raged in Asia Minor in the time of Domitian and which is mentioned in the Apocalypse, vi. 6: καὶ ἤκουσα ὡς φωνὴν ἐν μέσῳ τῶν τεσσάρων ζῴων λέγουσαν· χοῖνιξ σίτου δηναρίου, καὶ τρεῖς χοίνικες κριθῶν δηναρίου· καὶ τὸ ἔλαιον καὶ τὸν οἶνον μὴ ἀδικήσῃς. It is very probable that this was the same (or belonged to the same series) as that which is recorded in a Latin inscription of Antioch in Pisidia (Galatia). See W. M. Ramsay, 'Studies in the Roman Province Galatia', *JRS* 14, 1924, pp. 179 ff. no. 6; cf. D. M. Robinson, ibid. 15, 1925, pp. 255 ff. [= *L'An. ép.* 1925, 126 (cf. 1926, p. 19)]. Ramsay inclines to believe that the famine was local, but this is an insoluble question. Whether local or widespread, the famine was a great calamity, to cope with which exceptional measures were necessary. Famine was raging in the city owing to an unusually severe winter (*propter hiemis asperitatem*). Prices rose enormously. The governor, L. Antistius Rusticus, being approached by the city council, ordered a requisition of grain which was to be sold at a fixed price to the σιτῶναι of the city and to them only: 'omnes qui Ant(iochensis) col(oniae) aut coloni aut incolae sunt, profiteantur apud duoviros col(oniae) Antiochensis intra tricensimum diem quam hoc edictum meum propositum fuerit quantum quisque et quo loco frumenti habeat et quantum in semen aut in cibaria annua familiae suae deducat et reliqui omnis frumenti copiam emptoribus [the σιτῶναι] col(oniae) Antiochens(is) faciat'. The price is fixed at one denarius per *modius*, i.e. double the current price before the famine (eight asses). Evidently conditions of transport rendered impracticable the idea of importing corn from outside into this inland city. The only way to improve the situation was to confiscate the grain which might be concealed by the landowners; cf. the well-known story of the famine at Prusa in the time of Dio, Chap. III, note 27, and that of Aspendos under Tiberius (see above). A similar calamity visited Italy in the reign of M. Aurelius. The richest part of the peninsula—the Po valley and the northern part of Central Italy—suffered most severely. A commission to help the cities of the Transpadana was given to the *IIIIvir viarum curandarum* C. Arrius Antoninus, 'qui providentia maximorum imperat(orum) missus, urgentis annonae difficul(i)tates iuvit et consuluit securitati fundatis reip(ublicae) opibus' (*CIL* v. 1874 [= *ILS* 1118]). In his capacity of *curator viarum* he certainly imported corn into the city of Concordia; cf. Fronto, *Ad amicos*, ii. 7 (Naber, p. 192; Haines, ii, p. 176 [; van den Hout, i, p. 181]). In the case of the city of Ariminum a similar part was played by P. Cornelius Felix Italus, *iuridicus per Flaminiam et Umbriam*: 'ob eximiam moderationem et in sterilitate annonae laboriosam erga ipsos fidem et industriam ut et civibus annona superesset et vicinis civitatibus subveniretur' (*CIL* xi. 377). He may have resorted to measures similar to those taken by Rusticus in Galatia. About the same time (A.D. 162) another terrible famine visited Asia Minor, this time affecting Phrygia, while conditions in Galatia were better; see Kaibel, 793, where a landowner flees with his cattle to Galatia to save his life, cf. Ramsay, *Studies in the Hist. and Art of the Eastern Provinces*, p. 128; *OGIS* 511 (of a later date, about the time of the great plague). Another famine raged in Italy about A.D. 175 (*CIL* xi. 379 = *ILS* 6664; ibid. 5635 = *ILS* 6640; J. Schwendemann, *Der hist. Wert der Vita Marci bei den S.H.A.* (1923), pp. 38 ff.). A full collection of the evidence about famines in the Roman Empire is highly desirable (the topic is not discussed by Abbott and Johnson, *Municipal Administration*). Even in the richest corn-growing provinces, like Africa Proconsularis and Numidia, cases of local famine were frequent, see S. Gsell, *I.L.Al.* i. 2145: 'ob insignem in se amorem et frumenti copiam t[emp]ore inopiae sibi largiter praestitam' (the donor, M. Cornelius Fronto, was certainly a rich landowner in the territory of the city and had corn stored in his granaries); cf. *CIL* viii. 1648, 9250, 15497, 25703–4, 26121 (examples quoted by S. Gsell) and A. Merlin and L. Poinssot, *Les Inscriptions d'Uchi Majus*, p. 33, no. 13. Thus famine was of frequent occurrence in the cities of Africa, and this can be explained only by the difficulties of transport. It is hardly necessary to mention that not even Egypt was safe from famine: it is sufficient to recall that mentioned by Pliny (*Paneg.* 31), and cf. the edict of Hadrian (see Chap. VIII, note 14), and for the 1st cent. that of the time of Germanicus. In Macedonia the frequent cases of famine were probably due to the heavy burden imposed on the cities of feeding the soldiers during the expeditions of Trajan, when troops were constantly being moved from and to Europe and Asia through Macedonia: M. Rostovtzeff, *Bull. of the Russian Arch. Inst. at Constantinople*, 4, 1899, pp. 184 ff. (in Russian); cf. Chap. VIII. The grave famine suffered in the 2nd cent. A.D. by the municipium Aelium Coela in the Thracian Chersonese may be attributed to the same cause: cf. *Forsch. Eph.* iii, p. 134, no. 48 = *L'An. ép.* 1924, 82, l. 16: καὶ ἐν τῇ μεγίστῃ ἐνδείᾳ τῶν τροφῶν | τηρήσαντα μετ' ἐκτενείας ἅπαντας.

It is to be noted that the benefactor of the city was the Roman governor: cf. Chap. VIII, note 21.

¹⁰ See the articles quoted in Chap. IV, note 33. It is interesting to note how the little city of Teos organized its own library and spent money to have books copied, to pay librarians and to restore books: see *SEG* ii. 584. Unfortunately this inscription is in a very bad condition, and cannot be dated with certainty. On οἱ ἀπὸ τοῦ γυμνασίου or οἱ ἐφηβευκότες in Egypt, see U. Wilcken, *Grundzüge*, p. 144; P. Jouguet, *La vie municipale*, &c., pp. 150 ff.; W. Schubart, *Ägypten*, &c., p. 143; H. I. Bell, *Jews and Christians*, p. 34, ll. 53 ff. (note); B. A. von Groningen, *Le gymnasiarque des métropoles de l'Égypte romaine* (1924), pp. 4 ff. and pp. 38 ff.; E. Bickermann, 'Beiträge zur antiken Urkundengeschichte', *Arch. f. Papyr.* 9, pp. 37 ff.; K. F. W. Schmidt, *Das griechische Gymnasium in Ägypten* (1926). We must not forget that many cities paid for the services of public doctors: see R. Pohl, *De Graecorum medicis publicis* (1915). In Egypt the papyri mention many such doctors: see, for example, *P.Oslo*, 53 and 54; for Ephesos see Chap. IV, note 34.

¹¹ On the expense of the cities in general, see W. Liebenam, loc. cit., pp. 68 ff.

¹² W. Liebenam, loc. cit., pp. 165 ff.; L. Friedländer–G. Wissowa, *Sitteng. Roms*, 9th–10th ed., ii, pp. 377 ff.; O. Toller, *De spectaculis, cenis, distributionibus in municipiis Romanis Occidentis imperatorum aetate exhibitis*(1889); O. Liermann,'Analecta epigraphica et agonistica', *Diss. phil. Hal.* 10, 1899; De Marchi, *La Beneficenza di Roma antica* (1899); J. J. Esser, *De pauperum cura apud Romanos* (Campis, 1902); Müller, *Jugendfürsorge in der römischen Kaiserzeit* (1903); B. Laum, *Stiftungen in der griechischen und römischen Antike*, 2 vols. (1914); M. Rostovtzeff, 'Römische Bleitesserae', *Klio*, Beiheft 3, 1905; cf. the important inscription from Beneventum of A.D. 231 in *Not. d. Scavi*, 1913, pp. 311 ff.: 'hic primus . . . tesseris sparsis in aurum, argentum, aes, vestem, lentiamen ceteraq(ue) populo divisit.' [*L'an. ép.* 1914, 164].

¹³ An enumeration of some rich men who were benefactors of cities (without discrimination of time and place), in W. Liebenam, loc. cit., pp. 165 ff. The increase in the number of large benefactors begins in the East with the second half of the 1st cent. A.D., and reaches its climax in the first half of the 2nd cent. This follows from the material collected by B. Laum (loc. cit, i, pp. 8 ff.), and can be corroborated by an historical investigation of the development of gifts in general. Almost the same may be observed in the West. The participation of the intellectual leaders in the movement to assist the cities is shown by the biographies of the sophists compiled by Philostratus; see the survey given by L. Boulanger, *Aelius Aristide*, &c., pp. 74 ff., especially the pages on Scopelianus (pp. 83 ff.), Polemon (pp. 87 ff.), and Herodes Atticus (pp. 97 ff.). We have met already with such men as Dio of Prusa and Plutarch of Chaeronea; their Italian counterpart was Pliny the Younger; see T. Gentile, 'Le Beneficenze di Plinio Cecilio Secondo ai Comensi', *Rend. R. 1st. Lombardo*, 1881, pp. 458 ff. Note, however, that Aristides tries hard to free himself from any municipal or provincial service. On Herodes Atticus, cf. P. Graindor, 'Marbres et textes antiques de l'époque impériale', *Rec. de trav., &c., de l'Univ. de Gand*, 50, 1912, pp. 81 ff.: 'Contribution à l'histoire d'Hérode Atticus et de son père'; id. *Un Millionaire antique, Herodes Atticus et sa famille* (1930); Muenscher, Pauly–Wissowa,viii, cols. 921 ff.; U. von Wilamowitz-Moellendorff, 'Marcellus von Side', *Sitzb. Berl. Akad.* 1928, pp. 3 ff.; N. Svensson, 'Réception solennelle d'Hérode Atticus', *BCH* 50, 1926, pp. 527 ff.; see especially Suet. *Vesp.* 13. It is evident that the millionaire Hipparchus mentioned by Suetonius ('Salvium Liberalem in defensione divitis rei ausum dicere: quid ad Caesarem, si Hipparchus sestertium milies habet? et ipse laudavit') was the father of Ti. Claudius Atticus and the grandfather of Herodes Atticus, as Graindor has suggested, cf. Philostr. *Vit. Soph.* 2. 1. 2. On Opramoas,

R. Heberdey, *Opramoas* (1897); cf. E. Ritterling, *Rh. Mus.* 73, 1920, pp. 35 ff.; and C. S. Walton, *JRS* 19, 1929, pp. 54 ff. On C. Julius Eurycles and his family, all benefactors of Greek cities, especially of Sparta, see Chap. II, note 17; cf. C. S. Walton, loc. cit., pp. 42 ff., and P. Graindor, *Athènes sous Auguste* (1927), pp. 90 ff. A second Opramoas, this time from Phrygia, was M. Ulpius Appuleius Eurycles (about A.D. 157): *OGIS* 504–9 = *IGRR* iv. 564, 573–6. From Cibyra we have Q. Veranius Philagrus, *IGRR* iv. 914, 915 (1st cent. A.D.). From Ephesus C. Vibius Salutaris and his family, R. Heberdey, *Forsch. Eph.* ii, nos. 27 and 28, cf. 60 and 61–63 (members of his family—L. Vibius Lentulus and T. Flavius Montanus?), all of the time of Domitian and Trajan; and from the same city P. Vedius Antoninus, ibid. ii, nos. 64 ff. and 19. The same type of rich men appears all over the Western provinces, especially in Africa, mostly in the 2nd but also partly in the 3rd cent.

¹⁴ A list of senators of the 2nd and 3rd cent., with an indication of the place of their origin, is given by G. Lully, *De senatorum Romanorum patria* (Rome, 1918). Most of the senatorial families are of provincial origin and belong to the upper strata of the aristocracy of the cities. The measures taken by Trajan and M. Aurelius, which imposed on senators the obligation of investing a part of their fortunes in Italian lands (Plin. *Ep.* vi. 19; *S.H.A.*, Marcus Aur. 11. 8, cf. *Dig.* 1. 9. 11), were intended probably at once to arrest the steady increase of waste land in Italy and to attach these foreigners to Italy by economic ties. See Mommsen, *Staatsrecht*, iii, p. 900, note 1. Mommsen thought that the 'third part' of Trajan's ordinance and the 'fourth part' of M. Aurelius' refer not to the actual fortunes of the senators, but to the minimum fortune required. Cf. M. Gelzer, 'Die Nobilität der römischen Kaiserzeit', *Hermes*, 50, 1915, p. 412; W. Otto, ibid. 51, 1916, pp. 86 f.; E. Groag, *Strena Buličiana* (1924), pp. 253 ff. Groag shows that in the reigns of Trajan and Hadrian there were no more than thirty senators who belonged to families which bore the names of families of the ancient nobility. It is striking that even these few relics of the past were almost completely excluded from the higher military posts.

¹⁵ On the funeral monuments, see the relative sections in R. Cagnat and V. Chapot, *Manuel*, &c., and in H. Stuart Jones, *Companion*, &c.; cf. on the monument of the two Secundinii in Trèves (the so-called 'Igeler Säule'), F. Drexel, 'Die Bilder der Igeler Säule', *Röm. Mitt.* 35, 1922, pp. 83 ff., and H. Dragendorff and E. Krüger, 'Das Grabmal von Igel', *Röm. Grabmäler des Mosellandes u. der angrenzenden Gebiete*, i (1924). On the funerary monuments of Neumagen cf. W. von Massow, 'Die Wiederherstellung des Neumagener Denkmäler' *JDAI* 42, 1927, *Arch. Anz.* pp. 182 ff.; *Germania Romana*, vol. iii²; W. von Massow and E. Krueger, *Die Grabmäler von Neumagen* (1932) (*Die röm. Denkmäler d. Mosellandes*, ii), cf. note 27. Very impressive are the beautiful monuments of Aquileia: see the careful restorations (very little known to students of classical antiquity) of K. Mayreder, 'Mitteilungen über eine Studienreise nach Aquileia', *Zeitschr. des oester. Ingenieur- und Architektenvereines*, 1905, no. 19; cf. G. Brusin, *Aquileia* (1929), pp. 56ff., and p. 251, fig. 290, p. 253, fig. 192, and p. 255, fig. 193. The plans and elevations of some of these monuments coincide with those of the monuments painted on the walls of Roman and Pompeian houses of the 1st cent. A.D., see my article 'Die hellenistisch-römische Architekturlandschaft', *Röm. Mitt.* 26, 1911. Compare the gorgeous roads, flanked by majestic monuments, which led to such a modest city as Assos in the Roman period, J. T. Clarke, &c., *Investigations at Assos* (1921). On the tomb at Brestovik (near Viminacium) see Vasič and Valtrovč, *Starinar* (1906), pp. 128 ff. The collection and study of the most notable mausolea of the various provinces would be an attractive and useful contribution to the social and economic history of the Roman Empire. One example out of hundreds showing how the rich equestrian *bourgeoisie* was formed from the ranks of the lower strata of the city popula-

tion is given by the inscription, S. Gsell, *I.L.Al.* i. 2195 (Madaurus): 'hoc est sepultus L. Aelius Timminus loco | patiens laborum, frugi, vigilans, sobrius, | qui rem paravit haud mediocrem familiae, | domumque tenuem ad equestrem promovit gradum'; cf. A. Stein, *Der römische Ritterstand*, pp. 107 ff.

[16] I have dealt with this subject in Chap. II, note 18. Conditions did not change in the 2nd cent. A.D. To the evidence of Juvenal, collected and explained by Miss Brewster (see ibid.), add Dio. Chr. *Or.* 34 (Tars. alt.), 34: καίτοι ναυκληρεῖν μὲν ἢ δανείζειν ἢ γεωργεῖν οὐδεὶς ἂν ἱκανῶς δύναιτο πάρεργον αὐτὸ ποιούμενος, πολιτεύεσθαι δὲ ἐπιχειροῦσιν ἐκ περιουσίας καὶ πάντα ἔμπροσθεν τούτου τιθέντες, cf. note 27.

[17] On the commerce with Germany and the Scandinavian lands, see H. Willers, *Neue Untersuchungen über die römische Bronzeindustrie von Capua und von Niedergermanien* (1907), p. 45; H. Willers, *Numism. Zeitschr.* 1899, pp. 329 ff.; K. Regling, 'Römischer Denarfund von Fröndenberg', *Zeitschr. f. Num.* 29, 1912, pp. 212 ff.; O. Almgren and B. Nerman, *Die ältere Eisenzeit Gotlands* (1923), ii, pp. 57 ff.; Mattingly, *Coins of the R.E.*, pp. xxii and lxxv ff.; J. Kostrzewski, 'Capuanisches Bronzegeschirr im Norden', *Reallex. d. Vorg.* iii, pp. 280 ff., pl. 132; St. Bolin, *Fynden av romerska mynt i det fria Germanien* (1926); *Ber. d. röm.-germ. Kommission* (1929), pp. 86 ff.; H. Schaal, *Vom Tauschhandel zum Welthandel* (1931), pp. 182 ff.; and the bibliography of Chap. III, note 19 (on the earliest trade-relations with Germany). I am confident that Almgren and Nerman are right in assuming that the trade of Gotland with the Danube provinces of Rome was carried on through the Goths who had settled in the Dnieper region in South Russia; cf. the works quoted in my *Iranians and Greeks in South Russia*, p. 234, note 16, especially T. Arné, *Det Stora Svitgod* (1917), pp. 16 ff. The trade came to an end when the Goths at the beginning of the 3rd cent. began their advance first against the kingdom of Bosporus and afterwards against the Roman Empire. The finds of coins in the other parts of the Scandinavian lands and in Western Germany are of a different character, and testify to commercial relations with Belgium and the Rhine. The beautiful treasure of silver and bronze vases of the 1st cent. A.D. recently found in Denmark seems to have come in the same way, see K. Friis-Johansen, *Hoby-Fundet* (1922). It is an interesting observation of W. Kubitschek and S. Frankfurter that the finds in Carnuntum attest the same commercial relations with the Rhine, while the finds in Pannonia in general prove that these regions were entirely dependent on Aquileia (W. Kubitschek and S. Frankfurter, *Führer durch Carnuntum* (6th ed. 1923), p. 48; cf. H. Dragendorff, *Westdeutschland zur Römerzeit*, p. 56). The observation is the more striking as Carnuntum in the 1st cent. A.D. (under Nero) was one of the *étapes* of the amber trade of Aquileia with Northern Germany and the Baltic lands, K. Regling, loc. cit., p. 215, note 2; H. Dragendorff, loc. cit., p. 57. Cf. note 26 of this chapter and Chap. III, note 19. Very important for tracing the routes taken by the Gallic commerce in Eastern Europe is the investigation of the distribution of enamelled *fibulae* of Gallic workmanship through Germany, the Danube lands, Southern and Central Russia. The Gallic *fibulae* were first imported and afterwards imitated by the Germans. Both the Gallic products and the imitations swept Central and Northern Russia. On the Gallic *fibulae* see my article in *Mon. Piot*, 26, 1923, p. 66 of the reprint; on the German imitations, A. Spizyn, 'Objects with the *champlevé* enamel', *Memoirs of the Arch. Soc., Section of Russian and Slavonic Arch.* 5 (1), pp. 149 ff., Petrograd (in Russian); A. M. Tallgren, *Zur Archäologie Eestis* (1922), pp. 120 ff.; id. 'L'Orient et l'Occident dans l'âge de fer Finno-Ougrien', *Journal de la Société finlandaise d'arch.* 35. 3, 1924; H. Aubin, 'Der Rheinhandel in römischer Zeit', *Bonn. Jahrb.* 130, 1925, pp. 28 ff., illustrated very well the gradual extension of the Rhine trade in the 1st and especially in the 2nd cent. A.D. on the one hand to Britain and on the other to the coasts of Germany. It is interesting to note how the Rhine merchants, hampered

by the existence of military boundaries in their trade with Germany, achieved their aim by transporting their articles along the northern coasts of Germany.

[18] See my *Iranians and Greeks in South Russia*, pp. 147 ff. and 234 ff. Part of the great silk-route which connected the Roman Empire with China, through Southern Russia and Parthia, has been discovered, re-traced, and accurately described by Sven Hedin and Sir Aurel Stein. It was established during the first period of the Han dynasty and lasted almost without interruption to the late Roman Empire. Its construction and form of defensive works in Chinese Turkestan recall the routes of the Roman *limes*. See the two great works of Sir Aurel Stein, *Serindia* (1921) and *Innermost Asia* (1928), and in particular his article 'Innermost Asia; its geography as a factor in history', *Geogr. Journal*, 1925, pp. 377 ff.; and the masterly work of A. Herrmann, *Lou-Lan* (1931) (with complete bibliography). Cf. H. Schaal, *Vom Tauschhandel zum Welthandel* (1931), pp. 149 ff.

[19] How much more regular and extensive the commerce with India was in the 2nd cent. as compared with the 1st cent. is shown by the description of the trade routes and harbours given by Ptolemy compared with the data of the *Periplus Maris Erythraei*; see M. Chwostow, *History of the Eastern trade of Greco-Roman Egypt* (Kazan, 1907, in Russian), pp. 381 ff., especially pp. 392 ff.; E. H. Warmington, *The Commerce between the Roman Empire and India* (1928), pp. 84 ff.; H. Kortenbentel, *Der ägyptische Süd- und Osthandel in der Politik der Ptolemäer und römischen Kaiser* (1931); cf. my article 'Foreign Commerce of Ptolemaic Egypt', *Journ. of Econ. and Business Hist.* 3, 1932, pp. 728 ff. The changed character of the trade is proved by the comparison of the articles imported into the Roman Empire in the early 1st cent. A.D.—as enumerated by the Roman poets of this time and by Strabo, Pliny, and the Revelation of St. John—and the catalogue of articles exported and imported, given by the *Periplus Maris Erythraei*, M. Chwostow, loc. cit., pp. 86 ff. (import) and pp. 162 ff. (export); cf. Chap. III, notes 15–18, and E. H. Warmington, op. cit. pt. ii: *The Substance of Rome's Commerce with India*, pp. 145 ff.; cf. A. Herrmann, *Die alten Seidenstraßen zwischen China und Syrien*, i (1911); 'Die alten Verkehrswege zwischen Indien und S. China', *Zeitschr. der ges. Erdkunde*, 1913, pp. 771 ff., and in Pauly–Wissowa, xi, cols. 46 ff.; W. H. Schoff, 'The Eastern Iron-trade in the Roman Empire', *Journ. of the Amer. Or. Soc.* 35, 1915, pp. 224–39. M. P. Charlesworth, *Trade-routes and Commerce of the R.E.*, pp. 68 ff. and note on p. 255, quotes some very interesting Tamil poems which speak of wares imported by the 'Javan' into their land, from Pillai, *The Tamils 1,800 Years Ago*, Chap. III (inaccessible to me). On the trade in ἀρώματα with Somaliland see the important documents of the 2nd cent. B.C. published by Wilcken, *Zeitschr. f. äg. Spr.* 60, 1925, pp. 90 ff. [= *SB* 7169]. Probably in the Roman period trade of the Red Sea both with Arabia and with Somaliland was even better organized than under the Ptolemies. A group of important inscriptions found in Southern Egypt and especially at Coptos, gives valuable information on the organization of this province; the so-called Tariff of Coptos, to which I refer in the text, is of particular interest. This inscription [*OGIS* 674] has been studied by L. Fiesel, 'Geleitzölle im griech.-röm. Ägypten', *Gött. gel. Nachr.* 1925, pp. 95 ff. (with bibliography); and so also has the evidence on the escort-duties which were collected in the various villages of the Fayyûm (ibid., pp. 57 ff.). Cf. the ostraca collected at Coptos by Flinders Petrie and published by J. G. Tait, *Greek Ostraca in the Bodleian Library* (1930); cf. M. Rostovtzeff, *Gnomon*, 7, 1931, pp. 24 ff. The protection of the caravan-trade between Coptos and Berenice was probably achieved by the same method as the Nabataeans used at Petra, the Palmyrenes at Palmyra, and later the great merchants of Mecca and Taifa (cf. F. Cumont, *Fouilles de Doura-Europos*, p. xli). The Coptos-tariff may be compared with the Palmyra-tariff (*OGIS* 629; cf. my *Staatspacht*, pp. 405 ff., and 'Seleucid Babylonia', *Yale Class. Stud.* 3, 1932). We know

from numerous inscriptions the important part played by Alexandrian and foreign tradesmen in the traffic of the Red Sea; the evidence for the active part played by the merchants of Palmyra is very interesting. As these enjoyed continuous and close relations with the ports of Syria and of Phoenicia, and with those of the Red Sea (through Petra), they naturally tried to enlarge the sphere of their activity by investing money in overseas trade with India and Africa and by transporting merchandise through the Egyptian desert to the Nile and perhaps to Alexandria. It is not surprising to find in an inscription of Coptos (A. J. Reinach, *Rapport sur les fouilles de Coptos* (1911), p. 17 = *L'An. ép.* 1912, 171) that some Ἀδριανοὶ Παλμυρηνοὶ ἔμποροι pay honours to an owner of a Palmyrene ship, who was their friend: Ἀδριανῶν Παλμυρηνῶν ναυκλήρων Ἐρυθραικῶν. Of a different type is an inscription of the 3rd cent. A.D. in Greek and Palmyrene (*CIS* ii. 3. 3910) which honours a Palmyrene merchant, probably because he had been of some service as συνοδιάρχης to the residents of a Palmyrene *fondûq*. This *fondûq* was probably in Mesopotamia, and the honorand had probably successfully led a Palmyrene caravan from Mesopotamia to Egypt. The inscription repeats in Egypt the formulae and the style of corresponding documents in Palmyra. This active participation of Palmyrene merchants in Egyptian trade probably explains why Palmyrene soldiers (mounted archers) were used to protect the caravans in their trips from Berenice to Coptos (*IGRR* i. 1169 (A.D. 216), found at Coptos = *OGIS* 639); cf. Monneret de Villard, *La Scultura ad Ahnas* (1923). Red Sea merchants resident in Alexandria are mentioned in a remarkable inscription found at Medamut near Thebes [*SEG* viii. 703]: it is a dedication to the goddess of the temple, erected by Αἰλία Ἰσιδώρα καὶ Αἰλί[α] | Ὀλυμπιὰς ματρῶναι | στολᾶται ναύκληροι καὶ | [ἔμπο]ροι Ἐρυθραϊκαὶ ἅμα | [. . . Ἀ]πολιναρίῳ | ἐπάρχ[ῳ κλάσση]ς, Ὀλυμ|πιάδος καὶ [Ἰσιδώρας] | ἀμφοτέρων [ἀδελφῷ]. If my restoration is correct we have here again the case that the trade of the Red Sea was conducted by Egyptian Greeks and not by foreigners (2nd or 3rd cent. A.D.). See P. Jouguet, 'Dedicace grecque de Médamoud', *Bull. Inst. franc d'arch. or.* 31, 1931, pp. 1–29; P. Graindor, ibid., pp. 31 ff.; A. Wilhelm, *Anz. Wien. Akad.* 1932, pp. 1–3 [= *SEG* viii. 703 = *SB* 7539]. The restorations of Jouguet and Wilhelm do not convince me. According to Graindor, Apollinarius would have been prefect of a private fleet of the two women, which seems very unlikely. Wilhelm read the end of the inscription thus: [Ἀ]πολλιναρίῳ | ἐπαρχ[ῳ ὑπὲρ τῆ]ς Ὀλυμπιάδος καὶ [Ἰσιδώρας] | ἀμφοτέρων [σωτηρίας] | ἀνέθηκαν [ἐπ' ἀγαθῷ]. But why would the two women have repeated their own names and omitted that of Apollinarius, who appears with them as a dedicant? Compare a damaged, and now lost, inscription of Alexandria, *IGRR* i. 1062, in which there is a reference to the mercantile fleet of the Red Sea (line 4: καὶ εὐπλοίας τοῦ στόλου Ἐρ[υθραϊκ]ο[ῦ]) and to a ναύκληρος: also another fragmentary inscription of Coptos which mentions a κυβερνήτης Ἐρυθραϊκὸς (reign of Macrianus and Quietus), *Arch. f. Papyr.* 2, p. 450, no. 90 [= *SB* 8821]. The most interesting point of the inscription of Medamut is the reference to a prefect, probably of the Erythraean fleet. In an article published in *Arch. f. Papyr.* 4, p. 305, I showed that in the late Ptolemaic period (*OGIS* 132, cf. *P.Ryl.* ii. 66; Wilcken, *Arch. f. Papyr.* 6, p. 372; cf. *OGIS* 186 (and *SB* 2264), and 190) the African and Indian commerce of the Red Sea was under the control of the general governor of Southern Egypt, who had at his disposal soldiers and some men-of-war. There was probably no change in the Roman period. The fact that the Romans collected certain customs in the ports of the Red Sea (Plin. *NH* vi. 84) and that Trajan built a road from Syria to the Red Sea after the annexation of Arabia (Dessau *ILS* 5834 and 5845a) compels us to admit that at least from the time of Trajan onwards there was a section of the Roman fleet in the Red Sea, a *classis Erythraica*, commanded by a special prefect (cf. the ἔπαρχος κλάσσης Φλ. Μυσικῆς Γορδιανῆς in the Black Sea, Dessau, *ILS* 8851, and my article in *Klio*, 2, 1902, pp. 80 ff., cf. *IOSPE* i², pp. 509 ff., and the τριήραρχος κλάσσης Περινθίας, *IGRR* i. 781 (Domitian)). Since there was a special capitalist contractor, who collected the *Vectigal Maris Rubri* (Plin. *NH* vi. 22. 84), there must also have been land and sea forces to protect the trade of that sea. Consequently I believe (the evidence of Eutropius viii. 3 and of Jerome, *ad Euseb. Chron.* 220 Olymp., on the construction of a fleet in the Red Sea on the orders of Trajan refers to ships of that emperor in the Persian Gulf: there was a Roman fleet in the Red Sea before Trajan) that Apollinarius was prefect of the Red Sea fleet (notice that the prefect of the fleet of Moesia, P. Aelius Ammonius, is also a Greek, and that under Hadrian a Syrian rhetorician named Avitus Heliodorus was prefect of Egypt: see A. Stein, *Der röm. Ritterstand*, pp. 133, 316, and 406). It is of interest that in an inscription of Hiera Sykaminos, *IGRR* i. 1370, dedicated to Isis and Serapis by one or two soldiers or officers of two auxiliary cohorts, the dedicants make a προσκύνη[μα — ὑπὲρ — ἐπ]άρχου κλάσσης. I incline to believe that these soldiers belonged to a *vexillatio* sent to protect the caravan-routes leading to the ports of the Red Sea, and that this prefect was the commander of the *classis Erythraica.*

[20] Chap. III, notes 15–18. Cf., on the trade of Palmyra, M. Chwostow, op. cit., pp. 283 ff.; H. Dessau, 'Der Steuertarif von Palmyra', *Hermes*, 19, 1884, pp. 486 ff.; Th. Mommsen, *Röm. Gesch.* v, pp. 428 f.; J. B. Chabot, *Choix d'inscriptions de Palmyre* (1922); H. Schaal, *Vom Tauschhandel zum Weltandel* (1931), pp. 157 ff.; A. Février, *Essai sur l'histoire polit. et écomom. de Palmyre* (1931); M. Rostovtzeff, 'Les Inscriptions caravanières de Palmyre', *Mélanges Glotz* (1932), ii, pp. 793 ff.; id. *The Caravan-Cities* (1932); id. 'The Caravan Gods of Palmyra', *JRS* 22, 1932, pp. 107 ff. The best general picture of the Palmyrene trade is given by Herodian, iv. 10. 4; τά τε παρ' ἐκείνοις φυόμενα ἀρώματα ἢ θαυμαζόμενα ὑφάσματα (cf. Marc. *Dig.* 39. 4. 16. 7; νόμος τελωνικός of Palmyra, Chap. IV, 1) καὶ ⟨τὰ⟩ παρὰ Ῥωμαίοις μεταλλευόμενα ἢ διὰ τὴν τέχνην ἐπαινούμενα μηκέτι μόλις καὶ σπανίζοντα λανθάνοντά τε δι' ἐμπόρων κομισθήσεσθαι, μιᾶς δὲ γῆς οὔσης καὶ μιᾶς ἐξουσίας κοινὴν καὶ ἀκώλυτον ἀμφοτέροις τὴν ἀπόλαυσιν ἔσεσθαι. Cf. Aristid., εἰς Ῥώμην (*Or.* xiv Dind.; xxvi Keil), 12: ἐσθῆτας δὲ αὖ Βαβυλωνίους καὶ τοὺς ἐκ τῆς ἐπέκεινα βαρβάρου κόσμους πολὺ πλείους τε καὶ ῥᾶον εἰσαφικνουμένους ἢ εἰ ἐκ Νάξου ἢ Κύθνου Ἀθήναζ' ἔδει κατᾶραι τῶν ἐκεῖ τι φέροντας. It is worthy of note that Palmyra was never in practice a Roman provincial city, not even after Hadrian and L. Verus, nor indeed even after Septimius Severus, when it received the title of a colony (cf. the Capitol on the coins of Panticapaeum). It always had a good deal of autonomy. Like the kingdom of Bosporus, the city with her territory was rather a vassal state of the Empire. The Roman state, however, included the city of Palmyra in the sphere of its military protection, as it had included the Crimea and the territory of the city of Chersonesus. Unfortunately, we know very little of the military organization of Palmyra. Probably in the earlier Roman period she had her own militia. From the age of Trajan or later, as we learn from inscriptions discovered at Palmyra, the city was occupied by Roman troops, detached from the Syrian army. The same happened at Dura after it was occupied by Roman troops in the expedition of Lucius Verus (see *Excavations at Dura Europos*, Prelim. Reports, *passim*). This does not mean that Palmyra may not have had her own militia to protect caravans and fight the nomads. In spite of her considerable autonomy Palmyra, like the kingdom of Bosporus, was bound to furnish auxiliaries to the Roman army. We find military units of Palmyrene origin throughout the Empire (compare the shield with a map painted on it, which shows the journey of one of these soldiers from Palmyra to the Danubian countries under Severus: F. Cumont, *Fouilles de Doura-Europos*, pp. 323 ff., pls. 109 ff., and introd., p. lv). It is probable that the city paid tribute to Rome, as is shown by the part played by Roman procurators in the organization of the taxation of Palmyra, especially the customs-duties: see my discussion in *Geschichte der Staatspacht*, pp. 405 ff.; O. Hirschfeld, *Die kais. Verwaltungsb.* p. 90, note 1. It is very likely that the tribute consisted of part of the customs-duties, and was used for

the maintenance of the garrisons of the city and of the fortresses in her territory. Similar conditions prevailed in Chersonesus in the Crimea under M. Aurelius and Commodus, as is proved by the interesting series of documents issued by the city of Chersonesus, *CIL* iii. 13750 = B. Latyshev, *IOSPE* i², 404; cf. my article in *Bull. of the Arch. Commission*, 60, pp. 63 ff. (in Russian). The soldiers who were stationed in the Crimea and had their headquarters at Chersonesus participated in the collection of the τέλος πορνικόν (*vectigal lenocinii*) and probably received part of the revenue of this tax, the other part being retained by the city. On the trade with Arabia through Bostra and Petra and the cities of the East-Jordan land, which were all enormously enriched by it after the annexation of Arabia Petraea by Trajan, see H. Guthe, 'Die griechisch-römischen Städte des Ostjordanlandes', *Das Land der Bibel*, ii. 5, 1918, pp. 36 ff.; cf. H. Tiersch, *An den Rändern des römischen Reiches*, pp. 29 ff.; M. P. Charlesworth, op. cit., pp. 53 f.; M. Rostovtzeff, *The Caravan-Cities* (1932). The extent of Palmyrene trade throughout the Empire is shown by the discovery of inscriptions which mention Palmyrene merchants everywhere, in Egypt (see note 19 of this chapter), in Rome (where the Palmyrene merchants had their own sanctuary outside the city), and in Dacia (see F. Cumont, op. cit. pl. LV, and my articles quoted in this note).

²¹ See Chap. II, note 29. The best proof of my statement may be found in the inscriptions of Lyons. The most influential groups of merchants there were the dealers in wine, olive-oil, and lumber, see V. Pârvan, *Die Nationalität der Kaufleute im römischen Kaiserreiche*, p. 44. So in the city of Trèves, see note 27, and in Arles, note 28; M. P. Charlesworth, op. cit., pp. 203 ff. On the export of wine from Gaul see Héron de Villefosse, 'Deux armateurs narbonnais,' &c., *Mém. Soc. Ant. de France*, 74, 1915, pp. 153 ff.; L. Cantarelli; *Bull. Com.* 42, 1915, pp. 41 ff., and 279 ff.; A. Jardé in Daremberg–Saglio, v, pp. 917 and 923; C. Jullian, *Hist. de la Gaule*, v, pp. 183 ff. On the oil trade of Africa see R. Cagnat, 'L'annone d'Afrique', *Mém. de l'Ac. d. Inscr.* 40, 1916, pp. 255 ff.

²² My conception of the nature of the professional *collegia* does not coincide with the accepted views on this subject as expounded in the classical works of J. Waltzing, *Étude historique sur les corporations professionnelles*, vols. i, ii (1895–6); E. Kornemann in Pauly–Wissowa, iv, cols. 391 ff.; E. Groag, *Vierteljahresschrift f. Soc. und Wirtschaftsg.* 2, 1904, pp. 481 ff., cf. Chap. VIII, note 39; and V. Pârvan, loc. cit. I am convinced that from the very beginning the corporations of merchants and shipowners who dealt in some of the necessities of life, and especially the latter, were recognized by the state because they were agents of the state—more or less concessionaires of the Roman government. (Callistratus, *Dig.* 50. 6. 6. 3 ff., is perfectly right in speaking of the corporations of this kind as organized by the state.) Along with these corporations which were recognized by the state there existed both in the East and in the West private organizations which were either tolerated or ignored by the state. Some of them, especially in the East, were of very ancient origin. The semi-official character of the corporations which were recognized by the state is shown by the fact that the inscriptions on the amphorae of Monte Testaccio speak of *navicularii* as working for the state under its control, see Héron de Villefosse, 'Deux armateurs narbonnais', &c., *Mém. Soc. Ant. de France*, 74, 1915, pp. 153 ff., and 'La Mosaïque des Narbonnais à Ostie', *Bull. arch. du Com. des trav. hist.* (1918), pp. 245 ff.; L. A. Constans, *Arles antique*, pp. 205 ff., especially p. 210, and my *Gesch. d. Staatspacht*, pp. 426 ff., and furthermore by the fact that in Egypt the owners of river-boats undoubtedly possessed great privileges, since they never sold their boats, but concealed sale under the guise of a lease (μισθοπρασία): see *BGU* 1157 (10 B.C.); *P. Lond.* 1164 (h), iii, p. 163 (A.D. 212); *P.Oxy.* 2136 (A.D. 291): cf. E. de Ruggiero, *Bull. d. Ist. di diritto rom.* 20, 1908, pp. 48 ff. The early date of *BGU* 1157 shows that the privileges granted to

the boatmen went back to Ptolemaic times, and that Claudius in granting individual privileges to shipowners and merchants (Suet. *Claud.* 19) followed a tradition which in Egypt had never lapsed. I am not at all convinced by the arguments of Héron de Villefosse in *Bull. arch.* &c., 1918, pp. 270 ff., that G. Calza was wrong in explaining the building at Ostia rather as an office of the *annona* than as a building designed for the promotion of their private interests by certain corporations of merchants and ship-owners. The building at Ostia did not contain offices for the foreign corporations only: it is clear to me that a place was also given to the corporations of Ostia which were employed by the *annona*. It is interesting to observe that only the Western and the Northern provinces (Sardinia, Africa, Gaul) indicated their offices by their names; the other provinces limited themselves to the representation of the corresponding symbols. On the date of the building see G. Calza, l.c., and F. Noack, *Die Antike*, 2, 1926, pp. 212 ff. On the interpretation of some abbreviations in the mosaic inscriptions in different parts of the building see W. Ensslin, *Rh. Mus.* 77, 1928, pp. 106 ff. The inscriptions have been collected by L. Wickert, *CIL* xiv. 4549. On the *statio annonae* at Rome and its position see M. de Dominicis, 'La Statio annonae urbis Romae', *Bull. Com.* 52, 1925, pp. 135 ff. In Rome there were large corn-stores (*horrea*): see P. Romanelli, *Diz. epigr.*, s.v. horrea; cf. R. Paribeni, *Optimus Princeps*, i, pp. 170 ff.; on the *horrea Agrippiana* see L. Wickert, *Röm. Mitt.* 40, 1925, pp. 213 f., ibid. 41, 1926, p. 229. On the *horrea* of the provinces see Chap. VIII, note 21. On the *stationes* of many provincial cities in Rome see L. Cantarelli, *Bull. Com.* 28, 1900, pp. 124 ff.; Cantarelli considers them similar to the later 'fondûqs'. Some of these stations were in the *horrea*: see S. G. Mercati, *Atti della Pont. accad. Rom. di arch.* 1924–5, pp. 191 ff. = *L'An. ép.* 1926, 16, a sepulchral inscription of a prominent trader in stones in Bithynia (i.e. trade in the marble of Synnada): στατίωνα ἴσχων ἐν ὁρίοις (*horrea*) Πετρωνιανοῖς. On the *annona militaris* see in general A. von Domaszewski, 'Die annona des Heeres im Kriege', 'Επιτύμβιον H. Swoboda, pp. 17 ff. On the *annona* of Africa see R. Cagnat, 'L'Annone d'Afrique', *Mém. d. l'Ac. d. Inscr.* 40, 1916, pp. 258 ff.; on that of Egypt, my article 'Frumentum' in Pauly–Wissowa, vii; cf. P. Sak, 'La Perception de l'annone militaire dans l'Égypte romaine', *Mélanges Ch. Moeller* (*Rec. de trav. etc. de l'Univ. de Louvain*, 40, 1917), and J. Lesquier, *L'Armée romaine d'Égypte*, pp. 350 ff. On the merchants and shipowners of Alexandria and their corporations under the Ptolemies, see my volume, *A Large Estate in Egypt* (1922), pp. 35, 125, 133 ff.; and my article 'The Foreign-trade of Ptolemaic Egypt', *Journ. of Econ. and Business Hist.* 3, 1932, pp. 728 ff.; cf. on the corporations of merchants in the Greek part of the Empire, Stöckle in Pauly–Wissowa, Suppl. iv, cols. 157 ff. It is a pity that Stöckle's quotations of the inscriptions are utterly antiquated: he never cites, e.g., *IGRR*. Cf. Chap. VIII, note 39.

²³ Pliny, in a well-known passage of his *Panegyric* (ch. 29), formulates very clearly the policy of the enlightened monarchy as regards the provision of corn for the cities and associations of merchants and shipowners. He says: ' nonne cernere datur, ut sine ullius iniuria omnis usibus nostris annus exuberet? quippe non ut ex hostico raptae perituraeque in horreis messes nequiquam quiritantibus sociis auferuntur. deuehunt ipsi, quod terra genuit, quod sidus aluit, quod annus tulit, nec novis indictionibus pressi ad vetera tributa deficiunt. emit fiscus, quidquid videtur emere. inde copiae, inde annona, de qua inter licentem vendentemque conveniat, inde hic satietas nec fames usquam.' Pliny, in thus contrasting the present and the past, is undoubtedly thinking of the time of Domitian (see note 9 of this chapter) and of the first years of Trajan. It would have been difficult for him to repeat these words at the time of the Dacian and Eastern wars, when Trajan was compelled to adopt some of the expedients of Domitian (see Chap. VIII, notes 3 ff.). On the passage of Pliny see R. Paribeni, *Optimus Princeps*, i, pp. 172 ff.

²⁴ On roads and trade within the provinces see O. Hirschfeld, 'Die römischen Meilensteine', *Kl. Schr.*, pp. 703 ff.; V. Chapot in Daremberg–Saglio, v, pp. 777 ff.; cf. E. Miller, *Itineraria Romana* (1916), and the severe, learned, and fully justified criticism of this book by W. Kubitschek, *Gött. gel. Anz.* 1917, pp. 1 ff.; id. Pauly–Wissowa, ix, cols. 2308 ff.; O. Cuntz, *Itineraria Romana*, i, *Itinerarium Antonini Aug. et Burdigalense* (1929), [–ii, ed. J. Schnetz, *Ravennatis Anonymi Cosmographia et Guidonis Geographica* (1940)]; G. H. Stevenson, 'Communications and Commerce', *Legacy of Rome* (1923), pp. 141 ff.; cf. Lefebvre des Noëttes, 'La Voie romaine et la route moderne', *Rev. arch.* 1925 (2), pp. 105 ff.; M. P. Charlesworth, *Trade-routes and Commerce of the Roman Empire*² (1926). There is as yet no special description of the customs (*publicum portorii*) of the Empire. General works on the subject are: O. Hirschfeld, *Die kais. Verwaltungsb.*², pp. 76 ff. and R. Cagnat, art. 'Portorium' in Daremberg–Saglio, iv, pp. 586 ff. Cf. my book, *Geschichte der Staatspacht in der röm. Kaiserzeit*, Philol. Suppl. ix (1904). After the publication of Cagnat's article new and important epigraphic evidence was discovered. For the province of Asia see *Forsch. Eph.* iii, p. 131, no. 45; J. Keil, *Oest. Jahresh.* 33, 1926, p. 270. On the Danubian provinces see in particular the series of documents concerning the rights of the city of Histria over the fish-ponds at the mouth of the Danube and over the timber of the island of Peuke, and concerning the disputes between the city and the contractors of the *portorium ripae Thraciae*: see V. Pârvan, *Histria*, 4, nos. 15, 16 (pp. 557 and 560) and H. Dessau, *Oest. Jahresh.* 23, 1926, Beibl., pp. 346 ff. = *SEG* i. 329. Another group of documents comes from Poetovio, which was for some time the headquarters of the administration of the *publicum portorii Illyrici*: see M. Abramič, *Führer durch Poetovio*, pp. 28 ff. New evidence concerning the customs of Aquileia occurs in an inscription of the age of Caracalla found in the harbour of this city. This inscription (G. Brusin, *Aquileia*, p. 47; id. *Roma*, 6, 1928, p. 431; A. Calderini, *Aquileia Romana*, Ricerche di storia e di epigrafia (1930), pp. 245 ff.) seems to show (*qq* probably means *quinquagesimae*) that the tariff of the *publicum portorii Illyrici* amounted to 2 per cent. and not 5 per cent. We learn also that two customs-offices were in the harbour of the city. For the province of Africa see *ILA* 455. For Egypt see L. Fiesel, 'Geleitzölle im griech-röm. Ägypten und im germanisch-romanischen Abendland', *Gött. gel. Nachr.* 1925, pp. 57 ff. Cf. N. Y. Clausen, 'A Customs-House Registry from Roman Egypt', *Aegyptus*, 8, 1928, pp. 240 ff. In the walls of the sanctuary near the gate of Dura, which is dedicated to the Tyche of the city, inscriptions were found attesting a family of customs-officials, τελῶναι, and another family of porters (πυλουροί); the custom-duties are sometimes called, as in Egypt, τέλος πώρτας (sic: in Egypt πυης). The inscriptions of Dura provide a good illustration of two well-known passages of Philostratus, in the *Life of Apollonius of Tyana*, i. 20 (the customs-station on the Euphrates and the customs-officers at the gate of Babylon). See my *Gesch. d. Staatspacht*, pp. 405 ff. (77 ff.), and J. Johnson, *Excav. at Dura-Europos*, Prelim. Rep. ii. pp. 156 ff. Cf. the τέλος εἰσαγωγῆς at Babylon (10 per cent.) re-established by Antimenes in the time of Alexander: Ps.-Arist. *Oecon.* ii. 39; A. Andreades, *BCH* 53, 1929, p. 7. The most interesting district, however, is certainly that of the Danube, Illyricum. I have never maintained, as Pârvan and Dessau assert, that this district had no regulation before Hadrian. In my *Staatspacht*, p. 394, I said that it cannot have been established in its definitive form as it appears in the inscriptions of the 2nd and 3rd cents. A.D., divided into eight or ten sections, before the annexation of Dacia and the reorganization of Moesia. No doubt customs existed in Illyricum before this; but we do not know in what way the customs-district was organized. Probably it was originally confined to what subsequently became the province of Dalmatia, and was then extended to the other Danubian provinces, as soon as they were annexed and organized. Two inscriptions in particular help towards the solution of the problem of the position of the German provinces in regard to frontier-customs. One belongs to an altar

dedicated *Matribus Aufaniis*, and was found in 1928–9 in the Münster Church of Bonn. The dedicant is *M. Pompeius Potens conductor XXXX Galliarum et portus Lirensis*: H. Lehner, 'Römische Steindenkmäler von der Bonner Münsterkirche', *Bonn. Jahrb.* 135, 1930, no. 23, pl. XIII, cf. p. 31, and *Germania*, 16, 1932, pp. 104 ff. The second inscription comes from Viminacium (Dessau, *ILS* 9019), and was published for the first time by N. Vulič, *Oest. Jahresh.* 8, 1905, Beibl., p. 3: it was erected in honour of a certain *M. Antonius M. f. Fabia Fabianus*, who was *pro(curator) XL Galliarum et portus, item argentiarar(um) Pannonicar(um)*, and also *c(onductor) portori Illyrici*. The two inscriptions illustrate the transition from direct to indirect taxation, or, better, the mutual relations between contractors of customs and imperial officials (cf. on this Steinwenter, 'Manceps', Pauly–Wissowa, xiv, cols. 987 ff.): it is difficult to draw a line between the procurators and the contractors (*conductores*). At the same time the two inscriptions prove that the Rhine customs were usually in the hands of the farmer of the *quadresima Galliarum*. The question therefore arises as to the meaning of *portus Lirensis*. In *C. R. Acad. Inscr.* 1930, pp. 256 ff., I examined the alternatives of the customs of the western coast of Italy and of the Rhine customs. On the trade of the British Isles and of Spain see L. C. West, *Imperial Roman Spain: the Objects of Trade* (1929), and *Roman Britain; the Objects of Trade* (1931).

[25] The correct explanation of the growth of Puteoli at the expense of Ostia was given by T. Frank, *Economic History*[2], pp. 305 ff., 411 ff.; *Roman History*, p. 398. On the decay of Puteoli see *IG* xiv. 830 = *IGRR* i. 421 = *OGIS* 595; Ch. Dubois, *Pouzzoles antique*, pp. 83 ff., cf. pp. 79 ff.; K. Lehmann-Hartleben, 'Die antiken Hafenanlagen des Mittelmeeres', *Klio*, Beiheft 14, 1923, pp. 163 ff. On Ostia, ibid., pp. 182 ff. On Portus Augusti or Traiani see R. Paribeni, *Optimus Princeps*, ii, pp. 101 ff. The Alexandrian corn-fleet in the time of Nero still put in at Puteoli (Seneca, *Ep.* 77. 1). Later it came to Ostia, as is proved by many inscriptions. The importance of Campania and of Puteoli in Nero's time is shown by the fact that many cities of Campania including Puteoli were Neronian colonies, see A. Sogliano, 'Colonie Neroniane', *Rend. Lincei*, 6, 1897, pp. 389 ff.; cf. id. *Nuova Rivista Storica*, 1921, pp. 424 ff.

[26] On the character of Roman commerce in Gaul, see C. Jullian, *Histoire*, v, pp. 318 ff.; cf. P. Courteault, *JRS* 11, 1921, pp. 101 ff., and *Rev. ét. anc.* 24, 1922, pp. 236 ff., an inscription of Bordeaux of A.D. 237, in which a *sevir Augustalis* of York and Lincoln in England thanks the *Dea Tutela Boudig(a)* for his safe journey from England to Bordeaux [= *L'An. ép.* 1922, 116]. On the wine-trade with Ireland see above Chap. III, note 12, and H. Schaal, *Vom Tauschhandel zum Welthandel* (1931), pp. 165 ff. On the almost complete emancipation from Italy, see V. Pârvan, *Die Nationalität*, &c., pp. 28 and 33. On the trade of the Alpine regions see H. Aubin, *Schmollers Jahrb.* 49, 1925, pp. 418 ff.; F. Staehelin, *Die Schweiz in röm. Zeit*[2] (1931), pp. 366 ff. [3rd ed. (1948), pp. 386 ff.]. On Aquileia and her ever-growing industrial and commercial importance, see the bibliography quoted in Chap. I, note 16. The annexation of Noricum and the gradual pacification of the Danube lands, as well as the creation of many large fortresses for the legions, raised the importance of Aquileia to a height never before reached. The legions were stationed first in Dalmatia (Burnum and Delminium) and in Pannonia on the Save, and were transferred later first to the Drave and afterwards to the Danube. This meant the creation of a series of new and large markets for all the products of the agriculture and industry of Northern Italy and especially Aquileia. The iron and lead mines of Noricum promoted the manufacture of steel, iron, and bronze weapons and utensils; its semi-precious stones and gold stimulated the jewellers of Aquileia to work on their own account; the increasing demand for glass-ware induced the city to create her own glass factories. I have spoken already of the manufacture of amber articles.

Widely spread were the tiles of the well-known Aquileian family of the Barbii, a big export house of which we know one important branch in Noricum at Virunum and another at Tergeste (see the indexes to *CIL*, v and iii). The export of wine from Aquileia attained also a much greater importance than it had previously had. One of the many examples of rich landowners of North Italy who exported their wine and oil into the Danube lands is the well-known Calvia Crispinilla (Tac. *Hist.* i. 73), as is shown by the amphorae stamps with her name found at Poetovio and at Tergeste, *CIL* iii. 12010. 2; M. P. Charlesworth, op. cit., p. 236 and note on p. 284. Cf., in addition to the bibliography quoted above, R. Schneider, *Arch.-ep. Mitth. aus Oest.* 9, 1885, p. 83; id. *Kunstgeschichtliche Characterbilder aus Oesterreich-Ungarn*, p. 31; M. Abramič, *Oest. Jahresh.* 12, 1909, Beibl. pp. 54, 96, 101; C. Patsch, *Historische Wanderungen im Karst und an der Adria*, vol. i, *Die Herzegowina einst und jetzt* (1922), p. 128. While the region and the port of Aquileia were the main centres of wine export to the Danube lands, Histria and its harbours (Parentium and Pola which form a unit with Tergeste) were the main centres for the trade in olive-oil, which was produced in great quantities all over the Histrian peninsula on the large estates and on the small farms of this fertile district: see A. Gnirs, 'Forschungen über antiken Villenbau in Südistrien', *Oest. Jahresh.* 18, 1915, Beibl., pp. 101 ff.; 17, 1914, Beibl., pp. 192 ff.; H. Schwalb, 'Römische Villa bei Pola', *Schriften der Balkankommission*, 2, 1902, pp. 9 ff.; J. Weiss in Pauly–Wissowa, ix, col. 2113. It is instructive to follow the spread of Italian and Histrian commerce and industry throughout Dalmatia and the Danube lands. One of the best indications is given by the factory stamps on the oil and wine jars, and on the tiles. See, e.g., the history of the jars fabricated by C. Laekanius Bassus first in Vercellae, later in Pola, which have been found in masses in Poetovio (Pannonia) and also at Virunum in Noricum (A. Gnirs, *Oest. Jahresh.* 13, 1910–11, Beibl., pp. 95 ff.; cf. the imperial factory of jars near Parentium, *CIL* v. 2. 8112, 1–4). Not less instructive is the history of the tiles which were produced in the (at first private and later imperial) factory of Pansa (Pansiana), one branch of which was transferred from Italy to a place near Tergeste, see C. Patsch, *Wiss. Mitt. aus Bosnien*, 9 (1904), pp. 278 ff., 280 ff., especially pp. 284 ff. There are also interesting data on the commercial relations between Dalmatia and Africa, ibid., pp. 298 ff.; cf. the same writer's *Historische Wanderungen im Karst*, &c., i (1922), pp. 110 ff.

[27] A good study of the pillar-monuments of the Moselle and of their sculptures is given by F. Drexel, 'Die belgisch-germanischen Pfeilergräber' and 'Die Bilder der Igeler Säule', *Röm. Mitt.* 35, 1920, pp. 26 ff. and 83 ff. All the sculptures of the Moselle type, including those of Arlon and of the Luxembourg, are published by E. Espérandieu, *Recueil des bas-reliefs, statues et bustes de la Gaule romaine*, vi (1913). Cf. H. Dragendorff and E. Krüger, 'Das Grabmal von Igel' (*Röm. Grabmäler des Mosellandes u. der angrenzenden Gebiete*, i) (1924); *Germania Romana*², iii, cf. W. von Massow, *JDAI* 42, 1927, *Arch. Anz.* pp. 182 ff. The sculptures of Neumagen, as we now see them collected and partially restored in the museum of Trèves, after years of work, have been splendidly described and illustrated in the excellent book, *Die röm. Denkmäler des Mosellandes*, ii; E. Krüger and W. von Massow, *Die Grabmäler von Neumagen* (1930). Cf. also A. Schober, 'Zur Entstehung und Bedeutung der provinzial-röm. Kunst', *Oest. Jahresh.* 26, 1930, pp. 9 ff. and S. Ferri, *Arte romana sul Reno* (1931). In his appreciation and explanation of the Rhine and Moselle sculptures F. Drexel is wholly mistaken. The leading idea of the graves of the Roman time, on which scenes of daily life are reproduced, is not the display by some *nouveaux riches* of their wealth and their power over their fellow men, as Drexel suggests. The main inspiration was the Stoic religious and moral ideal, in general influenced by neo-Pythagoreanism, of the cultured classes of the Empire: by a model life crowned with success, by the strict

fulfilment of their duty, as depicted on the monuments, the owners of them acquired the right to the final 'apotheosis'. The same leading idea dictated the choice of the reliefs on the wonderful columns of Trajan and M. Aurelius; it also inspired the selection of the sculptures and paintings on the funeral monuments of the soldiers and officers of the Roman army and of the municipal magistrates, e.g. the set of paintings on the walls of the funeral monument of an aedile at Pompeii discovered many years ago near the Vesuvian Gate and not yet published; finally, the same idea prevailed in all the funeral inscriptions and the *elogia* of the Roman imperial aristocracy, with their minute enumeration of the military and civil offices of the deceased. Both the gorgeous monuments of the Moselle magnates and the modest *cippi* of Gallic artisans, with their realistic sculptures representing the daily toil of the departed, are typical expressions of a high appreciation of labour, as being not a bitter necessity but a social and religious duty—an ideal diametrically opposed to some ideas of the Roman aristocracy of the 1st cent. B.C., e.g. Cicero, who regarded trade and industry as occupations which have a degrading influence on human character and considered leisure to be the main goal of human life. Without doubt the ideal of the 'consecration of labour', which was not new to the Greek world (see T. Zielinski, *The Religion of Ancient Greece* (1918), pp. 27 ff., in Russian; English trans. *Religion of Greece* (1926), pp. 39 ff.), corresponded strictly to the Cynic and Stoic ideal of the imperial power, of which I have spoken in the fourth chapter, and which was itself a creation of the Stoic and Cynic teachings adapted to the aims and methods of the enlightened monarchy. It would be easy to corroborate this statement by quotations from the works of the Stoic philosophers of the imperial period. On the other hand, the tendency towards realistic painting and sculpture is in no way a peculiarity of the Gallic regions and of the Celtic nation. The Ionian Greeks (not to speak of the Oriental world), especially in the archaic period, liked to reproduce such scenes on different types of the products of their art. They transmitted this predilection to the Etruscans and to the Samnites, from whom it passed to the Romans, to become one of the leading features of Roman art. The Orient, however, in Hellenistic and Roman times did not maintain the realistic tradition, but concentrated on other fields of artistic creation. The fact that funeral monuments showing scenes of daily life, especially scenes connected with economic life—agriculture, commerce, and industry—are one of the outstanding features first of Southern and Central Italy and later of the Western branch of Roman provincial art, particularly that of Northern Italy and of Gaul (Gummerus in *JDAI* 28, 1913, pp. 67 ff.), does not indicate a peculiarity of artistic conception in these lands, but reflects the characteristic phenomena of life there, that is, its industrial and commercial aspect. The funeral monuments of Northern Italy and Gaul form, therefore, one of our most important sources of information about the economic and social life of these parts of the Roman Empire. The choice of episodes of daily and business life is, of course, influenced not only by the character of that life but also by the traditions of funeral art in general. Scenes of travel and of meals are prevalent, having been used from time immemorial to symbolize the last journey and the meal of the *beati*, just as scenes of battle prevail on the stelae of soldiers and officers in accordance with the ancient Greek tradition which liked to show the great and victorious battle of the divinized hero. The art of the Rhine and Moselle funeral monuments is not at all an art of *parvenus* (Drexel's expression), but a sound and vigorous attempt to create a realistic art on Etruscan and Italian models. On 'Apotheosis' and the ideas connected with it, see A. Della Seta, *Religione ed arte figurata* (1912), pp. 175 f.; Mrs. A. Strong, *Apotheosis and After Life* (1915), pp. 174 ff., and the masterly sketches of F. Cumont, *After Life in Roman Paganism* (1922).

A proof that Trèves was also a centre for clothes-making is provided by a badly damaged inscription of the main altar of the temple of Mercury found in the valley of the Altbach in the 'sacred' district of Trèves: mi[les clas]sis Germanice ⟨Do|mitianae p. f.⟩ neg[otiator cervesa]rius artis offec[ture exvoto pro]meritis posuit (S. Loeschke, *Die Erforschung des Tempelbezirkes im Altbachtale zu Trier* (1928), p. 22) [= *L'An. ép.* 1928, 183]. The interpretation of the inscription is doubtful: but, whether this marine had his private business while he was still in service, or whether he took it up only when he was a veteran, and whether *negotiator cervesarius* means simply a beer-dealer, and not also a dealer in some colouring-matter (the colour of beer?), one thing is clear: the man was closely connected with the corporation of *offectores* (dyers), and was probably a member of it himself. If he is to be considered the beer-dealer of the corporation, we should infer that the corporation had a compact organization and many members who probably lived near each other in a special quarter of the city: see my article, *C. R. Acad. Inscr.* 1930, pp. 250 ff. A second Trèves, on a smaller scale, was the capital of Raetia, Augusta Vindelicorum, the modern Augsburg (see Chap. VI, note 55). The Maximilian Museum there gives a full picture of the development of the ancient city which is in many ways similar to that of Trèves. The first colonizers were people of modest means; their funerary monuments are simple stelae and altars. The wealth of some families, who still played an active part in military service, grew: the altars and stelae became larger, the ornamental sculpture richer, with statues, portraits, and mythological scenes predominating. The climax is reached with the large and sumptuous tombs with pilasters similar to those at Trèves, on which the whole economic life of the family is represented. Here too the prevailing element is banking and trade: next come the making of clothes and trade in wine and beer. Is it pure chance that Augusta became the city of the Fugger family? Conditions in the German Rhineland are even more modest; but the psychology of the Roman and Celtic *bourgeoisie* is the same. Compare, for instance, the famous tombstone of Blusso, the wealthy shipowner, who is there, proud of himself, with wife and children, in a half-national dress, holding ostentatiously his purse. Another such, if we are to believe Koerber (*Mainz. Zeitschr.* 3, 1908, p. 3, fig. 4), has a heap of coins on his lap. No less typical are the 'brother' of Blusso, the man of Weisenau, and his beautiful, haughty, wife, as they appear on their funerary monument: see *Mainz. Zeitschr.* 22, 1927, pp. 41 ff., and pl. 1: cf. G. Behrens, 'Fibel-Darstellungen auf römischen Grabsteinen', ibid., pp. 51 ff., who also reproduces (p. 55, fig. 8) the monument of Blusso and others of the same kind, and studies the dresses, and more especially the *fibulae* and round German medallions, represented on them (cf. Drexel, *Das Schwäb'sche Museum* (1927), fasc. 2, p. 39, fig. iv). At Cologne, of course, the conditions of life were less restricted and the *bourgeoisie* wealthier: see Chap. VI, note 43.

²⁸ On Arelate and Narbo and their *bourgeoisie*, see the articles of Héron de Villefosse and the book of L. A. Constans quoted in note 22.

²⁹ See note 25.

³⁰ A good survey of the inter-provincial and foreign trade of Egypt has been given by Louis C. West, 'Phases of Commercial Life in Roman Egypt', *JRS* 7, 1917, pp. 45 ff. It is to be regretted that this study is only a fragment. It gives only a list of the articles which were exported from Egypt to foreign lands, and this list is itself less complete than that of Chwostow. There is also no list of objects exported from Egypt to the other provinces of the Empire. Cf. M. P. Charlesworth, op. cit., pp. 16 ff. On the roads of the Egyptian desert see G. W. Murray, 'The Roman Roads and Stations in the Eastern Desert of Egypt', *JEA* 11, 1925, pp. 138 ff.

³¹ V. Pârvan, op. cit., pp. 79 ff. The classical example of a shrewd and successful Oriental merchant is Flavius Zeuxis of Hierapolis in Phrygia. He sailed to Rome from Asia Minor seventy-two times, Dittenberger, *Syll.*³ 1229. Less well known is another

sea merchant and *navicularius* Flavius Longinus of Dyrrhachium. In his inscription adorned with a picture of a sailing-boat he says: ἐγὼ δὲ] πολλὰ περειπλεύ[σας κὲ] πολλὲς ἐξουσείες | [ὑπ]ηρετήσας (C. Praschniker and A. Schober, 'Archäologische Forschungen in Albanien', *Schriften der Balkankommission*, 8, 1919, p. 45, nos. 57 and 57a, ll. 9 ff.) [= *SEG* ii. 384]. His Greek is poor and he was certainly not an educated man, but he was rich and influential, as is shown by his remark on his services to his city in the capacity of magistrate. Another rich shipowner was L. Erastus of Ephesus, who repeatedly lent his services to the Roman governors of Asia, and twice carried the Emperor Hadrian to and from Ephesus in his own ship, *Syll.*³ 838 (A.D. 129). An inscription from Aedepsus (*IG* xii. 9. 1240; cf. Preuner, *JDAI* 40, 1925, pp. 39 ff.) is amusing. It refers to a ναύκληρος of Nicomedia, who died as a κυβερνήτης (or does he mean that he is sailing to the other world?). He says of himself (cf. pl. vii, 2): Διογενιανὸς Νεικομηδεὺς — — — πολλὰ περιπλεύσας πρότερον ναυκληρῶν εἶτα τὸ νῦν κυβερνῶν, κ.τ.λ., and adds the advice: ζῶν κτῶ χρῶ. A fine testimony to the lively maritime commerce of the imperial period is furnished by the inscriptions on the rocks of a little harbour in the region of the Acroceraunian mountains in Macedonia, where sailors saved by the Dioscuri recorded their thanks in scores of inscriptions both in Greek and in Latin, *CIG* 1824–7; *CIL* iii. 582–4; Heuzey and Daumet, *Mission archéologique en Macédoine*, p. 407; C. Patsch, 'Das Sandschak Berat in Albanien', in *Schr. d. Balkankomm.* 3, 1904, pp. 91 ff.

³² On the *étatisation* of internal commerce in Egypt under the Ptolemies see my *Large Estate in Egypt*, pp. 117 ff. For the Roman period there are some remarks in Wilcken, *Grundzüge*, pp. 262 ff., and W. Schubart, *Einführung*, p. 430; cf. E. Schönbauer, *Zeitschr. d. Sav.-St.* 46, 1926, pp. 199 ff. On the commerce in textiles and in paper, see my review of M. Chwostow's *Studies in the Organization of Industry and Commerce in Greco-Roman Egypt*, i, *The Textile Industry* (Kazan, 1914), in *Journ. of the Min. of Educ. of Russia*, 53, 1914, no. 10, pp. 362 ff. (in Russian). A revival of *étatisation* began in the time of Septimius Severus, as is shown by his creation of a special branch of the *ratio patrimonii*—the 'Anabolicum'. A certain part of the produce of the most important industries of Egypt (glass, papyrus, linen, hemp) was levied from the producers by the state and exported *en bloc* to Rome and partly to Gaul, probably for the use of the Rhine army. Thus a large part of the export trade was monopolized by the state, and these conditions affected also the organization of commerce within the province. I must add that I still consider it likely that the *anabolicum* or the *anabolica* (ἀναβολικά) are already mentioned in the edict of Tib. Iul. Alex., though many have doubted this: see now also W. Graf Uxkull-Gyllenband, *Arch. f. Papyr.* 9, p. 200. However, no monopoly was introduced even by the emperors of the 3rd cent. See my articles in *Röm. Mitt.* 11, 1896, pp. 317 ff.; in *Woch. kl. Phil.* 1900, p. 115; my *Catalogue des plombs de la Bibl. Nationale*, p. 10; F. Zucker, *Philol.* 70, 1911, pp. 79 ff.; Axel W. Persson, *Staat und Manufaktur im römischen Reiche* (Lund, 1923), p. 35. The inscriptions on lead seals are also in *CIL* xiii. 3. 2, no. 10029, 43; cf. Chap. IX, note 60.

³³ P. Girard, *Manuel élémentaire du droit romain*⁶ (1918), pp. iii–iv, titre i, Ch. II, 3; E. Cuq, *Manuel d'institutions romaines* (1917), pp. 493 ff.; W. W. Buckland, *A Text-book of Roman Law from Augustus to Justinian* (1921), p. 504 (without quotation of modern works on the subject); Manigk, Pauly–Wissowa, iii, A, cols. 772 ff., s.v. 'societas'.

³⁴ The inscriptions of the merchants of Palmyra may be found in *OGIS* 632, 633, 638, 646; *IGRR* iii. 1050–2, cf. 1538; *CIS* iii. 2; M. Rostovtzeff, 'Les inscriptions caravanières de Palmyre', *Mél. G. Glotz*, ii (1932), pp. 793 ff. It is not impossible that the same Babylonian and Persian traditions persisted in Asia Minor, see *IGRR* iv. 796 (Apamea in Phrygia): Ἡσύχῳ ἐμποριάρχῃ . . . σπουδασάντων κὲ τῶν συμβιωτῶν κὲ λβ' ἄλλων. Apropos of the Palmyrene merchants, we should bear in mind what a

peculiar system the caravan-trade is and what a marvel of organization a caravan represents, see P. Havelin, *Essai historique sur le droit des marchés et des foires* (1897), pp. 49 ff., esp. p. 50: 'La caravane forme un groupement distinct des groupements qu'elle traverse; elle constitue un organisme social complet; elle a en elle tous les éléments de défense, d'administration, d'autorité, de justice, qui constituent le marché et la ville. . . . Les difficultés qui peuvent surgir parmi les voyageurs sont tranchés par-devant le chef ou par-devant un tribunal particulier,' and P. H. Lammens, 'La Mecque à la veille de l'hégire', *Mél. Univ. St. Joseph de Beyrouth*, 9, 1924, pp. 304 ff. (excellent description of the organization of caravan-trade and of the life of a caravan-city). Such a peculiar social and economic body certainly established special laws and a special organization in the places which were its headquarters and formed the starting-points of its journeys. To Italy and Greece the caravan system was wholly alien, and therefore neither Greek nor Roman law says anything about it. It is interesting to see that the Syrian merchants who settled in Dacia under Trajan also appear organized in associations: see Chap. VI, note 83. The parchments and papyri from Dura give an idea of the Greco-Babylonian law prevalent in the cities of Mesopotamia in the Greek and Parthian periods: see F. Cumont, *Fouilles de Doura-Europos*, pp. 282 ff.; M. Rostovtzeff and C. B. Welles, 'A Parchment Contract of Loan from Dura-Europos on the Euphrates', *Yale Class. Stud.* 2, 1931, pp. 3 ff.; *Excav. at Dura-Europos*, Prelim. Rep. ii (1931), pp. 201 ff.; P. Koschaker, 'Über einige griechische Rechtsurkunden aus den östlichen Randgebieten des Hellenismus', *Abh. d. sächs. Ges.* 42 (1), 1931.

35 The great importance of commerce by sea is shown by the enormous sums which the emperors and the cities spent on the improvement of the old ports and the creation of new ones, with all the novel devices introduced by the perfected engineering technique of the Hellenistic period. The greatest activity in this field was displayed by Trajan: see R. Paribeni, *Optimus Princeps*, ii, pp. 101 ff. On the works of the port of Ephesus see *Forsch. Eph.* ii, pp. 174 ff., no. 61, II, 14; iii, pp. 149, no. 66, 14 ff.; 71, 11 ff. Note also that hundreds of lighthouses were built on the most important points of the Mediterranean shores. On the harbours, see K. Lehmann-Hartleben, 'Die antiken Hafenanlagen des Mittelmeeres', *Klio*, Beiheft 14, 1923. On the lighthouses, R. Hennig, *Abhandlungen zur Geschichte der Schiffahrt* (1927), ch. vii, with bibliography, which however does not quote the work of H. Thiersch, 'Griechische Leuchtfeuer', *JDAI*, 30, 1915, pp. 213 ff., and also in *Arch. Anz.* 1915, p. 52. Hennig has not convinced me that the invention of lighthouses is something we owe to the Romans; but he is correct in maintaining that the systematic building of lighthouses for the benefit of navigators was an innovation of the 1st cent. A.D. On navigation in general see the work of Hennig already quoted, and A. Köster, *Das Antike Seewesen* (1923); a complete and exhaustive treatment of the subject by Köster is expected [see A. Köster, 'Studien zur Geschichte des antiken Seewesens', *Klio*, Beiheft 32, 1934]. To realize the great development of river commerce, note the detailed differentiation of the various types of river-boats and river-ships in the well-known mosaic of Althiburos in Africa (P. Gauckler, 'Un catalogue de la batellerie gréco-romaine', *Mon. Piot*, 12, 1905, pp. 113 ff., cf. Aßmann, *JDAI* 21, 1906, pp. 107 ff.; H. Dessau, *ILS* 9456; *Inv. d. mos.* no. 576). It is very probable that the pictures of this mosaic (reproduced on our pl. xxix) were taken from an illustrated catalogue of ships, of which remains still exist in the works of A. Gellius, Nonius, and Isidorus of Seville. In the same way the mosaics which represent Orpheus charming the animals, the upper part of the famous mosaic of Palestrina, and of some paintings in a tomb of the Hellenistic period at Marissa in Palestine (J. P. Peters and H. Thiersch, *Painted Tombs in the Necropolis of Marissa* (1905), pls. vii–xv), were all influenced by illustrated treatises on zoology; and the fish mosaics

all over the Greco-Roman world drew the figures of the fishes from illustrated treatises of ichthyology. The fact that in the mosaic of Althiburos there are no special names of Egyptian boats but many names of Celtic and Italian boats shows that the ship-catalogue had been compiled in Italy from a Hellenistic, not an Alexandrian, source, by a man who knew both Italy and Gaul. I should suggest a man like Verrius Flaccus rather than Varro. On the river-trade of Mesopotamia, Egypt, Gaul, and Germany see H. Schaal, 'Flußschiffahrt und Flußhandel im Altertum', *Festschr. zur 400 Jahrfeier des alt. Gymn. zu Bremen* (1928), pp. 370 ff.; on that of Egypt see M. Merzagora, 'La Navigazione in Egitto nell' età greco-romana', *Aegyptus*, 10, 1930, pp. 105 ff.; of Gaul, C. Jullian, *Histoire*, v, pp. 161 ff., and L. Bonnard, *La navigation intérieure de la Gaule à l'époque romaine* (1913). Navigation on Celtic lakes (e.g. that of Geneva) is mentioned in the inscription of a certain Q. Decius Alpinus, honoured by the *nautae lacus Lemanni*, *Rev. ét. anc.* 28, 1926, p. 43 [= *L'An. ép.* 1926, 2]. On the importance of the Rhine trade for the economic history of Gaul and Germany see H. Aubin, 'Der Rheinland in röm. Zeit', *Bonn. Jahrb.* 130, 1925, pp. 1 ff. A brief synthesis of our information on the Rhine traffic is given by Joh. Ledroit, 'Die röm. Schiffahrt im Stromgebiet des Rheins', *Kulturgesch. Wegweiser durch das röm.-germ. Zentral-Museum*, 12, 1930.

36 A good survey of the importance of industry in the economic life of the early Empire, especially for the end of the 1st cent. and the first half of the 2nd cent. A.D., based on a careful collection of evidence from the novelists and poets of this time (especially Petronius, Martial, and Juvenal) is given by Miss E. H. Brewster, *Roman Craftsmen and Tradesmen of the Early Roman Empire* (1917), pp. 94 ff. The author is right in assigning a large part in economic and social life to industry and commerce (I should say 'to commerce and industry'). But the levelling policy of the emperors had nothing to do with the growing importance of the bourgeois class. It was the result of the existence of the Roman World-Empire and of the reign of peace which had lasted about two centuries: note in this connexion that the well-known statement of Pliny about papyrus-production in Babylonia, that is, in the Parthian Kingdom (*NH* xiii. 11, 73), was confirmed by the discovery of papyri at Dura.

37 C. Jullian, *Histoire*, v, pp. 216 ff.; on pottery, pp. 264 ff.; on glass, pp. 290 ff.; on metals, pp. 300 ff., with a complete up-to-date bibliography; cf. also R. Lantier, *La verrerie*, 'Musée des Art. Nat.' (1929). One of our most important sources of information is the innumerable funeral monuments of Gaul, which reproduce the portraits of the deceased and of the members of their families, with the attributes of their craft, and very often a *genre* scene showing the deceased in his workshop (see our plates xxv, xxix, and xxxvii). The characteristics of the economic life of Gaul are illustrated by a comparison of these bas-reliefs, as collected by E. Espérandieu, with the funeral monuments of the Rhine and the Moselle (see note 27). The Moselle and Rhine lands were centres of a lively commerce *en gros*; the cities of Gaul were centres of a prosperous industry, which worked both for the local market and for export. The scenes on the tombstones may suggest that the industrial work was done mostly in small shops by artisans, but the facts that the reliefs were modelled on existing patterns borrowed from Italy, and that they repeated everywhere the same types, prevent us from laying too much stress on this point. The character of the scene represented on the funeral stelae indicates the craft of the deceased in general, and does not necessarily imply that he was an artisan rather than an owner of a large workshop or of many workshops. We know, moreover, that the centres of pottery production in Gaul show the characteristic features of a large industrial settlement organized on capitalistic lines (note 39). It is noteworthy that, while scenes of industrial life form the outstanding feature of the Gallic tombstones, they are much less common in the Danube lands and in Spain, and never appear in Africa or Britain. Evidently this proves the leading part played by

Gaul and Northern Italy in the industrial life of the Roman Empire, and testifies to a much slower development of industry in the other provinces of the West. In the East the fashion of representing the craft of the deceased on his tombstone never took firm root, and this reflects the difference in the conceptions of labour and in its organization, cf. note 44.

[38] On the history of the African lamp-making industry, see the excellent article of L. Carton, 'Les fabriques de lampes dans l'ancienne Afrique', *Bull. de la Soc. de Géogr. et d'Archéologie de la province d'Oran*, 36 (144), 1916, cf. id. 'L'art indigène sur les lampes de la colonia Thuburnica', *Mém. Soc. Ant. de France*, 1913, pp. 141 ff. The same story is repeated in Gaul, see S. Loeschke, *Lampen aus Vindonissa* (1919); cf. F. Fremersdorf, *Römische Bildlampen* (1922). On the factory of bas-relief vases, see A. Merlin, 'Note sur des vases à figures provenant de la fabrique romaine d'El Aouja', *Bull. arch. du Com. des trav. hist.* 1920, pp. 21 ff.; cf. our plate LX. It would be easy to follow the same movement of emancipation both in Britain and in Belgium and Germany, as has been done by F. Haverfield, F. Cumont, H. Dragendorff, and F. Koepp; see the books quoted in note 4.

[39] T. Frank, 'Some Economic Data from *CIL.*, vol. xv', *Class. Phil.* 13, 1918, pp. 155 ff., repeated both in his *Economic History* and in his *History of Rome*; H. Gummerus in Pauly–Wissowa, ix, cols. 1483 ff. Cf. note 36. A very important source of information for the organization of big industrial concerns in Gaul is the *graffiti* of La Graufesenque, Aveyron (accounts of the pottery delivered by the individual workmen), Abbé F. Hermet, *Les Graffites de la Graufesenque près Millau, Aveyron* (1923); A. Oxé, *Bonn. Jahrb.* 130, 1925, pp. 38 ff. (the best study of these documents); A. Nicolai, *Les Officines des pottiers gallo-romaines et les graffites de la Graufesenque* (1927). For similar accounts at Arezzo, Hurta, Montans, Blickweiler (cf. Loth, *C. R. Acad. Inscr.* 1924, pp. 67 ff.), and Rheinzabern, see A. Oxé, l.c., pp. 51 ff.; cf. the accounts at Montenach on the Moselle (ii. A.D.), *Rev. ét. anc.* 29, 1927, pp. 205 ff. The most interesting items from the economic point of view in the accounts at La Graufesenque are the large quantity of different types of vessels, and the large scale production on big factories. The names of the potters suggest that the account is to be dated to the middle of the 1st cent. A.D. (between 40 and 55) (Oxé). The history of the *terra sigillata* of Gaul and Germany is also (cf. Chap. III, note 13) the best-known example of the gradual transference of the centres of production towards the markets of consumption. While at the beginning of the 1st cent. A.D. the centre of production was in Southern France, towards the end of that century there is a movement northwards and eastwards: the first region to be affected is the basin of the Allier in Central Gaul, then, in the Flavian period, Eastern Gaul and Raetia, still later, about A.D. 90, Alsace, and finally, in the 2nd cent. A.D., Rheinzabern on the Rhine and Trèves. See H. Aubin, *Bonn. Jahrb.* 130, 1925, pp. 21 ff., and the map to p. 10; on the diffusion of the terracottas of Cologne see ibid. p. 25.

[40] On the villa of Chiragan in Gaul, see L. Joulin, 'Les établissements gallo-romains de la plaine de Martres Tolosanes', in *Mém. prés. à l'Acad.* 11, 1902, pp. 287, 367, pl. l, nos. 63–72; H. Gummerus in Pauly–Wissowa, ix, col. 1461; G. Lafaye in Daremberg–Saglio, ix, p. 888. The villa of Darenth in Britain: G. Payne, 'The Roman Villa at Darenth', *Arch. Cantiana*, 22, 1897, pp. 49 ff. The villa of Chedworth: G. E. Fox, 'The Roman Villa at Chedworth, Gloucestershire', *Arch. Journ.* 44, 1887, pp. 322 ff.; cf. his 'Notes on some probable Traces of Roman Fulling in Britain', *Archaeologia*, 59, 2, 1905, pp. 207 ff. I accept Fox's conclusions and cannot believe that the large rooms of the villa were a laundry or a fullery for the use of a big villa, see F. Haverfield, *Trans. Bristol and Gloucestershire Arch. Soc.* 41, 1918–19, p. 161. Cf. the

interesting villa, with some industrial buildings (peculiar T-shaped kilns) inside the walls of a large courtyard, in the Hambleden Valley, Bucks., see A. H. Cocks, *Archaeologia*, 71, 1921, pp. 142 ff. For other villas see the reports of Collingwood and Miss Taylor in *JRS* from 1921 onwards. It is very likely that the famous Batavian and Frisian cloths, which were widely distributed throughout the Roman Empire, were produced on the large estates of the Batavian and Frisian landowners, see G. Girke, *Mannus Bibliothek*, 24, 1922, p. 11. Assuming that the management of a fullery required no particular technical skill and that cheap labour was available, especially in winter time, it is easy to understand why the rich landowners preferred to manufacture the wool produced by their estates and that which they purchased from shepherds in the vicinity rather than sell the raw material to the merchants of the city. The same observation applies to pottery. Potteries were found in some Belgian villas, e.g. in the Ville des Bois de la Louvrière in Hennegau, *Bulletin des Musées royaux du Cinquantenaire*, 4, 1904–5, pp. 57 ff., and 6, 1906–7, pp. 45 ff.; Baron De Loë, *Notions d'archéologie préhistorique belgo-romaine et franque* (n.d.), p. 201, and in the villa at Hoste (Basse Wavre), of which the Musée du Cinquantenaire has a good map in relief. Some maps of villas, prepared by M. Mahien, are also exhibited in the Museum of Namur (Baron de Loe, op. cit., p. 192). For Germany see K. Schumacher, *Siedlungs- und Kulturgeschichte der Rheinlande*, ii (1923), p. 199. For Britain, Sir George MacDonald, 'Forschungen in römischen Britannien 1914–21', *Ber. d. röm.-germ. Kommission*, 1929 (cf. H. Summer, *Excavations in New Forest Pottery Sites* (1927)). The same phenomenon, it may be noted, can also be observed in Africa: one of the largest factories of African lamps may have been situated on one of the estates of the family of the Pulaieni. The same combination of a large estate and a pottery-factory was very common in Italy in the 1st and 2nd centuries A.D.: cf. note 35. On the villa of Anthée (a geographical, not a personal, name) and its metal industry see A. Bequet, *Ann. de la Soc. arch. de Namur*, 26, 1900–4, pp. 262 ff.; F. Cumont, *Comment la Belgique fut romanisée*, pp. 75, 80. It is likely that the production of enamelled bronzes in the villa of Anthée was due to the existence, in the neighbourhood, of the raw materials necessary for both bronze and glass. On mines on private estates, worked by slave-labour, and sometimes (as in the villa of Anthée) connected with a factory of metal-implements see *Dig.* 39. 4. 16. 11. In Belgium many factories of metal implements have been discovered, for instance, one near Narville, at a place called Bois-des-Dames, E. del Marmol, *Ann. de la Soc. arch. de Namur*, 25, 1881, pp. 220 ff., and that described by V. Tahon, *Les Origines de la métallurgie du pays d'Entre-Sambre-et-Meuse*, p. 31. Baron De Loë, op. cit., p. 192, rightly says that 'many Belgian villas were undoubtedly occupied by the first Belgic *maîtres de forges*'. The most brilliant period for the development of industrial concerns on large estates was, of course, the late Roman Empire. See the material collected by P. Allard in *Rev. d. quest. hist.* 81, 1907, pp. 12 ff.

41 F. Oswald and T. D. Pryce, *An Introduction to the Study of Terra Sigillata* (1920), cf. the bibliography in K. Schumacher, op. cit., p. 346, note 60. On technical progress in the ancient world see the article by Gina Lombroso Ferrero, quoted Chap. VII, note 107. Very interesting contributions to our knowledge in this field have been made by the remarkable recovery of the ships of Nemi. On the work done at Nemi and its results see U. Antonelli, 'La prima nave imperiale del lago di Nemi', *Pegaso*, 2, 1930, pp. 419 ff.; id. 'Ancora sulle navi di Nemi', ibid., pp. 744 ff.; G. C. Speziale, 'Della navi di Nemi e dell' archeologia navale', *Nuov. Antol.* 9, 1930, pp. 87 ff. The new machines found in the ships are thus listed by Speziale: (1) rotating planes on roller-spheres; (2) pump worked by two cylinders; (3) large valve for intercepting water; (4) anchor of a very modern type. See also W. Technau, *Arch. Anz.* 1931, p. 646 ff.

⁴² On the labour employed in industry (both slave and free) see H. Gummerus in Pauly–Wissowa, ix, col. 1496 ff. It is probable that the amount of free labour gradually increased, especially in the West, in the 2nd cent. A.D. as compared with the 1st. On the East, see notes 43–45. On the *collegia tenuiorum*, see the works quoted in note 22.

⁴³ Lists of these corporations may be found in F. Oehler, 'Genossenschaften in Kleinasien und Syrien', *Eranos Vindobonensis* (1893), pp. 276 ff.; V. Chapot, *La province romaine d'Asie*, pp. 168 f.; Poland, *Geschichte des griechischen Vereinswesens* (1909), pp. 116 ff.; Stöckle in Pauly–Wissowa, Suppl. iv, cols. 162 ff. (antiquated and inadequate; he ignores the articles of Keil and Buckler, and *IGRR*). The treatment of the corporations in existing works is wholly inadequate, being merely systematic and not historical. The professional corporations in Greece, Asia Minor, Syria, Mesopotamia, and Egypt cannot be treated historically as a unit even in the period of the Roman Empire. The main centres of woollen industry were Laodicea ad Lycum (W. M. Ramsay, *Cities and Bishoprics*, i, pp. 40 ff.), Hierapolis (C. Cichorius, *Die Altertümer von Hierapolis*, pp. 49 ff.), and Thyatira (the inscriptions of its professional associations have been fully collected and enriched by some new texts by W. H. Buckler, 'Monuments de Thyatire', *Rev. de phil.* 1913, pp. 289 ff.; the most important was that of the βαφεῖς). Cf. L. Robert, *Rev. de phil.* 1929, esp. p. 136, no. 2, an inscription dedicated to the emperor by οἱ [πρα]γματευόμενοι τὸ τρίπυλον (note the use of these buildings for trade, as at Palmyra, Gerasa, and elsewhere) καὶ τὰς στοὰς τάς τε καταγωγὰς καὶ τὰ ἐν αὐταῖς ἐργαστῶν οἰκητήρια, κ.τ.λ. On the ἐργασταί or ἐργαζόμενοι—owners or tenants of shops—see A. Wilhelm, *Glotta*, 14, 1925, pp. 73 ff., and L. Robert, *Rev. ét. gr.* 42, 1929, p. 33 (with a list of the most important evidence). For Lydia see Bürchner, Pauly–Wissowa, xiii, cols. 2134 ff. To the lists already quoted add those by J. Keil and A. von Premerstein, *Dritte Reise* (*Denkschr. Wien. Akad.* 57 (1), 1914), p. 14, no. 15: τῆς συμβιώσεως προσόδῳ ἡ ψιλαγνάφω[ν συνεργασία]: βαφεῖς at Pergamon, *Ath. Mitt.* 27, 1902, p. 102, no. 102; εἱματο-πῶλαι at Ephesus, see *Forsch. Eph.* iii, p. 146, no. 63, cf. Wood, *Hermes*, 8, 1873, p. 34 (συνεργασία τῶν λαναρίων). In general a good picture of the associations of a relatively large city is offered by the inscriptions of Ephesus. The latest excavations have added more to those already known: see *SEG* iv. 522. 539–41; cf. *Forsch. Eph.*, ii, pp. 79–82, iii, p. 63; J. Keil, *Oest. Jahresh.* 24, 1929, Beibl. pp. 31 ff. [= *SEG* iv. 539–40]. That trade in Asia Minor was connected with ancient institutions is demonstrated by οἱ ἐν τῷ τόπῳ πραγματευόμενοι Ἀνδροκλεῖδαι of the Ephesian inscription, *Forsch. Eph.* iii, p. 161, no. 79. *IGRR* iv. 1414—long known but correctly interpreted only by A. Wilhelm, *Wien. Anz.* 1924, p. 115—with its reference to the φορτηγοί of the ἐμπόριον of Smyrna is noteworthy. To these 'porters who are under the protection of Asclepius and are therefore called Ἀσκληπιασταί, a deliberation of the Council, towards the end of the 2nd cent. A.D., con-firmed by the proconsul Lollianus Avitus, has granted four βάθρα . . . . I believe the βάθρα were blocks of stone similar to that on which the inscription is carved, which they could sit on when waiting for customers, and on which they could place their loads in passing' (p. 116). The various corporations which worked in the harbour at Chios have a similar organization; the inscriptions have been studied by L. Robert, *Rev. ét. gr.* 42, 1929, pp. 35 ff. The labour employed by the shopowners was to a great extent servile. This is shown by the embassy sent by the province of Asia to the emperor to ask for the reduction of the *vectigal vicesimae* (probably *libertatis*), *IGRR* iv. 1236, found at Thyatira (cf. V. Chapot, *La Province*, &c., p. 335), and by a similar embassy from Rhodes under-taken by a sophist P. Aurelianus Nicostratus (A. Maiuri, *Ann. d. R. Sc. arch. di Atene*, 2, 1916, p. 146, no. 19), as well as by another inscription of Thyatira, *OGIS* 524 = *IGRR* iv. 1257: οἱ τοῦ σταταρίου ἐργασταὶ καὶ προξενηταὶ σωμάτων ἐτίμησαν καὶ ἀνέθηκαν Ἀλέξανδρον Ἀλεξάνδρου σωματέμπορον. The age-old organization of trades in Asia Minor, with special hereditary presidents of the various crafts, is attested by the

inscription of Thyatira, *IGRR* iv. 1265: ἐπιστησάμενον τοῦ ἔργου βαφέων ἀπὸ γένους. On the λινουργοί in Tarsus, Dio Chr. *Or.* 34. 21–23; H. von Arnim, op. cit., p. 491. The λινουργοί were freeborn people, residing in the city for generations, and yet they had not the city franchise and were despised by the rest of the population. The reputation of the textile-industry of Asia Minor is well known; it seems, however, not superfluous to remember the remarkable inscription of Pessinus, in which the emperor Trajan (and Nerva?) in four letters thanks a certain Claudius for having sent him woollen clothes (see A. Körte, *Ath. Mitt.* 22, 1897, pp. 44 ff., no. 25 [= ‡W. H. Buckler, *Rev. Plub.*, 1937, pp. 105 ff.], cf. G. Perrot, *Galatie et Bithynie*, pp. 214 ff.). The wool of the sheep and goats of Ankara is still famous.

⁴⁴ The best study of the organization of a trade in Egypt is M. Chwostow, *The Textile Industry in Greco-Roman Egypt* (Kazan, 1913) (in Russian); cf. T. Reil, *Beiträge zur Kenntnis des Gewerbes im hellenistischen Ägypten* (1913); W. Schubart, *Einführung*, pp. 428 f.; W. L. Westermann, 'Apprentice Contracts and the Apprentice System in Roman Egypt', *Class. Phil.* 9, 1914, pp. 295 ff.; Axel W. Persson, *Staat und Manufaktur im römischen Reiche* (1923). Important evidence on the regulations of the textile industry and the corporation of weavers in Egypt is provided by some papyri of Philadelphia (now in Berlin). *P.Teb.* 703, of the reign of Euergetes I, proves that the weavers worked chiefly, if not exclusively, for the state. Although there were corporations of weavers at that time, we have no proof that the state held them responsible for the work of their members: the state dealt directly with each member. The Berlin papyri prove that in the Roman period the obligations of the weavers towards the state remained the same, and that they were required to complete the tasks assigned to them by the state in return for payment, but that the corporation, and not the individual weaver, was now responsible both for the execution of the work and for the payment of the taxes (*BGU* 1591). In *BGU* 1614 (A.D. 84) we have a list of weavers divided into groups of three each: each group is bound to produce a certain number of ἱμάτια. There are thirty weavers, while in the almost contemporary list *P.Lond.* ii. 257, p. 19 (A.D. 94) we find forty names (and the list is not complete). In *P.Corn.* 23 (of the early 1st cent. A.D.) the number is eighty-eight and in *BGU* 1572 (A.D. 139) eighty-one—nearly the same. This shows that Philadelphia was an important centre of the textile industry, which had been introduced there by Apollonius, the dioiketes of Ptolemy Philadelphus. In *BGU* 1564 (A.D. 138) the corporation works actively for the army. It is interesting to see that part of the product went to the army in Cappadocia, although Asia Minor had famous wool manufactures; another part went to the hospital of the *ratio castrensis* (?) of the emperor; cf. Chap. XI, note 42. In *BGU* 1572 (A.D. 139) twelve members of the corporation receive from it the order to furnish a certain quantity of δημόσιος ἱματισμός (probably the regular yearly assignment): four of them were subjected to a liturgy and brought to Alexandria: eight were left at home, and a new (extraordinary?) assignment was made to their group. The weavers are desperate and beg to be exempted from other χρεῖαι. We do not know how much time the weavers had to work for themselves, but it is likely that they did not always work for the state. Cf. E. Schönbauer, *Zeitschr. d. Sav.-St.* 46, 1926, p. 199 (on Wilcken, *Chrest.* 251), and Wilcken, *Arch. f. Papyr.* 8, pp. 290 and 292, and for the professional Egyptian corporations, M. San Nicolò, *Aegyptisches Vereinswesen* (2 vols., 1913–15); id. 'Zur Vereinsgerichtbarkeit in Ägypten', 'Επιτύμβιον H. Swoboda dargebracht (1927), pp. 255 ff.; E. H. Brewster, 'A weaver of Oxyrhynchus', *TAPA* 48, 1928, pp. 132 ff. Information on the monopoly of papyrus is provided by three papyri; one published by Hunt and Smyly, *P.Teb.* 709 (159 B.C.), and two by A. Calderini, *Pap. Mil.* i, pp. 26 ff.; (cf. Wilcken, *Arch. f. Papyr.* 9, p. 240): *Pap. Mil.* 6 (A.D. 25), and *BGU* 1180 (14–13 B.C.), published ibid. p. 27,

note 2. From these documents we learn that not all the papyrus-yielding marshes were owned by the state; but it seems that the processing of papyrus for a large number of objects (not only paper), and the sale of these products, were leased by the state; they constituted, that is, a monopoly. Only the concessionaires, for example, had the right to produce papyrus-articles and to sell them in a given νομός. I am not sure if the ξύλα παπυρικά of the Berlin papyrus were capable of being further processed into some other object. Calderini in his commentary quotes all the literature on the monopoly of papyri: the fundamental works are still, Wilcken, *Grundzüge*, pp. 255 ff.; Zucker, *Philol.* 70, 1911, pp. 79 ff.; Reil, *Beiträge zur Kenntniss d. Gewerbe*, pp. 15 ff. Cf. Chap. IX, note 60 and Chap. X, note 39. On the ἀρωματική see A. Lucas, *JEA* 16, 1930, pp. 41 ff. 'Cosmetics, Perfumes and Incense in Ancient Egypt'. A branch of industry typical of Alexandria and Egypt has been investigated by A. Schmidt, *Drogen und Drogenhandel im Alterum* (1924). On the Phoenician glass industry, R. Dussaud in *Syria*, 1, 1920, pp. 230 ff. (concerning a new glass factory, that of Jason, to be added to those of Ennion and Artas). I may remind the reader that the marks of the Sidonian glass found in Italy were collected by Drexel, *CIL* xv. 6957–6963, cf. also *CIL* xiii. 3. 2. 10025.

⁴⁵ Dio Chr. *Or.* 34. 21–23 (Tarsus) and the Bithynian speeches *passim*; Polemon as peacemaker between the men of 'the upland' (οἱ ἄνω) and those of 'the shore' at Smyrna, Philostr. *Vitae Soph.* i. 25. 1; bread-riot at Aspendos quelled by Apollonius, Phil. *Vita Apollonii*, i. 15; Ael. Arist. Ῥοδίοις περὶ ὁμονοίας (*Or.* 24 Keil), 5 and *passim*, cf. *Or.* 22, Πανηγ. Κυζ. (*Or.* 27 Keil), 44. The social problem as such, the cleavage between the poor and the rich, occupies a prominent place in the dialogues of Lucian; he was fully aware of the importance of the problem, see C. Guignebert, *Tertullien* (1901), pp. 312 ff. See also the inscription of Pergamon quoted above, *Ath. Mitt.* 24, 1899, pp. 197 ff. = *IGRR* iv. 444; cf. ibid. iv. 914 (about A.D. 74), 9 f.: καταλῦσαν|τα συν[ω]μοσίαν μεγάλην τὰ μέγιστα λυποῦσαν τὴν πόλιν. Is συνωμοσία a strike? The evidence on strikes in Asia Minor has been collected, and the epigraphical texts thoroughly revised, by W. H. Buckler, 'Labour Disputes in the Province of Asia Minor', *Anatolian Studies presented to Sir William Ramsay* (1923), pp. 27 ff. Of the four texts which are dealt with by Buckler, the inscription of Ephesus (p. 30, cf. *Inschr. von Magnesia*, no. 114, Waltzing, *Corporations professionelles*, &c., iii, pp. 49 f.) deals with a strike of the bakers, i.e. of the owners of bakeries; the ἐργαστηριάρχαι of l. 16 means the shop-managers, who were mostly identical with the shopowners. The disturbance was of the same kind as those connected with the activity of the bankers at Pergamon and at Mylasa (see note 47), the bakers being, like the bankers, concessionaires of the city, or working under a special authorization of the city magistrates and the city council. The same relations existed between the shipowners of Arelate (*navicularii*) and the *praefectus annonae*, i.e. the state, as is shown by the inscription quoted by Buckler on p. 29, on which see Chap. VIII, note 39, and Chap. IX, note 20. A real strike of workmen seems to be recorded in the inscription of Pergamon quoted above, while the case of Miletus (*Sitzb. Berl. Akad.* 1904, p. 83; Buckler, op. cit., pp. 34 ff.) remains obscure to me and does not necessarily imply a strike. The inscription of Sardis (Buckler, ibid., pp. 36 ff.) of A.D. 429 belongs to a time when the corporations both of employers and of workmen had already become enslaved. Buckler has not paid due attention to the form of oath (ὅρκος θεῖος καὶ σεβάσμιος, see P. Meyer, *Jurist. Pap.*, no. 51) which the agreement assumes, a form which seems to have originated in Egypt and reflects the peculiar position of labour there. Cf. the ὅρκοι βασιλικοί, which were sworn by the Egyptian *coloni*, a peculiar form of contract between the king or emperor and the humble tenants (see my *Studien z. Gesch. röm. Kol.*, pp. 50 and 213; Wilcken, *Grundz.*, p. 275, and *Chrest.*, no. 327). The oath taken by the tenants represented a special agreement which entitled them

to receive seed-grain and contained many obligations which restricted their freedom. Similar restrictions are usual in the relations between all those ἐμπεπλεγμένοι ταῖς προσόδοις and the state. On the oath in the papyri, see L. Wenger, *Zeitschr. d. Sav.-St.* 36, 1902, p. 240; Wilcken, *Zeitschr. f. äg. Spr.* 48, 1911, p. 171; E. Seidl, *Der Eid im ptolemäischen Recht* (1929). As regards our special case, I may quote an interesting papyrus of A.D. 286 from Oxyrhynchus (*PSI* 162), where a workman engaged in the building trade takes an oath to work at the construction of a bath in Alexandria, l. 10: καὶ παραμεῖναι ἐν τῷ ἐκῖσαι κατασκευαζομένῳ βαλα|νέῳ ποιούμενος τὴν αὐτὴν οἰκο|δομικὴν τέχνην ἐπὶ τὸν ὡρισ|μένον χρόνον καὶ μὴ ἀπολειφθή|σεσθαι ἔστ' ἂν ἀπολυθῶ, cf. *P.Oxyr.* 1426 (A.D. 332). This formula can be traced back to the Ptolemaic period: see some documents of the Zeno-archive: *PSI* 1002, *P.Cair.Zen.* 59113.

⁴⁶ On the banks in Egypt, see F. Preisigke, *Girowesen im griechischen Ägypten* (1910); id. 'Zur Buchführung der Banken', *Arch. f. Papyr.* 4, p. 95; W. Schubart, *Einführung*, pp. 426 ff. and 433 f.; cf. L. Mitteis, 'Trapezitica', *Zeitschr. der Sav.-St.* 19, 1898, pp. 198 ff., and B. Grenfell, *P.Oxyr.* xiv, pp. 59 ff., who is certainly right in assuming that all the banks in Egypt even in the 1st and 2nd cent. A.D. were to a certain extent working on behalf of the state. On the banks in Rome and in Italy, M. Voigt, 'Über die Bankiers, die Buchführung und die Litteralobligation der Römer', *Abh. d. sächs. Ges.* 23, 1888, pp. 513 ff.; R. Beigel, *Rechnungswesen und Buchführung der Römer* (1904); R. Herzog, *Aus der Geschichte des Bankwesens im Altertum. Tesserae nummulariae* (1919); cf. M. Cary, *JRS* 13, 1923, pp. 110 ff. On ancient banks in general, see Ch. Lecrivain in Daremberg–Saglio, v, pp. 407 ff., E. Weiss in Pauly–Wissowa, xi, cols. 1694 ff. and B. Laum, ibid., Suppl. iv, cols. 68 ff.; cf. cols. 9 ff. (art. 'Agio'), and Kiessling, ibid. cols. 696 ff. (art. 'Giroverkehr'). The most interesting representation of a banker in his office has been published by myself in *Röm. Mitt.* 26, 1911, pp. 278 ff., fig. 2; cf. the bas-relief of Arlon in E. Espérandieu, *Bas-reliefs de la Gaule romaine*, v, p. 228, no. 4037. Banking operations were also transacted by the big merchants and landowners of the Rhine and of the Moselle, see F. Drexel, *Röm. Mitt.* 35, 1920, pp. 97, 113, and 115. See our plates xxxII and xxxVIII. An interesting feature of the economic life of the Empire is the survival of the large and influential temples as banking concerns. The importance of their banking activities alike in the period of the Oriental monarchies and in the age of the Greek city-states is well known. In the Hellenistic period this importance was at least maintained (witness the banking business transacted at Delos, Delphi, the temple of Artemis at Sardis, and the temple of Jerusalem, Macc. II. 3; IV. 4). On Hellenistic banks in general see E. Ziebarth, 'Hellenistische Banken', *Zeitschr. f. Num.* 34, 1923, pp. 36 ff.; *Beiträge zur Gesch. des Seeraubes* (1929), pp. 87 ff. Under the Roman Empire a decline set in. But the temple of Jerusalem continued to be the place where Jews, both rich and poor, kept their money on deposit, Jos. *Bell, Iud.* vi. 282; H. Drexler, *Klio*, 19, 1924, p. 284, note 1. On the banks of Ephesus, *Forsch. Eph.* iii, no. 65.

⁴⁷ On the Roman coinage in the time of the early Empire, see Regling in Fr. von Schroetter, *Wörterbuch der Münzkunde* (1930); H. Mattingly, *Roman Coins, from the Earliest Times to the Fall of the Western Empire* (1928); M. Bernhardt, *Handbuch zur Münzkunde der röm. Kaiserzeit* (1926); and the masterly work of H. Mattingly and E. A. Sydenham [and others], *Roman Imperial Coinage*, vols. i–iii; iv. 1, 2, 3; v. 1, 2; ix [in progress]. The rescript of Hadrian (?) to the traders of Pergamon who complained about the illegal exactions of the city bankers: *OGIS* 484, cf. Add., p. 552 = B. Keil, *Ath. Mitt.* 29, 1904, pp. 73 ff. = *IGRR* iv. 352. The address of the city of Mylasa to the emperor Septimius Severus, containing the decree of the council and the people of Mylasa regulating the activity of the city bankers, *OGIS* 515 (cf. Th. Reinach in *BCH* 20, 1896, p. 523, and in *L'Histoire par les monnaies* (1902), pp. 194 ff.).

Reinach's article gives the best survey of our knowledge about the activity of the banks in the Greek cities both in the Hellenistic and in the Roman period. Cf. on the banks as money-changers *P. Oxyr.* 1411 (A.D. 260), and Epict. *Diss.* iii. 3. 3: τὸ τοῦ Καίσαρος νόμισμα οὐκ ἔξεστιν ἀποδοκιμάσαι τῷ τραπεζίτῃ οὐδὲ τῷ λαχανοπώλῃ, ἀλλ' ἂν δείξῃς, ἐθέλει οὐ θέλει, προέσθαι αὐτὸν δεῖ τὸ ἀντ' αὐτοῦ πωλούμενον, cf. H. Willers, *Geschichte der römischen Kupferprägung*, pp. 190 ff.; H. Mattingly, op. cit., i, p. xxii.

⁴⁸ M. Rostovtzeff, *The Roman Leaden Tesserae* (St. Petersburg, 1903) (in Russian); id. *Tesserarum plumbearum Urbis Romae et suburbi Sylloge* (1903), and Suppl. i (1904); id. 'Römische Bleitesserae', *Klio*, Beiheft 3, 1905; G. Lafaye in Daremberg–Saglio, v, pp. 132 ff. On the Egyptian leaden tokens, J. G. Milne, *Num. Chr.* 1908, pp. 287 ff., cf. id. in *JEA* 1, 1914, pp. 93 ff., and in *Ancient Egypt* 2, 1915, pp. 107 ff. The leaden tesserae in Egypt served the same purpose as in Rome and were issued both by the different districts of Egypt and by the temples and large estates; some were certainly used by private business men. On the scarcity of small currency in the early Roman Empire, see H. Mattingly, *Coins of the R.E.* i, p. cl, cf. p. clxiii.

⁴⁹ *Scr. Hist. Aug.*, Hadr. 7. 5 ff.: 'ad colligendam autem gratiam nihil praetermittens, infinitam pecuniam quae fisco debebatur privatis debitoribus in urbe atque Italia, in provinciis vero ex reliquiis ingentes summas remisit, syngraphis in foro divi Traiani quo magis securitas omnibus roboraretur incensis'; cf. Cass. Dio, 69. 8. The remark on the arrears of the provincials and on the *syngraphae* shows that the debts to the *fiscus* which Hadrian had in view were private debts, and these imply credit operations on its part: cf. *Scr. Hist. Aug.*, Marcus Aur. 23. 3, a very brief remark which implies gifts rather than loans. On the loan of Tiberius, Tac. *Ann.* vi. 17: 'eversio rei familiaris dignitatem ac famam praeceps dabat, donec tulit opem Caesar disposito per mensas milies sestertio factaque mutuandi copia sine usuris per triennium, si debitor populo in duplum praediis cavisset'; cf. the notes of H. Furneaux and K. Nipperdey, and Frank, *Economic History*², p. 409, and Cass. Dio, 58. 21. 5. The *mensae* are certainly *mensae fiscales*, i.e. offices of the *fiscus* in various parts of the city, which received payments due to the *fiscus*. They strictly corresponded, therefore, to the Egyptian τράπεζαι of the Ptolemaic period, which also were at once branches of the Treasury and banks, and which partly survived in Roman times, see O. Hirschfeld, *Die kais. Verwaltungsb.*², pp. 58 ff., 72 f., and 126, and also my article 'Fiscus' in Ruggiero, *Diz. epigr.*, where the evidence on the provincial *mensae* is collected. On the money which was given by Augustus to found the *aerarium militare*, see *Mon. Ancyr.* 3, pp. 35–39, and the other references to this gift collected by Th. Mommsen, ad loc.; cf. O. Hirschfeld, op. cit., p. 2. We shall speak of the *alimenta* in the VIIIth chapter. It is worthy of note that Cassius Dio in the well-known speech of Maecenas (52. 14 ff.) advocates the creation of a state bank which would lend money at a moderate rate of interest to everybody, especially to landowners. The capital of the bank should consist of the money which would be realized by the sale of all the properties of the state.

⁵⁰ L. Mitteis, 'Römisches Privatrecht bis auf die Zeit Diokletians. I. Grundbegriffe und Lehre von den juristischen Personen', in Binding, *Handbuch d. deutschen Rechtswiss.* I. 6, i (1908). On L. Mitteis, see L. Wenger, *Ludwig Mitteis und sein Werk* (Vienna, 1923).

⁵¹ L. Mitteis, *Reichsrecht und Volksrecht in den östlichen Provinzen des römischen Kaiserreichs* (1891). In a lecture delivered in Vienna in 1917 Mitteis strongly emphasized that he never thought of replacing the study of Roman law by the study of an imaginary Greco-Roman law taken as the law of the ancient world in general: his studies were concerned with the historical development of Roman law. The influence of the various forms of Hellenistic law and of the provincial juridical traditions on Roman law of the

Imperial age in general—an influence which had appeared so strong to Mitteis at the beginning of his career—was consequently reduced, in this his last work, almost to insignificance. I must state that such a radical statement seems to me a pessimistic exaggeration. See L. Mitteis, 'Ant. Rechtsgesch. u. röm. Rechtsstudium', *Mitt. des Vereins d. Freunde d. hum. Gymn.* (Wien) 18, 1918, pp. 56 ff.; see also the Italian translation of this work with a long and learned commentary by S. Riccobono, *Annali del sem. giuridico di Palermo*, 12, 1928, pp. 477 ff.; Riccobono fully shares the scepticism of Mitteis's last years. The problem attacked by Mitteis and Riccobono is discussed by L. Wenger, *Der heutige Stand der Rechtswissenschaft. Erreichtes und Erstrebtes* (1927), cf. his articles 'Juristische Literaturübersicht', *Arch. f. Papyr.* 9 to 10 [; 12–15]. See also Taubenschlag, *Mélanges de droit romain dédiés à G. Cornil* (1926), pp. 499 ff., and his 'Gesch. der Rezeption der röm. Privatrechtes in Ägypten', *Studi in hon. P. Bonfante*, i (1929), pp. 369 ff., where the author demonstrates the coexistence and reciprocal influence of Roman and peregrine law in Egypt both in the period before and after Caracalla, and in the post-Justinian period. In Egypt (as also in Syria) Roman law never wholly replaced Hellenistic law. See also the valuable study by F. de Zulueta, 'L'Histoire du droit dans l'Antiquité', *Mélanges Fournier* (1929), pp. 787 ff. (with full bibliography); A. I. Boyé, 'Le Doit romain et les papyrus d'Égypte', *L'Égypte contemporaine*, 20, 1929, pp. 529 ff.; E. Lévy, 'Westen und Osten in der nachkl. Entwicklung des röm. Rechts', *Zeitschr. d. Sav.-St.* 49, 1929, pp. 230 ff. A remarkable instance of survival of a Celtic law in Asia Minor (the *peculium* of a married woman) has been noticed by W. M. Calder, *Class. Rev.* 37, 1923, pp. 8 ff. The document found by F. Cumont at Dura (the law on succession of the Seleucid period) is of fundamental importance for our understanding of the Syriac version of Hellenistic law, which is in part collected in the 'Syriac Law-Book': see B. Haussoullier, *Rev. histor. du droit franç. et étranger*, 1923, pp. 515 ff.; F. Cumont, *Fouilles de Doura Europos* (1926), pp. 309 ff., and the other Dura documents ibid., pp. 281 ff.; compare also the three parchments (two in Greek, one in Pehlvi) from Avroman, published by E. H. Minns, *JHS* 35, 1915, pp. 22 ff. On the interesting document of the late Parthian period (A.D. 121) found at Dura in 1928 see C. B. Welles and M. Rostovtzeff, 'A Parchment Contract of Loan from Dura-Europos on the Euphrates', *Yale Class. Stud.* 2, 1931, pp. 3 ff., cf. *C.R. Acad. Inscr.* 1930, pp. 158 ff., and *Excavs. at Dura-Europos*, Prelim. Rep. ii (1931), pp. 201 ff. On all the Syrian parchments see P. Koschaker, *Über einige griechischen Rechtsurkunden aus den östlichen Randgebiet des Hellenismus, Ath. d. sächs Ges.* 42 (1), 1931. On Babylonian law and its survival in Hellenistic and Parthian times see M. San Nicolò, *Zeitschr. d. Sav.-St.* 48, 1928, pp. 45 ff.; id. *Beiträge zur Rechtsgeschichte im Bereiche der keilschriftlichen Rechtsquellen* (1931). On the 'Syriac Law-Book' see A. Nallino, 'Sul Libro Siro-romano e sul presento diritto siriaco', *Studi Bonfante*, i, pp. 201 ff.

52 P. Collinet, 'The General Problems Praised by the Codification of Justinian', *Tijdschrift voor Geschiedenis*, 37, 1922; id. *Histoire de l'école de droit de Beyrouth* (1925), and for the controversy on the influence of the Classical Roman and Byzantine juridical schools, see L. Wenger, *Der heutige Stand*, &c., pp. 25 ff.

53 The best general surveys may be found in L. Wenger, 'Über Papyri und Gesetzrecht', *Sitzb. Bayr. Akad.* 1914, 5, and in W. Schubart, *Einführung*, pp. 277 ff. Cf. P. M. Meyer, *Juristische Papyri* (1920); A. B. Schwarz, 'Die öffentliche und private Urkunde im römischen Ägypten', *Abh. d. sächs. Ges.* 31, no. 3, 1920, and Fr. von Woess, *Untersuchungen über das Urkundenwesen und den Publizitätsschutz im römischen Aegypten* (1924). Cf. L. Wenger, 'Die rechthistorische Papyrusforschung, Ergebnisse und Aufgaben', *Arch. f. Kulturgesch*, 19, 1928, pp. 10 ff., and 'Juristische Literaturübersicht', *Arch. f. Papyr.* 9, pp. 104 ff., 254 ff.; 10, pp. 98 ff. [; 12–15]; further the valuable accounts of new material and publications by P. Meyer, 'Juristischer Papyrusbericht', *Zeitschr. d.*

Sav.-St. On the βιβλιοθήκη ἐγκτήσεων see P. Meyer, ibid. 46, 1926, pp. 336 ff.; E. Schönbauer, *Beiträge zur Gesch. des Liegenschaftsrechts im Altertum* (1924), p. 64; Fr. von Woess, op. cit., pp. 229 ff. One of the most instructive documents, which shows the gradual adaptation to each other of the local Greco-Egyptian and the Roman civil law, is the 'Gnomon idiou logou' (Γνώμων 'Ιδίου Λόγου), a 'Code of Regulations which Augustus issued for one of the financial departments which he found already existing, the ἴδιος λόγος or Department of Special Revenues derived from fines, escheats and confiscations' (H. Stuart Jones, *The Legacy of Rome*, p. 113). On this document, which was first published by E. Seckel and W. Schubart, 'Der Gnomon des Idios Logos', *BGU* v. 1 (no. 1210)=P. Meyer, *Jurist. Pap.* 93 [=*Sel. Pap.* 206], cf. Plaumann, 'Der Idios Logos', *Abh. Berl. Akad.* 1918 (17), there exists a large literature: W. Schubart, 'Rom und die Ägypter nach dem Gnomon des Idios Logos', *Zeitschr. f. äg. Spr.* 56, 1920, pp. 80 ff.; Th. Reinach, 'Un Code fiscal de l'Égypte romaine', *Nouv. Rev. hist. du droit fr. et étr.* 1921 (cf. J. Carcopino, *Rev. ét. anc.* 24, 1922, pp. 101 ff. and 211 ff.); H. Stuart Jones, *Fresh Light on Roman Bureaucracy* (Oxford, 1920); V. Arangio-Ruiz, 'Un "liber mandatorum" da Augusto ad Antonino', *Atene e Roma*, 3, 1922, pp. 216 ff.; O. Lenel and J. Partsch in *Sitzb. Heid. Akad.* 1920, no. 1. The character of the *Gnomon* has been exactly described by Graf. W. Uxkull-Gyllenband, 'Zum Gnomon des Idioslogos', *Arch. f. Papyr.* 9, pp. 183 ff., 'it is an extract from the real γνώμων τοῦ ἰδιολόγου, which contains in abridged form those paragraphs which, because of new regulations or of false applications and so on, no longer agreed with the original text, and had thus become uncertain and had to be redefined' (op. cit., p. 190): cf. Ed. Tib. Iul. Alex. *OGIS* 669, § 9 (end): καὶ καθόλου δὲ ἐ[π]ικελεύσομαι τὸν γνώμονα ἰδίου λόγου [ἀεὶ] τα καινοποιηθέντα παρὰ τὰς τῶν Σεβαστῶν χάριτας ἐπανορθῶσαι (quoted by Uxkull-Gyllenband).

54 A short general survey of Roman law, both the *ius civile* and the *ius gentium*, may be found in F. de Zulueta, 'The Science of Law', *The Legacy of Rome*, pp. 173 ff.; cf. B. Kübler, *Gesch. d. röm. Rechts* (1925) and P. De Francisci, *Storia del Diritto Romano* (1926). On commercial legislation, L. Goldschmidt, *Universalgeschichte des Handelsrechts*, i. 1 (1891, 3rd ed.), pp. 58 ff.; P. Rehme, 'Geschichte des Handelsrechts', in Ehrenberg, *Handbuch des Handelsrechts*, i (1913), pp. 4–21; P. Huvelin, *L'Histoire du droit commercial* (1904); id. *Études d'histoire du droit commercial romain* (*Histoire Externe. Droit Maritime*) (1929). Unfortunately there is no adequate recent treatment by a specialist of the important subject of the development of ancient commercial law. Valuable as they are, the short surveys of Goldschmidt, Rehme, and Huvelin are antiquated and do not take account of the vast amount of information which has been furnished by inscriptions and papyri as well as by some archaeological material (viz. the inscriptions on the so-called 'instrumentum domesticum', which should be studied in connexion with the 'instrumentum' itself). But it will be useful to quote here the excellent summary given in 1891 by Goldschmidt, which shows how thoroughly adequate the Roman civil law was to the requirements of the most complicated business life. 'The ordinary civil law was universal and elastic, it had been worked out to the last detail with the utmost technical skill, and it was based on the *highest ethical principles*. In the administration of justice the general rule was to decide according to *bona fides*, with the result that account could freely be taken of changes in commercial practice and of the intention of the parties so far as discoverable. On the one hand, practice was scientific; and, on the other, legal theory was *steadily directed to practical application*, and derived its materials from a careful and penetrating observation of actual life. Hence, though no system of "political economy" had as yet been propounded, there was a clearer recognition than is often shown today of the *essential functions* of value, money, credit, and transactions based on credit, barter, loans of specific things and loans of capital, partnership, and

so forth. The cities, at least outside Italy, still enjoyed a wide autonomy, and commercial practice as well as local and provincial customary law were unreservedly recognized. The jury-system of the civil procedure was excellent, the division between *ius* and *iudicium* happy; methods of proof were unfettered by rules, and the execution of judgements was thoroughly effective. Such being the ordinary civil law, there was neither room nor need for a special commercial code, nor for a special commercial court. Cases where state interests demanded special consideration were, however, governed by a well-developed and appropriate *system of administrative law*.' On the regulation of sea commerce, see R. D. Benedict, *What do we know of the Rhodian Maritime Law?* (Discourse delivered before the Law Department of the Brooklyn Institute) (1897); R. Dareste, 'La Lex Rhodia', *Nouv. Rev. hist. du droit fr. et étr.* 29, 1903, pp. 429 ff., and id. *Rev. de Philol.* 19, 1903, pp. 1 ff.; H. Kreller, 'Lex Rhodia, Untersuchungen zur Quellengesch. des röm. Seerechts,' *Zeitschr. f. d. ges. Handelsrecht und Konkursrecht*, 85, 1921, pp. 257 ff. (in this excellent work Dareste's articles are not mentioned). Kreller established that Roman legislation only developed traditional rules of commercial maritime law which were known in the Hellenistic age under the name of the 'Rhodian Sea-Law', and which were accepted by all who were involved in maritime commerce. Cf. *CAH* viii, p. 636 (cf. pp. 651 ff.); cf. L. Mitteis, *Röm. Privatrecht*, i, p. 18; L. Goldschmidt, *Zeitschr. f. d. ges. Handelsrecht*, 35, pp. 37 ff.

55 R. H. Lacey, *The Equestrian Officials of Trajan and Hadrian* (1917). The policy of Hadrian in regard to the equestrian offices is well traced in this book from the political point of view. It is a pity that, in his useful prosopography of knights of the time of Trajan and Hadrian, Lacey says nothing of the families to which the officers belonged and of the history of these families.

56 See the facts collected by M. Gelzer, 'Das Römertum als Kulturmacht', *Hist. Zeitschr.* 126, 1921, p. 204; cf. Hasebroek, *Untersuchungen zur Geschichte des Kaisers Septimius Severus* (1921), p. 116. I cannot accept the theory of von Domaszewski and Hasebroek that the statement in the biography of Severus is a forgery. I see no reason whatever for such a forgery, and the statement contains many facts which could not have been invented. The fact that Severus himself spoke 'African Latin' does not imply that the women of his family used Latin in their domestic life. The father of Ausonius spoke Greek only (Aus. *Epic. in patr.* 9, ed. Peiper); the stepson of Apuleius spoke Punic only (Apul. *Apol.* 95 ad fin.). Cf. E. Hohl in Bursian's *Jahresber.* 200, 1924, p. 205. An investigation of the families of the city of Timgad, a colony of Trajan, carried out by my pupil R. Johannesen, showed that most of those whose history we are able to trace lasted for no more than two generations, just like the families of the emperors of the 2nd cent.

57 On the *collegia tenuiorum* see the works quoted in note 22; cf. F. F. Abbott, *The Common People of Ancient Rome* (1911). On the conditions of life among the lower classes of the population of Rome, see L. Homo, *Problèmes sociaux de jadis et d'à présent* (1922), pp. 37 ff.

VI. *The Roman Empire under the Flavians and the Antonines. The City and the Country in Italy and in the European Provinces of Rome*

1 Persistence of the native languages in Asia Minor: K. Holl, 'Das Fortleben der Volkssprachen in Kleinasien in nachchristlicher Zeit', *Hermes*, 43, 1908, pp. 240 ff.; H. Dessau, *Gesch. d. röm. Kais.* ii. 2, p. 576, note 3; W. M. Ramsay, *Oest. Jahresh.* 8, 1905, pp. 79 ff.; W. M. Calder, *JHS* 31, 1911, pp. 161 ff. (Phrygia); id. *MAMA* i, p. xii; J. G. C. Anderson, *JHS* 19, 1899, pp. 314 ff.; W. M. Ramsay, *Hist. Comm. to*

Galatians (1900), pp. 147 ff., F. Staehelin, *Gesch. kleinas. Galater*[2] (1907), p. 104 (Galatia); F. Cumont, *Anatolian Studies presented to Ramsay*, p. 115, note 1 (Armenia); in Celtic lands: F. Haverfield, *Romanization of Roman Britain*[4], p. 18; F. Cumont, *Comment la Belgique fut romanisée*, p. 95; C. Jullian, *Histoire de la Gaule*, iii, p. 521. Important data are to be found in the accounts of the potters of La Graufesenque (cf. above, p. 617, note 39). From the best of the studies on these Celto-Latin inscriptions (A. Oxé, *Bonn. Jahrb.* 130, 1925, p. 64) it is clear that the degree of Romanization of the potters was very slight, and their knowledge of Latin very superficial; in the Illyrian regions: C. Patsch, 'Historische Wanderungen im Karst und an der Adria. I. Herzegowina einst und jetzt', *Osten und Orient*, Zw. R. i, 1922, Wien, p. 95 (Hieronymus, *Comment. vii in Isaiam*, 19, 292); in Africa: W. I. Snellmann, *De interpretibus Romanorum*, &c. (1914), i, pp. 47 ff. (on Apuleius, Septimius Severus, and Augustinus), cf. p. 50; ii, pp. 108, 110, 112, 113, 119, 120, 129, 140, cf. A. Schulten, *Das römische Afrika* (1899), pp. 12, 25 ff., 98; S. Gsell, *Khamissa* (1914), pp. 31 ff.; and Chap. V, note 56. The persistence of Syrian and Arabic in the Near East and of the native language in Egypt is proved by the well-known Syrian, Arabian, and Coptic renaissance as soon as the Roman domination was nearing its end; on the Coptic renaissance see L. Wenger, 'Über Papyri und Gesetzesrecht', *Sitzb. Munch. Akad.* 1914 (5), p. 17.

[2] J. Toutain, *Les Cultes païens dans l'empire romain*, vol. iii.

[3] On the measures taken by the government to help the population and restore the buried cities, see Cass. Dio, 66. 24. In fact, none of the buried cities was rebuilt.

[4] F. G. de Pachtère, *La Table hypothécaire de Veleia* (1920), cf. O. Kromayer, *Neue Jahrb. kl. Alt.* 33, 1914, pp. 145 ff., and against his calculations M. Besnier, *Rev. ét. anc.* 24, 1922, pp. 118 ff.; J. Carcopino, 'La Table de Veleia', ibid. 23, 1921, pp. 287 ff.

[5] W. Heitland, *Agricola*, the chapters on Juvenal and Pliny the Younger.

[6] See my *Studien z. Gesch. röm. Kol.* pp. 326 ff.; Dessau, *Gesch. d. röm. Kaiserzeit*, ii. 2, p. 418 is perhaps right in maintaining that Pliny, in his well-known passage on *latifundia*, is referring essentially not to his own age, but to the past. However, this interpretation involves serious difficulties.

[7] On the colonies of Nero see Chap. V, note 24; cf. T. Frank, *Economic History*[2], p. 438. On the colonies of Vespasian see T. Frank, ibid.; compare the colony of marines settled at Paestum and mentioned in some military diplomas (*CIL* iii, p. 1959, dipl. ix [= *CIL* xvi. 15]; *L'An. ép.* 1912, 10 [= *CIL* xvi. 12]; 1921, 48 [= *CIL* xvi. 16]; J. Welkow, *Bull. de l'hist. arch. bulgare*, 2, 1923–24, pp. 95 ff. = *L'An. ép.* 1925, 68 [= *CIL* xvi. 13], ll. 3 ff.

[8] Cass. Dio, 68. 2. 1; Plin. *Ep.* vii. 31. 4; Dessau, *ILS* 1019; *Dig.* 47. 21. 3. 1; cf. O. Seeck, *Gesch. d. Unterg. d. ant. Welt*, i, pp. 324 ff. (345 ff., 2nd ed.).

[9] See note 4; cf. H. Schiller, *Gesch. d. röm. Kaiserzeit*, p. 566, note 4.

[10] See my article 'Frumentum' in Pauly–Wissowa, vii, col. 137.

[11] Le Bas–Waddington 1213 = Petersen and Luschan, *Reisen*, nos. 242 and 242a = B. Laum, *Stiftungen*, ii, no. 162, ll. 9 ff. = *IGRR* iv. 915; καὶ ἐ[ξ] αὐτῆς ἀ[γ]οραζέτω κτήσεις σειτο[φ]όρους, εἰς ἄλλο δὲ μ[η]|δὲν [ἐ]ξ[έστ]ω καταχρῆσθαι τῇ προσόδ[ῳ] | [τα]ύτ[η], ὡς [πε]ρὶ τούτου τῷ αὐτοκράτ[ο]|ρι καὶ τῇ συγκλήτῳ [λ]ό[γ]ου ἀπο[δ]οθ[η]σομέ[νου], cf. *IGRR* iv. 914. On Cibyra, Ruge in Pauly–Wissowa, xi, cols. 374 ff. The measure is easily understood if we take into consideration how much the cities, and not only the inland cities, of the Roman Empire depended on local grain production, especially in times of frequent famine; see Chap. V, note 9, and cf. Chap. VIII, note 21.

[12] All the evidence on the ordinance of Domitian and an ingenious explanation of the ordinance have been given by S. Reinach, 'La Mévente des vins sous le Haut Empire romain', *Rev. arch.* 1901 (2), pp. 350 ff.; cf. M. Besnier, ibid. 1919 (2), p. 34. On the *lex Manciana* and the *lex Hadriana*, see my *Studien z. Gesch. röm. Kol.* p. 321, note 1, and p. 323; T. Frank, *AJP* 47, 1926, pp. 55 ff., 153 ff.; id. *Economic History*[2], p. 447. Though the law of Hadrian speaks of vineyards being planted on waste land, it does not grant any privileges to the planters of vines, but such privileges are given to the planters of both olive and fruit trees. The permission of Probus to cultivate vines in the provinces (*Scr. Hist. Aug.* Prob. 18; Eutrop. ix. 17; Aurel. Vict. *de Caes.* 37. 2) cannot be a mere invention. It must be emphasized, however, that vines were planted both in Dalmatia and in the Danube provinces long before the time of Probus; see, e.g. *CIL* iii. 6423 (Lissa) and 14493 (Celei in Dacia). We have abundant evidence for the large-scale production of wine in Italy, which need not be repeated here. It is interesting to see that even in south Italy, where agriculture was supposed to have been abandoned in the Imperial age, wine was still produced in bulk. In the ruins of a large villa discovered on the site of the ancient Sybaris by Commendatore Galli, an ingenious wine-pipe was found, which corresponds to the description given by Athenaeus, 519 D— see W. Technau, *Arch. Anz.* 1930, pp. 411 ff.

[13] Bruns-Gradenwitz, *Fontes*[7], pp. 300 ff., no. 115 [= Riccobono, *FIRA*[2] 102], 3, ll. 6 ff.; no. 116 [= Riccobono, *FIRA*[2] 101], 3, ll. 9 ff. Africa as a producer of olive-oil, R. Cagnat, 'L'Annone d'Afrique', *Mém. d. l'Ac. de Inscr.* 40, 1916, pp. 258 ff. Cf. the remarkable receipts and accounts on ostraca (A.D. 373) discovered at Carthage and concerning the delivery and transport of oil for the *annona*: R. Cagnat and A. Merlin, *Journ. Sav.* 1911, pp. 514 ff. [=*L'An. ép.* 1912, 61–70].

[14] W. Heitland, *Agricola*, the chapters on Martial and Pliny.

[15] W. Heitland, *Agricola*, p. 325 and *passim*.

[16] What has been said in the text as to the prevalence of the peasant-plot in the system of husbandry of the 2nd cent. is based on well-known evidence which has often been collected, most recently by W. Heitland, *Agricola*, and E. Kornemann in Pauly–Wissowa, Suppl. iv, cols. 103 ff. (art. 'Bauernstand'), and cols. 240 ff. (art. 'Domänen'); cf. the bibliography in the article 'Latifundia' by Ch. Lecrivain, in Daremberg–Saglio, iii, p. 971, and the inscription of Ostia published by G. Calza in *Not. d. Scavi*, 1921, p. 236 [= *L'An. ép.* 1922, 93]: the 'cultores Larum et imaginum dominorum nostrorum invictissimorum Augustorum praediorum Rusticelianorum' were probably the tenants of this imperial estate. Cf. L. Wickert, *Sitzb. Preuss. Akad.* 1928, pp. 43 ff., and *CIL* xiv. 4570 (commentary). On the *coloni* and the habit of letting land to them together with some slaves, see 'Tabula alimentaria Veleias' in Dessau, *ILS* 6675, xliii: 'deductis reliquis colonorum et usuris pecuniae et pretis mancipiorum, quae in inemptione eis cesserunt'; cf. B. Kübler, *Festschrift für Johannes Vahlen* (1900), pp. 564 ff. It is striking that the title *colonus* is added in funeral inscriptions to the names of slaves, not of freemen, which shows that a slave *colonus* was not a common feature in the life of Italy in the 2nd and 3rd cent., see *CIL* vi. 9276 ('Iaso colonus fundo Mariano') = Dessau, *ILS* 7453 and x. 7957 ('Proculus colonus'); cf. ix. 3674, 3675 = Dessau, *ILS* 7455, 7455*a*: *colonus f(undi) Tironiani quem coluit ann(os) n.L.*; cf. O. Seeck in Pauly–Wissowa, iv, col. 487; P. Sticotti, *Atti e Mem. della Soc. Istriana di Arch. e Storia Patria*, 22, 1905, p. 11. Mentions of slave-managers of an estate are more frequent; *CIL* x. 6592 = Dessau, *ILS* 7451: *actor et agricola optimus*; *CIL* x. 5081; ix. 3028 = Dessau, *ILS* 7367 ('Hippocrati Plauti vilic(o) familia rust(ica) quibus imperavit modeste'); ix. 3651 ('vilicus et familia de fundo Favilleniano'); cf. P. Sticotti, op. cit., p. 11, note 3. A full collection and investigation of all the inscriptions bearing on the agricultural life of Italy in imperial times is a pressing need.

[17] See the *Edictum Claudii de Anaunis*, *CIL* v. 5050 = Dessau, *ILS* 206 = Bruns-Gradenwitz, *Fontes*[7], p. 253, no. 79 [= Riccobono, *FIRA*[2] 71], and the inscription of Tergeste, *CIL* v. 532 = Dessau, *ILS* 6680. Cf. J. S. Reid, *The Municipalities*, pp. 166 ff., and on the date, A. Puschi and P. Sticotti, *Wiener Stud.* 1902, pp. 252 ff.; O. Cuntz, *Oest. Jahresh.* 18, 1915, pp. 98 ff.; cf. also Chap. III, note 5, and E. Pais, *Dalle guerre puniche a Cesare Augusto*, ii (1918).

[18] A. Schulten, 'Die Landgemeinden im römischen Reiche', *Philol.* 53, 1894, p. 645; A. Grenier in Daremberg–Saglio, v, pp. 854 ff. In Veii, e.g., the *municipes extramurani* are opposed to those *intramurani*, *CIL* xi. 3797 and 3798; cf. E. de Ruggiero, *Diz. epigr.* ii, p. 2195. A common feature of the terminology of our juridical sources is the contrast between the *intramurani* and the *pagani*, see *Dig.* 50. 1. 35; 50. 1. 27; 10. 40. 3, where *pagani* are small landowners and tenants, cf. *Dig.* 11. 4. 3: 'praedia Caesaris, senatorum, paganorum'; Schulten, loc. cit.

[19] On Sicily see the bibliography quoted in Chap. I, note 27; cf. T. Frank, '*Dominium in solo provinciali* and *Ager publicus*', *JRS* 27, 1927, pp. 141 ff.; Libertini, *Le Isole Eolie nell' antichità greca e romana* (1921).

[20] We have two descriptions of Sicily in the imperial period, that of Strabo, 265 C ff., and that of Pliny, *NH* iii. 8. 88–91. I see no contradiction between the first and the second part of the description of Strabo. In the first he points out (probably following Posidonius) the decay of the Greek cities, a description which held good even for the time of Augustus, as very few cities regained prosperity; in the second he speaks of Sicily in general and emphasizes its role as the granary of Rome. The description of Pliny contrasts with the evidence of Cicero in many points, and shows how thorough was the reorganization of Sicily by Augustus and how short-lived the grants of Caesar and Antony, if they were real grants and not only intentions. Pliny committed many mistakes in characterizing the status of the various cities of Sicily, but his description of Sicily as a whole holds good. To one *oppidum civium Romanorum* (Messana), to five colonies (Tauromenium, Catina, Syracusae, Thermae, and Tyndaris), to three cities of Latin right (Centuripae, Neetum, Segesta) are opposed forty-six *civitates stipendiariae* and thirteen *oppida*, some of which had no city organization at all; cf. A. Holm, *Gesch. Siciliens*, iii, pp. 228 ff., 469 ff.; J. Beloch, *Die Bevölkerung der griechisch-römischen Welt*, pp. 325 ff.; O. Cuntz, *Klio*, 6, 1906, pp. 466 ff.; E. S. Jenison, *The History of the Province Sicily* (1919), pp. 101 ff.

[21] See my *Gesch. d. Staatspacht*, p. 425, and my article in Pauly–Wissowa, vii, col. 153. The fact is attested by the inscriptions of C. Vibius Salutaris of Ephesus, *CIL* iii. 14195. 4–13 = R. Heberdey, *Forsch. Eph.* ii, no. 28 (cf. no. 60 and no. 27). On the importance of Sicilian corn see Chap. I, note 27. Miss M. Blake refers the mosaic of Ostia, on technical grounds, to about the middle of the 1st cent. A.D., that is, the period immediately following the construction of the harbour by Claudius.

[22] On the large estates in Sicily, see *CIL* x. 7041 (Catina): 'd. m. s. Gallicano fidelissimo qui fuit vilicus Afinianis'; cf. the note of Mommsen, who quotes such place-names in Sicily as Calloniana, Calvisiana, Capitoniana, Comitiana, Corconiana, Philosophiana, Pitiniana, and *IG* xiv. 283, 284 = *IGRR* i. 502 (Drepanum)—two procurators, one freedman, and one slave of C. Asinius Nicomachus Flavianus (3rd cent.). A village and an estate in the territory of Catina are attested by a bilingual Greco-Latin inscription, *Not. d. Scavi*, 1922, pp. 494 ff.; R. Sabbadini, *Boll. di fil. cl.* 30, pp. 19–23 [= *L'An. ép.* 1923, 75]. The imperial and public estates were managed by imperial slaves, who are frequently mentioned in the inscriptions of Sicily: *CIL* x. 6977, 7189; [*IG* xiv. 272 =] *IGRR* i. 498 (near Selinus); cf. *CIL* x. 2489 (Lipara). On the revolt in Sicily under Gallienus, see *Scr. Hist. Aug.*, Gall. duo, 4. 9: 'denique quasi

coniuratione totius mundi concussis orbis partibus etiam in Sicilia quasi quoddam servile bellum extitit latronibus evagantibus qui vix oppressi sunt.' Note that the text does not speak of a slave war: it says 'a war which might be compared with a slave war', alluding no doubt to the two famous wars of the Republican period. It is very likely that the *latrones* who devastated Sicily were mostly peasants, *coloni* and shepherds of the large estates, some of them slaves.

²³ The evidence for the romanization of Sardinia and Corsica, for the cities, the tribes, and the large estates has been carefully collected and commented on by E. Pais, *Storia della Sardegna e della Corsica durante il dominio Romano*, i (1923), pp. 313 ff., especially pp. 329 ff. 'La dominazione Romana', he says, 'intensificò probabilmente centri di abitazione nelle varie parte dell' Isola, ma, fatta eccezione per Uselis e Valentia, per Turris, per Gurulis Nova e qualche altre località, non creò molte e nuove città di schietto tipo romano. Essa, seguendo assai probabilmente le norme dell' antica signoria punica, favorì invece la costituzione di aggregati rurali, di "vici" e di "villae", che **s**pesso, come ad esempio nel caso del castello e della cinta del Nuraghe Losa, si andarono svolgendo ed intensificando intorno alle vetustissime costruzioni megalitiche.' Cf. ibid. ii, pp. 499 ff. on the economic conditions which prevailed in Sardinia, and E. S. Bouchier, *Sardinia in Ancient Times* (1917); H. Philipp in Pauly–Wissowa, Zw. R. i, col. 2480. The rescript of Vespasian to the Vanacini is typical for Corsica (*CIL* x. 8038 = [Bruns⁷, p. 254, no. 80 = Riccobono, *FIRA*² 72] = Abbott and Johnson, *Mun. Adm.*, p. 363, no. 59, cf. Abbott, *Class Phil.* 10, 1915, p. 374). The Vanacini had bought some land from the emperor (who thus had imperial estates in Corsica), a dispute arose between them and a Roman colony (*Colonia Mariana*, that is the colony founded in Corsica by C. Marius) as to the boundaries of this land, and the question was settled, by order of the emperor, by an imperial procurator. The inscription mentions certain privileges which had been granted to the Vanacini by Augustus. It is to be noted that they had a temple of Augustus, which implies some sort of municipal constitution; but its priests were not Roman citizens.

²⁴ A. Schulten, *Tartessos* (1922); cf. his articles 'Hispania' and 'Lusitania' in Pauly–Wissowa, and 'Avienus in Spanien', *Zeitschrift f. Auslandskunde*, 1921, pp. 97 ff., and the reports on the excavations at Tartessos, *Arch. Anz.*, the last in 1927, pp. 1 ff.; [ibid. 1933, pp. 514 ff.; ibid. 1940, pp. 75 ff.; ibid. 1941, pp. 201 ff.]; cf. id. 'Forschungen in Spanien', ibid. 1927, pp. 198 ff. [*Tartessos*, 2ᵗᵉ Umgearb. Auflage, Hamburg, 1950]; O. Jessen, 'Südwest-Andalusien', *Petermanns Mittheilungen*, Ergänzungsh. 186, 1924, and *Arch. Anz.* 1927, pp. 236 ff. Cf. A. Schulten, *CAH* vii, pp. 769 ff., and the bibliography on p. 927. On the Phocaeans and Massaliotes in Spain, see Rhys Carpenter, *The Greeks in Spain* (Bryn Mawr Notes and Monographs, vi) (1925). Compare the important discovery of bronze weapons at Huelva, which testify to a large export from Huelva of bronze implements, to France and Britain and even to Italy, and suggest that at that period not only copper but also tin was mined in Spain in large quantities. See J. Albeda, 'Bronzes de Huelva', *Rev. arch.* 1923 (2), pp. 222 ff.; P. Bosch-Gimpera, ibid. 1925 (2), pp. 206 ff.

²⁵ On Spain in the Augustan age see T. Frank, *Economic History*², pp. 359 ff. For Gades see Strabo, 169C; 143C ff. The development of Emporium is typical (Liv. xxxiv. 9): the city was composed of two *oppida*, one Greek and the other Iberian, separated by a wall. *Tertium genus* (ibid., § 3) *Romani coloni ab divo Caesare post devictos Pompeii liberos adiecti, nunc in corpus unum confusi omnes Hispanis prius, postremo et Graecis in civitatem Romanam adscitis*. Notice the slower romanization of the Greeks. Cf. Sallust, *Hist.* iii. 6 (ed. Maurenbrecher), and A. Schulten, *Bulletì de l'Associació Catalana d'Antropologia*, 3, 1927, pp. 36 ff. On Spain see further Chap. V, note 4; on Portugal, A. Mesquita de Figueiredo, 'Monuments romains du Portugal', *Rev. arch.* 1913 (1),

pp. 345 ff., F. Pellati, 'I monumenti del Portogallo romano', *Historia*, 5, 1931, pp. 196 ff.

[26] A good survey of the economic resources of Spain is given by R. Knox McElderry, *JRS* 8, 1918, pp. 53 ff.; cf. M. Marchetti in E. de Ruggiero, *Diz. epigr.* iii, pp. 754–938; L. C. West, *Imperial Roman Spain, The Objects of Trade* (1929). On the export of oil from Spain to Germany see Bohn, *Germania*, 9, 1925, p. 78. We do not know what filled the pots, the sherds of which formed Monte Testaccio in Rome—probably not only oil and wine: see my *Gesch. d. Staatspacht*, p. 429.

[27] Hübner in Pauly–Wissowa, v, cols. 2493 ff.; cf. W. Barthel, *Bonn. Jahrb.* 120, 1911, p. 78, note 1. On Merida and her Roman ruins, see Don Maximiliano Macias, *Merida monumental y artistica* (1913); A. Schulten, 'Merida', *Deutsche Zeitung für Spanien* (1922); José R. Mélida, 'Merida', *IV Congrès internat. d'archéol.* 1929 (in Spanish and French). It is to be noted that Emerita remained a military settlement and administrative centre throughout her history—a Roman fortified post among the half-pacified tribes of the warlike Lusitanians. On the different social and economic aspects of the various parts of Spain, the division of the land into small cantonal units (as contrasted with the large cantons of Gaul), and the persistence of clans and *gentes*, see the valuable book of E. Albertini, *Les divisions administratives de l'Espagne romaine* (1923). He points out that the Romans never thought of increasing the division of the land, but on the contrary promoted the formation of larger units.

[28] O. Hirschfeld, 'Der Grundbesitz der römischen Kaiser', *Klio*, 2, 1902, p. 307 and *Kl. Schr.* p. 570. On the *ager publicus* in Spain, see my *Gesch. d. Staatspacht*, pp. 426 ff., and O. Hirschfeld, *Die kais. Verwaltungsb.*[2], pp. 140 ff. Add to the references quoted in these books *CIL* ii. 1438 = Dessau, *ILS* 5971 (restoration of the boundaries of the *agri decumani* in Baetica in A.D. 49). On the mines, O. Hirschfeld, op. cit., pp. 145 ff.; E. Schönbauer, *Zeitschr. d. Sav.-St.* 46, 1925, pp. 181 ff.; 47, 1926, pp. 352 ff.; T. A. Rickards, 'The Mining of the Romans in Spain', *JRS* 18, 1928, pp. 129 ff.

[29] Reid, *The Municipalities*, pp. 241 ff.; McElderry, loc. cit., especially pp. 62 ff., on the opposition at Rome to Vespasian and his barbarization of the Roman Empire. It is to be noticed that under Trajan some of the Spaniards who took a share in the war against the Dacians, particularly the Asturii, were treated as barbarians; they were called *symmachiarii*, a word used for the military units of the non-romanized peoples of the empire (H. Dessau, *Klio*, 20, 1925, p. 227).

[30] A. Schulten, 'Die peregrinen Gaugemeinden des römischen Reiches', *Rh. Mus.* 50, 1895, pp. 495 ff.; id. *Numantia*, i, *Die Keltiberer und ihre Kriege mit Rom.*; id. in Pauly–Wissowa, xi, col. 156; F. Behn, *Numantia u. seine Funde* (1931). On Asturia and Callaecia, see McElderry, op. cit., pp. 85 ff. On the relations between the original and the Roman divisions of the land, E. Albertini, op. cit., pp. 105 ff.

[31] The charter of Malaca, chs. 51 and 66 (*CIL* ii. 1964 = Dessau, *ILS* 6089; Bruns-Gradenwitz[7], p. 147, no. 30 [= Riccobono, *FIRA*[2] 24]; cf. Dessau, *ILS* 6898. Another sign of the poverty of the cities is the fact that a rich citizen of Ebuso left his town a legacy to pay the tribute (probably the poll-tax) of the citizens (Dessau, *ILS* 6960). It is noteworthy that similar gifts are found only in the poverty-stricken Greek lands, see *IG* xii. 5, 946, ll. 19 f. (cf. A. Wilhelm, Ἐπιτύμβιον *H. Swoboda dargebracht*, (1927), p. 341 (Tenos)); ibid. 724 (Andros), and the inscription of Macedonia, M. Rostovtzeff, *Bulletin of the Russian Arch. Inst. of Constantinople*, 4, 1899, pp. 171 (in Russian); [= *L'An. ép.* 1900, 131] (Beroea in Macedonia; gift of a rich citizen to pay the poll-tax for the population of the province, by which is probably meant the tax payable by the citizens of the towns only).

32 Dessau, *ILS* 6921; cf. the 'epistula Vespasiani Saborensibus', ibid. 6092. We shall meet with the same phenomenon in Dalmatia. In Gaul it was quite common. There is no doubt that in some cases the transfer of cities from the hills to the plain was due to an order of the Roman administration. Cities on the tops of hills were less safe from the government's point of view than those in the plains.

33 For the distinction between the *municipes* and the *incolae*, see Dessau, *ILS* 6902, 6908, 6916 (a rare case of an *incola* becoming a *decurio*), 6917, and frequently in the laws both of Malaca and of Salpensa and in the *lex coloniae Genetivae Iuliae* (Bruns, *Fontes*[7], 122 ff. no. 28 [= Riccobono, *FIRA*[2] 21]), cf. especially cap. 103: 'colon(os) incolasque contributos.' I regard the *incolae* as being mostly the country population of the territory attached to a city; see Dessau, *ILS* 6921: 'mutatione oppidi municipes et incolae pagi Tran[s]lucani et pagi Suburbani'; cf. E. de Ruggiero, *Diz. epigr.* ii, p. 2195; E. Pais, *Dalle guerre puniche a Cesare Augusto*, ii (1918), pp. 397 ff.; Berger, Pauly–Wissowa, ix, cols. 1249 ff. The two classes of *incolae*—those living in the cities and those which cultivate a part of the territory belonging to it—are distinguished in the classic definition of *incola*, in *Dig.* 50. 16. 239. 2: 'incola est, qui aliqua regione domicilium suum contulit: quem Graeci πάροικον appellant'. nec tantum qui in oppido morantur incolae sunt, sed etiam qui alicuius oppidi finibus ita agrum habent, ut in eum se quasi in aliquam sedem recipiant.' I cannot agree with Berger that this latter class was formed by the inhabitants of the suburbs of the town; the owners of portions of land belonging to the territory, to the *ager* of the city are evidently meant. It is very probable that the *vectigalia*, of which the Saborenses spoke to Vespasian, were payments of the *incolae* to the city (Dessau, *ILS* 6092). Cf. McElderry, op. cit., p. 77; Reid, *Municipalities*, p. 239.

34 C. Jullian, *Histoire*, vols. i, ii (pre-Roman Gaul), iv–vi (Roman Gaul), F. Cumont, *Belgique romanisée*[2] (1918), and Baron de Loë, *Notions d'archéologie préhistorique, belgo-romaine et franque* (n.d.) (a short but valuable picture of the social and economic conditions of the present territory of Belgium in the Roman period). A good archaeological survey of a part of Gaul is in M. Toussaint, *La Lorraine à l'époque gallo-romaine* (1928). On the progress of archaeological studies in France see R. Lantier, 'Ausgrabungen u. Funde in Frankreich (1915–1930)', *Ber. d. r.-g. Komm.* 20, 1930, pp. 119 ff. ('Die Römerzeit'). We have an excellent survey of Switzerland in antiquity in F. Staehelin, *Die Schweiz in röm. Zeit.*[2] (1931) [3rd ed. (enlarged) 1948]. The most important excavations in Switzerland are those of the legionary camp at Vindonissa, a general survey of which is not yet available. There is a short, but useful, summary in two works by R. Laur-Belart, *Anz. f. schweizer Altertumsk.* N.F. 31, 1929, pp. 181 ff., and *Die Erforschung Vindonissas unter S. Neuberger, 1897–1927* (1931) (with excellent bibliography), and in the same author's *Aargauische Heimatgeschichte. II: Römerzeit* (1930). This last work contains, beside a detailed account of the excavations at Vindonissa, two sketches on the antiquities of Baden (*Aquae Helveticae*) and of Augst (Augusta Raurica). It is well known that this part of Switzerland belonged administratively to Gallia Belgica. I call attention here to a discovery at Vindonissa, which, if it were better preserved, would excellently illustrate the daily life of the Roman legionary soldiers of the first part of the 1st cent. A.D.: namely, a group of letters in Latin, all by Roman soldiers, written on wood, which were found in the famous 'Schütthügel' of Vindonissa. They are published by O. Bohn, 'Hölzerne Schrifttafelchen aus Vindonissa', *Anz. f. Schweizer. Altertumsk.* 27, 1925, pp. 8 ff. and 133 ff.

35 A. Meitzen, *Siedelung und Agrarwesen der Westgermanen und Ostgermanen*, i (1895), pp. 221 ff.; O. Hirschfeld, *Gallische Studien*, i, pp. 289 ff. (*Kl. Schr.* pp. 62 ff.); *CIL* xii, pp. 160 ff.; E. Kornemann, *Zur Städtentstehung in den ehemals keltischen und germanischen Gebieten des Römerreiches* (1898), pp. 5 ff.; C. Jullian, op. cit., iv, pp. 352 ff.

³⁶ For the villa of Chiragan see Chap. V, note 40; on the sherds of Monte Testaccio, the articles of Héron de Villefosse cited ibid., note 22.

³⁷ Possessores Aquenses: *CIL* xii. 2459–60, 5874; C. Jullian, op. cit., iv, p. 353; cf., however, *CIL* xiii. 8254: 'possessor(es) ex vico Lucr(e)tio scamno primo' of Cologne; there is no doubt that these last were owners of houses in the city of Cologne; see W. Barthel, *Bonn. Jahrb.* 120, 1911, p. 48 (cf. A. Schulten, ibid. 103, 1898, pp. 17 ff.). The same must be said of the map of Arausio, A. Schulten, *Hermes*, 41, 1906, pp. 25 ff.; cf. ibid. 33, 1898, pp. 534 ff.; J. Formige, *Bull. Soc. Ant. de France*, 1929, pp. 167 ff. A curious type of organization is that of the 'neighbours' (*vicini, vicinia*), see Dessau, *ILS* 9413; Gerin-Ricard, *Rev. ét. anc.* 12, 1910, p. 74; cf. *CIL* xiii. 3652. The evidence on the *vicini* is worth collecting; cf. F. Sprater, *Die Pfalz unter den Römern*, i (1929).

³⁸ A description of a typical agricultural town of Gallia Comata is given by J. Matthière, *La Civitas des Aulerci Eburovices* (Evreux) (1925). On the Gallic villas and houses, see A. Grenier, *Habitations gauloises et villas latines dans la cité des Mediomatrices* (1906); id. in Daremberg–Saglio, v, pp. 877ff.; cf. C. Jullian, op. cit., v, pp. 174ff. and 351 ff., and vi, pp. 202 ff. Another type is represented by the commercial cities of the western and northern coast. Burdigala (Bordeaux) is familiar, C Jullian, *Inscriptions romaines de Bordeaux*, i–ii (1887–90). Less known are the cities of the northern coast. We can get an idea of them from the excavations of Noviomagus in Holland: J. H. Holwerda, 'Die Römer in Holland', *Ber. d. r.-g. Komm.* 15, 1926, pp. 1 ff. On Belgium, F. Cumont, *Belgique romanisée*, pp. 40 ff. (with bibliography); Baron de Loë, op. cit., pp. 189 ff. In the territory of present-day Belgium no ruins of ancient cities survive. Besides the *villae* there were only *vici*. The largest and best-known *vicus* is Orolaunum vicus (mod. Arlon): see J. P. Waltzing, *Orolaunum vicus, Arlon à l'époque romaine. I. Les inscriptions* (1905); J. B. Sibenaler, *Guide illustrée du Musée lapidaire romain d'Arlon* (1905). As is known, the Museum of Arlon is full of sculpture reproducing the daily life of the population. Another *vicus* of the same type was Turnacum (mod. Tournai). The same conditions obtained in the land of the Frisii: the characteristic habitations were *villae*, not cities. See Tac. *Ann.* iv. 73, and the contract of purchase of the early 2nd cent. A.D., found at Franeker, near Harling (mod. Olanda). The vendor, a Frisian peasant (the purchaser and the witnesses are Roman soldiers), lives at the *villa Lopetei*: see Vollgraff, *Mnemos.* 1917, pp. 343 ff.; A. G. Roos, ibid. 1918, pp. 201 ff.; E. Weiss, *Oest. Jahresh.* 23, 1926, Beibl. cols. 331 ff. [= *L'An. ép.* 1919, 51].

³⁹ C. Jullian, *Histoire*, vi, pp. 154 ff.; K. Schumacher, *Siedelungs- und Kulturgeschichte der Rheinlande*, ii, p. 185.

⁴⁰ An excellent short survey may be found in H. Dragendorff, *Westdeutschland zur Römerzeit*² (1919), pp. 7 ff.; more detailed on this subject is F. Koepp, *Die Römer in Deutschland*³ (1926), pp. 1 ff.; cf. the bibliography quoted by K. Schumacher, *Siedelungs- und Kulturgeschichte der Rheinlande*, ii, pp. 332 f.; F. Hertlein, *Die Geschichte der Besetzung des röm. Württemberg* (1928).

⁴¹ An excellent survey of the settlement of the Rhine-lands by the Romans, illustrated with instructive maps of various cities and sections of the country, and containing a full bibliography of all the local publications, is given in Schumacher's work quoted in the preceding notes; cf. E. Sadée, 'Gutsherrn und Bauern im römischen Rheinland', *Bonn. Jahrb.* 126, 1923, pp. 109 ff. On the 'Decumates agri', E. Hesselmeyer, *Klio*, 19, 1924, pp. 253 ff.; F. Hertlein, 'Klassikerstellen zur Archäologie', *Germania*, 9, 1925, pp. 18 ff.; E. Hesselmeyer, 'Was ist und was heißt Dekumatland', *Klio*, 24, 1931, pp. 1 ff.; cf. ibid. 20, 1926, pp. 344 ff., and F. Hertlein, ibid. 21, 1927, pp. 20 ff. I must confess that no satisfactory Celtic etymology of the word *decumates* has yet been found. F. Oelmann, 'Gallo-römische Straßensiedelungen und Kleinhaus-

bauten', *Bonn. Jahrb.* 128, 1923, pp. 77 ff., has proposed the interesting theory that inhabited centres developed in Gaul, Germany, and Britain from shops along the routes (good parallels to this are provided not only by the caravan-cities of Syria, but also by the development of many villages in modern Russia).

[42] K. Schumacher, op. cit., pp. 106ff., and bibliography on p. 339, note 38. A good description of Rhine trade is given by H. Aubin, 'Der Rheinhandel in römischer Zeit', *Bonn. Jahrb.* 130, 1925, pp. 1 ff. It is based on an exhaustive survey of the archaeological material, and shows how the larger cities of Germany gradually ceased to limit their commercial activity to goods first from Italy, and then, later, from Gaul, and promoted agricultural and industrial development in their own areas. The history of pottery, metal-working, and glass-production is especially instructive.

[43] On the pillar-monuments see Chap. V, note 27. For the villas, see the relative sections in F. Cumont, *Belgique romanisée*, pp. 40 ff., and K. Schumacher, op. cit., pp. 201 ff. (both with full bibliography). Cf. P. Steiner, *Römische Landhäuser (villae) im Trierer Bezirk* (1923); cf. H. Mylius, 'Die Rekonstructionen der röm. Villen von Nennig und Fliessem', *Bonn. Jahrb.* 129, 1924, pp. 109ff., and F. Oelmann, *JDAI* 43, 1928, *Arch. Anz.*, pp. 228 ff. (Mayen, Stahl, Blankenheim, Fliessem, Nennig), and the bibliography compiled by C. Blümlein, *Bursian's Jahresb.* 49 (197), 1924, pp. 21 ff. Nennig with its beautiful mosaics represents the type of wealthy country-house like the Italian villas. The best example of a villa where a luxurious residential house is associated with a large agricultural concern is furnished by the villa of Otrang near Fliessem, in the district of Bitburg in the Eifel, see von Behr, *Trierer Jahresberichte*, 1, 1908, pp. 74 ff.; E. Krüger, ibid. 4, 1911, pp. 1 ff.; cf. *Germania Romana*, pl. 17, 6 (plans and elevations of different types of villas, ibid., pls. 16 and 17). Not so large nor so luxurious, and more like the villas of Pompeii and Stabiae, are the villas of Stahl (F. Oelmann, 'Die villa rustica von Stahl und Verwandtes', *Germania Romana*, 5. 2) and of Bollendorf (P. Steiner, *Die villa von Bollendorf* (1922), cf. G. Wolff, *Phil. Woch.* 1923, cols. 924ff.). These villas were not houses of peasants, not even houses of 'Großbauern', as they are usually called. They were centres of comparatively large estates, of agricultural capitalistic concerns, which produced corn and other things for sale, not for consumption. Of the same type are the villas of Pforzheim and Dautenheim (K. Schumacher, op. cit., pp. 198ff. and figs. 49 and 50). The third type of villas (e.g. Mayen) is more or less similar to the houses of peasants, but even these cannot be explained as self-sufficient units, as instances of 'house-economy', see P. Oelmann, 'Ein gallo-römische Bauernhof bei Mayen', *Bonn. Jahrb.* 133, 1928, pp. 51 ff. and H. Mylius, ibid., pp. 141 ff.; cf. note 46. A good parallel to the gorgeous tombs of the merchants of Trèves is supplied by the fragments of sepulchral monuments of the 1st cent. A.D. which had been utilized to fill an ancient quarry near Kraft (district of Mayen) (H. Mylius, 'Die Kräften Grabdenkmäler und ihre Rekonstruction', *Bonn. Jahrb.* 130, 1925, pp. 180 ff.), and by the grave of a rich merchant and landowner of Cologne with a beautiful sarcophagus, together with busts of the deceased and an enormous wealth of small objects, Espérandieu, *Recueil*, viii (1922), pp. 375 ff.; *Bonn. Jahrb.* 114–15, 1906, pp. 368 ff.; K. Schumacher, loc. cit., p. 202.

[44] F. Drexel, *Röm. Mitt.* 35, 1920, p. 93, fig. 5; cf. above p. 205 and note 13.

[45] F. Drexel, loc. cit., pp. 133 f.; K. Schumacher, loc. cit., p. 287; *Germania Romana*, pl. 43, 5 (bas-relief of Worms).

[46] See S. Loeschke, *Die Erforschung des Tempelbezirkes im Altbachtale zu Trier* (1928); cf. 'Von den Ausgrabungen im großen Tempelbezirk in Trier', *Heimat*, 5 (May, 1930).

⁴⁷ See H. Lehner, 'Römische Steindenkmäler von der Bonner Münsterkirche', *Bonn. Jahrb.* 135, 1930, pp. 1–48 (and separately, Bonn, 1930).

⁴⁸ K. Schumacher, loc. cit., pp. 149 ff.; cf. F. Hertlein, O. Paret, and P. Goessler, *Die Römer in Württemberg*, i–iii (1928–32). Excellent work in investigating the gradual settlement of the land by agriculturists, mostly former soldiers or immigrants, has been done by G. Wolff for the Wetterau (Hessen-Nassau): see *Die südliche Wetterau* (1913) (supplements in 1921); id. *Arch. für hessische Gesch. u. Alt.* 13, 1920, pp. 1 ff. He points out as the main features of the settlement of the Wetterau: (1) the rapid increase during the 1st and 2nd cent. A.D. in the number of medium-sized farms of almost the same size and type; (2) the distribution of land among military settlers according to a definite plan; and (3) the existence of a native, mostly German, population which lived in poor huts and some of whose graves have been found. Cf. the map, pl. 16, in Schumacher's book and G. Wolff's notes on the map, pp. 342 ff. The size of the smaller estates, those granted to the soldiers by the government, can be calculated by measurements; it appears to be about one square kilometre. The estates to which belonged villas of the type of the Stahl, Bollendorf, Pforzheim, and Dautenheim examples (K. Schumacher, loc. cit., pp. 198 f., figs. 49 and 50) were certainly much larger; cf. F. Hertlein, *Klio*, 21, 1927, pp. 20 ff. I have some difficulty in admitting that the German Suebi were the colonizers of the *Decumates agri*. Tacitus, *Germ.* 29, says definitely that the land was occupied by mixed settlers.

⁴⁹ It is very tempting to explain the *coloni Crutisiones* of the inscription which was found near Pachten on the Saar (*CIL* xiii. 4228) and the *coloni Aperienses* of the inscription of Kollhausen in Lothringen: 'i[n] h[onorem] d(omus) d(ivinae) deae I[u]non(i) coloni Aperienses ex iussu' (B. Keune, *Lothr. Jahrb.* 26, 1914, pp. 461 ff.; id. *Röm.-Germ. Korrespondenzblatt*, 8, 1915, pp. 71 f., and in Pauly–Wissowa, Suppl. iii, col. 132) [*L'An. ép.* 1916, 128] as the tenants of certain large estates (cf. K. Schumacher, op. cit., p. 209). Similar expressions are to be found in Sardinia (note 22) and in Africa (see Chap. VII). Cf. also the lead tablets with the names of the staff of a large estate near Pola (mentioning a *colonus* and an *adiutor coloni*) in *Atti e Mem. della Soc. Istriana di arch. e storia patria*, 1905, pp. 213 ff.; A. Gnirs, *Führer durch Pola* (1915), p. 137. Some votive stones to the Matronae in the region of Düren (K. Schumacher, op. cit., p. 207) testify to small settlements of natives who worked on behalf of large landowners. On the progressive forms of agriculture which prevailed to some extent in the Rhine-lands and are attested by the frequent finds of agricultural implements, see K. Schumacher, *Der Ackerbau in vorrömischer und römischer Zeit* (1922).

⁵⁰ F. Haverfield, *Romanization of Roman Britain*⁴, revised by G. Macdonald (1923), and *The Roman Occupation of Britain* (1924); Cornelii Taciti, *De vita Agricolae*, ed. by H. Furneaux, 2nd ed. revised and largely rewritten by J. G. C. Anderson (1922); R. G. Collingwood, *Roman Britain* (1931), cf. id. 'The Roman Evacuation of Britain', *JRS* 12, 1922, pp. 76 ff.; and D. Atkinson, 'The Governors of Britain from Claudius to Diocletian', ibid., pp. 60 ff.; L. C. West, *Roman Britain: The Objects of Trade* (1931). For subsequent discoveries see the annual reports by R. G. Collingwood and M. V. Taylor, 'Roman Britain', *JRS* (with bibliography) and Sir G. Macdonald, *Roman Britain 1914–1928* (British Academy Suppl. Paper, vi, 1930).

⁵¹ Important evidence on the development of the British *civitates* is provided by an inscription found at Wroxeter, the *civitas Cornoviorum* (R. G. Collingwood and M. V. Taylor, *JRS* 14, 1924, p. 244) [*L'An. ép.* 1925, 1]. It shows that 'the local government of Roman Britain was carried out by tribal authorities classified and arranged just like the magistrates of a municipality' (Haverfield, *Romanization*, p. 58); cf. the

inscription of Caerwent (*Eph. Ep.* ix. 1012) and the inscriptions of the Dumnonii (*CIL* vii. 775–6) and of the Catavellauni (*CIL* vii. 863).

52 F. Haverfield, *Romanization*, pp. 38 ff. and 65 ff. Haverfield treated the evidence furnished by the villas in two different chapters of his work and from two different points of view. I venture to say that he was too pessimistic as regards the conclusions which may be drawn from it. Examined from the comparative point of view in connexion with the Gallic and the German parallels, the evidence fully justifies the conclusions which I have suggested in the text. It is to be regretted that, despite the efforts of many scholars, above all Haverfield himself, investigations in Britain have not in the past usually attained the same degree of accuracy and thoroughness, nor have they been carried on in the same systematic manner, as in Germany.

53 The sketch given in the text is of course hypothetical, but it is supported by the similar development of Gaul and Germany.

54 On the villages and the graves of the natives see F. Haverfield, ibid., pp. 45 ff. and 55 ff. It is idle to speculate about the degree of romanization reached by Britain. Without doubt the higher classes and the soldiers were partly Roman (in civilization) when they first came to Britain, and partly became romanized by constant contact with the army and afterwards in the Roman atmosphere of the cities. Without doubt also everybody in the cities spoke, and many wrote, Latin. It was natural also that the cheaper articles of industry imported from Gaul and produced locally in the cities of Britain should penetrate into the native villages and oust those made locally in the houses. This does not, however, mean that the villages were romanized in thought and life. One cannot, however, go all the way with R. G. Collingwood, 'Town and Country in Roman Britain', *Antiquity*, 1929, pp. 261 ff., who denied that the natives possessed any scientific knowledge of agriculture before the coming of the Romans, and claimed that the Romans introduced no new agricultural methods. The comparison with Gaul shows that the first contention cannot be maintained; the ruins of villas and Roman cities in Britain prove that the second is exaggerated. Against Collingwood see H. J. Randall, ibid. 1930, pp. 80 ff., and R. E. M. Wheeler, ibid. pp. 91 ff. Of course any attempt to calculate the size of the population on the basis of the area cultivated is purely hypothetical. Wheeler, however, with his figure of a million and a half is probably nearer than Collingwood to the truth. See also the very interesting observations of Sir George Macdonald, 'Forschungen in römischen Britannien 1914–1921', *Ber. d. r.-g. Komm.* 1929, pp. 735 ff., on the difference between the Celto-Roman agrarian system and the Anglo-Saxon as revealed by aerial photographs: see his figs. 59 and 60 on p. 80.

55 A general survey of the results of local research and excavations in Raetia is to be found in the excellent book of F. Wagner, *Die Römer in Bayern*[4] (1928). On the excavations of Cambodunum, see ibid. pp. 58 ff., with a map of the ruins of the town and complete bibliography. A good account of the ethnology of the land and of its political and military history is given by Haug in Pauly–Wissowa, Zw. R. i, cols. 42 ff. The inscriptions of Raetia have been collected and republished by F. Vollmer, *Inscriptiones Baivariae Romanae sive Inscriptiones provinciae Raetiae* (1915). The importance of trade for the citizens of Augusta Vindelicum is shown by a fragment of sculpture in a pillar-tomb, where the preparation for the transport of a gigantic bale, probably cloth (see F. Wagner, op. cit., pl. XIV), is portrayed.

56 *Negotiatores artis vestiariae, lintiariae, purpurariae* and others are frequently mentioned in the not very numerous inscriptions of Augusta Vindelicorum, and the fact certainly attests their social and economic prominence in the life of the city, see *CIL* iii. 5800 (Vollmer, *Inscr. Baiv.* 111), 5816 (Vollmer, 127; the brother of the merchant

is a soldier); 5824 (Vollmer, 135), cf. 5833 (Vollmer, 144) 'negotiator artis cretariae et flaturariae', 14370 (Vollmer, 175) 'negotiator porcarius', 5830 (Vollmer, 141) 'negotiator'. The inscription of Castra Regina is ibid. 14370, 10 (Vollmer, 361): 'Volk(ano) sacr(um) Aur. Artissius aedil(is) territor(i) contr(ibuti) et k(anabarum) R(eginensium)'. Note that the aedile seems to have been a native.

57 An excellent short survey of the social and economic conditions in Noricum may be found in R. Egger, *Führer durch die Antikensammlungen des Landesmuseums in Klagenfurt* (1921) (Introduction); cf. the chapters on Noricum in the books of J. Jung (see below, note 58) and in the fifth volume of Mommsen's *Roman History* (The Roman provinces), and R. Egger, *Teurnia. Die römischen und frühchristlichen Altertümer Oberkärntens*² (1926); id. 'Civitas Noricum', *Wiener Studien*, Festheft, 1929, and E. Klose and M. Silber, *Iuvavum. Führer durch die Altertumssammlungen des Museum Carolino-Augusteum in Salzburg* (1929). On the military occupation and the administration of Noricum and Raetia, see M. B. Peaks, 'The General and Military Administration of Noricum and Raetia', *Univ. of Chicago Studies in Class. Phil.* 1908. An interesting feature of Norican social life was the associations of young men (*iuvenes*) comparable with those in the cities and the villages of the Rhineland. Since the recruiting of the legions after the Flavians chiefly depended upon the loyalty and the warlike spirit of the population of the romanized cities in the provinces, the emperors promoted the formation of military associations of young men (which had been for a time a peculiarity of Italy) in the Spanish and Celtic cities, with the aim of educating a new stock of brave and loyal officers, non-commissioned officers, and soldiers, especially officers. A splendid field for the development of these associations was afforded by the cities and villages of the frontier with their population of former soldiers, still warlike natives, and pioneers. Hence the spread of the *collegia iuvenum* in the 2nd and the 3rd cent. to the cities and villages of Upper Germany (see K. Schumacher, *Siedelungs- und Kulturgeschichte*, p. 221), especially after the reforms of Septimius Severus. It is probable that both in the half-Celtic and in the half-German cities the institution was promoted by the existence of similar tribal institutions among the Celts and the Germans. It seems that the *Iuventus Manliensium* of Virunum, which celebrated the military games in honour of the emperor and of the gods, was based to a certain extent on the Celtic *gentes* of the native population of Noricum, see R. Egger, op. cit., p. 24, and fig. 5; and in *Oest. Jahresh.* 18, 1915, pp. 115 ff. Cf. Chap. II, note 5. An interesting glimpse into the social and ethnological constitution of one of the cities of Noricum and Pannonia is furnished by the inscription of the *centonarii* (firemen) of Solva in the time of Caracalla (A.D. 205). The text of an imperial rescript which confirms the privileges of the *collegium centonariorum* is followed by a list of members of the association given, as it seems, in full. Out of ninety-three members about one-half are *peregrini*, the rest are Latin or Roman citizens, and seventeen names are Celtic. The men represent not only the poorer class, the *tenuiores*, but also the well-to-do and the rich members of the community. This is expressly stated in the rescript of the emperor; they are described as 'ii quos dicis diviti(i)s suis sine onere [uti]' or 'qui maiores facultates praefi(ni)to modo possident'. O. Cuntz, *Oest. Jahresh.* 18, 1915, pp. 98 ff.; A. Steinwenter, *Wiener Studien*, 40, 1918, pp. 46 ff. [= Riccobono, *FIRA*² 88, with list of members omitted].

58 The excellent survey of the Danube lands given by Th. Mommsen in the fifth volume of his *Roman History* and the valuable books of J. Jung, *Römer und Romanen in den Donauländern* (1877), pp. 56 ff., and *Die romanischen Landschaften des römischen Reiches* (1881), pp. 314 ff., are now antiquated. The careful investigations of A. Gnirs in Histria, of C. Patsch in Dalmatia, of Bulič in Salona, of the Vienna Academy and of the Austrian Archaeological Institute in the Danube lands in general and especially on the Roman *limes* of the Danube, and the efforts of various scholars, Hungarian

(J. Hampel), Rumanian (G. Tocilescu and V. Pârvan), Bulgarian (G. Kazarow and B. Filow), and Serbian (M. M. Vassich and N. Vulič), have brought together so much new material and new points of view that the pictures of both Mommsen and Jung need a thorough revision. No such revision, and not even an attempt at a good bibliography, is to be found in the short article 'Illyricum' by N. Vulič in Pauly–Wissowa, ix, col. 1085 ff. An excellent general survey of those lands which formed part of Austria as it was before the First World War is given by W. Kubitschek, 'Die Römerzeit', *Heimatkunde von Nieder-Oesterreich*, Heft 8, 1924, cf. E. Nischer, *Die Römer im Gebiet des ehemaligen Oesterreich-Ungarn* (1923).

⁵⁹ J. Weiss in Pauly–Wissowa, viii, cols. 2111 ff.; A. Gnirs, *Führer durch Pola* (1915). The imperial estates in Pola are attested by many inscriptions of imperial freedmen and slaves found in Pola and elsewhere, e.g. *CIL* v. 37–39, 40, 41, 42, 475. A full list is given by P. Sticotti, 'Nuova Rassegna di Epigrafi Romane', *Atti e Mem. della Società Istriana*, 30, 1914, pp. 122 ff., cf. ibid., p. 124, no. 19; 'C. Coelius Halys col(onus).' A curious list of names is recorded on two leaden tablets found in a grave near Pola and published by P. Sticotti (see note 49). I cannot help thinking that the lists enumerate persons connected with a large (probably private) estate, partly slaves, partly free men. Some of the slaves were, or had been, managers of the estate ('dispensator' or 'qui dispensavit' or 'qui vilicavit'). One is *colonus*, another *adiutor coloni*. The free men bear no titles. I am inclined to suggest that the free men were the tenants of the estate, the *colonus* and the *adiutor coloni* being either slave supervisors of the agricultural work done on it or slaves who were assigned a parcel of land and were treated like free tenants. A large imperial property was probably located in the neighbourhood of Abrega in the territory of Parentium; see P. Sticotti, *Atti e Mem. della Società Istriana*, 30, p. 122, note 111. Here also, along with many slave managers of the emperor, we have one *colonus*, *CIL* v. 8190.

⁶⁰ On the Histrian villas see A. Gnirs, 'Forschungen über antiken Villenbau in Südistrien', *Oest. Jahresh.* 18, 1915, pp. 101 ff. (which quotes the author's previous articles on the villa on Brioni Grande and the other Histrian villas). Cf. J. Weiss, loc. cit., and H. Schwalb, 'Römische Villa bei Pola', *Schriften der Balkankommission*. Ant. Abt. 2.

⁶¹ The evidence is collected by J. Weiss, loc. cit.

⁶² Piquentum, *CIL* v. 433, 434, 436, 450, 452, cf. E. Pais, *Suppl. Italica* (to *CIL* v; (1888)), nos. 42–51. Nesactium: dedications to the local goddesses Eia and Trita, E. Pais, loc. cit., 1; *Atti e Mem. della Società Istriana*, 1902 ff.; A. Gnirs, *Führer durch Pola*, pp. 162 ff. The inscriptions and other finds of Nesactium are preserved in the Museum of Pola. On other local gods and goddesses of Histria, P. Sticotti, *Atti e Mem. della Società Istriana*, 25, 1909, pp. 7 ff., especially p. 10.

⁶³ A survey of the prehistoric discoveries in Illyria and of the history of the Greek settlements was given by S. Casson, *Macedonia, Thrace and Illyria* (1926), pp. 287 ff. (with an extensive bibliography). Casson's work is based on the excellent work which has been done in Histria and Dalmatia and in Bosnia and Herzegovina both by the Austrian Archaeological Institute and by the 'Bosnisch-Herzegovinisches Institut für Balkanforschung' in Sarajevo. Consequently the best explored Illyrian lands are Histria and Dalmatia on the one hand and Bosnia and Herzegovina on the other. The best general survey of the work done in Dalmatia is to be found in the short but substantial introduction of M. Abramič to the *Führer durch das K. K. Staatsmuseum in St. Donato in Zara* (1912), pp. 1 ff. On the excavations at Salona, see the bibliography quoted in Chap. V, note 4. An excellent general survey of the exploration of Bosnia and Herzegovina was given by C. Patsch, for many years the moving force of archaeological research in these lands, in his two books 'Bosnien und Herzegowina in römischer Zeit', *Schriften zur Kunde der Balkanhalbinsel*, xv, and 'Historische Wanderungen im Karst

und an der Adria. I. Die Herzegowina einst und jetzt', *Osten und Orient*, Zweite Reihe: *Schriften zur Kunde der Balkanhalbinsel* (1922); cf. his article 'Dalmatia' in Pauly–Wissowa, iv, cols. 2448 ff. A very valuable collection of evidence concerning Serbia, the Sanjak, and Montenegro, has been published by N. Vulič, 'Die antiken Denkmäler unseres Landes', *K. Serb. Akad., Spomenik*, 71, 1931; cf. the bibliography, pp. 247 ff. New and interesting data on the relations between Greek and Illyrian in the 5th cent. B.C. in the borderland between Macedonia and Greece were revealed by the series of rich Illyrian tombs excavated during the First World War at Trebenischte: see B. Filow, *Die archäische Nekropole von Trebenischte* (1927). On the redistribution of land every eight years among the tribe of the Dalmatians see Strabo, 315C; Steph. Byz. s.v. *Δάλμιον*; cf. C. Patsch in Pauly–Wissowa, iv, col. 2448, and E. Weiss, ibid. xi, col. 1086. A similar custom existed among the Vaccaei in Spain, Diod. v. 34. It is noteworthy that the tribe of the Ardiaeans ruled over an enslaved population of Thracians numbering about 300,000 (?), who tilled the soil for their Illyrian masters and are compared by Theopompus to the helots of the Spartans: Theopompus, in Athen. vi. 271, and x. 443 [= *FGrHist*. 115, F40]; Polyaen. vii. 42; C. Patsch, *Oest. Jahresh.* 10, 1907, pp. 171 ff. A typical Roman settlement, situated on the route from Salona to Servitium, was investigated by D. Sergejevski, 'Roman Stone Monuments Discovered at Glamoč', *Glasnik of the Museum of Bosnia and Herzegovina*, 39, 1927, pp. 255 ff.; cf. ibid. 49, 1928, pp. 79 ff. (in Serbian).

[64] On the well-known story of the Roman occupation of the Illyrian lands and on the Illyrian wars, see G. Zippel, *Die römische Herrschaft in Illyrien bis auf Augustus* (1877); M. Holleaux, *Rome, la Grèce et les monarchies hellénistiques au IIIme siècle av. J. Chr.* (1921), pp. 22 ff. and 98 ff.; id. *CAH* vii, p. 822, and bibliography, p. 932; G. de Sanctis, *Storia dei Romani*, iv, 1, p. 316, and the survey of C. Patsch, 'Die Herzegowina einst und jetzt' (see above, note 63), pp. 40 ff.; cf. R. Rau, *Klio*, 19, 1924, pp. 313 ff.; and C. Patsch, 'Aus dem albanischen Nationalmuseum', *Oest. Jahresh.* 23, 1926, Beibl. pp. 216 ff. The main centre of business activity in Dalmatia was Salona, which stood in the closest relations with Narona: C. Patsch, 'Die Herzegowina, &c.', pp. 88 ff. Many families of Italian origin like the Agrii, the Artorii, the Mescenii, the Obultronii, the Papii, the Ravonii, and the Umbrii resided in both these places. On the land behind Narona see C. Patsch, 'Archäologisch-epigraphische Untersuchungen zur Geschichte der römischen Provinz Dalmatien, viii', *Wiss. Mitt. aus Bosnien*, 12, 1912, pp. 92 ff., and 'Aus Narona', *Oest. Jahresh.* 15, 1912, Beibl. pp. 75 ff. Two men of Narona (C. Papius Celsus and M. Papius Kanus) built, probably on their own estate, a monument commemorating the victory of Augustus over Sex. Pompey. This family is represented also at Salona and Dyrrachium: see note 96. To the 1st cent. A.D. belong the ruins of a large villa in the valley of the Naro: C. Patsch, 'Untersuch. vi', *Wiss. Mitt.* 9, 1904, pp. 278 ff., cf. pp. 280 ff. on the families of the Livii and the Safinii, the first belonging to Narona, the second to Salona, established in the same region. On the fertile land behind Salona occupied by Roman settlers, see C. Patsch, 'Untersuch. v', *Wiss. Mitt.* 8, 1902, pp. 71 ff. and 84 ff. I feel certain that the first parts of the land to be exploited by the new settlers were the mining regions, the forests, and the pasture lands. Of the mines I shall speak later. Besides iron, lumber and cheese were the chief articles of export from Dalmatia as late as the time of the *Expositio totius mundi et gentium*, 53. Corn and cattle, however, were the staple products of Dalmatia as early as 158 B.C. (Polyb. 32. 18. 5, cf. C. Patsch, 'Die Herzegowina', p. 138). A large production of wine and olive-oil is a feature of the imperial period and was confined mostly to the lands near to the sea, C. Patsch, op. cit., pp. 119 ff. The statistics of Patsch, p. 121, show that wine may have been imported into Dalmatia both from South and from North Italy. It is hard to believe that all the jars were imported into Dalmatia empty.

[65] See the inscription *CIL* iii. 13250 = Dessau, *ILS* 5968, boundaries drawn between the pasture lands in the former territory of the legion and a private landowner. Many documents of the same kind have been found in Spain (Dessau, *ILS* 2454, 2455, 5969, 5970). On the extent of romanization of the maritime cities of Dalmatia see E. Weigand, 'Die Stellung Dalmatiens in der röm. Reichskunst', *Strena Buličiana* (1924), pp. 77 ff.

[66] C. Patsch, 'Die Herzegowina', pp. 105 ff. The city of Delminium was certainly transferred from the top of the hill to the plain: C. Patsch, 'Untersuch. vi', *Wiss. Mitt.* 9, 1904, pp. 172 ff.

[67] C. Patsch, 'Untersuch. vii', *Wiss. Mitt.* 11, 1909, pp. 121 ff. In *CIL* xiii. 6358 two soldiers of an auxiliary cohort give their place of origin as the *municipium* Salvium. This shows that the soldiers, though living in the territory of a Roman *municipium*, were *peregrini*, i.e. not citizens of the city but *incolae*. Cf. C. Patsch, 'Die Herzegowina', p. 107, who refers to *CIL* xiii. 7507, and iii, Dipl. xvi, p. 859, cf. xxiii, p. 1966 [= *CIL* xvi. 38], where two Thracians of the tribe of the Daorsi, which had formerly been enslaved by the Illyrians, indicate as their place of origin the territory of a city which occupied the site of the modern Stolac.

[68] C. Patsch, 'Untersuch. vii', *Wiss. Mitt.* 11, 1909, p. 155, figs. 63 and 64.

[69] See, e.g., the inscriptions of Skelani, C. Patsch, 'Untersuch. vii', *Wiss. Mitt.* 11, 1909, pp. 155 ff. Cf. *CIL* iii. 8350: Flavia Prisca 'c(larissima) f(emina)' sets up the stele to her nurse and to the manager of her estate (*vilicus*). The lady was certainly born in Dalmatia and owned land in this province.

[70] P. Sticotti, 'Die römische Stadt Doclea in Montenegro', *Schr. d. Balkankommission*, 6, 1913; C. Praschniker and A. Schober, *Archäologische Forschungen in Albanien und Montenegro* (1919), pp. 1 ff.; C. Patsch, 'Die Herzegowina', p. 89. Typical of conditions in Doclea, which became the main commercial centre of what is now Montenegro, is the personality of M. Flavius Fronto. He was connected with all the leading commercial cities of South Dalmatia—Narona, Epidaurum, Risinium, and Scodra: see *CIL* iii. 12692, cf. 13819; 12693, cf. 13820, 13821; P. Sticotti, op. cit., pp. 164 ff., 197 ff. On Asseria see *Oest. Jahresh.* 11, 1908, Beibl. pp. 17 ff.; M. Abramič, *Führer durch das K. K. Staatsmuseum in St. Donato in Zara*, pp. 16 ff. (Corinium, Nedinum, Asseria) and pp. 14 ff. (Aenona).

[71] On the organization of the Illyrian tribes of the province of Dalmatia, see the inscriptions found in the sanctuary of a local god Bindus Neptunus near the capital of the tribe of the Iapudes (Raetinium, modern Bihac?): C. Patsch, 'Untersuch. iii', *Wiss. Mitt.* 6, 1899, pp. 155 ff., cf. 'Untersuch. iv', *Wiss. Mitt.* 7, 1900, pp. 33 ff. On the tribe of the Maezaeans, C. Patsch, 'Untersuch. iv', *Wiss. Mitt.* 7, pp. 55 ff., cf. 'Die Herzegowina', p. 104. The tribes were subdivided into *decuriae* (clans, *gentes*), Plin. *NH* iii. 142. In the earlier period of the Roman occupation the tribes were ruled by Roman officers (*praefecti*), military commanders of the tribe, which was regarded as a military unit (*CIL* v. 3346, praefect of Iapudia and Liburnia; ix. 2564, praefect of the Maezaeans). Later the praefects lost their military character and became *praepositi*, civilians, and mostly natives, chosen from the local elders (*principes*), *CIL* iii. 14323–8, cf. 15062 ff. The fact that many cities were created in the territory of a tribe (e.g. Arupium, *CIL* iii. 3066, and Monetium, iii. 3022, in the territory of the Iapudes) and that many tribal *principes* became residents of the cities (*CIL* iii. 2774; 2776; N. Vulič, *Oest. Jahresh.* 12, 1909, Beibl. pp. 201 f. = Dessau, *ILS* 9411, 9412; P. Sticotti, *Doclea*, pp. 19 and 191; C. Praschniker and A. Schober, *Arch. Forsch. in Albanien und Montenegro*, p. 100; C. Patsch, *Wiss. Mitt.* 7, 1900, p. 156) does not imply the disappearance of the tribe as such and the urbanization of the whole territory occupied by it. This is

shown by the numerous boundary stones between the *municipia* and the tribes, Dessau, *ILS* 9378, 9379, 5948–53, 5953*a*, 5953*b*. The attitude of the government towards the tribes is shown, e.g., by the fact that Trajan transferred many Dalmatian clans to the newly created province of Dacia, *CIL* iii. 1332; C. Patsch, *Wiss. Mitt.* 6, 1898, p. 110 (of the reprint). The same phenomena and the same development may be observed in Spain and Africa. On the persistence of the native elements, native names, and native dress, as well as native religious beliefs, see C. Patsch, 'Die Herzegowina', pp. 92 ff.

⁷² See note 70.

⁷³ See the publication of the Academy of Vienna *Der römische Limes in Oesterreich*, i–xix, 1900–49 [in progress], and especially the excellent notes on the inscriptions by the late E. Bormann; cf. A. Alföldi, *Der Untergang der Römerherrschaft in Pannonien*, i–ii ('Ungar. Bibliothek', Erste Reihe, 10 (1924), and 12 (1926)). On Aquincum and Carnuntum see above Chap. V, note 5. The systematic excavations which were undertaken by the Czechoslovak government at Roman castles north of the *limes* in the territory of the Quadi and Marcomanni are very instructive. It is interesting to note the continuous advance of the Romans into the country of their vassals during the 2nd cent. A.D., and how Roman camps were superimposed on Celtic and German fortresses. The capitulation of Commodus to the barbarians put an ignominous end to this process. See A. Gnirs 'Limes und Kastelle der Römer vor der norischpannonischen Donaugrenze', *Sudeta*, 4, 1929, pp. 120 ff. A general report on the excavations of the Arch. Inst. of Vienna in Austria by E. Reisch, *Oest. Jahresh.* 16, 1913, Beibl. pp. 89 ff. On Poetovio (Pettau) see M. Abramič, *Oest. Jahresh.* 17, 1914, Beibl. pp. 89 ff.; id. *Poetovio. Führer durch die Denkmäler der röm. Stadt* (1925). On Intercisa, *Oest. Jahresh.* 15, 1912, pp. 174 ff. and S. Paulovič, 'Die röm. Ansiedlung von Dunapentele (Intercisa)', *Archaeologia Hungarica*, ii (1928) [see *Intercisa, I* (*Archaeol. Hung.*, ser. nov., 33, 1954)]. On Pannonian civilization and art see A. Hekler, 'Kunst und Kultur Pannoniens in ihren Hauptströmungen', *Strena Buličiana* (1924), pp. 107 ff. Cf. Chap. V, notes 4 and 5.

⁷⁴ On the *territorium* and the *prata* of a legion see A. Schulten, *Hermes*, 29, 1894, pp. 481 ff., and also in Pauly–Wissowa, iii, col. 1455; E. Bormann, *Der römische Limes in Oesterreich*, 2, 1901, pp. 142 ff. (*CIL* iii. 14356, 3*a*, cf. p. 2328, 193, A.D. 205); A. von Domaszewski, *Westd. Zeitschr.* 14, 1895, pp. 112 ff.; A. von Premerstein, *Klio*, 3, 1903, pp. 28 ff., cf. J. Lesquier, *L'Armée romaine d'Égypte* (1919), pp. 229 f. Cf. note 65. Delimitation of the territory near Viminacium, *CIL* iii. 8112 (cf. 12656) of A.D. 228.

⁷⁵ E. Bormann, *Der röm. Limes in Oesterreich*, 12, 1914, pp. 314 ff., figs. 37 and 38 (1st cent. A.D. or the beginning of the 2nd). Cf. A. Schober, 'Die römischen Grabsteine von Noricum und Pannonien', *Sonderschr. d. oest. Inst.* 10 (1923), p. 50, no. 105, fig. 45. Detachments (*vexillationes*) of soldiers sent out to cut wood in the forests (*lignarii*) are attested by three inscriptions of Germany, all found near Osterburken, *CIL* xiii. 6618, 6623; *Der obergermanischraetische Limes*, 33, p. 96; cf. K. Schumacher, *Siedelungs- und Kulturgeschichte*, ii, p. 161; R. Cagnat in Daremberg–Saglio, v, p. 776.

⁷⁶ *CIL* iii. 10570 (Vörösvár near Aquincum): dedication of an altar to the Capitoline Triad by the *possessores vici Vindoniani*, all Roman citizens, some of them Roman knights (all Aurelii, 3rd cent. A.D.), '[i]n possessi[o]n(e) Aureli Vettiani eq(uitis) R(omani) permissu eius'. A large villa, which was adorned with beautiful frescoes, has been discovered at Balácza: its earliest ruins date from the 1st cent. A.D. See Hornig-Rhé, *Balácza* (Veszprém, 1912) (with coloured plates); A. Hekler, *Strena Buličiana* (1924), p. 111 and figs. 2 and 3.

⁷⁷ One of the most interesting documents found on the Danube is a fragment of the municipal charter given to the city which developed in the neighbourhood of the camp of Lauriacum in Noricum (time of Caracalla). This fragment is almost an exact copy of

the corresponding part of the statute of Salpensa, see E. Bormann, *Oest. Jahresh.* 9, 1906, pp. 315 ff. [= *L'An. ép.* 1907, 100]; *Der röm. Limes in Oesterreich*, xi (1910), pp. 137 ff.

78 In the broad sense of the word a whole province (e.g. Numidia) formed the territory of one legion (legio III Augusta). On the Colapiani and their praefect L. Antonius Naso, see *CIL* iii. 14387 *ff* and *fff* = Dessau, *ILS* 9199; A von Domaszewski, *Philol.* 66, 1907, p. 162, note 4; A. Stein in Pauly–Wissowa, Suppl. i, col. 97, cf. C. Patsch, in Pauly–Wissowa, iv, col. 362. Many other tribes are named in the inscriptions of Pannonian soldiers, e.g. the Varciani and Latobici near Siscia; G. A. Reisner, C. S. Fisher, D. G. Lyon, *Harvard Excavations at Samaria*, i (1924), p. 20, no. 30, cf. p. 175; the soldiers of these tribes are called *cives Sicci(ani)*.

79 Colonies of veterans sent out to already existing cities, some of which had been military forts, are attested for Savaria, *CIL* iii. 8199 and 10921; for Scupi, iii. 8197, 8199, 8200; for Poetovio, iii. 4057: 'deduct(us) ... mission(e) agr(aria) II.'; cf. the corresponding 'missio nummaria', W. Kubitschek, *Jahrb. f. Altertumsk.* 3, 1909 (publ. 1910), p. 169: 'L. Gargilius C. f. Quirina Felix Tacapis vet(eranus) leg. I ad. p. f. missus missione nummaria'. On the veterans settled at Scupi, see also N. Vulič, *Oest. Jahresh.* 13, 1910–11, Beibl. col. 219, no. 31: 'hic situs est in praedio suo.' On the city of Savaria (mod. Steinamanger), a Claudian colony, see in general N. Vulič in Pauly–Wissowa, Zw. R. ii, cols. 249 ff. On Scarbantia, id. ibid., pp. 355 ff. Note the presence at Scarbantia of agents of the well-known Barbii of Aquileia, *CIL* iii. 14068. On Solva, W. Schmid, *Oest. Jahresh.* 19–20, 1919, Beibl. pp. 135 ff.; L. Wickert in Pauly–Wissowa, iii, A, cols. 987 f. In this city was found the fragment of the very important imperial rescript dealing with the association of the *centonarii*; see note 57. On Scupi, N. Vulič in Pauly–Wissowa, Zw. R. ii, col. 909. The best survey of the military colonies of the Roman emperors has been given by E. Ritterling in Pauly–Wissowa, xii, cols. 1214 ff. and 1239 ff. (Augustus), col. 1243 (Tiberius), col. 1251 (Claudius), col. 1263 (Nero), col. 1273 (the Flavians), col. 1287 (Trajan).

80 On the centuriation of Pannonia, Hyginus, pp. 204 ff. [Lach.]: 'multi huius modi agrum [the 'ager publicus' in the provinces] more colonico decimanis et kardinibus diviserunt, hoc est per centurias, sicut in Pannonia', cf. J. Jung, *Die romanischen Landschaften*, p. 358; W. Barthel, *Bonn. Jahrb.* 120, 1911, p. 46; cf. notes 65 and 73. On the measurement of provincial land see A. Oxé, 'Die römische Vermessung Steuerpflichtiger Bodens', *Bonn. Jahrb.* 128, 1923, pp. 20 ff.

81 A. von Premerstein, *Oest. Jahresh.* 6, 1903, Beibl. pp. 26 ff.; E. Groag in Pauly–Wissowa, vii, col. 358, no. 73, cf. no. 72; *CIL* iii. 8169, cf. 8238, 8240; Ulpianus, *Fr. Vat.* 220; *CIL* vi. 1423; and ix. 338 (legatus of Moesia in A.D. 222). Is it not possible to recognize in the *pratum Furianum* of Carnuntum (note 74) land assigned to the legion by the same C. Furius Octavianus? On the painted tomb of Brestovik near Belgrade, see Miloje M. Vassich, *Starinar* (1906), pp. 128 ff. (in Serbian).

82 On the dress of Pannonian women see Margarete Lang, 'Die pannonische Frauentracht', *Oest. Jahresh.* 19–20, 1919, pp. 208 ff. On the dress of the men, J. Hampel, *Arch. Értesitő*, 1881, pp. 308 ff.; 1906, pp. 257 ff.; 1907, pp. 289 ff.; 1910, pp. 311 ff. The basis of the dress is Celtic. Cf. A. Schober, *Die römischen Grabsteine von Noricum und Pannonien* (1923), p. 176. Some Celtic cults were retained by the Pannonians, e.g. the cult of the Mother Goddesses, who were worshipped in Pannonia under the name of Nutrices. A sanctuary of these 'Nurses' was recently discovered at Poetovio, K. Wigand, *Oest. Jahresh.* 18, 1915, pp. 189 ff.; cf. my article in *Archaeologia*, 69, 1920, pp. 204 ff. (Appendix III to F. Haverfield's article on 'Roman Cirencester'). On the peculiarities of art and culture in Pannonia, K. Hekler, *Strena Buličiana* (1924), pp. 107 ff.

83 On the province of Dacia in general see J. Jung, *Die romanischen Landschaften*, p. 378; id. *Die Römer und Romanen in den Donauländern*², pp. 114 ff., and the

excellent articles of Brandis in Pauly–Wissowa, iv, cols. 1967 ff. (cf. ibid., Suppl. i, col. 263) and N. Feliciani in E. de Ruggiero, *Diz. epigr.* ii, pp. 1440 ff., cf. V. Vaschide, *Histoire de la conquête romaine de la Dacie* (1903); R. Paribeni, *Optimus Princeps*, i, ch. xii, pp. 309 ff.; N. Vulič, 'Les Deux Dacies', *Mus. Belge*, 27, 1923, pp. 253 ff.; V. Christrescu, *Viaţa economică a Daciei Romane* (1929) (with French summary). On the Banat (which, according to the author, corresponds to Dacia Maluensis) see C. Patsch, 'Beiträge zur Völkerkunde von Westeuropa. II. Banater Sarmaten', *Wien. Anz.* 62, 1925, pp. 181 ff. On the Dacian *limes* see Em. Panaitescu, 'Le Limes dacique', *Acad. Roumaine, Bull. de la sec. hist.* 15, 1929, pp. 1 ff. On pre-Roman Dacia see Ioan G. Andriesescu, *Contribuţie la Dacia înainte de Romanii* (1912); V. Pârvan, *Getica* [1926] (in Romanian) and *Dacia* (1928). On Pârvan's conception of 'romanità' in Dacia see 'R. S.', *JRS* 19, 1929, p. 102. The native population which was not absorbed by the cities lived in villages, *CIL* iii. 7633 (827) and 8060. The territory of the cities was divided into *pagi*, *CIL* iii. 7847, cf. 7852, 7853, and 7868. It is very probable that at least a part of the native population rose in revolt against the Romans in the difficult times under M. Aurelius: the rebels massacred some members of the city *bourgeoisie* of Dacia, see *CIL* iii. 1579, 8009, 8021, and C. Patsch, 'Untersuch. v', *Wiss. Mitt.* 8, 1902, pp. 123 ff. One of the most influential families of Apulum was the family of the Aelii Marcelli, *CIL* iii. 974, 1001, 1104, 1181, 1182, 1208; a male member of this family was adopted by a high Roman officer of Italian (Umbrian) origin, *CIL* iii. 1180, cf. 7795 and xi. 5215. A record of a business manager belonging to the same family was found in the vicus ad Mediam near Drobeta (*CIL* iii. 1573*a*). Other business men on a large scale were the farmers of salt-mines, pasture lands, and customs-duties (*CIL* iii. 1209, cf. 1363 and 7853). They remind one of the well-known family syndicate of Julii, who farmed the customs, see my *Gesch. d. Staatspacht*, p. 395. Gold and silver mines were exploited by the state directly. On the town of Sarmizegetusa, capital of Dacia, see C. Daicovici, 'Fouilles et recherches à S.', *Dacia*, 1, 1924, pp. 224 ff. The town of Sarmizegetusa was the largest economic centre of Dacia and in general of the East Danubian countries. Two Palmyrene sanctuaries were discovered in the city, one of which is still visible (*CIL* iii. 7954–5; Daicovici, op. cit., p. 228, cf. *CIL* iii. 7956; Daicovici gives a bibliographical survey of these interesting discoveries). Apparently there were at least two groups of Palmyrene traders in the town: they can hardly have been soldiers or veterans. Two Syrian merchants in Dacia are recorded in an inscription found at Augusta Traiana in Thrace, of the reign of Alexander Severus: G. Kazarow, *Ann. du musée nat. de Sofia, 1922–26* (1926), p. 121 (in Bulgarian) = *SEG* iii. 537. One of these merchants is called in the inscription ννέμπορος τῆς Δακίας, where Kazarow read [σ]ννέμπορος, and Wilhelm (in *SEG*) (οἱ)νέμπορος. Since the omission of the *sigma* would be strange and inexplicable, I accept the reading of Wilhelm. The second merchant is called βλ τῆς Δακίας, which should perhaps be expanded as β(ου)λ(ευτής) τῆς Δακίας. In this βουλευτής (if he is one) should we recognize a member of a βουλή established in the West, according to Eastern usage, by an association of business-men? The Syrian merchants had their centre in Thrace, but maintained brisk trade-relations with Dacia. If Wilhelm's reading is correct, the inscription indicates that the production of wine in Thrace was important in the Roman age as well, and that Thrace at that time exported wine to Dacia. Compare the association of merchants on the Greek model at Perinthus, Kalinka, *Oest. Jahresh.* 23, 1926, Beibl. col. 172, no. 121 (Hellenistic); cf. J. Dobiaš, 'Les Syriens dans le bassin du Danube', *Bidluv Sborník* (Prague, 1928), pp. 15 ff.

[84] On the Thracians in general see the excellent book of G. Kazarow, 'Beiträge zur Kulturgeschichte der Thraker' (Sarajevo, 1916), in *Zur Kunde der Balkanhalbinsel*, II, *Quellen und Forschungen*, 5, cf. id. 'The Celts in Ancient Thrace and Macedonia', *Papers*

of the Bulgarian Academy of Science, 18, 1919, pp. 41 ff. (in Bulgarian); id. *Bulgaria in Antiquity* (1926) (in Bulgarian); id. *CAH* viii, pp. 534 ff., and pls. iii, 52–76; N. Vulič, 'Les Celtes dans le Nord de la Peninsule Balcanique', *Mus. Belge*, 30, 1926, pp. 231 ff.; S. Casson, *Macedonia, Thrace and Illyria* (1926). It is probable that in the tribal life of the Thracians the leading part was played by a ruling feudal aristocracy. The mass of the population lived in conditions which might be compared with those of the helots and of the *penestae* (G. Kazarow, op. cit., p. 17). It is hard to say whether the well-known description of the social and economic system of the Getae by Horace, *Carm.* iii. 24, is based on real information or on a vague idealized picture of 'barbarian' life in general, arbitrarily attributed to them. His words, 'campestres melius Scythae | . . . vivunt et rigidi Getae, | inmetata quibus iugera liberas | frugus et Cererem ferunt, | nec cultura placet longior annua, | defunctumque laboribus | aequali recreat sorte vicarius', | vague as they are, seem to imply that the Thracians held the land in common and that private property in land was unknown among them, which in fact is not incompatible with the conditions of serfdom. I am not as confident as G. Kazarow that Horace is merely reproducing a commonplace (op. cit., pp. 43 ff., with a good bibliography). Cf. the similar conditions both in Illyria and in Spain, note 63. I incline rather to believe that Horace got his evidence from an earlier source which represented conditions in Thrace before it was subject to strong Greek and Roman influence. Probably the subjects of Burebista and Decebalus in Dacia and those of the vassal Odrysian kings of Thrace lived a less primitive life On the social and economic conditions of the Thracians, see G. Kazarow, op. cit., pp. 26 ff. (Siedelungen und Befestigungen) and pp. 36 ff. (Ackerbau, Weinbau, &c.), and for the Roman period id. *Bulgaria in Antiquity*, pp. 59 ff.

[85] On the history of the Thracian regions in general (other than Dacia) in the Roman period see G. Kazarow, *Bulgaria in Antiquity* (1926) (in Bulgarian), pp. 48 ff.; B. Filow, 'Roman Rule in Bulgaria', *Bull. Bulg. History*, 1, 1928 (in Bulgarian). On the history of the province Moesia see A. von Premerstein, 'Die Anfänge der Provinz Moesien', *Oest. Jahresh.* 1, 1898, Beibl. pp. 146 ff.; S. E. Stout, *The Governors of Moesia* (1911). On the military occupation of Moesia, see Beuchel, *De legione prima Italica* (1903); B. Filow, 'Die Legionen der Provinz Moesia', *Klio*, Beiheft 6, 1906; H. van de Weerd, *Étude historique sur trois légions romaines du Bas Danube* (1907); J. Wolko, *Beiträge zur Geschichte der legio XI Claudia* (1908); B. Filow, 'The Roman Auxiliary Troops in Moesia', *Memoirs of the Bulgarian Hist. Soc.* 1906, pp. 11 ff. (in Bulgarian); E. Ritterling, Pauly–Wissowa, s.v. *Legio* (under the respective legions); cf. R. Paribeni, *Optimus Princeps*, i, pp. 335 ff. and B. Filow, *Bull. Soc. Arch. Bulg.* 5, 1915, pp. 191 ff. (in Bulgarian). On the military occupation of South Russia, see my *Iranians and Greeks*, pp. 152 and 234. New light was thrown on the social and economic life of the province of Moesia by the systematic and successful excavations of the late V. Pârvan. Reports on these excavations are printed in the Annals of the Romanian Academy (*Analele Academiei Romane*). They are quoted, and the new evidence is used, in Pârvan's articles *Sulle origini della civiltà Romana* (Rome, 1922), and 'I primordi della civiltà Romana alle foci del Danubio', *Ausonia*, 10, 1921, pp. 187 ff., cf. his Romanian book *Începuturile vieţii Romane la gurile Dunării* (1923), in *Ţara Noastră*. New readings of some passages of the inscriptions published by him were suggested by A. Wilhelm, *Anzeiger der phil.-hist. Klasse d. Akad. d. Wiss. in Wien*, 59, 1922, pp. 30 ff. On the pre-Roman conditions in Moesia and the Hellenic civilization, see Pârvan, 'La Pénétration hellénique et hellénistique dans la vallée du Danube', *Bulletin de la Section Historique de l'Académie Roumaine*, 10, 1923; cf. his book *Getica* (1926) and the English summary of it, *Dacia* (1928). On religion see J. Todorov, *Paganism in Moesia, pagan Cults and Deities* (1928) (in Bulgarian, with English summary).

[86] On these cities see *Die antiken Münzen Nordgriechenlands*, i. 1 (1898); 2 (1910), and

the corresponding articles in Pauly–Wissowa. Cf. the articles of Pârvan on Tomi, Histria, and Callatis in *Anal. Acad. Rom.* 1915, 1916, and 1920, and Pârvan, 'Fouilles d'Histria: Inscriptions: troisième série: 1923–25', *Dacia*, 2, 1925, pp. 198 ff.; id. 'Une nouvelle inscription de Tomi', ibid. 1, 1924, pp. 273 ff.; Th. Sauciuc-Saveanu, 'Callatis', ibid. 1, pp. 108 ff., 2, pp. 104 ff.; O. Tafrali, 'La Cité pontique de Callatis', *Rev. arch.* 1925 (1), pp. 238 ff., and *Arta si archeol.* 1, 1927. On Dionysopolis and environs see O. Tafrali, *La Cité pontique de Dionysopolis*, &c. (1927). The inscription in Tafrali, ibid., p. 71, no. 10 [Kalinka, *Antike Denkmäler*, 116], is interesting: it attests at Cavarna the existence of inhabitants of Scythian origin, and of a mysterious θίασος of Tauroi (Bacchae?). On Odessos (Varna) see A. Salač and K. Škorpil, 'Několik Archeologických Památek z Východního Bulharska', *Česká Akad. Věd a Umění*, 1928, cf. L. Robert, *Rev. de Phil.* 1929, p. 150, no. xviii (series of interesting inscriptions). It is interesting to see how strong the oriental element was in the new colonies of Trajan: see the inscriptions of Ratiaria, in I. Welkow, *Annuaire du mus. nat. de Sofia, 1922–26* (1926), p. 138, no. 1.

[87] This is the reason why South Russia was protected by detachments of the Moesian legions and by auxiliary troops. For the army of Moesia the foodstuffs came from Tyras and Olbia. The Bosporan kingdom was the hinterland of the Cappadocian and Armenian armies, see my *Iranians and Greeks*, pp. 147 ff.; cf. Tac. *Ann.* xiii. 39, and Chap. VIII, note 5. On the Dobrodgea (or Dobrudja) see J. Weiss, 'Die Dobrudscha in Altertum', *Zur Kunde der Balkanhalbinsel*, I. *Reisen und Beobachtungen*, vol. 12.

[88] V. Pârvan, 'Descoperiri novă în Scythia Minor', *Anal. Acad. Rom.* 1913, p. 491 (25 ff.) on the territory of Troesmis (legio V Macedonica), and p. 502 (36 ff.) on the territory of Noviodunum, which before Diocletian was the headquarters of the Classis Flavia Moesica, cf. *CIL* iii. 14448 (A.D. 178): 'c(ives) R(omani) v(eterani) vico Nov(o)', cf. 14447 and 12487. Cf. his article in *Riv. fil.* 52, 1924, pp. 307 ff., on the development of the municipium Aurelium Durostorum out of the canabae of the leg. xi Claudia. In the time of Antoninus Pius it was still a settlement of 'cives Romani et consistentes in canabis Aeliis legionis xi Claudiae', *CIL* iii. 7474; in the first year of M. Aurelius we have a dedication by 'veterani legion is xi Claudiae p. f. missi iiii co(n)s(ulatuum)' (first published by Pârvan, loc. cit.); in 169–76 it is styled municipium Aurelium (inscription published by Pârvan, loc. cit.). Cf. J. Todorov, *Durostorum* (1927) (in Bulgarian). The best-studied city is Nicopolis ad Istrum, which was excavated in 1900 and 1905. It was founded by Trajan about A.D. 114–16 and has almost the same plan as the contemporary African colony of that emperor—Timgad. At Nicopolis, however, a strong castle was added to the town, which is itself in the form of a military camp with buildings for the civil population (the forum, the theatre, and the curia (?) have been excavated). It may be noticed in passing that the Romans did the same also in the Chersonese and the Crimea, where a strong Roman garrison was stationed, at least from the time of Hadrian and Antoninus Pius. The best plans of Nicopolis, and the best attempts at reconstruction, are in S. Bobčev, 'Nicopolis ad Istrum', *Bull. Inst. Arch. Bulg.* 5, 1928–9, p. 56 (with full bibliography); cf. Chap. V, note 4.

[89] Most of the citizens of the Greek cities had the imperial *gentilicia*, Flavii, Cocceii, Ulpii, and Aelii, just as in Olbia, Chersonesus, and Panticapaeum. This fact, together with their Greek *cognomina*, shows that they were not immigrants from Italy or from the romanized provinces, but mostly natives of the Black Sea cities or immigrants from Asia Minor: see *CIL* iii. 7532, where Greeks from the Black Sea, Galatia, Cappadocia, Pontus, and Bithynia all have Roman *gentilicia*, cf. V. Pârvan, *I primordi*, &c., p. 196. Pârvan exaggerates somewhat the degree of romanization of the Greek cities of the Black Sea; cf., however, his just remarks in 'Histria vii' (*Mém. d. Ac. Rom.* Sect. Ist., iii. 2. 1), pp. 42 and 114 (in regard to a list of names, perhaps of members of the *gerousia* of Histria). Despite their Roman names, the residents in these cities, like

those of Chersonesus and Olbia in South Russia, remained Greek, at least in their language. It may be useful to enumerate some of the villages (*vici*) which were attributed to the cities, as far as our geographical knowledge goes. The best known are the territories of Histria and Tomi. Six inscriptions, almost all of the time of Antoninus Pius and M. Aurelius, are dedicated to the supreme god of the Roman Empire by the 'veterani et cives Romani et Bessi consistentes' of the Vicus Quintionis (Pârvan, 'Histria iv', p. 617, no. 24 [= *L'An. ép.* 1919, 13] and 'Histria vii', p. 55, nos. 46–52). The village was ruled by two *magistri*, one Roman and one Thracian, and by one quaestor. Two inscriptions of the same period (*CIL* iii. 7526, and Pârvan, 'Histria vii', no. 53 [= *L'An. ép.* 1924, 147]) speak of a Vicus Celeris and name one *magister*. Vicus Casianus occurs in two inscriptions (Pârvan, 'Desc. novă în Scythia Minor', *Anal. Acad. Rom.* 1913, pp. 534 ff.). Vicus Secundini: Pârvan, 'Histria vii', no. 61 [= *L'An. ép.* 1924, 148]. Vicus Narcisianus: Pârvan, *Începuturile vieţii Romane la gurile Dunării* (1923), p. 147; *IGRR* i. 599: ἔργον τοῦ ἀβιτωρίου (latrine) κατεσκεύασαν . . . τῇ κώμῃ ὑπὲρ μαγιστράτης. Vicus turre Muca(poris or -tralis): *CIL* iii. 7533; cf. 7536. Vicus Amlaidina: ibid. 13743. Vicus Hi . . . , ibid. 12494. Territory of Carsium: Vicus Verobrittianus: ibid. 12479 (14440). Territory of Aegyssus: ibid. 14441 and 14442; of Callatis, Asbolodeini and Sardeis, *vici* or tribes (?): ibid. 14214, 33. Cf. Pârvan, 'Cetatea Ulmetum', *Anal. Acad. Rom.* 1912–14, i, pp. 591 ff., and ii, 2, pp. 397 ff. (a list of *vici*). It is easy to recognize that some of these *vici* were named after a prominent Roman resident—Quintio, Secundinus, Narcissus, Celer, &c.—the owner of a large estate in the territory of the *vicus*; some had geographical names; some had a special descriptive epithet, like the Vicus Casianus: in the boundary inscriptions of its territory (ὅροι Κασιανῶν σπηλούχων) the residents are named cave-dwellers, which they probably were. (I do not believe in the religious explanation given by Pârvan.) In some inscriptions of the territory of Tomi and Histria (*CIL* iii. 7533, and Pârvan, 'Histria vii', no. 61, pp. 96 ff. [see above], both of the 3rd cent.; cf. Pârvan, *Dacia*, 2, 1925, p. 241, nos. 41 [= *L'An. ép.* 1927, 62] and 43 [= ibid. 64]) the residents are described as 'cives consistentes et Lai' (Histria) or 'Lae' (Tomi). It is certain that the name *Lai* (as also that of Bessi, Dacii, &c., see note 90) is that of a tribe; as has been shown by Pârvan and Casson (see Pârvan, 'Fouilles d'Histria. Inscriptions: troisième série: 1923–1925', *Dacia*, 2, 1925, pp. 241 ff., and S. Casson, *JRS* 17, 1927, pp. 97 ff.) it occurs as the name of a Paeonian tribe in Thucydides (ii. 96. 3; 97. 2), in the form Λαιαῖοι, and in Stephanus of Byzantium as Λάινοι. It is interesting to observe, with Casson, that the Romans moved some warrior-tribes to the steppes of the Dobrudja, including the Bessi of Haemus (see next note) and the Lai of Paeonia, who there learnt to lead the peaceful life of the peasant. Cf. L. Wickert, *JDAI* 44, 1929, *Arch. Anz.*, p. 193.

90 The best example of a tribal territory with a Roman *castellum* as its centre is afforded by the territory of Capidava, with the large and prosperous village Ulmetum. The population of this district consisted of Dacians and Bessi and of Roman citizens, *CIL* iii. 14214. 26 (A.D. 140), 'cives Romani et Bessi consistentes vico Ulmeto'; cf. Pârvan, 'Descoperiri novă în Scythia Minor', *Anal. Acad. Rom.* 1913, pp. 471 ff., 'cives Romani et Bessi consistentes regione Capidavae' (cf. p. 539), and *CIL* iii. 12492 (A.D. 150); V. Pârvan, *Începuturile*, p. 199. Other villages of the same territory were the Vicus Clementianus (*CIL* iii. 7565; V. Pârvan, op. cit., p. 203, cf. *CIL* iii. 12488) and the Vicus Ultinsium (Pârvan, *JDAI* 30, 1915, *Arch. Anz.*, p. 239 = *L'An. ép.* 1922, 65). One of the rich Romans of Capidava, C. Iulius C. f. Quadratus, *princeps loci* and *quinquennalis territori Capidavensis* (*CIL* iii. 12491, cf. Pârvan, *Inceputurile vieţii Romane la gurile Dunării*, pp. 52 ff., figs. 31–33), represented on his funeral altar himself (?) in the local dress (shirt, trousers, cloak), the god Silvanus, protector of his fields and pastures, and two scenes of the life of his estate: his sheep grazing in a forest (?), and one of his

coloni ploughing his field in the vicinity of a forest. It is worthy of note that the inhabitants of the territory formed a religious association in honour of Silvanus Sator under the name *consacrani*, Pârvan, *JDAI* 30, 1915, *Arch. Anz.*, pp. 204 f. = *L'An. ép.* 1922, 67 and 70. Other well-to-do local landowners: L. Iulius Iulianus qui et Rundacio (Pârvan, 'Castrul dela Poiana', *Anal. Acad. Rom.* 1913, pp. 103 ff.); L. Pompeius Valens from Ancyra in the territory of Histria (*CIL* iii. 12489); M. Ulpius Longinus buried *in praedio suo* in the territory of Tomi (*CIL* iii. 770); M. Atius T. f. Firmus, *loci princeps*, in the territory of Tomi (*CIL* iii. 772); Cocceius Vitales and Cocceia Julia, *obiti ad villam suam*, from Ulmetum and Capidava (*CIL* iii. 13737); Cocceius Elius who built a grave for Titia Matrina, *obita ad vila(m) sua(m)* (*CIL* iii. 14214, 20). Some men of higher standing are mentioned in inscriptions: *CIL* iii. 12463 names a 'vilicus L. [A]eli Marcelli c. v.'; *CIL* iii. 12419, 14447, and Pârvan, 'Histria iv', *Anal. Acad. Rom.* 1916, pp. 633 (101) ff., no. 30 [= *L'An. ép.* 1919, 14]: 'termin(i) positi inter [G]essi Ampudi [vil]|lam et vicanos B . . eridavenses' (I prefer the well-known name Gessius to the awkward Bessus). Besides the Bessi, other native tribes are mentioned on the boundary stones: Moesi et Thraces (*CIL* iii. 749; 12345; 12407; 14422, 1; I agree with Pârvan that these stones do not mark the boundary between the provinces of Thracia and Moesia), Daci (*CIL* iii. 14437, 2). It is probable that the Trullenses (on the Oescus) did not belong to a city territory (*CIL* iii. 14409 and 14412, 3) any more than did the vicus mentioned in iii. 7466; E. Kalinka, 'Antike Denkmäler in Bulgarien', *Schr. d. Balkankom.* 4, 1906, no. 128 (A.D. 153).

⁹¹ On the province of Thrace, D. Kalopothakes, *De Thracia provincia Romana* (1893); A. Stein, *Römische Reichsbeamte der Provinz Thracia* (Sarajevo, 1921); E. Kalinka, 'Antike Denkmäler in Bulgarien', *Schr. d. Balkankom.* 4, 1906; G. Kazarow, *Bulgaria in Antiquity* (1926) (in Bulgarian), pp. 48 ff. Reports on current excavations are published in the *Bulletin of the Bulgarian Arch. Soc.* and from 1923 in the *Bull. de l'Inst. arch. bulg.* (in Bulgarian with French résumés) and in the *Arch. Anz.* of the German Arch. Institute, cf. the useful bibliography by B. Filow, *Ann. du musée nat. de Sofia, 1922–25*, 1926, pp. 618 ff. (Classic period), 628 ff. (ancient Thracians). On the Greek cities of Thrace, F. Münzer and M. Strack, 'Die antiken Münzen von Thrakien', 1912, in *Die antiken Münzen Nordgriechenlands*, ii. On the first Roman settlers in Thrace (when it was still a vassal state under Rome) see E. Kalinka, 'Altes und Neues aus Thrakien', *Oest. Jahresh.* 23, 1926, Beibl. p. 118, no. 1. A very good survey of the activity of Trajan in urbanizing the Danube lands may be found in A. von Domaszewski, *Gesch. d. römischen Kaiser*, ii, pp. 177 ff., and in B. Filow, *Bull. Soc. Arch. Bulg.* 5, 1915, pp. 189 ff.

⁹² *IGRR* i. 721 = E. Kalinka, *Ant. Denkm.*, 55: κωμαρχία Ζηρκο[λη]νὴ καὶ κω[μ]αρχία Ζ[ελ.]οβαστηνὴ εὐχαριστοῦμεν διὰ κω[μη]τῶν Βρεντοπάρων καὶ Μωσυγην[ῶ]ν, εὐχαριστοῦμεν Αὐρηλί[ῳ] Καρδένθῃ Βειθυνικο[ῦ] γενομένῳ φυλάρχῳ φυλῆς Ἑβρηίδος ἄρξαντι ἐν ἡμεῖν ἁγνῶς καὶ ἐπιεικῶς κατὰ τοὺς νόμους, cf. ibid. 728 = E. Kalinka, ibid., 100 and 677 = E. Kalinka, ibid., 135: Ti. Cl(audius) Theopompus στρατηγὸς Ἀστικῆς περὶ Π[έ]ρινθον, Σηλητικῆς ὀρεινῆς, Δενθ[ελ]ητικῆς πε[δια]σί[α]ς. Note the close relation of the villages to soldiers, ibid. 738: ἀγα]θῇ τύχῃ | [κ]ωμῆτε Ζυλου|ζηνὺ Αὐρηλίῳ Μο|υκιανῷ Εἰουλανοῦ π|ρητοριανῷ· ἐλαβ|εν εὐχαριστήρια|παρὰ κωμητῶν. On the *strategiai* of the Thracians, see G. Kazarow, *Beiträge zur Kulturgeschichte der Thraker*, p. 19, note 1. Some of the *strategiai* may have been incorporated in the 2nd cent. A.D. in the territories of the new cities (Pliny, *NH* iv. 11. 40, knows of fifty of them, while Ptolemy, iii. 11. 6, enumerates only fourteen). It would be superfluous to produce evidence regarding the rural character of economic life in Thrace in the Roman period: observe the rustic type of nearly all the divinities worshipped in the shrines of this region and the part played by deities like Dionysus and the Nymphs in local cults. Further the Thracian Rider-God is essentially a god of fertility, see note 95. In this context I may recall the very interesting

inscription which attests the breeding of livestock, and particularly perhaps horses, in southern Thrace: it was found at Cillae (*Κίλλαι*) on the road between Philippopolis and Hadrianople (*Bull. Inst. Arch. Bulg.* 5, 1928–9, p. 379; G. Kazarow, *Eos*, 27, 1929, p. 143). It is a dedication to the great 'Heros' erected by a certain [Aurelius] Proculus ἐπικτηνείτης σὺν Εὐτυχιανῷ κόλληγα — ὑπὲρ τῆς ἐνθή[κης κ]αὶ αὐτῶν ἐλπίδος, cf. *BCH* 36, 1912, p. 592, no. 48; G. Kazarow, Pauly–Wissowa,. Suppl. iii, col. 1141 (Kadikeni): Ποσιδώνις Γλύκωνος γεωργὸς θ[ε]ῷ ἥρωι περὶ αἰαυτοῦ καὶ τῶν κτηνέων, εὐχήν. From the letters of the archive of Heroninus from Egypt (*P.Flor.* 121; 126, 13; 322, 81, cf. pp. 254, 255; *P.Ryl.* 236, 18) it seems certain that in the 3rd cent. the ἐπικτηνίτης superintended the transport-beasts in a large estate. This is also the case in our inscription, which is probably concerned with a large, perhaps an imperial, estate, where the excellent mounts of the Thracian cohorts and alae were probably bred. 'Ενθήκη probably means the whole number of beasts under the charge of the two ἐπικτηνῖται. See Chap. VIII, note 40.

⁹³ *IGRR* i. 766 = Dittenberger, *Syll.*³ 880. The villages contributed inhabitants to the new market-places. Near Augusta Traiana (mod. Gostilitza) we find one such emporium: Δισκοδουρατέραι ἐμπόριον ('double strong fortress'). We know of this fortified emporium from some inscriptions, the earliest of which belongs to the time of Marcus Aurelius, the latest to that of Aurelian, see I. Welkow, *Annuaire du musée nat. de Sofia, 1922–25*, pp. 129 ff., nos. 1–4, cf. *IGR* i. 591. Another place of the same type was Dia in Bithynia, ibid. iii. 1427; cf. iv. 863 (Laodicea ad Lycum). The inhabitants of these market-places were not citizens of a city but are called ἐνοικοῦντες or οἰκήτορες or κατοικοῦντες, which corresponds to the Latin *incolae*. The new town is therefore not a city (πόλις). It is probable that the emporium Nauna near Gallipoli in Italy had the same or a similar constitution, *CIL* ix. 10; Pliny, *NH* iii. 11. 105; G. Lugli in E. de Ruggiero's, *Diz. epigr.* ii, p. 2108. Cf. also the emporium near Placentia, Liv. xxi. 57. 10. The Greek name ἐμπόριον, which was used in Thrace, shows that in organizing new market-places of a permanent character the Romans followed the already existing Greek (probably Hellenistic) practice. The ἐμπόρια of the Greek half of the Empire may be compared with the early Italian *fora* and *conciliabula* (E. de Ruggiero, *Diz. epigr.* iii, p. 198; A. Schulten in Pauly–Wissowa, vii, col. 62): the difference was that the inhabitants of the provincial ἐμπόρια were not Roman citizens, and that the new settlements were to a large extent artificial creations, the ultimate object being to establish a new city around a market-place which was a centre of seasonal fairs; cf. the next note. It is interesting to observe that the establishment of ἐμπόρια, like the institution of seasonal fairs, is confined to the almost purely agricultural regions of the Empire, for the purpose was to organize a regular exchange of goods in places where commercial intercourse was handicapped by the slowness and (in winter time) the irregularity of communications. Cf. Chap. IX, note 51 (on the military character of these settlements).

⁹⁴ *CIL* iii. 12336 = *IGRR* i. 674 = Dittenberger, *Syll.*³ 888 (cf. Dessau, *Hermes*, 62, 1927, pp. 205 ff.; Wilcken, *Arch. f. Papyr.* 9, pp. 15 ff.). It is to be noted that in l. 14 the peasants of Scaptopare call themselves landowners of the village: οἰκοῦ|μεν καὶ κεκτήμεθα ἐν τῇ προγεγραμ|μένῃ κώμῃ, cf. l. 57. In l. 26 they mention a seasonal fair which was celebrated every year two miles from the village. On the seasonal fairs see P. Huvelin, *Essai historique sur le droit des marchés et des foires* (1897), pp. 80 ff. It would be worth while to collect the evidence about the fairs of the ancient world more fully than has been done by Huvelin, whose chief purpose was to characterize the fairs of the Middle Ages and of modern times. Very interesting, for instance, are the allusions to the *nundinae* at Pompeii, particularly the recently discovered *graffito* enumerating fairs at Pompeii itself, Nuceria, Atella, Nola, Cumae, Puteoli, and even at Capua and Rome (M. Della Corte, *Riv. Indo-Greco-Italica*, 8, 1924, p. 118). Seasonal fairs have

been very important factors in the economic history of almost all agricultural countries; witness their development in modern Russia before she became industrialized. Their persistence in such countries as Asia Minor and Syria (in connexion with the large temples and the large estates, see my *Stud. z. Gesch. röm. Kol.*, p. 274, and Chap. VII, note 6), and their development in Thrace and Africa (Chap. VII, note 81) during the period of the early Roman Empire, as well as the careful legislation of the late Roman Empire regarding them (Huvelin, loc. cit.), show that, while they came to play a secondary part in the more progressive and more industrialized regions of the Empire and during periods of progressive economic life in general, they were institutions of great and growing importance in the purely agricultural districts, and regained importance in every part of the Empire when economic life became everywhere simplified. Quite different from the seasonal fairs which developed in agricultural districts were those connected with the regular caravan-trade, to which such flourishing cities as Palmyra and Petra owed their origin and prosperity. These fairs are comparable with the great (and still surviving) fair of Nijnij-Novgorod in Russia, at least in its early days, or to the smaller one of Orenburg, which was a rallying point for caravans, before the construction of the Turkestan railway.

[95] On the funeral chariots of Thrace, from the 2nd to the 4th cent. A.D., see G. Seure 'chars thraces', *BCH* 49, 1925, pp. 347 ff., cf. ibid. 25, 1901, pp. 181 ff., and ibid. 28, 1904, pp. 210 ff.; cf. also, on certain clay chariots found in tombs of the same period, G. Seure, *RA* 1925 (2), pp. 3 ff. The metal parts of the chariots found in some *tumuli* in Bulgaria are in excellent preservation; some are plated with silver, others enamelled. They recall Sarmatian tombs. It is to be borne in mind that Sarmatians were settled in the Balkan lands from the 1st cent. A.D. (see the inscription of Titus Plautius Silvanus, Dessau, *ILS* 986 (A.D. 57), cf. ibid. 852–3: P. Aelius Rasparaganus, king of the Roxolani, captured by Hadrian, interned at Pola), and that the first migratory waves of Sarmatians may have adopted the Scythian custom (unknown to later Sarmatians) of burying the chariots. The Scythians lived for centuries in the Danubian countries, and even in the time of Ovid were still neighbours of the city of Tomi. It is also interesting to observe that at least one of the tombs of the Iazyges, a Sarmatian tribe which settled between the Danube and the Theiss in the period A.D. 20–50, namely the tomb of Jászalsószentgyörgy (see Hild, *Arch. Értesítő*, 1901, pp. 120 ff.; A. Alföldi, *Der Untergang der Römerherrschaft in Pannonien*, ii (1926), p. 8; N. Fettich, *Seminarium Kondakovianum*, 2 (1928), p. 108, pl. xv, 3 (cf. id. in M. Rostowzew, *Skythien und Der Bosporus*, i (1931), pp. 498 ff.), shows traces of Scythian funeral rites (including the chariot). We must not, however, forget that the Celts also buried their dead in chariots (cf. H. Lehner, *Bonn. Jahb.* 128, 1923, pp. 28 ff.). On the cults of the Thracian 'Heros', and on the local shrines of the Thracians (many of which have been excavated), where native gods were worshipped under a Greek or Roman disguise, see G. Kazarow, Pauly–Wissowa, Suppl. iii, cols. 1132 ff.; id. *Bulgaria in Antiquity* (1926) (in Bulgarian), pp. 78 ff.; id. *JDAI* 41, *Arch. Anz.* 1926, pp. 1 ff., and *Klio*, 22, 1928, pp. 232 ff.; cf. A. Buday, 'Thrak lovas istan problemaja' ('Das Problem des sogenannten thrakischen Reiters': in Hungarian with a German summary), *Arbeiten des arch. Inst. d. k. Ungar. Franz Josephs-Universität von Szeged (Dolgozatok*, &c.), ii (1926); iv (1928); v (1929); G. Seure, 'Le Roi Rhèse et le héros chasseur'. *Rev. d. phil.* 1928, pp. 101 ff. I cannot give my opinion here regarding the theory of Professor A. Buday, who believes that the rider represented on the votive and sepulchral reliefs is the dedicant or the dead person, heroized, not the divinity: the reliefs would thus be monuments of a religion of salvation. The sanctuaries are all modest village shrines, full of votive bas-reliefs of the same shape as many modern Greek-Orthodox 'icons'. The Thracian 'Heros' must not be confounded with the Oriental mounted god who was worshipped mostly by the soldiers of the

Danubian army and by veterans and their families, see my article in *Mém. prés. à l'Acad.* 13, 1923, and G. Kazarow, *JDAI* 38, 1922, p. 184, on an early Roman sanctuary of this Oriental god and the corresponding goddess near Razgrad.

96 On Macedonia, besides the chapter in Mommsen's *Roman History* and his introduction to the Latin inscriptions of Macedonia in *CIL*, iii, see J. Jung, *Die romanischen Landschaften*, pp. 377 ff.; M. G. Demitsas, 'Η Μακεδονία ἐν λίθοις φθεγγομένοις, &c. (Athens, 1896); H. Gaebler, *Die antiken Münzen Nordgriechenlands*, iii, *Makedonia und Paionia* (1906); and cf. his 'Beiträge zur Münzkunde Makedoniens', *Zeitschr. f. Num.* (the last in 36, 1927, pp. 183 ff., and 37, 1928, pp. 223 ff.). On Paeonia, see G. Kazarow, *Paeonia* (Sofia, 1921, in Bulgarian); cf. id. *Klio*, 18, 1922, pp. 20 ff. On Thessalonica see O. Tafrali, *Théssalonique des origines au XIVe siècle* (1919). On Lissus, Apollonia, and Dyrrhachium, see C. Praschniker and A. Schober, 'Archäologische Forschungen in Albanien und Montenegro', *Schr. d. Balkankom.* 8, 1919, pp. 14 ff., 32 ff., 69 ff.; C. Praschniker, 'Muzakhia und Malakastra, *Oest. Jahresh.* 21–22, 1922, Beibl. pp. 6 ff.; cf. C. Patsch, 'Das Sandschak Berat in Albanien', *Schr. d. Balkankom.* 3, 1904, and M. N. Tod, *JHS* 42, 1922, p. 171, and C. Patsch, 'Aus dem Albanischen Nationalmuseum', *Oest. Jahresh.* 23, 1926, pp. 210 ff. It is interesting to observe that Apollonia and Dyrrhachium, though officially cities of Macedonia, are socially and economically connected with the Roman cities of Dalmatia: see note 64. On the earlier history and archaeology of Macedonia see S. Casson, *Macedonia, Thrace and Illyria* (1926). On the excavations at Stobi see B. Saria, *Oest. Jahresh.* 26, 1930, pp. 64 ff., with bibliography. New discoveries in Albania are recorded in *Albania, Rev. d'arch. d'hist., d'art*, &c. 1–6 (1925–39). An archaeological survey of the region is given by L. M. Ugolini, *Albania Antica: I. Ricerche archeologiche* (1928); [*II. L'Acropoli di Fenice* (1932); *III. L'Acropoli di Butrinto* (1942).]

97 On the municipal aristocracy of Macedonia, the presidents of the Macedonian κοινόν, see my article 'Inscriptions from Macedonia', *Bulletin of the Russian Arch. Inst. at Constantinople*, 4, 1899, pp. 166ff. (in Russian), especially the inscriptions nos. 2 and 2a relating to C. Popillius Python of Beroea, of the time of Nerva and Trajan [=*L'An. ép.* 1900, 131]; cf. M. G. Demitsas, op. cit., p. 71, no. 62. His contemporary was Paulus Caelidius Fronto from Heraclea Lyncestis (P. Perdrizet, *BCH* 21, 1897, pp. 161 ff.; cf. M. Holleaux, *Rev. ét. gr.* 11, 1898, pp. 273ff. [= *Études*, i, pp. 271 ff.]). At Philippi a prominent part was played by the family of the Opimii, rich landowners and benefactors of the city (*CIL* iii. 656). Rich Thracian landowners of Philippi are mentioned in *CIL* iii. 703, 707. On the Roman character of Philippi see Ch. Picard, *C. R. Acad. Inscr.* 1923, p. 395; P. Collart, *BCH* 52, 1928, pp. 74ff. (with bibliography), cf. ibid., pp. 492ff. (The French excavations at Philippi are reported in *BCH* [P. Collart, *Philippes, Ville de Macédoine* (1937)].) A prominent man of the end of the 2nd cent. and the beginning of the 3rd was T. Aelius Geminius Macedo of Thessalonica, the first president of the Panhellenion from this city (M. N. Tod, *JHS* 42, 1922, pp. 167ff.). His gift of 10,000 feet of lumber for the construction of a *basilica* may indicate that he owned a large forest estate. In *CIL* iii. 14206, 4 (Dessau, *ILS* 5981) an estate of Claudianus Artemidorus s.p.c. and in iii. 14206, 12, another of a certain Caesius Victor are mentioned. The large landowners in the cities which were not Roman colonies, e.g. Beroea, belonged mostly to the class of ἐνκεκτημένοι Ῥωμαῖοι (M. G. Demitsas, op. cit., p. 70, no. 58). The persistence of the tribal and rural organization of Macedonia is attested by the division of the large territory of Beroea into φυλαί, which had geographical names and corresponded probably to the *pagi* of the Danube provinces. In the above-mentioned inscription of Heraclea the cost of repairing the roads is imposed by the emperor, in his letter, on the landowners of the city (two-thirds) and on the tribe of the Ἄντανοί (one-third); in the latter M. Holleaux recognizes the well-known Ἀτιντανοί. In another inscription on the

same stone Caelidius Fronto performs the gymnasiarchy both for the city and for the tribe of the Lynkesti (ἔθνος Λυγκηστῶν). It is therefore probable that the city of Heraclea included in her territory the country of the Lynkesti, who were not citizens of the city, one part of the tribe of the Ἀτιντανοί being attached to the city in the same way as the Carni and Catali were attached to Tergeste. A very curious distinction between the ἐπαρχικοί and the πολῖται is made in the most interesting of the inscriptions of the Orestis (A. M. Woodward, *JHS* 33, 1913, pp. 337 ff., 2nd cent. A.D.). As a third category of landowners, not indentical either with the ἐπαρχικοί or the πολῖται, are named the Oresti (l. 23). I cannot help thinking that the aggressive ἐπαρχικοί were the Roman landowners of the territory (οἱ ἐνκεκτημένοι), who belonged to the province but did not belong to the city, while the Oresti were the members of a tribe attached to the city. They were entered in the census rolls of the city as holders of parcels of public land. Cf. the κοινὸν Ὀρέστων (A. J. B. Wace and A. M. Woodward, *BSA* 18, 1911–12, p. 179, no. 23 [= *L'An. ép.* 1914, 216]) and the Dassaretii and their προστάτης, M. G. Demitsas, op. cit., p. 371, no. 330 (2). Both in Macedonia and in the neighbouring districts of Thessaly life seems to have been mostly rural, as is shown by the frequent mention of *vici* in the documents recording a delimitation between the city territories in Macedonia and Thessaly. We have three imperial decisions on this subject, all of the time of Trajan and Hadrian, *CIL* iii. 591 (Trajan), 586 (12306) (Hadrian), and A. J. B. Wace and M. S. Thompson, op. cit., 17, 1910–11, pp. 193 ff. [= *L'An. ép.* 1913, 2], where in ll. 14 ff. reference is made to the delimitation first made by Amyntas, father of Philip II: 'inscriptos esse f(i)nes convenientes defini(t)ione regiae factae ab Amynta Philippi patr⟨a⟩e inter Dolichanos et Elemiotas', cf. A. Rosenberg, *Hermes*, 51, 1916, pp. 499 ff. On another stone of the same time recording a delimitation between Geneatae and...xini, cf. G. Kazarow, *BCH* 47, 1923, pp. 275 ff. [= *L'An. ép.* 1924, 57]. Mentions of *vici*: *CIL* iii. 656; A. Salač, *BCH* 47, 1923, p. 63, no. 23: 'M. Bietius Cerius vet(eranus) vicanis d(e) s(uo)'; and, ibid., p. 65, no. 24, a votive stone to a local goddess set up by 'vicani Sc . . . Nicaenses et Coreni et Zcambu . . . ', followed by the names of *curatores*, all Thracian [= *L'An. ép.* 1924, 50].

⁹⁸ Dio Chr. *Tars. pr.* (*Or.* 33), 25 (on Thessaly and Arcadia); 26 (on Macedonia); cf. the well-known statement of Plutarch, *De def. or.* 8, 414, and O. Seeck, *Gesch. d. Unterg. d. ant. Welt*, i, p. 321, note 32.

⁹⁹ Dittenberger, *Syll.³* 827; E. Bourguet, *De rebus Delphicis imperatoriae aetatis* (1905), pp. 74 ff. (letter of Hadrian); cf. ibid., pp. 94 ff. (general conclusions). There was no doubt a revival of the sanctuary in the 2nd cent. A.D., especially under Hadrian (the worst time had been the 1st cent. A.D.), but this revival was based almost wholly on gifts of the Roman emperors and of some members of the Roman and provincial nobility (especially Herodes Atticus and his family).

¹⁰⁰ Dittenberger, *Syll.³* 800; cf. A. von Premerstein, *Oest. Jahresh.* 15, 1912, pp. 200 ff.; see especially ll. 12 ff.: ἐπεδέξατο δὲ καὶ τὰν ἱερατείαν Νικάσιππος τᾶς Δεσποίνας ὄντος Ὀλυμ|πικοῦ ἐνιαυτοῦ μηθενὸς θέλοντος προσελθεῖν, τῶν τε χρημά|των μὴ πεσόντων τοῖς μυστηρίοις ἀπέδωκε ἐκ τοῦ ἰδίου βί|ου τῷ φίσκῳ.

¹⁰¹ I cannot undertake here the task of putting together the rich material on the economic life of Greece in the imperial period which is stored in the volumes of *IG*. The work is worth doing. One part of this material, concerning Athens in the early Roman period, has been investigated in a masterly way by S. Shebeleff, *History of Athens from 229 to 31 B.C.* (St. Petersburg, 1898, in Russian), cf. id. Ἀχαικά, *Studies in the History of the Province of Achaea*, 1903 (in Russian); P. Graindor, *Athènes sous Auguste* (1927), esp. pp. 159 ff.; id. *Athènes de Tibère à Trajan* (1931). The half-romantic attitude of the cultivated Romans towards Greece is well-illustrated by Plin. *Ep.* viii. 24, addressed to Maximus, the friend of Epictetus and at that time *corrector civitatium*

liberarum of Achaea: see the article of F. Zucker, 'Plinius Epist. viii, 24–ein Denkmal antiker Humanität', *Philol.* 84, 1928, pp. 209 ff. I see no indication in the sources that the conditions of agriculture in Greece in the 2nd cent. A.D. were desperate. It seems as if there had been a notable improvement as compared with the conditions of the 1st cent. B.C. described by Cicero, *ad Fam.* iv. 5. 4 (we can place complete confidence in what Dio Chryst. says in the *Εὐβοικός*). Such an impression may be derived from a careful study of the inscription of Thisbe (Dittenberger, *Syll.*³ 884), and is confirmed by the fact that Greece had sufficient numbers of wealthy citizens to support the institution of the Panhellenion created by Hadrian (see M. N. Tod, *JHS* 42, 1922, pp. 173 ff., who quotes the bibliography of the question and gives a full survey of the epigraphical and literary evidence). The main feature of the Panhellenion was the great games, and they were supported and financed by the presidents and members of the council (σύνεδροι) of the Panhellenion. It is noteworthy that in the list of these presidents and σύνεδροι or Πανέλληνες (compiled by Tod, ibid., p. 177) there are also wealthy men from Greece (cf. C. S. Walton, *JRS* 19, 1929, p. 62). A wealthy Spartan, a landowner, appears as a benefactor of his city during a period of famine under Hadrian: see the inscription in A. M. Woodward, 'Sparta: the Inscriptions', *BSA* 27, 1925–6, pp. 22 ff., no. 3 [= *SEG* xi. 492]. He is C. Julius Theophrastus, who sold cheap corn to the citizens of Sparta (probably from his own estate, or else imported by him: instead of 40 denarii per medimnus, the price was 1 denarius per hemiekton, the twelfth part of the medimnus). Subsequently he distributed oil and, often, corn at a price below that of the market. Cf. Chap. V, note 9, and Chap. VIII, note 21, and H. Box, 'Roman Citizenship in Laconia', *JRS* 21, 1931, pp. 200 ff. However, A. Stein and C. S. Walton are right in emphasizing that very few senators came from Greece proper, and in attributing this to the fact that Greeks were not wealthy enough to become senators. This is because the most energetic Greeks did not stay in Greece where there was very little to do. It cannot be denied, however, that economic conditions in Greece improved under the Empire; this was due, in part, for example, to the continued or resumed export of wine to Italy. At Pompeii, amphorae which had once been filled with wine, have been discovered, and Scyros exported large quantities of wine to Ravenna (the dome of the baptistery of the Arians is built of wine-amphorae, the inscriptions of which indicate that they came to Ravenna from Scyros: see P. Graindor, *Byzantion*, 3, 1929, pp. 281 ff.; id. *Athènes sous Auguste*, p. 165). The prosperity of Corinth and Patrae (Dessau, *Gesch. d. röm. Kaiserzeit*, ii. 2, p. 553) also implies a flourishing trade, which was not only one of transit. The American excavations at Corinth have shown how magnificent the Roman city was. Even Athens was a fairly wealthy city, though naturally not because of her trade or industry (Graindor, *Athènes sous Auguste*, pp. 159 ff.). It is to be noted that Greece continued to have at all times an industry working for the export market. The army of the Danube sent its agents there to purchase clothing: see the papyrus published by Hunt, *Racc. Lumbroso*, pp. 265 ff., l. 34: *in Grecia vest[itum]*; cf. Chap. V, note 43.

VII. *The Roman Empire under the Flavians and the Antonines. The City and the Country in the Asiatic and the African Provinces of Rome*

¹ *Studien z. Gesch. röm. Kol.* (1910), pp. 283ff. Fresh documents and valuable observations bearing on the social and economic conditions of Lydia in imperial times were subsequently contributed by J. Keil and A. von Premerstein, 'Bericht über eine dritte Reise in Lydien', *Denkschr. Wien. Akad.* 57, 1914; cf. the inscriptions of Lydia in *IGRR* iv. The agrarian history of Asia Minor in the Republican period and in the early Empire is hardly known. Sir William Ramsay and I proposed the following hypotheses. The royal land (γῆ βασιλική) and the private estates (οὐσίαι) of the Pergamene kings,

and also those of the kings of Bithynia, Pontus, Galatia, Cappadocia, Commagene, &c., became *ager publicus* when these regions were transformed into Roman provinces. Subsequently those parts of the land which had not passed into the ownership of Roman citizens were united in some way with the private patrimony of the Roman emperors (in some parts of Asia Minor, for instance in Galatia, the crown-lands may have passed directly into the hands of the emperors). This hypothesis was challenged by T. Frank, *JRS* 17, 1927, pp. 148 ff., and 156 ff. (followed by H. Dessau, *Gesch. d. röm. Kaiserzeit*, ii. 2, p. 592, note 1); he believes that only the private estates of the Pergamene kings were declared *ager publicus*. The γῆ or χώρα βασιλική remained, according to him, in its previous condition, namely in the hands of γεωργοί who became free tenants (whose?). If by this we are to understand that nothing changed in Asia Minor after its transformation into a Roman province, save that the royal estates were called *ager publicus* and the χώρα βασιλική *ager stipendiarius*, I have no objection to this slight modification of my theory; but if Frank believes that the Roman state recognized a juridical title for the tenants, and recognized their land as their private property, I must reject his theory. Undoubtedly the Roman state claimed exactly the same right of free disposition for the lands which had previously been χώρα βασιλική as for the *ager publicus*; and if such a right was seldom enforced, this was for political and not for juridical reasons. I do not understand how Frank manages to reach the conclusion that the imperial estates were limited to Galatia: we know of large imperial estates in Lydia (Keil–Premerstein, *Dritte Reise*, pp. 287 ff.) and we know that here the tenants said that they were bound to the land by birth: see the petition found at Aga Bey, Keil–Premerstein, 55, l. 47: ἑστίας πατρῴας καὶ τάφους προγονικούς, and ll. 51 ff., τῶν δεσποτικῶν χωρίων ἐν οἷς ‹κ›αὶ ἐγεννήθημεν καὶ ἐτράφημεν. On the origin of the later imperial estates in Lydia, I previously conjectured (*Kolonat*, p. 290) that Augustus inherited large estates in Asia Minor from Antony, and that these later were either sold or became imperial properties. My suggestion was determined by the large number of people in Lydia, both in the cities, and more particularly in the villages, who bear the name Antonius. Dessau, l.c., considered it unlikely that a frivolous wastrel like Antony could have thus administered his estates in Asia Minor: in his opinion the Asiatic Antonii were individuals to whom Antony in a moment of good humour granted citizenship. I cannot share this opinion. His Asiatic possessions were of the greatest importance for Antony, and he could not have granted the citizenship to the inhabitants of villages only because he was personally attracted to them. In general I cannot accept the theory of T. Frank with regard to the *dominium in solo provinciali*. The fact that the provincial land paid *decuma* or *stipendium* in money, when Italy was exempted from direct taxes, shows that there was a fundamental difference between *solum Italicum* and *solum provinciale*. Cf. the observations of E. Schönbauer, *Beiträge zur Geschichte des Bergbaurechtes* (1929), pp. 123 ff., which illustrates the peculiarities of the provincial land-law by analysing the chapter of the *lex agraria* of 111 B.C. referring to Africa. Cf. also M. A. Levi, 'La Sicilia e il dominium in solo provinciali', *Athenaeum*, 7, 1929, pp. 514 ff. Cf. Chap. I, note 20.

² See the inscription of Ephesus belonging to the time of the Emperor Valens, A. Schulten, *Oest. Jahresh.* 9, 1906, pp. 40 ff.; R. Heberdey, ibid., p. 182; Bruns–Gradenwitz, *Fontes*, 7th ed., p. 270, no. 97 [= Riccobono, *FIRA²* 108]. The inscription speaks of the public land of Ephesus which became the property of the *ratio privata*. It is worthy of note that in this late time the land was cultivated to a great extent either by small tenants, who were citizens of the city of Ephesus, or by rich farmers.

³ The description of the territory of a city of Asia Minor (Aphrodisias in Caria), contained in a letter in which Julius Caesar confirmed freedom and *ateleia* on the city,

is typical: *OGIS* 455, l. 14: μεθ' ὧ]ν κωμῶν χωρίων ὀχυρωμάτων ὀρῶν προσόδων ... [ταῦτα ἔχωσ]ιν κρατῶσιν χρῶνται καρπίζωνταί τε πάντων πραγμάτων ἀτε[λεῖς ὄντες ...]. Cf. R. Vagts, *Aphrodisias in Karien* (Diss., Hamburg, 1920). On the peculiar constitution of Caria, with her two leagues, that of Zeus Chrysaor and that of Zeus Panamaros, see H. Dessau, *Gesch. d. röm. Kaiserzeit*, ii. 2, p. 601; H. Oppermann, *Zeus Panamaros* (Religionsgeschicht. Versuche und Vorarbeiten, xix. 3, 1924). The inscriptions of the sanctuary are published by J. Hatzfeld, *BCH* 51, 1927, pp. 57 ff. [= *SEG* iv. 243–387]; cf. *Amer. Journ. Arch.* 32, 1928, p. 517, and P. Roussel, *BCH* 51, 1927, pp. 123 ff. and 55, 1931, pp. 1 ff.

4 Dio Chr. ἀπολογισμός (*Or.* 45), 3: οὐκ ἔξαρνός εἰμι τὸ καὶ συνοικίζειν ἐθέλειν τὴν πόλιν καὶ πλῆθος ἀνθρώπων εἰς αὐτὴν ὅσον δύναμαι συναγαγεῖν, καὶ οὐ μόνον τῶν ἐπιχωρίων ἀλλ' εἰ δυνατὸν ἦν καὶ ἑτέρας πόλεις συνελθεῖν ἀναγκάσαντα (cf. H. von Arnim, *Leben und Werke*, p. 341). Id. *Or.* 35. 14 (on Celaenae): καὶ τοῦτο μὲν πολλὰς τῶν ἀνωνύμων πόλεων, τοῦτο δὲ πολλὰς εὐδαίμονας κώμας ὑπηκόους ἔχετε. Cf. *Or.* 38. 26 on the δεκάται τῶν Βιθυνῶν which the inhabitants of Prusa were obliged to pay to the treasury of the Nicomedians. An admirable documentary illustration of the endeavours of Dio is given by some inscriptions of Prusias ad Hypium in Bithynia, *IGRR* iii. 69 (distributions by a certain T. Ulpius Aelianus Papianus; cf. *PIR* iii, p. 458, nos. 537, 538), l. 19: πᾶσιν τοῖς ἐνκεκριμ[ένοις κ]αὶ τοῖς ἀγρ[ο]ικίαν κατοικοῦσι (cf. l. 26, where the same expression is used except that παροικοῦσι is substituted for κατοικοῦσι); cf. *IGRR* iv, 808 (Hierapolis): καὶ διὰ τ]ῆς τῶν ἰδίων ἀγροίκων βοηθείας. The situation of these πάροικοι or κάτοικοι of Prusias is illustrated by another inscription of the same place (ibid. iii, 65). We meet here with special magistrates called φύλαρχοι (ll. 12 ff.), and we are told that they were ἐπὶ τῆς ὁμονοίας ᾑρημένοι. I am convinced that A. Körte (*Ath. Mitt.* 24, 1899, p. 437) is right in suggesting that these φύλαρχοι were carrying out a συνοικισμός in Dio's sense, including the peasants in the roll of citizens. It is noteworthy that the inscription of Prusias belongs to the times of Septimius Severus, see Chap. IX. On the social and economic standing of the πάροικοι and κάτοικοι, see my *Studien z. Gesch. röm Kol.*, pp. 260 ff.; cf. A. Asboek, *Das Staatswesen von Priene* (1913), pp. 66 ff., and my article in *Anatolian Studies presented to Sir William Ramsay* (1923), p. 376. Their situation in imperial times was no different from what it had been in the Hellenistic period. In the well-known Ephesian inscription of the time after the first Mithradatic war, Dittenberger, *Syll.*[3] 742, ll. 45 f.: εἶναι δὲ καὶ τοὺς ἰσοτελεῖς καὶ παροίκους καὶ ἱεροὺς καὶ ἐξελευθέρους καὶ ξένους, they rank, just as in the equally well-known inscription of Pergamon (*OGIS* 338, l. 20), a little above the public (i.e. the royal or sacred) slaves and the freedmen. The same position was held by the κάτοικοι or πάροικοι in Syllium of Pamphylia in the 2nd cent. (?) A.D., as is shown by the three inscriptions of Menodora, daughter of Megakles, *IGRR* iii. 800–2: in a public distribution the πάροικοι received the same sum or the same amount of corn as the freedmen and the *vindictarii*, while the members of the senate, those of the gerousia, the members of the public assembly (ἐκκλησιασταί), and the common citizens received much more; in no. 802 the πάροικοι are not mentioned at all. In the island of Cos we have almost the same division of the residents of one of the *demoi* of the city, *IGRR* iv. 1087, ll. 4 ff.: τοὶ κατοικεῦντες ἐν τῷ δάμῳ Ἀλεντίων καὶ το[ὶ] | ἐνεκτημένοι καὶ τοὶ γεωργεῦντε[ς] | ἐν Ἀλεντι καὶ Πέλῃ, τῶν τε πολιτᾶν καὶ Ῥωμαίων καὶ μετοίκων. Thus the κατοικεῦντες are the citizens, the ἐνεκτημένοι the Romans, and the γεωργεῦντες the μέτοικοι. It would be worth while to collect all the evidence on the subject, which of course cannot be done here. A good beginning has been made in the excellent article Κώμη of H. Swoboda in Pauly–Wissowa, Suppl. iv, cols. 950 ff.; on the κῶμαι in Asia and in Syria, pp. 961 ff. Of course, the evidence I have quoted concerns especially the political and social condition of the κάτοικοι: of

their economic condition we hear little. We do not know the fate in Roman times of the λαοί of the Hellenistic age. Juridically and politically they, as well as the inhabitants of the cities, were subjects of the Roman state. Dessau, however (*Gesch. d. röm. Kaiserzeit*, ii. 2, p. 599, note 1), did not manage to prove that all trace of personal serfdom had disappeared in the Roman period. It is difficult to accept that the πάροικοι and κάτοικοι of the Roman period were landowners. They were probably still, as they had been in the Hellenistic age, tenants of the cities or the landowners, perhaps better defended against the abuses of the landlords by the Roman government than they had been in the Hellenistic age. I do not agree with Dessau that the δεκάται of the Bithynians in Dio Chryostom (see above) were taxes paid to the state by provincials; but the passage is obscure.

⁵ See my *Studien z. Gesch. röm. Kol.*, pp. 269 ff. (the temples), pp. 287 ff. (the emperors), p. 311 (private landowners). In Roman times the first of these three classes survived only in the remotest parts of Asia Minor; that it ever totally disappeared is uncertain: see note 6. I give here some additional evidence on the third class. At Zelea in Phrygia lived a certain Myrinus (*BCH* 17, 1893, p. 530 = *IGRR* iv. 186). In his funeral inscription his career is described as follows (according to my own restoration of the text):
. . . Μυρίνου πραγματευ[τοῦ] Κλ(αυδίας) Βάσσης· ἐπιδεδ[εγμένος πλόας εἰς] Ἰταλίαν Ῥώμην ις', Γε[. . . . .] β', ἐπὶ τὴν ὄχθην δ', Δαλμα[τία]ν, Ἰστρίαν, Λιβυρνίαν β', Ἀλεξάνδρειαν τὴν κατ' Αἴγυπτον β', καὶ τὰ τούτων ἀνὰ μέσον, φορικὰ χρήματα πράξας ἔτη λε', αὐτῷ ἐποίησε ζῶν.
Ziebarth, in note 1 to Dittenberger, *Syll.*³ 1229, suggests that Myrinus was a merchant. According to my restoration he was an *actor* of a noble woman Claudia Bassa (the family is known as a senatorial family of the 2nd cent.: *CIL* vi. 3829 and 31697, Claudius Bassus Capitolinus, cons. suff. in an unknown year), who was certainly a rich landowner in Asia Minor; cf. the inscription of Tralles, *Ath. Mitt.* 21, 1896, p. 113, no. 3, set up in honour of a woman who was perhaps the wife or a relative of Cl(audius) Capitolinus. It is evident that Myrinus, the *actor* of Claudia Bassa, collected the rent of her estates all his life long (thirty-five years). He undertook journeys to Italy and to other places to convey the money to his mistress, and to manage her affairs in other provinces where she had economic interests. Other instances of faithful managers of rich families: Trophenius, manager or private tutor of the wealthy Ephesian family of the famous sophist Flavius Damianus, *Forsch. Eph.* iii, pp. 163 ff., nos. 82–85; a προοικος of Telmessus, who died at the age of 110, *SEG* ii. 690; cf. ibid. 747; a πραγματεύτης of Sardis, *Ath. Mitt.* 21, 1896, p. 112, no. 1, who, in honour of a distinguished lady, τὸν ἀνδριάντα| ἀνέστησεν ἐν τῷ ἔρ[γ]ῳ τῷ ἰδίῳ αὐτῆς (l. 16); an οἰκονόμος of another lady described as κρατίστη, to whom the κώμη Ὀκαηνῶν in Bithynia pays honour (L. Robert, *BCH* 52, 1928, p. 412, no. III), cf. *CIG* 4258 [= *TAM* ii, 518] (Pinara in Lycia). Other examples in P. Landvogt, *Epigraph. Untersuchungen über den Οἰκονόμος* (Diss., Strassburg, 1908), and L. Robert, l.c., p. 414. Cf. *Cod. Th.* vi. 2. 11 (A.D. 395): 'omnes senatores qui in sacratissima urbe consistunt, licet habeant per longinquas provincias atque diversas possessiones, aurum oblaticium in urbe persolvant quod a procuratoribus et actoribus suis ad urbem reditus perferuntur.' This provincial aristocracy of landowners was probably mostly of local origin, descendants of rich municipal landowners. We know scores of them, e.g. *IGRR* iii. 422 (Ariassus); 451 (Termessus) [= *TAM* iii, 185]; 498, 499, and 1506 (well restored by L. Robert, *BCH* 52, 1928, pp. 416 ff., no. V) (Oenoanda); 477 (in Lycia); cf. 478; 528 (Lydae) [= *TAM* ii, 157]; 576 [= ibid. 532] (Pinara); 583 [= ibid. 188] (Sidyma); cf. 585 [= ibid. 190]; 679 (Patara; the famous Opramoas, whom the inscription shows to have been a rich landowner) [= ibid. 578]; iv. 1302 (the landowner L. Vaccius L. f. Aem. Labeo of Kyme); W. M. Calder, *MAMA* i, 24 (*praedia Quadratiana*: estates of the first Roman consul from Asia Minor, Antius Quadratus: in the 3rd cent. imperial estates); R. d'Orbeliani,

JHS 44, 1924, p. 42, no. 76 = *L'An. ép.* 1924, 21 (C. Aelius Flavianus Simplicius Protus, *Galetarches*, especially ll. 9 ff.: ἐν [το]ῖς ἰδίοις αὐτοῦ κτίσμασιν, &c.). Cf. A. Stein, 'Zur sozialen Stellung der provinzialen Oberpriestern' in Ἐπιτύμβιον *H. Swoboda dargebracht* (1927), pp. 300 ff. Cf. L. Robert, loc. cit., and W. M. Calder, 'A Galatian Estate of the Sergii Paulli', *Klio*, 24, 1930, pp. 59 ff.

[6] Some examples may be quoted of temples in Asia Minor which were attached to cities and yet owned large tracts of land. I leave aside the temples of the former kingdom of Pergamon enumerated in my article in *Anatolian Studies presented to Sir William Ramsay*, pp. 370 f. A full list would be useful and easy to compile, but cannot be given here. (1) The Ephesian temple had large lands of its own, see J. Keil and A. von Premerstein, *Dritte Reise*, pp. 82 ff.; p. 96, no. 137; p. 98, no. 146. Cf. Dittenberger, *Syll.*³ 742, l. 34; *Forsch Eph.* iii, p. 137, no. 50 (with references to other inscriptions). (2) Athena at Ilion possessed land, *OGIS* 440 = Dessau, 8770 = *IGRR* iv. 194 and 197; cf. Dittenberger, *Syll.*³ 747 (Amphiaraus at Oropus, A.D. 73). (3) Pergamon, temple of Athena and of Dionysos, *IGRR* iv. 304 and 397. (4) Temple of Zeus at Aezani, *CIL* iii. 356 (14191) = *OGIS* 502 = *IGRR* iv. 571. (5) Aegae in Lydia, *IGRR* iv. 1117. (6) Hierocaesarea in Lydia, ibid. 1306. (7) Castabala (Hierapolis) in Cilicia, ibid. iii. 904. (8) Stratonikeia in Caria (Zeus-Hekate), Le Bas–Waddington, 518 (cf. above, note 3). All these temples were attached to a city and yet owned extensive tracts of land. Still more extensive were the estates of the independent temples, of which I have spoken at length in my book on the Colonate. Other smaller temples of Asia Minor also still preserved under the Romans their ownership of one or more villages. A noteworthy group of inscriptions is that consisting of the so-called 'expiatory inscriptions' of Maeonia, which have been much studied (most recently by J. Zingerle, 'Heiliges Recht', *Oest. Jahresh.* 23, 1926, Beibl. pp. 6 ff., with bibliography; the same scholar studies another group of similar inscriptions ibid. 24, 1929, Beibl. pp. 107 ff.). Apparently some of the ancient temples of this region still preserved in the first centuries of our era a form of jurisdiction over the peasants of the villages on their estates; it is, however, certain that such jurisdiction was never recognized as such by the government, and the sanctions had only a religious character. The inscription, no. 1 in Zingerle, l.c., is of considerable interest: in it Anaitis (not her companion, Men Tiamu) appears as Ἄζιτα (the name of the village) κατέχουσα, and the individuals who are engaged in a law-suit are ἀπὸ Σύρου μάνδρων: cf. the other instances quoted by Zingerle; Keil–Premerstein, *Zweite Reise*, p. 103, no. 204: Men and Anaitis Δώρου κώμην βασιλεύοντες; ibid., p. 105: μέγας [Μὴν] Πετραείτην [τὴν κώμην βα]σιλεύων. Cf. W. M. Ramsay, 'Anatolica Quaedam'; x, Temples in Anatolia', *JHS* 50, 1930, pp. 275 ff.

[7] I shall return to the subject of village life in the eleventh chapter. Modern books contain no list of the villages which existed in Asia Minor in imperial times. Those which could be identified with existing remains are enumerated in the text to the large map of Asia Minor by H. Kiepert, *Formae Orbis Antiqui*, map IX, cf. VIII, and are recorded on the maps. A good list of κατοικίαι may be found in the article 'Κάτοικοι' by F. Oertel in Pauly–Wissowa, xi, cols. 1 ff. The terminology of rural life in Asia Minor is complicated: κατοικία, κώμη, τρικωμία, τετρακωμία, πεντακωμία, τετραπυργία, &c., are of frequent occurrence. A group of villages, e.g., which formed one δῆμος (cf. *CIL* iii. 14191) [= *OGIS* 519] is attested at Girindi, *CIL* iii. 282 = *IGRR* iii. 154 (near Ancyra); the centre of this group is formed by a μεσοκώμιον (A.D. 145). As in Gaul, we meet also the *vicini* in Bithynia: ἡ . . . οτα . |ηνῶν γειτοσ[ύ]νη (*IGRR* iii. 50), not to be confounded with the *vicini* of the city of Antioch in Syria. A typical example of a flourishing village is afforded by the κώμη Φιλαδελφέων in the famous Καστωλοῦ πεδίον (*OGIS* 488). It is important to note that the κώμη as such owns land:

γενο|μένης ἐκκλησίας ὑπὸ τῆς γερουσίας | καὶ τῶν λοιπῶν κωμητῶν πάντων καὶ βουλευσαμέ-
νων αὐτῶν διελέσθαι τὸν ὑπ[άρ|χ]οντα αὐτοῖς ἀγρὸν ἐν τοῖς ἰδίοις ὅροις | [τό]πῳ τῷ λεγομένῳ
Ἀγάθωνος μά[νδ]ραις | [ὄ]ντα ὀρινόν. This shows that not all villages were situated on
imperial land or on the land of a city. Some may have formed independent territories. In any case many of them, as in Africa, had the right of a juristic person, see
E. Weiss, *Zeitschr. d. Sav.-St.* 36, 1915, p. 170; F. Preisigke, *Girowesen* (1910), p. 80;
M. San Nicolò, *Ägyptisches Vereinswesen*, i (1913), pp. 166 ff.; L. Mitteis, *Röm. Privatrecht*,
i, p. 376; L. Wenger, *Stellvertretung*, p. 113. A good instance of villages attached to
cities is *OGIS* 527, or, again, *IGRR* iv. 1237, where a magistrate of Thyatira was
honoured with an altar and a statue by the Ἀρηνοί and Νάγδημοι ἐπὶ τῷ ἐ[κ]δικῆσαι
καὶ ἀποκαταστῆσαι τὰ τῶν κωμῶν. Clearly the villages were inhabited by natives.
Another prosperous village, probably belonging to the city of Perga, was the
Kome Lyrboton in Pamphylia (see J. Keil, 'Die Lyrboton Kome in Pamphylien',
Oest. Jahresh. 23, 1926, Beibl. pp. 89 ff.). A wealthy family of the district which owned
much land in the territory of the village, and was particularly prominent in olive-
growing, built a tower which served as a place of refuge (πύργος ἀσύλωτος) for the
village; later, under Domitian (Keil, loc. cit., no. 1), the building was repaired; still later,
under Hadrian, the same family dedicated two plots of land to the temple of the local
God Apollo (Keil, l.c., nos. 2 and 3). It is interesting to note that the territory of this
village, like that of Philadelphia, was divided into τόποι, and that the corporation
which controlled it was composed of γεραιοί. From time to time the place was visited
by soldiers, who at times behaved in a positively friendly manner (Keil, l.c., no. 4).
Good examples of imperial villages are the Χαρμιδεανοί, *IGRR* iii. 17, set up ὑπὲρ τῶν
δεσποτῶν (the emperors), cf. 18 and 36 (A.D. 138–61); and Karalar in Galatia, ibid.
iii. 153: Αὐρ[η]λι[α]|[νοὶ] ὑπὲρ | νίκη[ς] | τῶν κυρί|ων [κ(αὶ)] ὑπὲρ ἑαυτῶν κ(αὶ) τῶν ἰδίων
τ[ε]τραπόδων. An important group of imperial estates had its centre in Laodicea
Combusta (see W. M. Calder, *MAMA* i, p. xiii). Compare the δῆμος Μοξεανῶν
in Phrygia, an imperial possession bordering on the great imperial estates of the
Tembrogius valley; this had two centres, Siocharax and Diocleia, which developed into cities (Siocharax coined for the δῆμος Μοξεανῶν), *JHS* 4, 1883, p. 422.
An instance of a village, the territory of which was apparently owned by a
private citizen, a prominent man of the province of Asia, Domninus Rufus, Asiarch
and *strategos* of the city of Sardis (*B.M. Catal. Coins of Lydia*, Sardes, nos. 206–11 belonging to A.D. 253–68), is furnished by an inscription of Kula, *IGRR* iv. 1381, recording
permission granted to Domninus by the proconsul to institute a monthly fair in
the village. As is well known, similar inscriptions are very frequent in Africa;
cf. A. Besnier in Daremberg–Saglio, iv, pp. 122 ff. Another case of a self-governing
village on a private estate in *IGRR* iv. 1492; cf. H. Swoboda in Pauly–Wissowa,
Suppl. iv, cols. 961 ff.

[8] On Cilicia, D. Vaglieri, *Diz. epigr.* ii, p. 222; cf. Chap. V, note 4. On Cappadocia,
id. ibid., pp. 95 ff., and Ruge in Pauly–Wissowa, x, cols. 1910 ff.; cf. my *Studien z. Gesch.
röm. Kol.*, p. 282, and W. E. Gwatkin, *Cappadocia as a Roman procuratorial province* (1930).
In this book, pp. 18 ff., Gwatkin has collected the texts which refer to the estates which
had belonged to Archelaus, the last king of Cappadocia, and which passed to the
Roman emperors; on p. 17 the author gives a general picture of the social structure of Cappadocia in the 1st cent. A.D. The social conditions of Cappadocia are
illustrated by the short notice in *Scr. Hist. Aug.* Hadr. 13. 7–10: 'deinde a Cappa-
docibus servitia castris profutura suscepit.' It is evident that *servitia* means serfs
of the native aristocracy and of the temples. On Commagene and its social and
economic constitution, see the well-known inscription of Nemrûd-Dagh (69–34 B.C.),
OGIS 383 = B. Laum, *Stiftungen*, ii, no. 210, ll. 94 ff. = R. Jalabert and R. Mouterde,

Inscr. gr. et lat. de la Syrie, i. 1: βασιλείας δὲ πλῆθος | εἰς συναγωγὰς καὶ πανηγύρεις | καὶ θυσίας ταύτας διελὼν κατὰ | κώμας καὶ πόλεις τοῖς ἔγγιστα | τεμένεσιν. Villages were assigned by the king to the gods, ll. 191 ff.: ὁμοίως δὲ | μηδὲ κώμας, ἃς ἐγὼ καθειέρωσα | δαίμοσιν τούτοις, μηδενὶ | ὅσιον ἔστω μήτε ἐξιδιά|σασθαι μήτε ἐξαλλοτριῶσαι | μήτε μεταδιατάξαι μήτε | βλάψαι κατὰ μηδένα τρόπον κώ|μας ἐκείνας | ἢ πρόσοδον ἢν ἐγὼ κτῆμα δαιμόνων | ἄσυλον ἀνέθηκα. Both passages show to what an extent life in Commagene was rural, and how largely the main form of social life was that of a village. The feudal structure of this kingdom, like that of the other half-Iranian kingdoms of Asia Minor, is made evident by ll. 171 ff., of the same inscription: μηδενὶ δὲ ὅσιον | ἔστω μήτε βασιλεῖ μήτε δυνάστει μή|τε ἱερεῖ μήτε ἄρχοντι τού|τους ἱεροδούλους, κ.τ.λ.; cf. l. 228, and Jalabert and Mouterde, op. cit., no. 47, col. iv, 5, and no. 51 [= *BSA* 47, 1952, pp. 96 ff.]. βασιλεύς and δυνάστης represent the regal power in the land, ἱερεῖς that of the priests, ἄρχοντες that of the cities. Cf. A. Wilhelm, 'Inschriften des Königs Antiochos von Kommagene aus Samosata', *Wiener Studien*, 47, 1929, pp. 127 ff.; Honigmann in Pauly–Wissowa, Suppl. iv, cols. 978 ff. On Armenia, see J. de Morgan, *Histoire du peuple arménien* (1919); J. Sandalgian, *Histoire documentaire de l'Arménie des âges du paganisme* (1917); my *Studien z. Gesch. röm. Kol.*, p. 282, and F. Cumont, *Anatol. Studies presented to Sir William Ramsay* (1923), pp. 109 ff.; cf. id. *C. R. Acad. Inscr.* 1905, p. 93, and Th. Reinach, ibid., p. 332. In the 4th and 6th cent. A.D. Armenia was still governed by satraps as it had been in the Persian and the Hellenistic periods. I cannot here enter into the interesting question of the social structure of the Iberians and of the Greek cities of Colchis. See my *Studien z. Gesch. röm. Kol.*, pp. 281 ff. (with bibliography); cf. S. Gargazé, 'Essais sur l'histoire de la Géorgie', *Mém. de la Soc. Géorg. d'hist. et d'ethnogr.* 1, 1909, pt. 2, pp. 43 ff.; T. von Margwelaschwili, *Colchis, Iberien und Albanien um die Wende des I. Jahrv. v. Chr.*, &c. (diss. Halle, 1914); D. Magie, *Ann. Rev. Amer. Hist. Ass. 1919*, 1 (1923), pp. 295 ff.; S. Kakabazé, 'Problème de l'origine de l'État géorgien', *Bull. Hist.* (Tiflis, 1924), pp. 9 ff.; A. Amiranscvili, *Bull. of the Acad. for Material Culture*, 5, 1927, p. 409 (in Russian).

⁹ M. Rostovtzeff, *Iranians and Greeks in South Russia* (1922).

¹⁰ The division of the land into κλῆροι with fortified villas, which occupied the fertile territory of the Heraclean peninsula and were protected by walls and small fortresses and towers against the inroads of the Taurians, is shown by the abundant remains of the delimitation-walls of the single κλῆροι, which date at least from the 4th cent. B.C. and form a well-organized system, see Z. Arkas, 'Description of the Heraclean Peninsula and its Antiquities', *Transactions of the Hist. Soc. of Odessa*, 2, 1845, reprinted in 1879, Nicolaev (in Russian, with map); P. Becker, *Die Herakleotische Peninsula* (Leipzig, 1856); N. M. Pechonkin, 'Archaeological Excavations on the Site of Strabo's Old Chersonese', *Bull. de la Comm. arch. de Russie*, pp. 108 ff. (in Russian); cf. *Arch. Anz.* 1911, p. 206, and K. Grinevič, *Exhibition of the Results of the Excavations in the Peninsula of Heraclea* (from 7 Aug. to 7 Sept. 1929) (in Russian). The remains of the country-houses excavated by N. M. Pechonkin attest an intensive cultivation of the vine, cf. *IOSPE* i², 343, ll. 10 ff. (procession of the citizens of Chersonesus with wives and children in honour of Dionysos). The fertile land near the city is called πεδίον in the well-known oath of the Chersonesites, ibid. 401, ll. 47 ff.; on its division into κλῆροι (ἑκατώρυγοι) and the sale or letting of these κλῆροι, ibid. 403.

¹¹ E. von Stern, 'Die politische und soziale Struktur der Griechenkolonien am Nordufer des Schwarzmeergebietes', *Hermes*, 50, 1915, pp. 161 ff. Conditions at Olbia at the end of the 1st cent. A.D. are excellently described in the Borysthenitic oration of Dio Chrysost. xxxvi. Unfortunately von Stern does not quote this work in his study (though he made use of it). The notices of Dio correspond exactly, some romantic exaggeration apart, with the picture of the Greco-Sarmatian city provided by the archaeological and epigraphical material from Olbia. The lack of security which

reigned before the arrival of a Roman garrison is admirably described. H. Dessau (*Gesch. d. röm. Kaiserzeit*, ii. 2, p. 534, note) over-emphasizes the fantastic element in Dio's picture: not even the Olbian 'Homerolatry' is an invention; this is shown by the use in the Roman period of such names as Achilles (*IOSPE* i², 237; note to the name Olbia Brizais, and the index of the names). Apart from the *Ex Ponto* of Ovid, Dio's description is the only literary evidence we have for the Sarmato-Greek cities of the Black Sea coasts. Although in the 2nd cent. A.D. Tyras and Olbia enjoyed comparative prosperity under the protection of Roman garrisons of the army of Moesia Inferior, the perpetual movement of the Sarmatian and Teutonic tribes in the steppes of South Russia hampered the development of these cities. We know of several attacks which were repulsed by the Roman forces. Already at the beginning of the 3rd cent. the situation was critical: see my article in *Bull. Comm. Arch.* 58, 1915 (in Russian), pp. 1 ff., and *SEG* iii. 584; an inscription in honour of an *evocatus*, who ὑπὸ τῶν ἡγουμένων (the governor? the emperor?) had been sent to Olbia περὶ πραγμάτων ἀναγκαίων (containing questions concerning the security of the city); cf. *IOSPE* i², 167, 236–7, 322, 687. On Tyras and its relations with Rome see P. Nicorescu, *Eph. Dacorom.* 2, 1924, pp. 394 ff. = *SEG* iii. 565, a fragment of a letter or imperial edict in which there is a reference to the barbarians and their assaults. In the same article some moulds of bricks of Roman legions are published, identical with those from Olbia published by me. On Olbia see further B. Krueger, *Bull. of Acad. for Mater. Culture*, 4, 1925, pp. 81 ff. (in Russian); *SEG* iii. 583, a decree for a man who in a moment of grave peril which threatened Olbia took part in an embassy, cf. *IOSPE* i², 687 and 223. The Roman military occupation of Tyras under Trajan is attested by the interesting *pridianum* of the *cohors I Hispanorum*: see A. Hunt, *Raccolto Lumbroso* (1925), pp. 265 ff., 1. 57; G. Cantacuzène, *Aegyptus*, 9, 1928, pp. 91 ff. A Roman military road led from the Danube (Porolissum) to Tyras, and later even to Olbia: see the interesting map which decorated a painted shield found at Dura: F. Cumont, *Fouilles de Doura-Europos*, pp. 323 ff.

¹² M. Rostovtzeff, *Iranians and Greeks* (1922), pp. 159 ff.; E. von Stern, op. cit., pp. 211 ff.; E. H. Minns, *Scythians and Greeks* (1913), pp. 612 ff.

¹³ This is attested by the well-known inscription of King Rhoemetalces, B. Latyshev, *IOSPE* ii, 353 (A.D. 151): Τιβέριος Ἰούλιος βασιλεὺς | Ῥοιμητάλκης, φιλόκαισαρ καὶ φι|λορώμαιος, εὐσεβής, τὰς ὑπὸ | Ληποδώρου ἀνατεθείσας γέας | ἐν Θιαννέοις καὶ τοὺς πελάτας | κατὰ τὸν παρακείμενον τελαμῶ|να χρόνῳ μειωθέντα συναθροί|σας ἅπαντα καὶ πλεονάσας ἀπε|κατέστησε τῆι θ[ε]ῶι σῶα, δι' ἐπι|μελεί[α]ς Ἀ[λ]εξάνδρου Μυρείνου | τοῦ ἐπὶ τῶν ἱερῶν. ημυ', μηνὶ | Ἀπελλαίωι κ', cf. E. H. Minns, op. cit., p. 655, no. 49 The word πελάτης is used in the same sense by Plutarch, *Crassus*, 21, with reference to the Parthians. On the προσπελάται of the Illyrians cf. Chap. VI, note 63. The word πελάτης was, of course, used to define the position of enslaved peasants in the time of Solon. With this inscription we may compare another discovered at Kytaea or Kytai, a little town near Panticapaeum (on the south), in which a former superintendent of the stables (πρὶν ἐπὶ τοῦ ἱππῶνος) of the Bosporan king Ininhimeus dedicates (in A.D. 234) a temple, with an οἶκος and a περίαυλον (the description recalls the plan of the temples of Atargatis and Artemis at Dura), and a sum of 22 *aurei*, to the god βροντῶν ἐπήκοος: B. Latyshev, *Bull. of Acad. for Mater. Culture*, 2, 1922, pp. 84 ff. (in Russian) = *SEG* ii. 481; a reproduction of the sacrificial table on which the inscription is written is given by J. J. Marti, 'Ruins of Cities of the Bosporan Kingdom on the South of Kertch: Cymmericum, Cytaia, Acra', *Bull. of the Tauric Soc. of History, Archaeology and Ethnology*, 2 (59), 1928, p. 12, fig. 12, cf. 13 (in Russian).

¹⁴ This picture is based wholly on archaeological material, M. Rostovtzeff, *Iranians and Greeks*, pl. xxviii, 1 (a landowner in the steppes), pl. xxix, 1, 2, 3 (battles between

Panticapaeans and Taurians and Scythians). Wagons: E. H. Minns, op. cit., pp. 50 ff., figs. 5, 6, cf. p. 310, and E. von Stern in *Bobrinskoy Miscellanea* (1911), pp. 13 ff. (in Russian).

¹⁵ B. Latyshev, *Bull. de la Comm. arch. de Russie*, 37, p. 38, no. 2; E. H. Minns, op. cit., p. 655, no. 51 (Sauromates II): dedication to Poseidon by the *thiasus* of the Gorgippian shipowners and merchants (ναύκληροι), which mentions that the king honoured the *thiasus* and the god by paying an entrance-fee of 1,000 artabae of corn (εἰσαγωγίου ἀρταβῶν χιλίων). The precise meaning of the word εἰσαγώγιον is not clear. The payment may have been made by the king as a new member of the association of the *naukleroi*, as a charge for initiation (Minns), or, as is more likely, the money was a gift of the king to the college, consisting of the remission of the εἰσαγώγιον—import-tax—on 1,000 artabae of corn, as a favour to the corn-importers (Latyschev). One must suppose that the tax was paid on the corn imported from the χώρα to one of the ports of the Bosporan kingdom. On Bithynia and Bosporus, M. Rostovtzeff, 'Pontus, Bithynia, and the Bosporus', *BSA* 22, 1916–18, pp. 1–22; cf. W. Schur, *Die Orientpolitik des Kaisers Nero, Klio*, Beiheft 15, 1923, pp. 85 ff.

¹⁶ I dealt with the Scythian kingdom of Skiluros and his successors in a special book on the political history of South Russia which was ready in 1914 but has never been printed. The capital of the Scythian kings in the Crimea has been partly excavated (*Extract from a Report on the Arch. Excavations of 1853* (Petersburg, 1895), pp. 129 ff. (in Russian); cf. *C. R. de la Comm. Arch.* 1889, pp. 20 ff., and 1895, p. 19 (also in Russian)). The inscriptions found during these excavations are dedications either by the kings or by a rich merchant of Olbia (Posideos), all of the 2nd cent B.C., *IOSPE* i², nos. 668–73 (from Neapolis), and the introduction of Latyschev; cf. ibid., nos. 77, 78, and 168 (from Olbia). There is no doubt that the relations between Olbia and the Scythian kingdom of the Crimea were the same in the Roman period. Large corn-export presumes a fair cultivation of the fertile land of the Northern Crimea. M. Rostovtzeff, *Iranians and Greeks*, p. 162.

¹⁷ On the war between the Romans and the Siracians (a Sarmatian tribe) see Tac. *Ann.* xii. 15–21. Zorzines, king of the Siracians, offered to deliver to Aquila 10,000 'slaves' in return for the lives of the free men, cf. M. Rostovtzeff, op. cit., p. 164. The slaves were of course the πελάται, the natives, like the προσπελάται of the Ardiaeans, cf. above, note 13.

¹⁸ M. Rostovtzeff, op. cit., pp. 167 ff. On the garrisons of Chersonesus and of the castle of Charax (Ai-Tudor), see *IOSPE* I², 404, 417, 547–562, and pp. 509 ff.

¹⁹ On archaeological investigations in Syria, see the works quoted in Chap. V, note 4. On the history of Syria as a Roman province see J. Dobiáš, *Histoire de la province Romaine de Syrie*, i (1929, in Czech, with a French summary).

²⁰ Jul. *Misop.* 362 C: μυρίους κλήρους γῆς ἰδίας κεκτημένη; cf. 370 D, where it is stated that 3,000 κλῆροι, alleged to be unsown (ἄσποροι), were taken by the rich landowners without payment of a rent, probably as emphyteutic land (i.e. tax-free for a certain time under the obligation of cultivating it). Julian also speaks repeatedly of the members of the Antiochean senate as very rich landowners who opposed the measures taken by him to establish normal prices for products of the first necessity, *Misop.* 350; cf. E. S. Bouchier, *Syria*, p. 63, and *Short History of Antioch*, p. 152.

²¹ A short description of the villas in the neighbourhood of Apamea and Antiochia may be found in E. Littmann, *Ruinenstätten und Schriftdenkmäler Syriens* (1917), p. 31; cf. H. C. Butler in the books quoted in Chap. V, note 4. The description of these villas

given by St. John Chrysostom (*In Acta Apost.* 45 [*PG* 60], p. 343 D) suits excellently the still existing and beautifully preserved ruins.

²² St. John Chrysostom, *In Matth.* 66 [*PG* 58], p. 657 E; 85 [*PG* ibid.], p. 810 A. A typical fortune of a rich senator of Antiochia is described by him in his sermon *In Matth.* 63 [*PG* ibid.], p. 633 C: large tracts of land, 10 to 20 houses and baths, 1,000 to 2,000 slaves, cf. J. Milton Vance, *Beiträge zur byzantinischen Kulturgeschichte* (1907), p. 66. The sermons *In Matth.* belong to the Antiochean period of the life of Chrysostom, M. von Bonsdorff, *Predigtthätigkeit des Johannes Chrysostomus* (Helsinki, 1922), pp. 14 ff.

²³ The classical passage is St. John Chrysostom, *In Matth.* 61 [*PG* 58], pp. 614 A ff.; cf. *In Acta Apost.* 18 [*PG* 60], p. 150 C, and J. M. Vance, op. cit., pp. 48 ff. (good translation of the passage). According to the picture of St. John (*In Matth.* 61) the tenants of the land were subject to heavy payments, which were exacted in the most merciless way (καὶ τελέσματα διηνεκῆ καὶ ἀφόρητα ἐπιτιθέασι), and to personal services (καὶ διακονίας ἐπιπόνους ἐπιτάττουσι). The exactors were the procurators of the owners (καὶ τοῦ λιμοῦ τούτου καὶ τοῦ ναυαγίου τὰς τῶν ἐπιτρόπων βασάνους καὶ τοὺς ἑλκυσμοὺς καὶ τὰς ἀπαιτήσεις καὶ τὰς ἀπαγωγὰς καὶ τὰς ἀπαραιτήτους λειτουργίας μᾶλλον δεδοικότες καὶ φρίττοντες). There is no hint of the peasants' being obliged to work for the landowners under the provisions of a general law. Their obligations seem to have been of a purely private character, the most powerful weapon of the rich being loans at high interest (καινὰ δὲ καὶ γένη τόκων ἐπινοοῦσι, καὶ οὐδὲ τοῖς Ἑλλήνων νόμοις νενομισμένα, καὶ δανεισμάτων γραμματεῖα πολλῆς γέμοντα τῆς ἀρᾶς συντιθέασι. οὐδὲ γὰρ ἑκατοστὴν τοῦ παντός, ἀλλὰ τὸ ἥμισυ τοῦ παντός, ἀπαιτεῖν βιάζονται). In the vineyards the peasants worked for money (ἀπὸ μὲν τῶν πόνων αὐτῶν καὶ ἱδρώτων ληνοὺς καὶ ὑπολήνια πληροῦντες, αὐτοῖς δὲ οἴκαδε οὐδὲ ὀλίγον εἰσαγαγεῖν ἐπιτρέποντες μέτρον . . . καὶ ὀλίγον αὐτοῖς ὑπὲρ τούτου προσριπτοῦντες ἀργύριον). Cf. the methods of the Turks in Syria before 1914 as described by C. L. Woolley (see Chap. III, note 25).

²⁴ Jul. *Or.* ii, p. 91 D; Lib. *Or.* iii. 328; Jul. *Misop.* 368 ff. (the πλούσιοι are the rich landowners); and St. John Chrysostom, *passim*. The position of a peasant was the lowest on the social ladder, less enviable than even that of the most despised city proletarian, as the peasants were the main taxpayers, Sozom. [*PG* 67], v. 4: τὸ δὲ πλῆθος τῶν Χριστιανῶν σὺν γυναιξὶ καὶ παισὶν ἀπογράψασθαι καὶ καθάπερ ἐν ταῖς κώμαις φόρους τελεῖν.

²⁵ Malalas, xvii, p. 420 (under Justinus): τινὲς δὲ ἐκ τῶν πολιτῶν τῶν σωθέντων (after the earthquake), εἴ τι ἠδυνήθησαν, ἀφείλαντο καὶ ἔφευγον· καὶ ὑπήντουν αὐτοῖς γεωργοὶ καὶ ἀπέσπων παρ' αὐτῶν φονεύοντες αὐτούς, cf. Sozom. vii, 15, about the peasants killing Marcellus bishop of Apamea; besides pagan feelings, their chief motive was hatred of the city lords, who interfered in their life.

²⁶ It would be useless to enumerate the names of the villages in the territories of Apamea and Antiochia. Some of these names are recorded by K. O. Müller, *Antiquitates Antiochenae*, p. 233, note; cf. E. Kuhn, *Städtische und bürgerliche Verfassung des röm. Reiches*, ii, p. 317, note 2781; cf. p. 321, note 2818, and Malalas, xiii, p. 347. Many are mentioned in the inscriptions of Roman soldiers (E. de Ruggiero, *Diz. epigr.*, s.v. Antiochia), some are recorded in the inscriptions of Syrian Christians, residing in Northern Italy (Keune in Pauly–Wissowa, x, cols. 1918 ff.); cf. R. Egger, *Forschungen in Salona*, ii, p. 100, no. 217, a Syrian family of Apamea at Salona. On the Syrian villages in general see G. McLean Harper, 'Village Administration in Syria', *Yale Class. Stud.* 1, 1928, pp. 105 ff.; A. H. M. Jones, 'The Urbanization of the Ituraean Principality', *JRS* 21, 1931, p. 265, who has not utilized Harper's work. There is no doubt that, besides small free landowners, these villages were inhabited by some rich men, and that some land attached to the villages was owned by rich landowners who lived in Antiochia or Apamea; see St. John Chrysostom, *In Acta Apost.* 18 [*PG* 60], p. 149 E. It is probable that the ancient village on the site of the modern Niha (*CIL* iii. 14384, 2;

cf. 14384, 1) with a temple of the local Baal (Hadaran) belonged to the territory of Berytus. A man who was a decurio, quaestor, and flamen of this city died in the village of Niha, which shows that he used to live in the village and had landed property there (ibid. iii. 14384. 3); cf. Strabo, 16. 756 C; R. Mouterde, *Mél. de l'Univ. St. Joseph*, 12, 1927, p. 287. Small landowners of northern Syria appear in an inscription of Il-Anderin, *Public. of the Princeton University Arch. Exped. to Syria*, Div. III, Sec. B (Northern Syria), no. 918: τὸ λουτρὸν Θωμᾶς τ[οῦτ]' αὖ πάντων πρὸς χάρι[ν] | [ἐγὼ] πᾶσιν δέδωκα τοῖς γεω[μόροις]; cf. ibid. 881: Abbosus the κωμάρχης, cf. 874, 875.

27 Baitocaece: *CIL* iii. 184, Addit., p. 972 = *IGRR* iii. 1020 = *OGIS* 262 [= ll. 1–17, Laum, *Stiftungen*, ii. 209 = Welles, *Royal Corresp.* 70]. One of the villages probably attached to the temple of Doliche, *CIL* iii. 3490. An interesting description of two villages in the territory of the northern Chalcis, Litarba and Batna, may be found in the well-known letter of the emperor Julian, *Ep.* 27 (J. Bidez and F. Cumont, p. 155, no. 98). A large and prosperous village near Baalbek, Κώμη Χάμων, is mentioned in *CIL* iii. 14162, 2 and p. 2328, 74 = *IGRR* iii. 1074 (A.D. 172). On Chalcis and Abila of the Lebanon district, see Benzinger in Pauly–Wissowa, i, cols. 98f., and iii, col. 2091; cf. Beer, ibid. ix, cols. 2378ff.; and A. H. M. Jones, in the article quoted in note 26. A delimitation of territory between the Caesarenses ad Libanum and the Gigarteni de vico Sidoniorum, *CIL* iii. 183.

28 Chap. III, note 15, and Chap. V, notes 20 and 34. The villages and estates of the Palmyrene territory are mentioned in the tariff of Palmyra, *IGRR* iii. 1056, IVa, ll. 47 ff.: τῶν βρωτῶν τὸ κα[τὰ] τὸν νόμον . . . ὅταν ἔξωθεν τῶν ὅρων εἰσ[άγηται] ἢ ἐξάγηται, τοὺς δὲ εἰς χωρία ἢ ἀπὸ τῶν [χω]ρίων κατακομίζοντας ἀτελεῖς εἶναι ὡς καὶ συνεφώνησεν αὐτοῖς. The χωρία of the tariff are probably villages in the second oasis of the desert and on the borders of the Euphrates. We do not know the extent of Palmyrene territory in the various stages of its development. It is not likely that Dura was an advance-post of Palmyra before the rise of the great Palmyrene empire in the 3rd cent. A.D., although it may have been commercially dependent on that city (cf., however, F. Cumont, *Fouilles de Doura-Europos*, p. xxxix, cf. xlii). The extension of the cultural influence of Palmyra is attested by the diffusion of the Palmyrene type of tower-tomb, which is found in a vast area in the region of Palmyra. See G. Bell, *Amurath to Amurath* (1911), pp. 49, 83; F. Cumont, op. cit., p. 273. However, the construction of squared stones found outside Dura on the main caravan-route was not a sepulchral tower, but, as at Jerash, a triumphal arch (fragments of the Latin dedication of Trajan's reign were found [= *Excavs. at Dura-Europos, Prelim. Rep.* iv, pp. 56 ff. [= *L'An. ép.* 1933, 225]; vi, pp. 480 ff.]. On the auxiliary *numeri* from Palmyra in the Roman army see G. L. Cheesman, *The Auxilia of the Roman Imperial Army* (1914), pp. 88 ff.; F. Cumont, *Mon. Piot*, 26, 1923, pp. 1–46; id. *Fouilles de Doura-Europos*, Introd., pp. xlvii ff.; M. Rostovtzeff, *Excav. at Dura-Europos, Prelim. Rep.* 1 (1929), pp. 53 ff. These *numeri* and the later *cohortes* always preserved their national character. On the Arabian and Syrian troops in general see Cichorius, Pauly–Wissowa, i, cols. 1223 ff.; iv, cols. 231 ff.; cf. G. L. Cheesman, op. cit., pp. 145 ff.; G. Cantacuzène, 'Le Recrutement de quelques cohortes syriennes', *Mus. Belg.* 31,1927, pp. 5–18. I shall revert in the following chapters to the important part which the Syrians and the Arabs played in the imperial army of the 2nd and 3rd cent. I may note in this connexion that their importance attests a low grade of urbanization and a purely rustic and tribal manner of life in the Syrian lands. After the fall of Dura and the decay of Palmyra, the mission of the latter in the work of civilization was inherited by the Romans and later by the Arabs. In the 4th cent. A.D. a certain Silvinus, *comes limitis*, is praised in a metrical Latin inscription found in Roman ruins five hours from Qarietein, the site of the tribe of the Ναζαληνοί (E. Kalinka in *Oest. Jahresh.* 3, 1900, Beibl., p. 19, nos. 1–4), for having rebuilt one of the forts of the Eastern *limes* (on the

road between Palmyra and Damascus) and for having made the whole district near the fort fertile and safe (*CIL* iii. 6660 (cf. 14161) = Buecheler, *Anthol. Lat.* 296 = ‡E. Kalinka, op. cit., p. 34, no. 54 [= ‡*Amer. Expedn. to Syria*, lii, p. 280, no. 355]). Cf. A. Gabriel, *C. R. Acad. Inscr.* 1926, pp. 294 ff., who has shown that the system of fortresses and towers between Palmyra and the Euphrates, built in the late Empire, was entirely restored by the Arabs in the 8th cent. One of the best Arabian palace-fortresses of this period (Kasr el Heir) was connected with a large garden which was abundantly irrigated.

²⁹ On the life of Dura in the Roman age, see my book *Caravan-Cities: Petra and Jerash, Palmyra and Dura* (1932); cf. C. B. Welles, 'The House of Nebuchelus', *Excavs. at Dura-Europos, Prelim. Rep.* iv (1933).

³⁰ On the Damascene soldiers in the Roman army, see E. de Ruggiero, *Diz. epigr.* ii, pp. 1463 ff.; cf. Benzinger in Pauly–Wissowa, iv, cols. 2042 ff.

³¹ The most eminent member of the Palmyrene aristocracy, who was entirely romanized and played a certain part in the history of the late 2nd cent. A.D., was L. Julius Vehilius Gratus Julianus, *praefectus praetorio* under Commodus: see *CIL* vi. 31856 = Dessau, *ILS* 1327; xiv. 4378; his Palmyrene origin is attested by *IGRR* iii. 1037 (cf. 1536) = Dessau, *ILS* 8869; cf. A. von Premerstein, *Klio*, 12, 1912, pp. 155 ff. and 168 f.; A. Stein, *Der römische Ritterstand* (1927), p. 408. The eminent position at Palmyra of Septimius Vorodes and the family of Septimius Odenathus is well known; cf. A. Stein, l.c. It is interesting to see that Vorodes, who was certainly a Parthian, and who is portrayed with Parthian clothes and arms on a Palmyrene relief shortly to be published by Dr. H. Ingholt [*Berytus*, 3, 1936, pp. 93–95; pl. xix. 1], receives two titles in his inscriptions, one Roman (*procurator*) and the other Parthian-Sassanian (*argapetes*, that is, commander or feudal lord of a city of the Parthian kingdom). He exercised this office of a Roman-Parthian functionary during the victorious war of Odenathus against the Sassanids. These titles of Vorodes, which correspond to the various titles which the rulers of Palmyra, Odenathus and his son Vaballathus, assumed successively, show the hybrid nature of the state and government of Palmyra, particularly in the 3rd cent. A.D., Roman on the one hand and Iranian, that is Partho-Sassanian, on the other. The inscriptions concerning Vorodes and Odenathus have now been collected by J. B. Chabot, *Choix d'Inscr. de Palmyre* (1922), pp. 51 ff.; cf. J. G. Février, *Essai sur l'histoire politique et économique de Palmyre* (1931). On the title of *argapetes* or *arkapetes*, and on conditions in Parthian Mesopotamia in the early Roman Empire, see M. Rostovtzeff, *Yale Class. Stud.* 2, 1931, pp. 33 ff. On the history of the king-priests of Emesa see Benzinger in Pauly–Wissowa, v, cols. 2496 ff. On the Sampsigerami, Stähelin in Pauly–Wissowa, Zw. R. i, col. 2226; cf. *CIL* iii. 14387a, and note = Dessau, *ILS* 8958, and id. *Gesch. d. röm. Kaiserzeit*, ii. 2, p. 632. The Sampsigerami are mentioned at Emesa even after their dethronement by Domitian, *IGRR* iii. 1023 (A.D. 78/79), 1025 (A.D. 108), Le Bas–Waddington, iii. 2564 (A.D. 182/3). I see no ground for disbelieving the notice of Malalas, xii, p. 296, that under Valerian one Sampsigeramus led the militia of Emesa against the Parthians; cf., however, A. von Domaszewski, *Arch. f. Rel.* 11, 1908, p. 230, whose identification of the Sampsigeramus of Malalas with the well-known usurper Uranius Antoninus (253/4) I cannot accept. On Edessa in Osroene, E. Meyer in Pauly–Wissowa, v, cols. 1933 ff. On the members of the senatorial and equestrian orders, who came from well-known families of hellenized and romanized towns of Syria and Phoenicia, see A. Stein, op. cit., pp. 405 ff. On the earliest instances of equestrian officers of Syrian origin (one from Tyre the other from Palmyra) see W. H. Buckler, W. M. Calder, and C. W. M. Cox, *JRS* 16, 1926, pp. 74 ff., no. 201 [= *L'An. ép.* 1927, 95] and E. Ritterling, *JRS* 17, 1927, pp. 28 ff.

³² The best survey of social and economic life in Palestine in the earlier period may be found in A. Bertholet, *Kulturgeschichte Israels* (1919), pp. 141 ff. The conditions did not

change in the Hellenistic and Roman periods, see the short survey of commerce and industry (no section devoted to agriculture) in E. Schürer, *Geschichte des jüdischen Volkes im Zeitalter Jesu Christi*[4] (1901–10), ii, pp. 67 ff.; cf. S. Dickey, *The Constructive Revolution of Jesus* (1924), pp. 85 ff. and 115 ff.; and on the coins cf. G. F. Hill, *Br. Mus. Catal. of the Greek Coins of Palestine* (1914). It might be worth while to collect the whole evidence, including that of the Talmud, on this subject. Note that according to Cassius Dio (69. 14. 1) Hadrian destroyed fifty Jewish φρούρια (forts or big villages, μητροκωμίαι) and 975 villages of importance. And how many unimportant hamlets? Cf. H. Swoboda in Pauly–Wissowa, Suppl. iv, col. 975.

The Roman veterans at Emmaus: Fl. Joseph., *Bell.* vii. 6. 6 [217], cf. E. Schürer, op. cit., i, pp. 640 ff., note 142. Estates of the Roman emperor in Galilee: Joseph., *Vita*, 13 (71): παρεκάλει γάρ με τὸν Καίσαρος σῖτον κείμενον ἐν ταῖς τῆς ἄνωθεν Γαλιλαίας κώμαις ἐξουσίαν αὐτῷ δοῦναι ἐκφορῆσαι. I do not think that the imperial corn stored in the villages was the proceeds of a tax in kind paid to the Roman government; it is more probable that it was the produce of the imperial estates in Galilee. Estates of the royal family: Joseph. *Vita*, 24 (119), cf. *Antiq. Jud.* xiv. 10. 6 (209). The εὐσχήμονες of the cities and the officers of the king as large landowners: *Vita*, 9 (32) and *passim* (John of Gischala, Philip of Gamala, Josephus himself, &c.). At Beit Gebrin (Bethogabra, called Eleutheropolis from Septimius Severus onwards), not far from Marissa, ruins were discovered of a villa of the 4th cent. A.D., with mosaics very similar to contemporary mosaics of Africa, which describe scenes of the owner's life. See L. H. Vincent, *Rev. bibl.* 31, 1922, pp. 259 ff. (It was perhaps a villa of this sort which Libanius owned.) The turbulent proletariate of the cities: *Vita*, 9 (32–36), cf. 12 (66) (Tiberias): it was composed mostly of ναῦται and ἄποροι, but also included peasants, id. *Ant. Jud.* xviii. 2. 3 (37–38), cf. my *Studien z. Gesch. röm. Kol.*, p. 305. The same picture applies to the other foundations of Herod. On the *Vita* of Josephus as an historical source, see H. Drexler, *Klio*, 19, 1924, pp. 293 ff., and his bibliography of other modern works on the subject. It is evident that the Jewish ruling aristocracy consisted mostly of large landowners who exercised a kind of protectorate over whole villages and smaller towns, being the owners of the largest part of their territory; cf. the conditions at Antioch as described in note 23. The ties which linked them to the kings and the Roman government were too strong to permit them to be real supporters of the national movement in Palestine, which was based almost wholly on the religious fanaticism and economic oppression of the peasants. On the aristocracy of Palestine in the time of the Idumaean dynasty, cf. E. Bevan, *Jerusalem under the High-Priests* (1904), pp. 155 ff.; J. Jeremias, *Jerusalem zur Zeit Jesu*, i. ii (1924). On the history of Judaea in the late Hellenistic and early Roman periods, and especially on the relations between Judaea and Rome, see M. S. Ginsburg, *Rome et la Judée* (1928), esp. ch. viii, pp. 107 ff., 'L'Époque du régime des rois vassaux et des procurateurs romains'. On large estates in Palestine in the time of Jesus see D. J. Herz, 'Grossgrundbesitz in Palästina im Zeitalter Jesu', *Palästina Jahrb.* 24, 1928, pp. 98 ff. A general sketch of the history of Palestine at the end of the Hellenistic and the beginning of the Roman period is given by H. Dessau, *Gesch. d. röm. Kaiserzeit.* ii. 2, pp. 706 ff., though he deliberately says nothing of social and economic conditions. Cf. E. Taübler, 'Staat und Umwelt: Palästina in der hellenistisch-römischen Zeit' in his book *Tyche*. On the urbanization of Palestine in the Roman period, see A. H. M. Jones, 'The Urbanization of Palestine', *JRS* 21, 1931, pp. 78 ff.

33 R. Dussaud and F. Macler, *Voyage archéologique au Safa* (1901), and 'Mission dans les régions désertiques de la Syrie Moyenne', *Arch. d. miss. scient.* 10, 1903; R. Dussaud, *Les Arabes en Syrie avant l'Islam* (1907) (my quotation is from this book, pp. 5 ff.); H. Guthe, 'Die griechisch-romischen Städte des Ostjordanlandes', *Das Land der Bibel*, ii, p. 5, (1918) (where the story of the gradual civilization of the Trachonitis is told on pp. 29 ff.

according to the narrative of Josephus; cf. the edict of Herod Agrippa, fragments of which have been found at Canatha, *OGIS* 424 = *IGRR* iii. 1223); G. F. Hill, 'The Mints of Roman Arabia and Mesopotamia', *JRS* 6, 1916, pp. 135 ff., and *B. M. Catal. of Coins of Arabia, Mesopotamia and Persia* (1923); cf. *IGRR* iii. 1341: protection of vineyards in the Auranitis near Gerasa by an imperial (?) order. Cf. A. H. M. Jones, 'The Urbanization of the Ituraean Principality', *JRS* 21, 1931, pp. 265 ff. Further light has been thrown on the history of the land beyond the Jordan by the discovery of the correspondence of Zenon, the agent of Apollonius, minister of Ptolemy Philadelphus: see M. Rostovtzeff, *A Large Estate*, pp. 25 f. and 114; cf. G. M. Harper, 'A Study of the Commercial Relations between Egypt and Syria in the Third Century B.C.', *AJP* 49, 1928, pp. 1 ff.; C. C. Edgar, *Zenon Papyri in the University of Michigan Collection* (1931) (Introduction). One of the most striking documents is the letter of the Transjordanian sheikh Tubias to Apollonius, sent with a party of exquisite slaves (noble boys and girls) to the influential minister of his suzerain. The extensive slave trade was evidently one of this Egyptian vassal's chief sources of income. See C. C. Edgar, *Annales du Service*, 23, 1924, p. 201, no. 84 = *P. Cairo Zen.* 59076, cf. 59075, and p. 95, no. 76 = ibid. 59015. Cf. F. M. Abel, *Rev. bibl.* 33, 1924, pp. 566 ff. On trade in Syria in the Roman period (except Palestine, Arabia, and Palmyra), L. C. West, 'Commercial Syria under the Roman Empire', *TAPA* 55, 1924, pp. 159 ff., cf. R. Mouterde, *Mél. de l'Univ. St. Josèphe*, 12, 1927, p. 288.

³⁴ The ruins of part of the Decapolis were investigated by H. C. Butler, *Public. of an American Arch. Expedition to Syria, 1899–1900*, vols. i–iv (1904–5), and *Public. of the Princeton University Arch. Exped. to Syria, 1904–5*, Divisions I–III (1907–16). One of the most characteristic places is the village of Si'a with its temple and theatre connected with it, H. C. Butler, op. cit., 'Ancient Architecture in Syria', Div. II, part 6, pp. 374 ff.; cf. Div. III, no. 772 (1916), and A. Kammerer, *Pétra et la Nabatène* (1930), pp. 436 ff., pls. 139–41. I give a small collection of texts concerning villages and tribes. Μητροκωμίαι: Phaenae, *IGRR* iii. 1119; μ. Ζοραουηνῶν, ibid. 1155. Κῶμαι: ibid. 1149, 1186, 1192, 1213, 1270, 1284, 1317, 1362; cf. *Princeton Expedition*, Div. III, Sec. A, 66, 714, 741, 744, 765, 11. Κοινὸν τῆς κώμης: *IGRR* iii. 1143, 1146, 1186, 1187, 1213, 1262; cf. *Princeton Expedition*, Div. III, Sec. A, 765, 12 and 13. Ἐποίκιον: *IGRR* iii. 1132 (Caracalla), Ἀρισηνοὶ καὶ Ἰαχφιρηνοὶ οἱ ἀπὸ ἐποικίου Ἀβιβηνῶν; B. W. Bacon, *Amer. Journ. Arch.* 11, 1907, pp. 315 ff. [= *L'An. ép.* 1907, 145]; ἐποίκιον Χρησιμιανὸν (is ἐποίκιον a private estate or just a hamlet?). Φυλαί: *IGRR* iii. 1171, οἱ ἀπὸ φυλῆς Ὀγνεδην[ῶν]; 1180, φ(υ)λ(ῆς) Ὀσαινηνῶν; 1276, φυλῆς Σομαιθηνῶν. Γεωργοί: ibid. 1154, Ζοραουηνῶν γεωργοί. Στρατηγοί: ibid. 1136 [στρατηγ]ὸς Νομάδων; 1213, στρατηγείας Οὐλ(πίου) Ζκαυριανοῦ; 1247, ἐθνάρχου στρατηγοῦ Νομάδων, cf. 1254, οἱ ἀπὸ ἔθνους Νομάδων. Πρόεδροι: ibid. 1235 (Canatha), πρόεδρος . . . εἰς τὸ κτίσμα τοῦ θεατροειδοῦς ᾠδείου (an *odeum* of this kind at Dura, F. Cumont, *Fouilles de Doura-Europos*, pp. 188 ff.). Γενεάρχης: Cumont, *C. R. Acad. Inscr.* 1924, p. 28, and *Fouilles de Doura-Europos*, p. 344 and p. 409, no. 52 [=*SEG*, ii, 818]; cf. the inscription of Pontus, *IGRR* iii. 90; cf. also the articles of G. M. McLean Harper and A. H. M. Jones (see note 26).

The delimitation-stones between the territories of the cities, the villages, and the private estates in Syria form an interesting series of documents. The earlier stones belong to the 2nd cent. A.D., *CIL* iii. 183; *Princeton Expedition*, Div. III, Sec. A, 666, 'fines M. Herp(i) iusso Avidi C(a)ssi cos. per Favonium Priorem pr(a)efectum;' (cf. A. von Domaszewski, *Korr.-Blatt d. Westd. Zeitschr.* 2, 1909, pp. 36 f. [=*L'An. ép.* 1909, 131]); ibid. 28, ἔνγεο[ν] ταμιακὸν ἐξ Αὐρηλιανοῦ (between an imperial estate and a certain Aurelianus). Cf. the delimitation of the imperial forests in the Lebanon, M. Rostovtzeff, 'Definitio u. Defensio', *Klio*, 11, 1911, pp. 387 ff., and 'Defensio', *Journ. of the Min. of Publ. Educ. of Russia*, 1912 (in Russian). Under Diocletian a general delimitation of Syria was carried out, *IGRR* iii. 1002, 1112, 1252, 1278, 1364; B. W. Bacon, *Amer. Journ. Arch.* 11, 1907, pp. 315 ff.; [*IGRR* iii. 1002 =] Jalabert and Mouterde, *Inscr. gr. et lat. de la Syrie*, i, no. 59. A similar delimitation was carried out in Thrace, *IGRR* i. 813. Note the fixing of boundaries between the territory of a city, Dionysias (Soada), and that of a village, the Ἀθελενοί, ibid. iii. 1278. This delimitation was no doubt connected with a general census, which is attested by many inscriptions. On this census and the document (fragments of census-lists), see in the last instance J. Keil and A. von Premerstein, 'Dritte Reise in Lydien', pp. 68 ff., no. 85 (with full bibliography). Transformation of a village into a city: W. Kubitschek, 'Zur Geschichte von Städten des röm. Kaiserreiches', *Sitzb. Wien. Akad.* 177, 1916, pp. 45 ff. (the tribe and the village of the Saccaei transformed into the city of Philippopolis); cf. *IGRR* iii. 1142 (also 1136–41) concerning the δῆμος Ἐειθηνῶν Καισαρέων.

35 I cannot collect here all the evidence on the veterans as the village aristocracy: a few examples must suffice. A veteran was the *patronus* of the tribe of the Μοζαιεδηνοὶ in A.D. 213/4, *IGRR* iii. 1298. Veterans appear as benefactors of the tribes and villages in many inscriptions, ibid. 1294 (A.D. 156), 1299 (A.D. 170/1), 1301, 1302, 1305, 1310, 1313, 1316, 1317 (ἐκτίσθη ἡ λίμνη . . . ἐ(κ) κοινῶν ἀναλωμάτων τῆς κώμης (δηναρίων) ιε′ μ(υριάδων) ἐκ προνοίας Φλ. Κορνηλιανοῦ π(ριμι)π(ιλαρίου) in A.D. 294/5), &c. The veterans seem to have formed a privileged class among the villagers: in ibid. 1187, two οὐιτρανικοί (descendants of veterans) are contrasted with a βουλευτής (member of the village council). We may say without exaggeration that most of the prominent members of a village community all over Syria were former soldiers. The cohorts of mounted archers, which were recruited in Syria and were called *cohortes civium Romanorum*, were probably composed of descendants of veterans settled in Syrian villages. See my observations in *Excavs. at Dura-Europos, Prelim. Report*, i (1929), p. 56, note 1. The well-known Stercoria Gallix from Rotomagus (Rouen) in Gaul may have come to Mothana, where her funeral stone has been found, with her husband, a veteran (Lebas–Waddington, 2036; cf. *Rev. arch.* 1901 (2), pp. 375 ff.). Cf. W. Kubitschek, 'Itinerarstudien', *Abh. d. Akad. d. Wiss. in Wien*, 61 (3), 1919.

36 I have already mentioned the Safaite inscriptions and drawings which illustrate the life of this Arabian tribe. They are much more numerous than the Greek texts of the same place. See the works of R. Dussaud quoted in note 33. It is interesting to observe among the numerous inscriptions of the main gate of Dura a series of Safaitic texts: see Ch. Torrey, *Excavs. at Dura-Europos, Prelim. Report*, ii (1931), pp. 172 ff., ibid. iii (1932), pp. 66 ff. It may be noted that the imperial procurators in dealing with the natives resorted to the help of interpreters, *IGRR* iii. 1191 (Saccaea), ἑρμηνεὺς ἐπιτρόπων; cf. W. I. Snellman, *De interpretibus Romanorum*, &c. (1914), pp. 120 f.

37 On the social and economic structure of Egypt in the Ptolemaic period see my summary in *CAH* vii, 1929, pp. 109 ff. (and bibliography on pp. 889 ff.). On slavery in Ptolemaic Egypt see W. L. Westermann, *Upon Slavery in Ptolemaic Egypt* (1929). The fragment of a royal διάγραμμα concerning taxation on trade in slaves, published by Westermann, and a series of contemporary documents with similar content, quoted by him, show that in Alexandria slaves were used not only in domestic service, but also in business life. As regards my view that there was no real private ownership of land in early Ptolemaic Egypt, see the facts and documents quoted and interpreted by V. Struve, *Journ. of the Min. of Publ. Educ. of Russia*, 1915, January, pp. 1 ff.; 1917, July–August, pp. 223 ff. (in Russian), and especially Sethe–Partsch, 'Demotische Urkunden zum ägyptischen Bürgschaftsrecht, vorzüglich der Ptolemäerzeit', *Abh. d. sächs. Ges.*, Phil.-hist. Kl. 32, 1920, cf. P. Meyer, 'Juristischer Papyrusbericht II', *Zeitschr. f. vergl. Rechtswiss.* 40, 1922, pp. 174 ff. esp. pp. 182, 198 (Pacht), 203, and 207 ff. (Lehnsrecht, Tempelland). I am convinced that these new documents do not

invalidate my theory, though I would now modify some of my statements in regard to details; cf. Partsch in *Arch. f. Papyr.* 7, pp. 259 f. The new evidence of these documents has been taken into account in the short sketch of Ptolemaic Egypt given in the text.

[38] See the brilliant sketch of A. Moret, 'L'Accession de la plèbe égyptienne aux droits religieux et politiques sous le moyen empire', *Recueil de J. F. Champollion* (1922), pp. 331 ff.

[39] *P.Oxyr.* 1681 (3rd cent. A.D.), ll. 4 ff.: ἴσως με νομίζετε, | ἀδελφοί, βάρβαρόν τι|να ἢ Αἰγύπτιον ἀνάν|θρωπον εἶναι. There has been very little change since the time of Ptolemy Philadelphus, Theocr. *Id.* 15. 50: ἀλλάλοις ὁμαλοί, κακὰ παίγνια, πάντες ἐρινοί (words used by Praxinoa to characterize the native Egyptians). Cf. U. Wilcken, *Arch. f. Papyr.* 7, p. 98. It is to be noticed that not even Philo was very enthusiastic about the Egyptians. Apart from his contempt for the Egyptian religion and the low opinion he has in general of the materialistic ideals of the Egyptians, he attacks in many places their passionate, unstable, rebellious, and unreasonable character. I cannot quote here all the passages in which he speaks of the Egyptians: I am indebted to Professor Goodenough for having called my attention to this point.

[40] On the Hellenization of Egypt and the part played by the Greeks in the economic, social, and cultural life of the country, see in addition to the bibliography quoted in note 37: W. Schubart, 'Hellenen in Ägypten', *Hellas, Organ der deutsch-griechischen Gesellschaft*, 1921, no. 8, pp. 4 ff.; P. Jouguet, 'Les Lagides et les indigènes Égyptiens', *Revue Belge de Philologie et d'Histoire*, 1923, pp. 419 ff.; H. I. Bell, 'Hellenic culture in Egypt', *JEA* 8, 1922, pp. 139 ff.; E. Bickermann, 'Beiträge zur antiken Urkundengeschichte', *Arch. f. Papyr.* 8, pp. 216 ff., and 9, pp. 24 ff.; F. Heichelheim, 'Die auswärtige Bevölkerung im Ptolemäerreich', *Klio*, Beiheft 18, 1925; id. *Arch. f. Papyr.* 9, pp. 47 ff.; [id. ibid. 12, pp. 54 ff.]; cf. the bibliography in *CAH* vii, pp. 896 ff. The most difficult question concerns the extent to which the Greeks were denationalized in the later Ptolemaic period by a gradual infiltration of the Egyptian (though Hellenized) element, or in other words the extent to which the upper class of the Egyptians was Hellenized. The fact itself is evident, but I greatly doubt whether the exclusiveness of the Greeks was seriously modified by some cases of intermarriage (never legally recognized) and by the efforts of some Greeks to take a more intimate part in the life of the Egyptians and even to learn their language. If such a tendency did exist in the later Ptolemaic period, the process was certainly stopped by Augustus, as is now shown by the *Gnomon idiu logu*, the main part of which dates from his time; cf. B. A. van Groningen, *Le Gymnasiarque des métropoles de l'Égypte romaine* (1924), pp. 6 ff. The causes of the discontent of the Egyptians and of their repeated revolts are well explained in the article of P. Jouguet quoted above. The main causes, however, were the fact that after Raphia a part of the Egyptians came into possession of arms, and the hostile attitude of the priests, who may have dreamed (and not without reason, had it not been for the Romans) that another Saitic period was approaching (see the two fragments of a trilingual decree of the Egyptian priests discovered at Memphis and Pithom, which glorifies the king, Ptolemy IV Philopator, and the victory of Raphia; note in this decree the Egyptian form of the protocol as compared with the decree of Canopus—H. Gauthier and H. Sottas, *Un Décret trilingue en l'honneur de Ptolémée iv* (1925); W. Spiegelberg, *Sitzb. Bayr. Akad.* 1925 (4), and Spiegelberg and W. Otto, ibid. 1926 (2) [Greek text; *SEG* viii. 467 = *SB* 7172]). Meanwhile they utilized the revolts to obtain important grants and privileges (see the inscription of Rosetta [*OGIS* 90], and *P. Tebt.* 5). It is hard to believe, as was suggested by W. Spiegelberg, *Das Verhältnis d. griech. und. ägypt. Texte in den Dekreten von Rosette und Kanopus* (Papyrus-institut Heidelberg, vol. v) (1923), that the original text not only of

the decree of Canopus but also of the Rosetta inscription, was the Greek one. I feel convinced that P. Jouguet's attack on the 'rehabilitators' of Euergetes II is fully justified. Euergetes made a virtue of necessity: his practice was probably very different from his words, which as a matter of fact were not even invented by him but assumed at a very early time the form of conventional expressions used for amnesty decrees, just like the decrees of the priests and similar Egyptian documents of the earlier period. The question of the self-government of Alexandria is treated in full by H. I. Bell, *Jews and Christians in Egypt* (1924), pp. 8 ff.; id. *Juden und Griechen im römischen Alexandrien* (Beihefte zum *Alten Orient*, Heft 9) (1926). The principal text is now the letter of Claudius [= *Sel. Pap.* 212], col. 4, 66 ff.: περὶ δὲ τῆς βουλῆς ὅτι μέν ποτε σύνηθες | ὑμῖν ἐπὶ τῶν ἀρχαίων βασιλέων οὐκ ἔχωι λέγειν, ὅτι δὲ ἐπὶ τῶν | πρὸ ἐμοῦ Σεβαστῶν οὐκ εἴχεται σαφῶς οἴδατε; cf. H. Dessau, *Gesch. d. röm. Kaiserzeit*, ii. 2, p. 655, and the articles of Oliver and Vitelli quoted in Chap. II, note 11.

⁴¹ On the social and economic conditions of Roman Egypt in general, see my *Studien z. Gesch. röm. Kol.*, pp. 85 ff.; U. Wilcken, *Grundz.*, pp. 237 ff.; W. Schubart, *Einführung*, pp. 403 ff.; id. *Ägypten*, pp. 227 ff.; F. Oertel, 'Der Niedergang der hellenistischen Kultur in Ägypten', *Neue Jahrb. kl. Alt.* 45, 1920, pp. 361 ff.; id. *Die Liturgie* (1917); H. I. Bell, 'The Byzantine Servile State in Egypt', *JEA* 4, 1917, pp. 86 ff.; V. Martin, *La Fiscalité romaine en Égypte aux trois premiers siècles de l'Empire* (1926); T. Frank, *An Economic History of Rome*² (1927), pp. 379 ff.; J. Grafton Milne, *A History of Egypt under Roman Rule*³ (1924); id. 'The Ruin of Egypt by Roman Mismanagement', *JRS* 17, 1927, pp. 1 ff.; id. 'Egyptian Nationalism under Greek and Roman Rule', *JEA* 14, 1928, pp. 230 ff.; M. Rostovtzeff, 'The Exploitation of Egypt in the First Century A.D.', *Journ. of Econ. and Business Hist.* 1, 1929, pp. 337 ff.; U. Wilcken, 'Zum Germanicus-Papyrus', *Hermes*, 63, 1928, pp. 48 ff.; H. Dessau, *Gesch. d. röm. Kaiserzeit*, ii. 2, pp. 650 ff. It is a pity that papyrologists, while giving full attention to the administrative and, in some cases, to the economic aspects of Egyptian life in the Roman period, still neglect the social problems. There are a few exceptions, for instance the articles of A. Calderini: see 'La Composizione della famiglia secondo le schede de censimento dell' Egitto Romano', *Pubblic. d. Univ. Catt. del Sacro Cuore*, Ser. III, Scienze sociali, i. 1, 1923; *Liberi e schiavi nel mondo dei papiri* (Milano, 1918), and 'Guarnigioni romane contro il nazionalismo egiziano', *Conferenze e prolusioni* (1919), pp. 309 ff. (the last two are inaccessible to me); cf. M. Hombert, 'Une Famille nombreuse en Égypte au IIᵐᵉ siècle', *Mélanges P. Thomas* (1930), pp. 440 ff.; W. L. Westermann, 'Entertainment in villages of Greco-Roman Egypt', *JEA* 18, 1932, pp. 16 ff.; W. Schubart, 'Griechische Briefe aus Ägypten', *Die Antike*, 8, 1932, pp. 113 ff. Cf. also the brilliant book of A. Deissmann, *Licht vom Osten*⁴ (1923). On the question how large a part of the Egyptian population was engaged in agriculture, see now, besides the article of Calderini cited above ('La Composizione della famiglia', &c., pp. 24 ff.), the excellent book of Michael Schnebel, *Die Landwirtschaft im hellenistischen Ägypten* (1925) (Münchener Beiträge zur Papyrusforschung und antiken Rechtsgeschichte, vii), pp. 2 ff. A good knowledge of modern Egyptian economic life, especially that prevailing among the Fellahin in the country, is very useful for the reconstruction of the ancient life of the country. Those unfamiliar with Egyptian life can consult with profit the book of W. S. Blackman, *The Fellahin of Upper Egypt, their Religious, Social, and Industrial Life Today with Special Reference to Survivals from Ancient Times* (1927).

⁴² See my article in *Gött. gel. Anz.*, 1909, pp. 606 ff., and my *Studien z. Gesch. röm. Kol.*, *passim*. My point of view has been justified by the discovery of the *Gnomon idiu logu*.

⁴³ The best survey of the Egyptian administrative machinery is F. Oertel, *Die Liturgie* (1917); cf. A. Stein, *Untersuchungen zur Geschichte und Verwaltung Ägyptens unter*

römischer Herrschaft (1915), especially pp. 132 ff. on the official languages in the administration of Egypt. On the higher officials of Egypt and their career, see Ballou, *TAPA* 52, 1921, pp. 96 ff. Unfortunately Miss Ballou has relied on antiquated editions of sources and on some antiquated modern books; cf. H. I. Bell, *JEA* 9, 1923, pp. 106 ff.; O. Hornickel, *Ehren- und Rangprädikate in den Papyrusurkunden* (1930), and A. Stein, *Gnomon*, 7, 1931, pp. 172 ff. See also, on the military organization of Egypt, the excellent book of J. Lesquier, *L'Armée romaine d'Égypte d'Auguste à Dioclétien* (1918); cf. H. A. Sanders, *TAPA* 55, 1924, pp. 21 ff.

⁴⁴ My *Studien z. Gesch. röm. Kol.*, pp. 85 ff., cf. Lesquier, *L'Armée romaine d'Égypte*, pp. 328 ff.; U. Wilcken, *Grundz.*, p. 300, cf. *Chrest.*, 368 and 369, and *Grundz.*, p. 403. An excellent general picture of Egypt in the time of Augustus is given by Strabo in his 17th book, see especially the parallel on p. 798: ὅπου οὖν ὁ κάκιστα καὶ ῥᾳθυμότατα τὴν βασιλείαν διοικῶν (Auletes) τοσαῦτα προσωδεύετο, τί χρὴ νομίσαι τὰ νῦν (Augustus) διὰ τοσαύτης ἐπιμελείας οἰκονομούμενα; cf. Ath. v. 206D; G. Lumbroso, *Aegyptus*, 5, 1924, pp. 31 f. An important testimony would be furnished to the efficient care which Augustus and his successors devoted to Egypt, and a further proof of the thorough application to Egypt of Greek achievements in technique, which developed but slowly after Euergetes I, if H. E. Winlock is right in maintaining that some of the technical inventions which are still used in Egypt, e.g. the threshing machine (*plostellum punicum*, nawraj) and the water-wheel (κάδος, qadus, saqiyeh), were first introduced into the country in the time of Augustus or a little later—no doubt by the new landowners, who poured into the country from all parts of the Roman world just as in the reign of Ptolemy Philadelphus; see H. E. Winlock and W. E. Crum, *The Monastery of Epiphanius at Thebes, The Metropolitan Museum Egypt. Explor.* (1926), i, pp. 61 ff. 96 ff.; cf. the description of pl. 43. 5, ibid. The careful collection of all the available material by M. Schnebel in his *Landwirtschaft im hellenistischen Ägypten* (1925) (see the general summary, p. 356) supports Mr. Winlock's view. But the scantiness of the information which we possess about the Hellenistic period prevents us from forming a final judgement on the question. Not long ago, for example, we were convinced that the Ptolemies did not make extensive use of camels: now we know that they did. A very instructive list of landowners may be found in *P.Ryl.* ii, 202 (late 1st cent. A.D.). Five are Romans, seven Greeks. The Romans are either soldiers or probably veterans. Some bear characteristic archaic names: C. Valerius, L. Bruttius. One is M. Antonius—one of the veterans of Antony? Of the Greeks one is certainly an Alexandrian ('Ωρίων Λύκου Μαρωνεύς). Does the document really belong to the *late* 1st cent.? For the κουφοτελεῖαι see also the evidence supplied by *P.Oxyr.* 1434.

⁴⁵ The evidence on the οὐσίαι collected and illustrated in my *Studien z. Gesch. röm. Kol.*, pp. 120 ff., has been enriched by a series of papyri of the early 1st cent. A.D., which were found in Euhemeria in the Fayyûm and probably belonged originally to the bureau of the chief of police of this village (ἀρχέφοδος). Most of these documents are petitions addressed to the chief of police of the νομός—the ἐπιστάτης. A few of them went to the British Museum (*P.Lond.* iii, pp. xliii and 129 ff.), the largest part to the Rylands Library at Manchester, see *P.Ryl.* ii. 124–52, introd. It is notable how many of these papyri mention the οὐσίαι in one form or another. Evidently they played a very important part in the life of Euhemeria in the first half of the 1st cent. The account of the distribution of them given in the text is based mainly on the papyri of Euhemeria. Another source of information on the οὐσίαι is the accounts of the σιτολόγοι of Theadelphia for A.D. 164/5, published by K. Thunell, *Sitologen-Papyri aus dem Berliner Museum* (Upsala, 1924). On pp. 72 ff. the editor gives a general survey of the οὐσίαι of the imperial period, and interprets the data of the Berlin accounts. In some cases parts of the οὐσιακὴ γῆ of the 2nd cent. A.D. were still listed as having formerly

been private property (οὐσία) of the Emperors Vespasian and Titus. This is a striking proof of the correctness of my hypothesis that, after Nero, Vespasian and Titus were the only Roman emperors who carried out vast confiscations of private οὐσίαι, and so laid the foundation of the department of the γῆ οὐσιακή, which was finally organized probably by Domitian. Another document of the same kind, and also very important for the history of land-ownership in the 1st and 2nd cents. A.D. and of the land-taxes, is the register with tax-roll of Hiera Nesos and four adjacent villages, compiled in A.D. 167, *Pap. Bouriant*, 42; see the excellent commentary by P. Collart. The earlier οὐσίαι play an important part in the document. As in the Berlin papyrus mentioned above, the majority of them are described as confiscations of Vespasian and Titus.

The list given in my *Studien z. Gesch. röm. Kol.* may be replaced by a new one arranged according to the social standing of the owners. The date of the corresponding papyrus is quoted only when it helps to identify the owner.

I. *Reigning emperors*: (1) Tiberius, *P.Ryl.* ii. 134 (A.D. 34), owner of an οὐσία which had formerly belonged to Germanicus. (2) Gaius Caesar, *P.Ryl.* ii. 148 (A.D. 40), joint owner with his uncle Claudius. (3) Claudius, *BGU* 650 = U. Wilcken, *Chrest.* 365 (A.D. 46/47), owner of an οὐσία which formerly belonged to C. Petronius. (4) Nero, *BGU* 191 (A.D. 52); *P.Lond.* ii, p. 195, no. 280 (A.D. 55); cf. C. Wessely, *Spec. Isag.* 20 f. = Wilcken, *Chrest.* 176 (1st cent.). (5) Vespasian, K. Thunell, *Sitologen-Papyri* (Pap. Berl. Inv., nos. 11537, 11541, 11540, 11545), no. 4 R. iii. 22 ff.: οὐσιῶν (πρότερον) θεοῦ Οὐεσπ(ασιανοῦ) Θεαδελ(φείας) Διονυσοδωρι(ανῆς) οὐσ(ίας); no. 1 R. iii. 5; no. 1 R. iii. 18; no. 4 R. iv. 2: οὐσιῶ(ν) Οὐεσπ(ασιανοῦ); Οὐεσπασιανὴ οὐσία, *BGU* 1646; and Titus: *P.Oxyr.* 62. 1–2; *BGU* 979. 5; 980. 5, 13 (Mendes); K. Thunell, *Sitologen-Papyri*, no. 1 V. ii. 6: οὐσιῶ(ν) (πρότερον) θεοῦ Τίτου, cf. R. iv. 13; vi. 15. A series of οὐσίαι which came to Vespasian or Titus: *P.Bouriant*, 42 (A.D. 167), pp. 162 ff. Whether Hadrian is named as owner of an οὐσία (*P.Fay.* 82, 14 ff., A.D. 145) is still a matter of controversy; see my *Studien Gesch. Kol.*, p. 121; Wilcken, *Arch. f. Papyr.* 1, p. 552; Thunell, op. cit., p. 74, note.

II. *Members of the imperial family*: (6) Livia, *P.Lond.* ii, p. 166, no. 445 (A.D. 14–15), joint owner with Germanicus; cf. a payment of A.D. 15, μέτρῳ τετραχοινείκῳ θησαυροῦ Λιβύιας Σεβαστῆς at Tebtunis, *PSI* 1028. (7) Agrippa, *BGU* 1047, col. ii. 14. (7 bis) Julia and the sons of Germanicus, *Pap. Mil.* 6: ἐγλήμπτωρ βίβλου Ἰουλίας Σεβάστης καὶ τέκνω(ν) Γερμανικοῦ Καίσαρος (A.D. 25): request for rent for the cutting of papyrus in papyrus-groves belonging to the οὐσία. Mats were also made with the papyrus, and these were undoubtedly sold in the district by the entrepreneur. Cf. Wilcken, *Arch. f. Papyr.* 9, p. 240. (8) Antonia Drusi, *P.Oxyr.* 244 (A.D. 23); *P.Ryl.* ii. 140 (A.D. 36); 141 (A.D. 37); 171. 4. Cf. Ἀντωνιανὴ οὐσία: *BGU* 212. 5; 199.9; 653. 11; 277.7; *P.Fay.* 60.6; *SB* 5670; Goodspeed, *P.Chic.* 7. 3; K. Thunell, *Sitologen-Papyri*, no. 1 V. ii. 16; iii. 5. It is more probable that the οὐσία Ἀντωνιανή belonged originally to Antonia Drusi than to the great M. Antonius or to the younger daughter of Claudius. (9) Ti. Claudius Germanicus (the future Emperor Claudius), *P.Ryl.* ii. 148 (A.D. 40), joint owner with the Emperor Gaius. (10) Germanicus, *P.Lond.* ii, p. 166, no. 445 (A.D. 14–15), joint owner with Livia (cf. no. 7a of this list); *P.Ryl.* ii. 134 (A.D. 34), his οὐσία owned by the Emperor Tiberius; C. Wessely, 'Karanis und Soknopaiu Nesos', *Denkschr. Wien Akad.* 47, 1902 (4), no. 13 (time of Emperor Gaius); *P.Hamb.* 3. 10. 12; *BGU* 160. 5; 441. 4; Goodspeed, *P.Chic.* 6. 4; 10. 4; 31. 7; 70. 5; 81. 5; cf. an unpublished Louvre papyrus (my *Studien z. Gesch. röm. Kol.*, p. 121), and *BGU* 810, col. ii. 7; *P. Bouriant*, 42, p. 162. (11) Children of Claudius (Antonia) by his first marriage with Urgulanilla and of Livia, the wife of Drusus son of Tiberius (Julia), *P.Ryl.* ii. 138 (A.D. 34), joint ownership. It is probable that the two estates of these minors were managed jointly by a special order of the emperor. (12) Antonia, the daughter of Claudius, *P. Fay.* 40; *P. Bouriant*, 42 (A.D. 167), p. 162; cf. *BGU* 280. 4 (?); Goodspeed, *P.Chic.* 4. 4 (?). The Ἀντωνία of these papyri may be Antonia Drusi.

(13) Livia Drusi, *P.Ryl.* ii. 127 (A.D. 29). (14) Messalina, *CPR* 243. 8 = Wilcken, *Chrest.* 367; *P.Flor.* 40. 8; C. Wessely, 'Karanis und Sokn. N.', no. 4; tessera, Dattari, *Numi Augustorum Alexandrini*, no. 6506.

III. *Members of the senatorial and equestrian classes*: (15) Falcidius, *P.Ryl.* ii. 138. 12 (A.D. 34): ἐν τοῖς πρότερον Φαλκιδίου in the estate no. 11. I am inclined to believe that our Falcidius belonged to the well-known family of the Falcidii of the late Republican period: see F. Muenzer in Pauly–Wissowa, vi. (16) C. Maecenas, *P.Lond.* iii. p. 89, no. 900, l. 5 (1st cent. A.D.); *BGU* 181. 7 (A.D. 57); 889; *P.Ryl.* ii. 171. 14 (A.D. 56/57); 207. 8. 26; 383; *P.Hamb.* 3. 4; 34. 10; *P.Tebt.* 343, col. iv. 76; *Class. Phil.* 1, 1906, p. 168, no. III; *P.Chic.* 81. 4; K. Thunell, *Sitologen-Papyri*, no. 1 V. ii. 18; iii. 16; iv. 5; *P.Osl.* ii. 26a, 9. Cf. Wilcken, *Hermes*, 54, 1919, pp. 111 ff. (17) C. and P. Petronii, probably members of the family of the well-known prefect of Egypt under Augustus, *P.Ryl.* ii. 127 (A.D. 29), 4 ff.: ἐν τοῖς ἀμμίνοις ἐποικίου Ποπλίου καὶ Γαίου Πετρωνίων; *BGU* 650 = Wilcken, *Chrest.* 365 (A.D. 46/47). On the two families of the Petronii of the 1st cent., see *PIR* iii, pp. 25 ff. Cf. also *P.Giss.*, 101. 6, and introd. (18) M. Aponius Saturninus, *P.Ryl.* ii. 131. 14 ff. (A.D. 31); 135. 9 f. (A.D. 34); *P.Osl.* ii. 33. 4–5 (A.D. 29); cf. *Klio*, 22, 1928, pp. 221 ff. (cf. Wilcken, *Symb. Osl.* 7, 1928, pp. 33 ff.). There is no doubt about the identity of this man with one of the members of the well-known family of the Aponii Saturnini, P. von Rohden in Pauly–Wissowa, ii, col. 172, nos. 8–10; *PIR* i², no. 937. (19) Gallia Polla, *P.Lond.* ii, p. 127, no. 195 (cf. *P.Ryl.* ii, p. 254) and K. Thunell, *Sitologen-Papyri*, no. 1 V. iv. 8 f.; cf. ibid., p. 88. The estate of Gallia Polla passed into the possession of M. Antonius Pallas. She belonged probably to the well-known family of the Gallii, partisans of M. Antonius. It is probable that the estate was originally formed out of lands given by M. Antonius to one of his partisans: see von der Mühll, Pauly–Wissowa, vii, col. 671, nos. 5 and 7. (20) Iucundus Grypianus, *P.Hamb.* 3. 7; *P.Ryl.* ii. 207. 5: Πάλλαντος (πρότερον) Ἰουκούνδ(ου); cf. Παλατ( ) οὐσία (πρότερον) Ἰουμερ( ), *P.Bouriant*, 42, p. 163. I should like to connect Iucundus Grypianus with the family of L. Plotius Grypus, one of the generals of Vespasian, *PIR* iii, p. 53, no. 385. (21) Norbana Clara, *P.Lond.* iii, p. 121, nos. 1213–15 (A.D. 65/66); cf. Norbanus Orestes, *P.Ryl.* ii. 180 (A.D. 124). The family of the Norbani was prominent at Rome in the 1st cent., *PIR* ii, p. 415, nos. 134–6. (22) Atinii, *P.Ryl.* ii. 427, fr. 22: Ἀτινιανῆς οὐσίας, cf. T. Atinius T. f. Fabia Tyranus, senator in 39 B.C., *PIR* i², no. 1316. (23) Lurii, *P.Hamb.* 3. 10; *BGU* 105; 284; *P.Chic.* 32, 36, 39, 41, 43, 48, 49, 50, 78, 87; K. Thunell, *Sitologen-Papyri*, no. 1 V. iv. 12; *P.Bouriant*, 42, p. 162. Two Lurii of the time of Augustus are known: one was commander of a portion of his fleet against both Sex. Pompeius and M. Antonius, *PIR* ii, p. 307, nos. 315, 316. (24) L. Septimius, *P.Lond.* ii, p. 127, no. 195 (cf. *P.Ryl.* ii, p. 255. 16), owner of the estate of Gallia Polla before it passed to her. Cannot he be connected with one of the early members of the family of the future emperor Septimius Severus and of the Septimius Severus, friend of Statius, *PIR* iii, p. 212, no. 345? An estate of a Severus is known from many papyri, *P.Lond.* iii, p. 89, no. 900 (1st cent.); *BGU* 31; *P.Ryl.* ii. 207. 25 and 28; *P.Chic.* 19. 47, &c.; K. Thunell, *Sitologen-Papyri*, no. 1 V. ii. 19; iii. 7. Statius speaks of his friend as a wealthy landowner. (25) L. Annaeus Seneca, *P.Ryl.* ii. 99; 207. 7, 15; *P.Hamb.* 3. 9; *P.Lips.* i. 115. 6; *BGU* 104, 172, 202; *P.Chic.*, see Index; *Class. Phil.* 1, 1906, p. 172, no. vi. 3; K. Thunell, *Sitologen-Papyri*, no. 1 V. ii. 20; iv. 11; cf. *P.Bouriant*, 42 (Σενέκου).

IV. *Freedman—favourites of the emperors*: (26) Narcissus, *P.Ryl.* ii. 171. 1 (A.D. 56/57); C. Wessely, *Spec. Isag.* 20–21 = Wilcken, *Chrest.* 176. (27) M. Antonius Pallas, *P.Lond.* ii, p. 127, no. 195; (cf. *P.Ryl.* ii, p. 255). K. Thunell, *Sitologen-Papyri*, no. 1 V. iv. 8 f. (28) Ti. Claudius Doryphorus, *P.Ryl.* ii. 171. 1 (A.D. 56/57): Εὐσχήμονι ο[ἰ]κονόμωι τῆς ἐν Ἀρσινοίτηι [Τιβερίου] | Κλαυδίου Δορυφόρου πρότερον Ναρκισσιανῆς οὐσίας; *P.Goodspeed*, 52. 6; *P.Osl.* ii. 21. 5.

V. *Rich Alexandrians*: (29) C. Iulius Theon, *archiereus* and *hypomnematographos* of Alexandria, *P.Oxy.* 1434 (7–4 B.C. and A.D. 10–11). On the family, see B. Grenfell, ibid., note to l. 10, and H. I. Bell, *Jews and Christians in Egypt*, p. 30; cf. *P.Oxy.* 1475. (30) Theon Theonis, *P.Ryl.* ii. 145 (A.D. 38); cf. *PSI* 315: Θέων ὁ καὶ Ἄνθος Ἀμμωνιανοῦ, former gymnasiarch and *agoranomos* of Alexandria in A.D. 137/8. (31) Anthus (οὐσία Ἀνθιανή), *BGU* 985; 199; 810; *P.Strassb.* 1108. Cf. no. 30; the name Anthus was popular among the Alexandrians. (32) M. Iulius Asclepiades, *P.Fay.* 82 and 87; *P.Hamb.* 36; *P.Lond.* no. 1912. 17. Probably the well-known philosopher, successor of Areius, friend of Augustus, E. Schwartz in Pauly–Wissowa, ii, col. 1627. One part of his estate was owned in the 2nd cent. by the city of Alexandria (οἶκος πόλεως Ἀλεξανδρέων: cf. Wilcken, *Grundz.* 308), another by the state. (33) Asclepiades Ptolemaei, *P.Ryl.* ii. 167 (A.D. 39). (34) C. Iulius Athenodorus and Ti. Calpurnius Tryphon, *P.Ryl.* ii. 128 (A.D. 30). (35) Apion, *BGU* 8, col. ii. 18 and 24. (36) Dionysodorus, *P.Lond.* iii, p. 89, no. 900 (A.D. 94/95 or 110/11); *P.Oxyr.* 986, cols. viii–ix; *P.Gen.* 38; K. Thunell, *Sitologen-Papyri*, no. 4 R. iii. 22 f.; no. 1 R. iii. 5 f.; V. ii. 17; iii. 6; iv. 10; *P.Bouriant*, 42, p. 163; *BGU* 1636; *P.Osl.* ii. 26a (*Klio*, 22, 1928, p. 224; Wilcken, *Symb. Osl.* 7, 1928, p. 32); *P.Giess. Univ. Bibl.* 12, pp. 28 f. It is evident from the Berlin accounts of the *sitologoi* that the οὐσία of Dionysodorus was confiscated by Vespasian. (37) Euander Ptolemaei, *P.Ryl.* ii. 132 (A.D. 32): ἱερεὺς Τιβερίου Καίσαρος Σεβαστοῦ, cf. 133 (A.D. 33) and 166, 9 ff. (A.D. 26). (38) Philodamus, *BGU* 512; 210. 4; 262. 3; *P.Chic.*, Index; *P.Bouriant*, 42, pp. 156 ff. (39) Onesimus, *P.Ryl.* 207. 23. (40) Theoninus, *BGU* 63 and 382. (41) Charmis or Charmos, K. Thunell, *Sitologen-Papyri*, no. 1 V. iv, 6; cf. p. 87; *BGU* 1636. Thunell points out that in *P.Lond.* ii, p. 127, no. 195. 17, Charmos is mentioned as owner of an estate and that a rich surgeon of the name of Charmis in the time of Nero occurs in Plin. *NH* 29. 22. (42) Socrates, K. Thunell, *Sitologen-Papyri*, no. 1 V. iv. 7. (43) Tigellius, probably M. Tigellius M. f. Ialysus (*BGU* 1168 (11–10 B.C.) and 1180 (14–13 B.C.)), *BGU* 1669 (age of Augustus). Cf. also the οὐσίαι Ἀνουβᾶ, *P.Lond.* ii, p. 161, no. 214; Ἐμβρῆ, *BGU* 106. 4; Λαεείνου καὶ Ἡρᾶτ[ος], *P.Ryl.* ii. 427, fr. 15; Καμηλιανή, *BGU* 104, 106, 204, 206, 211, 438; *P.Chic.*, Index; *P.Osl.* ii. 26a. 10 (cf. villa Camilliana, Plin. *Ep.* vi. 30); Προφητιανή, *P.Strassb.* i. 74. 4 f. and 78. 5 f. (A.D. 126–8); Thermutharion Lycarionis, *P.Ryl.* ii. 146 (A.D. 39), and 152 (A.D. 42), cf. Plin. *Ep.* x. 5. 2. Ἀλεξανδριανή, *P.Bouriant*, 42, p. 162; Μακ( ), ibid. (perhaps Μαικηνετιανή). In the Collection Froehner, at the Cabinet des Médailles, there is a wooden tablet with the inscription Κτῆσις Ἀμμω. It may be the seal of an estate which belonged to an Ἀμμωνιανός; perhaps the father of Θέων ὁ καὶ Ἄνθος (no. 30, above) (?). More evidence on these οὐσίαι is needed to assign them to one of our classes. Lycarion may have been an Alexandrian.

VI. *Noble foreigners*: (44) C. Iulius Alexander, *P.Ryl.* ii. 166 (A.D. 26). I should suggest the identification of this man with the son of Herodes and Mariamne the Hasmonaean, Groag in Pauly–Wissowa, x, col. 151. Cannot the word after his name in the papyrus be read βα]σι[λέω]ς? Is the οὐσία Ἀλεξανδριανή of *P.Bouriant*, 42, p. 162 perhaps his estate? Or should we rather think of the celebrated Prefect, Ti. Julius Alexander? (45) Iulia Berenice, *P.Hamb.* 8 (A.D. 136), probably a descendant of the mistress of the Emperor Titus.

[46] The Euhemeria documents of the 1st cent. A.D. give us a deeper insight into the questions concerning the constitution and the exploitation of the οὐσίαι of that century. It is certain that the οὐσίαι were formed mostly of abandoned and waste κλῆροι confiscated by the government, some of them probably owned by the temples: see, e.g. *P.Ryl.* ii. 166 (A.D. 26), κλῆρος of the 5th γύον, cf. ibid., ii. 148 (A.D. 40), 18: εἰ⟨ς⟩ ἣν ἔχωι θήκην | ἀννήσου ἐν τοῖς κατοικικ[οῖς] ἐδάφε[σι] and *P.Oxyr.* 1434; *P.Lond.* iii, p. 127, no. 195 (cf. *P.Ryl.* ii, pp. 254 ff.) : the three estates which are described in this

last document consisted of parcels of γῆ κληρουχική and ἰδιόκτητος. An excellent illustration of the manner in which an οὐσία was formed is given by *P.Oxyr.* 1434 (A.D. 107/8), where the story of an estate of C. Iulius Theon is told in full. This man applied to C. Tyrannius, prefect of Egypt in 7–4 B.C., for land ἀπὸ λόγου Καίσαρος. The request was granted, but land was probably not assigned. A second application was sent to C. Iulius Aquila, prefect in A.D. 10–11, in which Theon asked for some land belonging to the sanctuary of Isis Taposiris to be granted to his son. This time the land was assigned: ἐφ' ᾧ τελέσει ἐπὶ πόλ(εως) (probably Alexandria, as Theon was an Alexandrian) ὑπὲρ τε | [ιμῶ]ν (B. Grenfell reads τε[λῶ]ν) καὶ ἑτέρων (τάλαντα) β, (δραχμὰς) .... This is exactly the same procedure as I have described in my *Studien z. Gesch. röm. Kol.*, p. 95. It was applied exclusively for the acquisition of land which after purchase became γῆ ἰδιωτική or ἰδιόκτητος. Theon's land, according to the original provisions recorded in the Edict of Ti. Iulius Alexander, was classed in respect of its payments under the heading of lands taxed at a reduced rate, see the heading of *P.Oxyr.* 1434: κουφο]τελειῶν ὧν τὰ ἀργυρικὰ καὶ σειτικὰ καθ(ήκοντα) [ἐν]θάδε λογίζεται. As regards provenance and legal status, the land of the οὐσίαι belonged therefore to the class of ἰδιωτική or ἰδιόκτητος. Individual concessions as regards *atelia* or *kouphotelia* may have been granted to some of the owners by a special charter. The emphyteutic character of the grants, which was an outstanding feature of grants of private land in general, applied also to the οὐσίαι. Even the irrigation work was done, as in the Ptolemaic period, to a large extent by the owners. In *P.Ryl.* ii. 171 (A.D. 56/57) the owner (Doryphorus) promised to his lessee to pay him a certain sum per aroura εἰς κατεργασίαν καὶ χωματισ[μόν]. Ibid. 132 (A.D. 32) an ἔμβλημα is described as οἰκοδομη-μένον | μετὰ δαπάνης οὐκ ὀ|λίγων κεφαλαίων | ἀργυρικῶν (ll. 13 ff.). The estates, like private land in general, were mostly cultivated as vineyards, orchards, and olive-groves, new plantations being a prominent feature of the management of the land. Thus, e.g. the οὐσίαι of Thermutharion (ibid. 152, A.D. 42) and of Doryphorus (ibid. 171, A.D. 56/57) consisted of vine and olive estates. Of the three estates (of which one at least belonged to M. Antonius Pallas) described in *P.Lond.* ii, p. 127, no. 195, (cf. *P.Ryl.* ii, pp. 254 ff.), one contains 65¼ ar. of ἄμπελος φόριμος and 126¾ ar. of ἄμπελος ἄφορος; in the second there are 57 ar. of ἀμπελῶνες, 50½ of νεόφυτα in one κλῆρος (for-merly the property of Gallia Polla), 6 ar. of the former class and 2½ of the latter and 2 ar. under a ληνών and χρηστήρια in the second κλῆρος (formerly belonging to Philox-enus, son of Theon); in the third estate 216¼ ar. of ἄφορος and probably 170$\frac{2}{32}$ ar. of φόριμος. No corn-land is mentioned. Along with vineyards, gardens (παράδεισοι), olive-groves (ἐλαιῶνες), reed-plantations (κάλαμοι), kitchen-gardens (λαχανεῖαι), plan-tations of μυροβάλανοι (see *P.Ryl.* ii, p. 255, note 4), and of fig-trees appear in each of the three estates. On the νεόφυτα see *P. Ryl.* ii. 138 (A.D. 34), 9; *P.Oxyr.* 1483; *P.Lond.* i, p. 175, no. 131 recto, l. 192, and p. 190 f., 131 verso, ll. 42, 83 (*P.Ryl.* ii, p. 244). The centres of the οὐσίαι were usually ἐποίκια, large farm-houses of the owner and adjacent houses of his tenants and workmen: *P.Ryl.* ii. 127 (A.D. 29) ἐποίκιον Ποπλίου καὶ Γαΐου Πετρωνίων; 171 (A.D. 56/57); 138 (A.D. 34): ἐποίκιον and πύργος (on πύργος as an agri-cultural building, see my article in *Anatolian Studies presented to Sir William Ramsay*, p. 374, note 1). As in Philadelphia in the 3rd cent. B.C., special buildings were devoted to the treatment of the grapes (ληνῶνες and χρηστήρια), to the making of olive-oil (ἐλαιουργεῖα), and to the grinding of corn (μύλα), *P.Ryl.* ii. 171; 128; Wilcken, *Chrest.* 176, &c. It is probable that free hired labour was mostly used on the estates; see, e.g. the recently published diptych, a day-book of an overseer of some estates (γῆ οὐσιακή or a private estate of the 3rd cent.), A. E. R. Boak, *JHS* 41, 1921, pp. 217 ff. [= *SB* 7013]; cf. *P.Lond.* i, pp. 166 ff., no. 131 (A.D. 78/79): a large private or imperial farm (accounts of the manager and cashier), and *P.Fay.* 102 (estate of the veteran Gemellus, see note 49). I studied the administration of the οὐσίαι in my *Studien z. Gesch. röm. Kol.*

New evidence shows that the administrators of the οὐσίαι (προεστῶτες, as in the Ptolemaic period), are often called γραμματεῖς (*BGU* 1669 and *P.Osl.* 2 (A.D. 71), in *Klio* 22, 1928, p. 224; cf. Wilcken, *Symb. Osl.* 7, 1928, p. 33). The owners of the οὐσίαι not only had their own granary, but used their own measures (*PSI* 1028). The θησαυρός of Livia, wife of Augustus, may be compared with the *arca* (or τράπεζα) she had in Asia Minor (Dessau, *ILS* 8853; cf., however, O. Hirschfeld, *Klio*, 2, 1902, p. 303 [= *Kl.Schr.*, p. 565]).

⁴⁷ The new policy is reflected both in the Edict of Ti. Iulius Alexander, which deals mostly with questions concerning the Alexandrians and therefore devotes a large space to discussing the οὐσίαι and the γῆ ἰδιωτική (*OGIS* 669 [= ‡H. G. Evelyn White and J. H. Oliver, *The Temple of Hibis*, ii (1939), pp. 23 ff., no. 3], cf. Wilcken, 'Zu den Edikten', *Zeitschr. d. Sav.-St.* 42, 1921, pp. 124 ff.), and in the papyri of the late 1st and early 2nd cent., especially *P.Amh.* 68 = Wilcken, *Chrest.* 374 (Domitian) and *BGU* 915 (1–2 cent. A.D.), cf. *P.Oxy.* 1434. The emperors of the end of the 1st cent., especially Vespasian and Domitian, probably ordered a general and thorough revision of existing titles, certainly with the aim of checking the illegal grabbing of land by the powerful magnates and of stopping the squandering of public money caused by letting good arable land become γῆ ἰδιωτική. And yet the prefect did not want to stop the selling of land altogether; in *BGU* 915. 9 ff. he says: ἦν | παραδεικνύουσι [γ]ῆν διὰ τῶ(ν) σπόρων καθ' ἔτος ἀναγραφέσθωσαν, τὴν δὲ συνήθ(ειαν) τὴν ἐμὴ(ν) [τ]ηρῶι, ἵνα μὴ δυσχερὴς οὖσα ἡ παράδειξις αὐτῆς τὴν πρᾶσειν ἐνποδίζηι. On the Edict of Ti. Iulius Alexander see my *Studien z. Gesch. röm. Kol.*, pp. 109 ff.; cf. Wilcken, *Chrest.* 375 (A.D. 246) as compared with 369 (A.D. 13/14). On the edict itself see the excellent article by Graf W. Uxkull-Gyllenband, *Arch. f. Papyr.* 9, pp. 199 ff. How deeply the Alexandrians were impressed and shocked by the reforms of Vespasian is shown by the well-known demonstrations of the population of the city against Vespasian, whom they had at first supported and helped to the throne. The sale of the old οὐσίαι was still going on in the 2nd cent. A.D., as is shown by *P.Bouriant*, 42: see the observations of P. Collart on the estate which had been owned by Antonia, Claudius's daughter (ibid., pp. 163, 174).

⁴⁸ M. Antonius Pallas, owner of a large οὐσία in the Hermupolites in A.D. 121 (*P.Lond.* iii, p. 139, no. 1223 = Wilcken, *Chrest.* 370), was probably a descendant of the famous M. Antonius Pallas and retained at least part of his estate. The οὐσία Προφητιανή of Claudia Athenais, also in the Hermupolites, is mentioned in *P.Strassb.* 78 (A.D. 127/8), cf. 74 (A.D. 126). Iulia Polla, *P.Lips.* 113 (A.D. 127/8), bears a cognomen which was used in many senatorial families. On the Athenaides of the family of Herodes Atticus see F. Münzer in Pauly–Wissowa, iii, col. 2889, no. 407; cf. ibid., col. 2677, nos. 71 and 72. Claudia Isidora, owner of a large estate in the Oxyrhynchites at the beginning of the 3rd cent., may have belonged to the same family, *P.Oxy.* 1630; cf. 919. 7, 1578, 1046, 1634, 1659, and the inscription *SB* 4961 (of the time of Domitian); cf. Tib. Claudia Eupatoris Mandane Atticilla, F. Münzer in Pauly–Wissowa, iii, col. 2889, no. 416.

⁴⁹ On the land owned by veterans, J. Lesquier, *L'Armée romaine d'Égypte*, pp. 328 ff. On L. Bellenus Gemellus of Aphroditopolis in the Fayyûm (about A.D. 100) and his correspondence, see W. L. Westermann, *An Egyptian Farmer* (in *Univ. of Wisconsin Studies in Language and Literature*, vol. 3); Bror Olsson, *Papyrusbriefe aus der frühesten Römerzeit* (1925), nos. 52–65. Exactly similar to him is L. Iulius Serenus, in A.D. 179, *summus curator* (treasurer) of the Ala Veterana Gallica, later *decurio*, finally a retired ex-*decurio* living on the income of his landed property. We possess part of his account-book of A.D. 179 (*P.Hamb.* 39) and a series of receipts for the payment of taxes for his estates (*P.Hamb.* 40–53, A.D. 213–19); cf. E. Grier, *Class. Phil.* 24, 1929, pp. 52 ff. The estate of Gemellus, besides producing corn, specialized in olive-growing; the estate of Serenus in viticul-

ture and sheep-breeding. Another veteran and big landowner, Iulius Horion, occurs in a declaration of uninundated land, *P.Oxyr.* 1459 (A.D. 226); his uninundated land alone amounted to at least 25 *arourae* in seventeen parcels. The declarations of uninundated land, confined to the owners of γῆ ἰδιόκτητος, are in general a good source of information on the private estates of the 2nd and 3rd cent.; see P. Meyer, *P.Hamb.* 11, intr., and V. Martin, 'Un Document administratif du nome de Mendès' in C. Wessely, *Studien zur Paläographie und Papyr.* 17 (1917), pp. 29 ff. Another excellent source is the numerous carbonized documents of Thmouis in the Mendesian nome; see V. Martin, loc. cit. and *P.Ryl.* ii. 213–22, intr. pp. 290 ff.; cf. *PSI* 101–8 and 229–35. Especially important for our purpose are the land-surveys in Geneva (V. Martin, loc. cit.; cf. M. Hombert, *Rev. belg. de phil. et d'hist.* 1925, pp. 634 ff.) and *P.Ryl.* ii. 216, both dealing with private and not with crown land. I cannot enter into details, but I lay stress on the preponderant part which is played in these documents by vineyards and olive-groves, of which some are new plantations. It must also be observed that the majority of the references to lands newly planted with vines and olives belong to the 1st cent. A.D., and refer to large estates. See Ch. Dubois, 'L'Olivier et l'huile d'olive dans l'ancienne Égypte', *Rev. de phil.* 1927, pp. 7 ff. (cf. ibid. 1925, pp. 60 ff.); C. Ricci, *La Cultura della vite nell'Egitto greco-romano* (1924). In the κωμογραμματεία of Hiera Nesos and four smaller villages, the total surface of which is reckoned at 12,600 *arurae*, 3,700 *arurae* are taken as γῆ ἰδιωτική or ἰδιωτικὰ ἐδάφη, 3,400 *arurae* as γῆ βασιλική, and the remainder (about half) belonged to various old οὐσίαι (P. Collart, *P.Bouriant*, 42, p. 159: A.D. 167). From this we can deduce the proportion between the land occupied by royal peasants and the private land on the border of the Fayyûm. The Flavian age represented a reaction against rapid increase in private property in Egypt, but, as I have shown, even under the Flavians the formation of new private estates, small and large, did not cease. This is probably because ability and energy were needed to make the borderlands useful and fertile, and the royal peasants certainly were not conspicuous for either of these qualities. If nobody was prepared to undertake the cultivation of derelict land voluntarily, such land was assigned to collective cultivation by peasants of other villages, by the procedure known as ἐπιμερισμός. See Wilcken, *Grundz.*, pp. 293 ff.; cf. *P.Bouriant*, 42. According to *P.Bouriant*, 42, out of 2,459 *arurae* of the village of Ptolemais, 859 did not find a lessee on the spot and were assigned to the village of Caranis. As a result a part of the inhabitants of Caranis were sent for a certain time to Ptolemais (P. Collart, *P.Bouriant*, p. 175). That explains why the authorities were in such a hurry to sell the old estates of Antonia—with small success (P. Collart, ibid., p. 173). Characteristic of the growth of large private fortunes is the fact that in the land-survey in Geneva three rich landowners grabbed one of not less than thirteen (Philoxenus), another of sixteen (Callimachus), and a third of nineteen parcels or farms. Note the two Greeks and one Roman as large landowners and the rare occurrence of Alexandrians, the μητροπολῖται prevailing (*P.Ryl.* ii. 216, intr. and notes; cf. *P.Bouriant*, 42). An interesting feature is the composition of the private estates. Like the οὐσίαι, they consisted mostly of γῆ κληρουχική and κατοικική; cf. the land-surveys of Naboo (Upper Egypt), *P.Giss.* 60 (A.D. 118), and Wilcken, *Chrest.* 341. In these documents the ancient terminology is kept in full, and this enables us to realize how densely populated and intensely exploited was the land in the Delta in the 3rd cent. B.C. I have no doubt that Ptolemy Philadelphus carried out in the Delta a no less important work of improvement than in the Fayyûm. One of the classes of cleruchic land, the enigmatic γῆ δεκαρούρων Ἰετηριτῶν, must certainly be understood as δεκαρούρων (δεκ)ετηριτῶν and testifies to a division of land in commemoration of the *deceteris* (*decennalia*) of one of the Ptolemies. As regards the nationality of the owners of the γῆ ἰδιωτική, the prevalence of Egyptians, holding mostly one parcel, is noticeable in *P.Ryl.* ii. 216. The prominent part played among the large landowners by actual and former officials is illustrated by the life and career of Apollonius, the *strategos* of Heptakomia in the time of Hadrian, as shown by his correspondence now at Giessen, see *P.Giss.* 3–27; A. G. Roos, *Apollonius strateeg van Heptakomia* (Groningen, 1923); cf. Kraemer, *Phil. Woch.* 1923, pp. 702 ff. and 727 ff. The quotation in the text is taken from *P.Amh.* 79 (A.D. 186); cf. *P.Ryl.* ii. 129 (A.D. 30), a *strategos* as owner of an estate in the Fayyûm. Other large landowners of the late 1st and of the 2nd cent.; Chaeremon, the gymnasiarch, *BGU* 248; cf. 249, 531, 594, 595, and 850 (Groningen, *Le Gymnasiarque*, p. 42*b*; cf. in general pp. 41 ff.); Valeria Gai ἀστή, *PSI* 31 (A.D. 164); cf. *BGU* 603, 604; Flavia Epimache, *P.Tebt.* 402 (A.D. 172); Ti. Claudius Irenaeus, P. Meyer, *Janus, Arbeiten zur alten und byzantinischen Geschichte*, 1, 1921, pp. 73 ff. [= *P.Hamb.* 64] (A.D. 104/5); cf. *P.Oxyr.* 727 (A.D. 154); *P.Fay.* 96 (A.D. 122) and 99 (A.D. 159), and *BGU* 390 (A.D. 148); cf. Bror Olsson, *Papyrusbriefe aus der frühesten Römerzeit* (1925), nos. 1–7 (Asclepiades and Isidora); 24 (Pausanias); 25–28 (Ammonius, a shipowner); 29–30 (a big trader of Alexandria); 34 (large villa) 41–47; (the above-mentioned Chaeremon); 50 (an individual escaped to Alexandria to avoid a liturgy).

50 On the stages through which passed the transformation of the private properties into οὐσιακὴ or βασιλικὴ γῆ see P. Collart, *P.Bouriant*, 42, pp. 156 ff. He conjectures, probably rightly, that the οὐσίαι or κτήσεις first became πρόσοδος or προσοδικὰ ἐδάφη, and then were incorporated in the γῆ οὐσιακή or the γῆ βασιλική: cf. *BGU* 1669. On the administration of the former οὐσίαι, which now formed a new class of state land, see my *Studien z. Gesch. röm. Kol.*, pp. 180 ff.; cf. F. Oertel, *Liturgie*, pp. 94 ff. and *P.Ryl.* ii. 168 (A.D. 120), intr. I have never denied that the οὐσιακοὶ μισθωταί were, in the earlier period, men who rented the land from the crown for exploitation. I doubt, however, even after the proofs produced by F. Oertel and the editors of *P.Ryl.*, if the farmers-general of an οὐσία had the right of sub-letting the land without at least officially informing the administration. The evolution of the system of exploitation of the γῆ οὐσιακή seems to have been as follows. In the earlier period (end of the 1st and beginning of the 2nd cent.) the land is leased by the administration of a given οὐσία mostly to small lessees (*P.Ryl.* ii. 207; cf. Wilcken, *Chrest.* 341). Gradually, however, the system arises of letting the οὐσία *en bloc* to one man, and develops, concurrently with the growth of the liturgical system in general, into a liturgical lease, while at the same time parcels of waste patrimonial land are assigned to farmers of state land and owners of private land; cf. F. Oertel, op. cit., and *P.Ryl.* ii. 202, note on p. 270, and *P.Ryl.* ii. 209 (on ἐπιμερισμός and ἐπιβολή); cf. Chap. XI and above, note 49. It is well known that the γῆ οὐσιακή was, side by side with the private and public land (γῆ βασιλική and δημοσία), one of the three large subdivisions of Egyptian land in general, see, e.g. *PSI* 807 (A.D. 280), ll. 8 ff.: ὑπὲρ γῆς | εἰς ἣν οὐκ ἐνφέρομαι | οὔτε κατὰ κληρονομί|αν (private land) οὔτε κατὰ | γεωργίαν (βασιλική and δημοσία γῆ) ἢ μίσθωσιν (οὐσιακὴ γῆ). How much waste land there was in Egypt after the great Jewish war of the time of Trajan, and how difficult it was to find lessees for this land, is shown by *BGU* 889 (Wilcken, *Hermes*, 54, 1919, pp. 111 ff.). From the last year of Trajan and the first of Hadrian to A.D. 145/6, land which became ἔρημος and ἄφορος ἐν τῷ Ἰουδ(αικῷ) ταράχῳ (A.D. 116/17), and which belonged to the οὐσία Μαικηνατιανή, remains in that condition and lessees cannot be found for it.

51 On the development of the *metropoleis* of Egypt in the 2nd cent. see P. Jouguet, 'Sur les métropoles égyptiennes à la fin du IIᵐᵉ siècle après J. C.', *Rev. ét. gr.* 30, 1917, pp. 294 ff.; cf. the bibliography for some *metropoleis* quoted in Chap. V, note 5, and H. Rink, *Strassen- und Viertelnamen von Oxyrhynchus* (Diss. Giessen, 1924). On the hellenization of the natives, J. Lesquier, *L'Armée romaine d'Égypte*, pp. 197 ff. On the service of the natives in the Egyptian army, suggested by a passage in the *Gnomon idiu logu*, J. Carcopino, *Rev. ét. anc.* 24, 1922, pp. 24 ff. Cf. H. A. Sanders, *TAPA* 55, 1924,

pp. 21 ff., and *P.Heidelb.* 72 (Hadrian): a native Egyptian called Psenamuris was enrolled in a legion and received the name of M. Longinus Valens. Of considerable importance is *PSI* 1026, a petition of twenty-two former soldiers of Egyptian origin, who had served in the fleet and later been incorporated in *legio X Fretensis* (A.D. 150). They beseech their commander to inform the prefect that they have received their *honesta missio* as legionaries and not previously as marines. L. Amundsen, 'A Latin Papyrus in the Oslo Collection', *Symb. Osl.* 10, 1932, pp. 16 ff., gives a list of papyri which contain lists of soldiers of the Egyptian army. Groningen, *Le Gymnasiarque*, &c., pp. 6 ff., attributes to Augustus the introduction of an organization of the Egyptian *metropoleis* on city lines, and E. Bickermann, *Arch. f. Papyr.* 9, pp. 35 ff., conjectures that about the Augustan age the old division of the population of Egypt between 'Greeks' and 'Egyptians' became obsolete, except in Alexandria, and was replaced by another division of inhabitants of a *metropolis* (subdivided into μητροπολῖται and κάτοικοι, *incolae*) and inhabitants of villages. He further supposes that the administration of the individual *metropoleis* was entrusted to a small group of inhabitants, the so-called οἱ ἀπὸ γυμνασίου. But it is possible that the social distinction between Greeks and Egyptians remained as it had been in the Ptolemaic period.

⁵² The ἀναχώρησις remained the characteristic feature of Egyptian life even in the comparatively happy period of the 1st and the beginning of the 2nd cent. It seems, however, as if the mentions of ἀναχωρήσεις in this period may all be explained by exceptional circumstances. In C. Wessely, 'Catal. P.R.' ii. 33 (1st cent.), in his *Studien*, &c., 22, 1923, a mass-ἀναχώρησις is explained by a plague, probably not a general but a local one (cholera and plague are still endemic in Egypt); cf. *P.Oxy.* 252 = Wilcken, *Chrest.* 215 (A.D. 19/20). The mysterious ἀνακεχωρηκότες of A.D. 103 (*PSI* 1043) are perhaps explained by the pressure exercised by the government on taxpayers during the effort of the Dacian war. The edict of M. Sempronius Liberalis (*BGU* 372 = Wilcken, *Chrest.* 19, A.D. 154) must be explained as a measure taken after general disturbances in Egypt in the time of Antoninus Pius: P. Meyer, *Klio*, 7, 1907, pp. 124; my *Studien z. Gesch. röm. Kol.*, pp. 207 ff.; Stein in Pauly-Wissowa, Zw. R. ii, cols. 1428 f.; cf. *P.Ryl.* ii. 78 (A.D. 157), col. i. 4; *P.Oxy.* 1438; *PSI* 822 (2nd cent. A.D.): strike (?) of workmen in alabaster mines. In general, Wilcken, *Grundz.*, p. 324 ff. It is not easy to decide whether the documents of Thmouis of the end of the 2nd cent. (*BGU* 902, 904, and *PSI* 101–8 and 229–35), which speak of mass-ἀναχωρήσεις and of a wholesale depopulation of some villages, are to be taken as a testimony to the incipient decay of Egypt in general, connected with the growing system of liturgies, compulsory work, and compulsory deliveries (see next chapter),.or whether they indicate some local cause (such as the plague of the time of M. Aurelius, the revolt of the Βουκόλοι, or a local inroad of the sea). Certainly the situation may have been aggravated by special circumstances. Yet the ultimate cause was undoubtedly the policy followed by the Roman government in the exploitation of Egypt: see my article in *Journ. of Econ. and Business Hist.* 1, 1929, pp. 337 ff. The only merit of the Roman government, its only service to the population, was that it maintained in good working order the irrigation system. Interruptions and cases of negligence there were, particularly in the middle of the 1st cent. A.D., but on the whole the work was done accurately and methodically: see *P.Ryl.* ii. 81 (A.D. 104), and the other documents quoted by the editors.

⁵³ On former researches on Nubia and the isle of Meroe see J. W. Crowfoot, 'The Island of Meroe', *Archaeological Survey of Egypt*, 19, 1911. The main works relating to the archaeology of Nubia are as follows (I do not intend to give a complete bibliography). *The Archaeological Survey of Nubia*: G. A. Reisner, *Report for 1907-8* (Cairo, 1910); Firth, *Report for 1908–9* (Cairo, 1912); id. *Report for 1909–10* (Cairo, 1915).

The Liverpool expedition. Town of Meroe: J. Garstang, A. H. Sayer, and F. Ll. Griffith, *Meroe, the City of the Ethiopians* (Oxford, 1911), report on the first campaign of excavations, 1909–10. Provisional reports of J. Garstang, A. H. Sayce, F. Ll. Griffith, and their assistants on the annual excavations at Meroe in *Liverpool Annals of Archaeology and Anthropology*, 3, 1910; 4, 1911–12; 5, 1912–13; 6, 1914; 7, 1914–16. The excavations, interrupted by the First World War, have never been completed. Archaeological investigations in the island of Meroe: see the report of J. W. Crowfoot, cited above, and in *Sudan Notes and Records*, published in Cairo from 1918 [in Khartoum from 1920]. The Oxford expedition. Excavations at Faras. F. Ll. Griffith, *Liverpool Annals*, 8, 1921; 10, 1923; 11, 1924; 12, 1925; 13, 1926, cf. the *Conspectus*, ibid. 15, 1928, pp. 82 ff. ibid. 13, 1926; 14, 1927; and 15, 1928, Griffith deals with the churches and Christian tombs of Faras; cf. id. *JEA* 11, 1925, pp. 259 ff., and J. W. Crowfoot, 'Christian Nubia', ibid. 13, 1927, pp. 141 ff. Pennsylvania expedition, *University of Pennsylvania, Egyptian Department of the University Museum*. Eckley B. Coxe, jr., *Expedition to Nubia*, vols. 1–6 (1910–11), especially vols. 3–4, *Karanog* by C. L. Woolley and D. Randall MacIver. Harvard–Boston expedition. Excavations of the necropolis of Napata and Meroe, at Kerma and Gammai. (*a*) Napata. G. A. Reisner, *Harvard African Studies*, 2, 1918, pp. 1–64; *Boston Museum, Fine Arts Bulletin*, nos. 97 and 112; *Sudan Notes and Records*, 2, 1919, pp. 237 ff.; 'Inscribed Monuments from Gebel Barkal', *Zeitschr. f. äg. Spr.* 56, 1931, pp. 76 ff.; (*b*) Meroe. G. A. Reisner, *Boston Mus. Fine Arts Bulletin*, no. 137, pp. 17 ff.; Dows Dunham, 'Two Royal Ladies of Meroe', *Boston Mus. of Fine Arts, Comm. to the Trustees*, 7, 1924; G. A. Reisner, 'The Meroitic Kingdom of Ethiopia. A Chronological Outline', *JEA* 9, 1923, pp. 34 ff. and 157 ff.; (*c*) Kerma. G. A. Reisner, 'Excavations at Kerma, i–iii', *Harvard African Studies*, 5, 1923; (*d*) Gammai, 'Excavations at Gammai', *Harvard African Studies*, 8, 1927. Austrian expedition. H. Junker, 'Turah', *Denk. Wien. Akad.* 56 (1), 1912; id. 'Kubanieh-Süd', ibid. 62 (3), 1919 and 'Kubanieh-Nord', 64 (3), 1920; id. 'Ermenne', ibid. 67 (1), 1925.

[54] General surveys of Nubian History: M. Chwostow, *History of the Oriental Trade of Greco-Roman Egypt* (1907) (in Russian), pp. 13 ff.; G. Roeder, 'Die Gesch. Nubiens und des Sudans', *Klio*, 12, 1912, pp. 51 ff. (antiquated); A. Kammerer, *Essai sur l'histoire antique d'Abyssinie. Le Royaume d'Aksum et ses voisins d'Arabie et de Méroé* (1926) (useful summary: see especially ch. x: 'Ezana, le Constantin de l'Abissinie', pp. 85 ff.); id. 'La Mer Rouge l'Abyssinie et l'Arabie depuis l'antiquité, I: Les pays de la mer Érythrée jusqu'à la fin du moyen âge', *Mém. de la Soc. roy. de Géographie d'Égypte*, 15, 1929; G. A. Reisner, 'Outline of the Ancient History of the Sudan', parts i–iii, in *Sudan Notes and Records*, 1, 1918, pp. 3 ff., 57 ff., 217 ff.; part iv, ibid. 2, 1919, pp. 35 ff.; id. 'The Pyramids of Meroe and the Candaces of Ethiopia', ibid. 5, 1922, pp. 173 ff. (cf. his reports quoted in note 53); F. Ll. Griffith, 'Oxford Excavations in Nubia', *Liverpool Annals*, 11, 1924, pp. 115 ff.; C. Conti-Rossini, 'Storia d'Etiopia', *Africa Italiana*, 3, 1928; id. *L'Abissinia* (1929); cf. D. Nielsen, Fr. Hommel, N. Rhodokonakis, *Handb. des altarab. Altertums*, 1, *Die altarab. Kultur* (1927). Meroitic inscriptions: F. Ll. Griffith, 'The Inscriptions from Meroe', *Meroe, the City of the Ethiopians* (1911), pp. 57 ff.; id. 'Meroitic Inscriptions, I', in Crowfoot, *The Island of Meroe* (1911), pp. 45 ff.; id. 'Meroitic Inscriptions, II', *Arch. Survey of Egypt*, 20, 1912; id. 'Karanog. The Meroitic Inscriptions of Shablul and Karanog', *Univ. of Pennsylvania Exped. to Nubia*, 6, 1911; id. 'Meroitic Studies', *JEA*, esp. 4, 1917, pp. 159 ff.; id. 'Faras', *Rec. Champollion*, pp. 565 ff.; id. 'Christian Documents from Nubia', *Proc. Brit. Acad.* 14, 1928; E. Gylarz, 'Das Meroitische Sprachproblem', *Anthropos*, 25, 1930. In his reconstruction of the list of kings of Meroe Reisner does not take into account the observation of Garstang that in the Ptolemaic period incineration was used instead of burial, and that the ashes of the kings and their families were put in urns within the citadel. If this observation is correct, Reisner's list needs revision.

[55] On Meroe and Nubia in the Ptolemaic period see the reports by J. Garstang in *Liverpool Annals*, quoted in note 53; cf. A. H. Sayce, ibid. 4, 1911–12, p. 63, and F. Ll. Griffith, ibid. 11, 1924, pp. 117 ff. The royal bath with its statues and Greco-Nubian frescoes is particularly interesting.

[56] This episode in Nubian history is well known. A beautiful head of a bronze statue of Augustus was found buried under the floor in the palace of Meroe. One may infer either that Candace did not give back to the Romans all the statues she took, or that there was a statue of Augustus for some time in the capital of the Ethiopian kingdom. See R. C. Bosanquet, *Liverpool Annals*, 4, 1911–12, pp. 66 ff., and J. Garstang, ibid. 6, 1914, pp. 1 ff. On the large stelae with Meroitic inscriptions, found at Meroe, and which according to A. H. Sayce (ibid. 7, 1914–16, p. 23) contain the Meroitic version of the expedition of Petronius, see F. Ll. Griffith, 'Meroitic Studies', *JEA* 4, 1917, pp. 159 ff. The text of the large stele, as Griffith attempted to interpret it, gives the name of the queen-mother, Amanineras, who seems to correspond to the one-eyed Candace of Strabo and the other Greek literary sources: her son is called Akinizaz. Both names appear again in other Meroitic inscriptions. It also seems certain that in the opening lines the names of Rome and the Romans appear frequently as enemies conquered by the queen and the royal prince. All this seems to show that in this stele we really have the Meroitic version of the victor of Petronius, here transformed into a victory of the queen of Meroe. If that is correct, Reisner's opinion that Strabo's Candace was a queen of Napata, and not of Meroe, must be reconsidered. On the Roman military occupation of Nubia see G. L. Cheesman, *Karanog*, text, pp. 106 ff. Kasr Ibrim (Primis or Premnis) was abandoned by the Romans after the conclusion of the peace between the queen of Meroe and Augustus. The terms of peace granted by Augustus in Samos show that Strabo probably exaggerated the successes of Petronius and that there is some truth in the boasts of the stele of Meroe. It looks as if we cannot speak any longer of a capture of Meroe by Petronius.

[57] On the gradual decay of Roman rule in the Dodecaschoenus see M. Chwostow, *History of the Oriental Trade of Greco-Roman Egypt* (1907) (in Russian), pp. 29 ff. Chwostow points out that Aelius Aristides, ii, p. 457 (Dind.) (Aristides may have visited Egypt more than once), expressly says that in his time the frontier had been withdrawn to the First Cataract. After this perpetual unrest reigned south of Thebes. On the Blemmyes and Nobades see Chwostow, op. cit., pp. 31 ff.; MacIver and Woolley, *Karanog*, text, pp. 85 ff.; F. Ll. Griffith, *Liverpool Annals*, 11, 1924, pp. 123 ff. On the later Christian history of Nubia see Griffith, ibid. 13, 1926; 14, 1927; 15, 1928. Cf. the work of Kammerer quoted in note 54. On the expeditions of Aeizanas see the inscription of Axum, *OGIS* 200 [= *Aksum*, iv (1913), p. 4, no. 4 = *SB* 6949]; cf. the fragment of a Greek inscription found at Meroe which probably refers to this king, Sayce, *Liverpool Annals*, 4, 1911–12, p. 64 [= *SB* 2055].

[58] On the ruins of temples, palaces, and water-reservoirs in the island of Meroe see J. W. Crowfoot, *The Island of Meroe* (cf. above note 53). On the tombs and ruins of Nubia see F. Ll. Griffith, *Liverpool Annals*, 13, 1926, pp. 17 ff. On the title of *peshates* (*psentes*) see Griffith, ibid. 12, 1925, p. 65, and 'Meroitic Inscriptions II' (cf. above note 54), p. 47, cf. *Liverpool Annals*, 13, 1926, pp. 17 ff.

[59] On the iron-mines of Meroe and the iron-foundries of the Meroitic centres see A. H. Sayce, *Liverpool Annals*, 4, 1911–12, p. 55. Sayce is wrong in believing that bronze was scarcely used in the kingdom of Meroe: Strabo, xvii. 2. 2, 821 c, speaks both of σιδηρουργεῖα and of χαλκωρυχεῖα in regard to the kingdom of Meroe, and his remark is confirmed by numerous discoveries of bronze furniture in the sepulchral zones of Nubia of the Meroitic period.

⁶⁰ J. W. Crowfoot, *The Island of Meroe* (see note 53).

⁶¹ The best description of the commerce between Greco-Roman Egypt and Nubia is to be found in M. Chwostow, *History of the Oriental Trade of Greco-Roman Egypt* (1907) (in Russian), pp. 4 ff.; cf. H. Kortenbeutel, *Der ägyptische Süd- und Osthandel in der Politik der Ptolemäer und römischen Kaiser* (1931), pp. 35 ff. Chwostow gives a complete list of the goods imported into Nubia and exported from it (pp. 4 ff.), and a valuable synthesis of the history of commercial relations between Nubia and Egypt (pp. 39 ff.). It is regrettable that his book is never cited by modern students of Nubian history. On gold see pp. 9 ff. with particular regard to the evidence of Strabo, xvii. 2. 2, 821 C, and Philostr. *Vita Apoll.* vi. 2. On the discovery of vases containing gold dust and nuggets see J. Garstang, *Liverpool Annals*, 4, 1911–12, pp. 49 ff. In one of the vases found under the walls of the royal palace near a completely empty treasure-room, were found some gold pyramids with the hieroglyphic names of two kings. According to Reisner, *JEA* 9, 1923, p. 75, these kings (successors of the famous Aspalta) ruled at Napata from 568 to 538 B.C. The vases may, however, have been buried much later.

⁶² The existence of commercial relations between Roman Egypt and Nubia is attested not only by the finds made in the Nubian towns and necropoleis, but also by the existence of a customs-house at Syene, and by the notice of Pliny, *NH* v. 59, that many Ethiopian boats reached the First Cataract. On the 'silent trade' see Philostr. *Vit. Apoll.* vi. 2. 1. The same sort of commerce characterized the relations between the Axumites and the Negroes (Cosmas Indic. *Top. Chr.* 139–40), and between the Carthaginians and the Negroes (Hdt. iv. 196). The better knowledge of central Africa which is displayed by Ptolemy and by the Anonymous [Hudson, *Geogr. vet. script. graec.* iv (1712), Ἀποσπασμάτιά τινα γεωγραφικά, pp. 38 ff, repeated in Müller–Fischer, Claud. Ptol. *Geogr.* ii, pp. 776–7], if compared with the very slight knowledge shown by Aristides and by the Anonymous with regard to Meroe, proves that Marinus of Tyre and the Anonymous derived their information not from Meroe, but from Axum: see M. Chwostow, op. cit., p. 694. On the commerce of Adulis see M. Chwostow, op. cit., pp. 32 ff., cf. pp. 194 ff. and 242 ff.

⁶³ On the excavations of the praetorium at Gortyn—not yet finished—see the preliminary reports in *Bolletino d'Arte*, the last by A. M. Colini, ibid. 5, 1926, pp. 413 ff. The inscriptions of the praetorium are published by M. Guarducci, *Riv. del r. Ist. d'arch. e Stor. d'Arte*, 1, 1929, pp. 193 ff.; ibid. 2, 1930, pp. 88 ff. [*Inscr. Cret.* iv, 10 and passim]. The name 'praetorium' for the building is established by an inscription of the time of Gratian, Valentinianus, and Theodosius, Guarducci, l.c., no. 7 [= *Inscr. Cret.* iv. 284a]; the name basilica occurs in nos. 19 and 25 [= *Inscr. Cret.* iv. 336a–b, 341].

⁶⁴ A good general description of the economic resources of Cyrenaica and Tripolitania may be found in the article of L. Homo, *Rev. des Deux Mondes*, 20, 1914 (2), pp. 389 ff. The material discovered after 1914 in the Italian excavations is to be found in the various Italian publications cited in Chap. V, note 4 and in Chap. II, note 6; cf. also note 98 of this chapter, and, in particular, G. Oliverio, *Africa Italiana*, 5, 1927, pp. 126 ff.; 6, 1928, pp. 296 ff. and 317 ff., and W. Uxkull-Gyllenband, *Gnomon*, 6, 1930, pp. 121 ff. The most important inscriptions relative to the organization of Cyrene both in the Classic and the Hellenistic and Roman periods are republished and illustrated in *Riv. fil.* 56, 1928; also by G. Oliverio, *Documenti antichi dell' Africa Italiana*, i–ii, 1932–6 [and *SEG* ix]. On the history of Cyrene in the Roman period see W. Rossberg, *Quaestiones de rebus Cyrenarum prov. Romanae* (1876); G. Oliverio, 'La Stele di Augusto rinvenuta nell'agora di Cirene', *Notiz Arch.* 4, 1927, pp. 33 ff.; J. Stroux and L. Wenger, 'Die Augustus-Inschrift auf dem Marktplatz von Kyrene', *Bayer. Abh.* 34 (2), 1928, pp. 44 ff.; H. Dessau, *Gesch. d. röm. Kaiserzeit*, ii. 2, pp. 560 ff.; A. von Premerstein, *Zeitschr. d. Sav.-St.*, 51, 1931, pp. 435 ff. (The article 'Kyrene' in Pauly-

Wissowa does not deal with the Roman period: see, however, the article in *Diz. epigr.* ii, pp. 1430 ff.): on the *bellum Marmaricum* see note 99 of this chapter. On the history of the *ager publicus* see Cic. *de lege agr.* ii. 50; Hygin, *de cond. agr.* ed Lachmann, i, p. 122; Tac. *Ann.* xiv. 18; cf. my *Studien z. Gesch. röm. Kol.*, pp. 326, 530; T. Frank, *JRS* 17, 1927, pp. 149 ff. Naturally, the *Ptolemaici Cyrenenses* of the late Republican inscription, Dessau, *ILS* 897, are not the tenants of the *agri regii*, as Frank, loc. cit., proposes, but the citizens of the well-known Ptolemais in Cyrene. On silphium and its disappearance in the Roman Imperial period see Plin. *NH* xix. 15. 38; Strab. xvii. 835; Solin. xxvii. 48; cf. E. Strantz, *Zur Silphionfrage* (1909). On attempts to identify silphium see C. Tedeschi, 'L'enigma del silfio cirenaico', *Notiz. Econ. d. Cirenaica*, 1929 (no. 4), pp. 50 ff.; B. Bonacelli, 'Il silfio non venne ancora ritrovato', *Rassegna Economica delle Colonie*, 1929, nos. 11–12. On the Hellenes in general see W. Uxkull-Gyllenband, op. cit., p. 131; A. von Premerstein, l.c. Vespasian's care in restoring the *ager publicus* to the Roman people is shown by the *cippi* found at Cyrene, erected in A.D. 71, which say that Q. Paconius Agrippinus, legate of the emperor *p(opulo) R(omano) Ptolmaeum* (in the Greek text Πτυλυμαῖον) *restituit*: see E. Ghislanzoni, *Notiz. Arch.* 2, 1916, pp. 165 ff. = *L'An. ép.* 1919, 91 and 93. The Πτολεμαιεῖον is undoubtedly a τέμενος, probably a park (ἄλσος) dedicated at Cyrene to Ptolemy and hence his own property: cf. Ditt. *Syll.³* 463 (Itanos, Crete, *c.* 246 B.C.): ἱαρὸν τέμενος | [ἱ]δρύσασθαι τὸν παράδισον τὸν πρὸς τᾶι πύλαι | βασιλέως Πτολεμαίου καὶ βασιλίσσης Βερενίκας κ.τ.λ. [*Inscr. Cret.* iii, p. 83, no. 4]. On such ἄλση or *luci* in Egypt see my article in *JEA* 12, 1926, pp. 28 ff. For the devastations effected by the Jews in Cyrenaica see the milestone of Hadrian, of A.D. 118–19, found in Cyrenaica: *viam quae tumultu Iudaico eversa et corrupta erat re-s(tituit)*, Ghislanzoni, l.c., pp. 195 ff. Cf. the inscription in honour of Hadrian, which speaks of the restoration of a bath, G. Oliverio, *Africa Italiana*, 1, 1927–8, p. 321: *balnea . . . quae tumultu Iudaico diruta et exusta erant* [cf. *JRS* 40, 1950, pp. 87 ff.; ibid. 42, 1952, p. 37]. For the repopulation of Cyrenaica by Hadrian see Orosius, vii. 12 (quoted Chap. VIII, note 12). From all this evidence one gathers that Hadrian considered this province an important possession. For the benefits conferred by him on Cyrene see the inscription in Ghislanzoni, l.c., pp. 195 ff. Stele with name of ephebes of Cyrene, Ghizlanzoni, *Notiz. Arch.* 4, 1927, pp. 189 ff. [= *SEG* ix. 128]. On the Roman troops in Cyrenaica and the Pentapolis see E. Ritterling, *JRS* 17, 1927, pp. 28 ff. Syrian soldiers at Cyrene: S. Ferri, *Riv. di Tripolitania*, 2, 1926, pp. 363 ff. On the action of Nero in Crete, comparable to that of Vespasian in Cyrene, see *L'An. ép.* 1919, 22.

⁶⁵ See the bibliography quoted in Chap. V, note 4. On the romanization of Africa Proconsularis, see T. R. S. Broughton, *The Romanization of Africa Proconsularis* (1929) (Johns Hopkins University, Studies in History and Political Science, Extra Volumes, N.S., no. 5). Broughton gives a useful survey of the cities in Africa, and of the development of the large estates.

⁶⁶ On pre-Roman Africa see the brilliant treatment of the scanty evidence in S. Gsell, *Histoire de l'Afrique*, iv (1920), pp. 1 ff. On the conditions of agriculture in the African territory and the influence of local tradition on the development of the African colonate, see Hesselmeyer, 'Das vorrömische Karthage in seiner Bedeutung für den spätrömischen Kolonat', *Korr.-Blatt. f. d. höh. Schulen Württembergs*, 32, 1916, pp. 393 ff.

⁶⁷ Th. Mommsen, *Röm. Gesch.* v, p. 623.

⁶⁸ On the early Roman organization of Africa and on the law of 111 B.C., see Mommsen, *CIL* i. 200, and his masterly introduction and commentary reprinted in his *Ges. Schr.* i, pp. 65 ff., especially pp. 119 ff.; M. Weber, *Die römische Agrargeschichte* (1891), pp. 152 ff.; my *Studien z. Gesch. röm. Kol.*, pp. 314 ff.; W. Barthel, *Bonn. Jahrb.* 120, 1911, pp. 76 ff.; S. Gsell, *Hist. de l'Afrique*, vii (1928), pp. 74 ff.; and the bibliography

quoted in Chap. I, note 20, especially W. Ensslin, *Neue Jahrb.* 54, 1924, pp. 15 ff., and Ch. Saumagne, *Rev. de phil.* 1927, pp. 50 ff. Barthel attributes the centuriation of Africa to the Gracchi, while Gsell, *Rev. Hist.* 156, 1927, p. 235, and cf. *Hist. de l'Afrique*, vii, pp. 47 ff., holds that it was probably carried out soon after 146 B.C. On the different types of refuge-castles and of cities in the kingdoms of Numidia and Mauretania see Gsell, *Hist. de l'Afrique*, v (1927), pp. 223 ff. On the *pagi* of the Muxsi, &c., see R. Cagnat, A. Merlin, L. Chatelain, *Inscriptions latines d'Afrique* (1923), 422 (quoted in the following notes as *ILA*) = Dessau, *ILS* 9482; cf. A. Merlin, *C. R. Acad. Inscr.* 1913, p. 166, and Dessau, *ILS* 901. On the pagus Gurzensis, *CIL* viii. 68, 69, and E. Kornemann, 'Die caesarische Kolonie Karthago', *Philol.* 60, 1901, p. 404. Pagus Assaritanus, *ILA* 501. Cf. Dessau, *ILS* 901.

⁶⁹ On the Roman *negotiatores* in Africa see E. Kornemann in Pauly–Wissowa, iv, cols. 1182 ff.; V. Pârvan, *Die Nationalität der Kaufleute* (1909). Of great interest is the inscription, *ILA* 306 = Dessau, *ILS* 9495: 'Augusto deo cives Romani qui Thinissut negotiantur, curatore L. Fabricio.' The Marian veterans received land both in the Uchi Majus (A. Merlin and L. Poinssot, *Les Inscriptions d'Uchi Majus* (1908), pp. 17 ff.) and in Thibaris (Dessau, *ILS* 6790). On Sittius, T. Rice Holmes, *The Roman Republic*, iii (1923), pp. 246 ff., 272 ff. The quotation in the text is from him; cf. Gsell, op. cit. viii (1928), pp. 157 ff.

⁷⁰ On the activity of Caesar in Africa see E. Kornemann, *Philol.* 60, 1901, pp. 402 ff. Of great importance is the well-known inscription *CIL* x. 6104, of 44 B.C., mentioning eighty-three *castella* attached to the city of Carthage; cf. a similar mention of a *praefectus* of seventy-two *castella* which may have belonged to the territory of Mactaris, an ancient Punic city, in *CIL* viii. 23599. The theory of the *coloniae Iuliae* attached to Carthage was first formulated by E. Kornemann, loc. cit. It is supported by the fact that three colonies were attached to Cirta (see note 82) and were called *coloniae contributae* (cf. Gsell, op. cit. vii, pp. 159 ff.), but the history of Cirta is a peculiar one and cannot be taken as normal for the rest of Africa. Furthermore the evidence for Carthage is meagre and far from convincing. The allegiance to the African capital of the cities which were originally attached to Carthage is attested by the cult of Carthage —the object of the cult is the Semitic god which corresponds to the Greek Τύχη, the goddess of the city—in the minor cities of the Proconsular province: see A. Merlin and L. Poinssot, *Inscr. d'Uchi Majus*, p. 24, no. 3 (statue of Carthage dedicated by the city of Uchi); cf. Dessau, *ILS* 9398 = *CIL* viii. 26239, and L. Poinssot, *Bull. arch. du Com. des trav. hist.* 1917, p. 31, note 2. This cult of Carthage is, of course, not only a reminiscence but also a testimony to the growing pride of the Africans in their own country. Carthage is now the capital, overshadowing Rome. On the rebuilding of the town by Caesar and Augustus see S. Gsell, 'Les Premiers Temps de la Carthage romaine', *Rev. hist.* 156, 1927, pp. 225 ff., and *Hist. de l'Afrique*, viii, pp. 173 ff.

⁷¹ Pliny, *NH* v. 1–4 (1–30). On the *coloniae Iuliae* in Africa, E. Kornemann, 'Colonia', in Pauly–Wissowa and the sensible judgement of Gsell, op. cit. viii, pp. 167 ff., 197 ff. On the colonies in Mauretania, J. Carcopino, *Bull. arch. du Com. des trav. hist.* 1919, pp. 170 ff. and Gsell, op. cit. viii, pp. 201 ff.

⁷² The colony of Thuburbo founded by Augustus existed for a time side by side with the *civitas* of natives. The *civitas* was granted the rights of a *municipium* by Hadrian. Finally, in the time of Commodus the two bodies coalesced into one *colonia Aurelia Commoda* or *Iulia Aurelia Commoda*, see L. Poinssot, *C. R. Acad. Inscr.* 1915, pp. 325 ff.; A. Merlin, *Le Forum de Thuburbo Majus* (1922), p. 13. On Carthage see W. Barthel, *Zur Geschichte der römischen Städte in Africa* (1904), pp. 19 ff. Cf. the writings of Gsell quoted in note 70. Gsell believes that the indigenous community, of which we have some coins, survived only a short time and was merged into the Roman colony. But R. Albizzati,

'Studi d'arch. Rom.', 1928, pp. 7ff., pl. 1 (*Ann. d. Fac. di Lett. della R. Univ. di Cagliari*, 1–2, 1926–27 (publ. 1928)), points out that the coins in question with the name of two suffetes and with the legend *Ex Kar* on the obverse are exactly like those of Metalla and Uselis in Sardinia and that a hoard of such coins was found in 1865 in the region of Cagliari (Caralis). Cf. L. Poinssot, *Bull. Soc. Ant. de France*, 1928, p. 266. Carthage thus disappears from the list of cities with two communities. On Hadrumetum, *CIL* viii, Suppl. p. 2319. On Hippo, ibid. 25417, cf. H. Dessau, *Klio*, 8, 1908, pp. 457 ff. Note that both Hadrumetum and Hippo were not *civitates* but *oppida libera*, and yet colonies were sent to these places. A similar case is that of Volubilis in Mauretania (E. Cuq, *C. R. Acad. Inscr.* 1920, pp. 339 ff.), though Volubilis was not a colony but a *municipium civium Romanorum*, *ILA* 634; cf. 608 and 613, and L. Chatelain, *C. R. Acad. Inscr.* 1924, p. 77. See also the bibliography on the inscription of Volubilis in Chap. III, note 5.

73 On the double communities of Africa see W. Barthel, *Zur Gesch. d. röm. Städte in Africa* (1904), and *Bonn. Jahrb.* 120, 1911, p. 81, note 1; A. Merlin and L. Poinssot, *Inscr. d'Uchi Majus*, pp. 17 ff.; L. Poinssot, *Nouv. Archives d. miss. scient.* 21. 8, pp. 65 ff.; 22, pp. 171 ff.; cf. on Thugga, *CIL* viii, p. 2615 (introduction to the inscriptions of Thugga). On Sutunurca, Dessau, *ILS* 9400=*ILA* 301: 'cives Romani pagani veter(ani) pagi Fortunalis quorum parentes beneficio divi Augusti. . . . Sutunurca agros acceperunt'; cf. *CIL* viii. 24003, 24004: 'civitas Sutunurcenses'. On Medeli, *CIL* viii. 885 (cf. 12387) = Dessau, *ILS* 6803: 'ex decreto pagi Mercurialis (et) veteranorum Medelitanorum'. On Sicca, Dessau, *ILS* 6783, 6805–7; *CIL* viii. 27823; cf. Dessau, *ILS* 444, and *CIL* viii. 17327: Aubuzza, Titulitanenses, Ucubi, &c., *castella* attached to Sicca. At Aubuzza many Roman citizens formed a pagus, Dessau, *ILS* 6783: 'Genio coloniae Iuliae Veneriae Chirtae novae . . . [cives Romani qui] Aubuzza consistunt paganicum pecunia sua a solo [resti]tuer[unt]'. Also an inscription of Rusgunii, *L'An. ép.* 1928, 23, probably confirms the same subdivision into natives and Roman immigrants: *Rusg(unienses) et Rusgunis consistentes* honour a magistrate of the city *ob merita aere collato, quod annonam frumenti passus non sit increscere*, cf. Chap. V, note 9. An interesting instance of a *castellum* (Roman citizens?) co-existing with a *civitas* is furnished by Thiges in Byzacena, *CIL* viii. 23165, 23166 (A.D. 83 and 97); cf. the *castellum* and the *civitas* Biracsaccarensium, *CIL* viii. 23849; cf. 23876. The same conditions prevailed in Mauretania, *CIL* viii. 20834 = Dessau, *ILS* 6885: 'veterani et pagani consistentes apud Rapidum'. Here, as at Medeli, not all the *pagani* were veterans. In many places the *civitas* is expressly stated to consist of natives, e.g. at Masculula, *CIL* viii. 15775: 'conventus civium Romanorum et Numidarum qui Mascululae habitant'; at Sua, *Bull. arch. du Com. des trav. hist.* 1894, p. 321: 'Afri et cives Romani Suenses'; at Chiniava, *CIL* viii. 25450: 'ordo Chiniavensium peregrinorum'.

74 W. Barthel, *Bonn. Jahrb.* 120, 1911. On the 'agrarian immigration' into Africa see Chap. I, notes 19 and 32; T. R. S. Broughton, *The Romanization of Africa Proconsularis* (1929), pp. 78 ff. Broughton, p. 83, does not believe there was a 'huge' immigration; but I never said there was. Does he possess statistics which allow us to establish how many Italians emigrated to Africa? Taking into account the general lack of evidence, and the traces which this immigration has left, we cannot fail to be convinced that in its time it was a factor of some importance. I am not even persuaded by the objections of H. Dessau, *Gesch. d. röm. Kaiserzeit*, ii, 2, p. 475, note 2. Why should those dispossessed in 30 B.C. all have gone to Macedonia (Dessau, op. cit., p. 565) and not also to Africa Proconsularis and to the rich valleys of Numidia? We cannot calculate how many Roman citizens there were among the African peasantry in the 2nd cent. A.D. (but see note 83), and, even if we could, that would not give a norm for conditions in the 1st cent.: clever farmers could become landowners, while the weak ones died out. One must also bear in mind the large number of *municipia Iulia* and *coloniae Iuliae*

created in Africa by Caesar and Augustus. Side by side with this planned emigration, which took not only veterans to Africa, there was certainly also a migratory current arising from the free initiative of the emigrants.

75 On the imperial land and the *saltus* of the senatorial aristocracy in Africa, my *Studien z. Gesch. röm. Kol.*, pp. 320 ff.; cf. E. Kornemann in Pauly–Wissowa, Suppl. iv, cols. 249 ff. Since the appearance of the former book no general work on the African *saltus* has been published nor have any important new inscriptions been found. The section on the African inscriptions in W. Heitland, *Agricola*, pp. 342 ff., contains a useful survey of the evidence. Cf. E. von Nostrand, *The Imperial Domains of Africa* (1925); T. Frank, 'Inscriptions of the Imperial Domains', *AJP* 47, 1926, pp. 55 ff., 153 ff., and *Economic History*[2], pp. 444 ff. The *Lex Manciana* and the inscriptions of Ain el Gemala and Ain Wassel are published in *CIL* viii. 25902 [= *FIRA*[2], 100], 25943, 26416, cf. J. Carcopino, *Quelques passages controversés du règlement d'Henchit Mettich* (1928). As is well known, the date and character of the *Lex Manciana* are controversial. S. Gsell, *Hist. de l'Afr.* vii, p. 86 and viii, p. 167 believes that the law is earlier than the Empire, and belongs to the period immediately after the large sale of *ager publicus* (the old domains of the kings of Numidia). It is interesting to find that the *Lex Manciana* was still operative in the time of the Vandals, as is shown by one of the very peculiar sale-contracts written on wooden tablets, which were found near Tebessa and published by E. Albertini, 'Actes de vente de l'époque vandale trouvés dans la région de Tébéssa', *Journ. Sav.* 1930, pp. 23 ff. [See *Tablettes Albertini*, ed. C. Courtois, L. Leschi, C. Perrat, and C. Saumagne (Paris, 1952).] This act, of A.D. 496, says that the land sold is *ex culturis suis mancianis d(e) p(raedio) Tuletanensis sub dominio Flabi G(emini) Catullini flam(inis) p(er)p(etui)* [= op. cit., no. xi, 22b]. I believe that the two vendors occupied plots of land belonging to Catullinus in conformity with the *Lex Manciana*. The *Lex Manciana* was certainly still in force in the 3rd cent. A.D.

76 S. Gsell, *Inscriptions latines de l'Algérie*, i. 2939, 2988, 2989; Dessau, *ILS* 5958 a–b and 5959: boundary stones between the Musulamii, the emperor, and the colonies of Ammaedara and Madaurus; cf. *CIL* viii. 28073 ff. A private estate in the territory of the Musulamii, owned by Valeria Atticilla, is mentioned in *Inscr. lat. de l'Alg.* 2986; cf. L. Carton, *C. R. Acad. Inscr.* 1923, pp. 71 ff. As is well known, the saltus Beguensis with the village Casae was situated 'territorio Musulamiorum', *CIL* viii. 23246; cf. L. Poinssot and R. Lantier, *Bull. Soc. Ant. de France*, 1923, pp. 147 ff. On the *praefecti gentium* in Africa, R. Cagnat, *L'Armée romaine d'Afrique*, 2nd ed., pp. 263 ff.; cf. *Not. d. Scavi*, 1895, p. 342 [= Dessau, *ILS* 9195], and *CIL* v. 5267 (time of the Emperor Nero).

77 S. Gsell et A. Joly, *Khamissa, Mdaourouch, Announa. I. Khamissa* (1914), pp. 13 ff. *Principes* of the Numidae: *CIL* viii. 4884 = Dessau, *ILS* 6800; *C. R. Acad. Inscr.* 1904, p. 479 = Dessau, *ILS* 9392 [= *Inscr. lat. de l'Alg.*, 1297]; cf. *C. R. Acad. Inscr.* 1904, p. 484 = Dessau, *ILS* 9391 [= *Inscr. lat. de l'Alg.* 1226]: 'Genio gentis Numidiae sacrum'. On the *principes* of the tribes in general, S. Gsell, op. cit., pp. 15 ff. The part played by the *principes* in Africa and their relation to the military *praefecti*, generally Roman officers, are exactly the same as on the Danube, see Chap. VI, note 70. Large private estates in the territory of Thubursicu Numidarum are enumerated by S. Gsell, op. cit., pp. 29 ff.

78 Nybgenii: R. Cagnat, *C.R. Acad. Inscr.* 1909, pp. 568 ff. [= *CIL* viii, 22787–8]; W. Barthel, *Bonn. Jahrb.* 120, 1911, pp. 87 ff. Musunii Regiani: *ILA* 102 = Dessau, *ILS* 9393; *ILA* 103; *CIL* viii. 23195. Suburbures: Dessau, *ILS* 9380, 9381. Nattabutes: J. Toutain, *Les Cités romaines de la Tunisie*, p. 344; S. Gsell, *Atlas archéologique de l'Afrique*, feuille 18, no. 135; *CIL* viii. 4836, cf. 16911: 'Flaminali[s] Saturi[f.] qui flamonium c(ivitatis) N(attabutum) c(onsecutus) item principatu(m) civitatis suae.' Nicivibus: S. Gsell, *Atlas*, feuille 26, no. 161. Zimizenses or Zimizes: *CIL* viii. 8369 = Dessau, *ILS* 5961 (A.D. 128): 'termini positi inter Igilgilitanos in quorum finibus kastellum Victoriae positum est et Zimiz(es)

ut sciant Zimizes non plus in usum haber(e) ex autoritate M. Vetti Latronis proc. Aug. qua(m) in circuitu a muro kast(elli) p(assus quingentos).' Saboides: *CIL* viii. 7041 (cf. 19423) = Dessau, *ILS* 6857: 'Florus Labaeonis fil(ius) princeps et undecemprimus gentis Saboidum.' Chinithi: *CIL* viii. 22729 = Dessau, *ILS* 9394. Gens Bacchuina: *CIL* viii. 12331 = Dessau, *ILS* 4440.

⁷⁹ On *definitio* and *defensio* see my articles quoted in note 34.

⁸⁰ S. Gsell and A. Joly, *Khamissa, Mdaourouch, Announa. III. Announa* (1916).

⁸¹ R. Cagnat, 'La Colonie romaine de Djemila', *Mus. Belge*, 1923, pp. 113 ff.; cf. id. *Rev. ét. anc.* 17, 1915, pp. 34 ff. and 183 ff.; *C. R. Acad. Inscr.* 1916, p. 593; E. Albertini, ibid. 1924, p. 253. In one of the inscriptions a veteran settled in Cuicul calls himself *acceptarius*, i.e. one who was granted land; cf. note 73 on Sutunurca and Chap. VI, note 78, on the *missio agraria* in Pannonia.

⁸² *CIL* viii. 8210 = Dessau, *ILS* 6864, cf. *CIL* viii. 7988 = Dessau, *ILS* 5648, and *CIL* 7963, cf. 19849 = Dessau, *ILS* 5473.

⁸³ My *Studien z. Gesch. röm. Kol.*, p. 369, and my article in *Oest. Jahresh.* 4, 1901, Beibl., p. 41, note 9, and p. 43, notes 12, 13. In the numerous inscriptions of the villages we meet almost everywhere with *magistri* and often even with a council of *decuriones*. Some inscriptions add much to our knowledge of the *vici*. Near Semta a certain Q. Geminius Q. fil. Arn. Sabinus, who had a long and brilliant military career under the Flavians and Trajan, bequeathed to the 'vicani vici Annaei' a certain sum of money with the obligation of erecting some statues to him in the *vicus*. The acting magistrate is D. Annaeus Arn. Advena (see L. Poinssot and R. Lantier, *C. R. Acad. Inscr.* 1923, pp. 197 ff. [= *L'An. ép.* 1923, 28]). It is evident that the *vicus* grew up on the private estate of a certain Annaeus (*CIL* viii. 23116 and 12065), was populated by Roman citizens partly from Carthage (the 'Arnensis' is the *tribus* of Carthage), and soon developed into a quasi-urban centre; it possessed apparently the *ius legatorum capiendorum*. Similar was the development of the 'vicus Haterianus', another settlement on a private estate. A statue to the Emperor Hadrian was erected here by the 'cives Romani qui vico Hateriano morantur' (*CIL* viii. 23125 = Dessau, *ILS* 6777). Many funeral inscriptions of the *vicus* give names of Roman citizens (*ILA* 78). Another *vicus* on a private estate is mentioned in the inscription *L'An. ép.* 1913, 226, where a certain Phosphorus has built a temple to Ceres, 'item vicum qui subiacet huic templo', and ends his inscription by saying 'et nundinas instituit qui vicus nomine ipsius appellatur'; cf. J. Carcopino, *Bull. arch. du Com. des trav. hist.* 1918, pp. 232 ff. In a *vicus* near, or of, Lambiridi two *magistri* who gave the village 'mensuras publicas frumentarias' were both Roman citizens (P. Albertini, *Bull. arch. du Com. des trav. hist.* 1921, juin, p. viii [= *L'An. ép.* 1922, 12]). A very instructive series of inscriptions comes from the 'vicus Verecundensis' near Lambaesis, which is called also 'vicus Augustorum Verecundensis' and therefore was a village of an imperial estate. One of these, belonging to the time of Antoninus Pius, mentions 'possessores vici Verecundensis', *CIL* viii. 4199 (cf. 18493) = Dessau, *ILS* 6850. Another (*CIL* viii. 4249 (cf. 18503) = Dessau, *ILS* 6852a) honours a citizen of the Ortani and Falerienses, 'Verecundensium incolae et flamini per(petuo) et principi'; cf. *CIL* 4205, cf. 18497 = Dessau, 5752. In *CIL* viii. 4192, cf. p. 1769 = Dessau, *ILS* 6851), the 'ordo Verecun(densis)' is mentioned; cf. also *CIL* viii. 4194 (cf. 18490) = Dessau, *ILS* 6852. It is worthy of note that most of these inscriptions date from the time of Hadrian. On the *nundinae* in the *vici* see the well-known inscription of the saltus Beguensis, the village of which bore the characteristic name 'Casae', i.e. 'Houses', comparable with the well-known 'Mappalia Siga'; *CIL* viii. 270, 11451 (cf. 23246); cf. 8280 (cf. 20077) = Dessau, *ILS* 6869, and note (vicus et nundinae' in the private estate of Antonia Saturnina); *CIL* viii. 20627 = Dessau, *ILS* 4490 ('nundinae' of the tribe Vanisnensium, or is it a *vicus*?);

CIL viii. 6357 = Dessau, *ILS* 6868: 'nundinae habentur in castello Mastarensi'. Cf. M. Besnier in Daremberg–Saglio, pp. 122 ff., and Chap. VI, note 93.

84 On the *praefecti iuvenum* and the organization of the *iuvenes* in Africa see *Inscr. lat. de l'Alg.*, 3080, note; cf. R. Cagnat, *Rev. ét. anc.* 22, 1920, pp. 97 ff., especially p. 100 (inscription of the well-known benefactor of the city of Cuicul C. Iulius Crescens Didius Crescentianus [=*L'An. ép.* 1920, 114–15]). Still more important is the inscription of Thuburnica, L. Carton, *Bull. arch. du Com. des trav. hist.* 1920, p. xl = *L'An. ép.* 1921, 21. It is interesting to see that here the *praefectus iuvenum* is a veteran who had the charge of enrolling recruits in Mauretania ('praefectus tironum in Mauretania'). On the *iuvenes* cf. Chap. II, note 34, and Chap. VI, note 57.

85 *ILA* 180, boundary 'inter colonos [of Ammaedara] et socios Tal(enses)'.

86 My *Studien z. Gesch. röm. Kol.*, pp. 320 ff.

87 Some inscriptions have supplied us with valuable information on the *conductores* of the imperial estates. An influential citizen of Thugga was A. Gabinius Quir. Datus, one of the members of the association of the 'conductores praediorum regionis Thuggensis', *ILA* 568, 569; the stone was set up to him by the association through a special *curator*, see J. Carcopino, *Rev. ét. anc.* 24, 1922, pp. 13 ff.; cf. *L'An. ép.* 1924, 28–30. Another association of the same type is attested by the inscription, *Inscr. lat. de l'Alg.* 3992: 'T. Flavio T. f. Quir. Macro II vir(o), flamini perp. Ammaedarensium, curatori frumen[ti] comparandi in annona(m) urbis facto a divo Nerva Traian(o) Aug., proc. a[d pr]aedia saltus Hippon[ensi]s et Theve[st]ini, proc. provinc[i]ae S[ic]iliae, collegium Larum Caesaris n. et liberti et familia item conductores qui in regione Hippon[ens]i consist⟨u⟩nt.' Note the similarity of the terminology of this inscription to that used by the *negotiatores* of Africa of the Republican and the early Imperial periods. The career of the man is noteworthy. He was probably himself a landowner or a *conductor* before he started his career. As an expert in corn-trade, he was appointed by Trajan *curator* of supplies which were destined for the city of Rome. Having shown himself a good and faithful officer, he was appointed chief of an important district of imperial and public lands, and finally procurator of one of the most important corn-provinces of Rome, Sicily. Cf. *Inscr. lat. de l'Alg.* 285 (Guelma, an inscription in honour of the same man). More evidence on the imperial estates: L. Poinssot, 'Un Domaine impérial voisin de Thubursicum Bure', *Bull. Soc. Ant. de France*, 1921, pp. 324 ff. and Ch. Saumagne, *Bull. arch. du Com. des trav. hist.* 1927 (February), p. xli.

88 It is not possible to collect here the new evidence on the different officials of the patrimonial department in Africa which has been published since 1910. It is interesting to find the two procurators of the *Lex Manciana* (*CIL* viii. 25902 [= *FIRA*², 100]) reappearing in an inscription of the time of Trajan, *ILA* 440. Copious fresh information on the *tractus* of Hippo has been afforded by the inscriptions found in this city, *ILA* 89, 92, 99, 100, 101, 102; cf. 323, 325, 476, 477 (Calama), and 3991. On the *regio Leptiminensis* see *ILA* 3062, 3063; cf. *ILA* 135, and 52.

89 On Pactumeius Fronto see A. Stein, *Der römische Ritterstand*, pp. 219 ff. On the Antistii see S. Gsell and A. Joly, *Khamissa, Mdaourouch, Announa. III. Announa* (1916).

90 R. Cagnat, *Bull. arch. d. Com. des trav. hist.* 1893, pp. 214 ff., no. 25 = *ILA* 280; A. Merlin and L. Poinssot, *Inscriptions d'Uchi Majus*, pp. 58 ff., nos. 40–41. Cf. the family of the Arrii, *CIL* viii. 23831 = *ILA* 279; cf. *CIL* viii. 23832; vi. 1478; iii. 6810–12; A. Merlin, *Bull. arch. d. Com. des trav. hist.* 1915, p. cxxxvii (and 1916, p. cxxxii).

91 L. A. Constans, 'Gigthis', *Nouv. Arch. d. miss. scient.* 14, 1916, pp. 16 ff.

⁹² *CIL* viii. 22729 = Dessau, *ILS* 9394. A good survey of Roman knights of African origin is given in A. Stein, *Der römische Ritterstand*, pp. 393 ff.

⁹³ *ILA* 2195.

⁹⁴ S. Gsell and A. Joly, *Khamissa, Mdaourouch, Announa, I. Khamissa*, p. 29, and in *Mél. de l'Éc. fr. de Rome*, 23, 1903, pp. 117 f.; cf. Plin. *Ep.* vii. 25. 2: 'diligens agricola'; Fronto, *ad M. Caes.* ii. 5 (Naber, p. 29; Haines, i, p. 116; [van den Hout, i, p. 29 (ii, 7)]): *agricola strenuus*.

⁹⁵ *CIL* viii. 11824 (cf. p. 2372) = Dessau, *ILS* 7457, ll. 3 ff.: 'paupere progenitus lare sum parvoq(ue) parente | cuius nec census neque domus fuerat. | Ex quo sum genitus, ruri meo vixi colendo; | nec ruri pausa, nec mihi semper erat', and ll. 23 f.: 'ordinis in templo delectus ab ordine sedi, | et de rusticulo censor et ipse fui.'

⁹⁶ The mosaics are enumerated by A. Merlin, 'La Mosaïque du seigneur Julius à Carthage', *Bull. arch. du Com. des trav. hist.* 1921, pp.ᶠ 95 ff.; see also P. Romanelli, 'La Vita agricola tripolitana attraverso le rappresentazioni figurate', *Afric. Ital.* 3, 1930, pp. 53 ff.; cf. note 103; cf. the descriptions of plates LVIII, LIX, LXI–LXIII, LXVI, 2, LXXIX, 1.

⁹⁷ *CIL* viii. 1641 = Dessau, *ILS* 6818; cf. 6775 and 6783: money was given to the city for the *alimenta*, 'legi autem debebunt municipes item incolae dumtaxat incolae qui intra continentia coloniae nostrae aedificia morabuntur'. It is, of course, possible that the *incolae* who did not live in the city were citizens of other cities, but the words used by the donor point rather to those who lived in the country. The *incolae* excluded from the foundation were probably those who lived in the country. The earliest instance of the incorporation of natives in a *municipium* is that of Volubilis, A.D. 45 [*FIRA*², 70]: Weuillemier, *Rev. ét. anc.* 28, 1926, pp. 323 ff.; cf. *CIL* viii. 30 (Gigthis); ibid. 9663 (Cartenna). On the *incolae* of the country see Chap. VI, note 33. On the *mapalia*, see E. Müller-Graupa, *Philol.* 73, 1914, pp. 302 ff. The most striking evidence of the persistence of the local cults is the sanctuary of Saturnus Balcaranensis, discovered and excavated by J. Toutain. No dated inscription is earlier than the 2nd cent. A.D. (*CIL* viii, pp. 2441 ff.). Cf. J. Carcopino, 'Salluste, le culte des Cereres et les Numides', *Rev. hist.* 158, 1928, pp. 1 ff., and J. Toutain, *Les Cultes païens dans l'Empire romain*, iii (1920), pp. 15 ff. One inscription illustrates in a surprising way the social and economic life of a small community in the recently annexed province of Mauretania. The document is a decree of the senate of Sala in honour of a Roman prefect, who was both the commanding officer of a body of troops stationed at Sala, and military governor of the district (A.D. 144). It has been published in an exemplary style by S. Gsell and J. Carcopino, 'La Base de M. Sulpicius Felix et le décret des décurions de Sala', *Mél. de l'Éc. fr. de Rome*, 48, 1931, pp. 1 ff. [=*L'An. ép.* 1931, 38]. In this inscription we see a group of Roman citizens, tenants of the city of Sala, farmers, cattle-rearers, and woodsmen of the dense forests of the area, living in imminent danger of native incursions, under the protection of Roman troops. Space does not permit me to discuss this inscription at length. One must read the inscription—written in perfect Latin with no Africanisms—together with the learned comments of the editors.

⁹⁸ Reports on the excavations in Tripolitania have been published periodically in the three periodicals which appeared successively after the opening of excavations: *Rivista di Tripolitania, Libya, Africa Italiana*. Some important information is also to be found in an official publication, the *Notiziario archeologico del Ministero delle Colonie*, of which *Africa Italiana* was a continuation. Cf. the bibliography in Chap. V, note 4. On the roads see S. Aurigemma, 'Pietre miliari tripolitane', *Riv. di Tripolitania*, 2, 1925/6, pp. 3 ff., 135 ff. The most important routes were (1) that which ran along the coast and led from Africa Proconsularis into Egypt, (2) that flanking the *limes* of

Tripolitania, which had been definitely established by Septimius Severus, (3) the great caravan-route from Oea to Fezzan.

99 On the history of Tripolitania see the works quoted in Chap. V, note 4. On the economic resources of the country: oil, S. Gsell, 'L'Huile de Leptis', *Riv. di Tripol.* 1, 1924/5, pp. 41 ff., cf. G. Salvioli, 'Sulla esportazione di grano e di olio dall'Africa nell'epoca romana', *Atti d. R. Acc. Pontaniana*, 42 (sec. series, no. 17), 1912; *La Missione Franchetti in Tripolitania* (1915), app. 2: 'Le risorse economiche della Tripolitania nell'antichità.' Trade: Gsell, *Hist. de l'Afr.* iii, pp. 138 ff.; id. 'La Tripolitaine et le Sahara au iiiᵉ siècle de notre ère', *Mém. de l'Acad. d. Inscr.* 43, 1926; P. Romanelli, 'Ricordi di Tripolitania a Roma e in Italia', *Bull. Com.* 55, 1921, pp. 69 ff. (the elephant of the *statio Sabrathensium* and the stamps with the name of Lepcis Magna on the rims of oil-amphorae). A dedication of elephant tusks to the great Tripolitanian god Liber Pater at Oea: *CIL* viii. 11001 (10488) [= *Inscr. Trip.* 231]; P. Romanelli, 'Iscrizione tripolitana che ricorda un'offerta di denti di avorio', *Rend. Acc. Lincei*, 1920, pp. 376 ff. I have verified the readings of the editors in Tripoli Museum, and I propose the following restoration of the four lines: 'Liber pater sanctissime | arcem [. . . q]ui possides | pro sa[lvis *or* lvo . . .] aram—urbis[. . . i]ugis | et hic [libens] votum dico | dentes duo[s] Lucae bovis.' This man dedicated an altar in the temple of Liber Pater, probably in the *arx* of the city on the top of a hill, for the safety of somebody (of his children, of the emperors, or of somebody else?); and the two tusks were originally inserted in the top of the altar, on which the inscription was carved, which was found in the square (the *forum* or market-place?). Note the archaic expression: *dentes Lucae bovis*. On the city of Lepcis in general and on the works undertaken by Septimius Severus see my article 'An Emperor's Dream', *Annales contemporaines* (Современныя записки) 1932 (in Russian). I think it likely that the arch of Septimius Severus at Lepcis was dedicated in the same year in which were dedicated the two arches to that Emperor at Rome, that is, probably, the year in which Septimius, accompanied by his sons, visited his native city. The sculptures of the *Arcus Argentariorum* can be regarded as expressions of the same political ideas which are reflected in the sculptures of the Lepcis arch. Cf. R. Bartoccini, 'L'Arco quadripartito dei Severi a Lepcis' (Lepcis Magna), *Africa Italiana*, 4, 1931, pp. 32 ff. On the war of the Marmaridae and Garamantes, and the inscription of Cyrene which mentions a *bellum Marmaricum* [*SEG* ix. 63], see S. Ferri, 'Firme di legionari della Siria nella gran Sirte', *Riv. di Trip.* 2, 1925/6, pp. 363 ff.; cf. Groag, Pauly–Wissowa, iv A, cols. 825 ff. The leader of the expedition was the famous Quirinius (Flor. ii. 31. 41). Domaszewski, *Philol.* 67, 1908, pp. 4 ff., thinks (cf. Cass. Dio, 55, 10a, 1) that Quirinius directed the war from his province of Syria. Note that Quirinius was the first to form cohorts of Ituraeans in Syria (Groag, op. cit., col. 840). Cf. the inscription of Cyrene in honour of a citizen of Cyrene, Phaos, *OGIS* 767: πρεσβεύσας ἐν τῷ Μαρμαρικῷ πολέμῳ ἐν χειμῶσι ἑαυτὸν ἐς τὸς κινδύνος ἐπιδὸς καὶ τὰν ἐπικαιροτάταν συμμα[χ]ίαν καὶ πρὸς σωτηρίαν τ[ᾶς] πόλιος ἀνήκοισαν ἀγαγών. The date of this expedition is controversial. Mommsen (*Röm. Gesch.* v, p. 631), Gardthausen (*Aug. u. s. Zeit.* i, pp. 702, 1137), Cagnat (*L'Armée rom. d'Afrique*, p. 7), and Ritterling (Pauly–Wissowa, xii, col. 1224, cf. ibid. iv. col. 1270) believe that it was the expedition of the year 21–20 B.C. led by Cornelius Balbus, proconsul of Africa, and Sulpicius Quirinius, propraetor of Crete and Cyrene, against the Garamantes and Marmaridae, while Boissevain (on Cass. Dio, 55, 10 a, 1) and Domaszewski (l.c.) think it refers to the year 1 B.C., when Quirinius was in Syria. Quirinius may have directed the war when he was in Syria with Gaius Caesar: cf. *Rev. bibl.* 38, 1929, pp. 448 ff.

100 On mines, quarries, fisheries, &c., see the excellent book by E. Schönbauer, *Beiträge zur Gesch. des Bergbaurechts* (Münchener Beiträge zur Papyrusforsch. 12, 1929), with good bibliography, which relieves me of the necessity of citing other works on this topic: cf. T. Frank, *Economic History*², pp. 198 ff. On quarries see Ch. Dubois

Étude sur l'administration et l'exploitation des carrières etc. dans le monde romain (1908); cf. Fiehn, Pauly–Wissowa, iii A, cols. 2241 ff. On the measures taken in the republican period by the Roman government with regard to the mines in Italy see E. Pace, *Rend. Lincei*, 1916, pp. 41 ff.; M. Besnier, 'L'Interdiction du travail des mines en Italie sous la Républ.', *Rev. arch.* 1919, pp. 31 ff. T. Frank, *Economic History*[2], p. 233, thinks that Pliny is referring to an exceptional measure, which was only in force for a short time, but I cannot accept this. Cf. Schönbauer, op. cit., p. 133. There are no special studies on forests, lakes, fisheries, &c. In my *Gesch. d. Staatspacht*, pp. 411 ff., I collected the references on the collection and sale of salt under the Republic and the Empire, as well as in the Hellenistic age: cf. M. Besnier, art. *Sal* in Daremberg–Saglio, *Dict. d. ant.* iv, pp. 1009 ff.; Blümner, Pauly–Wissowa, ii A, cols. 2096 ff., and my article 'Seleucid Babylonia', *Yale Class. Stud.* 3, 1932, pp. 1–114. A new *conductor pascui et Salinarum in Dacia* is mentioned in the inscription published in *Anuarul Comisiuni monumentalor istoria pentru Transilvania*, 1929, p. 208 [= *L'An. ép.* 1930, 10]. Relatively plentiful information exists regarding fishing: see my *Gesch. d. Staatspacht*, pp. 414 f. and G. Lafaye, *Piscatio et Piscatus* in Daremberg–Saglio, iv, pp. 492 ff. According to this evidence it looks as if the state, at least in certain parts of the Roman Empire, claimed a right on fishing in sea, lake, and river. The inscription from Holland, Dessau, *ILS* 1461, a dedication of the *conductores piscatus*, under a *manceps*, to the *dea Hludana*, is particularly interesting. As the fishing-rights, however, were an ancient privilege of many temples and cities, numerous disputes arose between these previous owners and the Roman *publicani*, and the Roman government frequently decided in favour of the former. This is shown, for example, at Istrus, by a bilingual Greek-Latin inscription (*SEG* i. 329), which contains the documents of the dispute. The importance of fishing for the cities of the Black Sea is well known. A *collegium* of the θυνεῖται Ἑρμᾶντος (a geographical name?) is attested for Odessus (Varna) by the inscription published by A. Salač and K. Škorpil, 'Několik Archeologických Památek, etc.', *Česká Akad. Věd a Umění*. 1928, p. 12, no. 4 [*L'An. ép.* 1928, 146]. Therefore it does not seem to me impossible that the *collegium* of Kallipolis (*IGRR* i. 817) is an Egyptian religious association. Another instance of litigation between the *publicani* and the old owners is that which arose at Ephesus. Here the city had the right to impose τέλη which were paid for the right of fishing in the λίμνη Σελινουσία. The kings of Pergamum had claimed this right for some time, but the Roman government restored it to the temple in spite of the claims of the *publicani* (Strab. xiv. 1. 26, 642 C). Two inscriptions which refer to a τελωνεῖον (cf. Dessau, *ILS* 8858) τῆς ἰχθυϊκῆς, *OGIS* 496, and J. Keil, *Oest. Jahresh.* 26, 1930, Beibl. col. 51 (of A.D. 54–55), must be considered with this passage of Strabo. Both inscriptions refer to a powerful association of fishermen and fishmongers, who have leased the undertaking from the temple (cf. *OGIS* 494). Such associations are also known in the West, Dessau, *ILS* 3624 (Carthago Nova in Spain) and 6146 (Ostia). It is, however, not clear who the *publicani* were who were engaged in litigation with the temple of Ephesus. At Istrus the *publicani* in question were the farmers of the *publicum portorii Illyrici et ripae Thraciae*. Were the *publicani* the farmers of the τεσσαρακοστὴ λιμένος at Ephesus also? What this had to do with fishing I do not understand, though the matter is certain for Istrus. An inscription discovered near Lake Egedir in Pisidia gives interesting information regarding the administration of the lakes and fisheries of Asia Minor: it is the funerary stele of a man who had been 'manager of the lake' (ἐπὶ λίμνης ἐπιστάτης) for twenty years: Pace, *Ann. R. Scuol. Arch. de Atene*, 3, 1921, p. 53, no. 42 [= *SEG* ii. 747]. The abundant material relative to fishing and fisheries in Egypt is partly collected by M. C. Besta, 'Pesca e pescatori nell'Egitto greco-romano', *Aegyptus*, 2, 1921, pp. 67 ff. Fishing was connected with hunting in Egypt: P. M. Meyer, *Klio*, 15, 1920, pp. 376 ff.; L. Wenger, *Arch. f. Papyr.* 10, p. 168. For the history of fishing in Italy and in the western provinces (Gaul and Spain), and not only from a technical point of view, the numerous ponds and salting-establishments, the ruins of which are still to be seen on the shores of the Mediterranean, mainly in Italy, Southern Gaul, and on the coasts of Spain and Portugal, are of great interest. Credit for the first scientific exploration of many of these, and for their identification as *piscinae in litore constructae* which belonged to Roman villas, must go to L. Jacono, 'Note di archeologia marittima', *Neapolis*, 1, 1913, pp. 353 ff., and 'Piscinae in litore constructae', *Notiz d. Scavi*, 1927, pp. 333 ff. On the ponds and on the establishments for preparing *garum*, &c., in Southern France (near Fréjus) see R. Lantier, *Ber. d. röm.-germ. Komm.* 20, 1931, p. 125. On those in Spain and Portugal, see F. Pellati, 'I monumenti del Portogallo Romano', *Historia*, 5, 1931, pp. 214 ff.; on those of Africa, Gsell, *Hist. de l'Afr.* iv, pp. 51 ff. New light has been thrown on the administration of the forests by the accurate researches carried out in the Pfalz by F. Sprater, who was able to show that some fortifications built in that region by the Romans in the late Empire had an economic rather than a military purpose. Such was, for instance, the Heidelsburg near Waldfischbach, where an inscription concerning a certain *T. Publicius Tertius Saltuarius*, and perhaps also the sepulchral relief of a *Saltuarius* and his wife (a very instructive product of the rough local art), were found. In the same mountain fortification several iron instruments were discovered, and from these it can be inferred that wood-cutting, cart-building, and sheep-rearing were practised. The same holds good also for Heidenburg near Krambach; see F. Sprater, 'Die Heidelsburg bei Waldfischbach, eine Bergbefestigung aus Konstantinischer Zeit', *Pfälz. Museum-Pfälz. Heimatkunde*, 1928; id. *Die Pfalz unter den Römern*, i (1929), pp. 59 ff., especially figs. 58 f., cf. fig. 61.

101 On the organization of mines and quarries in the Roman Empire, see my *Gesch. d. Staatspacht*, pp. 445 ff.; O. Hirschfeld, *Die Kais. Verwaltungsb.*², 1905, pp. 144 ff.; my *Studien z. Gesch. röm. Kol.*, pp. 353 ff. and 408 f. On Spain see E. Schönbauer, *Zeitschr. d. Sav.-St.* 46, 1925, pp. 181 ff.; 47, 1926, pp. 352 ff.; T. A. Rickard, 'The Mining of the Romans in Spain', *JRS* 18, 1928, pp. 129 ff. On Egypt, K. Fitzler, *Steinbrüche und Bergwerke im ptolemäischen und römischen Ägypten* (1910). On the lead mines of Sardinia, Spain, and Britain, M. Besnier, 'Le Commerce du plomb à l'époque romaine', *Rev. arch.* 1920 (2), pp. 211 ff.; 1921 (1), pp. 36 ff.; 1921 (2), pp. 98 ff. Cf. L. Maistre, ibid. 1919 (1), pp. 234 ff., and 1926 (2), pp. 25 ff. (on the iron and tin mines of Aquitania). On tin in Spain and Britain see the excellent survey of F. Haverfield and Miss M. V. Taylor, 'Romano-British Remains', *Victoria County History of Cornwall* (1924), pp. 10 and 15 ff.; cf. F. Haverfield, *Cornelii Taciti de vita Agricolae*, ed. by H. Furneaux (2nd ed. by J. G. C. Anderson, 1922), pp. 173 ff., and C. Clement Whittick, *JRS* 21, 1931, pp. 256 ff. Export of tin from Britain stops at about A.D. 50, and the mining is resumed not earlier than the 3rd cent. A.D. The main reason probably was the competition of Spain in the early Roman Empire (after its pacification by Augustus) and the troubled state of that province in the 3rd cent., which, together with a partial exhaustion, made tin-mining difficult there, and therefore profitable once more in Britain. On the many mines of the Danubian regions see G. Cantacuzène, 'Un papyrus Latin relatif à la défense du Bas Danube', *Aegyptus*, 9, 1928, pp. 75 ff. An inscription published several times, more or less exactly, is of some interest: *AEMÖ* 1891, p. 153, no. 36 = G. Seuré, *RA* 1908 (1), pp. 48 ff., no. 51 = K. Škorpil, *Description of the Ancient Monuments in the Region of the Black Sea*, ii (1927) (in Bulgarian), p. 72, fig. 93. The inscription was discovered at Malko-Tirnovo in Eastern Thrace in the northern part of the plain of Strandza (district of Burgas). I owe a photograph of the inscription to the kindness of Professor G. Kazarow. Škorpil and Kazarow read the inscription correctly as follows: Ἀγαθῆι τύχηι. | Ἀπόλλωνι Αὐλαριό|κῳ θεῷ ἐπηκόῳ | Στράτων Στράτωνο[ς] ἄρξας τῶν ἐν τοῖς σιδ[η]ρείοις Ἑλλήνων τῷ η' ἔτει τῆς Ἀντωνείνου βα|σιλείας ὑπέρ τε ἑαυτοῦ | καὶ τῶν ἰδίων | καὶ τῶν ἐργαστῶν σωτηρίας τε κ|αὶ εὐεργεσίας εὐξάμε|νος τὸν βωμὸν | ἀνέθηκα. Straton was

then the ἄρχων of a group of Greeks, who were connected with the local mines. I think that he was the president of an association both national and professional in character, rather than director of the mines: a magistrate, not an official. I also think that the Greeks employed in the mines, and whose president he was (ll. 5 ff.), were the same as the ἐργασταί mentioned later on (l. 10), who, as in Spain, used to lease one or more pits of the mines. On the ἐργασταί see the inscriptions quoted in Chap. V, note 43. Mines of Africa: Gsell, 'Vieilles explorations minières dans l'Afrique du Nord', *Hespéris, Archives Berbères*, 1928, pp. 1 ff.

On the quarries of Teos see Y. Béguignon, *Rev. arch.* 1928 (2), pp. 185 ff., 203 ff. E. Schönbauer, in his book (quoted in the preceding note), tried to demonstrate that the theory according to which half the production belonged to the state *more antiquo* had its roots in the *colonia partiaria*, that is, the division of the produce of the land between landlord and farmer. He is also inclined to think that the theory according to which half any treasure found in land belonging to the state belongs to the discoverer is the result of a decision of Hadrian, influenced in this matter by the practice of the mines. This theory, however, though acute, has not convinced me. In the terms of the Spanish mine law I still see a fusion of the theory of the right of ownership of treasures discovered in the soil, and of the principle—essentially Hellenistic—that public lands are administered on behalf of the state and the emperor. I cannot admit that Hadrian invented the theory concerning treasures; probably he did no more than legalize a *mos antiquus*. On the contrary I agree with Schönbauer in his interpretation of the second paragraph of the mine laws of Vipasca [*ILS* 6891] which contain Hadrian's rules on the sale to a contractor of that half of the product which belonged to the state. Very probably the 'generosity' of Hadrian had the aim of stimulating the contractors in the exploitation of the exhausted silver mines. We do not know the part which had to be given to the state from those mines which were sold to contractors. Schönbauer is probably right in calculating it at much less than 50 per cent. The inscription found at Aljustrel in 1907, and republished by L. Wickert, *Sitz. Preuß. Akad.* 1931, pp. 9 ff. (835 ff.), is of considerable interest. The inscription was on the base of a statue of a *procurator metallorum* who also has the title of *vicarius rationalium*: it was erected by the *coloni* of the *metallum Vipascense*. The procurator is called *restitutor metallorum*. That shows that in A.D. 173 or 235 (the date of the inscription) the mines were in full decline, in spite of Hadrian's reforms.

102 It seems certain that in the 2nd cent. A.D. the silver mines, especially those of Spain, were partially exhausted. We may connect this fact with the measures taken by Hadrian regarding silver mines, and the revival of the mining industry in Britain in the 3rd cent. A.D. (see note 101). But to speak of general exhaustion of the mines in the Roman Empire (O. Seeck, *Gesch. d. Untergangs*, &c., ii, pp. 200 ff.; H. Delbrueck, *Gesch. d. Kriegskunst*, ii (1921), p. 283) is undoubtedly an exaggeration, without foundation in the evidence. The principal cause of the decline in mining activity must be assigned to the anarchy of the 3rd cent., because the richest mines were in the Danubian regions. One of the best mining regions, Dacia, was lost under Aurelian; in the other mines work fell into disorder. In any case the frequent mention of mines in the legal sources of the early 3rd cent. (esp. Ulpian, '*de offic. procon.*' *Digest*, 48, 19, 8, 4), the great care bestowed on the mines by the emperors of the 4th cent. (Schönbauer, op. cit., pp. 147 ff.), and the efforts made by the barbarians to master the mining districts, show that the mines had still sufficient quantities of metals, and that the main difficulty was to ensure the labour necessary for extraction. The spectacle is the same as we are familiar with in the field of agriculture. The mines remained unexploited without being exhausted. Notice that silver ornaments of the 2nd and 3rd cent. A.D. are not at all rare in our museums.

[103] See *CIL* iii. 6660 (cf. 14161) = ‡E. Kalinka, W. Kubitschek, and R. Heberdey, *Oest. Jahresh.* 3, 1900, Beibl. p. 34, no. 54 = ‡W. Prentice, 'Greek and Latin Inscriptions', *Amer. Exped. to Syria*, iii, p. 280, no. 355, an inscription in verse in honour of a certain Silvinus (3rd cent. A.D.?), who transformed large tracts of desert land between Damascus and Palmyra by means of cisterns (*lymfae celestes*) into rich fields and vineyards. On the Trachonitis see note 33. On the culture of olives in Africa, R. Cagnat, 'L'Annone d'Afrique', *Mém. de l'Ac. d. Inscr.* 40, 1916, pp. 256 ff. For a period as late as the 4th and 5th cent. A.D. the flourishing state of African olive culture is attested by many mosaics which reproduce the beautiful villas that formed the centres of the agricultural estates of the large African landowners (cf. note 96). One of the best was found at Carthage (A. Merlin, 'La mosaïque du seigneur Julius à Carthage', *Bull. arch. du Com. des trav. hist.* 1921, pp. 95 ff., and plate). The mosaic shows in the centre a beautiful villa, in the four corners the four seasons as illustrated by the agricultural work characteristic of each season (winter represented by the gathering of olives, summer by cornfields and herds, spring by flowers, autumn by grapes), on the sides the main occupations of the landowners (hunting expeditions and dealings with the *coloni* for the master, toilet scenes, and inspection of the poultry for the mistress). The scenes where the master is represented receiving a petition or a written compliment and gifts from a *colonus*, and the mistress receiving a kid from a daughter of a *colonus*, remind one vividly of the scenes depicted by Juvenal and Martial (Mart. iii. 58, and x. 87; Juv. iv. 25–6; *Dig.* 32. 99; 33. 7, 12, and 13). The other mosaics (beginning with the 2nd cent. A.D.) are enumerated by A. Merlin, op. cit.; cf. the mosaics of Zliten in Tripolitania (1st cent. A.D.) discovered by the Italians (S. Aurigemma, 'I mosaici di Zliten', *Africa Italiana*, 2, 1926; cf. the description of our pl. LIX, and P. Romanelli, *Africa Italiana*, 3, 1930, pp. 53 ff.). On one of the mosaics we see in the background a farm; before the farm Libyan *coloni* are threshing corn on a threshing-floor and near the threshing-floor is an olive tree. Cf. our pls. LVIII, LIX, LXII, LXIII. On the progress of the cultivation of olive and vine in Egypt see above, notes 46 and 49, and the book by M. Schnebel, *Die Landwirtschaft im hellenistischen Ägypten* (1925). I have dealt with the progress made in this field in the other provinces in this and the preceding chapter. It would be very interesting to collect the evidence on beekeeping in Italy and the provinces. On beekeeping in Italy see P. d'Héronville, 'Virgile Agriculteur', *Mus. Belg.* 1926, pp. 161 ff.; 1927, pp. 37 ff. There is abundant evidence for Egypt, especially for the Ptolemaic period: see my *Large Estate*, pp. 105 ff., and M. Schnebel, op. cit. Cf. Olck, Pauly–Wissowa, ii, cols. 431 ff., and H. Malcolm Frazer, *Beekeeping in Antiquity* (1931) (not available to me).

[104] On the *dediticii* see *P.Giss.* 40 = P. Meyer, *Jur. Pap.*, no. 1 (with a good bibliography); cf. id. *Zeitschr. f. vergl. Rechtswiss.* 39, p. 224, and G. Segré, *Bull. d. Ist. di Dir. Rom.* 32, 1922, pp. 207 ff. P. Meyer, *Zeitschr. d. Sav.-St.* 48, 1928, pp. 595 ff., surveys the position, starting with the valuable dissertation of E. Bickermann, *Das Edikt des Kaisers Caracalla in P.Giess.* 40, 1926; cf. below, Chap. IX, note 38. On the *peregrini* in the Western provinces, O. Cuntz, *Oest. Jahresh.* 18, 1915, pp. 98 ff.; cf. Th. Mommsen, 'Schweizer Nachstudien', *Ges. Schr.* v, pp. 418 ff. It is probable that the free peasants who lived in the villages both in East and West, the *possessores*, had a higher legal status than the former serfs in the East, and that the same status was given to the *coloni* of the imperial domains, at least in Africa. This, however, is purely hypothetical, and cannot be proved because of the almost complete lack of evidence. The lists of names of the tenants of the Phrygian imperial estates unfortunately belong to the period after Caracalla. On the peasants in general, especially on their relations to the large landowners, see E. Kornemann, 'Bauernstand', in Pauly–Wissowa, Suppl. iv, cols. 83 ff.; cf. 'Domänen', ibid., cols. 238 ff.

¹⁰⁵ On the strikes in Egypt see note 52. On the Jewish war of the last years of Trajan and the first years of Hadrian, see A. von Premerstein, *Hermes*, 57, 1922, pp. 305 ff. Our tradition emphasizes that the government was supported in Egypt by the Hellenes, not by the Egyptians. The general statement of *Scr. Hist. Aug.* Hadr. 5. 2, 'Aegyptus seditionibus urgebatur', cannot be referred to the Jewish revolt only. The religious character of the sedition in Alexandria in A.D. 122 shows that the participants were probably not the Greeks but the Egyptians (*Scr. Hist. Aug.* Hadr. 12. 1; Cass. Dio, 69. 8. 1*a* (iii, p. 229, ed. Boissevain); W. Weber, *Untersuchungen zur Geschichte des Kaisers Hadrianus* (1907), pp. 113 ff.). The reforms of Hadrian, which will be treated in the next chapter, were certainly intended to pacify the Egyptian peasants. On Antoninus Pius see *Scr. Hist. Aug.* Ant. Pius, 5. 5, 'in Achaia etiam atque Aegypto rebelliones repressit'; cf. note 63. On the Βουκόλοι, J. Lesquier, *L'Armée romaine d'Égypte*, pp. 29 ff.; cf. above pp. 348 and 454.

¹⁰⁶ On Asia Minor see note 3. H. Dessau, *Gesch. d. röm. Kaiserzeit*, ii, 2, p. 577, thinks that there was complete security in Asia. But the well-known letter of Fronto to Antoninus Pius (*ad Ant. Pium*, 8; Naber, p. 169, Haines, ii. p. 236; [van den Hout, i. p. 161]), of 153–4, is against this. Fronto states that he is ready to assume the proconsulate of Asia, and he has secured the assistance of his friend Julius Senex of Mauretania, *cuius non modo fide et diligentia sed etiam militari industria circa quaerendos et continendos latrones iuvarer*. Mauretania, as is well known, was a nest of brigands. The fact that Fronto wanted to have with him a specialist in repressing brigandage certainly does not suggest that, after so many years of profound peace in the Empire, conditions were very normal in Asia Minor: cf. Chap. XI, note 17. On Palestine, S. Dickey, *The Constructive Revolution of Jesus* (1924), pp. 122 ff. On Mariccus, C. Jullian, *Histoire de la Gaule*, iv, pp. 192 ff. On the revolt in Dacia and Dalmatia see Chap. VI, note 82.

¹⁰⁷ K. Bücher, *Die Entstehung der Volkswirtschaft* (16th ed. 1922); G. Salvioli, *Il capitalismo antico* (1929) (also in French and German editions; note the change of mind of the author in his article, 'La Città antica e la sua economia', *Atti d. R. Accad. di Sc. Mor. della Soc. Reale di Napoli*, 1925, pp. 195 ff.); cf. W. Sombart, *Der moderne Kapitalismus* (2nd ed. 1916); L. Brentano, *Anfänge des modernen Kapitalismus* (1916); Sigwart in Pauly–Wissowa, x, cols. 1899 f.; M. Weber, *Wirtschaft und Gesellschaft* (*Grundriss der Sozialökonomik*, iii. 2), ii (1921), pp. 211 ff.; Passow, *Kapitalismus* (1928); O. von Zwiedineck, 'Was macht ein Zeitalter kapitalistisch', *Zeitschr. f. ges. Staatsw.* 90, 1931, pp. 482 ff.; cf. M. Rostovtzeff, ibid. 92, 1932, p. 334. Cf. the criticism of Bücher's division into periods by W. Sombart, *Econ. Hist. Rev.* 2, 1929, pp. 11 ff. Cf. also my article 'The Decay of the Ancient World and its Economic Explanation', ibid. 2, 1930, pp. 197 ff.; C. Barbagallo, 'Economia antica e moderna', *Nuova Riv. Stor.*, 12, 1928, pp. 415–85, and 13, 1929; id. 'Dalla economia antica alla irrazionalità della storia', ibid. 13, 1929, pp. 385–97; E. Ciccotti, 'Il problema economico nel mondo antico', *Nuova. Riv. Stor.* 16, 1932, pp. 1–51, 145–87. An interesting, although antiquated, review of the progress made in antiquity in the technical and scientific fields, together with a good explanation of the causes which retarded the development of industry in antiquity, is to be found in G. L. Ferrero, 'Le machinisme dans l'antiquité', *Rev. du Mois*, 21, 1920, pp. 448 ff.

¹⁰⁸ H. Gummerus in Pauly–Wissowa, ix, col. 1454.

VIII. *The Economic and Social Policy of the Flavians and Antonines*

¹ On Trajan see the excellent, but antiquated, monographs of Dierauer and C. de la Berge; further, the book of B. W. Henderson, *Five Roman Emperors* (1927), and that of Paribeni, *Optimus Princeps*, vols. i–ii (1928). Paribeni has collected the literary.

epigraphical, and archaeological evidence regarding Trajan's activity, but he has not perceived the great consumption of energy imposed by his wars on the Empire. For a certain time the immense expenditure necessitated by the war and by the organization of the new provinces was covered by the rich Dacian booty and by the product of the Dacian gold and silver mines (J. Carcopino, 'Les Richesses des Daces sous Trajan', *Dacia*, 1, 1924, pp. 28 ff.); but no war booty, however large, lasts long, and no amount of silver and gold can ultimately give vigour to a weakened economic structure. Cf. R. Syme, 'The Imperial Finances under Domitian, Nerva and Trajan', *JRS* 20, 1930, pp. 55 ff.; F. Heichelheim, 'P.Bad. 37, ein Beitrag zur römischen Geldgeschichte unter Trajan', *Klio*, 25, 1932, pp. 124 ff. The monetary policy of Trajan in Syria, as revealed by Dura parchment X, is of interest: see M. Rostovtzeff and C. B. Welles, *Yale Class. Stud.* 2, 1930, pp. 60 ff.; A. Bellinger, *Excavs. at Dura Europos, Prelim. Rep. 3* (1932), pp. 146 ff.

² *Scr. Hist. Aug.*, M. Aurel. 11. 7: 'Hispanis exhaustis Italica adlectione *contra Traiani quoque praecepta* verecunde consuluit'; Peter and Hohl suspect a lacuna after *contra*. It follows that Trajan and another emperor before him granted some relief to the Spaniards in the matter of recruiting; cf. Hadr. 12. 4: 'omnibus Hispanis Tarraconem in conventum vocatis dilectumque iociariter, ut verba ipsa ponit Marius Maximus, retractantibus Italicis vehementissime, ceteris prudenter et caute consuluit.' It is evident that Trajan made extensive use of Spain for recruiting purposes, although he exercised prudence, and Hadrian was not able to grant the Spaniards any important relief in this respect. Not even Marcus Aurelius could do much. The two texts show what a heavy price Spain had to pay for the privileges granted her by Vespasian. Cf. Chap. III, note 8, and Chap. IV, note 36.

³ Judgement on Trajan's building activity will be possible when the excavations of the imperial forum, so successfully begun, are completed. It is no exaggeration to say that Trajan entirely changed the appearance of the centre of the city by uniting the most magnificent architectural complexes in Rome—the *Campus Martius* and the Imperial fora with the capitolium, by means of the vast works undertaken by him on the slope of the Quirinal from which resulted the beautiful forum and the recently excavated market. Paribeni has some excellent pages on Trajan's building activity. On 'Trajan's market' see C. Ricci, *Il Mercato di Traiano* (n.d.) and A. Boethius 'Appunti sul mercato di Traiano', *Roma*, 10, 1931, pp. 447 ff. The market into which Apollodorus, Trajan's brilliant architect, transformed the supporting wall of the slope of the Quirinal, is the first instance of a market, not of a little provincial town, of which we have many examples, but of the capital of the world. The shops are fine and roomy, and were probably not inferior to modern ones. Another big market was built by Hadrian near the Forum of Julius Caesar, with the entrance from the *Clivus Argentarius* (*basilica Argentaria?*). The ruins of this market have been discovered in the excavations of Caesar's Forum. On its back wall there are numerous interesting graffiti: see C. Ricci, 'Il foro di Cesare', *Capitolium*, 13, 1932, pp. 157 ff. Boethius makes the good suggestion that Trajan's market derives from oriental prototypes (a street with two lines of shops).

⁴ P. Perdrizet, *BCH* 21, 1897, pp. 161 ff.; cf. M. Holleaux, *Rev. ét. gr.* 11, 1898, pp. 273 ff. [= *Études*, i, pp. 271 ff.]: τίνα | [δὲ δεῖ τρ]όπον στόρνυσθαι τὰς ὁδοὺς κοινῷ διατάγματι ἐδήλωσα· | [κε]λεύω καὶ Ἀντανοὺς συντελεῖν ὑμεῖν εἰς τὰ ἀναλώματα | τὸ τρίτον συνεισφέροντας· ἡ δὲ συνεισφορὰ γενέσθω ἀπὸ | τῶν ἐν Μακεδονίᾳ ὄντων Ἀντανῶν· εὐτυχεῖτε· | πρὸ ιγ' Καλανδῶν Ἰουνίων ἀπὸ Δυρραχίου, and M. Rostovtzeff, *Bull. of the Russ. Arch. Inst. at Constantinople*, 4, 1899, pp. 171 ff. (in Russian): inscription in honour of C. Popillius Python, a contemporary of Nerva and Trajan, who paid for the city the poll-tax καὶ ὁδοὺς ἐκ τῶν ἰδίων ἐπισκευάσαντα and sold corn for moderate prices ἐν καιροῖς ἀναγκαίοις. It is probable that in the fragment of a letter of Hadrian to the city of Beroea granting remission

of some arrears to the συνέδριον of the Macedonian κοινόν, the arrears alluded to were for the construction of roads and the feeding of the troops, see A. Plassart, *BCH* 47, 1923, pp. 183 ff. [= ‡*JRS* 30, 1940, pp. 148 ff.]. Services similar to those of Python were rendered to Heracleia by Paulus Caelidius Fronto, whose inscription was engraved on the same stone as the above-mentioned letter of Trajan. So also M. Salarius Sabinus was honoured in the time of Hadrian (A.D. 121–3): ἐν τε σειτενδείαις | πλειστάκις παραπεπρακότα πολὺ | τῆς οὔσης τιμῆς εὐωνότερον καὶ ταῖς | τοῦ κυρίου Καίσαρος τῶν στρατευ|μάτων διοδείαις παρασχόντα εἰς τὰς | ἀννώνας σείτου μεδ(ίμνους) υ΄, κριθῶν μεδ. ρ΄, κυάμου μεδ. ξ΄, οἴνου μετρητὰς ρ΄ πολὺ τῆς | οὔσης τειμῆς εὐωνότερον (M. N. Tod, *BSA* 23, 1918–19, pp. 67 ff.) [= *SEG* i. 276]. Cf. Chap. VI, note 96. A very characteristic general statement, which refers both to Italy and to the provinces, is given by Siculus Flaccus (*Grom. vet.* Lachm.), p. 165. 4: 'nam et quotiens militi praetereunti aliive cui comitatui annona publica prestanda est, si ligna aut stramenta deportanda, quaerendum quae civitates quibus pagis huius modi munera prebere solitae sint.' A good monograph on this subject is much wanted. The archaeological monuments, especially the columns of Trajan and of M. Aurelius and the 'triumphal' arches of this period, furnish ample illustration, which, like the epigraphic evidence, has never been collected in full: cf. Chaps. IX and X and our pls. LXIX and LXXIV. We find the situation described above reflected in the coins. In Asia Minor many cities coined money to pay troops in passage. Military insignia are represented on these coins. The accurate collection of these coins by Cl. Boesch, *JDAI* 46, 1931, *Arch. Anz.*, p. 422, shows clearly the routes followed by the troops and the stations where they stopped. The large finds of coins at Dura would enable one to undertake a similar study for Syria: see A. Bellinger, *Two Roman Hoards from Dura-Europos* (*Numismatic Notes and Monographs*, no. 49, 1931). An excellent illustration of the manner in which the *annona* for the emperor and his soldiers was collected in Egypt is furnished by *PSI* 683. Wilcken, *Arch. f. Papyr.* 7, pp. 84 f., was the first to recognize that the document refers to the visit of Septimius Severus to Egypt in A.D. 199. Cf. Chap. IX.

⁵ M. Rostovtzeff, 'Pontus, Bithynia and the Bosporus', *BSA* 22, 1916–18, pp. 1 ff.; cf. U. Wilcken, *Hermes*, 49, 1914, pp. 120 ff. Pliny was in Bithynia and Pontus from A.D. 111 to 113. Similar conclusions on Pliny's mission in Bithynia are reached by O. Cuntz, 'Zum Briefwechsel des Plinius und Traian', *Hermes*, 61, 1926, pp. 192 ff., and p. 352 (he did not know of my article). Against Cuntz see R. P. Longden, 'Notes on the Parthian Campaigns of Trajan', *JRS* 21, 1931, pp. 19 ff. Longden's arguments have not convinced me. It would be odd if Trajan, who knew the situation in Parthia well, had made no preparation for this war, after the end of the Dacian war. It is true that Pliny does not say so *expressis verbis*: but secret letters are not published, and published letters do not contain political secrets.

⁶ *IGRR* iii. 173 = *OGIS* 544, inscription in honour of Ti. Iulius Severus, a descendant of the royal houses of Pergamon and of Galatia, governor of Syria under Hadrian, and sent by him on a special mission to Bithynia to improve the financial situation of the province, *IGRR* iii. 174, 175; cf. Cass. Dio, 69. 14. In the inscription *IGRR* iii. 173, he is praised as καὶ τῷ αὐτῷ ἔτει καὶ ἐλαιοθετήσαντα διηνεκῶς ἐν τῇ τῶν ὄχλων παρόδῳ (l. 17) and ἀποδεξάμεν[όν] τε στρατεύματα τὰ παραχειμάσα[ν]τα ἐν τῇ πόλει καὶ προπέμψαντα παροδεύοντα ἐπὶ τὸν πρὸς Πά[ρ]θους πόλεμον (ll. 29 ff.). The date is A.D. 114/15 and the occasion the great expedition of Trajan. The fact that Severus took over the heavy burden of feeding and quartering a huge army through a whole winter is proof both of his immense fortune and of the conditions prevailing in Bithynia. It is no less symptomatic of the financial situation of the state that Trajan gratefully accepted such a gift. A special officer of equestrian rank entrusted with the task of providing the Oriental armies with food when in Mesopotamia is mentioned

in an inscription from Alabanda in Caria, A. von Premerstein, *Oest. Jahresh.* 13, 1911, pp. 204 ff. [= *L'An. ép.* 1911, 161]; cf. A. von Domaszewski, *Rh. Mus.* 58, 1903, pp. 224 ff. Practically the same thing occurred when the army was on its way back, under Hadrian, after the end of the war in A.D. 117, *IGRR* iii. 208 = ‡R. d'Orbeliani, *JHS* 44, 1924, p. 26, no. 9: Latinius Alexander, father of Latinia Cleopatra, another member of the royal Galatian family, is praised for his services (ll. 3 ff.): ἐπὶ τῇ τοῦ μεγίστου | αὐτοκράτορος Καίσαρος Τραιανοῦ | Ἀδριανοῦ Σεβαστοῦ παρόδῳ καὶ τῶν | ἱερῶν αὐτοῦ στρατευμάτων δόντος διανομὰς τῇ πόλει; cf. W. Weber, *Untersuch. z. Gesch. des Kaisers Hadrianus* (1907), pp. 56 ff. It is evident that the city was so exhausted by the passage of the 'holy army' that Alexander came to her rescue with distributions of food. There is no doubt that the special mission of Ti. Iulius Severus to Bithynia under Hadrian had almost the same purpose as that of Pliny. The latter had to get the country ready for the heavy task; the former was sent to restore the shattered finances of the province after the war. How burdensome the travels of Trajan were for the population of the provinces (despite his moderation, so highly praised by Pliny in his well-known description of Domitian's travels, *Paneg.* 20) is shown by the letter of the procurator, Caelius Florus, to Opramoas, the Lycian magnate (R. Heberdey, *Opramoas* (1897), inscrr. nos. 8, 9, and 13 = *IGRR* iii. 739 (iv. Chap. XIII) [= *TAM* ii. 905]; and E. Ritterling, *Rh. Mus.* 37, 1920, pp. 35 ff.). Caelius Florus endeavours to spur Opramoas to give the emperor, on his last journey of A.D. 117, the same reception as had been given to him by his Galatian rival three years before. Later, a rich man of Palmyra entertained the Emperor Hadrian and his troops during his stay in 130, *IGRR* iii. 1054; cf. Weber, op. cit., pp. 122 and 237. Similarly, on the occasion of the Parthian war of L. Verus, entertainment was provided at Ephesus for Verus himself by Vedius Gaius in A.D. 162 or 164 (*Forsch. Eph.* iii, p. 155 f., no. 72) and for the imperial army on its way back in A.D. 166 or 167 by T. Flavius Damianus, the famous and fabulously rich sophist of that city (*Forsch. Eph.* iii, p. 161 f., no. 80). Cf. also *IG* iv. 759; Weber, op. cit., p. 183: repair of roads near the city of Troezen in Greece before Hadrian's visit. On the officials who were responsible for the *annona* for the emperor, when travelling, and for the army, see A. von Domaszewski, 'Die Annona des Heeres im Kriege', Ἐπιτύμβιον *H. Swoboda dargebracht*, (1927), pp. 17 ff. It seems that this service was systematically organized for the first time by Trajan, who entrusted it to people of the equestrian order. The municipal magistrates had to furnish them with the necessary supplies. Cf. the *pridianum* of the *cohors I Hispanorum* in the papyrus published by A. S. Hunt, *Racc. Lombroso* (1925), pp. 265 ff., ll. 54–57, 67, 69, 71; cf. G. Cantacuzène, *Aegyptus*, 9, 1928, pp. 89 ff.

---

7 Nerva: Cass. Dio, 68. 2. 1; Plin. *Ep.* vii. 31. 4; Dessau, *ILS* 1019; *Dig.* 47. 21. 3. 1; H. Schiller, *Gesch. d. röm. Kaiserzeit*, i, 2, p. 540; O. Seeck, *Gesch. d. Unterg. d. ant. Welt.* i, p. 324; Th. Mommsen, *Röm. Staatsrecht*, ii, p. 955; cf. p. 846; A. Merlin, *Les Revers monétaires de l'empereur Nerva* (1906). Trajan: prohibition of emigration, and foundation of colonies in Italy or assignation of land in Italy to veterans, *Scr. Hist. Aug.*, M. Aur. 11. 7 (see above, note 2); *Liber Coloniarum* (ed. E. Pais, *Mem. Linc.* 1920–3), p. 68 (p. 223, Lachmann, *Schr. röm. Feldm.* i): Veii, *CIL* xi. 3793, *Lib. Colon.* 67 (Pais, p. 220, Lachm.); Lavinium, *Lib. Colon.* 93 (Pais, p. 234, Lachm.), *CIL* xiv. 2069; Ostia, *Lib. Colon.* 379–80 (Pais, p. 236, Lachm.). E. Kornemann in Pauly–Wissowa, iv, s.v. 'Colonia', does not mention the colonies of Trajan in Italy. This is due to the unjustified disbelief in the evidence of the *Liber Coloniarum* first expressed by Mommsen, but Pais seems to be right in assuming that most of its statements are based on good sources. One of the most important and trustworthy of these sources belongs to the time of Trajan. On the military colonies of Trajan, cf. Ritterling in Pauly–Wissowa, xii, cols. 1287 ff.; on the slaves and the manumissions, V. Macchioro, 'L'impero

Romano nell' età dei Severi', *Riv. di st. ant.* 10, 1906, pp. 201 ff. The development began early in the 2nd cent. One of the most important questions connected with the status of freedmen after manumission is their right to acquire property in the territory of provincial cities; the question needs new treatment; see A. Calderini, *La Manomissione e la condizione dei liberti in Grecia* (1908), p. 318 f.; cf. A. Maiuri, *Ann. d. R. Sc. Arch. di Atene*, 4–5, 1924, p. 485. On the *alimenta* see Chap. VI, note 4. I agree with the point of view set forth by J. Carcopino in his interesting review of F. de Pachtère's book in *Rev. ét. anc.* 23, 1921, pp. 287 ff., and I cannot accept the theory of G. Billeter, *Gesch. des Zinsfußes* (1898), pp. 187 ff., that Trajan regarded his loans as a burden imposed on the munificence of the rich landowners of Italy. On the economic and social policy of Trajan see R. Paribeni, *Optimus Princeps*, ii, pp. 150 ff.

The activity of Trajan is summarized in the symbolical reliefs which adorn the arch in Beneventum, voted to him by the Roman senate in 114 but completed in the first years of Hadrian. The sculptural ornaments of the arch represent, therefore, both a summary of Trajan's activity and the programme of Hadrian, who appears twice in the bas-reliefs as Trajan's associate and heir to his power: once in the scene of the reception of Trajan by the gods and the city of Rome at the entrance to the Capitol (bas-relief 2 of the attica), and again in the bas-relief representing the subjection of Mesopotamia, where Hadrian shows his disapproval of a policy of further conquests in the East. The symbolism of the arch is perfectly clear and has been finely explained both by E. Petersen and by A. von Domaszewski, even if the precise significance of some scenes is not quite clear. This symbolism, as I understand it, is as follows. The main motive is to glorify peace and prosperity established by the great military activity of Trajan, and maintained and promoted by Hadrian. The inner front of the arch, turned towards the city of Beneventum and therefore towards Rome, is devoted to the city of Rome. It depicts the triumphal reception of the emperor by all classes of the population of Rome and Italy: the gods and the city of Rome, the senatorial, equestrian, and municipal aristocracy, the *cives Romani*, the business men of the Forum Boarium, and the veterans of the praetorian guard and of the legions. The outer front depicts the victories of Trajan over Mesopotamia, Parthia, and the North, the *honesta missio* given to the veterans, and the peace and prosperity established by Trajan throughout the Empire, a peace and prosperity based on agriculture, which creates *Abundantia*, and on the success of the policy of repopulation symbolized by the children. The figures in the background are the Roman provinces. The two bas-reliefs inside the arch relate to the city of Beneventum: one shows the institution of *alimenta* and the other the sacrifice of the emperor in the city. The leading idea is, therefore, the same as that which dominates the coinage of Hadrian with its new types and new legends such as *Felix Roma, Italia Felix, Saeculum aureum, Tellus stabilita, Temporum felicitas*, and the coins with the figures of the provinces (Weber, *Unters.*, pp. 87 and 92). Cf. H. Mattingly, 'Some Historical Coins of Hadrian', *JRS* 15, 1925, pp. 209 ff., esp. pp. 214 and 219. Mattingly proves that the four great series issued in A.D. 134–5—the provinces, *adventus, exercitus, restitutor*—were 'neither the announcement of a new policy nor a running commentary upon one: they serve rather to crown an achievement. The Empire appears not only as a domain of Rome, but as a great family of peoples.' Cf. the interesting analysis of these series in Mattingly–Sydenham, *The Roman Imperial Coinage*, ii (1926), pp. 331 ff. The coinage of Hadrian can undoubtedly be used to understand his leading ideas in the same way that the numerous monuments of the Augustan age can be used to reconstruct Augustan policy. On the arch of Beneventum see E. Petersen, *Röm. Mitt.* 7, 1892, pp. 240 ff.; A. Meomartini, *Benevento* (1909), pp. 82 ff.; A. von Domaszewski, *Oest. Jahresh.* 2, 1899, pp. 173 ff. (= id. *Abhandlungen zur römischen Religion* (1909), pp. 25 ff.); W. Weber, *Unters.*, pp. 4 ff. and 21 ff.; Bellissima, *Arco di Trajano in Benevento* (1905), and *Brevis descriptio arcus*, &c. (1910); Mrs. A. Strong,

La Scultura Romana, ii (1926), pp. 191 ff.; S. Reinach, *Rép. d. rel.* i, pp. 58 ff.; G. A. S. Snijder, *JDAI* 41, 1926, pp. 94 ff.; R. Paribeni, *Optimus Princeps*, ii, pp. 255 ff. The tendency towards a strict maintenance of the privileges of the upper classes of the population, especially of the Roman citizens both in the East and in the West, remained throughout the leading principle of the policy of the enlightened monarchy. This tendency is, e.g., strongly emphasized in the newly discovered *Gnomon idiu logu*; see the just remarks of J. Carcopino, *Rev. ét. anc.* 24, 1922, pp. 19 ff. The tendency to protect the weak against the strong (see note 20) has nothing to do with the sharp division of the population into two classes or castes: the Romans and romanized (or hellenized) men and the natives, the barbarians. The protection of the weak meant the endeavour to establish justice in economic relations and to make it possible for the lower classes gradually to reach the standards which would allow of their assimilation by the higher, privileged inhabitants of the Roman Empire.

[8] A good survey of the provincial policy of Trajan is given by A. von Domaszewski, *Abhandlungen zur römischen Religion* (1909), pp. 40 ff.; cf. *Oest. Jahresh.* 2, 1899, pp. 173 ff., and W. Weber, 'Trajan und Hadrian', *Meister der Politik* (1923), pp. 69 ff.

[9] Weber, *Unters.*, pp. 50 ff.; B. W. Henderson, *The Life of Hadrian*, p. 34.

[10] The standard work on Hadrian, a book replete with facts and acute observations, is W. Weber's *Untersuchungen zur Geschichte des Kaisers Hadrianus* (1907); cf. E. Kornemann, *Kaiser Hadrian und der letzte grosse Historiker Roms* (1905); G. Mancini and D. Vaglieri in E. de Ruggiero, *Diz. epigr.* iii, pp. 640 ff., and W. Weber, *Trajan und Hadrian* (1923); L. Perret, *La titulature impériale d'Hadrien* (1929). On his military policy, E. Kornemann, *Klio*, 7, 1907, pp. 88 ff. On the question of Hadrian's wall in Britain, see the lucid short statement of R. G. Collingwood in Henderson's *Hadrian*, p. 166, and his article in *JRS* 11, 1921, pp. 37–66. It is interesting to note that Hadrian's policy of purchasing peace, if necessary—a policy which was freely adopted by his successors and particularly by Commodus and the Severi, and which was opposed by the senate and the most prominent men of the Empire—was supported by some philosophers; see Philostr. *Vita Apoll.* ii. 26.

[11] On the administrative reforms carried out by Hadrian see the valuable book of R. H. Lacey, *The Equestrian Officials of Trajan and Hadrian: their Careers, with some Notes on Hadrian's Reforms* (Princeton, 1917); A. Stein, *Der römische Ritterstand* (1927), pp. 447 ff. On the *curatores*, E. Kornemann in Pauly–Wissowa, iv, cols. 1806 ff. On the λογισταί in the East, M. N. Tod, *JHS* 42, 1922, pp. 172 ff. The inscriptions concerning M. Ulpius Eurycles, and his appointment as λογιστής, first of the *gerousia* of Ephesus and afterwards of a city (Aphrodias), *OGIS* 508 ff.; cf. *Forsch. Eph.* ii, pp. 119 ff., no. 23 (age of M. Aurelius and Commodus). One of the most pernicious novelties of Hadrian was the use of special soldiers, presumably agents of their detachments for the purchase of food (*frumentarii*), in the capacity of special agents (as spies of the emperor and for other purposes), see Dessau, *ILS* 9473, 9474; A. von Domaszewski, *Die Rangordnung des römischen Heeres*, pp. 63 and 109. The subject of the *frumentarii* has been treated in *JRS* 13, 1923, pp. 168 ff., by P. K. Baillie Reynolds, who comes to the same conclusion as regards their original duties. It is unfortunate that in his valuable collection and investigation of the epigraphical material Mr. Reynolds has wholly disregarded both the work of Domaszewski quoted above, and the contributions of O. Hirschfeld, see Chap. IX, note 7, and Chap. XI, note 26. On Hadrian's reforms in the collection of taxes, see my *Staatspacht*, pp. 395 ff., 418 ff., and *passim*.

[12] Stratoniceia-Hadrianopolis, Dittenberger, *Syll.*³ 837 = *IGRR* iv. 1156 = Abbott and Johnson, *Munic. Admin.*, p. 405, no. 83, ll. 8–10: δίκαια ἀξιοῦν μοι δοκεῖτε καὶ ἀναγκαῖα ἄ[ρ]τι γεινομένῃ πόλει· τά τε οὖν τέλη τὰ ἐ[κ] | τῆς χώρας δίδωμι ὑμεῖν. Τέλη means

of course the payments of the rural population of the territory of the newly created city. On Hadrianuthera, W. Weber, *Unters.*, p. 131. The repopulation of Cyrenaica, a counterpart to the repopulation of Dacia by Trajan, is mentioned by Orosius, vii. 12: 'per totam Libyam adversus incolas atrocissima bella gesserunt [the Jews], quae adeo tunc interfectis cultoribus desolata est, ut nisi postea Hadrianus imperator collectas aliunde colonias deduxisset, abraso habitatore mansisset.' The other allusions to the same fact are collected by Weber, ibid., p. 119. The friendly attitude of Hadrian towards the villages of Asia Minor is attested, e.g., by the inscription, *IGRR* iv. 1492. On the work done by Hadrian in Africa see Weber, ibid., p. 203; L. Poinssot, *C.R. Acad. Inscr.* 1915, p. 6; cf. A. Merlin, *Forum et maisons d'Althiburos*, p. 30, and F. de Pachtère, *Bull. arch. du Com. des trav. hist.* 1911, p. 390; T. R. S. Broughton, *The Romanization of Africa Proconsularis* (1929), pp. 171 ff. Privileges granted to villages: Dessau, *ILS* 6777 (vicus Haterianus); *Bull. arch. du Com. des trav. hist.* 1896, p. 296, no. 13 = *CIL* viii. 23896: the men who honour Hadrian in this inscription were probably not members of the community of Thabbora, which later became a *municipium* (*CIL* viii. 23897 = Dessau, *ILS* 8941), but the inhabitants of a *vicus* near Thabbora, or a group of imperial *coloni* living not far from Thabbora.

¹³ *P.Giss.* 60, ii. 25–31; Wilcken, *Chrest.* 341, l. 15. The papyrus of Giessen is dated A.D. 118. The offers of the peasants: *P.Giss.* 4–7; *P.Brem.* 36; *P. Lips.*, inv. 266, published by Wilcken, *Arch. f. Papyr.* 5, p. 245; *P.Ryl.* ii. 96; cf. Wilcken, op. cit., pp. 248ff., and *Chrest.* 351; my article in *Arch. f. Papyr.* 5, pp. 299 f., and my *Studien z. Gesch. röm. Kol.*, pp. 165 f., 175 ff.; E. Kornemann, *P.Giss.* 4–7, intr.; W. L. Westermann, *Class. Phil.* 16, 1921, pp. 185 ff.; *JEA* 11, 1925, pp. 165 ff. Westermann sees in Hadrian's πρόσταγμα, to which the peasants appeal in their offers of a rent, an administrative regulation introduced by the officials of Egypt in the name of the emperor, but without his direct participation. He believes that this regulation was simply the application of a very ancient law according to which land which was in danger of becoming barren was let as grassland for a very small rent. I cannot, however, accept this interpretation: the peasants speak of the πρόσταγμα as if it were the grant of a new and important privilege, and call it a favour. The rent paid is exactly that of the γῆ ἐν τάξει ἰδιοκτήτου. We know how Hadrian liked to concern himself with the minutest details of the economic life of the provinces: at the beginning of his reign (A.D. 118) he was particularly anxious to help the provinces by remission of taxes and rents (*CIL* vi. 967, quoted by Westermann).

¹⁴ P. Jouguet, 'Un édit d'Hadrien', *Rev. ét. gr.* 33 ,1920, pp. 375 ff.; Wilcken, *Arch. f. Papyr.* 7, pp. 110 ff.; S. Eitrem, *Symb. Osl.* 10, 1932, pp. 153 ff. [= *SB* 6994 = ‡*P.Oslo* 78 = *FIRA*², 81]; cf. *P.Hamb.* 93 (A.D. 121–4), a memorandum of some προσοδικοὶ γεωργοί to the prefect Haterius; are not the προσοδικοὶ γεωργοί the newly created half-landowners, and the ἀργυρικοὶ φόροι, of which the edict speaks, their payments? On the γῆ προσόδου see the bibliography in the article of Jouguet, op. cit., pp. 392 ff., and P. Collart, *P.Bouriant*, 42, pp. 156 ff.; cf. Chap. VII, note 50.

¹⁵ On the African inscriptions, see Chap. VII, note 75.

¹⁶ See Chap. VI, note 96.

¹⁷ My *Studien z. Gesch. röm. Kol.*, p. 386; cf. p. 275. The inscription regarding lake Copais is mentioned by Papadakis, Ἀρχ. Δελτ. 5, 1919. παράρτ. p. 34.

¹⁸ See Chap. VII, notes 100 and 101.

¹⁹ On the *Euboicus* of Dion, H. von Arnim, *Leben*, &c., p. 500 f.

²⁰ Ivo Pfaff, 'Über den rechtlichen Schutz des wirtschaftlich Schwächeren in der römischen Kaisergesetzgebung', *Sozialgeschichtliche Forschungen* (*Ergänzungshefte zur Zeitschr. f. Soz.- u. Wirtschaftsg.*), 1897; cf. I. Greaves, *Studies in the History of Roman*

Land-tenure, i, pp. 534 ff. (in Russian), and V. Duruy, *Histoire des Romains*, v, Appendix: 'Sur la formation historique des deux classes de citoyens, désignés dans les Pandectes sous les noms d'*honestiores* et d'*humiliores*.' Mommsen, *Strafrecht*, p. 225, note 5, and p. 481, note, in dealing with the different treatment of the two classes from the point of view of criminal law, points out that the terms *honestiores* and *humiliores* date from the 3rd cent. A.D.

²¹ Oil-law, *IG* ii², 1100. Fish-regulations, A. Wilhelm, *Oest. Jahresh.* 12, 1909, pp. 146 ff. [= *IG* ii², 1103]: the letter of Hadrian drew its inspiration from some laws in the spirit of Plato, *Leg.* xi, p. 917, B–C; see e.g. Alexis, in Kaibel, *Fr. Com. Gr.* ii, p. 8 (Athen., p. 226, A–B): τίθησι γὰρ νυνὶ νόμον | τῶν ἰχθυοπωλῶν ὅστις ἂν πωλῶν τινι | ἰχθὺν ὑποτιμήσας ἀποδῶτ' ἐλάττονος | ἧς εἶπε τιμῆς εἰς τὸ δεσμωτήριον | εὐθὺς ἀπάγεσθαι τοῦτον. The bankers of Pergamon: *OGIS* 484. The problem of the food supply, as I have often pointed out in this volume, was one of the most difficult questions with which the Roman Empire had to deal, the difficulty being largely due to the slowness and the high cost of land transport. The conditions certainly led to much profiteering and speculation, and consequently to the oppression of the poor by the rich. It is not surprising that Hadrian was not the first to interfere with free trade in foodstuffs by means of special regulations. I have collected the evidence bearing on the regulation of corn-prices in my article 'Frumentum' in Pauly–Wissowa, vii, col. 143 (Tiberius, Tac. *Ann.* ii. 87; Nero, Tac. *Ann.* xv. 39; in Asia Minor, Euseb. *Chron.* ii. 152, Schöne). Measures of a more general, though local, character were taken frequently by the emperors in connexion with local famines. In Chap. V, note 9, I have referred to the evidence of a Latin inscription of Antioch of Pisidia, belonging to the time of Domitian, which speaks of measures adopted by the governor against profiteering in time of famine, and to the steps taken by M. Aurelius in Northern Italy under similar conditions. The examples of Domitian and M. Aurelius were frequently followed in later times: see *Dig.* 7. 1. 27. 3; 50. 4. 25 (cf. my article in Pauly–Wissowa, vii, col. 186), where permission is granted to the cities to buy from the *possessores* of their territory a certain quantity of corn at reduced prices (the *frumentum emptum* of the time of Verres in Sicily, the σῖτος ἀγοραστός of Egypt). A similar measure is recorded at Cibyra in *IGRR* iv. 914 (time of Claudius): ἃ δὲ ἦν ἀναγκαιότατα τῶν ἐν ταῖς πρεσβείαις ἐπιτευχθέντων, ᾐτημένον ἀπὸ Τιβερίου Κλαυδίου Καίσαρος ἀπεσκευάσθαι Τιβέριον Νεικήφορον πράσ[σο]ντα τὴ[ν] πόλιν καθ' ἕκαστον ἔτος δηνάρια τ[ρι]σχείλια καὶ λαμβάνοντα, καὶ τὴν τοῦ σείτου πρᾶσιν γεινέσθαι ἐν τῇ ἀγορᾷ κα[τὰ] ζεύ[γ]ος μοδίων ἑβδομήκοντα πέντε ἐκ πάσης τῆς χώρας. It is not easy to guess the reasons of the dismissal of the procurator and to judge whether there was any connexion between his exactions and the ordinance regarding the corn trade in the city. We may suppose that the procurator favoured illicit speculations in corn. With the emperor and his chief assistant in this department, the *praefectus annonae*, lay the final decision of questions connected with the victualling of the cities, which affected not only the cities concerned, but to some extent the whole state. One of the most important was that of granting or withholding permission to import corn into the cities from outside. To the evidence on this subject which is quoted in my article 'Frumentum' in Pauly–Wissowa, vii, add Epict. i. 10. 2 and 9–10 (speaking of the *praefectus annonae*): ὅμοιον οὖν ἐστιν ἐντευξίδιον παρά τινος λαβόντα ἀναγιγνώσκειν ' παρακαλῶ σε ἐπιτρέψαι μοι σιτάριον ἐξαγαγεῖν ', and *Forsch. Eph.* iii, no. 16 (corn from Egypt for Ephesus) and the parallels collected by J. Keil (Tralles); cf. B. Laum, *Ath. Mitt.* 38, 1913, pp. 23 ff.; *Syll.*³ 839 = Abbott and Johnson, *Munic. Adm.*, p. 407, no. 86. Information regarding the granaries of Alexandria and the policy followed by the early emperors in regard to Egyptian grain is to be found in Wilcken, 'Zum Germanicus Papyrus', *Hermes*, 63, 1928, pp. 48 ff. An excellent example of profiteering on a large scale to the detriment of a city is afforded by the well-known

oil speculation of John of Gischala, which is told by Josephus, *Vita*, 13 (75). John bought up the oil in his own town for a ridiculously low price (four drachmae for 80 *xestai*) and sold it in Caesarea at the rate of one drachma for 2 *xestai*. We do not, however, know how much he paid for transporting the oil to the city. We may note in this connexion that the emperors of the 2nd and 3rd cent. A.D. were extremely active in building large granaries in the provinces, especially the corn-producing provinces, of the Empire. Their main purpose was, of course, to facilitate the victualling of the capital and of the troops. But the fact that in A.D. 199 the city of Cuicul in Numidia built extensive *horrea* (*Bull. arch. du Com. des trav. hist.* 1911, p. 115 [= *L'An. ép.* 1911, 106]) testifies to the interest which the provincial population had in the construction of such inland storehouses. Cf. the inscriptions published (with parallel examples) by E. Albertini, *C. R. Acad. Inscr.* 1924, pp. 253 ff. [= *L'An. ép.* 1925, 73–74]. On the *horrea* of Lycia see Benndorf and Niemann, *Reisen in Lykien und Kasien*, i (1884), p. 116; Petersen and von Luschau, *Reisen in Lykien, Milyas u. Kibyratis*, ii (1889), p. 41; cf. R. Paribeni, *Optimus Princeps*, i, pp. 174 ff. The sale of bread, not only of corn, was probably controlled in the cities of the Roman Empire. An investigation carried out by my pupil Yeo, on the ruins of the Pompeian bakeries, has shown that they are distributed regularly in the town, and that almost all have dimensions corresponding to those of a normal bakery in Rome. The inscriptions (*CIL* vi. 22 and 1002) and the reliefs of the sepulchral monument of Eurysaces show that in Rome the baking and sale of bread was controlled by the state. Cf. T. Frank, *Economic History*[2], p. 256. This problem would profit from further study.

[22] The evidence on the rule of Antoninus Pius is carefully collected and fully treated by E. E. Bryant, *The Reign of Antoninus Pius* (1895).

[23] On the military activity of M. Aurelius see the text to the excellent publication of the bas-reliefs of the column of M. Aurelius by E. Petersen, A. von Domaszewski, and A. Calderini, *Die Reliefs der Marcussäule* (1904); cf. A. von Premerstein, 'Untersuchungen zur Geschichte des Kaisers Marcus', *Klio*, 11, 1911, pp. 355 ff., and 12, 1912, pp. 139 ff.; P. E. Matheson, *Marcus Aurelius and his Task as Emperor* (1922); J. Schwendemann, *Der historische Wert der Vita Marci bei den Scriptores Historiae Augustae* (1923). The calamities which befell Asia Minor as a result of the plague of A.D. 166 are brought out by two oracles of Apollo Clarius, one for Pergamon and the other for Caesarea Trocetta: Picard, *BCH* 46, 1922, pp. 190 ff.

[24] *IGRR* iv. 1290, with the reading of the inscription by A. von Premerstein in *Klio*, 12, 1912, p. 165 (cf. J. Keil–A. von Premerstein, *Zweite Reise*, pp. 34 and 36): δεκ]απρωτεύσαντα τὴν β[αρυτ]έραν πρᾶξιν Βαστερ[νικ]ήν.

[25] Cass. Dio, 72. 32. 2–3; 72. 19. 1–2 (p. 274, Boiss.); *Scr. Hist. Aug.* M. Aur. 23. 1 and 11. 3. Cf. J. Schwendemann, *Der hist. Wert. der Vita Marci*, p. 50.

[26] Cass. Dio, 71. 3. 2 (A.D. 168).

[27] *Scr. Hist. Aug.* M. Aur. 11. 7.

[28] *Scr. Hist. Aug.* Comm. 16. 2, Pesc. Niger, 3. 3 f.; Herodian i. 10.

[29] Cass. Dio, 72. 4. 1–2; cf. J. Lesquier, *L'Armée romaine d'Égypte*, p. 29 f., and pp. 391 and 402.

[30] Ivo Bruns, 'Marc Aurel', *Vorträge und Aufsätze* (1905), pp. 291 ff.; W. W. Buckland, *The Roman Law of Slavery* (1908); Ph. Lotmar, *Zeitschr. d. Sav.-St.* 33, 1912, pp. 340 ff.; H. D. Sedgwick, *Marcus Aurelius, a Biography* (1921). Similar was his attitude towards the tenants of the large imperial estates in Italy. We learn from the *Scr. Hist. Aug.* M. Aur. 11. 9, that the *curatores viarum* received from him a commission to inspect the revenues of the imperial estates situated in the districts through which the roads under their care passed. Was not the aim of this measure to protect the *coloni* against the

farmers-general of the estates? Cf. Mommsen, *Staatsr.* ii, p. 1081, note 1; Schwende-mann, op. cit.; and the well-known inscription of the saltus Burunitanus (Chap. IX, note 8) [= *FIRA²*, 103]. The beginning of the trouble with which this inscription deals dates from the reign of M. Aurelius. The oppressive behaviour of the *conductores* was cer-tainly due to the pressure put on them by the imperial administration, a pressure occa-sioned by the ever-increasing demand for corn and money for the troops. The measures of M. Aurelius were intended to prevent an outbreak of discontent among the tenants.

³¹ O. Seeck, *Gesch. d. Unterg. d. ant. Welt*, i, pp. 318 ff.; G. Sigwart, 'Die Fruchtbar-keit des Bodens als historischer Faktor', *Schmöllers Jahrb.* 39, 1915, pp. 113 ff.; id. in Pauly–Wissowa, x, cols. 1899 ff.; V. G. Simkhovitch, 'Rome's Fall reconsidered', *Polit. Sc. Quart.* 31, 1916; cf. id. *Toward the Understanding of Jesus*, &c. (1921), pp. 84 ff.; T. Frank, *Economic History*¹ (1920), pp. 288 ff.; Abbott and Johnson, *Munic. Adm.*, pp. 210 ff.; cf. J. N. L. Myres, *Econ. Hist. Rev.* 2, 1929, pp. 143 ff. As Myres observes I made no allusion to the climatological theories of Brueckner and Huntingdon accord-ing to which, after 400 B.C. (except for a temporary return of dampness between A.D. 180 and 300), the climate of the Mediterranean became increasingly dry. The problem is far from solved, and its importance for the economic history of the ancient world demands that it be investigated by a scholar equally versed in climatology and history. Was the change so general as to affect every region of the Empire? The experiments of the French in Africa and Syria and the agricultural revival in Palestine show that prosperous agriculture is still possible without vast efforts. I must admit that the historical chapters in the very interesting books of Professor E. Huntingdon, *Civilization and Climate* (1924), and especially *World Power and Evolution* (1920), ch. xi, 'The Example of Rome', pp. 186 ff., did not persuade me. I am certainly not competent in matters of historical climatology. See my article 'The Decay of the Ancient World and its economic explanation', *Econ. Hist. Rev.* 2, 1930, pp. 212 ff.

³² *C.Theod.* xi. 28. 13 (A.D. 422), a statistical survey of the cultivated land of the *ratio privata* in Africa Proconsularis and in Byzacena. The careful investigation of this text by W. Barthel, *Bonn. Jahrb.* 120, 1911, p. 50, shows that the statistics attest a very small percentage of waste land and indicate an intensive cultivation of the soil. If the population was poor and labour scanty, it was therefore not due to the exhaustion of the soil. Cf. Chap. VII, note 103.

³³ The idea of the supremacy of the interests of the state or the community over those of the individuals is repeatedly emphasized by M. Aurelius, see vi. 44; vii. 55; xi. 4; cf. iv. 29 (those who are opposed to it are ξένοι κόσμου). To the observations made by G. de Sanctis in his review of the first edition of this book in *Riv. fil.* 54, 1926, pp. 536 ff., regarding the predominant position of the state as a fundamental factor in the economic decline of the Roman Empire, I would reply that naturally the idea of the superiority of the interests of the state over those of the individual in general is sound in itself; but that an irresponsible government is only too liable to consider the interests of the state as the only predominant motive, and to attempt to 'save' the state at the expense of the community and of individuals. That is precisely what happened in the Roman Empire.

³⁴ The growth of the imperial estates, an outstanding fact of the economic develop-ment of the Roman Empire, does not affect the accuracy of the picture given in the text. The imperial estates, so far as the land owned by the emperor did not belong to the territory of the cities, grew at the expense, not of the cities and their territories, but at the expense of the great landowners of the 1st cent. B.C. and A.D., who were mostly extra-territorial. Imperial land-holding within city territories was minimal. More-over, as we have seen, the emperors of the 2nd cent. A.D. were not unwilling to trans-

form their estates into city territories. However, even on the imperial estates a class of landlords was in process of formation, and there existed the same differentiation as in the cities. I refer to the numerous farmers-general, of whom I spoke in the preceding chapter. The importance of the phenomenon of which we are speaking was fully recognized by W. L. Westermann, 'The Economic Basis of the Decline of Ancient Culture', *Amer. Hist. Rev.* 20, 1915, pp. 724 ff.; cf. E. Kornemann in Pauly–Wissowa, Suppl. iv, cols. 240 ff.

35 On the *angareiae* (ἀγγαρεῖαι) in Egypt see the collection of material and a good bibliography in F. Oertel, *Die Liturgie* (1917), pp. 24 ff., 88 ff.; cf. W. Schubart, *Einführung*, p. 431, and *PSI* 446, an edict of M. Petronius Mamertinus, A.D. 133–7 [= Hunt–Edgar, *Sel. Pap.* 221]. It is characteristic of the discipline of Trajan's time that Mamertinus expressly mentions the soldiers as the chief offenders and insists on the evil influence of the exactions on the morals and the discipline of the army. Oertel also gives the evidence about the compulsory deliveries of foodstuffs, &c.

36 F. Oertel, *Die Liturgie*, pp. 62 ff. On πρᾶξις ἐκ τῶν σωμάτων see E. Weiss, *Griech. Privatrecht*, i (1923), pp. 495 ff., cf. the bibliography of note 43 of this chapter. Unfortunately the jurists who have studied this question have not extended their investigations to public law, and have not studied how the system was applied by the state for its own ends. Cf. my article 'The Roman Exploitation of Egypt in the First Century A.D.', *Journ. Econ. and Bus. Hist.* 1, 1929, pp. 337 ff.

37 My articles in *Klio*, 6, 1906, pp. 249 ff., and in *JRS* 8, 1918, p. 29, note 3, and p. 33, note 1; P. Fiebig, *Zeitschr. f. Neutest. Wissenschaft*, 18, 1917, pp. 64 ff. For the spread of the institution over the whole Roman Empire in the 2nd cent. A.D. see Epict. *Diss.* iv. 1. 79: ἂν δ' ἀγγαρεία ᾖ καὶ στρατιώτης ἐπιλάβηται, ἄφες, μὴ ἀντίτεινε μηδὲ γόγγυζε· εἰ δὲ μή, πληγὰς λαβὼν οὐδὲν ἧττον ἀπολεῖς καὶ τὸ ὀνάριον, to be compared with the well-known story of the gardener and the soldier in Apuleius [*Met.* ix. 39 ff.]. Cf. L. Poinssot, *Bull. Soc. Ant. de France*, 1924, pp. 196 ff.: a bronze plaque with a Greek inscription, which shows that a horse or a donkey belonging to the imperial postal service is exempt from *angaria* [= *SEG*, ii, 871 = ‡L. Robert, *Hellenica*, iii (1946), pp. 170 ff.].

38 On the system prevailing in the ancient world (including India and China) of using beasts of burden as driving-power see Commandant Lefebvre des Noëttes, *L'Attelage de cheval de selle à travers les âges. Contribution à l'histoire de l'ésclavage* (1931) (a new edition of his book *La Force motrice animale à travers les âges* (1924)), and for the Roman roads his article in *Rev. arch.* 1925 (2), pp. 105 ff. The evidence of the Roman period, in so far as it is known to me, confirms on the whole the author's views on the Roman transport system. There are, however, exceptions. The relief of Vaison (id., *La Force motrice*, pl. xxxiii, fig. 88) cannot be a modern forgery: that is quite certain (cf. our pl. lxxiv, 1, and the bibliography). Thus I cannot admit that the harness of the horses on this relief is simply modern work. A new and accurate survey of the enormous archaeological material of the Roman period is urgently necessary. Monuments such as those represented in my plates xxxiii, 3, and xlvi, 3, do not agree with Lefebvre's system. I may recall that the loads of the carts in modern Russia are mostly about the same weight as those mentioned in the *Codex Theodosianus*, partly because of the miserable breed of horse used by the peasants, and partly because of the bad roads. The same considerations undoubtedly apply to the Roman Empire. The peasants' horses, mules, donkeys, and oxen were not better than those of Russia, and the Roman roads exacted a heavy toil from the beasts of burden. We must not forget that the greater part of the roads close to the Roman roads were simply paths in very bad condition, like the roads of Asia Minor and the northern Balkan lands today. The

whole question of transport in the Roman Empire requires fresh and accurate investigation. On the gradual improvement of transport in the ancient world see W. L. Westermann, 'On Inland Transportation and Communication in Antiquity', *Polit. Sc. Quart.* 43, 1928, pp. 364 ff.

³⁹ On the associations of shipowners see Chap. V, note 22. It is characteristic of the conditions of the 2nd cent. that the *praefectus annonae* of A.D. 201, Claudius Iulianus, in a letter addressed to the procurator of Narbo gives strict orders to comply with the demands of the *navicularii Arelatenses* who had bitterly complained of the bad organization of the service and threatened a strike; see *CIL* iii. 14165, ll. 11 ff. (Dessau, *ILS* 6987): 'et cum eadem querella latius procedat ceteris etiam implorantibus auxilium aequitatis cum quadam denuntiatione cessaturi propediem obsequisi permaneat iniuria, peto ut tam indemnitati rationis quam securitati hominum qui annonae deserviunt consulatur', &c. On the identity of the Iulianus of the inscription with the *praefectus annonae* of 201, cf. Hähnle in Pauly–Wissowa, x, col. 23, no. 20; *CIL* vi. 1603; Pauly–Wissowa, s. v. 'Claudius', no. 189; cf. also Chap. IX, note 53. As the legislation of Septimius Severus in regard to the associations was rather liberal (see next chapter), there can be no doubt that the incidents described in the inscription occurred every time that the pressure of war demanded of the shipowners an intensified compulsory service. We must bear in mind that after Claudius' grant of certain privileges to the *navicularii* and merchants, all of them given to individuals, not to the associations (Suet. *Claud.* 18. 19; Gaius, *Inst.* i. 32; Ulp. *Fragm.* iii. 6), the first general measures favouring the *navicularii* and the merchants in the service of the state were taken by Hadrian and developed and made specific by his successors Antoninus and M. Aurelius. The main privilege which was granted to these associations was exemption from the municipal liturgies, a privilege which shows how heavy this burden was after Trajan; see *Dig.* 50. 6. 6. 5; cf. 8 (Hadrian); ibid. 9 (Antoninus); ibid. 6 (M. Aurelius and L. Verus).

⁴⁰ O. Hirschfeld, *Die Kais. Verwaltungsb.*², pp. 190 ff. It is very probable that the management of the messenger-service by the state involved the organization of some state depots of horses and other draught animals at the stations. The animals were brought from the imperial estates and were state property. This is shown by an inscription of Dacibyza in Bithynia, *IGRR* iii. 2, which has been restored and brilliantly explained by J. Keil, *Oest. Jahresh.* 21, 1921, pp. 261 ff. [=*SEG* ii. 666]: Ἀγαθῇ Τύχῃ. Μάρκος Στάτιος Ἰουλιανὸς καὶ Σ[....]λιος Ῥοῦφος στρατιῶται σπείρης ἕκτης ἱππικ[ῆς] οἱ ἐπὶ τῶν στατιώνων τῶν ἄκτων καὶ νουμέρων καὶ οἱ [μ]ουλίωνες οἱ ἐπεστῶντες συνωρία εὐχαριστοῦσιν Λευ[κο]ύλλῳ ˙Ηδυος ἐπιμελητῇ κτηνῶν Καίσαρος. The inscription belongs to the 3rd cent. It enumerates the officers of a post-station: two *actarii et numerarii stationum*, cavalry soldiers, a certain number of drivers, and the manager of the imperial herds, whose duty it was to provide the stations with draught animals. It is very tempting to refer this organization to Septimius Severus, but its beginnings may have been earlier, its first introduction into Italy being due to Nerva and its gradual extension to the provinces to Hadrian, Antoninus, and Severus. By 'gradual' I mean an increase in the number of roads and stations provided with a supply of draught animals and drivers. But there is no doubt that the provisions of the government never met all needs, and that the state stations remained an exception. I must, however, point out that the above interpretation is not the only one possible (see Keil, loc. cit.). The *stationes* may have been military posts for horse-troops or special posts for the requisitioning and purchase of horses required by the army. Bithynia and Cappadocia were famous centres of horse-breeding, cf. the papyrus published by A. S. Hunt in *Racc. Lumbroso*, p. 265, l. 56: *trans M(a)r(u)m equatum*, which shows that the cavalry units used to send special commissioners to get horses. Cf. G. Cantacuzène, *Aegyptus*, 9, 1928, pp. 72–73. Dar-

dania and Moesia superior on the two banks of the Morava also produced good horses. It appears that the *stratores* of the governors, under the ἀρχιστράτωρ, were responsible for remounts: see the inscription of Termessos of A.D. 142, published by F. Schehl, *Oest. Jahresh.* 24, 1928, Beibl. pp. 97 ff., where an ἀρχιστράτωρ of Val. Eudaemon, prefect of Egypt in A.D. 142, is mentioned [= *SEG* vi. 628 = *TAM* iii. 52]. A funerary inscription found at Belgrade in Jugoslavia speaks of a slave born at Cibyra in Asia Minor who died in Pannonia and was ὀρεωκόμος. Hades took from his hands ἡνίας συνωρίδων. The stone was erected by Hiera, his σύνδουλος. I believe that the dead man worked in the postal service. See N. Vulić, 'Ancient Monuments of our Country', *Royal Acad. Serb.*, Mem. 71, 1931, p. 8, no. 8 (in Serbian). Near Trèves a large estate surrounded by walls, which was used in the 4th cent. A.D. as a stud, was discovered: see J. Steinhausen, 'Die Langmauer bei Trier und ihr Bezirk: eine kaiserliche Domäne', *Trier Zeitschr.* 6, 1931 pp. 41 ff. Cf. Chap. VI, note 91.

[41] There is no adequate treatment of the history of the liturgies in the urbanized Eastern and Western parts of the Empire. The best (but now wholly antiquated) survey is that given by E. Kuhn, *Die städtische und bürgerliche Verfassung des römischen Reichs bis auf die Zeiten Justinians* (1864). Kuhn, however, gave a systematic, not an historical, treatment of the problem based on our juridical sources and representing therefore in the main the situation as it existed in the period after Diocletian. The first attempt at an historical treatment is W. Liebenam's *Städteverwaltung im römischen Kaiserreiche* (1900), which is still the best book on the subject. Liebenam carefully collected the epigraphical evidence and endeavoured to arrange his material according to historical requirements, but he did not grasp the very great importance of the introduction of the principle of personal, not collective, responsibility in the field of tax-collection, &c. Since Liebenam nothing of importance (except for Egypt) has been written on the liturgies as they developed in the cities of the Empire. On the Spanish cities see Chap. VI, note 31. Some new and interesting points of view concerning the development of the liturgies, and the meaning of the word, are suggested by J. Partsch, *Arch. f. Papyr.* 7, pp. 264 ff., in a review of Oertel's book, *Die Liturgie* (1919).

[42] My *Gesch. der Staatspacht*, pp. 415 ff.; O. Hirschfeld, *Die kais. Verwaltungsb.*[2], pp. 68 ff.; my articles in E. de Ruggiero's *Diz. epigr.* iii, pp. 107 ff., and in Pauly–Wissowa, vi, cols. 2385 ff. Within the territories of the cities, i.e. in the country parts, the responsibility for the collection of taxes lay on the representatives of the villages: see J. Keil–A. von Premerstein, *Dritte Reise*, p. 69.

[43] My *Gesch. der Staatspacht*, pp. 374 ff.; O. Hirschfeld, *Die kais. Verwaltungsb.*[2], pp. 77 ff.; and my article 'Fiscus' in Pauly–Wissowa. The transition from the collection of the taxes by companies (*societates publicanorum*) to collection by half-farmers, half-officials is illustrated by two inscriptions of Africa: one is *ILA* 257, a dedication to Venus Augusta by two *promagistri soc*(*iorum*) *IIII p*(*ublicorum*) *Afric*(*ae*) (1st cent. A.D., time of Claudius?), the other is an inscription of the time of Septimius Severus in honour of M. Rossius Vitulus who ended his career (at least at the time of the erection of his statue in Bulla Regia) with the post of a *procurator IIII p. A.* (*ILA* 455). Cf. for Asia *Forsch. Eph.* iii, pp. 131 f., no. 45—a *promag*(*istro*) *duum p*(*ublicorum*) *XXXX p*(*ortuum*) *Asiae*—and another inscription relating to the same individual, *Oest. Jahresh.* 1, 1898, Beibl. p. 76; A. Stein, Pauly–Wissowa, suppl. i, col. 332, no. 7*a* (the Greek translation of *promagistro* is here ἀρχώνης). Cf. the fragment published in *Forsch. Eph.* iii, p. 132. The inscription is of A.D. 103–14. M. Aurelius Mindius Matidianus belongs to a later period (under M. Aurelius and Commodus); in the latter stages of his life he was a *procurator* of high rank, and had previously been ἀρχώνης τεσσαρακοστῆς λιμένων Ἀσίας. It is not impossible that he was both *procurator* and ἀρχώνης, that is *pro magistro*. See Dessau, *ILS* 8858, and J. Keil., *Oest. Jahresh.* 23, 1926, Beibl. p. 269 = *L'An. ép.* 1928, 97. It is to be

noticed that under Trajan the *vectigal ferrariarum* was still (in Italy?) managed by a company (*socii*), *CIL* xiv. 4326 and *Add.* p. 773. At Letnica, in the district of Lorech, an inscription has been found referring to a *conductor p.p. Illyrici et ripae Thraciae* (*L'An. ép.* 1928, 133). Cf. Chap. V, note 24. My remarks on Nero's proposal concerning the *vectigalia* are based on the well-known passage of Tacitus (*Ann.* xiii. 50), and the interpretation of it which has been suggested to me by J. G. C. Anderson. 'According to Tacitus', he writes, 'the reason why Nero considered the question was "crebrae populi flagitationes", and Nero's action was an *impetus*, on which the Senate had to throw cold water, by pointing out that an empire cannot be run without revenue. "Pulcherrimum id donum generi mortalium daret" are manifestly Nero's own words. Nero was bored by the constant complaints and had a fit of his characteristic irresponsible benevolence, a benevolence typical of Bohemians of his sort.' Nero's advisers, however, through an edict of the emperor, took some important steps to improve the collection of taxes (ibid. 51), and later a special commission was created for this purpose (ibid. xv. 18). Cf. my *Gesch. der Staatspacht*, p. 387 (59), and my article 'Fiscus' in Pauly–Wissowa, vi, col. 2391; O. Hirschfeld, *Die kais. Verwaltungsb.*², p. 81, note 3, and p. 89, note 3.

⁴⁴ This is the famous *cessio bonorum*, additional material for the study of which has been provided by many important papyri from Egypt; to it may also refer Caracalla's rescript to the *centonarii* of Solva [= Riccobono, *FIRA*² 87]. See E. Weiss, *Zeitschr. d. Sav.-St.* 36, 1915, p. 168; L. Guenoun, *La Cessio bonorum*, 1913 (1920); P. Meyer, *Zeitschr. f. vergl. Rechtswiss.* 39, 1921, p. 282; A. Steinwenter, *Wiener Stud.* 40, 1918; ibid. 42, 1920, pp. 88 ff.; A. G. Roos, *Mnemosyne*, 1919, pp. 371 ff.; F. von Woess, *Zeitschr. d. Sav.-St.* 43, 1922, pp. 485 ff.; Siro Solazzi, *Racc. Lumbroso*, pp. 246 ff.; E. Weiss, *Griechisches Privatrecht*, i (1923), pp. 495 ff.; A. Segrè, *Aegyptus*, 9, 1928, pp. 30 ff. Cf., however, the acute suggestion for the restoration of the critical word in the inscription from Solva, l. 7, made by J. Kampstra, *Mnemosyne*, 1923, pp. 1 ff. (disputed for formal reasons by O. Cuntz, *Oest. Jahresh.* 23, 1926, Beibl. pp. 361 ff.). Whatever restoration one accepts, however, the inscription shows that the cities as well as the government worked to prevent wealthy members of the privileged corporations from escaping the municipal liturgies.

⁴⁵ O. Seeck, *Klio*, 1, 1901, pp. 147 ff., especially pp. 173 f. I must confess that the evidence on the *decemprimi*, who should not be identical with the *decemviri*, is very scanty for the early Empire. A large number of the allusions to the *decemprimi* and *undecimprimi* refer not to cities but to village and tribal communities. It may be that an institution which existed in some cities of the West was later generalized and legalized in accordance with the practice which took firm root in the East. Cf. Brandis in Pauly–Wissowa, iv, cols. 2417 ff., and O. Hirschfeld, *Die kais. Verwaltungsb.*², p. 74, note 6.

⁴⁶ See preceding note; cf. my *Gesch. der Staatspacht*, p. 417; E. Hula, *Oest. Jahresh.* 5, 1902, pp. 197 ff.; W. Liebenam, *Städteverwaltung*, pp. 421, 490, and 552 (list of δεκάπρωτοι).

⁴⁷ In the early imperial inscriptions of the East the δεκάπρωτοι never appear. O. Seeck, it is true, speaks of the *decaprotia* as existing in Asia Minor as early as M. Antonius (*Klio*, 1, 1901, p. 150, note 4), but the games (μεγάλα Ἀντώνια) mentioned in the inscription, *BCH* 10, 1886, p. 415, which he quotes, were instituted in honour of the Emperor M. Antonius Gordianus, not of M. Antonius the triumvir. In *CIG* 3732, the mention of an Antonius and of an Asinnia does not help us in dating the inscription, as these names were very common in Asia Minor. Leaving aside the vague and doubtful allusions of Fl. Josephus, the earliest mention of a δεκάπρωτος which we have occurs at Gerasa in A.D. 66 (*IGRR* iii. 1376 [= *OGIS* 621 = *Gerasa*, no. 45]; the reckoning of the date as A.D. 98 is wrong, as the era of Gerasa is that of Pompey (another copy of the same inscription confirms the date)). As the δεκάπρωτος of Gerasa is also ἄρχων at the

same time, and as he is called δεκάπρωτος διὰ βίου τῆς πόλεως, it seems probable that in the East, as in the West (note 45), the office, or rather the title, of δεκάπρωτος was purely honorary in the 1st cent. A.D. The office is mentioned much more frequently in and after the time of Hadrian. So in Lycia, *IGRR* iv. 640 (Arneae) [= *TAM* ii. 765], δεκα-πρωτεύσαντα ἀπὸ ἐτῶν ιη'; ibid. 649 (Idebessus) [= *TAM* ii. 838]; (cf. E. Hula, *Oest. Jahresh*. 5, 1902, p. 198, note 3, and p. 206): the forefathers of the man were δεκάπρωτοι, he himself was εἰκοσάπρωτος; cf. ibid. 539; perhaps in Phrygia (Hierapolis), ibid. 818, C. Agellius Apollonides δεκαπρωτεύσαντα καὶ κονβενταρχήσαντα τῶν Ῥωμαίων καὶ ἐλαιοθετή-σαντα καὶ ἐξεταστὴν γενόμενον καὶ ἐργεπιστατήσαντα καὶ εἰς χρίας κυριακὰς εὔχρηστον γενόμενον, cf. 870 (Colossae), καὶ εἰς κυριακὰς (scil. χρείας) (ὑπηρετήσας?); certainly in Lydia, especi-ally in Thyatira, ibid. 1228, Asclepiades δεκαπρωτεύσαντα ἔτη ι' καὶ ἐπιδόσει καὶ κυριακαῖς ὑπηρεσίαις χρησιμεύσαντα τῇ πατρίδι (probably not later than the 2nd cent.) and Laevianus, ibid. 1290, [δεκ]απρωτεύσαντα τὴν β[αρυτ]έραν πρᾶξιν Βαστερ[νικ]ήν, cf. A. von Premerstein, *Klio*, 12, 1912, p. 165: Laevianus was certainly a contemporary of M. Aurelius; in Andros, *IG* xii. 5. 724 (Antoninus) and in Palmyra, *IGRR* iii. 1056. i. 8 [= *OGIS* 629]. Note that in many of these inscriptions the rank of the δεκάπρωτος is not very high, and that the office is often connected with the performance of κυριακαὶ χρεῖαι, i.e. responsibility for compulsory work and compulsory deliveries by the people. However, the bulk of the inscriptions (see the list in W. Liebenam, *Städteverw.*, p. 552) belongs to the early and late 3rd cent.: cf., e.g., the series of inscriptions of Prusias ad Hypium, *IGRR* iii. 60, 63, 64, 65, 67, and most of the inscriptions of Thyatira; and at this time the *decaprotia* appears as the highest office of the city.

[48] In A.D. 73 a rich citizen of Cibyra gave a capital sum to the city to cover the cos of the gymnasiarchy, *IGRR* iv. 915 = B. Laum, *Stiftungen*, ii, no. 162. Trajan: Bithynia, Plin. *Ep.* x. 113; Aquileia, *CIL* v. 875 = Dessau, *ILS* 1374. Hadrian: exemption of the new city of Antinoupolis from liturgies, *P.Oxy.* 1119 = Wilcken, *Chrest.* 397, l. 15: ὅτι πρῶτον μὲν θεὸς Ἀδριανὸς . . . ἐνομοθέτησεν σαφῶς παρὰ νόμοις μὲν ἡμῖν ἄρχειν καὶ λειτουργεῖν, πασῶν δὲ ἀπηλλάχθη τῶν παρ' ἄλλοις ἀρχῶν τε καὶ λειτουργιῶν. Hadrian also freed the philosophers, the rhetors, the teachers, and the doctors from ἀγορανομιῶν, ἱεροσυ-νῶν, ἐπισταθμιῶν, σιτωνίας, ἐλαιωνίας, καὶ μήτε κρίνειν, μήτε πρεσβεύειν, μήτε εἰς στρατείαν καταλέγεσθαι ἄκοντας, μήτε εἰς ἄλλην αὐτοὺς ὑπηρεσίαν ἐθνικὴν ἤ τινα ἄλλην ἀναγκάζεσθαι, *Dig.* 27. 1. 6. 8. This shows that Hadrian realized how heavy the burden of liturgies had become. But granting privileges was not a remedy. It aggravated the situation of those who had no privileges, and it was, of course, a compensation for other services ren-dered by the privileged to the state. This was the reason why the same privileges were granted to members of some associations which worked for the state: the 'fabri et centonarii', *Dig.* 27. 1. 17. 2; cf. the inscription of Solva, O. Cuntz, *Oest. Jahresh.* 18, 1915, pp. 98 ff. [= Riccobono, *FIRA²* 87]; cf. *Dig.* 50. 6. 6. 12; the 'negotiatores qui annonam urbis adiuvant, item navicularii', *Dig.* 50. 6. 6. 3; the 'frumentarii negotia-tores', ibid. 50. 5. 9. 1; the 'conductores vectigalium publicorum', ibid. 50. 6. 6. 10. Antoninus Pius: *CIL* v. 532. 2. 1 ff., especially 11, '[e]t sin[t] cum quibus numera decurionibus iam ut pauci[s one]rosa honeste de pl[e]no compartiamur'. Cf. the endeavours of Aelius Aristides to free himself from the municipal burdens with the help of his Roman connexions. *Latium maius*: O. Hirschfeld, *Die kais. Verwaltungsb.²*, p. 74. M. Aurelius: the *senatus consultum de sumptibus ludorum gladiatoriorum minuendis*, *CIL* ii. 6278 (cf. p. 1056) = Dessau, *ILS* 5163 = Bruns, *Fontes⁷*, no. 63 (p. 207) [= Riccobono, *FIRA²* 49], ll. 23 ff.: 'censeo igitur inprimis agendas maximis impp. gratias qui salutaribus remedis, fisci ratione post habita, labentem civitatium statum et praecipitantes iam in ruinas principalium virorum fortuna(s) restituerunt', &c. Another copy of this *SC*. was found in Sardis: J. Keil–A. von Premerstein, *Zweite Reise*, p. 16 = Dessau, *ILS* 9340.

IX. The Military Monarchy

¹ The best monograph on Commodus is J. M. Heer, 'Der historische Wert der Vita Commodi', *Philol.*, Suppl. 9 (1904); cf. O. Th. Schulz, *Das Kaiserhaus der Antonine und der letzte Historiker Roms* (1907). On the mood of the senate after the conclusion of peace on the Danube, J. M. Heer, op. cit., pp. 41 ff.

² A. von Domaszewski, 'Der Truppensold der Kaiserzeit', *Neue Heid. Jahrb.* 10, 1901, p. 230.

³ *Scr. Hist. Aug.* Comm. 16. 2; Pesc. Nig. 3. 3 f.; Herod. i. 10 (Gaul and Spain); for Africa *Scr. Hist. Aug.* Pert. 4. 2; J. M. Heer, op. cit., p. 107. On the revolts of a military character see Ritterling in Pauly–Wissowa, xii, col. 1307 (Britain, Germany, and Dacia).

⁴ On the 'classis Africana Commodiana Herculea', *Scr. Hist. Aug.* Comm. 17. 7; J. M. Heer, op. cit., pp. 108 ff.; A. Audollent, *Carthage romaine*, p. 359; R. Cagnat, 'L'Annone d'Afrique', *Mém. de l'Ac. d. Inscr.* 40, 1916, pp. 25 ff.; J. Vogt, *Die alexandrinischen Münzen* (1924), pp. 154 ff. It is evident both from the literary and from the numismatic evidence (especially that of Alexandria) that Commodus organized the corn fleet of the second greatest corn-producing province of the Empire, Africa, on the pattern of the oldest and best organized corn fleet of Rome—the Alexandrian. This fleet was organized for the service of the state as early as the Ptolemaic period. The creation of the African fleet followed on the revolt of part of Africa, and was caused by bad crops and disturbances in Egypt. This conclusion of mine has been recently corroborated by the investigations of J. Vogt, loc. cit. How far the service of the two fleets was compulsory, we do not know. But Callistratus, *Dig.* 50. 6. 6. 5, emphatically insists upon the public and compulsory character of the service of the shipowners in general, whether organized on the Alexandrian model or not. In any case it was a *munus publicum*; and it was no doubt a λειτουργία in Alexandria as early as the Ptolemies. See M. Rostovtzeff, 'Foreign Commerce in Ptolemaic Egypt', *Journ. Econ. and Business Hist.* 3, 1932, pp. 728 ff.

⁵ The metrical inscription (*CIL* vi. 9783 = Dessau, *ILS* 7778) runs 'd. m. s. Iulio Iuliano viro magno, philosopo (*sic*) prirо. Hic cum lauru(m) feret Romanis iam relevatis, reclusus castris inpia morte perit'. I think M. Bang in *Hermes*, 53, 1918, pp. 211 ff., is right in connecting the death of Iulianus with the events after Commodus' death. It is very probable that the philosopher was one of the street-preachers known to the mob and was therefore seized and killed by the praetorians; cf. Tertullian, *Apol.* 46: 'quis enim philosophum sacrificare aut deierare aut lucernas meridie vanas prostituere compellit? Quin immo et deos vestros palam destruunt et superstitiones vestras commentariis quoque accusant laudantibus vobis. *Plerique etiam in principes latrant sustinentibus vobis.*' The words of Tertullian remind one of Cassius Dio's description of the behaviour of the philosophers in the time of Vespasian and Domitian. Did Tertullian meet such philosophers in Carthage? It was A. von Premerstein, 'Zu den sogenannten alexandrinischen Märtyrerakten', *Philol.*, Suppl. 16 (1923), who connected the trial in Rome before the Emperor Commodus, of which the so-called 'Acts of Appian' speak, with that emperor's persecution of the family of Avidius Cassius. I am inclined to think that Tertullian speaks of the same event, which happened in the last years of Commodus, when he says (*ad Scap.* 2): 'sic et circa maiestatem imperatoris infamamur, tamen nunquam Albiniani, nec Nigriani, vel Cassiani inveniri potuerunt Christiani.' It is hard to believe that in mentioning the Cassiani he alludes to the time of M. Aurelius. It is well known that M. Aurelius did not persecute the members of the family of Avidius Cassius, whereas it was natural for Tertullian to mention the Cassiani after the Nigriani in inverse chronological order if the persecution of Commodus, in which many other men were involved, took place on the eve, so to say, of the persecution of

the partisans of Niger and Albinus. The visit of Septimius Severus to Alexandria may have been connected with this affair. I cannot believe with Premerstein that Appian was a mere witness in the trial of Heliodorus. The city of Alexandria was probably involved in the affair and accused of having supported the Cassiani. Appian was both a delegate of the city and one of the prosecuted. Was not the affair of Alexandria part of the widespread conspiracy against Commodus, and Heliodorus one of the candidates for the throne? Appian endeavoured to show that in his attacks on Alexandria Commodus was actuated by mere greed. Cf. J. Schwendemann, *Der hist. Wert der Vita Marci*, pp. 107 ff.

⁶ I deal with the religious policy of Commodus in a special article in *JRS* 13, 1923, pp. 91 ff.; cf. J. M. Heer, op. cit., p. 70, note 158*a*; A. von Domaszewski, *Die Religion des röm. Heeres* (1895), p. 54; J. M. Heer, op. cit., pp. 94 ff. The concessions of Commodus were made in connexion with the revolt of the army of Britain, which was quelled, not without difficulties, about A.D. 187; cf. M. Platnauer, *The Life and Reign of the Emperor L. Septimius Severus* (1918), p. 101, and R. G. Collingwood, *JRS* 13, 1923, pp. 69 ff.

⁷ J. M. Heer, op. cit., pp. 47 and 68; cf. Cass. Dio, 79. 14. 1, on the career of Oclatianus Adventus, who was a *miles frumentarius* and advanced under Macrinus to be *princeps peregrinorum*, with O. Hirschfeld, *Die kais. Verwaltungsb.*², p. 309, note 3. Cf. also Cass. Dio, 78. 14. 3, on the career of Marius Maximus who ἐν τῷ μισθοφορικῷ ἐστράτευτο καὶ τὰ τῶν δημίων ἔργα καὶ προσκόπων καὶ ἑκατοντάρχων [of the *frumentarii*?] ἐπεποιήκει. Cf. the inscription of Aphrodisias (Th. Reinach, *Rev. ét. gr.* 19, 1906, p. 145 = Dessau, *ILS* 9474, cf. *CIG* 2802): ἑκατόνταρχον φρουμεντάριον ἁγνῶς καὶ ἀνδρείως ἀναστραφέντα ἐν τῷ τῆς Ἀσίας ἔθνει. The inscription (of the time of the Severi?) shows that a *centurio frumentarius* had to deal with the whole of the province of Asia, and that he had various opportunities of oppressing the population (ἁγνῶς) and had to face dangers (fighting those who took to robbery?). Cf. the letter of Fronto quoted in Chap. VII, note 106. On these police agents see below note 45.

⁸ On the inscription of the 'saltus Burunitanus' see the bibliography quoted in my *Studien z. Gesch. röm. Kol.*, p. 321, note 1; the text is given in *CIL* viii. 10570 and 14464 (cf. 14451) = Dessau, *ILS* 6870 = Bruns–Gradenwitz, *Fontes*⁷, no. 86 = P. Girard, *Textes de droit Romain*⁴, no. 10, pp. 199 ff. [= Riccobono, *FIRA*² 103]. My quotation is a translation of Chap. III, ll. 18 ff.: 'subvenias, et cum homines rustici tenues manum nostrarum operis victum tolerantes conductori profusis largitionib(us) gratiosis(si)mo impares aput proc(uratores) tuos simu[s], quib(us) [pe]r vices succession(is) per condicionem conductionis notus est, miser[eari]s ac sacro rescripto tuo,' &c. The inscription of Gazr-Mezuar, *CIL* viii. 14428; cf. W. Heitland, *Agricola*, pp. 342 ff.

⁹ The best monographs on the rule of L. Septimius Severus are J. Hasebroek, *Untersuchungen zur Geschichte des Kaisers Septimius Severus* (1921); cf. id. *Die Fälschung der Vita Nigri und Vita Albini in den Scr. Hist. Aug.* (1916); and M. Platnauer, *The Life and Reign of the Emperor L. Septimius Severus* (1918). These books give a full and up-to-date bibliography. Add V. Macchioro, 'L'impero Romano nell' età dei Severi', *Riv. di st. ant.* 10, 1905, pp. 201 ff., and 11, 1906, pp. 285 ff. and 341 ff.; G. A. Harrer, 'The Chronology of the Revolt of Pescennius Niger', *JRS* 10, 1920, pp. 155 ff.; Fluß in Pauly–Wissowa, Zw. R. ii, cols. 1940 ff.; and on Iulia Domna, M. G. W. Williams, *Amer. Journ. Arch.* 6, 1902, pp. 259 ff., and G. Herzog in Pauly–Wissowa, x, cols. 926 ff. For the history of Septimius Severus and his family, and especially for knowledge of the ideas which moved him, the bas-reliefs of the various arches erected to him in Rome (those of the Forum and the Forum Boarium) and at his birthplace Lepcis (particularly the latter) have the same importance as the column of the Forum

and the arch of Beneventum have for the reigns of Trajan and Hadrian. The reconstruction of the Lepcis arch is not complete, and consequently it cannot be said with certainty what the political ideas expressed on it were. It seems to me that Severus wanted to stress particularly the hereditary, dynastic character of his power—*vis-à-vis* the Senate—and the *Concordia principum*, in which was included his wife, the mother of Caracalla and Geta, Iulia Domna— *vis-à-vis* his own sons. From the artistic point of view the rigid frontality in which the Emperor and his family are portrayed on the three arches is interesting: this is a clear case of oriental influence. Cf. R. Bartoccini, *Africa Italiana*, 4, 1931, pp. 321 ff., and above, Chap. VII, note 99.

¹⁰ On the controversy see M. Platnauer, op. cit., pp. 162 ff.; cf. his article in *JRS* 10, 1920, p. 196. From the time of Gibbon (*History of the Decline and Fall of the Roman Empire*, i, p. 125, ed. Bury) the general conviction has been that Septimius' rule was fatal for the Roman Empire. The last to emphasize this point of view was A. von Domaszewski, *Gesch. d. röm. Kaiser*, ii, p. 262. Platnauer calls his pointed and, of course, exaggerated statement 'little more than nonsense'. His own point of view is summarized in the quotation given in the text from *JRS* 10, 1920, p. 196. There is no doubt that he is utterly mistaken in idealizing the personality and the rule of Septimius. In basing his personal power, which he wanted to pass on to his sons, on the support of the army, in bribing and spoiling the troops, Septimius broke definitely with the traditions of the Antonines. It is a different question whether it was possible to maintain their traditions any longer and whether sooner or later the Roman Empire was not bound to become a military autocracy. In any case, by his usurpation of power and by the treachery which he committed towards the senate and Albinus, Septimius entered consciously on the new path and inaugurated the new phase in the history of the Empire which led directly, through a prolonged military anarchy, to the Oriental despotism of Diocletian and Constantine. I see no reason why another pair of emperors of the type of Trajan, Hadrian, and M. Aurelius should not have prolonged the quiet and comparatively prosperous period in the history of the Empire for some scores of years, had it not been for the ambition and the unscrupulous policy of Septimius Severus.

¹¹ Large confiscations after the victory over Pescennius: Cass. Dio, 74. 8. 4 and 9; *Scr. Hist. Aug.* Sev. 9. 7, 'multas etiam civitates eiusdem partis iniuriis adfecit et damnis'; cf. Cass. Dio, 74. 9. 4; Herod. iii. 4. 7. On the policy of Septimius after the victory over Albinus, J. Hasebroek, op. cit., pp. 101 ff.

¹² On the policy of barbarizing the army, A. von Domaszewski, *Rangordnung*, pp. 83 ff. and 122 ff. Against his exaggerations see H. Dessau, *Hermes*, 45, 1910, pp. 1 ff., and M. Platnauer, op. cit., pp. 158 ff. (where Dessau's article is ignored). Cf. A. Stein, *Der röm. Ritterstand* (1927), p. 413. Stein demonstrated that although Domaszewski's theory that Italians and Roman citizens of the West (Spain, Gaul) were entirely excluded from the *militia equestris* is exaggerated, Domaszewski rightly defined the general trend of Severus' policy, which reached its climax in military anarchy. In his chronological survey of the rule of Septimius, Hasebroek has often occasion to speak of the emperor's military reforms. In the main he shares the views of Domaszewski. However exaggerated some statements of Domaszewski may be, he has proved that Septimius took a decisive step towards the barbarization of the army, and especially the corps of officers. Dessau may be right in emphasizing that this barbarization was not achieved at one stroke. But it is almost absurd to deny, against the direct evidence of our sources, the difference between the provincial troops and the pre-Severan praetorian guard. The Noricans, the Spaniards, and the Macedonians of this guard were the descendants of Roman colonists, who were either of Italian origin or wholly Romanized provincials, most of them city residents, while the Danubian legions were composed of Thracian and Illyrian peasants who hardly spoke Latin at all: yet they now became

the seminary of the centurians and officers. In the eyes of the population of Rome these men were pure barbarians (there is no sense in the remark of O. Schulz, *Vom Prinzipat zum Dominat*, pp. 25 ff., note 48). There is no doubt, too, that Septimius demoralized the soldiers both by lavish gifts and an increase of their pay and by lowering the standards of discipline. It is enough to pass in review the donatives by which he quelled the frequent revolts and bribed the soldiers (*Scr. Hist. Aug.* Sev. 7. 6; Cass. Dio, 46. 46. 7, and *Scr. Hist. Aug.* Sev. 8. 9; J. Hasebroek, op. cit., pp. 41 and 46 on the revolts, and pp. 24 and 129 on the gifts) and to note the behaviour of the soldiers in Rome (*Scr. Hist. Aug.* Sev. 7. 2–3, 'tota deinde urbe milites in templis, in porticibus, in aedibus Palatinis quasi in stabulis manserunt, fuitque ingressus Severi odiosus atque terribilis, cum milites inempta diriperent vastationem urbi minantes') and before Hatra (Platnauer, op. cit., p. 121). Striking also is the emphasis laid by the biographer of Pescennius on his strict discipline and the model behaviour of his troops in contrast to the lack of discipline in the army of Severus, *Scr. Hist. Aug.* Pesc. Nig. 3. 6; 4. 6, &c. As regards the 'equestrianizing' of the administration, add to the facts collected by Platnauer and Hasebroek the substitution of procurators for proconsuls (C. W. Keyes, *The Rise of the Equites in the Third Century of the Roman Empire* (1915), pp. 3 ff., and J. Keil, *Forsch. Eph.* iii, pp. 139 f., no. 54, and pp. 110 f., no. 20). We cannot, however, speak of any radical change in the constitution of the body of senators. The predominance, in that body, of men of Italian origin over provincials (F. Sintenis, *Die Zusammensetzung des Senats unter Septimius Severus und Caracalla* (1914), Diss., p. 29, cf. A. Jardé, *Études critiques sur la vie et le règne de Sévère Alexandre* (1925), Appendice, pp. 119 ff.: *L'Album sénatorial sous Sévère Alexandre*), in contrast to the policy of Trajan and the Antonines, shows his distrust of the representatives of the provincial aristocracy. Of two evils he chose the lesser. The Italians were at least nearer and less opulent. Among the provincials he preferred the Orientals to the senators of the West, and in this preference he was certainly guided by other considerations than mere regard for the sympathies of his wife. The only democratic step which he took was the introduction of some *primipili* into the senate (A. von Domaszewski, *Rangordnung*, p. 172; Fluß in Pauly–Wissowa, Zw. R. ii, col. 1981). For the marriage of soldiers and residence in the *canabae*, J. Hasebroek, op. cit., p. 127, and Fluß in Pauly–Wissowa, Zw. R. ii, col. 1992. There is no doubt that the majority of the soldiers were unmarried and continued to live in the camps; cf. Cass. Dio, 78. 36. 2, and Herod. iii. 8. 5, and Stuart Jones, *Companion*, p. 240.

[13] J. Hasebroek, op. cit., pp. 44 f. (early period), pp. 88 f. (consecration of Commodus), pp. 92 ff. (the religious character of his reverence for the Antonines). The main point in the policy of Septimius was his effort to legitimatize not only his personal power but his dynasty by emphasizing his descent from M. Aurelius, who left his power to his son, and his reverence for Commodus. That is why he gave the name of Antoninus to Caracalla and why he ruthlessly exterminated all the partisans of his presumptive heir, Albinus. On the dynastic policy of Septimius cf. J. Vogt, *Die alexandrinischen Münzen* (1924), pp. 166 ff. How firmly the senatorial aristocracy clung to the idea of adoption as opposed to the idea of the hereditary transmission of the imperial power is shown by the part played by this idea in the writings of Vopiscus, the biographer of the later emperors of the 3rd cent.: see E. Klebs, *Hist. Zeitschr.* 61 (N. F. 25), 1889, p. 231, note 6; cf. E. Hohl, *Klio*, 11, 1911, pp. 292 f. On the crowns of the *flamines* of a province adorned with busts of the imperial family, G. F. Hill, *Oest. Jahresh.* 2, 1899, pp. 245 ff.; cf. id., *Catal. of Coins of the Br. Mus.*, Lycaonia, p. xvii, and in *Anatolian Studies pres. to Sir W. Ramsay*, p. 224. In the mosaic of Aquileia published by G. Brusin in *Not. d. Scavi*, 1923, pp. 224 ff., with appended plate, fig. 6, the old man with the diadem is probably the flamen of Aquileia, the three busts which adorn the diadem

are those of Juppiter, Juno, and Minerva, not those of Septimius Severus and his sons, as I first thought. But it is to be noticed that Severus wanted to be identified with Jupiter in his dynastic cult, and his wife with Juno. See one of the bas-reliefs of the Lepcis arch: R. Bartoccini, *Africa Italiana*, 4, 1931, p. 96, fig. 67. It is very probable that he was worshipped with the attributes of Juppiter, and his wife with those of Juno, in the temple of his forum, the new Septimianum of Lepcis. It is worthy of note that it is from the 3rd cent. that the *domus divina* appears along with the emperor in all dedications. Earlier it was rather exceptional.

¹⁴ M. Platnauer, op. cit., p. 181. As regards the protection of the *humiliores* we may quote the opinion of Ulpian. Ulpian's ἀκμή belongs of course to the time of Alexander, but his opinions were formed earlier and reflect the tendency of the military autocracy in general. *Dig.* 1. 18. 6. 2 (Ulp. l. i, *Opinionum*): 'ne potentiores viri humiliores iniuriis adficiant neve defensores eorum calumniosis criminibus insectentur innocentes, ad religionem praesidis provinciae pertinet', and ibid. 4: 'ne tenuis vitae homines sub praetextu adventus officiorum vel militum lumine unico vel brevi suppellectili ad aliorum usus translatis iniuriis vexentur, praeses provinciae providebit' (the text is sound: *lumine unico vel brevi suppellectili* is a picturesque way of describing the arbitrary behaviour of the soldiers: they would use even the single lamp and the few pots of the household as if they were their own).

¹⁵ On the edict of Subatianus Aquila see *BGU* 484 (A.D. 201–2); *P.Gen.* 10; *P.Catt.* ii. 1–7 [= *SB* 4284]; *P.Flor.* 6; my *Studien z. Gesch. röm. Kol.*, pp. 209 ff.; Wilcken, *Chrest.* 202, p. 235 (Einl.). The edict was certainly connected with the regular census, but the frequent references to it show that the conditions of the land were very bad and that ἀναχωρήσεις became a real plague. The expressions used by the peasants of Sokopaiu Nesos quoted in the text (*SB* 4284 (A.D. 207); cf. *P.Gen.* 10; my *Studien z. Gesch. röm. Kol.*, pp. 167 ff.; F. Zucker, *Philol.* 69, 1910, pp. 455 ff.) and their appeal directly to the emperor suggest that Septimius during his stay in Egypt (A.D. 199–200), like Caracalla later (*P.Giss.* 40. ii. 15–29), published one or more edicts endeavouring to liquidate the state of anarchy in the country after the revolt of Avidius Cassius, which was followed by the persecutions of Commodus, and after the war between Pescennius and Severus, which led to extensive confiscations and exactions. Cf. the ἀπόφασις of Severus and Caracalla, H. Frisk, *Aegyptus*, 9, 1928, pp. 281 ff. [= *SB* 7366]. A Florentine papyrus, *PSI* 683 (cf. Wilcken, *Arch. f. Papyr.* 7, pp. 84 f.), furnishes important evidence on this subject. During his visit to Egypt Severus intended to inspect the whole country. Preparations were made for his journey. It meant a heavy additional burden for the population. As usual, the maintenance of the emperor, of his suite, and of his soldiers was imposed on the cities and villages of Egypt, which had to make proportionate payments in the form of cows, calves, goats, corn, hay, wine, &c. Our document is the report of the village scribes to the *strategos* regarding the distribution of the payments (ἐπιμερισμός) among the villages. But, before dealing with the main subject of their report, the village scribes quote in full a special letter of Arrius Victor, the *epistrategos*, to the *strategoi* of the Arsinoite nome. The mere fact of this quotation shows how unusual the document was. And in fact it is a peculiar piece of official literature. The *epistrategos* asks first, in the usual way, for a report from the *strategoi* on the distribution of the payments εἰ[ς τὴν] ἀννῶναν τοῖς | κ[υ]ρίοις ἡμῶν (l. 12). With the next paragraph the novelties begin. It is stated in ll. 14 f. that money had been advanced by the treasury to the governor for the payment of the goods, probably those which had been delivered by the people (προσθέντες τοῖς γράμμασι καὶ τὸ ἐξωδιασθὲν | ἀργύριον ἐν προχρείᾳ ἐκ τοῦ ἱερωτάτου | ταμείου εἰς πόσα καὶ τίνα εἴδη ἐχώρησε). With l. 17 begins a new sentence expressing very peculiar ideas. 'As the natives, I think', says Arrius Victor, 'have shown care in providing supplies for the most noble soldiers, it is like-

wise necessary for us to take care of (or "to protect") them' (ὥσπερ γὰρ οἶμαι π[ρ]όνοιαν ἐποιήσαντο | [οἱ ἐ]νχώριοι τοῦ τὰ ἐπι⟨τ⟩ή[δ]εια παρεσχηκέναι | [τ]οῖ[ς] γεννεοτάτοις στρα- τιώ⟨τα⟩ις, οὕτω καὶ | αὐτῶν [ἐπι]μεληθῆ[ναι ἀ]ναγκαῖόν ἐστι). It is a pity that the end of the document is in such a bad state of preservation. No doubt in the following lines Arrius Victor specified what he meant by protecting the people. One of the measures in question, however, is intelligible (ll. 26 ff.). The ἐπιμερισμός, or distribution of payments, must be published (προθεῖναι) in every village, and if anybody has any complaint to make he may come forward (καὶ εἴ τις μέμψασθαι ἔχει | προσέλθῃ). Wilcken thinks that all these humanitarian phrases and acts were means adopted by the governor-general to protect himself against complaints to the emperor during his visit. I am inclined, however, to believe that Arrius was acting in accordance with special orders issued by the emperor himself, who wished the people to be protected against needless oppression when it was necessary to resort to the unavoidable evil of ordering the levy of an *annona*. Arrius, of course, makes no mention of imperial instruc- tions, but such instructions might have been communicated to the prefect of Egypt verbally and transmitted by him to his chief assistants—the governors-general of the *epistrategiai*. However, even if we assume that Arrius acted on his own initiative— which is most improbable as the money for the προχρεία could not have been assigned without a special order of the prefect—the fact that he assumes such a humanitarian tone shows that he desired to act in the spirit of the emperor and by his order to protect the *humiliores* against the *potentiores*. But in spite of the emperor's efforts the condition of the country did not improve. Two documents illustrate the conditions of the land at the beginning of Caracalla's reign. One is the Caranis papyrus of A.D. 214 (Boak, *Ann. Serv.* 29, 1930, p. 51, no. 3 = *SB* 7360): it is an ἀπογραφή in which the owner declares three lots of land. Two of them had been olive-groves, but had now become corn-land; the third—a silted-up canal (?)—had become barren. Another papyrus of the same series (Boak, ibid., no. 4 = *SB* 7361) of A.D. 211–12 illustrates the steps taken by the emperor and by the prefect in order to restore agriculture and, first of all, to repair and maintain embankments and canals. It was not apparently a great success, because the papyrus contains a petition of two land-owners (γεοῦχοι), who were at the same time state-lessees (δημόσιοι γεωργοί). They complain to the ἐπιστρατηγός that the κατασπορεῖς, in spite of repeated warnings from the prefect, had not provided the materials necessary for the construction of a very important ἔμβλημα: Cf. Chap. XI, notes 33–35.

[16] J. Keil–A. von Premerstein, *Dritte Reise*, nos. 9, 28, and 55; cf. *Zweite Reise*, no. 222 = *IGRR* iv. 1368. The first quotation in the text is from no. 28 (pp. 24 ff.), ll. 9 ff.: καὶ τοῦτο δεόμεθ' ἀπιδόντας ὑμ[ᾶς, μέ|γιστ]οι καὶ θειότατοι τῶν πώποτε αὐτοκρατόρων, πρός τε τοῦ[ς | ὑμετέ]ρους νόμους τῶν τε προγόνων ὑμῶν καὶ πρὸς τὴν εἰρηνικὴ[ν | ὑμῶ]ν περὶ πάντας δικαιοσύνην, μεισήσαντας δέ, οὓς ἀεὶ με[ι|σήσ]ατε αὐτοί τε καὶ πᾶν τὸ τῆς βασιλείας προγονικὸν ὑμ[ῶν | γένο]ς, &c. The words are in remarkable conformity with the leading ideas of Septimius. The peasants appeal to the beneficent laws of the emperors and to their justice, and insist upon the fact that in this policy Septimius follows the example of the Antonines, his ancestors. The second quotation is from ibid. no. 55 (pp. 37 ff.), l. 51: φυγάδας ⟨τε⟩ γενέσθαι τῶν δεσποτικῶν χωρίων, ἐν οἷς | (κ)αὶ ἐγεννήθημεν καὶ ἐτράφημεν καὶ ἐκ προγόνων | διαμένοντες γεωργοὶ τὰς πίστεις τηροῦμεν τῷ | δεσποτικῷ λόγῳ. There is a striking similarity between the tone and the expressions of this petition and those of the saltus Burunitanus.

[17] M. Platnauer, op. cit., pp. 189 ff., covers the policy of Septimius towards the pro- vinces with a rose-coloured veil when he speaks of its 'beneficent character' and of 'an era of peace and prosperity for the provincials'. J. Hasebroek, op. cit., p. 132, in em- phasizing the prosperity of Africa and Syria, keeps closer to the facts (cf. G. A. Harrer,

Studies in the History of the Roman Province of Syria (1915)). In addition to the evidence adduced by Hasebroek, we may remind the reader of the great care which Septimius took of his own native city. The excavations of the Italians at Tripoli show that with Septimius a new era began for the modest cities of the African coast, especially for Lepcis. We should add the Danubian lands. It is, however, to be observed that the city of Nicopolis ad Istrum, which erected a series of statues to Septimius Severus and his family, made a voluntary gift of 700,000 denarii, which the emperor accepted gladly. See M. Britschov, *Ath. Mitt.* 48, 1923, p. 99, no. 7 [= *L'An. ép.* 1926, 95]. In announcing the gift the city of Nicopolis extols the benefits of peace which she is able to enjoy thanks to the victories of Septimius Severus: this praise is obviously in good faith. Compare the numerous inscriptions in honour of Septimius Severus and his family published by Britschov in the same article. See the enumeration of the cities which possessed the *ius Italicum* and colonial rights in *Dig.* 50. 15. 1 (Ulp. l. i, *de censibus*) and 8 (Paulus, l. ii, *de censibus*). I would not attach too much importance to the well-known picture of Tertullian, *de pallio*, 2: 'quantum reformavit orbis saeculum istud! quantum urbium aut produxit, aut auxit, aut reddidit praesentis imperii triplex virtus! Deo tot Augustis in unum favente quot census transcripti! quot populi repugnati! quot ordines illustrati! quot barbari exclusi! revera orbis cultissimum huius imperii rus est, eradicato omni aconito hostilitatis et cacto et rubo subdolae familiaritatis convulso, et amoenus super Alcinoi pometum et Midae rosetum.' This rosy picture has a special purpose and probably refers to Africa only. Note especially the emphasis laid on the further urbanization of Africa and on the privileges granted to the cities. But in some other passages Tertullian uses different colours and predicts the near collapse of the Roman Empire, see Tert. *ad Scap.* 3; cf. 5, and especially the picture of the ruthless persecutions of Septimius' enemies throughout the Empire and of the spirit of protest which these aroused even in the city of Rome, in *Ad nat.* i. 17; *Apol.* 35, 6: 'Ipsos Quirites, ipsam vernaculam septem collium plebem convenio an alicui Caesari suo parcat illa lingua Romana: testis est Tiberis et scholae bestiarum': '. . . (35, 11) sed et qui nunc scelestarum partium socii aut plausores cottidie revelantur, post vindemiam parricidarum racematio superstes', &c. The last remark refers to the punishment applied to the sharp tongues of Rome. The policy of Septimius Severus towards Syria was not a new departure. M. Aurelius and Commodus granted colonial rights freely to the cities of Mesopotamia, and so did the immediate successors of Septimius. Almost all the important cities of Mesopotamia received such rights (Carrhae, Edessa, Nisibis, Rhesenae, Singara, Dura). This, of course, is explained by the situation of these cities on the border of the enemy's land, and the grant probably implied not only the bestowal of the title but also the settlement of veterans of the Roman army as colonists, cf. note 53. On the Italian excavations in Tripolitania see the bibliography given in Chap. V, note 4 and Chap. VII, note 98.

[18] In book 50 of the *Digest*, which deals with the organization of municipal life in general and particularly with the liturgies, most of the regulations date from the earlier part of the 3rd cent. On some points reference is made to the *constitutiones* of the Antonines. The earliest systematic treatment of the relations between the cities and the state, especially in regard to the *munera*, is that of Papirius Justus, who collects the regulations drawn up by M. Aurelius and Verus. It is evident, however, that the real work was done by the jurists of the time of the Severi. In the title 'de muneribus et honoribus', *Dig.* 50. 4, most of the quotations are taken from Ulpian and some of the fundamental ideas from Callistratus and Papinian. Later, a final systematic survey was given by Hermogenianus and Arcadius Charisius, although the institution, which grew up gradually, was never thoroughly and methodically organized from the theoretical point of view. The distinction between *munera personalia, patrimonii*, and

mixta remains vague. The origin of this distinction certainly goes back to the great Severan jurists and was based on municipal practice and probably on experience in Egypt. The great part played by Ulpian in systematizing the *munera* is shown by many of his 'Opinions'. One of the most interesting is *Dig.* 50. 4. 3. 15: 'praeses provinciae provideat munera et honores in civitatibus aequaliter per vices secundum aetates et dignitates, ut gradus munerum honorumque qui antiquitus statuti sunt, iniungi, ne sine discrimine et frequenter isdem oppressis simul viris et viribus res publicae destituantur'; cf. the attempt at a classification of the *munera* by Callistratus, *Dig.* 50. 4. 14. 1 ff. It is worthy of note that Ulpian (l. 2, *Opinionum, Dig.* 50. 2. 1) also records for the first time the theory of the ἰδία as applied to the *decuriones* and the practice of forcing them to remain in their places of residence: 'decuriones quos sedibus civitatis ad quam pertinent relictis in alia loca transmigrasse probabitur, praeses provinciae in patrium solum revocare et muneribus congruentibus fungi curet.'

¹⁹ *Dig.* 50. 12. 10 (Herennius Modestinus); 50. 4. 3. 10 (Ulpianus); 50. 4. 1. 1 (Hermogenianus); 50. 4. 18. 26 (Arcadius Charisius quoting Herennius Modestinus). The first inscriptions of Asia Minor to show the changed aspect of the *decaprotia*, after it became a regular liturgy in the 2nd cent. A.D., are those of Prusias ad Hypium, all of them of the time of Caracalla or a little later, *IGRR* iii. 60, 61, 63, 64, 65, 67. To the same time belong similar inscriptions from Syllion, ibid. 801, and Aspendus, ibid. 804, and those of Thyatira, another abundant source of information on the history of the *decaprotia, IGRR* iv. 1248; cf. 1228 (after Caracalla), 1261, 1265, 1273 (all of the 3rd cent. A.D.). It is no accident that the first dated mention of δεκάπρωτοι in the role of presidents of the municipal council is in A.D. 207, *IG* xii. 7. 240. 2: γνώμῃ στρατηγῶν καὶ δεκαπρώτων ἐχόντων δὲ καὶ τὴν πρυτανικὴν ἐξουσίαν ; cf. 239. 12: θυγάτηρ ἀνδρὸς δεκαπρώτου καὶ ἀρχικοῦ (member of the same family) (both from Minoa, Amorgos) and 395 (Aegiale, Amorgos, the same time). The position of the δεκάπρωτοι at Chalcis (Euboea) after A.D. 212 is identical, *IG* xii. 9. 906. 5: εἰσηγησαμένων τοῦ δεκαπρώτου Κλ. Ἀμύντου καὶ Οὐλπίου Παμφίλου: cf. ibid. l. 14: στρατηγοῦντος τοῦ δεκαπρώτου Λ. Νοουίου Λυσανίου; cf. ibid., no. 295 (Eretria) and xii. 8. 646 (Peparethus). On the δεκάπρωτοι in Egypt, see F. Oertel, *Die Liturgie*, pp. 211 ff. and 432 f.

²⁰ *Dig.* 50. 6. 6. 3 ff. (Callistratus, l. 1, *de cognitionibus*): 'negotiatores *qui annonam urbis adiuvant*, item navicularii, *qui annonae urbis serviunt*, immunitatem a muneribus publicis consequuntur, quamdiu in eiusmodi actu sunt, nam remuneranda pericula eorum, quin etiam exhortanda praemiis merito placuit, ut qui peregre muneribus et quidem publicis cum periculo et labore fungantur, a domesticis *vexationibus* et sumptibus liberentur: cum non sit alienum dicere etiam hos rei publicae causa, dum annonae urbis serviunt, abesse. Immunitati, quae naviculariis praestatur, *certa forma* data est,' &c. We cannot speak of an enslavement or complete *étatisation* of the corporations, even those of shipowners, in the 2nd and the early 3rd cent., but the pressure on them was hard and became ever harder. The fact that the *navicularii Arelatenses* threaten a strike does not mean that strikes were either allowed or forbidden. As a matter of fact, strikes are always the last resource of those who have no other means at their disposal. But the fact shows that membership in the 'collegia naviculariorum' was not yet *de iure* compulsory and hereditary (though it may have been *de facto*). I do not see how one can speak of a collective responsibility of the *navicularii* either in the early or in the later Empire. The responsibility always remained personal. In the development of the 'collegia naviculariorum' there was no such thing as collective responsibility being replaced by individual (as in the case of the city councils), or *vice versa*. The movement was in the direction of making the service of individual *navicularii* to the state, which in fact was of secondary importance in the early life of the corporations, more and more prominent and therefore compulsory. I cannot believe that

the corporation was responsible for the activity of its members: every member was responsible for himself. The corporate organization was due, so far as the members were concerned, to the natural desire to act together in cases of emergency, and, so far as the state was concerned, to the wish to have good lists of men on whom it could rely in case of need. Cf. E. Groag, *Vierteljahrsschr. f. Soc.- u. Wirtschaftsg.* 2, 1904, pp. 483 f.

²¹ Cf. Chap. V, note 22, and especially Chap. VIII, note 39.

²² Chap. VIII, note 42.

²³ Chap. VII, note 87. *Dig.* 49. 14. 3. 6 (Callistratus, rescript of Hadrian), and 50. 6. 6. 10 (Callistratus, rescript of M. Aurelius).

²⁴ *Dig.* 50. 6. 6. 11 (Callistratus, l. 1, *de cognitionibus*): 'coloni quoque Caesaris a muneribus liberantur, ut idoniores praediis fiscalibus habeantur'; cf. the rescript of M. Aurelius and L. Verus, *Dig.* 50. 1. 38. 1: 'colonos praediorum fisci muneribus fungi sine damno fisci oportere, idque excutere praesidem adhibito procuratore debere'; my *Studien z. Gesch. röm. Kol.*, p. 374, note 1, with pp. 292 f.; Keil–von Premerstein, *Dritte Reise*, pp. 42 ff. How heavily the municipal liturgies bore on the *coloni* is illustrated by the following words of the petition found at Aga Bey, Keil–von Premerstein, ibid. p. 38, no. 55, ll. 33 ff.: κωλῦσαι δὲ τὴν εἰς τὰ χωρία δεσποτικὰ ἔφοδον καὶ τὴν εἰς ἡμᾶς ἐν[ό]|χλησιν γεινομένην ὑπό ⟨τ⟩ε τῶν κολλητιώνων καὶ τῶν ἐπὶ προφάσει ἀρχῶν ἢ λειτουργιῶν τοὺς ὑ|μετέρους ἐνοχλούντων καὶ σκυλλόντων (sic) γεω[ρ]|γούς, &c.

²⁵ *Dig.* 50. 6. 6. 12, see especially the end of the paragraph: 'sed ne quidem eos qui augeant facultates et munera civitatium sustinere possunt, privilegiis, quae tenuioribus per collegia distributis concessa sunt, uti posse plurifariam constitutum est.' Callistratus in this passage certainly refers to documents similar to the rescript of Septimius and Caracalla to the city of Solva (on which see Chap. VIII, note 44); cf. especially the following words of this rescript: 'ii quos dicis diviti(i)s suis sine onere [uti publica subire m]unera compellantur', and 'alioquin [tenuiores perfr]uantur vacatione quae non competit beneficiis coll(egiorum) derogari'.

²⁶ See the articles of P. Jouguet and others quoted in Chap. VII, note 51. Light has been thrown on this question by the investigations of Hasebroek, *Untersuchungen*, pp. 118 ff., and by the papyrus *PSI* 683, which show that Septimius visited Egypt, not in A.D. 202, but in 199–200, and that therefore the grant of a βουλή to Alexandria may have dated from the same year; cf. Wilcken, *Zeitschr. d. Sav.-St.* 42, 1921, p. 138, note 2, and *Arch. f. Papyr.* 7, p. 85; cf. ibid. 9, pp. 21 ff. and 83. The fragment of a document discovered in Egypt, published by H. B. van Holsen and A. C. Johnson, *JEA* 12, 1926, pp. 118 ff. [= *SB* 7261], does not belong to the beginning of the 3rd cent. A.D., but to the early fourth: see Wilcken, *Arch. f. Papyr.* 8, p. 314.

²⁷ Chap. VII, note 3.

²⁸ The material is fully collected by J. Hasebroek, op. cit., pp. 102 ff. I need not enumerate the documents again. M. Platnauer, *Septimius Severus*, p. 205, has collected only part of the evidence and endeavours to minimize its importance. I would draw the attention of the reader to the utterances of Tertullian, *ad Scap.* 5: 'parce provinciae quae visa intentione tua obnoxia facta est concussionibus et militum et inimicorum suorum cuiusque.' The persecutions of Christians assumed the same forms of arbitrariness and corruption.

²⁹ One of the most efficient agents of Septimius in the matter of war exactions was M. Rossius Vitulus, whose inscription has been found at Bulla Regia, *ILA* 455. This man had a brilliant military career and was twice *praepositus*, or *procurator*,

annonae expeditionis, once during the march of Septimius on Rome, and again during his war against Albinus; cf. J. Hasebroek, op. cit., p. 29, note 5. At the time of the 'march on Rome' Vitulus was first master of supplies and later chief of the exchequer (*procurator arcae expeditionalis*), i.e. he first extorted the supplies and later the money from the cities and the people of Italy.

³⁰ *Dig.* 49. 16. 2 and 4–6, *de re militari*, especially 4. 9–13, and 5 (Arrius Menander, *de re militari*); cf. the treatise *de re militari* of Aemilius Macer, a contemporary of Caracalla and Alexander, *Dig.* 49. 16. 12 and 13. The other quotations under the title *de re militari* are taken from Aelius Marcianus (time of Septimius), Papianus, Paulus, Ulpian, and Herennius Modestinus. Many of the robbers (*latrones*) who devastated Italy and the provinces in and after the time of Septimius were probably deserters; compare especially the war of some detachments of the army of Germany 'adversus defectores et rebelles', *CIL* iii. 10471–3 = Dessau, *ILS* 1153 (found at Aquincum). The inscription of Lydia runs as follows [Keil–von Premerstein, *Dritte Reise*, p. 87]: Ἀγαθῇ Τύχῃ | ἐπὶ πρυτάνεως Λ. Σεπτ(ιμίου) Αὐρ(ηλίου) | Ἀχιλλείδη νε(ωτέρου) μη(νὸς) ε΄ Αὐρ(ήλιος) Ἑρμόλαος | Ῥουστίκου ἔδωκεν ὑπὲρ ἀρχῆς | λογιστείας καθὼς ἔδοξε τοῖς | κωμήταις (δηνάρια) διακόσια πεντή|κοντα προσχωρήσαντα εἰς τὴν τῶν τειρώνων συντέλειαν. I cannot help thinking that the inscription belongs to the time soon after 212; cf. my article in *JRS* 8, 1918, pp. 26 ff.

³¹ Keil–von Premerstein, *Dritte Reise*, no. 9, ll. 16 ff.: ἀγαθοῦ μὲν οὐδενὸς γεινόμενοι αἴτ|ιοι, ἀνυποίστοις δὲ φορτίοις κ(αὶ) ζημιώμα|σιν ἐνσείοντες τὴν κώμην ὡς συμβαί|νειν ἐξαναλου-μένην αὐτὴν εἰς τὰ ἄμε|τρα δαπανήματα τῶν ἐπι[δη]μούντων | κ(αὶ) ε[ἰς τ]ὸ πλῆθος τῶν κολλη-τιώνων ἀ|πο[στερεῖσθ]α[ι] μὲν λουτροῦ δι' ἀπορίαν, | ἀποστερεῖσθ]ε [δὲ κ(αὶ)] τῶν πρὸς τὸν βί|ον ἀ[ν]ανκέ[ω]ν, &c. Ibid., no. 55, ll. 21 ff.: ἱκέται δὲ τῆς ὑμετέ|ρας γεινόμεθα, θειότατοι τῶν πώποτε αὐτοκρα|[τ]όρων, θείας καὶ ἀνυπερβλήτου βασιλείας, καὶ | [το]ῖς τῆς γεωργίας καμά-τοις προσέχειν κεκωλυ|[μ]ένοι τῶν κολλητιώνων καὶ τῶν ἀντικαθεστώ|των ἀπειλούντων καὶ ἡμεῖν τοῖς καταλειπομέ|νοις τὸν περὶ ψυχῆς κίνδυνον καὶ μὴ δυνάμενοι{ς} | ἐκ τοῦ κωλύεσθαι τὴν γῆν ἐργάζεσθαι μηδὲ ταῖς δε|[σ]ποτικαῖς ἐπακούειν ἀποφοραῖς καὶ ψήφοις πρὸς | [τ]ὰ ἑξῆς, καὶ δεόμεθα εὐμενῆ (sic) ὑμᾶς προσέσθαι τὴν | δέησιν ἡμῶν, &c. On the *colletiones*, who appear only in the Lydian inscriptions and in the papyrus of A.D. 206, *P.Oxy.* 1100, see Keil–von Premerstein, op. cit., pp. 43 ff.; M. Rostovtzeff, *JRS* 8, 1918, p. 33; A. Garroni, *Rend. Lincei*, 25, 1918, pp. 66 ff. The chief offenders were the military police force, and in the atmosphere of lawlessness created by the civil war and by the policy of Sep-timius it was probably impossible even for the emperors, not to speak of the procura-tors and the governors of the provinces, to prevent them from doing mischief. On execution against the person in connexion with *cessio bonorum* see F. von Woess, 'Personalexekution und cessio bonorum im römischen Reichsrecht', *Zeitschr. der Sav.-St.* 43, 1922, pp. 485 ff. (cf. Chap. VIII, note 44). The abuses practised by police officers in the provinces did not, of course, begin in the reign of Septimius, nor was that emperor the first to create new names for the agents of the police force, see Epict. iii. 24. 117: ἂν δ' ἅπαξ περιποιήσῃ τὸ ἄλυπον καὶ ἄφοβον, ἔτι σοι τύραννος ἔσται τις ἢ δορυφόρος ἢ Καισαριανοὶ ἢ ὀρδινατίων δήξεταί σε ἢ οἱ ἐπιθύοντες ἐν τῷ Καπιτωλίῳ ἐπὶ τοῖς ὀπτικίοις (ὀφφικίοις?) τὸν τηλικαύτην ἀρχὴν παρὰ τοῦ Διὸς εἰληφότα; The term ὀρδινατίων is certainly provincial slang, derived from the Latin *ordinatio* (or *ordinatus*), just as κολλητίων is probably derived from *collatio*. The same methods were used by the municipal police in villages belonging to the territory of a city. In an inscription of a village belonging to the territory of Hierapolis (Anderson, *JHS* 17, 1897, p. 411, no. 14 = *OGIS* 527) the city tries to check the illegal exactions of her own παραφύλακες, whom she had sent to her dependent villages. This inscription probably belongs to the 2nd cent. A.D. No doubt the behaviour of the policemen was no better in the atmosphere of the 3rd cent. A.D. On the municipal police see O. Hirschfeld, 'Die

Sicherheitspolizei im röm. Kaiserreiche', *Kl. Schr.*, pp. 605 ff.; cf. Chap. IX, note 45, and Chap. XI, note 54.

[32] On prices see the bibliography in Chap. XI, note 3. On the Roman coinage in general see the bibliography in Chap. VII, notes 47 and 48, and Chap. XI, note 2. Cf. E. A. Sydenham, *Num. Chr.* 1918, pp. 182 ff.; 1919, pp. 114 ff. and 168 ff. The gradual depreciation of coinage in the 3rd cent. is variously explained. H. Delbrueck, *Gesch. der Kriegskunst*, ii³ (1921), p. 223, attributes it to the exhaustion of the silver-mines; K. Regling, *Münzkunde*, in the *Einleitung* of Gercke and Norden, ii³ (1922), p. 110, and others emphasize the 'subsidies' paid to foreign 'allies', and the foreign trade. Cf. A. Segrè, 'Circolazione e inflazione nel mondo antico', *Historia* [Milano], 3, 1929, pp. 369 ff.; F. Heichelheim, 'Zum Ablauf der Währungskrise des röm. Imperiums im 3. Jahrh. n. Chr.', *Klio*, 26, 1933, pp. 96–113; cf. id. *Schmollers Jahrb.* 55, 1931, p. 760. (A papyrus of the 3rd cent. A.D., *P. Giss. Univ.-Bibl.* 22, dealing with money sent in large quantities to Cnidos, is interesting.) In my opinion all these factors are secondary and without decisive importance. I believe that the fundamental cause lay in the general insecurity and disorganization of economic life, which grew apace with the increase in expenditure necessitated by the maintenance of a corrupted army, by external wars, and by the bureaucracy. The emperors had urgent need of money, while the population hid it and withdrew it from circulation. From all this resulted that state of monetary economy which corresponds to the inflation of modern times: the gradual and systematic deterioration of coinage. On the mines see Chap. VII, notes 100–1.

[33] There are no good monographs on Caracalla. O. Th. Schulz, *Der römische Kaiser Caracalla* (1909); cf. id. *Beiträge zur Kritik unserer literarischen Überlieferung für die Zeit von Commodus' Sturze bis auf den Tod des M. Aurelius Antoninus (Caracalla)* (1903), and *Das Kaiserhaus der Antonine und der letzte Historiker Roms* (1907), are based on the literary evidence only; cf. W. Reusch, 'Der historische Wert der Caracallavita in den Scriptores Historiae Augustae', *Klio*, Beiheft 24, 1931. All the 'Syrian' emperors are treated, from the point of view of their relations to the Christian church, by K. Bihlmeyer, *Die 'Syrischen' Kaiser zu Rom (211–235) und das Christentum* (1916).

[34] I cannot deal here with the much-vexed problem of the sources, and especially with the question of the origin and the character, of the well-known collection of biographies of the Roman emperors known under the name of *Scriptores Historiae Augustae* (see Chap. X). Whoever the authors or the author of these biographies were and to whatever time they or he belonged, it is evident that in the earlier lives (with the exception of the secondary ones, the so-called *Nebenviten*, which are notoriously a late compilation) an historical Latin work of the early 3rd cent. was used. Whether this work ended with the reign of Septimius or included the period down to Alexander, is a matter of controversy. I am inclined to think that large parts of the lives of Caracalla, Elagabalus, and Alexander were based on the narrative of this last 'great' historian of the Roman Empire or of a similar source of the 3rd cent. A.D. The opposite point of view, however, seems to prevail: see the summary of A. von Domaszewski, 'Die Topographie Roms bei den Scr. Hist. Aug.', *Sitzb. Heid. Akad.* 1916 (7), pp. 4 ff., and cf. the monographs of O. Th. Schulz (quoted in the preceding note) and K. Hönn, *Quellenuntersuchungen zu den Viten des Heliogabalus und des Severus Alexander* (1911), and W. Thiele, *De Severo Alexandro imperatore* (1909). Cf., however, the accurate study by A. Jardé, *Études critiques sur la vie et le règne de Sévère Alexandre* (1925), especially p. 109. On Herodian see E. Baaz, *De Herodiani fontibus et auctoritate* (1909); E. Sommerfeldt, *Philol.* 73, 1915–16, pp. 568 ff.; A. G. Roos, *JRS* 5, 1915, pp. 191 ff. On the relation between Cassius Dio, Herodian, and Dexippus, on the one side, and the *Script. Hist. Aug.* on the other, see A. Jardé, op. cit., pp. 95 ff.

³⁵ Cass. Dio, 77. 10. 4 (iii, p. 383, Boiss.): καὶ γὰρ ἔλεγε πολλάκις ὅτι ' οὐδένα ἀνθρώπων πλὴν ἐμοῦ ἀργύριον ἔχειν δεῖ, ἵνα αὐτὸ τοῖς στρατιώταις χαρίζωμαι'. καί ποτε τῆς Ἰουλίας ἐπιτιμησάσης αὐτῷ ὅτι πολλὰ ἐς αὐτοὺς ἀνήλισκε, καὶ εἰπούσης ὅτι ' οὐκέθ' ἡμῖν οὔτε δίκαιος οὔτ' ἄδικος πόρος ὑπολείπεται', ἀπεκρίνατο, τὸ ξίφος δείξας, ὅτι ' θάρσει, μῆτερ· ἕως γὰρ ἂν τοῦτ' ἔχωμεν οὐδὲν ἡμᾶς ἐπιλείψει χρήματα'. On Caracalla's attitude towards education and the educated classes, Cass. Dio, 78. 11. 2–3 (iii, p. 413, Boiss.). On his tendency to pose as a common soldier, Herod. iv. 7. 6: καὶ πάντων μὲν τῶν πολυτελῶν ἀπείχετο· ὅσα δὲ εὐτελέστατα καὶ τοῖς πενεστάτοις τῶν στρατιωτῶν εὐμαρῆ, τούτοις ἐχρῆτο· συστρατιώτης τε ὑπ' αὐτῶν μᾶλλον ἢ βασιλεὺς καλούμενος χαίρειν προσεποιεῖτο. On the enormous expense of the pay and the *praemia* of the soldiers, Cass. Dio, 77. 24. 1 (iii, p. 402, Boiss.); A. von Domaszewski, *Neue Heid. Jahrb.* 10, 1901, p. 236; id. *Rh. Mus.* 58, 1903, p. 223, especially the inscription of Varius Marcellus, Dessau, *ILS* 478.

³⁶ Even in the excerpts of Xiphilinus and the so-called Exc. Val. we have a full and substantial summary of the system of taxation and exactions adopted by Caracalla: see Cass. Dio, 77. 9 (iii, pp. 381 ff., Boiss.): οὗτος οὖν ὁ φιλαλεξανδρότατος Ἀντωνῖνος ἐς μὲν τοὺς στρατιώτας φιλαναλωτὴς ἦν, τοὺς δὲ λοιποὺς πάντας ἀνθρώπους ἔργον εἶχε περιδύειν ἀποσυλᾶν ἐκτρύχειν, οὐχ ἥκιστα τοὺς συγκλητικούς (Xiphil.). χωρὶς γὰρ τῶν στεφάνων τῶν χρυσῶν οὓς ὡς καὶ πολεμίους τινὰς ἀεὶ νικῶν πολλάκις ᾔτει (λέγω δὲ οὐκ αὐτὸ τοῦτο τὸ τῶν στεφάνων ποίημα· πόσον γὰρ τοῦτό γε ἐστίν; ἀλλὰ τὸ τῶν χρημάτων πλῆθος τῶν ἐπ' ὀνόματι αὐτοῦ διδομέ-νων, ⟨οἷς⟩ στεφανοῦν αἱ πόλεις τοὺς αὐτοκράτορας εἰώθασιν), τῶν τε ἐπιτηδείων (annona) ἃ πολλὰ καὶ πανταχόθεν τὰ μὲν προῖκα τὰ δὲ καὶ προσαναλίσκοντες ἐσεπρασσόμεθα, ⟨ἃ⟩ πάντα ἐκεῖνος τοῖς στρατιώταις ἐχαρίζετο ἢ καὶ ἐκαπήλευεν, καὶ τῶν δώρων ἃ καὶ παρὰ τῶν ἰδιωτῶν τῶν πλουσίων καὶ παρὰ τῶν δήμων προσῄει, τῶν τε τελῶν τῶν τε ἄλλων ἃ καινὰ προσκατέ-δειξεν, καὶ τοῦ τῆς δεκάτης ἣν ἀντὶ τῆς εἰκοστῆς ὑπέρ τε τῶν ἀπελευθερουμένων καὶ ὑπὲρ τῶν καταλειπομένων τισὶ κλήρων καὶ δωρεᾶς ἐποίησε πάσης, κ.τ.λ. (Exc. Val. and Xiphil.).

³⁷ See the remarks of A. von Premerstein, 'Alexandrinische Märtyrerakten', *Philol.*, Suppl. 16 (1923), p. 75, and Ritterling in Pauly–Wissowa, xii, col. 1318. Cf. the edicts of Caracalla, *P. Giss.* 40. ii. 16 ff. = Wilcken, *Chrest.*, 22 [= P. Meyer, *Jurist. Pap.*, 1], and *P. Oxy.* 1406 = Meyer, op. cit. 72. Compare the behaviour of the soldiers of Elagabalus toward Antioch: to save the city from being sacked, a huge donative was given by the new emperor, which was afterwards exacted from the city in the form of a capital levy, Cass. Dio, 79. 1. 1.

³⁸ On the *Constitutio Antoniniana* see the bibliography quoted by P. M. Meyer, *Jurist. Pap.*, no. 1. R. von Scala, *Aus der Werkstatt des Hörsaals* (1914), pp. 30 ff., endeavours to show that Caracalla's grant was the completion of the great work done by the emperors for the Roman Empire, inasmuch as it put an end to all political distinctions between the various groups of the population of the Empire. He forgets that in the 3rd cent. Roman citizenship did not mean very much, that it was probably not extended to everybody, and that the extension did not affect the social problem. G. Segrè pointed out that the usual explanation of the text of the *P. Giss.* not only contra-dicts the explicit statements of Dio (77. 9. 4 and 5, cf. 52. 19. 6) and Ulpian (*Dig.* 1. 5. 17) but is not derived from the text as it stands (*Bull. d. Ist. di dir. Rom.* 32, 1922, pp. 191 ff.; cf. Bonfante, *Storia del dir. Rom.*³ (1923), i, p. 358). Dio and Ulpian emphatically state that Roman citizenship was granted to all the inhabitants of the Empire, while the text of the papyrus emphasizes the same point and adds that the new grant would not change the legal status of the various πολιτεύματα except those of the *dediticii* (cf. A. Beltrami, *Riv. fil.* 45, 1917, pp. 16 ff.). The matter must remain obscure so long as we do not know exactly who the *dediticii* were; even after the disser-tation of E. Bickermann, and the discussion which that aroused (see Chap. VII, note 104), the problem is not solved. Firstly it must be observed that Bickermann was not able to demonstrate that *P. Giss.* 40 is not the *Constitutio Antoniniana*; and his reconstruction

of the text is no more convincing than that of the first editor and G. Segrè. But in any case, whether we have here an amendment of the *Constitutio* or its original text, the papyrus proves that the *dediticii* were excluded from Caracalla's concession. Bickermann's definition of the *dediticii* must however be seriously considered. It seems evident that the *dediticii* were not identical with the *peregrini*, that is, the inhabitants of the provinces, not even with that part of them which did not belong to a city or to urban territory in the provinces. It seems that the country population both of the urban territories and of the extraterritorial rural groups were included in the grant. But if the *dediticii* were not the *peregrini* of the provinces, who were they? I cannot accept the thesis of Bickermann that they were barbarians incorporated into the Roman army, but not stationed on Roman soil, while the foreign *gentes* living within the provinces or on the confines of the Roman Empire were not *dediticii* and consequently profited from Caracalla's grant. This view is contradicted by the conditions which existed in the territory of Palmyra: see *Excavs. at Dura-Europos, Prelim. Rep.* i (1929), pp. 57 ff., and cf. Dessau, *ILS* 9184 and Mommsen, *Ges. Schr.* vi, pp. 166 ff. On the other hand, if Mommsen is right in maintaining that after M. Aurelius the auxiliary soldiers who were not already Roman citizens at the time of their enrolment did not receive the citizenship even after their *honesta missio*, with the exception of decurions and centurions (see the interesting list of soldiers promoted decurions between A.D. 217 and 245, all of whom are Egyptians and all Roman citizens, published by H. A. Sanders, *Class. Stud. in hon. J. C. Rolfe* (1930), pp. 265 ff. = *P.Mich.* [164]), and that even these last, at least in the 3rd cent., obtained the citizenship for their sons only when these were settled as *castellani* (see *CIL* iii, pp. 2002 and 2015), there must have been many people in the provinces even after Caracalla who did not possess Roman citizenship, and who were precisely in the position of the *dediticii* of the Giessen papyrus. It seems likely that the members of the *gentes* dwelling within the frontiers of the Empire, and also, probably, at least some of the barbarians settled by the emperors on Roman territory, *laeti*, *tributarii*, *cultores*, *coloni*, were in this condition. In Egypt, undoubtedly, a large part of the native population did not receive Roman citizenship after Caracalla. This is shown by *P.Mich.* 164, and by another papyrus published by L. Amundsen, *Symb. Osl.* 10, 1932, pp. 16 ff. [= *P.Osl.* iii, 122], a list of *duplicarii* and *sesquiplicarii* of a *turma*, who began their service in the years between A.D. 217 and 230. All the *duplicarii* in this list are noted as *c(ivitate) do(na)t(i)*, apparently while still serving. All *sesquiplicarii* are Roman citizens, one excepted. As all these soldiers have Egyptian cognomina, it is clear that they did not possess Roman citizenship before their service, and belonged to the class of *dediticii*. A further step in the process of degrading Roman citizenship was taken by Alexander Severus when he allowed Roman citizens to make their last wills and testaments in Greek. A Roman citizen was no longer supposed to know Latin. Wessely, *Stud. Pal.* xx (*Cat. P.R.* i), no. 35; cf. Kreller, *Erbrechtliche Untersuchungen* (1919), p. 331.

39 On Macrinus and his son Diadumenianus, H. J. Bassett, *Macrinus and Diadumenianus* (Diss., Michigan, 1920). The low standard of military discipline under Macrinus is striking, see e.g. Cass. Dio, 78 (79). 27. 1. Despite his flirting with the senate, he followed in the main the policy of his predecessors, as is shown by his appointments of men of humble origin to the highest posts; see H. J. Bassett, op. cit., p. 57.

40 On Elagabalus there are many monographs which are mostly of no historical value: G. Duviquet, *Héliogabale* (1903); O. F. Butler, *Studies in the Life of Heliogabalus*, (*University of Michigan Studies*, 4, 1910); J. Stuart Hay, *The Amazing Emperor Heliogabalus* (1911); J. Cl. Smits, *De fontibus e quibus res a Heliogabalo et Alexandro Severo gestae colliguntur* (1908). On Julia Soaemias, G. Herzog in Pauly–Wissowa, x, cols. 948 ff. The behaviour of the soldiers during the short rule of Elagabalus was as violent as under

Caracalla and Alexander: see the account in Cass. Dio, 80. 2. 3, of a violent fight in the city of Rome between them and the people.

⁴¹ On Alexander Severus see W. Thiele, *De Severo Alexandro imperatore* (1909); K. Hönn, *Quellenuntersuchungen zu den Viten des Heliogabalus und des Severus Alexander im Corpus der Scr. Hist. Aug.* (1911); A. Jardé, *Études critiques sur la vie et le règne de Sévère Alexandre* (1925). In analysing the biography of Alexander, Hönn goes too far in his scepticism, especially in regard to the accuracy of its statements on the emperor's reforms. Many of the items in this list are corroborated by Dio and Herodian and receive still more important confirmation from the inscriptions and the juridical sources, of which Hönn makes very little use. The parallels which he cites from the *Codex Theodosianus* to prove the late origin of the corresponding chapters in the biography are mostly unconvincing. I believe that most of the data about the reforms of Alexander are genuine and trustworthy. Jardé is nearer the truth. On Julia Mamaea see M. G. Williams, *Studies in the lives of the Roman Empresses: Julia Mammaea* (*Univ. of Michigan Studies*, 1, 1904), pp. 67 ff.; G. Herzog in Pauly–Wissowa, x, cols. 916 ff. On the administrative policy of Alexander and on the personality of his assistants and officials, A. Stein, 'Die kaiserlichen Verwaltungsbeamten unter Severus Alexander (222–235)', *51 Jahresb. der I. Deutschen Staatsrealschule in Prag*, 1912, and Jardé, loc. cit.

⁴² Cass. Dio, 79 (80). 3 and 80. 4. 1; Zos. i. 12; K. Hönn, op. cit., p. 70. On the repeated levies of soldiers in Italy and the formation of a new legion (*IIII Italica*), see E. Ritterling in Pauly–Wissowa, xii, col. 1326.

⁴³ Herod. ii. 4. 6.

⁴⁴ O. Seeck, *Gesch. d. Unterg. d. ant. Welt*, i, p. 384, 12, and p. 532, 21. Interesting projects relating to the depopulation of the Empire and especially of Italy were again in the air in the reign of Alexander (as in the time of Trajan and of Hadrian). Cassius Dio in the well-known speech put into the mouth of Maecenas advocates, e.g., the creation of a state land-bank (52. 28. 3 ff.): φημὶ τοίνυν χρῆναί σε πρῶτον μὲν ἁπάντων τὰ κτήματα τὰ ἐν τῷ δημοσίῳ ὄντα (πολλὰ δὲ ταῦτα ὁρῶ διὰ τοὺς πολέμους γεγονότα) πωλῆσαι, πλὴν ὀλίγων τῶν καὶ πάνυ χρησίμων σοι καὶ ἀναγκαίων, καὶ τὸ ἀργύριον τοῦτο πᾶν ἐπὶ μετρίοις τισὶ τόκοις ἐκδανεῖσαι. οὕτω γὰρ ἥ τε γῆ ἔνεργος ἔσται, δεσπόταις αὐτουργοῖς δοθεῖσα, καὶ ἐκεῖνοι ἀφορμὴν λαβόντες εὐπορώτεροι γενήσονται, τό τε δημόσιον διαρκῆ καὶ ἀθάνατον πρόσοδον ἕξει. Cf. *Scr. Hist. Aug.* Alex. Sev. 40. 2, and note 56 to this chapter. For the disappearance of livestock in Italy, *Scr. Hist. Aug.* ibid. 22. 7. *Penuria hominum*, both in the cities and in the country, is the outstanding feature of the times of the Severi, *Dig.* 50. 6. 3. 1 (Ulp. l. iv, *de officio proconsulis*): 'impuberes quamvis necessitas penuriae hominum cogat, ad honores non esse admittendos rescripto ad Venidium Rufum, legatum Ciliciae, declaratur.' On Venidius Rufus see *PIR* iii, p. 395, no. 245.

⁴⁵ For requisitions of camels, *P.Basel* (E. Rabel, *Papyrusurkunden der öffentlichen Bibliothek der Universität Basel*), no. 2, dating A.D. 190; *BGU* 266 (A.D. 215–16), cf. *P.Gen.* 35; *P.Flor.* 278 (A.D. 203); J. Lesquier, *L'Armée romaine d'Égypte*, pp. 370 and 372; F. Oertel, *Die Liturgie*, pp. 88 ff. Exaction of hides: *BGU* 655 (A.D. 215); cf. *PSI* 465 (A.D. 265). Exaction of palm wood for spears: C. Wessely, *Cat. P.R.* ii. 92 (3rd cent.). Compulsory purchase of corn: *P.Amh.* 107 = Wilcken, *Chrest.* 417 (A.D. 185) ibid.; 108; ibid. 109 = Wilcken, *Chrest.* 418 (A.D. 185); *BGU* 807; *P.Ryl.* ii. 85; cf. 274, 275; *P.Oxy.* 1541; *P.Tebt.* 369; *BGU* 842; *P.Grenf.* i. 48 = Wilcken, *Chrest.* 416 (A.D. 191). Delivery of cows, calves, goats, hay, and wine for the soldiers: *PSI* 683 (A.D. 199), cf. note 15. A Göteborg papyrus is very typical for conditions in Egypt during Caracalla's stay there: H. Frisk, *P.Göt.* 3 (Panopolis, A.D. 215–16). In it a fisherman goes surety for another fisherman: εἰσοδοθέντα ἐπὶ τῆς ἑτοιμα|σίας γάρου τε καὶ ταριχείου λεπτοῦ καὶ | ἰχθύος πρὸς εἰς τὴν εὐκλειστάτην | ἐπι[δ]ημίαν τοῦ κυρίου ἡμῶν, κ.τ.λ.: cf. *Scr. Hist. Aug.* Carac. 6; Cass. Dio, 77. 22; Herod. iv. 6. Liturgies compulsory

on the propertied classes: in *P.Ryl.* ii. 77, col. ii. 35 ff. (A.D. 192), one of the members of the Greek community of Hermupolis agrees to undertake the στεφανηφόρος ἐξηγετεία and to pay two talents a year, if he should be freed from the compulsory lease of imperial land; cf. my *Studien z. Gesch. d. röm. Kol.*, p. 189, note 1. The habit of giving up one's property to escape the burden of liturgies became widespread in the time of Septimius: see the rescript of Septimius and Caracalla (A.D. 200) in Mitteis, *Chrest.* 375 (cf. *P.Ryl.* ii. 75 (2nd cent.)), and the rescript of the same emperors on the *cessio bonorum* in *P.Oxyr.* 1405; cf. *CPR* 20 = Wilcken, *Chrest.* 402. Note the promise in *P.Oxyr.* 1405, l. 10: ἡ δὲ ἐπιτειμία σου ἐ|κ τούτου οὐδὲν βλαβήσεται, οὐδὲ εἰς τὸ | σῶμα ὑβρεισθήσει which implies a very brutal practice. In l. 23 read οὐκ ἀναλογῶν οὐδὲ πρὸς [ἐν] | μέρος τῆς λειτουργίας. On the *cessio bonorum* in general see the bibliography quoted in Chap. VIII, note 44. The obligation of cultivating the waste land becomes one of the heaviest burdens in the 3rd cent. In *PSI* 292 (3rd cent. A.D.) Aurelius Hermias surrenders his property and humbly begs the procurator (ll. 18 ff.): ἀναγκαίως παρὰ τὰ σὰ ἴχνη καταφεύγω ἐξιστανόμενος αὐτοῖς . . . | ἔχειν με τὸ σῶμα ἀνεπηρέαστον καὶ ἀνύβριστον, ἵνα διὰ τ[ὴν σὴν φιλανθρω]|πίαν ἀόχλητος ἐν τῇ πατρίδι συνεστάναι δυνηθῶ. In the new councils of the cities there was a constant fight between the presidents and the members, and between the members themselves. It is easy to understand that the bone of contention was the liturgies. See the edict of Caracalla, *P.Oxyr.* 1406. 6 (A.D. 213–17): ἐὰν βουλευτὴς τὸν [πρύτανιν ἢ βουλευ]|τὴν τύψῃ ἢ μέμψ[ητα]ι[...] | ὁ μὲν βουλ[ε]υτὴς τῆς βουλῆς ἀ[παλλά]|ξεται καὶ εἰς ἄτιμον χώραν [καταστή]|σεται. Under such conditions the country was far from safe. Robbers abounded, as is shown by the letter of Baebius Juncinus to the *strategoi*, *P.Oxyr.* 1408 (A.D. 210–14), in which the prefect repeats an order to all the magistrates, [τὴ]ν τῶν λῃστῶν ἀναζήτησ[ιν] ποιήσασθαι (l. 13). To the letter is appended an edict which fulminates against those who shelter the robbers, ll. 23 ff.: τὸ τοὺς λῃστὰς κα]θαι[ρ]εῖν χωρὶς τῶν ὑποδεχομένων μὴ δύνασθαι πᾶ[σι] φανερόν . . . εἰσὶ] δὲ ὑποδεχομένων πολλοὶ τρόποι· οἱ μὲν γὰρ κοινων[οῦντες τῶν ἀδικη]μάτων ὑποδέχονται, &c.; cf. Ulp. c. vii, 'de off. proconsulis', *Dig.* 1. 18. 13 pr. (in almost the same words), and Marc. *Dig.* 48. 13. 4. 2; O. Hirschfeld, 'Die Sicherheitspolizei im römischen Kaiserreich', *Kleine Schriften*, p. 593, note 4. It is worthy of note that a special river-police force (ποταμοφυλακία), which first appears in the second half of the 2nd cent., assumes ever-increasing proportions and importance in the period of the Severi, see *P.Flor.* 91; *PSI* 734 (A.D. 218–22); cf. *P.Gen.* 1, and *CIL* ii. 1970; Wilcken, *Grundz.*, p. 392; Oertel, *Liturgie*, p. 272; P. Meyer, *Griechische Texte aus Ägypten*, p. 160. The fact shows how unsafe was the river and what a serious handicap this insecurity was to the sound economic development of Egypt. A benefaction of Aurelius Horion to lighten the burden of the inhabitants of some villages in the Oxyrhynchite nome, especially the burden of παραφυλακή (the obligation to act as guards, φύλακες, of various kinds): *P.Oxyr.* 705 = Wilcken, *Chrest.* 407 (A.D. 202). In his request Horion says: κῶμαί τινες τοῦ ᾿Οξυρυγχείτου νομοῦ . . . σφ[ό]δρα ἐξησθένησαν ἐνοχλούμενοι ὑπὸ τῶν κατ᾿ ἔτος λειτουργιῶν τοῦ τε ταμείου καὶ τῆς παρα[φ]υ[λ]ακῆς τῶν τόπων, κινδυνεύουσί τε τῷ μὲν ταμείῳ παραπολέσθαι, τὴν δὲ ὑμετέραν γῆν ἀγεώργητον καταλιπεῖν (ll. 69 ff.). The important part played by police officials in the life of the cities is shown by two objects, both probably from Asia Minor (I know παραφύλακες only from Asia Minor: see above, note 31): one is a silver seal with a portrait of the emperor Hadrian, and with the inscription Κλέων Ἀρτεμιδώρου παραφύλαξ, and the other is a lead weight on the recto of which there is the inscription λεῖτρα, and on the verso Δημητρίου παραφύλακος: see F. H. Marshall, *JHS* 29, 1909, p. 106 (I owe this reference to Professor Wolters). It is also significant that in the Fayûm there existed many watch-towers (μάγδωλα), from which special watchers, μαγδωλοφύλακες, kept a look-out for robbers, who were not only desert-brigands. Cf. E. Kiessling, 'Magdolophylax', Pauly–Wissowa, xiv, col. 300. *P.Fayûm*, 108, quoted by Kiessling, is a very good example. Cf. also note 17 of this chapter.

[46] Παραπομπή (*prosecutio*) of the troops and of military supplies, and the repair of roads: *IGRR* iv. 1247 = *OGIS* 516 (Thyatira), A.D. 215; ibid. 1251, of the same period; *OGIS* 517, A.D. 218–22 (near Thyatira); cf. *Dig.* 49. 18. 4. 1 (Ulp. l. iv, *de officio proconsulis*), where no immunity is to be granted to veterans in respect of the roads and the *angariae*. In the first of the inscriptions quoted above Julius Menelaus entertained Caracalla, and was sent three times as ambassador to the emperors; in the second C. Perelius was sent to Caracalla περὶ ὁδῶν; in the third, as in the first, Caracalla's ἐπιδημία at Thyatira is mentioned. In *IGRR* iii. 714, one of the residents of Sura in Lycia repeatedly entertained the 'imperials' (κυριακοί). A series of inscriptions of Prusias ad Hypium speaks of παράπεμψις στρατευμάτων in the time of Septimius, Caracalla, and Elagabal, ibid. iii. 60 (Septimius), 62 (Septimius, Caracalla, and Elagabal), 66 (Septimius and Caracalla), 68 (of the same period), and 1421, l. 8: παραπέμψαντα τὰ ἱερὰ στρατεύματα πολλάκις. *Prosecutio annonae*: ibid. iii. 407 (Pogla), in or after the time of Caracalla; cf. 409, l. 8: πέμψαντα ἀννῶναν εἰς τὸ Ἀλεξανδρέων ἔθνος and M. Rostovtzeff, *Num. Chr.*, 1900, pp. 96 ff.; ibid. 1412, l. 8: ἀννωναρχήσα[s] | λεγιῶσι α' καὶ β' διόδοις [ἐπὶ] Πέρσας, cf. Ritterling in Pauly–Wissowa, xii, col. 1322; ibid. 1033 = *OGIS* 640 (Palmyra, under Alexander Severus). See also *IG* xiv. 235 = *IGRR* i. 497 (Acrae in Sicily), where a certain Alfius Clodius is praised for his embassies to the emperor καὶ γ' παραπονπες, which I am inclined to explain as καὶ (τρὶς) παραπομπε(ύσα)s. The management of the supplies was generally entrusted to the most skilful and most loyal officers, A. von Domaszewski, *Rh. Mus.* 58, 1903, pp. 218 ff. The exactions of the imperial officers have already been spoken of, but some further facts may be added. In one of the villages of Syria the visits of the soldiers became such a nuisance that Julius Saturninus was obliged to protect the village by a special letter, *OGIS* 527; the inscription shows that the soldiers were wont to take up their quarters in the houses of the provincials; cf. Cass. Dio, 78. 3. 4 (iii, p. 405, Boiss., of Caracalla's Parthian war): αὐτόν τε οὖν τοιοῦτον οἱ βάρβαροι ὁρῶντες ὄντα, καὶ ἐκείνους πολλοὺς μὲν ἀκούοντες εἶναι, ἐκ δὲ δὴ τῆς προτέρας τρυφῆς (τά τε γὰρ ἄλλα καὶ ἐν οἰκίαις ἐχείμαζον, πάντα τὰ τῶν ξενοδοκούντων σφᾶς ὡς καὶ ἴδια ἀναλίσκοντες) καὶ ἐκ τῶν πόνων τῆς τε ταλαιπωρίας τῆς τότε αὐτοῖς παρούσης οὕτω καὶ τὰ σώματα τετρυχωμένους καὶ τὰς ψυχὰς τεταπεινωμένους ὥστε μηδὲν τῶν λημμάτων ἔτι, ἃ πολλὰ ἀεὶ παρ' αὐτοῦ ἐλάμβανον, προτιμᾶν αἰσθόμενοι ἐπήρθησαν ὡς καὶ συναγωνιστὰς αὐτοὺς ἀλλ' οὐ πολεμίους ἕξοντες. The passage illustrates the complete demoralization of Caracalla's soldiers, who were accustomed to behave as if the province were a conquered land. The same attitude on the part of the troops is attested by the episode related by Dio, 79. 4. 5 (iii, p. 458, Boiss.), in speaking of the murder of M. Munatius Sulla Cerialis by Elagabal (A.D. 218–19): ὅτι μεταπεμφθεὶς ὑπ' αὐτοῦ ἐκ τῆς Ῥώμης ἀπήντησε τοῖς στρατιώταις Κελτικοῖς οἴκαδε μετὰ τὴν ἐν τῇ Βιθυνίᾳ χειμασίαν ἐν ᾗ τινα ὑπετάραξαν ἀπιοῦσιν, Ritterling in Pauly–Wissowa, xii, col. 1323. Cf. Chap. VIII, note 5.

[47] *Dig.* 50. 5. 2. 8 (Ulp. l. iii, *Opinionum*): 'qui pueros primas litteras docent, immunitatem a civilibus muneribus non habent: sed ne cui eorum id quod supra vires sit indicatur, ad praesidis religionem pertinet *sive in civitatibus sive in vicis* primas litteras magistri docent.' On the role of the village schools in Egypt see C. H. Oldfather, 'The Greek Literary Texts from Greco-Roman Egypt', *Univ. of Wisconsin Studies in Soc. Sc. and History*, 9, 1923.

[48] J. Carcopino, 'Les Castella de la plaine de Sétif', *Revue Africaine*, no. 294, 1918; cf. id. *Rev. ét. anc.* 25, 1923, pp. 33 ff., in *C. R. Acad. Inscr.* 1919, p. 386, and in *Syria*, 6, 1925, pp. 30 ff., esp. p. 52. Life on an estate situated on the border of the desert is excellently illustrated by the sculptures on a funeral monument of a local landowner at Ghirza in the Tripolitana (a few of which were published by H. Méheir de Mathuisieulx in *Nouv. Arch. d. miss. scient.* 12, 1904, pp. 3 ff., pls. x and xi); cf. the

complete publication by P. Romanelli, 'La Vita agricola tripolitana attraverso le rappresentazioni figurate', *Africa Italiana*, 3, 1930, pp. 53 ff. The type of husbandry recalls that which prevailed in South Russia (see our pls. LXI and XLVII). An estate of the same sort, which was owned by the father of St. Melania, is described by St. Augustine, ch. 46; cf. P. Allard, *Rev. d. quest. hist.* 81, 1907, p. 11, note 2. Carcopino has produced evidence which shows that the Severi did not confine their policy to the region of Sitifis but extended it to the southern regions of modern Algeria (*Rev. arch.*, 1924 (2), pp. 316 ff., especially p. 324). He quotes numerous inscriptions (partly unpublished) which speak of *coloni* and *conductores* in these areas and one (*ILA* 9) which mentions a *numerus colonorum* at Si-Aoun in Southern Tunisia at the beginning of the reign of Septimius.

⁴⁹ On the new settlements and on the relations of the settlers to the land see the evidence collected in my *Studien z. Gesch. d. röm. Kol.*, pp. 383 ff. The land was either granted to, or bought by, the new settlers, just as in Egypt at the same time; cf. note 53.

⁵⁰ *Scr. Hist. Aug.* Al. Sev. 58. 3: 'sola quae de hostibus capta sunt limitaneis ducibus et militibus donavit, ita ut eorum essent, si heredes eorum militarent, nec umquam ad privatos pertinerent, dicens attentius eos militaturos, si etiam sua rura defenderent. addidit sane his et animalia et servos, ut possent colere, quod acceperant, ne per inopiam hominum vel per senectutem possidentium desererentur rura vicina barbariae, quod turpissimum ille ducebat.' Cf. K. Hönn, *Quellenuntersuchungen*, &c., pp. 103 ff., especially notes 207 and 208, and the military diploma, *CIL* iii, p. 2001, no. xc [=*CIL* xvi, 132]: 'praeterea [liberis eorundem] decurionum et centurio[num qui cum filiis in] provinc(ia) ex se procreatis [milites ibi castell]ani essent.' The passage from the *Scr. Hist. Aug.* and the inscription illustrate one side of the policy of the Severi—the transformation of the soldiers on the frontiers into peasants, a phenomenon which we meet both in Africa (the *burgi*) and on the Rhine and Danube *limites* (the *burgi* of the Danube and the *castella* of the Rhine), cf. notes 51 and 52. The inscriptions of Africa quoted above reveal another aspect of the same policy—the militarization of the peasants, the creation in the border-lands of the provinces of groups of militarized peasants who should defend themselves and their settlements, and at the same time furnish the troops of the province with a large number of good and reliable soldiers devoted to the emperor and to his house. In Africa and in Thrace, as well as in Egypt, the chief importance was attached to these elements—the *castellani seminaria militum*, as in Germany to the *milites castellani*, themselves soldiers and fathers of future soldiers.

⁵¹ On Thrace see the inscription of Pizus, Dittenberger, *IGRR* i. 766 = *Syll.*³ 880. There is no doubt that the ἐμπόριον of Pizus, of which we possess the charter, was one of a series of similar foundations planned and, to a certain extent, established by Septimius during his stay on the Danube: see the beginning of the letter of Q. Sicinnius Clarus, appended to the charter and to the list of residents in the new ἐμπόριον, ll. 15 ff.: τῇ προόψει τῶν σταθμῶν ἠσθέ[ν]|τες ὁ[ἱ] κύριοι ἡμῶν μέγιστοι | καὶ θειότατοι αὐτοκράτορες | διὰ παντός τε τοῦ ἑαυτῶν αἰῶ|νος βουληθέντες ἐν τῇ αὐτῇ εὐπρε|πείᾳ διαμεῖναι τὴν αὐτῶν | ἐπαρχείαν, προσέταξαν τὰ ὄν|τα ἐνπόρια ἐπιφανέστερα ὑπ[άρ]ξαι, καὶ τὰ μὴ πρότερον ὄντα γενέσθ[α]ι· καὶ γέγονεν. The term ἐμπόριον means, of course, a market-place (the Latin *forum*), which was neither a village nor a city. Ἐμπόρια are also σταθμοί, *stationes*, in the military sense of that word. The numerous favours granted to the inhabitants of these ἐμπόρια, ll. 49 ff.: τουτέστιν | πολειτικοῦ σείτου ἀνεισφορίαν | καὶ συν[τελ]είας βουργαρίων καὶ [φ]ρουρῶν καὶ ἀνγαρειῶν ἄνεσιν, show that the new settlers formed a privileged class in the province. The only reason which I see for the grant of such privileges was the military importance of the new centres of half-urban life thus created. I feel no doubt, therefore, that the ἐμπόρια of Thrace corresponded to the *castella* of Africa and were intended to provide the Empire with good soldiers, who in their fortified towns should form the

bulwarks of the Roman Empire against the barbarians, and so play the part of the colonies of the old glorious times of Rome. This view is confirmed by the fact that the new settlements received no municipal organization, but were ruled by special presidents (τόπαρχοι βουλευταί) who received the right of jurisdiction by letter, in this respect resembling the *praefecti* of the earlier Roman colonies in Italy (ll. 25 ff.). It is evident that the burdens from which the new settlers were relieved pressed the more heavily on the villages and the cities of the province. The ἐμπόρια were free from payments of municipal taxes in kind, from conscription for the various bodies of military and civil police—a burden which lay so heavily, for instance, on the villages of Egypt—and from the obligation to furnish drivers and draught cattle for the *cursus publicus*. On these privileges see M. Rostovtzeff, *JRS* 8, 1918, pp. 29 ff.; on the πολειτικὸς σεῖτος, id. *Studien z. Gesch. d. röm. Kol.*, p. 302. The ἐμπόρια must not be confounded with the *burgi*, the small forts and towers on the frontier, manned by special soldiers settled there and combined with special corps of native cavalry used for the post-service—the *veredarii*. We find such forts on the Danube, on the Rhine, and in Africa (*JRS*, loc. cit.). In the charter of Pizus it is stated explicitly that the inhabitants of the ἐμπόρια are not required to perform the duties either of the *burgarii* or of the *veredarii*. Cf. the inscription of Kara-Kutuk near Burgas, from which it appears that the system of *burgi* and *praesidia* is earlier than Commodus, see G. Kazarow, *Bull. Inst. Arch. Bulg.* 4, 1926–7, p. 108 = *L'An. ép.* 1927, 49, an inscription of the age of Antoninus Pius. Cf. A. Salač and K. Škorpil, 'Několik Archeologických Památek', &c., *Česká Akad. Věd a Umění*, 1928, p. 61, no. 26. The last effort of the Roman Empire to urbanize the provinces and to create a new class of privileged citizens was strikingly different from the efforts made by the enlightened monarchy. The emperors of the 3rd cent. recurred to the methods of the Roman Republic and of the early Principate, and renewed, in modified forms, the attempts to Romanize the Empire by means of military colonies. Septimius and Alexander were the last emperors to send out real colonies to already existing cities, e.g. to Uchi Majus and Vaga in Africa (A. Merlin and L. Poinssot, *Les Inscriptions d'Uchi Majus*, p. 21).

[52] On Germany see E. Fabricius, *Hist. Zeitschr.* 98 (2), 1907, pp. 23 ff.; A. von Domaszewski, 'Die Schutzgötter von Mainz', *Abhandlungen zur römischen Religion* (1909), pp. 129 ff.; id. 'Die Juppitersäule in Mainz', ibid., pp. 139 ff.; E. Sadée, *Bonn. Jahrb.* 128, 1923, pp. 109 ff. Cf. Chap. VI, note 48.

[53] On the κολωνίαι in Egypt, E. Kornemann, *Klio*, 11, 1911, p. 390; Wilcken, *Grundz.*, p. 403; id. *Chrest.*, 461; J. Lesquier, *L'Armée romaine d'Égypte*, pp. 328 ff. Note the parallel phenomenon in the *civitates* of Gaul in the 1st cent. A.D., emphasized by Kornemann. The policy of Septimius, as I have said, was, *mutatis mutandis*, a renewal of the policy of Sulla, Marius, Caesar, and Augustus. Septimius indeed refrained from creating in this way any real urban centres; his measure was intended, not to promote the development of town-life in the Empire, but to create apart from, or along with, the municipal elements a new privileged aristocracy of military settlers, closely connected with the members of the new dynasty and with its policy. Yet, in the main, the purpose of the colonies of Sulla, Marius, Caesar, and Augustus was the same. In this connexion I may emphasize the fact that Septimius, during his stay in Alexandria (A.D. 199–200), closely studied the economic situation of the country, and started afresh the policy of reclaiming temporarily unproductive land by distributing it and selling it to the soldiers and by revising the conditions on which crown land was leased to the large and small tenants. The confiscations of which we have previously spoken may have increased the area of the estates directly owned by the emperors in Egypt. It was probably for this purpose, and to check the influence of the prefect of Egypt, that Septimius created the new post of financial manager of the Egyptian land, the

καθολικός or *rationalis,* to whom he granted the title of *vir perfectissimus* or διασημότατος. The first καθολικός of Egypt, Claudius Julianus (from A.D. 202), had been *praefectus annonae* in 201 and therefore was well acquainted with the resources and the administration of the country. See *P.Giss.* 48; F. Zucker, *Sitzb. Berl. Akad.* 1910, p. 713; A. Stein, *Arch. f. Papyr.* 5, p. 418; Wilcken, *Grundz.,* p. 157. Cf. Chap. VIII, note 39. I shall return to this policy of Septimius in dealing with certain documents of a similar kind belonging to the time of Philip; see Chap. XI, note 57. It is striking that in both series of documents the καθολικός appears in association with his assistant, a Roman procurator. In the reigns of Septimius and Julianus the holder of this office was Claudius Diognetes, who acted on behalf of Julianus and appears in documents which deal with the uninundated land, both private and imperial, *P.Hamb.* 11, cf. 12, intr. On the land sold to private proprietors, mostly soldiers or veterans, see Chap. VII, note 44. On the uninundated land, W. L. Westermann, *Class. Phil.* 16, 1921, pp. 169 ff. Westermann has made it very probable that, by taxing the uninundated land highly, the Roman emperors intended to force the owners and the tenants of the land to irrigate it artificially and not let it unsown. This policy may have been started at an early date and may already have been employed by the late Ptolemies. But it was not till the second half of the 2nd cent. A.D. that it was vigorously pursued, as is shown by the extant declarations of uninundated land (see Chap. VII, note 49), which all belong to the second half of the 2nd cent. and to the 3rd, and in every case mention special orders of the prefects (or, after Septimius, of the καθολικός). These orders made such a declaration obligatory and were certainly a novelty. This category of land was the *bête noire* of the Egyptian peasants, who were accustomed to easy work on flooded land, and it is very probable that one of the chief duties of the new official appointed by Septimius was to find cultivators who should be willing to invest money and labour in it. Such cultivators were to be found among the soldiers and the veterans of the Roman army, who were enriched by the emperors of the 3rd cent. at the expense of the rest of the population. Have we not here the same principle which so clearly marks the policy of the Ptolemies in regard to the dry and uninundated land? See W. L. Westermann, *Class. Phil.* 17, 1922, pp. 21 ff., and M. Rostovtzeff, *A Large Estate* (1922). The difference was that the land put under cultivation by the Ptolemies was virgin land, while the Roman emperors endeavoured to reclaim waste and abandoned areas which had been under cultivation before.

⁵⁴ The account given in the text is based on the discoveries at Dura. The general lines of the process have already been described by F. Cumont, *Fouilles de Doura-Europos,* pp. xlvii ff. The excavations at Dura have considerably increased our knowledge. After Lucius Verus detachments of the regular army of Syria, among which was the *Cohors Secunda Ulpiana equitata civium Romanorum Sagittariorum,* were sent to Dura, which became one of the most important Roman fortresses on the Euphrates. Under Alexander Severus we find in Dura the *XX Cohors Palmyrenorum* formed with mounted archers. At the same time Dura received the title of Roman colony together with other cities of the Euphrates (cf. note 17). The new situation was probably created by Septimius Severus during his Parthian war. See *Excavs. at Dura-Europos, Prelim. Rep.,* i (1929), pp. 50 ff.; ii (1931), pp. 82 ff.; iii (1932), p. 51. The discovery during the campaign of 1931–2 of a praetorium with many inscriptions, and of the archives of the garrison, containing papyri and parchments, greatly adds to our knowledge of conditions at Dura and in Mesopotamia in the Severan age: see Chap. VII, note 28, and Chap. V, note 20.

⁵⁵ See Chap. VI, note 57.

⁵⁶ Cass. Dio, 78. 6. 1 (iii, p. 708, Boiss.); Herod. iv. 7. 3.

57 See Chap. VII, note 84, especially the inscription of Thuburnica [*L'An. ép.* 1921, 21]: 'C. Herennius M. f. Quir. Festus veteranus leg. x Fretensis honesta missione dimissus, *praefectus tironum* in Mauretania, praef[ec]tus iuventutis, ɪɪvir bis'. Evidently there was an intimate connexion between the recruitment of soldiers and the associations of young men. Compare also the emphasis laid by the Severi on the *iuventus imperii* on their coins (H. Cohen, *Monn. imp.*, Caracalla, nos. 115f., 405ff., 411f.; Geta, 217f.). Caracalla and Geta, like Gaius and Lucius in the reign of Augustus, were honorary presidents of the newly armed youth of the Empire. The close relation between the ideas of Augustus and those of Septimius and the difference in the conditions are equally striking.

58 H. Delbrueck, *Gesch. d. Kriegskunst*, ii³ (1921), p. 240, explains the new policy of settlements, initiated by the Severi, by the financial difficulties and particularly by the fall in the value of money. He is followed by E. Stein, *Gesch. d. spätröm. Reiches*, i (1928), p. 90. Of course Delbrueck's interpretation of Herod. iii. 8. 4 is mistaken, but it is possible that the measures taken by the Severi were to a certain extent influenced by financial considerations: but these would only be of secondary importance. The principal reasons were political, social, and military.

59 On the *aurum coronarium*, see J. G. Milne, *History of Egypt* (1898), pp. 228 ff., 3rd ed., pp. 158 f.; Wilcken, 'Zu den Edikten', *Zeitschr. d. Sav.-St.* 42, 1921, pp. 150 ff.; B. P. Grenfell and A. S. Hunt, *P.Oxyr.* 1441 (A.D. 197–200), intr., and 1659, an account of the sums paid as στεφανικόν by the nome of Oxyrhynchus under Elagabalus (A.D. 218–21); P. Meyer, *P.Hamb.* 80, 81 intr.; *PSI* 733 (Alexander), and *P.Oxyr.* 1433 (Pupienus, Balbinus, and Gordianus). Mentions of the στεφανικόν are remarkably rare in the Egyptian papyri of the 1st and the early 2nd cent. A.D., while they become frequent in the period of M. Aurelius, Commodus, and the Severi, especially under and after Elagabal, when the crown gold becomes a regular tax. However, even in this period and still more later, supplementary and extraordinary taxes under the same name were a common feature. The careful investigation of *P.Fay.*, no. 20, by Wilcken, loc. cit., shows that we must date this papyrus—an imperial edict on the partial remission of the *aurum coronarium*—to the reign of Alexander Severus; cf. J. Bidez and F. Cumont, *Imp. Caesaris Flavii Claudii Juliani Epistolae, Leges*, &c. (1922), p. 83, no. 72 (where the article of Wilcken is overlooked and the edict is still ascribed to the Emperor Julian); C. Barbagallo, *Aegyptus*, 1, 1920, pp. 348 f., and Ensslin, *Klio*, 18, 1922–3, pp. 128 ff. Wilcken has pointed out how characteristic this edict is of the ideas and ideals that marked Alexander's rule and of its liberal tendencies. The more striking was the contrast afforded by the brutal reality. Against the σωφροσύνη, the benevolence and the economy, of the court of Alexander there was ranged the stubborn force of the imperial troops determined to insist upon their desires, and the brutal conduct of governors and procurators. Compare Alexander's letter to the Bithynian κοινόν, of which we possess the text in *Dig.* 49. 1. 25 (from the *Responsa* of Paulus, lib. xx), and in a papyrus, *P.Oxyr.* 2104. The letter is a general order to procurators and governors forbidding the obstruction, through βία (*vis*), ὕβρις (*iniuria*) or φρουρὰ στρατιωτική (*custodia militaris*), of persons who wish to appeal to the emperor's tribunal. The reason given is very interesting: ll. 13 ff.: εἰδότες ὅτ[ι το]σοῦ[τόν μοι μέλει τῆς τῶν ἀρχο]μένων ἐλευθερί[ας ὅσον καὶ τῆς εὐνοίας αὐτῶν καὶ πείθους]. It is to be noted that ἐλευθερία refers to Roman citizens, εὔνοια and πειθώ to the subjects. See P. M. Meyer, 'De epistula Severi Alexandri, *Dig.* 49. 1. 25 = *P.Oxyr.* xvii. 2104', *Studi in hon. di P.Bonfante*, ii (1929), pp. 341 ff. Reduction of taxes: *Scr. Hist. Aug.* Al. Sev. 39. 6, a passage not mentioned by K. Hönn. The statement is, of course, very general and the amount of the reduction is probably exaggerated, but I feel certain that the statement is based on real facts. In 40. 2 the biographer speaks of subsidies granted to landowners to improve their position: the object of making grants of livestock, of agricultural

implements, and of slaves was to keep the agricultural concerns of the landowners going (cf. the passage of Maecenas' speech quoted in note 44). The measure was in the spirit of the enlightened monarchy, and the means adopted reflected the bad state of the imperial treasury. Help for the cities: ibid. 21. 2. It took the form, not of subsidies, but only of permission to use the local *vectigalia* for the improvement of the towns.

⁶⁰ A. W. Persson, *Staat und Manufaktur im römischen Reiche* (1923), pp. 58 ff. I cannot believe that the statements of the *Scr. Hist. Aug.* referring to these measures are mere forgeries. They represent a natural advance along the path which had been traced by the emperors of the 2nd cent. The remission of the tax on merchants and the introduction of a tax on production were local measures intended only for the city of Rome. Of the same kind were the later measures of Aurelian connected with the *anabolicum* of Egypt; cf. A. W. Persson, ibid., pp. 35 f. The *anabolicum* as a special tax is, no doubt, earlier than the time of Aurelian, as is shown by the leaden seals (from the time of Septimius onwards) found at Lyons and investigated and published by myself (in *Röm. Mitt.* 11, 1896, pp. 317 ff.; *Woch. kl. Phil.* 1900, p. 115; *Étude sur les plombs*, &c. (1900), ch. i; P. Dissard, *Coll. Récamier*, pp. 1 ff., nos. 1–3) and by the many mentions of this tax in the papyri of the early 3rd cent. (Reil, *Beiträge*, &c., pp. 9 and 17, note 7; F. Zucker, *Philol.* 70, 1911, p. 100; Jouguet, *P.Thead.* 34. 25, p. 184; *PSI* 779). Persson explains *anabolicae species* as 'Stapelwaren' in contrast to the *annonariae species* (year's goods). I am inclined to think that *anabolicae species* are the '*species* subject to the *anabolicum*' and to explain *anabolicum* as a special tax in kind or a delivery of goods of which the manufacture in the Ptolemaic period was monopolized by the state (flax, hemp, glass, papyrus). Ἀναβάλλειν, from which ἀναβολικόν is derived, probably means, as a *terminus technicus* of taxation, to 'deal out', i.e. to deal out a portion of a certain kind of goods for export to Rome and to the other capitals of the Empire, the portion which was 'dealt out' being a new additional or an old reformed payment imposed on the producers of raw material (e.g. flax and hemp) and on the manufacturers (glass, papyrus). At Rome the produce of the tax was used for the population of the capital and for the praetorians, at Lyons for the needs of the Rhine army. To a certain extent the *anabolicum* was similar to the *annona*, inasmuch as it meant the transformation of payments in money into payments in kind or, better, the addition of payments in kind to the regular payments which were effected in money. Since the *anabolicum* as a special tax is first mentioned in the reign of Septimius, it may have been introduced by him, or by the last Antonines, under the pressure of financial difficulties. Alexander resumed a practice which had existed before him. The measures concerning the corporations may have had a more general application, though the tenor of the passage in the biography (Al. Sev. 33) again suggests a local measure. The decisive step towards nationalizing some of the corporations, alike in Rome and throughout the Empire, was not taken before Aurelian; see E. Groag, 'Collegien und Zwangsgenossenschaften im dritten Jahrundert', *Vierteljahrsschr. f. Soc.- und Wirtschaftsg.* 2, 1904, pp. 491 ff. How far the state advanced towards replacing money economy by natural economy is difficult to say. Most of the passages in the biography of Alexander and in those of his successors which refer to natural economy are late forgeries.

⁶¹ On robbery at sea, see the inscriptions of P. Sallustius Sempronius Victor, a contemporary of Alexander Severus (*PIR* iii, p. 160, no. 69; Pauly–Wissowa, Zw. R. i, col. 1958). In his reign he held an extraordinary command described as τῆς ἐπὶ πᾶσαν θάλασσαν ἡγησάμενος εἰρήνης μετ' ἐξουσίας σιδήρου. Another prominent man of the same period, C. Sulgius L. f. Pap. Caecilianus, began his career as one of the bodyguards of the emperor (*optio peregrinorum*) and instructor of the secret military police (*exercitator militum frumentariorum*). Later, he was promoted to the command of

the division of the fleet which was left at Misenum to protect Italy, with the duty of transporting the emperor's baggage and of providing supplies for his court during imperial journeys: 'praepositus reliquationi classis praetoriae Misenatium piae vindicis et thensauris domini[cis e]t bastagis copiarum devehendar(um)', Dessau, *ILS* 2764; A. von Domaszewski, *Rh. Mus.* 58, 1903, pp. 782 ff. On the fugitives and the measures taken against them, *Dig.* 11. 4. 1. 2 (A.D. 228, Ulp. l. i, *ad edictum*); cf. analogous measures under M. Aurelius, *Dig.* 11. 4. 3; 11. 4. 1. 1. How deeply rooted was the system of spies and how intolerable they were to the people may be gathered from the description of their activity in the famous speech of Maecenas, see Dio, 52. 37. 2 ff.:

καὶ ἐπειδή γε ἀναγκαῖόν ἐστι καὶ διὰ ταῦτα καὶ διὰ τἆλλα καὶ ὠτακουστεῖν τινας καὶ διοπτεύειν πάντα τὰ τῇ ἡγεμονίᾳ σου προσήκοντα, ἵνα μηδὲν τῶν φυλακῆς τινος καὶ ἐπανορθώσεως δεομένων ἀγνοῇς, μέμνησο ὅτι οὐ χρὴ πᾶσιν ἁπλῶς τοῖς λεγομένοις ὑπ' αὐτῶν πιστεύειν, ἀλλ' ἀκριβῶς αὐτὰ διασκοπεῖν. συχνοὶ γάρ, οἱ μὲν μισοῦντές τινας, οἱ δ' ἐπιθυμοῦντες ὧν ἔχουσιν, ἄλλοι χαριζόμενοί τισιν, ἄλλοι χρήματα αἰτήσαντές τινας καὶ μὴ λαβόντες, ἐπηρεάζουσιν αὐτοὺς ὡς νεωτερίζοντας ἢ καὶ ἄλλο τι ἀνεπιτήδειον κατὰ τοῦ αὐταρχοῦντος ἢ φρονοῦντας ἢ λέγοντας. οὔκουν εὐθὺς οὐδὲ ῥᾳδίως προσέχειν αὐτοῖς δεῖ, ἀλλὰ καὶ πάνυ διελέγχειν, cf. Chap. X, note 23. On the general situation of the Roman Empire see Cyprianus, *ad Demetrianum*, 3 (*Corp. Scr. Eccl.* iii. 1, pp. 352 f., ed. Hartel): 'hoc etiam nobis tacentibus . . . mundus ipse iam loquitur et occasum sui rerum labentium probatione testatur. non hieme nutriendis seminibus tanta imbrium copia est, non frugibus aestate torrendis solita flagrantia est nec sic verna de temperie sua laeta sunt nec adeo arboreis fetibus autumna fecunda sunt. minus de ecfossis et fatigatis montibus eruuntur marmorum crustae, minus argenti et auri opus suggerunt exhausta iam metalla et pauperes venae breviantur in dies singulos. et decrescit ac deficit in arvis agricola, in mari nauta, miles in castris, innocentia in foro, iustitia in iudicio, in amicitiis concordia, in artibus peritia, in moribus disciplina.'

x. *The Military Anarchy*

[1] On Eutropius, Aurelius Victor, and the Epitome de Caesaribus see A. Enmann, *Philol.*, Suppl. 4 (1884), pp. 337 ff.; cf. E. Hohl, *Klio*, 11, 1911, p. 187. On the Byzantine Chronicles and Eunapius, F. Gräbner, *Byzant. Zeitschr.* 14, 1905, pp. 87 ff.; cf. E. Hohl, op. cit., p. 191.

[2] It is impossible to give here a full bibliography of the much-vexed question of the *Scr. Hist. Aug.* It must suffice to quote the two articles of H. Dessau in *Hermes*, 24, 1889, pp. 337 ff., and 27, 1892, pp. 561 ff., cf. his last contribution in *Janus*, 1, 1921, pp. 124 ff., and the excellent surveys of Diehl in Pauly–Wissowa, viii, cols. 2051 ff., of E. Kornemann in Gercke and Norden, *Einleitung in die Altertumsw.*[2] (1914), pp. 255 ff. [= 3rd ed. (1933), pp. 155 ff.], and of A. Rosenberg, *Einleitung und Quellenkunde zur römischen Geschichte* (1921), pp. 231 ff. Cf. also the reports of E. Hohl in Bursian's *Jahresberichte*, 171, 1915, and 200, 1924, pp. 165 ff. Hohl is a warm partisan of Dessau and violently attacks the latest work of von Domaszewski and some of his pupils. In no field of ancient history is so much animosity displayed in the discussion of scientific problems as in the investigation of the *Scr. Hist. Aug.* Hohl's reports are one of many examples. The theory of A. von Domaszewski is briefly summarized in his paper 'Die Topographie Roms bei den Scriptores Historiae Augustae', *Sitzb. Heid. Akad.* 1916, (7), pp. 4 ff., and is stated more fully, and with important modifications based on some rather fantastic suggestions, in 'Die Personennamen bei den Scr. Hist. Aug', ibid. 1918, (13), cf. also 'Der Staat bei den Scr. Hist. Aug.', ibid. 1920, (6). O. Seeck's theory is emphasized again in his *Geschichte des Untergangs der ant. Welt*, vi (1920), pp. 33 ff. and 309 f. J. Geffcken's point of view is stated in *Hermes*, 55, 1920, pp. 279 ff.; cf. E. Hohl,

ibid., pp. 296 ff., and in *Klio*, 12, 1912, pp. 474 ff. A new theory on the date of composition and the character of the *Scriptores Historiae Augustae* was proposed by N. H. Baynes, *The Historia Augusta, its date and purpose* (1926) (with a large bibliography); and cf. his answer to the criticisms of G. de Sanctis and Ch. Lécrivain, *Class. Quart.* 22, 1928, pp. 1 ff. According to Baynes the series of biographies is a 'Tendenz-Schrift' inspired by the Emperor Julian, and has a popular character. Cf. A. Alföldi, 'Zur Kenntnis der röm. Soldatenkaiser, 2', *Zeitschr. f. Num.* 38, 1928, p. 167, note. On the 'documents' in the *Scrip. Hist. Aug.* see L. Homo, *Rev. hist.* 1927 (1), pp. 161 ff.; ibid. (2), pp. 1 ff. The more conservative standpoint is represented by Ch. Lécrivain in his volume, *Études sur l'histoire Auguste* (1904), by Diehl, op. cit., and by W. Soltau, 'Die echten Kaiser-biographien', *Philol.* 74, 1917, pp. 384 ff. Cf. the monographs on the emperors of the 3rd cent. quoted in Chap. IX and in the following notes.

3 The best general surveys of the history of the 3rd cent. A.D. are those of A. von Domaszewski, *Geschichte der römischen Kaiser*, ii, pp. 284 ff., and H. Stuart Jones, *The Roman Empire*, pp. 279 ff. The coins from Valerian to Florian are collected in H. Mattingly and E. A. Sydenham, *The Roman Imperial Coinage*, v, 1 (1927) (by P. H. Webb). On the composition of the senate in the period between A.D. 244 and 284 see A. Parisius, *Senatores Romani qui fuerint inter a. 244 et a. 284* (Diss., Berlin, 1916). The constitutional history is given by O. Th. Schulz, *Vom Prinzipat zum Dominat* (1919). On the social and economic crisis cf. my article in *Mus. Belge*, 27, 1923, pp. 233 ff.

4 On the period after Alexander Severus and on the reigns of Maximinus, Pupienus, Balbinus, and Gordian III, see O. Seeck, 'Der erste Barbar auf dem römischen Kaiserthron', *Preuß. Jahrb.* 56, 1885; cf. id. *Die Entwicklung der römischen Geschichtsschreibung und andere populäre Schriften* (1898); A. Sommer, *Die Ereignisse des Jahres 238 n. Chr.* (Progr. Gymnasium Aug. zu Görlitz, 1888); K. F. W. Lehmann, *Kaiser Gordian III, 238–244 n. Chr.* (1911); L. Homo, 'La Grande Crise de l'an 238 après J. Chr. et le problème de l'Histoire Auguste', *Rev. hist.* 131, 1919, pp. 209 ff., and 132, 1919, pp. 1 ff.; E. Hohl in Pauly–Wissowa, x, cols. 852 ff.; P. W. Townsend, 'The Chronology of the Year A.D. 238', *Yale Class. Stud.* 1, 1928, pp. 231 ff.; A. Calderini, *Aquileia Romana* (1930), pp. 52 ff. An inscription found in Rome gives the name and *cursus honorum* of Rutilius Pudens Chrispinus who, according to the inscription, was *dux ex s.c. bello Aquileiensi*: Paribeni, *Not. d. Scav.* i, 1928, pp. 343 ff.; J. Dobiaš, *Listý Filologické*, 56, 1929, pp. 16 ff. [= *L'An. ép.* 1929, 158].

5 On Philip see E. Stein in Pauly–Wissowa, x, cols. 755 ff. On his brother, C. Julius Priscus, *praefectus* of Mesopotamia and afterwards *rector Orientis* and *praefectus praetorio*, cf. ibid., cols. 781 ff.; E. Groag, *Wiener St.* 40, 1918, pp. 20 ff., and A. Stein, *Der röm. Ritterstand* (1927), p. 410.

6 On Decius, G. Costa in E. de Ruggiero's *Diz. epigr.* ii, pp. 1486 ff.; F. S. Salisbury and H. Mattingly, 'The Reign of Trajan Decius', *JRS* 14, 1924, pp. 1 ff.

7 On Valerianus and Gallienus, see R. Paribeni in de Ruggiero's *Diz. epigr.* iii, 1905, pp. 425 ff.; A. von Domaszewski, *Bonn. Jahrb.* 117, 1908, p. 196; L. Homo, 'L'Empereur Gallien et la crise de l'empire romain', *Rev. hist.* 113, 1913, pp. 248 ff. L. Wickert, *RE* xiii, s.v. 'Licinius' (46), (47), (84), (172), (173), (195) (on the members of the Imperial house of the Licinii); A. Alföldi, 'Zur Kenntnis der römischen Soldaten-Kaiser, 1: Der Usurpator Aureolus und die Kavallerie-Reform des Gallienus; 2: Das Problem des "verweiblichten" Kaisers Gallienus', *Zeitschr. f. Num.* 37, 1927, pp. 198 ff.; 38, 1928, pp. 156 ff.; id. 'Die Vorherrschaft der Pannonier im Römerreiche und die Reaktion des Hellenentums unter Gallienus', *Fünfundzwanzig Jahre Römisch-Germanische Kommission*, 1929, pp. 11 ff.; id. 'The Numbering of the Victories of the Emperor

Gallienus and the loyalty of his Legions', *Num. Chr.* 1929, pp. 218 ff. Some important inscriptions and coins connected with the history of the Danubian lands and of Gaul in the time of Gallienus are dealt with by B. Saria, 'Zur Geschichte der Provinz Dacien', *Strena Buličiana* (1924), pp. 249 ff.; N. Vulič, *Mus. Belge*, 27, 1923, pp. 253 ff.; A. Blanchet, ibid., pp. 169 ff. Alföldi has shown in his brilliant writings that the Danubian population saved the unity of the very Empire in the most difficult period of Roman history, by their attachment to the Empire and their bravery. He must not however forget that the patriotic activity of these people began only in the second part of the 3rd cent. A.D. Before that time they, like the other sections of the Roman army, contributed to the dissolution and economic ruin of the Empire. At all events it is not wholly a matter of chance that the saviours of the unity and security of the Empire came from the Danubian lands. Military colonists of differing origins were stationed there, and these formed large, compact groups well fitted to spread Romanism among the natives. No wonder that in the decisive moment the inhabitants of the Danubian countries were the first to perceive the magnitude of the danger to the Empire, and to contribute strongly to its defence. Gallienus, as Alföldi pictures him, with his philhellenism and his interest in cultural matters, is undoubtedly one of the most interesting figures who ever sat on the Roman throne. Cf. C. Daicovici, 'Gli Italici nella provincia di Dalmatia', *Ephem. Dac.* 5, 1932, pp. 57–122.

8 On the 'thirty tyrants' of the time of Gallienus, H. Peter, 'Die römischen sogenannten dreißig Tyrannen', *Abh. d. sächs. Ges.* 57, 1909, pp. 179 ff. On Postumus and the *imperium Galliarum*, C. Jullian, *Hist. de la Gaule*, iv, pp. 570 ff. There can be no doubt that the Empire of Postumus was not a German Empire, as has been suggested by A. von Domaszewski in Pauly–Wissowa, viii, cols. 611 ff.; cf. id. *Gesch. d. röm. Kaiser*, ii, p. 303. Hercules, the god of Postumus' predilection, is not the German Donar but the god of the Antonines, who fights against barbarism and protects the Roman Empire. The same reverence was paid to Hercules, for example, by the Bosporan king Sauromates II, the contemporary of Commodus, Septimius, and Caracalla, and in the same spirit: see M. Rostovtzeff, *Strena Buličiana* (1924), pp. 731 f. Genuine separatist tendencies, associated with a revival of Oriental nationalism, were shown by the native dynasts of Palmyra. On the Palmyrene dynasty, see Chap. VII, notes 29 and 31: cf. Chap. IX, note 54 and note 10 of this chapter. Cf. J. G. Février, *Essai sur l'histoire politique et économique de Palmyre* (1931). On Aemilianus see J. Grafton Milne, *JEA* 10, 1924, pp. 80 ff. Milne has shown that Aemilianus endeavoured at first, like Odaenathus in Syria and like Valens and Piso after him in Greece, to save Egypt for Gallienus and was forced later by the troops to declare himself emperor, an act which led to his deposition by Gallienus. On the Herulian incursion into Athens see *SEG* i. 62 with bibliography ibid. [= *IG* ii². 5201].

9 M. Ancona, *Claudio II e gli usurpatori* (1901); L. Homo, *De Claudio Gothico Romanorum imperatore* (1904).

10 L. Homo, *Essai sur le règne de l'empereur Aurélien* (1904); E. Groag in Pauly–Wissowa, v, cols. 1347 ff.

11 E. Hohl, *Vopiscus und die Biographie des Kaisers Tacitus* (1911) (also in *Klio*, 11, 1911). Cf. *Forsch. Eph.* iii, no. 20.

12 E. Dannhäuser, *Untersuchungen zur Geschichte des Kaisers Probus* (1909); J. H. E. Crees, *The Reign of the Emperor Probus* (1911). On the serious war in Africa, comparable with the war of Gallienus against Faraxen, *ILA* 609, 610; L. Chatelain, *C. R. Acad. Inscr.* 1919, p. 352.

13 P. Bianchi, *Studi sull'imperatore M. Aurelio Caro* (1911).

¹⁴ On Carinus, Henze in Pauly–Wissowa, ii, col. 2455; D. Vaglieri in de Ruggiero, *Diz. epigr.* ii, p. 125.

¹⁵ The speech Εἰς βασιλέα was incorporated in the collection of the orations of Aelius Aristides (no. 9 Dindorf, no. 35 B. Keil), and was for a long time believed to have been delivered by this sophist. B. Keil was the first to recognize that Aristides could not possibly have been the author of the speech, and proved this in the most convincing way (see 'Eine Kaiserrede', *Gött. gel. Nachr.* 1905, pp. 381 ff.). He suggested that Macrinus is the emperor addressed in the speech, and was supported by I. Turzevich, *Bulletin of the Hist.-Phil. Institute of Niejin*, 1907, pp. 49 ff. (in Russian). In *Philol.* 65, 1906, pp. 344 ff., A. von Domaszewski rejected this identification and proposed Gallienus. The real solution is given by E. Groag, *Wiener St.* 49, 1918, pp. 20 ff. It is evident that the emperor is Philip. Possibly the author of the speech was Nicagoras, the great Athenian sophist of this period. See A. Wilhelm, Ἀρχ. Ἐφ., 1924, pp. 57 ff., no. 5 [= *IG* ii². 4831].

¹⁶ O. Th. Schulz, *Vom Prinzipat zum Dominat*, pp. 51 ff., insists on the fact that Maximinus did not seek recognition by the senate; cf., however, O. Seeck, *Preuß. Jahrb.* 56, 1885, pp. 267 ff., and E. Hohl in Pauly–Wissowa, x, cols. 852 ff.

¹⁷ Herod. vii. 3. 1: τί γὰρ ἦν ὄφελος βαρβάρων ἀναιρουμένων, πλειόνων γενομένων φόνων ἐν αὐτῇ τε Ῥώμῃ καὶ τοῖς ὑπηκόοις ἔθνεσιν; ἢ λείας ἀπάγειν τῶν ἐχθρῶν, γυμνοῦντα καὶ τὰς οὐσίας ἀφαιρούμενον τῶν οἰκείων; *Scr. Hist. Aug.* Max. 8. 7: 'audiebant enim alios in crucem sublatos, alios animalibus nuper occisis inclusos, alios feris obiectos, alios fustibus elisos, atque omnia haec sine dilectu dignitatis'; cf. Herod., loc. cit. Naturally, one cannot put much faith in the *SHA*.

¹⁸ Ps.-Aristid., Εἰς βασιλέα, § 7 (58): ἐκεῖνοι μὲν γὰρ μετὰ πολέμων καὶ φόνων πολλῶν εἰσῆλθον εἰς τὰ πράγματα, πολλοὺς μὲν τῶν ἐν τάξει ἀπολέσαντες, πολλοῖς δὲ ἀνηκέστων συμφορῶν αἴτιοι γενηθέντες, ὥστε πολλὰς μὲν ἐρημωθῆναι πόλεις ὑπηκόους, πολλὴν δὲ χώραν ἀνάστατον γενέσθαι, πλεῖστα δὲ ἀναλωθῆναι σώματα. Cf. § 9 (58): καὶ μὴν οὐδ' ὡς ἔσχε τὴν ἀρχὴν οὐδὲν ἔπραξε σκυθρωπὸν οὐδὲ ἐμιμήσατο, οὐδὲ ἐζήλωσε τούτων οὐδέν, οὐδὲ ὥσπερ ἄλλοι τῶν πρὸ αὐτοῦ βασιλέων τῶν ἐν τέλει τινὰς φοβηθέντες ἐπιβουλεύειν αὐτοῖς αἰτιασάμενοι τοὺς μὲν φυγαῖς, τοὺς δὲ θανάτοις ἐζημίωσαν, οὐδὲν τούτων ἐποίησεν.

¹⁹ *CIL* viii. 2170 = Dessau, *ILS* 8499.

²⁰ *Scr. Hist. Aug.* Max. 9. 6; Herod. vii. 1.

²¹ Herod. vii. 3. 3 ff.; cf. Zosim. i. 13.

²² B. Laum, *Stiftungen*, &c.; i, pp. 8 ff. The diagram on p. 9 shows an abrupt fall in the 3rd cent. It is a pity that most of the documents which deal with donations and foundations are not dated, so that it is impossible to trace the evolution in the 3rd cent.

²³ Ps.-Aristid., Εἰς βασιλέα, § 21 (62): καὶ περὶ δικαιοσύνης τοσαῦτα. φιλανθρωπία γε μὴν τίς μείζων ταύτης καὶ φανερωτέρα; ᾗ κατεπτηχὸς ἅπαν τὸ ὑπήκοον καὶ ὑπὸ φόβου δεδουλωμένον, πολλῶν τῶν κατηκόων περιόντων καὶ ὠτακουστούντων κατὰ πάσας τὰς πόλεις εἴ τις φθέγξαιτό τι, ἐλεύθερον δὲ οὐδὲν οὔτε φρονῆσαί τι οὔτε εἰπεῖν οἷόν τε ὄν, ἀνῃρημένης τῆς σώφρονος καὶ δικαίας παρρησίας, τρέμοντος δὲ ἑκάστου σκιάν, ἀπήλλαξε τοῦ φόβου τούτου καὶ ἠλευθέρωσε τὰς ἁπάντων ψυχάς, ἐντελῆ καὶ ὁλόκληρον ἀποδιδοὺς τὴν ἐλευθερίαν αὐτοῖς. Cf. Herod. vii. 3. 1 and Chap. IX, notes 31 and 60.

²⁴ Ps.-Aristid., Εἰς βασιλέα, § 16 (60): καὶ πρῶτόν γε τὴν εἰς χρήματα δικαιοσύνην αὐτοῦ θεασώμεθα. τῆς γὰρ συντάξεως ὑπερβαλλούσης τῆς εἰς τὴν διοίκησιν συντεταγμένης καὶ φόρων ἐπιταχθέντων πλειόνων καὶ οὐδὲ τούτων ἀρκούντων, ἀλλὰ κεκενωμένων μὲν τῶν πανταχοῦ ταμιείων, ἀεὶ δὲ μείζονος ὄντος τοῦ περὶ μέλλοντος φόβου, οὐ τοῦ πλείονος ἐδεήθη οὐδ' ἐζήτησεν οὐδὲ διὰ

χρήματα κακὸς ἐγένετο, ἀλλ᾽ ἀνῆκε καὶ ἐπεκούφισεν, οὐ μόνον δικαιότατος, ἀλλὰ καὶ φιλανθρω-
πότατος βασιλεὺς περὶ ταῦτα γενόμενος.

25 Ps.-Aristid., Εἰς βασιλέα, § 30 (64–65): καὶ μὴν τὰ μὲν πρὸς πολεμίους ἀνδρείοις πολλοῖς
ὑπῆρξε γενέσθαι, ὑπὸ δὲ τῶν σφετέρων στρατιωτῶν αὐτοὺς ἄρχεσθαι· ὁ δὲ οὕτως ῥᾳδίως ἐκράτησε
καὶ κατεστήσατο ὥστε πολλῶν μὲν καὶ ἀπείρων ὄντων τῶν διδομένων αὐτοῖς, χαλεπῶν δὲ καὶ
φοβερῶν, εἰ μὴ τοσαῦτα λαμβάνοιεν, καὶ ἔτι πλείω [τῶν διδομένων αὐτοῖς], ... οὐχ ὅπως ἐπηύξησεν
τὰς ἐπιθυμίας αὐτῶν, ἀλλ᾽ ὁρίσας τὸ δέον τοὺς μὲν στρατιώτας πρὸς τοὺς πόνους καὶ τὴν ἄσκησιν
τῶν σωμάτων ἀμείνους ἐποίησεν, οὐκέτι τῷ λαμβάνειν αὐτοὺς ἐάσας προσέχειν, ἀλλὰ τὴν μελέτην
τῶν πολεμικῶν αὐτοῖς συνήθη ποιήσας, οὐδὲ ἐν ἡδυπαθείᾳ καὶ τρυφῇ ὄντας διάγειν, ἀλλ᾽ ὅπως
μηδένα καιρὸν ἕξουσιν ἐπιθυμίας τῆς τοιαύτης. τοῦτο ποιήσας ἐπήμυνε μὲν ταῖς τῶν ἀρχομένων
ἐνδείαις, ἐπεμελήθη δὲ τῆς εὐταξίας τῶν στρατιωτῶν, τῶν δὲ χρημάτων βεβαιοτέραν ἐποίησε τὴν
πρόσοδον.

26 The mood of the population and the opinion of the educated classes on the
general condition of the Empire are clearly expressed in the same speech, § 14 (60): ὃς
ἁπάντων μὲν κεκινημένων καὶ μεθισταμένων, ὡς ἔπος εἰπεῖν, εἰς ἑτέραν γῆν, σαλευούσης δὲ τῆς
ἀρχῆς ὥσπερ ἐν μεγάλῳ χειμῶνι ἢ σεισμῷ, κᾆτα ὥσπερ νεὼς καταδύεσθαι μελλούσης ἀποφερο-
μένης πρὸς ἔσχατα γῆς, οὗ καὶ πρότερον ἀπεπλανήθησάν τινες τῶν ἐν ἀρχαῖς καὶ βασιλείαις γενομένων κἄπειτα ὥσπερ ἐν λαβυρίνθῳ πολλαῖς καὶ χαλεπαῖς ἀπορίαις ἐντυχόντες τελευτῶντες αὐτοὺς
ἀπεῖπον, ἀποκλεισθέντες τῆς ὀπίσω ὁδοῦ ἐπανελθεῖν μὴ δυνηθέντες, ταῦτα ὁρῶν, κτλ. This rhe-
torical digression probably refers both to the time before the senatorial restoration
and to the reign of Gordian III. We know very little about the policy of this boy,
or rather about that of his father-in-law Timesitheus, one of the most faithful and able
assistants of Maximin. I am inclined to think, with von Domaszewski, that he followed
the policy of his former master rather than that of Maximin's immediate predecessors.
Philip's rule represented a reaction against the resumption of the methods of Maximin; see A. von Domaszewski, *Rh. Mus.* 58, 1903, pp. 218 ff.

27 A. von Domaszewski, ibid., p. 229.

28 Herod. vii. 4. 2 ff., especially § 3, καὶ νεανίσκους τινας τῶν παρ᾽ ἐκείνοις εὖ γεγονότων
καὶ πλουσίων καταδίκαις περιβαλὼν εἰσπράττειν τὰ χρήματα εὐθέως ἐπειρᾶτο, πατρῴων τε
καὶ προγονικῶν οὐσιῶν αὐτοὺς ἀφαιρεῖσθαι. Cf. *Scr. Hist. Aug. Gord. Tres,* 7. 4: 'tunc quidam
Mauricius nomine, potens apud Afros decurio, iuxta Thysdrum maxima posthac
oratione apud plebem vel urbanam vel rusticanam in agro suo velut contionabundus
est locutus.' Mauricius, as well as his speech, may be an invention, but the standing
given to him shows that the biographer was well aware to whom the revolution in
Africa was due.

29 Herod. vii. 6. 2 (Gordian at Carthage): εἵπετο δὲ αὐτῷ πᾶσα ἡ βασιλικὴ πομπή, τῶν
μὲν στρατιωτῶν οἵτινες ἦσαν ἐκεῖ, καὶ τῶν κατὰ τὴν πόλιν ἐπιμηκεστέρων νεανίσκων ἐν σχήματι
τῶν κατὰ τὴν Ῥώμην δορυφόρων προϊόντων. Id. vii. 9. 5: γενομένης δὲ συμβολῆς οἱ μὲν
Καρχηδόνιοι ὄχλῳ πλείους ἦσαν, ἄτακτοι δὲ καὶ πολεμικῶν ἔργων ἀπαίδευτοι ἅτε ἐν εἰρήνῃ
βαθείᾳ τεθραμμένοι ἑορταῖς τε καὶ τρυφαῖς σχολάζοντες ἀεί, γυμνοί τε ὅπλων καὶ ὀργάνων πολε-
μικῶν· ἕκαστος δὲ ἐπεφέρετο οἴκοθεν ἢ ξιφίδιον ἢ πέλεκυν δοράτιά τε ἐκ κυνηγεσίων. There is
no doubt that this description excludes the peasants, and points to the lower, and still
more to the higher, classes of the city population. Cf. our pl. LXXVI. The promises of
Gordian, which attracted soldiers to his army, are described by Herod. vii. 6. 4:
συκοφάντας τε πάντας φυγαδεύων καὶ παλινδικίαν διδοὺς τοῖς ἀδίκως κατακριθεῖσι. They
meant the end of the system of spies and the restoration of confiscated property.

30 Herod. vii. 10: ὁ δὲ Καπελιανὸς ἐς Καρχηδόνα εἰσελθὼν πάντας τε τοὺς πρωτεύοντας
ἀπέκτεινε, εἴ τινες καὶ ἐσώθησαν ἐκ τῆς μάχης, ἐφείδετό τε οὔτε ἱερῶν συλήσεως οὔτε χρημάτων
ἰδιωτικῶν τε καὶ δημοσίων ἁρπαγῆς· ἐπιὼν τε τὰς λοιπὰς πόλεις ὅσαι τὰς Μαξιμίνου τιμὰς
καθῃρήκεσαν, τοὺς μὲν ἐξέχοντας ἐφόνευε, τοὺς δὲ δημότας ἐφυγάδευεν, ἀγρούς τε καὶ

κώμας ἐμπιπράναι λεηλατεῖν τε τοῖς στρατιώταις ἐπέτρεπε. This was a regular persecution of the propertied classes, and particularly the class of large landowners.

31 My point of view agrees with that of Herodian, and is based on facts which he reports. In vii. 12. 1 he says στρατηγοί τε οὖν κατελέγοντο ἔκ τε πάσης 'Ιταλίας λογάδες, ἥ τε νεολαία πᾶσα ἠθροίζετο, ὅπλοις τε αὐτοσχεδίοις καὶ τοῖς προστυχοῦσιν ὡπλίζετο. Italy, as we know, was thoroughly urbanized, and the greater part of her population was a city-population. Besides, she still remembered the days of her supremacy, and she was naturally angry with a Thracian barbarian and his barbarian soldiers. Compare the story of the fight put up by the people of Rome against the new praetorians, who used this opportunity to pillage the rich, Herod. vii. 12. 7. On Emona, id. viii. 1. 4. On the attitude of the people of Italy after the victory of the senate, see id. viii. 7. 2: αἵ τε [ἀπὸ] 'Ιταλίας πόλεις πρεσβείας ἔπεμπον τῶν πρωτευόντων παρ' αὐτοῖς ἀνδρῶν οἳ λευχειμονοῦντες καὶ δαφνηφόροι θεῶν πατρίων ἕκαστοι προσεκόμιζον ἀγάλματα καὶ εἴ τινες ἦσαν στέφανοι χρυσοῦ ἐξ ἀναθημάτων. Very different was the mood of the soldiers, οἱ πλεῖστοι γὰρ αὐτῶν ἠγανάκτουν καὶ λανθανόντως ἤλγουν (ὁρῶντες) τὸν μὲν ὑπ' αὐτῶν ἐπιλεχθέντα βασιλέα καθῃρημένον, κρατοῦντας δὲ τοὺς ὑπὸ συγκλήτου ᾑρημένους (id. viii. 7. 3, cf. 8. 1). I see no reason to assume that the report of Herodian is biased. He was not a senator and had no reason whatever to rejoice in the victory of the senate, if it were a victory of the senate alone; but in fact it was a victory of the educated classes, and Herodian represents the standpoint and the ideals of the majority of those classes. I do not doubt that Maximin was an honest man and an able general. But his aim was to destroy the main fabric of the Roman state, as based on the cities. No wonder that he was hated by those who saw in such destruction the fall of ancient civilization as a whole—which indeed it really was. How could they believe in the necessity of it, if even modern scholars are not all convinced that it was necessary to crush the educated classes in order to bring about an alleged equality that was never achieved? These considerations are to be set against the attempt of E. Hohl (in Pauly–Wissowa, x, cols. 852 ff.) to 'save the memory' of Maximin.

32 Chap. IX, note 58.

33 Above, note 26.

34 On his attitude towards the senate see E. Groag, *Wiener St.* 40, 1918, p. 38. On the foundation of new colonies, which was one of the last attempts to urbanize the Empire, E. Stein in Pauly–Wissowa, x, col. 760: W. Kubitschek, 'Zur Geschichte von Städten des röm. Kaiserreiches', *Sitzb. Wien. Akad.* 177, 1916, pp. 3 ff.; E. Groag, op. cit., p. 35. On Decius, J. R. Knipfing, 'The *Libelli* of the Decian Persecution', *Harv. Theol. Rev.* 16, 1923, p. 352; cf. L. Homo, 'La Disparition des privilèges administratifs du sénat romain', *Rev. Hist.* 137, 1921, pp. 162 ff.

35 See the careful dissertation of C. W. Keyes, *The Rise of the Equites in the Third Century of the Roman Empire* (1915); cf. M. Rosenberg, *Hermes*, 55, 1920, pp. 319 ff., and L. Homo, *Rev. hist.* 137, 1921, pp. 162 ff., and 138, 1921, pp. 1 ff. Homo gave a very fine picture of the struggle between the senate and the emperors for the key positions in the state, but I agree with N. H. Baynes, *JRS* 15, 1925, pp. 195 ff., that his interpretation is illusory. The senate had no force with which to fight against the Emperor. Gallienus was determined in his action not by the wish to deprive the senate of any rights (*de facto* it no longer had any rights) but by the desire to obtain the best possible service and to satisfy the soldiers. It is, however, clear that the elimination of the senate from the provinces was effected by individual appointments, not by a general measure. Homo has done valuable work in analysing the equestrian *cursus honorum* in the time of Gallienus, and showing how thoroughly military it was. 'Le cursus équestre nouveau exclut tout emploi civil: il est strictement militaire et, par les grades de sous-officier,

de centurion, de tribun, éventuellement de "dux ducenarius", conduit le simple soldat des rangs les plus humbles de la milice jusqu'aux gouvernements des provinces' (*Rev. hist.* 138, 1921, p. 19). His conclusions are naturally based on the collection and investigation of the epigraphical material in the brilliant study of A. von Domaszewski, 'Die Rangordnung des römischen Heeres', *Bonn. Jahrb.* 117, 1908, pp. 1 ff. With the control of the provinces the senate lost also its financial functions, and the *aerarium Saturni* gradually became the municipal treasury of the city of Rome.

³⁶ The religious beliefs of the army of the Danube in the 3rd cent. are illustrated by many hundreds of little *icones* (compare those used in the Greek Orthodox Church) found only in the Danubian lands, which were either votive offerings or amulets of the soldiers. These tablets (made of stone or lead) show a curious mixture of solar monotheism and of the worship of a triad of divinities, half-Thracian, half-Persian, with some admixture of the religious beliefs of Asia Minor. The triad consists of two gods on horseback (a syncretism of Mithras and the Thracian hero) and the Great Mother. The mystic character of this worship is illustrated by some scenes representing the various ceremonies of the cult. See my article 'Une Tablette votive thraco-mithriaque du Louvre', *Mémoires des savants étrangers de l'Académie des Inscriptions*, 13, 1924, pp. 167 ff.; cf. G. Kazarow, *JDAI* 37, 1922, *Arch. Anz.*, pp. 184 ff. The cult of Mithras played a great part in the religious life of the Danube provinces. Sanctuaries of the god appear in almost every fort occupied by Roman troops there. The best known are the three or four *Mithraea* of Carnuntum (*Führer durch Carnuntum* (6th ed. 1923), pp. 52 ff.) and the *Mithraeum* of Poetovio, which was flourishing in the time of Gallienus (B. Saria, *Strena Buličiana* (1924), pp. 249 ff.). In this respect, however, there was no difference between the Danube lands and those of the Rhine. We must bear in mind that the Syrian and Arabian soldiers were the second best in the Roman army, and that they had an enormous influence on politics from the time of Septimius Severus. The purely Oriental character of this army is splendidly illustrated by the monuments of the 3rd cent. found at Salihiyeh (Doura) on the Euphrates: see F. Cumont, *Mon. Piot*, 26, 1923, pp. 1–46, and cf. J. Carcopino, *Syria*, 6, 1925, pp. 30 ff.; cf. Chap. IX, note 54.

³⁷ For M. Aurelius, Cass. Dio, 71. 3. 2 (iii, p. 252, Boiss.) (A.D. 168). When the soldiers demanded an increase of pay, Marcus refused: αὐτὸ τοῦτο εἰπὼν ὅτι ὅσῳ ἂν πλεῖόν τι παρὰ τὸ καθεστηκὸς λάβωσι, τοῦτ' ἐκ τοῦ αἵματος τῶν τε γονέων σφῶν καὶ τῶν συγγενῶν ἐσπεπράξεται· περὶ γάρ τοι τῆς αὐταρχίας ὁ θεὸς μόνον κρίνειν δύναται. For Aurelian, Petr. Patr., Fr. 10. 16 (*Fr. Hist. Gr.* iv. 197; Cass. Dio, iii, fr. 178, p. 747, Boiss.); ὅτι Αὐρηλιανὸς πειραθείς ποτε στρατιωτικῆς ἐπαναστάσεως, ἔλεγεν ἀπατᾶσθαι τοὺς στρατιώτας, εἰ ἐν ταῖς αὐτῶν χερσὶ τὰς μοίρας εἶναι τῶν βασιλέων ὑπολαμβάνουσιν· ἔφασκε γὰρ τὸν θεὸν δωρησάμενον τὴν πορφύραν (καὶ ταύτην ἐπεδείκνυ τῇ δεξιᾷ) πάντως καὶ τὸν χρόνον τῆς βασιλείας ὁρίσαι. Did Aurelian know the saying of Marcus? Or has Petrus Patricius misread 'Aurelianus' for 'M. Aurelius'? Or is the saying a pure fiction?

³⁸ *CIL* xi. 6308.

³⁹ In the books and articles quoted in note 10 the reader may find a detailed discussion of the economic and social policy of Aurelian. The professional corporations are treated in the article of E. Groag in *Vierteljahrsschr. f. Soc.- u. Wirtschaftsg.* 2, 1904, pp. 493 ff. It is very probable that Aurelian militarized and nationalized some of the corporations, especially some of those connected with the city of Rome. This was a result of the great difficulty of victualling Rome, with private commerce in a dying condition and the productivity of Italy decaying. The rations of bread, oil, and pork introduced by Aurelian must be regarded, not as a bribe to the people, but as a measure adopted to save the huge city from starvation. A similar purpose underlay the measure

by which Aurelian reserved for the people of Rome the products which were delivered to the state by the hemp- and flax-producers, and by the papyrus and glass industries of Egypt. These *anabolicae species*, which had previously been sold by the state in various places (e.g. at Lyons), were now all brought to the capital and probably sold to the population (see Chap. IX, note 59). Another measure of the same type, showing the difficult position in which the city of Rome found herself in regard to supplies of the necessities of life, was the attempt to nationalize the production and sale of wine. I shall return to these measures in the next chapter.

[40] We have little evidence regarding the composition of the senate in the second half of the 3rd cent.: A. Parisius, *Senatores Romani qui fuerint inter a. 244 at a. 284* (Diss. Berlin, 1916), was able to collect only 151 names of senators of this period, while the age of Severus Alexander has yielded no less than 280 senators (W. Thiele, *De Severo Alexandro imperatore* (1909), pp. 77 ff.; cf. A. Jardé, *Études critiques sur la vie et le règne de Sévère Alexandre* (1925), pp. 119 ff. But even this scanty material shows that the new provincial families were a majority in comparison with those belonging to the senatorial aristocracy of the 2nd cent. A.D. On the new landed aristocracy see the fine remarks of C. Jullian, *Histoire de la Gaule*, iv, pp. 552 ff. and 605 ff. The phenomenon was, of course, not confined to Gaul.

[41] On the reforms of the Roman army, besides the books which deal with the reigns of Gallienus and Aurelian, see R. Grosse, *Römische Militärgeschichte von Gallienus bis zum Beginn der byzantinischen Themenverfassung* (1920), and the bibliography quoted by him. It is unfortunate that the evidence on the system of conscription is so desperately meagre for the 3rd cent. Our knowledge is mostly limited to the 2nd cent. and to the period after Diocletian. My view, as set forth in the text, is based on the masterly article of Th. Mommsen, 'Die Conscriptionsordnung der römischen Kaiserzeit', *Ges. Schr.* vi, pp. 20 ff.; cf. also my article in *JRS* 8, 1918, pp. 26 ff.

XI. *The Roman Empire during the Period of Military Anarchy*

[1] *Scr. Hist. Aug.* Probus, 20. 5 and 23; cf. Aur. Vict. *de Caes.* 37. 3; Eutr. ix. 17. 3. The coincidence between the Latin biographer, Aurelius Victor, and Eutropius shows that the saying of Probus, if not genuine, was invented in the 3rd cent. Cf. Th. Mommsen, *Hermes*, 25, 1890, p. 259; Dannhäuser, *Unters. z. Gesch. d. Kais. Probus*, pp. 84 ff.; J. H. E. Crees, *The Reign of the Emperor Probus*, p. 139; G. Costa, 'L'opposizione sotto i Costantini', *Racc. Lumbroso*, pp. 293 ff. I find as little reason to think that the saying reflects the state of mind of Rome in A.D. 306, before the conflict between Constantine and Galerius, as to see in it an invention of the time of Theodosius.

[2] On the *Antoninianus* in the 3rd cent. see A. Cesano in de Ruggiero, *Diz. epigr.* iii, pp. 1624 ff.; E. Babelon, *Traité des monnaies*, i, pp. 610 ff.; A. Segrè, Καινὸν Νόμισμα, *Rend. Lincei*, 16, 1920, pp. 4 ff.; P. H. Webb, *Num. Chr.* 1927, pp. 314 ff.; H. Mattingly, ibid., pp. 219 ff.; P. H. Webb in Mattingly and Sydenham, *The Roman Imp. Coinage*, vi (1927), pp. 8 ff. and 248 ff.; cf. Mattingly, ibid., p. 14. Cf. Chap. IX, note 32, and on the value of the Antoninianus at Dura, C. B. Welles, *Excav. at Dura-Europos*, Prelim. Rep. iv (1933), pp. 140 ff. [See *Excavations at Dura-Europos*, Final Report vi, The Coins, by A. R. Bellinger (New Haven, 1949)].

[3] F. Oertel, 'Der Niedergang der hellenistischen Kultur in Ägypten', *Neue Jahrb.* 45, 1920, pp. 375 f.; A. Segrè, *Circolazione monetaria e prezzi nel mondo antico* (1922); J. Kell, *Forsch. Eph.* iii, pp. 102 ff., nos. 10–12 (bread price doubled between A.D. 100 and 200).

[4] See Chap. V, note 47.

⁵ *P.Oxyr.* 1411 (A.D. 260). It is possible that the troubled conditions of the short rule of Macrianus and Quietus contributed to the general insecurity which prevailed in Egypt throughout the 3rd cent. On the preference for Ptolemaic silver in the 3rd cent. A.D. see C. Wessely, *Mitt. P.R.* iv, pp. 144 ff. The earlier orders probably emphasized the principle embodied in the utterance of Epict. *Diss.* iii. 3. 3, which is quoted in Chap. V, note 47.

⁶ G. Billeter, *Geschichte des Zinsfusses im griechisch-römischen Altertum bis auf Justinian* (1898), pp. 211 ff. Cf. A. Segrè, 'Il mutuo e il tasso d'interesse nell'Egitto greco-romano', *Atene e Roma*, 1924, pp. 119–38.

⁷ B. Laum, *Stiftungen in der griechischen und römischen Antike*, i (1914), pp. 8 ff.; cf. p. 255.

⁸ See Chap. III, notes 15–18, and Chap. V, note 19; cf. Chap. V, note 20, on the trade through Palmyra. The destruction of Palmyra by Aurelian was fatal to the Eastern land-trade in general, and so was the conquest of South Russia, and especially of Panticapaeum, by the Goths. Cf. the articles quoted in note 2.

⁹ On Dacia see the articles quoted in Chap. X, note 7, and cf. the paper of Jorga read before the French Academy on 22 Feb. 1924, *C.R. Acad. Inscr.* 1924, p. 66. Jorga's conclusions, however, which were opposed at the meeting by F. Lot, cannot be accepted. On Panticapaeum, M. Rostovtzeff, *Iranians and Greeks in South Russia*, p. 155, and in *Mon. Piot*, 26, 1923, pp. 99 ff.

¹⁰ *Scr. Hist. Aug.* Prob. 16. 4; Zos. i. 69; J. H. E. Crees, *Reign of Probus*, pp. 106 ff. and 159. It is worth noting that Probus settled many of his veterans in Isauria with the same purpose of pacifying the land and securing a constant supply of well-trained soldiers as the Severi had in founding similar settlements in Africa, on the Danube, and on the Rhine; see Chap. IX, notes 48–52.

¹¹ *Scr. Hist. Aug.* Prob. 17; Zos. i. 71. 1. The advance of this wild tribe probably coincided with the fall of the kingdom of Meroë and with the rise of the kingdom of Axûm. They were allies of the Palmyrenes and supporters of the usurper Firmus (*Scr. Hist. Aug.* Firm. 5). The victory of Probus over them was only a temporary success. Diocletian was forced to cede to them the Dodecaschoinos, and the Blemmyes remained the terror of Egypt for many centuries to come: see Wilcken, *Grundz.*, pp. 30 f. and 68 ff., cf. *Chrest.* 6; W. Schubart, *Einführung*, p. 241, cf. p. 147; J. Lesquier, *L'Armée romaine d'Égypte*, pp. 33 ff., and the literature concerning Nubia given in Chap. VII, notes 53 ff.

¹² R. Cagnat, *L'Armée romaine d'Afrique*², i, pp. 53 ff.; *ILA* 609, 610; L. Chatelain, *C. R. Acad. Inscr.* 1919, pp. 352 ff. The last extension of the frontier to the South was carried out by Gordian III: cf. J. Carcopino, *Rev. ét. anc.* 25, 1923, pp. 33 ff. [cf. *L'An. ép.* 1923, 95–98], *Rev. arch.* 1924 (2), pp. 316 ff., and *Syria*, 6, 1925, pp. 30 ff.

¹³ Such at least is the opinion of the best authority on Roman Britain, the late F. Haverfield, *Romanization of Roman Britain*⁴ (1923), pp. 76 f. What he says, however, about Gaul cannot be accepted. For Gaul the 3rd cent. was a time of great disasters. A sort of peace and stability came later, after Diocletian.

¹⁴ *Scr. Hist. Aug.* Aur. 7. 4 and 5.

¹⁵ A careful enumeration of plagues may be found in Zos. i. 26, 36, 37, 45, and 46. His description of the plague under Gallienus is striking (i. 37): ἐν ἐσχάτῳ δὲ καὶ τῶν ἐν Ἰλλυριοῖς πραγμάτων ἐκ τῆς τῶν Σκυθῶν ἐφόδου διακειμένων καὶ πάσης τῆς ὑπὸ Ῥωμαίους ἀρχῆς ἐς τὸ μηκέτι λοιπὸν εἶναι σαλευομένης, λοιμὸς ἐπιβρίσας ταῖς πόλεσιν, οἷος οὔπω πρότερον ἐν παντὶ τῷ χρόνῳ συνέβη, τὰς μὲν ἀπὸ τῶν βαρβάρων συμφορὰς μετριωτέρας ἀπέφηνεν, τοῖς δὲ τῇ νόσῳ κατειλημμένοις εὐδαιμονίζειν ἑαυτοὺς ἐδίδου καὶ τὰς ἑαλωκυίας ἤδη πόλεις, ἀνδρῶν παν-

τάπασι γενομένας ἐρήμους. Th. Reinach, *Rev. ét. gr.* 19, 1906, p. 142, no. 75; a citizen of Aphrodisias λουτροῖς καὶ σιταρχίαις λοιμὸν καὶ λιμὸν ἀπελάσαντα (time of the Severi or later?). The baneful practice of the exposure of children and of procured abortions, of little importance in prosperous times, may have been one of the causes of depopulation in the 3rd cent. See C. Appleton, *La Longévité et l'avortement volontaire aux premiers siècles de notre ère* (Lyons, 1920); H. Bennet, *Class. Journ.* 18, 1923, pp. 341 ff.; cf. *TAPA* 53, 1922, pp. xvii–xviii; F. Maroi, 'Intorno all'adozione degli esposti nell'Egitto romano', *Racc. Lumbroso*, pp. 377 ff.; J. Carcopino, 'Le Droit romain d'exposition des enfants et le Gnomon de l'idiologue', *Mém. Soc. Ant. de France*, 77, 1928, pp. 59 ff. If Severus issued a special edict against exposure, this means that matters were serious enough; but the edict probably achieved little.

¹⁶ I shall quote later certain papyri from Egypt which refer to flights as a quite common and almost natural occurrence. Measures against decurions leaving their place of residence and trying to settle down in other cities were taken as early as the time of the Severi: see Ulp. *Dig.* 50. 2. 1.

¹⁷ Brigandage raged all over the Roman Empire. A detachment of sailors was sent to Umbria to fight bandits in the time of Philip, *CIL* xi. 6107 = Dessau, *ILS* 509 (A.D. 246). Compare the two *praefecti arcendis latrociniis* in Germany, *CIL* xiii. 5010 = Dessau, *ILS* 7007 (Noviodunum) and 6211 (Treveri); cf. O. Hirschfeld, 'Die Sicherheitspolizei im römischen Kaiserreich', *Kl. Schr.*, p. 610. Some tribes in the mountains resumed their inborn habit of organized robbery and practised it on a large scale. I have mentioned the Isaurians in Asia Minor; the same is true of some tribes in the Maritime Alps, *Scr. Hist. Aug.* Proc. 12. 1–3. On the revolt of peasants in Sicily, which took the form of a regular pillage of the province, *Scr. Hist. Aug.* Gall. 4. 9. On robbery at sea, *IGRR* iii. 481 [= Dessau, *ILS* 8870: quoted in full, note 24, below] (A.D. 253). On robbery in general, O. Hirschfeld, *Kl. Schr.*, pp. 591 ff.; L. Friedländer–G. Wissowa, *Sitteng. Roms*⁹, i, pp. 350 ff. (without discrimination of time); see also G. Cantacuzène, *Aegyptus*, 9, 1928, p. 69. A soldier (l. 46) is said to have been *occisus a latronibus* in a *pridianum* of the First Spanish Cohort, in the time of Trajan. Conditions were of course exceptional. In this recently occupied and barely appeased country, the task of maintaining order was the responsibility of the military garrisons rather than of the cities: cf. Chap. VI, note 82. Though most of the inscriptions which mention robbers cannot be dated, it is to be noted that most of the literary sources which speak of robbery as a common thing belong to the end of the 2nd or to the 3rd cent. A.D. (e.g. Apuleius and the novels). We may admit that the improved organization of the military police—the development of the institution of *frumentarii, colletiones, speculatores, beneficiarii,* and *stationarii,* who all played their part in combating brigandage—was due to the political preoccupations of the emperors and was used for the purpose of hunting out political suspects. Nevertheless, the fact that it was in the 3rd cent. that the institution of field *gendarmes* was systematically developed, and a well-planned network of military posts (*stationes*) of *beneficiarii* and of *stationarii* was devised and methodically established, shows how bad were the conditions and how powerless the cities to fight the plague of brigandage. On the *beneficiarii* see A. von Domaszewski, *Westd. Zeitschr.* 21, 1902, pp. 158 ff., and in *Röm. Mitt.* 17, 1902, pp. 330 ff.; J. Schwendemann, *Der hist. Wert der Vita Marci,* pp. 70 ff., and Chap. IX, note 7; cf. note 26 below. On the *speculatores* and their journeys, see my article in *Röm. Mitt.* 26, 1911, pp. 267 ff.; on the insignia and the functions of the *beneficiarii* and *speculatores,* E. Ritterling, *Bonn. Jahrb.* 125, 1920, pp. 9 ff.; M. Abramič, *Starinar* (1922) (in Serbian); cf. on the *beneficiarii* and *statores* my article in *Excavations at Dura-Europos,* Prelim. Rep. i (1929), pp. 56 ff.; on the *stationarii* and their quasi-judicial activity, especially in Asia Minor, O. Hirschfeld, 'Sicherheitspolizei',

in *Kl. Schriften*, pp. 596 ff., and on the *stationarii* on the imperial estates, id. *Die k. Verwaltungsb.*², p. 134, note 3; J. Keil–A. von Premerstein, *Erste Reise*, p. 50, no. 101; *Zweite Reise*, p. 115, no. 222; *Dritte Reise*, p. 28, no. 28, and p. 11, no. 9. A special quasi-municipal εἰρηνάρχης (the slave of an emperor) appears in *OGIS* 550. A group of εἰρήναρχοι and διωγμῖται is mentioned in inscriptions recorded by them in the sanctuary-cave of In-Daghinda Qogia-in in Pamphylia: see G. Moretti, *Ann. d. R. sc. arch. di Atene*, 6–7, 1923–4, pp. 509 ff., esp. no. 3, where I read εἰρήναρ|χος Μόσ|χος διω|γμῖται Εὔκαρ|πος Μεννέ |ας Ἔρως; cf. no. 5, where I would read Ἀννιανὸς διω|γμείτης Σύν|τροφος | διω[γμεί]της (after the first ΔΙΩ Moretti reads ΕΡΜΕΤΗΣ) [= *SEG* vi. 688, 690]. The same readings are given by L. Robert, *BCH* 52, 1928, pp. 407 ff., who also gives, p. 408, note 3 and p. 409, note 2, a complete bibliography concerning εἰρήναρχοι and διωγμῖται. Cf. Chap. VII, note 106, and pl. LXXIV. My impression is that in the 1st and 2nd centuries the cities were fairly successful in combating robbery, and that it was the misery of the second half of the 2nd cent. and of the 3rd that revived the plague and forced the emperors to organize strong corps of military police, and to insist that the cities should take a more active part in suppressing brigandage by introducing new municipal offices of a liturgical character with a wide-reaching responsibility. Such were the 'guardians of the peace' (εἰρηνάρχαι) in Asia Minor, an institution which gradually spread to other Eastern provinces, like the institution of the *decaprotia* (O. Hirschfeld, 'Sicherheitspolizei', *Kl. Schr.*, pp. 605 ff., and *Forsch. Eph.* iii, no. 70; cf. the special police of the temple of Ephesos: *L'An. ép.* 1926, no. 15) and the *praefecti arcendis latrociniis* in some provinces of the West. On Egypt see Chap. IX, note 45, and note 54 below. In Syria in the 3rd and 4th cent. A.D. the police were called δεκαδάρχαι and had several villages under their supervision: see Mouterde, *Syria*, 6, 1925, pp. 243 ff. (commentary on the funerary inscription of a man who had been killed περὶ μηδενός by a δεκαδάρχης). Cf. F. Cumont, *Rend. Pont. Accad. Arch.* 5, 1927, pp. 73 ff., and W. Vollgraff, *Syria*, 7, 1926, p. 283. Cf. also Ch. Torrey, *Excavs. at Dura-Europos*, Prelim. Rep. i, p. 63, and M. Rostovtzeff, ibid., p. 59, note 1. The same is true of Italy; see Mommsen, *Röm. Staatsr.*³ ii, p. 1075, notes 1 and 2. The conditions did not change in the early 4th cent.: see the inscription of Thuburbo Majus in Africa, *ILA* 269, an imperial letter in reply to complaints about the *beneficiarii*.

¹⁸ There is no other explanation of the repeated settlements of captured barbarians and the assignment of land to barbarian tribes, which were so common in the 3rd cent. The fact that it was possible to evacuate Dacia and to find room for its population in other provinces of the Danube region attests the depopulation both of Dacia and of the other Danube lands. See, further, the quotations made below from the plaint of the villagers of Scaptopare, *Syll.*³ 888, especially ll. 53 ff.: 'We have declared that we can endure no longer, and we intend to leave our ancestral homes because of the violence of our visitors. For in truth we have been reduced from many householders to a very few' (ἐδηλώσαμεν γὰρ μηκέτι ἡμᾶς δύνασθαι ὑπομένειν, ἀλλὰ καὶ νοῦν ἔχομεν ἐγκαταλιπεῖν καὶ τοὺς πατρῴους θεμελίους διὰ τὴν τῶν ἐπερχομένων ἡμεῖν βίαν. καὶ γὰρ ὡς ἀληθῶς ἀπὸ πολλῶν οἰκοδεσποτῶν εἰς ἐλαχίστους κατεληλύθαμεν). Cf. the inscription of Araguë (quoted in note 26), l. 34: καὶ τὰ χωρία ἐρημοῦσθαι καὶ ἀν[άστατα γίγνεσθαι]. The evidence for the settlements of barbarians has been often collected; see, e.g. O. Seeck, i, p. 384, 12 and 21 (p. 532), and, for the time of M. Aurelius, J. Schwendemann, *Der hist. Wert der Vita Marci*, p. 53; cf. E. Bickermann, *Das Edikt des Kaisers Caracalla in P.Giss. 40* (Diss., Berlin, 1926), pp. 23 ff. Barbarians were very early settled in Roman territory; see for instance the inscription of Plautius Silvanus Aelianus, Dessau, *ILS* 986 = *CIL* xiv. 3608 (Neronian age), and the settlement of 50,000 barbarians on the Roman border of the Danube ordered by Augustus, Strab. vii. 310 c, and A. von Premerstein, *Öst. Jahresh.* 1, 1898, Beibl. pp. 145 ff.

[19] On malaria see H. Nissen, *Italische Landeskunde*, i, pp. 413 ff.; W. H. S. Jones, *Liverpool Annals of Archaeology and Anthropology*, 2, 1909, pp. 97 ff., and the articles 'Febris' in Pauly–Wissowa, Daremberg–Saglio, and de Ruggiero. There is, however, no sufficient evidence for the spread of malaria in Italy in the 2nd and 3rd centuries, and it is a question whether the depopulation of Latium, Etruria, and South Italy was due chiefly to malaria or whether the spread of malaria was due to depopulation.

[20] Everybody who is familiar with the work of excavation in the Roman provinces, and with the local museums of antiquities, knows what an enormous contrast there is between the archaeological material of the 2nd cent. and the second half of the 3rd. One of the most striking features of the 3rd cent. is the further decentralization of manufacturing activity, the gradual disappearance of imported articles (even when there were industrial centres near at hand), and the predominance of local ware. Another feature is the poverty of the graves of this period. The insecurity of the times is attested by the frequency of the so-called 'coin hoards'. But the most convincing and the simplest test is a comparison of the coins of the period of the Antonines and of the Severi with those of the second half of the 3rd cent. We find an almost complete lack of new types, frequent mistakes in the inscriptions, and a bald and rough style—a real desert in comparison with the still blossoming coinage of the earlier times. The same observation applies to the monumental art of the period, apart from the portraits. We have only to compare the bas-reliefs of the column of M. Aurelius and the monuments of Septimius Severus with such later products as the bas-reliefs of the arch of Constantine and of the arch of Galerius at Salonica. It is to be noted that the second half of the 3rd cent. produced no important public monuments, except those of Aurelian.

[21] The measure by which Aurelian made the cities responsible for waste and abandoned land is well known (*Cod. Just.* 11. 58. 1). I doubt whether it was the first measure of the kind. The practice at least was much older (my *Studien z. Gesch. röm. Kol.*, p. 395). The increase of waste land, and especially the decay of viticulture, in Italy is also attested by Aurelian's well-known attempt to revive this branch of husbandry by distributing families of war-captives among the owners of abandoned vineyards (*Scr. Hist. Aug.* Aurel. 48. 2; L. Homo, *Aurélien*, p. 150; E. Groag in Pauly–Wissowa, v, col. 1410). We have already mentioned that the economic decay of Italy affected the food-supply of the city of Rome, and forced the emperors (especially Aurelian) to nationalize this branch of the administration of the capital. The hopeless decay of the culture of the vine in Italy explains the liberal policy of Probus in regard to its cultivation in the provinces (*Scr. Hist. Aug.* Prob. 18. 8). The measures adopted for the protection of viticulture in Italy were futile, as there was now very little to protect. The reform of Probus enabled Gaul at least to revive again; cf. C. Jullian, *Histoire de la Gaule*, iv, p. 609; J. H. E. Crees, *Reign of Probus*, pp. 142 f. His ordinance, attested as it is not only by the Latin biographer but also by Victor and Eutropius, is certainly genuine. How far the early restrictions on viticulture in the provinces were still in force before his reign cannot be ascertained; but there is no doubt that neither South Gaul nor Spain nor Dalmatia was subject to any such restrictions, to say nothing of the Oriental provinces, including Thrace.

[22] Chap. VII, note 31.

[23] See above, note 17. The Lydius of Zosimus (Palfurius of the Latin biographer) was probably one of the local chiefs, a member of the local aristocracy and a Roman citizen. His full name perhaps was Palfurius Lydius: the Palfurii Surae were a good Roman family, which still survived in the 3rd cent. (*Scr. Hist. Aug.* Gall. 18. 6). If so, the Isaurian hero would appear in quite a different light, as a local dynast, like the

dynasts of Palmyra, Emesa, Edessa, &c., and not as a common robber. The colonization of the land by Roman soldiers after the death of Lydius shows that separatist tendencies were very strong in the country of the Isaurians.

24 *IGRR* iii. 481 = Dessau, *ILS* 8870 (cf. A. von Domaszewski, *Rh. Mus.* 58, 1903, pp. 382 ff., and *Gesch. d. röm. Kaiser*, ii, p. 297; *PIR* iv, p. 378, no. 137): Οὐαλέριον Στατείλιον Κᾶστον τὸν κράτιστον σύμμαχον τῶν Σεβαστῶν, πραιπόσιτον βιξιλατιώνων Τερμησσέων τῶν πρὸς Οἰνοάνδοις ἡ βουλὴ καὶ ὁ δῆμος καὶ ἡ γερουσία τὸν εὐεργέτην προνοησάμενον τῆς εἰρήνης κατὰ θάλασσαν καὶ κατὰ γῆν, ἐπιδημήσαντα τῇ λαμπρᾷ ἡμῶν πόλει μετὰ πάσης εὐκοσμίας ἡμερῶν ιβ', ἀγαγόντα δὲ καὶ ἱππέριον φιλοτίμως ἐν τῷ λουσωρίῳ τῇ πρὸ ε' εἰδ(ῶν) Νοεμβρίω[ν] ἐν ᾗ [ἡ]μέρᾳ ἐκομίσθη [ε]ἰκὼν ἱερὰ τοῦ κυρίου ἡμῶν Οὐαλεριανοῦ νέου Σεβαστοῦ. Cf. *Forsch. Eph.* iii, no. 38.

25 *Scr. Hist. Aug.* Proc. 12. 1–3: 'Proculo patria Albingauni fuere, positi in Alpibus maritimis. domi nobilis sed maioribus latrocinantibus atque adeo pecore ac servis et is rebus, quas abduxerat, satis dives. fertur denique eo tempore quo sumpsit imperium duo milia servorum suorum armasse. . . .' 5: 'idemque fortissimus, ipse quoque latrociniis adsecutus, qui tamen armatam semper egerit vitam.'

26 The inscription was found and first published by J. G. C. Anderson in *JHS* 17, 1897, pp. 417 ff., cf. A. Schulten, *Röm. Mitt.* 13, 1898, pp. 231 ff.; J. G. C. Anderson, *JHS* 18, 1898, pp. 340 ff. = *OGIS* 519 = *CIL* iii. 14191; my article in *Klio*, 6, 1906, pp. 249 ff.; J. Keil–A. von Premerstein, *Dritte Reise*, p. 12. The attempts to restore this inscription have not taken into account the fact that the lines of the document (the right border is mutilated) were much shorter than has usually been supposed. This is shown by the first lines, which can be restored with full certainty. The numbers of letters missing, according to my calculation, are approximately 12 to 13 in the first 14 lines; 15 to 16 in ll. 15–17; 18 in ll. 18–20; 21 in ll. 21–23, and about 23 to 25 in the last lines of the document. I may, therefore, suggest a new restoration of the inscription. Considerations of space forbid a discussion of the former attempts; Ἀγαθῇ Τύχῃ | Imp. Caes. M. [Julius P]hi[lippus p. f. Aug.] et [M. Julius Philippu]s n[o]bi[l]issimus Caes. M. Au[r. Eglecto] | pe[r] Didymum mil(item) cen(tenarium) frum(entarium): proco[n]sule v. c. perspecta fide eorum quae [adlegastis si] | quid iniuriose geratur, ad sollicitudinem suam revocabit. [v]a[l]e. | Αὐτοκράτορι Καίσαρι Μ. Ἰουλίῳ Φιλίππῳ Εὐσεβεῖ Εὐτυχεῖ Σεβ(αστῷ) κ[αὶ Μ. Ἰουλίῳ] | Φιλίππῳ ἐπιφανεστάτῳ Καίσαρι δέησις παρὰ Αὐρηλίου Ἐγλέκτ[ου περὶ τοῦ κοι]|νοῦ τῶν Ἀραγουηνῶν παροίκων καὶ γεωργῶν τῶν ὑμετέρων [τοῦ ἐν τῇ Ἀππια]νῇ δήμου κοινο(ῦ Τ)οττεανων Σοηνων τῶν κατὰ Φρυγίαν τόπων διὰ Τ. Οὐ[λπίου Διδύμου] | στρατιώτου· πάντων ἐν τοῖς μακαριωτάτοις ὑμῶν καιροῖς, εὐσεβέσ[τατοι καὶ ἀλυ]|πότατοι τῶν πώποτε βασιλέων, ἤρεμον καὶ γαληνὸν τὸν βίον διαγ[όντων πάσης πο]|νηρίας καὶ διασεισμῶν πε[π]αυμένων, μόνοι ἡμεῖς ἀλλότρια τῶν ε[ὐτυχεστά]|των] | καιρῶν πάσχοντες τήνδε τὴν ἱκέτειαν [ὑ]μεῖν προσάγομεν. ἔχε[ται δὲ τὸ τῆς δε]|ήσεως ἐν τούτοις· χωρίον ὑμέτερον [ἐ]σμεν, ἱερώτατ[οι αὐτοκράτορες, δῆ]|μος ὁλόκληρος οἱ καταφεύγοντες κ(αὶ) γεινόμενοι τῆς ὑμετέρας [θειότητος ἱκέται· δια]|σειόμεθα δὲ παρὰ τὸ ἄλογον καὶ παραπρασσό|μεθα ὑπ' ἐκείνων ο[ἷς σώζειν τὸ δημό]|σιον ὀφ(ε)ίλει· μεσόγειοι γὰρ τυγχάνοντες καὶ μ[ή]τε (read μηδὲ) παρὰ στρατα[ρχίαις ὄντες πάσ]|χομεν ἀλλότρια τῶν ὑμετέρων μακαριωτάτων καιρων· [διοδεύοντες γὰρ] τὸ Ἀππιανῶν κλίμα παραλιμπάνοντες τὰς λεωφόρους ὁ[δοὺς στρατάρχαι τε κ(αὶ) στρα]|τιῶται κ(αὶ) δυνάσται τῶν προυχόντων κ[ατ]ὰ τὴν πόλιν [Καισαριανοί τε ὑ]|μέτεροι ἐπεισε[ρ]χόμενοι καὶ καταλιμπάνοντες τὰς λε[ωφόρους ὁδοὺς καὶ ἀπὸ τῶν] | ἔργων ἡμᾶς ἀφιστάντες καὶ τοὺς ἀροτῆρας βόας ἀνγ[αρεύοντες τὰ μηδὲν ὀφει]|λόμενα αὐτοῖς παραπράσσουσι· καὶ συμβαίνει οὐ [τὰ τυχόντα ἡμᾶς ἐκ τ]|ούτου ἀδικεῖσθαι διασεισμένους· περὶ ὧν ἅπα[ξ ἤδη κατήλθομεν ἐς τὸ σόν, ὦ] | Σεβαστέ, μέγεθος, ὁπότε τὴν ἔπαρχον διεῖπε[ς ἀρχὴν ἐμφαίνοντες τὸ γεγο]|νός. καὶ ὅπως περὶ τούτων ἐκειν[ή]θη σου ἡ θε[ία ψυχή, ἐπιστολὴ δηλοῖ ἡ] | ἐντεταγμένη· quae libe[l]lo complexi esti[s, ad procos. misimus] | qui dabit operam ne d[iu]tiu⟨i⟩s querell[is locus sit]. ἐπειδὴ οὖν οὐδὲν ὄφελο[ς ἡ]μεῖν ἐκ ταύτης τ[ῆς δεήσεως γέγονε, συνβέ]|βηκεν

δὲ ἡμᾶς κατὰ τὴν ἀγροικίαν τὰ μὴ ὀφει[λόμενα παραπράσσεσθαι, ἐ]|πενβαινό[ν]των τινῶν
καὶ συνπατούντων ἡμᾶς [παρὰ τὸ δίκαιον, ὡσαύτως δ]|ὲ ὑπὸ τῶν Καισαριανῶν οὐ τὰ τυχόντα
δι[ασ]είεσ[θαι καὶ τὰ ἡμέτερα εἰς αὐτοὺς] | [ἐξαναλί]σκεσθαι καὶ τὰ χωρία ἐρημοῦσθαι καὶ ἀν[άσ-
τατα γίγνεσθαι· μεσόγειοι γὰρ] | [τυγχάνοντε]s καὶ οὐ παρὰ τ[ὴν ὁ]δὸν κατοικοῦντες. . . . .
(There follow a few remains of two more lines, below which the stone is fractured.)
In this short note I cannot defend the new suggestions which I have introduced into
the text, but a word may be said on the new reading which I have suggested in l. 2:
mil(*item*) *cen*(*tenarium*) *frum*(*entarium*). It follows exactly the facsimile given in Anderson's second article. The title *centenarius* applied to a *frumentarius* is new for the 3rd cent.
A.D., but in the 4th cent. it is commonly applied to the successors of the *frumentarii*, the
agentes in rebus. On the *frumentarii* see O. Hirschfeld, 'Sicherheitspolizei', *Kl. Schr.*,
pp. 588 and 592; D. Vaglieri in de Ruggiero, *Diz. epigr.* iii, pp. 221 ff.; Fiebiger
in Pauly–Wissowa, vii, cols. 122 ff.; P. K. Baillie Reynolds, *JRS* 13, 1923, pp. 177
and 183 ff.; cf. Chap. VIII, note 11, and Chap. IX, note 7. On the *agentes in rebus* and
the title *centenarius* applied to them, cf. O Hirschfeld, 'Die agentes in rebus', *Kl. Schr.*,
pp. 624 ff., especially pp. 626 ff.

27 *CIL* iii. 12336 = *IGRR* i. 674 = *Syll.*³ 888; cf. F. Preisigke, 'Die Inschrift
von Skaptoparene in ihrer Beziehung zur kaiserlichen Kanzlei in Rom', *Schr.
d. Wiss. Ges. in Strassburg*, 1917 (30); M. Rostovtzeff, *JRS* 8, 1918, p. 33; Wilcken,
Hermes, 55, 1920, pp. 1 ff.; cf. H. Dessau, *Hermes*, 62, 1927, pp. 205 ff., and Wilcken,
Arch. f. Papyr. 9, pp. 15 ff. In the early 4th cent. the police agents remained as
troublesome as they used to be in the 3rd cent. The reforms of Diocletian and of
Constantine effected no improvement in their behaviour. See the fragments of a letter
of an emperor in reply to complaints about the exactions of the *beneficiarii*, found at
Thuburbo Majus in Africa (A.D. 315–18?). At the end there comes a curious tariff of
fees which the *beneficiarii* were entitled to receive.

28 *P.Oxyr.* 1477. In the introduction to this papyrus Grenfell quotes the other
papyri of the same type, all of an earlier date.

29 C. Wessely, *Catal. P.R.* 75 (3rd–4th cent. A.D.).

30 P. Jouguet, *Papyrus de Théadelphie* (1911).

31 Unpublished *P.Wis.*, inv. 56. I owe a transcription of the text to the kindness of
Prof. A. G. Laird of the University of Wisconsin. On the territory of Philadelphia,
cf. M. Rostovtzeff, *A Large Estate*, pp. 13 f.

32 C. Wessely, *Catal. P.R.* 58 (A.D. 265/6) from Hermupolis Magna, col. ii, ll. 13 ff.:
ὀλίγην μὲν ἄμπε|λον ζωφυτοῦσ[αν] καὶ [τ]αύτην ἐν [..].ωτάτῳ ἀμελίᾳ οὖσαν καὶ ἔνθρυον, κύκλῳ
δὲ τοῦ | χωρίου χέρσον πολλὴν καὶ θρύ[ον]; cf. col. iii, l. 4: γενάμ[ενοι δὲ ε]ἰς ἕτερον χω[ρίον]
ἐπεθεωρήσαμεν αὐτὸ μὲν [κείμενον ὅ]λον ἐν χέρσῳ [..] καὶ ἄχρηστον. Compare, also, the
well-known *P.Rain.* xix = Mitteis, *Chrest.* 69 (A.D. 330) of Hermupolis; cf. C. Wessely,
Catal. P.R. p. 86, and my *Studien z. Gesch. röm. Kol.*, pp. 198 ff. The description of one
part of the estate is as follows, ll. 3 ff.: ὧν τὸ | καθ' ἐν οὕτως ἔχει· ἀμπελικὸν χωρίον ὑπὸ τέλους
(ἀρουρῶν) ηLῑsλβ′, καλαμίας (ἄρουραι) γη′, πωμαρίου (ἄρουρα) Lῆ, ἅπαντα νυνὶ | ἐν χέρσῳ
καὶ τὰ ἐν αὐτῷ οἰκόπεδα καὶ ἐκ νότου τούτου γεώργιον καλούμενον Πώλυπον, ὅσου ἐστὶν ἀρουρηδοῦ |
καὶ οὐσιακῆς γῆς ὑπὸ τέλους (ἄρουραι) μβ Lῆ καὶ τὴν πᾶσαν χέρσον κα ἄσπορον τὴν ἐν αὐτῇ. The
property consists of parcels of private vineyards and gardens and of a large plot of
imperial land. See also *SB* 7630, an ἀπογραφὴ of abandoned olive-groves.

33 *Scr. Hist. Aug.* Prob. 9. 3.

34 *P.Oxyr.* 1409 (A.D. 278); cf. W. L. Westermann, *Aegyptus*, 1, 1920, pp. 297 ff. See
especially the sanction: ἐὰν γὰρ τοιοῦτο ἐπιχειρ[ῆσ]αι τολμή[σ]η ἢ τῶν πρ[οστετα]γμένων
ἀμελήσῃ, ἴστω ὅτι ὡς λυμαινόμενος τοῖς ἐπὶ τῇ σωτηρίᾳ συνπά[ση]s τῆς Αἰγύπτου προηρ[ημέ]-

νοις οὐ μόνον περὶ χρημάτων ἀλλὰ καὶ περὶ αὐτῆς τῆς ψυχῆς τὸν ἀγῶνα ἔξε[ι. Cf. Chap. IX, note 15.

35 *P.Oxyr.* 1469 (A.D. 298).

36 *P.Oxyr.* 1413 (A.D. 270–5), ll. 25 ff. I have not been able to make use of the book of S. Singalevich, *The Senate of Oxyrhynchus in the 3rd Cent. of our Era* (Kharkoff, 1913) (in Russian), dealing with the important papyri which illustrate the activity of the βουλή of Oxyrhynchus in the 3rd cent.; cf. U. E. P(aoli), *Riv. fil.* 43, 1913, pp. 178 f. Cf. a similar document of the 4th cent., *P.Oxyr.* 2110 (A.D. 370), and the Princeton papyrus of the early 4th cent., H. B. van Hoesen and A. Ch. Johnson, *JEA* 12, 1926, pp. 118 ff. [= *SB* 7261]; cf. U. Wilcken, *Arch. f. Papyr.* 8, p. 314.

37 *P.Oxyr.* 1419 (A.D. 265).

38 *P.Oxyr.* 1194 (A.D. 263).

39 *P.Oxyr.* 1115 (A.D. 281).

40 *P.Oxyr.* 1543 (A.D. 299): πρὸς διάδοσιν τοῖς διοδεύουσιν γεννεοτάτοις στρατιώταις.

41 C. Wessely, *Catal. P.R.* 84, col. i, ll. 1 ff.: Ἑρμοπολείτου | βρέουιον ἐκταγέντων ἀνακο-μι|σθῆσαι εἰδῶν εὐθενιακῶν καὶ τῶν ἀπ' αὐτῶν ἀνακομισθέντων εἰς τὴν | ι' τὴν ἐνεστῶσαν ἡμέραν. The stuffs are corn, chaff, wine, and meat. Special προπομποί were appointed.

42 On compulsory deliveries of various kinds in the 2nd cent. and in the first years of the 3rd see Chap. VIII, note 35, and Chap. IX, note 45. There is no doubt that, as a rule, the forced delivery was regarded as a compulsory purchase and that money was really paid for the stuffs, J. Lesquier, *L'Armée romaine d'Égypte*, pp. 258 ff. One of the most striking examples is the delivery of clothes by the weavers of Soknopaiu Nesos for the soldiers of the army of Judaea in A.D. 128 (*P.Ryl.* ii. 189); cf. *P.Tebt.* 347. 12, and P. Gradenwitz quoted in *P.Hib.* 67. 10, note. Similar provisions for the army of Cappadocia and for the hospital of the *ratio castrensis* of Rome are mentioned in A.D. 238 at Philadelphia (*BGU* 1564), cf. Chap. V, note 44. As late as A.D. 232 the officials of Alexander Severus paid for the clothes which were delivered to the soldiers in accordance with an order of the prefect, *PSI* 797. Compare this practice with the deliveries of ἐσθὴς στρατιωτική in the 4th cent., *P.Lips.* 45, 46, 48–60; Wilcken, *Grundz.*, p. 362, and of clothing for the gladiators, *P.Lips.* 57. 6–11. Cf. also *P.Oxyr.* 1424 (about A.D. 318), 1428, and 1448, and *PSI* 781. On the organization of the collection of the *annona* in the 3rd cent. see P. Jouguet, *La vie municipale*, pp. 387 ff.; Wilcken, *Grundz.*, p. 360; *P.Oxyr.* 1115 and 1419; C. Wessely, *Catal. P.R.* 84; *PSI* 795. The fact that payments for the *annona militaris* were sometimes made in the 4th cent. does not prove that such was the regular practice in the 3rd cent. The same practice, i.e. probably requisition without actual remuneration, seems to have been introduced into the other provinces of the Roman Empire and into Italy; see, e.g. the interesting inscription of A. Vitellius Felix belonging to the time of Gallienus found in Thugga, *CIL* viii. 26582. All the offices held by this man are connected with transportation and with the collection of rents from imperial estates, especially in Africa. One of the most important offices was 'p(rae)p(ositus) agens per Campaniam, Calabriam, Lucaniam, Picenum annonam curans militibus Aug. n.'

43 *P.Oxyr.* 1490 (late 3rd cent. A.D.).

44 I have dealt with the transportation of state goods in Egypt in three special articles, in *Arch. f. Papyr.* 3, 215 ff., in *Klio*, 6, 1906, pp. 253 ff., and in Pauly–Wissowa, vii, cols. 169 ff.; cf. Wilcken, *Grundz.*, p. 370, and F. Oertel, *Die Liturgie*, pp. 115 ff. I have since modified the views expressed in these articles in regard to transport by land. Transportation from the local storehouses to the river or to the canal was certainly carried out by the guilds of ὀνηλάται and of καμηλοτρόφοι. Responsibility for the transport rested either with the municipal magistrates, to whom the village administration was responsible in its turn for payments due from the villages, or with the municipal magistrates and the great landowners. I find it hard to explain the receipts of Theadelphia in the names of Appian (a big landowner, one of the chiefs of Heroninus, see below, note 59) and Sodikes as receipts given to ναύκληροι, agents of the government for land-transport. I now regard both Appian and Sodikes as large landowners and lessees of imperial lands, who were responsible for the transportation of their payments to the landing-places. For this purpose they used either their own donkeys and camels or, as a rule, those of the guilds. See F. Preisigke, *Arch. f. Papyr.* 3, pp. 44 ff.; my own articles, ibid., pp. 223 ff., in *Klio*, 6, 1906, p. 253, and in Pauly–Wissowa, vii, col. 163; F. Oertel, *Die Liturgie*, pp. 117, 122, note 6, 431. Cf. *P.Oxyr.* 2131 (A.D. 207) and the documents of *c.* A.D. 163 concerning the affairs of a group of καμηλοτρόφοι, studied by C. W. Keyes, *JEA* 15, 1929, pp. 160 ff. Compare the responsibility of special *curatores frumenti Alexandrini* (ἐπιμεληταὶ σίτου Ἀλεξανδρείας), who were members of the municipal councils, for the river-transport from the Nile to Alexandria in the 4th cent., *P.Flor.* 75 (Wilcken, *Chrest.* 433, A.D. 380); Wilcken, ibid. 434 (A.D. 390); *P.Lond.* iii, p. 220; *Stud. Pal.* i. 34; Wilcken, *Grundz.*, p. 371. Transportation by river was done chiefly by the shipowners and the ship-lessees, the ναύκληροι. Was the ναυκληρία a liturgy? A strict control over the ναύκληροι (who, at least in Alexandria, were organized as a corporation) was certainly exercised by the government as early as the Ptolemaic period (cf. my article, *Journ. Econ. and Business Hist.* 3, 1932, pp. 728 ff.). It had been inherited by the Romans. The ναυκληρία, however, was in the main a good business proposition, and there were plenty of ναύκληροι who were prepared to invest their money in the transport trade. In the 3rd cent. it was different. There is no doubt that the state then resorted to compulsion in order to secure a sufficient number of ναύκληροι, and that the ναυκληρία became a liturgy. This is proved by many documents, especially by *P.Oxyr.* 1418 (A.D. 247), 8: [τῆς πληρω]θείσης ὑπ' ἐμοῦ ναυκληρίας καὶ ὧν ἄλλω[ν λειτουργιῶν (?) . . ., cf. B. Grenfell, *P.Oxyr.* 1412. 14, note. Grenfell is undoubtedly right in explaining *P.Oxyr.* 1261—a declaration concerning the transport of produce for troops at Babylon, made by a senator who certainly fulfilled a liturgy—as an exact parallel to the declarations of a ναύκληρος χειρισμοῦ Νέας πόλεως (*P.Oxyr.* 1259, A.D. 211) and of a κυβερνήτης (*P.Oxyr.* 1260), cf. F. Preisigke, *P. Cairo*, 34. 3–4. The purport of these documents has not been grasped by F. Oertel, *Die Liturgie*, p. 431. Cf. also *P.Oxyr.* 1553–5 (A.D. 214, 251, 260), which contain declarations on oath by κυβερνῆται, who are shipowners, with a registration of their sureties. I do not maintain that in the 3rd cent. the ναυκληρία was a pure *munus*, and that it might not be regarded as profitable, because of the privileges connected with it (see *P.Lond.* iii, p. 163, 1164 [h], of A.D. 212 and *P.Oxyr.* 2136, of A.D. 291), but in case of necessity compulsion was resorted to, and men were forced to keep on their business, even against their will. Sometimes, perhaps, even those who had ceased to be shipowners, or were not shipowners and transporters by profession at all, were forced to undertake responsibility for the transportation of a certain freight by river. In the light of the new conclusions on the Alexandrian granaries provided by Wilcken's very interesting article, *Hermes*, 63, 1928, pp. 48 ff., the regulations concerning the ναύκληροι of Alexandria must be carefully re-examined.

⁴⁵ On the *prosecutio annonae* see my article in Pauly–Wissowa, vii, cols. 163, 170. We have shown in the ninth chapter how widespread the *prosecutio annonae* was in other parts of the Empire at the beginning of the 3rd cent., and in the eighth chapter that recourse was had to it as early as the first decades of the 2nd cent. in cases of emergency. What, however, in the 2nd cent. was a voluntary service of rich provincials

gradually became a compulsory *munus*. In Egypt in the second half of the 3rd cent. it appears as a normal institution. Men were specially and regularly appointed for the purpose by the city councils and were made responsible for the shipments. See *P.Oxyr.* 1414. 19 ff.: καταπομπὴ ζῴων, and 1415. 4 ff., especially 7: βουλευταὶ εἶπον· μὴ προ[τρα-πήτωσαν (?) ἵν]α μὴ φεύγωσιν. In the 4th cent. the institution flourished, Wilcken, *Chrest.* 43, intr. (*P.Oxyr.* 60, A.D. 323).

⁴⁶ *PSI* 298 (4th cent. A.D.).

⁴⁷ *P.Oxyr.* 1414 (A.D. 270–5); cf. Wessely, *Cat. P.R.* i, no. 53; Wilcken, *Arch. f. Papyr.* 7, p. 103; and above, note 42.

⁴⁸ C. Wessely, *Catal. P.R.* ii. 177. 24: οὐκ ἐξέσται δὲ οὐδενὶ ἄλλῳ | κοτυλίζειν ἐν τῷ ἐποικίῳ εἰ μὴ ἐμοὶ καὶ τοῖς | σύν μοι [μόν]ῳ, cf. *P.Oxyr.* 1455 (A.D. 275), a declaration of an oil-dealer. Cf. Chap. X, note 39, and above, note 21.

⁴⁹ On *cessio bonorum* see Chap. VIII, note 44, and cf. Chap. IX, note 45. The rescript of Severus: *P.Oxyr.* 1405, 10 ff., ἡ δὲ ἐπιτειμία σου ἐ|κ τούτου οὐδὲν βλαβήσεται, οὐδὲ εἰς τὸ | σῶμα ὑβρισθήσει, cf. *BGU* 473 = Mitteis, *Chrest.* 375 (A.D. 200), 6: νομοθετῆσαι ὅτι οὐ χρὴ τοὺς τὴν ἔ[κστασιν ποιησαμένους (?)] ἐνέχεσθαι οὔτε πολειτικοῖς οὔτε ἰδιωτι[κοῖς πράγμασιν. . .]. Hermophilus' appeal to this or a similar rescript: *CPR* 20 = Wilcken, *Chrest.* 402 (A.D. 250), 15 ff. My quotation is from *PSI* 292 (the Greek text is given in Chap. IX, note 45). Equally explicit is *PSI* 807 (A.D. 280), a petition addressed by Aurelius Heracleius to a *beneficiarius* of the prefect, i.e. to a police officer. Heracleius was made responsible by the *decaproti* for some land which did not belong to him. To his complaint he adds, ll. 21 ff.: ἀναγκαίως ἐπιδίδω|μι τὰ βιβλείδια ἀξιῶν | ἔχειν τὸ σῶμα ἐλεύθερον καὶ ἀνύβριστον (he fears imprisonment and corporal punishment).

⁵⁰ *P.Oxyr.* 1663 (3rd cent. A.D.); cf. *P.Oxyr.* 2107 (A.D. 262): an instruction to the chief of police (εἰρηνάρχαι) of the Oxyrhynchite nome to send a certain person to the ἐπιστρατηγός, after he had done what was necessary, if not to the prefect.

⁵¹ *P.Oxyr.* 62 = Wilcken, *Chrest.* 278 (after A.D. 242).

⁵² *P.Oxyr.* 64 (= Wilcken, *Chrest.* 475), and 65; and cf. Wilcken, *Grundz.*, p. 414.

⁵³ *P.Flor.* 137. 7; 151. 10, 12; 250. 4; cf. *P.Gen.* 16 = Wilcken, *Chrest.* 354 (A.D. 207). Very instructive is the private letter *PSI* 842, ll. 7 ff.: διὸ γνώτωσαν ὅτι ἐὰν ἀμελήσωσιν ἐλθεῖν . . . Σαραπίων αὐτοῖς πράγματα κεινήσει· ἤμελλε γὰρ στρατιώτην πέμψαι, κτλ.

⁵⁴ *P.Flor.* 2 = Wilcken, *Chrest.* 401 (A.D. 265); cf. Wilcken, *Grundz.*, p. 349, *BGU* 325 = Wilcken, *Chrest.* 472 (3rd cent. A.D.): κώμης Σοκνοπ[αίου Νήσ]ου. [πα]ραγγέλ-λεται τοῖς ὑπ[ο]|γεγραμμένοις λῃστοπιασταῖ[ς προσε]λθεῖν τοῖς τῆς κώμης | δημοσίοις καὶ ἀναζητῆσαι τοὺ[ς ἐπ]ιζητουμένους κακούργους. | ἐὰν δὲ ἀμελήσωσι, δ[ε]δ[ε]μένοι πεμφθήσον[τ]αι ἐπὶ τὸν λαμπρό(τατον) | ἡμῶν ἡγεμόνα, and *P.Oxyr.* 80 = Wilcken, *Chrest.* 473 (time of the Gordians). O. Hirschfeld, 'Die ägyptische Polizei der römischen Kaiserzeit nach Papyrusurkunden', *Kl. Schr.*, pp. 612 ff. Cf. Chap. IX, note 45.

⁵⁵ The average fortune of a member of the city *bourgeoisie* cannot be estimated in the absence of statistics. What we hear occasionally does not lead us to overestimate the wealth of the *bourgeoisie*. Most of them were well-to-do, but not rich men. In *P.Ryl.* ii. 109 (A.D. 235), the heirs of Aurelius Hermias value their father's estate at 10 tal. Σεβαστά; in *P.Amh.* 72 (A.D. 236), we have another valuation of the same kind amounting to 3 tal.; in *P.Oxyr.* 1114 (A.D. 237), a third one of 200,000 sest. We must not forget how depreciated the currency of this period was.

⁵⁶ The confiscated land which was assigned to a city was called τὰ ὑποστέλλοντα τῇ δεκαπρωτείᾳ or τὰ ὑπάρχοντα τῇ δεκαπρωτείᾳ, the *decaproti* being responsible for the revenues of such land. Another designation was τὰ ὑπάρχοντα οἴκου πόλεως. See *PSI*

187; *P.Flor.* 19, cf. *P.Fay.* 87. 5; 88. 5; *P.Oxyr.* 122. 1; 54. 1; *CPR* 39. 8. On the πολιτικά, as opposed to the κωμητικά, and on the special municipal treasury of the city, as opposed to the governmental one, see B. Grenfell, *P.Oxyr.* 1419. 2, note. Cf. above, note 32. On the activity of the *decaproti* and their violence, see *P.Ryl.* ii. 114 (A.D. 280), and *PSI* 807 (A.D. 280).

57 The attempt of Philip is well attested by many documents. The best known is *P.Lond.* iii, pp. 109 ff. no. 1157 = Wilcken, *Chrest.* 375 (A.D. 246), a sale of land by the government to a *beneficiarius* of the prefect in accordance with the order of Claudius Marcellus the καθολικός (*rationalis*) and Marcius Salutarius the procurator. The same order of the same two men is referred to in *P.Oxyr.* 78. 11 ff., containing a list of parcels of private land, one of which is bought in accordance with the order. I have no doubt that the same order is mentioned in *P.Wis.*, inv. 56. 22 ff.: ὅθεν οὐκ ὀλίγου ὄντος τοῦ ἀδικήματ[ο]ς τὴν ἐπίδοσιν τῶν βι|βλειδίων ποιούμεθα μαρτυρο[ύ]μενοι κατὰ τὰ κελευσθέντα ὑ|π[ὸ] Κ[λ]αυδίου [Μ]αρκέλλου τοῦ διασημοτ[ά]του καθολικοῦ καὶ Μ[α]ρκίου Σαλο[υ]ταρίου [το]ῦ κρατίστου ἐπ[ι]-τρόπου [τ]ῶν Σεβαστῶν. It is evident that the three veterans from Antinoupolis have been attracted by the proclamation of Philip's officials to buy the land, and, being cheated, now refer to this proclamation, which probably contained some clauses designed to protect purchasers against the carelessness or dishonesty of the local officials. I suspect that some of the land owned by Aurelius Serenus was acquired in the same way and at the same time, *P.Oxyr.* 1636 (A.D. 249), 6: ἀπὸ τοῦ ὑπάρξαντός μοι ἀγορα|[στικῷ δικ]αίῳ περὶ [τ]ὴν αὐτὴν Σερῦφιν; cf. *P.Wis.*, inv. 56. 30: τηρουμέν[ου ἡ]μῶν τοῦ δικαι|[ο]υ τῆς κτήσεως. Cf. Chap. IX, note 53.

58 *P.Oxyr.* 1662 (A.D. 246), 11: ἕνεκα πρεσβεί|ας περὶ τῆς ἐπιβληθείσης | ἐπιβολῆς τῷ ἡμετέρῳ | νομῷ τοῦ ἱεροῦ ἀποτάκτου, cf. 1187. 13–15, and 1630. The protection of small landowners was also the policy of Philip in Africa, where he likewise took over the practice of the Severi, see S. Gsell, *Bull. arch. du Com. des trav. hist.* 1909, p. 183, and J. Carcopino, *C. R. Acad. Inscr.* 1919, pp. 379 ff.

59 On the correspondence of Heroninus see D. Comparetti, *P.Flor.* ii, pp. 41 ff.; cf. *P.Ryl.* ii, pp. 236–40, and F. Oertel, *Die Liturgie*, pp. 231 ff. It is not easy to decide whether Alypius, Appian, &c., acted as λειτουργοί, being forced to take on themselves the responsibility for large tracts of γῆ οὐσιακή, or as men who, confident of their influence, were willing to try their luck and added by their own choice parcels of γῆ οὐσιακή to the land which they owned privately. I am inclined to think that in the 3rd cent. both government pressure and private initiative contributed to the creation of such large holdings as the estate of Alypius, Appian, &c. Cf. my *Studien z. Gesch. röm. Kol.*, pp. 198 ff.; Wilcken, *Grundz.*, pp. 310 ff. and 314 ff.

60 On the estate of Aurelius Serenus (A.D. 249–80) see *P.Oxyr.* 1209, 1276, 1558, 1631, 1633, 1646, 1689, 1763. No. 1633 (A.D. 275) is specially important: Aurelius Serenus is bidding for some unsold state land (l. 8: ἀπὸ ἀπ[ράτ]ων τῆς δι[οικήσε]|ως πρότερο[ν] Σαραπίωνος [τοῦ] Ζωίλου) and outbids another offer (of a member of his own family?). Another way of increasing one's estate was by renting land from other persons: in *P.Oxyr.* 1646 (A.D. 268/9) Aurelius Serenus rents land from the heirs of Vibius Publius, a veteran, ἀπὸ ὀφφικιαλίων ἐπάρχου Αἰγύπτου, and formerly a βουλευτής of Alexandria. We can understand this grabbing of land by rich, energetic, and influential men. The most important part of Serenus' income came from vineyards and orchards (*P.Oxyr.* 1631, A.D. 280). *P.Oxyr.* 1631 is one of the most important documents which show how elaborate and minute were the devices for cultivating vineyards and orchards scientifically; see the introduction to this papyrus and the comments of B. Grenfell and myself; cf. *P.Oxyr.* 2153 (iii. A.D.), a report made by Didymus to the 'very honourable Apollon' whose estates be administered, on the good harvest of one of his vineyards.

⁶¹ Claudia Isidora ἡ ἀξιολογωτάτη ἡ καὶ Ἀπία, *P.Oxyr.* 919; 1578; 1046. 8; 1630; 1634; 1659 (A.D. 214–22). *P.Oxyr.* 1630 suggests that the estate of Claudia Isidora was managed on a system which differed from that applied to ordinary γῆ ἰδιόκτητος, and approximated to that employed on state οὐσίαι. It is probable that a large part of Isidora's land was γῆ οὐσιακή. See *P.Oxyr.* 1630, introd. If so, we must regard Claudia Isidora as another instance of a rich and powerful landowner managing large tracts of crown land in Egypt. Aurelia Thermutharion, ἡ καὶ 'Ηραΐς: C. Wessely, *Mitt. P.E.R.* ii. 33 = *SB* 5126; cf. for the agricultural details *P.Oxyr.* 1631. In the 3rd cent. there was in general a sharp discrimination between the landowners and the peasants, the γεοῦχοι or γεουχοῦντες and the κωμῆται, *P.Oxyr.* 1531 (3rd cent., before A.D. 258) and 1747 (3rd to 4th cent. A.D.). In the 4th cent. large emphyteutic οὐσίαι are typical in Egypt, Wilcken, *Grundz.*, pp. 316 f.; cf. *PSI* 820 (A.D. 312 and 314).

⁶² See note 60.

⁶³ The theory that the crisis of the 3rd cent. was caused by the struggle of the emperors against the state—or vice versa—is defended by many scholars, including G. Ferrero (see Chap. XII, note 12) and, to a certain extent, L. Homo in his brilliant articles and books (see Chap. X, notes 4, 7, 10). Also the other theory, that the barbarization of the army and of the leading class was the principal cause, has many supporters, for instance H. Delbrück, *Gesch. d. Kriegskunst*, ii³ (1921), pp. 219 ff. Many who reviewed the first edition of this book have expressed the same opinion, in particular G. de Sanctis, *Riv. fil.*, 54, 1926, pp. 531 ff.

⁶⁴ O. Seeck, *Gesch. d. Unter. d. ant. Welt²*, i, pp. 420 ff. So far as I know, he was the only scholar who emphasized the changed mood of the peasantry in the 3rd cent. A.D. He ascribed the change to the emperors' policy of settling barbarians in the Empire. I greatly doubt whether this factor was of any moment in creating the attitude which I have described above. There were many provinces of the Empire which were not affected by the settlement of barbarians, e.g. Asia Minor, Syria, Africa, Spain, and even the larger part of Gaul. On the other hand, the barbarians did not yet play an important part in the imperial army. The bulk of the army consisted of peasants levied in the provinces from the old stock of the population. I am convinced, therefore, that the change of mood in the peasants was due, not to any infiltration of new blood, but to the policy of the emperors of the 2nd and the early 3rd cent. and to the natural process which led to the spread of a higher standard of culture among the masses of the peasants. I have not the slightest doubt that the emperors and the leading men of the 3rd cent. fully realized the change that was taking place. See Cass. Dio, 52. 19. 6 (pretended speech of Maecenas): ὥστε καὶ τῆς πολιτείας πᾶσί σφισι μεταδοθῆναί φημι δεῖν, ἵνα καὶ ταύτης ἰσομοιροῦντες, πιστοὶ σύμμαχοι ἡμῖν ὦσι ὥσπερ τινὰ μίαν τὴν ἡμετέραν πόλιν οἰκοῦντες· καὶ ταύτην μὲν ὄντως πόλιν τὰ δὲ σφέτερα ἀγροὺς καὶ κώμας νομίζοντες εἶναι. It is evident that in the reign of Alexander Severus the peasants of the provinces did not regard the city of Rome as *their* city.

⁶⁵ The evidence about this episode has been fully collected and brilliantly illustrated by C. Jullian, *Hist. de la Gaule*, iv, pp. 587 ff.

⁶⁶ Petr. Patr., fr. 10. 4 (Cass. Dio, ed. Boiss., 176, iii, p. 746). Aurelian promised the soldiers not to leave a dog in the city of Tyana, if it were captured. After the capture he ordered all dogs to be killed, καὶ μετὰ ταῦτα συγκαλέσας αὐτοὺς εἶπεν ὅτι ' ἡμεῖς ὑπὲρ τοῦ ἐλευθερῶσαι τὰς πόλεις ταύτας πολεμοῦμεν· καὶ ἐὰν μέλλωμεν πραιδεύειν αὐτάς, οὐκέτι ἡμῖν πιστεύουσιν· ἀλλὰ μᾶλλον τὴν πραῖδαν τῶν βαρβάρων ζητήσωμεν καὶ τούτων ὡς ἡμετέρων φεισώμεθα '.

⁶⁷ Petr. Patr., fr. 9. 2 (Cass. Dio, ed. Boiss., 170, iii, p. 745): ὅτι οἱ Σκύθαι πρὸς τοὺς ἐν πόλεσι ἐγκεκλεισμένους ἀπέσκωπτον, ὅτι οὗτοι οὐκ ἀνθρώπινον βίον ζῶσιν, ἀλλ' ὀρνίθων ἐν

καλιαῖς εἰς τὸ ὕψος καθημένων καὶ ὅτι καταλιπόντες τὴν γῆν τὴν τρέφουσαν αὐτοὺς ἀκάρπους πόλεις ἐπιλέγονται καὶ ὅτι τοῖς ἀψύχοις θαρροῦσι μᾶλλον ἤπερ ἑαυτοῖς.

⁶⁸ Lib. *de patrociniis* (or. 47, ed. R. Foerster, iii, pp. 404 ff.). An admirable analysis of the speech is given by F. de Zulueta, *De patrociniis vicorum*, in P. Vinogradoff's *Oxford Studies in Social and Legal History*, i (1909), pp. 28 ff. It is to be regretted that the author did not pay more attention to the first eleven chapters of the speech, where a special type of *patrocinium* is described—not that of one powerful officer, as in the case of Libanius himself, but that of a whole detachment of soldiers. The fact that the patrons of the villages were to a large extent officers is explained not only by the important position which the military commanders held in the provinces but also by the tendency of the peasants to seek protection from those whom they supposed to be in sympathy with them. I would again remind the reader of the feelings of allegiance which the villagers of the provinces show to their successful countrymen, their natural protectors. On the *patrocinia vicorum* see F. Martroye, 'Les Patronages d'agriculteurs et de vici', *Rev. hist. du droit fr. et étr.* 1928, pp. 201 ff. (in speaking of Egypt the author overlooks the evidence of papyri).

⁶⁹ F. Preisigke, *P.Cairo*, 4 = Wilcken, *Chrest.* 379 (A.D. 320); cf. id. *Grundz.*, p. 311. The sharp discrimination between the γεοῦχοι and the κωμῆται (to which I have referred above, note 61) amounted to a division of the population into two classes or castes. In the 3rd cent. many γεοῦχοι were degraded and became κωμῆται, but hardly any κωμήτης became a γεοῦχος except through the army.

XII. *The Oriental Despotism and the Problem of the Decay of Ancient Civilization*

¹ The best general history of the late Roman Empire which takes account of the social and economic conditions is O. Seeck's *Geschichte des Untergangs der antiken Welt*, vol. ii (1901), with abundant references to the sources; cf. his numerous articles in Pauly–Wissowa, and in various periodicals, quoted by the author himself, and by J. B. Bury, *History of the Later Roman Empire*² (1923), vol. i, chaps i and ii (the best short description of the general conditions which prevailed in the late Roman Empire). Cf. L. M. Hartmann, *Der Untergang der antiken Welt. Geschichte in gemeinverständlicher Darstellung*, iii (1919), pp. 201 ff., and E. Stein, *Gesch. d. spätrömischen Reiches*, i (1928) [ii (1949), *Histoire du Bas-Empire* (476–565)]. Stein's book deals in the introduction with conditions in the earlier empire: the following chapters pay little attention to the social and economic conditions which developed after Diocletian and Constantine. This theme is better covered by the general book by F. Lot, *La Fin du monde antique et le début du moyen âge*, 1927 (in the series *Évolution de l'humanité* edited by H. Berr). It is needless to remind the reader of the brilliant pages of Gibbon on the same subject, and of the masterly comments of Godefroy in his edition of the *Codex Theodosianus*. A good bibliography is appended to the article of J. S. Reid, 'The Reorganization of the Empire', *Cambridge Medieval History*, i (1911), pp. 24 ff., and to the book of Lot. On Diocletian see K. Stade, *Der Politiker Diokletian und die letzte grosse Christenverfolgung* (1926). On Constantine see J. Maurice, *Constantin le Grand et l'origine de la civilisation chrétienne* (1924), and N. H. Baynes, *Constantine the Great and the Christian Church* (1931). My short sketch of the economic and social evolution of the period after Diocletian given here has been considered too black and hostile by some eminent scholars, for example M. Gelzer, *Byzant. Zeitschr.* 27, 1927, pp. 387 ff.; K. Stade, *Der Politiker Diokletian*, Appendix; F. Heichelheim, *Hist. Zeitschr.* 137, 1927, pp. 289 ff. I agree with these reviewers that the idea of the 'ruin of the ancient world' is antiquated. Undoubtedly the late Roman Empire is not merely a period of decay:

it is one phase in the evolution of humanity and gave many contributions of lasting value in the field of art, literature, theology, and so on. I can to this extent agree with the views expressed by M. Gelzer in his interesting article 'Altertumswiss. u. Spät-antike', *Hist. Zeitschr.* 135, 1926, pp. 173 ff. Moreover, I agree with Gelzer that there is no sharp break between the early and the late Roman Empire. But my sketch aimed at indicating how, from a social and economic point of view, the Roman Empire entered a new phase in the period after Diocletian, and how this phase was prepared by the evolution of the early Empire and the crisis of the 3rd cent. Gelzer and Heichelheim are right in observing that there is throughout the Roman Empire a certain awakening of economic life between Diocletian and Theodosius, and that the inhabitants of the Empire were not then in a worse position in this respect than at the end of the 2nd cent. (see note 6 of this chapter, where I quote the evidence and the modern writings on this question). But this awakening was short-lived and limited. Pressure exerted from above continued to be the hall-mark of the age; it is sufficient to read the complaints of the *curiales* of Egypt and of the other parts of the Empire to be convinced of this. I cannot but think that the cause of the brevity of the improve-ment lies not in the incompetence or ill-intent of the emperors, but, *inter alia*, in the fiscal system created by Diocletian and Constantine.

² The point of view from which I regard the imperial power of Diocletian and Con-stantine nearly agrees with that of E. Schwartz, *Kaiser Constantin und die christliche Kirche* (1913); cf. the works quoted above in note 1.

³ R. Grosse, *Römische Militärgeschichte von Gallienus bis zum Beginn der byzantinischen Themenverfassung* (1920); cf. E. Ch. Babut, 'Recherches sur la garde impériale', *Rev. hist.*, 114, 1913, pp. 225–60 and 116, 1914, pp. 225–93. The survey of the work done both by Diocletian and by Constantine in reorganizing the Roman army, by E. Nischer, *JRS* 13, 1923, pp. 1 ff., is superficial. Cf. P. Coussin, *Les Armes romaines* (1926), who offers an interesting picture of the barbarization of the Roman army so far as weapons are concerned.

⁴ See the article of J. S. Reid quoted in note 1, and cf. A. E. R. Boak, 'Roman *magistri* in the civil and military service of the Empire', *Harvard Stud. in Class. Phil.* 26, 1915, pp. 73–164.

⁵ A. Piganiol, *L'Impôt de capitation sous le Bas-Empire romain* (1916), and the good bibliography there given, especially the articles of O. Seeck; cf. the works quoted in note 1 and F. Lot, 'Le *caput* du Bas-Empire et sa valeur fiscale', *Nouvelle Rev. hist. du droit*, 1925. I have not seen H. Bott, *Die Grundzüge der diocletianischen Steuerverfassung* (Diss., Frankfurt, 1928). On the edict of Diocletian, K. Bücher, 'Die Diokletianische Taxordnung vom Jahre 301', *Zeitschr. f. ges. Staatsw.* 50, 1894, pp. 189–219, 672–717. On the situation of the middle class, Sir S. Dill, *Roman Society in the Last Century of the Western Empire* (1899), pp. 227 ff.

⁶ On the economic and social conditions of the late Roman Empire see (besides the works quoted in note 1) P. Vinogradoff, 'Social and Economic Conditions of the Roman Empire in the Fourth Century', *Cambridge Medieval History*, i (1911), pp. 543 ff. A brilliant account of the Western provinces, especially of Gaul, is given by Sir S. Dill, op. cit. Good information about Syria is supplied by Libanius, the Emperor Julian, St. John Chrysostom, Johannes of Antioch, and Zosimus; see Chap. VII, pp. 264 ff., where I have collected the evidence and quoted recent works. The picture given by these writers does not differ greatly from that which Ausonius, Paulinus of Pella, Sidonius Apollinaris, and Salvian draw of the province of Gaul; on Salvian cf. R. Thouvenot, 'Salvien et la ruine de l'empire romain', *Mél. de l'Éc. fr. de Rome*, 38, 1920, pp. 145 ff. For Africa remarkable evidence is furnished by the mosaics of the

4th and 5th cent. A.D., which give representations of some large villas of the period and indicate the main sources of their owners' income. Some of these mosaics are reproduced on pls. LXIII. 2; LXXVII; LXXIX. 1; LXXX; cf. P. Romanelli, 'La Vita agricola tripolitana attraverso le rappresentazioni figurate', *Africa Italiana*, 3, 1930, pp. 53 ff.; another example of the same type is the well-known mosaic of Pompeianus (Oued Atmenia near Constantine: S. Reinach, *Rép. d. peint.*, p. 359. 1). From the economic point of view the mosaics are important as showing that agriculture on the large estates was not in any way decaying. While the production of corn was left to the *coloni*, the more profitable and more progressive branches of husbandry were concentrated round the central villa of the estate—the production of wine and oil, horse-breeding (a profitable activity owing to the enormous development of circus-races), cattle-raising, poultry-farming, and probably also fruit and vegetable growing. In the earlier period the owners of the estates dwelt in the cities. Now, as the mosaics show, they dwell as a rule on their estates, living the life of real country squires—hunting, supervising the agricultural work, acting as patrons of the *coloni*, reading, and even entertaining scholars, philosophers, or philologists (see the mosaic of Pompeianus, with the inscription *filosofi*, or *filologi*, *locus*). Note also that in the mosaic of Julius (pl. LXXIX. 1) the main occupation of the landowner is to receive payments, mostly contributions in kind made by *coloni*; see the description of the plate. In this period Egypt is not so well known as Syria and Gaul. The documents of the 4th and 5th cent. are few. They depict the life of those centuries almost in the same colours as the earlier documents depict the life of the 3rd cent. In the second half of the 4th cent. and in the 5th conditions improved somewhat, or at least became more stable. But economic decay was steadily advancing, and the pressure of the state became more and more heavy. See H. I. Bell, 'The Byzantine Servile State in Egypt', *JEA* 4, 1917, pp. 86 ff., and 'An Epoch in the Agrarian History of Egypt', *Recueil Champollion* (1922), pp. 261 ff.; A. Heisenberg and L. Wenger, *Byzantinische Papyri in der K. Hof- und Staatsbibliothek zu München* (1914); L. Wenger, *Volk und Staat in Ägypten am Ausgang der Römerherrschaft* (1922) (with an excellent bibliography); F. Oertel, *Die Liturgie* (1917), and 'Der Niedergang der hellenistischen Kultur in Ägypten', *Neue Jahrb. kl. Alt.* 45, 1920, pp. 361 ff.; A. S. Hunt and H. I. Bell, *P.Oxyr.* vol. xvi (documents of the 5th to 7th cent. A.D.); H. I. Bell, *Jews and Christians in Egypt* (1924). Two very instructive series of documents illustrate the prosperous life of soldiers in Elephantine, and the oppressed life of peasants in the village Aphrodito: the former may be found in *P.Lond.* v, pp. 169 ff., and in *Byz. Pap. Münch.* (fully quoted above), the latter in J. Maspero, *Papyrus grecs d'époque byzantine*, 3 vols. (1910–16); *P.Flor.* iii, nos. 279 ff.; and *P.Lond.* v, pp. 21 ff. Of great interest, too, are the documents referring to the family of Apion, a family of local origin which belonged to the imperial aristocracy and held large estates in Egypt, *P.Oxyr.* 1829 (note to l. 24); see the very useful book of E. R. Hardy, *The Large Estates of Byzantine Egypt* (1931); cf. W. Hengstenberg, 'Die griechisch-koptischen μουλον Ostraka', *Zeitschr. f. äg. Spr.* 66, 1931, pp. 51 ff. and 122 ff. On the economic and social conditions of the Byzantine Empire in general see L. Brentano, 'Die byzantinische Volkswirtschaft', *Schmollers Jahrb.* 41, 1917, pp. 11 ff.; cf. C. Roth, *Sozial- und Kulturgeschichte des byzantinischen Reiches²* (1919). Cf. H. I. Bell, 'The Decay of a Civilization', *JEA* 10, 1924, pp. 207 ff. and the 'Bulletin papyrologique' by M. Hombert, published in *Byzantion* from 1926.

[7] On the different types of land-tenure in the late Roman Empire, see my *Studien z. Gesch. röm. Kol.*, pp. 393 ff. A very instructive picture of a great fortune of the 5th cent. A.D. is furnished by the various sources for the life of St. Melania, P. Allard, *Rev. d. quest. hist.* 81, 1907, pp. 6 ff.; cf. his articles on serfdom and slavery, ibid. 89, 1911, pp. 1–22; 90, 1911, pp. 28–53; 91, 1912, pp. 5–35.

⁸ On the old and the new mentality, see the brilliant book of J. Geffcken, *Der Ausgang des griechisch-römischen Heidentums*² (1929), with references to the sources and a good bibliography; for the Western Roman Empire the subject is treated in the volume of Sir S. Dill, which has been quoted in the preceding notes. The growth of the Church and the development of the Christian mentality are described in Ed. Schwartz's *Kaiser Constantin und die christliche Kirche* (1913). The abundant bibliography of the subject need not be quoted. A good bibliography may be found in the *Cambridge Medieval History*, i, chaps. 4–6, 17, 18, 20, and 21; cf. the general works quoted in note 1.

⁹ It is impossible to give here a complete enumeration of all the books and articles which have been written on the subject. In most of the articles and books which are quoted in the following notes the reader will find general surveys of the various theories expressed by the scholars of the 19th cent. It is sufficient for our purpose to cite some more recent attempts to solve the problem. I regret my inability to consult the article of M. Weber, 'Die sozialen Gründe des Untergangs der antiken Kultur', *Die Wahrheit*, 6, 1896, pp. 59–77 (Stuttgart) [= *Ges. Aufs.* (1924), 289–311]. Cf. by the same author, *Wirtschaft und Gesellschaft* (*Grundr. der Sozialökonomie*, iii. 2), 1921, ii, pp. 211 ff., and 'Agrarverhältnisse im Altertum' [= *Ges. Aufs.*, pp. 1–288].

¹⁰ J. Beloch, 'Der Verfall der antiken Kultur', *Hist. Zeitschr.* 84, 1900, pp. 1 ff.

¹¹ E. Kornemann, 'Das Problem des Untergangs der antiken Welt', *Vergangenheit und Gegenwart*, 12, 1922, 5, 6.

¹² G. Ferrero, *La Ruine de la civilisation antique* (1921) (first printed in the *Revue des Deux Mondes*).

¹³ W. E. Heitland, *The Roman Fate, an Essay in Interpretation* (Cambridge, 1922); *Iterum, or a further Discussion of the Roman Fate* (1925); *Last Words on the Roman Municipalities* (1928).

¹⁴ Chap. VII, note 107; cf. O. von Zwiedineck, 'Was macht ein Zeitalter kapitalistisch?', *Zeitschr. f. ges. Staatsw.* 90, 1931, pp. 482 ff., and M. Rostovtzeff, ibid. 92, 1932, pp. 334 ff.

¹⁵ His well-known theory is fully stated in his general work, *Gesch. d. Untergangs d. ant. Welt*, i.

¹⁶ T. Frank, 'Race Mixture in the Roman Empire', *Amer. Hist. Rev.* 21, 1916, pp. 689 ff., and *A History of Rome* (1922), pp. 565 ff. His view, as expressed in the latter book, combines the economic and the biological theories. I add a short bibliography of some modern studies on race-mixture in Italy and Gaul: A. Solari, 'Delle antiche relazioni commerciali tra la Siria e l'occidente, I. In Roma e in Gallia', *Ann. del. Univ. tosc.* 6, 1916, pp. 1 ff.; id. 'I Siri nell'Emilia antica', *Riv. Indo-Greco-Italica*, 1921, pp. 165 ff.; R. Vulpe, 'Gli Illiri dell'Italia imperiale romana', *Ephem. Daco-rom.* 3, 1925, pp. 129 ff.; G. C. Mateescu, 'I Traci nelle epigrafi di Roma', ibid. 1, 1923, pp. 57 ff.

¹⁷ A very good survey of the problem from the biological point of view was given by a young Russian scholar, N. A. Vassiliev, *The Problem of the Fall of the Western Roman Empire and of Ancient Civilization* (Kazan, 1921) (in Russian). The theory of O. Spengler on the natural decay which is bound to overtake every civilization belongs to a certain extent to the same class, see *Der Untergang des Abendlandes. Umrisse einer Morphologie der Weltgeschichte*, i–ii (1920–2).

¹⁸ M. Rostovtzeff, 'The Decline of Ancient Civilization', *Russkaja Mysl*, 1922, vols. vi–xii (in Russian; a translation into Bulgarian by G. Kazarow was published in 1924). A new attempt (from a neo-Marxist, Bolshevik point of view) to lay the blame for the ruin of the Roman Empire on Christianity has been made in the second edition of G. Sorel, *La Ruine du monde antique* (1925). This book is without value for the historian.

LIST OF EMPERORS FROM AUGUSTUS TO CONSTANTINE

Augustus (C. Octavius, *after his adoption* C. Iulius Octavianus).—Imp.
Caesar Augustus . . . . 27 B.C.–A.D. 14
Tiberius (Ti. Claudius Nero, *after his adoption* Ti. Iulius Caesar).—Ti
Caesar Augustus . . . . A.D. 14–37
Caligula (C. Iulius Caesar).—C. Caesar Augustus Germanicus . 37–41
Claudius (Ti. Claudius Nero Drusus Germanicus).—Ti. Claudius
Caesar Augustus Germanicus 41–54
Nero (L. Domitius Ahenobarbus, *after his adoption* Ti. Claudius Drusus
Germanicus Caesar).—Nero (*later* Imp. Nero) Claudius Caesar
Augustus Germanicus 54–68
Galba (Ser. Sulpicius)—Ser. (Sulpicius) Galba imp. Caesar Augustus 68–69
Otho (M. Salvius Otho).—Imp. M. Otho Caesar Augustus . . 69
Vitellius (A. Vitellius).—A. Vitellius imp. (*or* Germanicus imp.) . 69
Vespasian (T. Flavius Vespasianus).—Imp. Caesar Vespasianus
Augustus 69–79
Titus (T. Flavius Vespasianus).—Imp. Titus Caesar Vespasianus
Augustus 79–81
Domitian (T. Flavius Domitianus).—Imp. Caesar Domitianus
Augustus 81–96
Nerva (M. Cocceius Nerva).—Imp. Caesar Nerva Augustus . . 96–98
Trajan (M. Ulpius Traianus).—Imp. Caesar Nerva Traianus
Augustus 98–117
Hadrian (P. Aelius Hadrianus).—Imp. Caesar Traianus Hadrianus
Augustus 117–138
Antoninus Pius (T. Aurelius Fulvus Boionius Arrius Antoninus, *after
his adoption* T. Aelius Hadrianus Antoninus Pius).—Imp. Caesar
T. Aelius Hadrianus Antoninus Augustus Pius . . . 138–161
Marcus Aurelius (M. Annius Catilius Severus, *after his adoption* M.
Aelius Aurelius Verus Caesar).—Imp. Caesar M. Aurelius
Antoninus Augustus 161–180
Lucius Verus (L. Ceionius Commodus Verus, *after his adoption* L. Aelius
Aurelius Commodus Verus).—Imp. Caesar L. Aurelius Verus
Augustus 161–169
Commodus (Imp. Caesar L. Aelius *or* L. (*or* M.) Aurelius Commodus
Antoninus Augustus).—Imp. Caesar M. Aurelius Commodus
Antoninus Augustus 176–192
Pertinax.—Imp. Caesar P. Helvius Pertinax Augustus . . . 193
Didius Julianus.—Imp. Caesar M. Didius Severus Iulianus Augustus 193
Septimius Severus.—Imp. Caesar L. Septimius Severus Pertinax
Augustus 193–211
Clodius Albinus.—Imp. Caesar D. Clodius Septimius Albinus
Augustus 193–197
Pescennius Niger.—Imp. Caesar C. Pescennius Niger Iustus Augustus 193–194
Caracalla (Septimius Bassianus, *named in* 196 M. Aurelius Antoninus).
—Imp. Caesar M. Aurelius Antoninus Augustus . . . 198–217
Geta (Lucius *or* Publius).—Imp. Caesar P. Septimius Geta Augustus 209–212
Macrinus.—Imp. Caesar M. Opellius Macrinus Augustus . . 217–218

Diadumenianus.—M. Opellius Antoninus Diadumenianus Caesar . A.D. 218

Elagabalus *or* Heliogabalus (Varius Avitus, *named* M. Aurelius
    Antoninus).—Imp. Caesar M. Aurelius Antoninus Augustus . 218–222

Severus Alexander (Alexianus Bassianus).—Imp. Caesar M. Aurelius
    Severus Alexander Augustus 222–235

Maximinus.—Imp. Caesar C. Iulius Verus Maximinus Augustus . 235–238

Gordian I.—Imp. Caesar M. Antonius Gordianus Sempronianus
    Romanus Africanus Senior Augustus 238

Gordian II.—Imp. Caesar M. Antonius Gordianus Sempronianus
    Africanus Iunior Augustus 238

Balbinus.—Imp. Caesar D. Caelius Calvinus Balbinus Augustus . 238

Pupienus.—Imp. Caesar M. Clodius Pupienus Augustus . . 238

Gordian III.—Imp. Caesar M. Antonius Gordianus Augustus . 238–244

Philip the Arab.—Imp. Caesar M. Iulius Philippus Augustus . . 244–249

Decius.—Imp. Caesar C. Messius Quintus Traianus Decius (*or* Decius
    Traianus) Augustus 249–251

Trebonianus Gallus.—Imp. Caesar C. Vibius Trebonianus Gallus
    Augustus 251–253

Volusianus.—Imp. Caesar C. Vibius Afinius Gallus Veldumianus
    Volusianus Augustus 251–253

Aemilianus.—Imp. Caesar M. Aemilius Aemilianus Augustus . . 253

Valerian.—Imp. Caesar P. Licinius Valerianus Augustus . . 253–260

Gallienus.—Imp. Caesar P. Licinius Egnatius Gallienus Augustus . 253–268

Claudius II, Gothicus.—Imp. Caesar M. Aurelius Claudius Augustus 268–270

Quintillus.—Imp. Caesar M. Aurelius Claudius Quintillus Augustus 270

Aurelian.—Imp. Caesar Domitius Aurelianus Augustus . . 270–275

Tacitus.—Imp. Caesar M. Claudius Tacitus Augustus . . 275–276

Florianus.—Imp. Caesar M. Annius Florianus Augustus . . 276

Probus.—Imp. Caesar M. Aurelius Probus Augustus . . 276–282

Carus.—Imp. Caesar M. Aurelius Carus Augustus . . 282–283

Carinus.—Imp. Caesar M. Aurelius Carinus Augustus . . 283–285

Numerianus.—Imp. Caesar M. Aurelius Numerius Numerianus
    Augustus 283–284

Diocletian.—Imp. Caesar C. Aurelius Valerius Diocletianus Augustus 284–305

Maximianus.—Imp. Caesar M. Aurelius Valerius Maximianus
    Augustus 286–305

Constantius I.—Imp. Caesar M. (*or* C.) Flavius Valerius Constantius
    Augustus 293–306

Galerius.—Imp. Caesar C. Galerius Valerius Maximianus Augustus 293–311

Constantine I.—Imp. Caesar Flavius Valerius Constantinus Augustus 306–337

INDEXES

I. INDEX OF NAMES AND SUBJECTS

Q

Commerce, decay of, in Italy, 99, 162, 195, 199, 203.

— — in the empire, 476, 515, 524.

— decentralization of, 162.

— development of, 94, 172, 179, 186, 271, 272.

— foreign, 3, 66, 67, 94–98, 153–7, 170, 172, 301, 352, 413, 473, 565–6, nn. 26, 27, 576–7, nn. 18, 19, 603–7, nn. 17–21, 613, n. 30, 718, n. 18, 737, n. 5.

— individualistic character, 171.

— inter-provincial, 67–70, 157–62, 165, 167, 170, 172, 613, n. 30.

— intra-provincial, 142, 162, 167.

— maritime, 3, 95, 141, 172, 185, 238, 431, 562, n. 18, 614, n. 31, 615, n. 35, 626, n. 54.

— nationalization, 54, 279, 462, 614, n. 32.

— organization, 567, n. 36.

— oriental, 94, 95, 155–7, 524.

— policy of the central government towards, 53, 54, 74, 145, 170.

— river, 141, 615–16, n. 35.

— ruin of, 432, 464, 505, 735, n. 39.

— slaves in, *see* Slaves.

— source of large fortunes, 153, 172, 219, 530.

— wholesale, 57, 158, 166, 167, 196 (2), 225, 616, n. 37.

— world, 153, 555, n. 33.

Commerce of ancient Egypt and Babylon, 538.

— Central African, 307, 335, 336 (2), 337, 338.

— of the Hellenistic monarchies, 5.

— of Histria, 611, n. 26.

— of Nubia, 306, 307, 680, nn. 61, 62.

— of Palestine, 664, n. 32.

— of the Punic cities, 10, 314.

— of Tripolitania, 688, n. 99.

— *See also* Africa; Alexandria; Aquileia; Arabia; Asia Minor; Britain; Campania; Carthage; Dalmatia; Danube provinces; Egypt; Gaul; Germany; Greece; Greek cities; Palmyra; Russia; Spain; Syria; *also* Merchants *and* Trade.

Commercial activity, 16, 66.

— buildings, 568, n. 36.

— capitalism, *see* Capitalism.

— cities, 67, 71, 141, 166, 172, 186, 211, 218, 533, 554, n. 31, 633, n. 38, 640, n. 70.

— class, 524.

— concerns, 578.

— fleet, 155, 386, 431, 605; *see also* Fleet.

— legislation, 625–6, n. 54.

— posts, 307.

— practice, 626, n. 54.

Commercial routes, 303; *see also* Routes.

Commodus, emperor, 122, 125, 126, 404, 535, 711, n. 13.

— army, 126, 128, 394, 397, 399, 411, 425, 496, 498, 708, n. 3.

— colonies, 714, n. 17.

— economic policy, 395, 397, 398, 405, 408, 423, 431, 462, 727, n. 59.

— opposition to, 393–5, 398, 399, 401, 590, n. 33, 709, n. 5.

— religion, 395, 507, 709, n. 6.

— revolts, 374, 394, 398, 412, 708, n. 3, 709, n. 6.

— struggle against senate, 394, 397.

— terror, 374, 394, 395, 712, n. 15.

— wars, 374, 394, 641, n. 73, 698, n. 10.

Communes (πολιτεύματα), 283, 427.

Communities, mixed, in Africa, 51, 319, 554, n. 32, 683, n. 73.

— — in Phoenicia, 554, n. 32.

— tribal, 107, 344, 706, n. 45.

Companies (*societates*), 171.

— of bankers, 181.

— of business men, 327.

— mining, 341.

— of tax-farmers, *see* Tax.

— trade, 170, 171; *see also* Associations.

Compita, 583, n. 32.

Compulsion, 171, 274, 384, 431, 449, 450, 472, 477, 482, 489, 491, 492, 509, 510, 520–2, 524, 531, 532, 744, n. 55, 745, n. 45.

Compulsory buying and selling, 382.

— contributions, 411, 412, 417, 474.

— — to cities, 148.

— deliveries, 424, 480, 505, 515, 519, 520, 677, n. 52, 707, n. 47, 728, n. 60, 743, n. 42.

— — of animals, 381, 384, 385, 519, 721, n. 45.

— — of drivers, 381, 384, 385.

— — of fodder, 381, 484, 721, n. 45.

— — of foodstuffs, 381, 412, 417, 474, 484, 515, 517, 703, n. 35, 743, n. 41.

— — of manufactured goods, 515, 517, 519.

— — of raw materials, 515, 517.

— — of wine, 480, 721, n. 45, 743, n. 41.

— enrolment of new members of the corporations, 463.

— gifts, 417, 470, 505.

— lease of land, 722.

— levies, 41, 295, 355, 374, 391, 412, 413, 418, 467, 474, 492, 503, 511, 591–2, n. 36, 721, n. 42; *see also* Conscription.

— loans, 387, 505.

— membership of a caste, 527.

— migration, 250.

— payments, *see* Payments.

— purchase, 381, 721, n. 45, 743, n. 42.

Corn, tribute, 301.

Corn-ears, representation of, 236 (2), 242, 312 (1, 2), 364 (*j, k, m*), 372 (*a*).

Cornelius Balbus, 688, n. 99.

— Felix Italus, P., 600.

— Fronto, M., 600.

— Gallus, 303.

— Marcellus, 573, n. 6.

— Primogenes, L., 92.

— Tages (or Teges), P., 579, n. 20.

Corporations, 383, 408, 409, 410, 431, 462, 463, 527, 546, n. 12, 579, n. 20, 619–21, n. 43, 706, n. 44, 715–16, n. 20, 728, n. 60.

— building, 462.

— of dyers, 226, 613, n. 27, 619, n. 43.

— of merchants, *see* Merchants.

— of priests in Egypt, 283.

— professional, 171, 178, 607–8, n. 22, 619, n. 43, 620, n. 44, 735, n. 39.

— of shipowners, *see* Shipowners.

— square of, 337.

— of weavers, 620, n. 44.

— *See also* Associations.

Corrector civitatium liberarum, 651, n. 101.

Corsica, 8, 30, 207, 210, 211, 311, 553, n. 27, 630, n. 23.

Corvées, *see* Compulsory work.

Cos, 598, n. 7, 654, n. 4.

Cotiaeum, 256 (2).

Cotton, 97, 155.

Councils of the cities, *see* City Councils,

— provincial (κοινά), 48, 149, 150, 650, n. 97, 695, n. 4, 727, n. 59.

Cowherds, *see* Βουκόλοι.

Cows, 30, 231, 306, 329 (1), 360 (3), 565, n. 23, 712, n. 15, 721, n. 45.

— representation of, 20 (2–4), 76 (1), 196 (1), 300 (1).

Crafts, *see* Trades.

Craftsmen, *see* Artisans.

Crassus, L. Licinius, 52.

Credit, 3, 31, 179, 359, 414, 431, 625, n. 54.

— cheap, 199.

— operations, 16, 180, 623, n. 49.

Cremona, 88, 89.

Crescens Didius Crescentianus, C. Julius, 686, n. 84.

Cretan cities, 2.

Crete, 2, 308, 681, n. 64, 688, n. 99.

Crimea, 97, 141, 154, 249, 258, 259, 260, 324, 473, 606–7, n. 20, 645, n. 88, 660, n. 16.

'Crinitus' (horse), 456 (2).

Crutisiones, coloni, 635, n. 49.

Ctesiphon, 157.

Cuicul (Djemila), 141, 323, 594, 685, n. 81, 686, n. 84, 701, n. 21.

Cults, local, 187, 647, n. 92, 687, n. 97.

Cumae, 648, n. 94.

'Cupido' (horse), 168.

Cupids, 92 (1, 2, 4), 96 (3, 4), 100 (2), 168, 578.

Curatores, 651, n. 97, 686, n. 87, 698, n. 11.

— *frumenti Alexandrini*, 744, n. 44.

— *kalendarii*, 391.

— of provincial cities (λογισταί), 362, 365, 390, 391, 698, n. 11.

— special, 482.

— *summi* (treasurers), 674, n. 49.

— *viarum*, 600, 701, n. 30.

Curiae, 142, 326, 523, 526, 645, n. 88.

— *iuniorum*, 326, 457.

Curiales, 501, 521, 523, 524, 526, 527, 749, n. 1.

Currency, 179–81, 423, 516.

— depreciation of, 413, 424, 431, 470–3, 505, 515–17, 718, n. 32, 745, n. 55.

— fiduciary, 471.

— gold, 470, 473.

— imperial, 472.

— new (καινὸν νόμισμα), 470.

— private, 623, n. 48.

— regulation of, 462.

— small, 623, n. 48.

— stabilization of, 3, 522.

— wine as, 490.

— *See also* Money.

Cursus publicus (postal service), 79, 372 (*b*), 385, 387, 416, (1), 570, n. 2, 703, n. 37, 704–5, n. 40, 725, n. 51.

Cushites, 305, 306.

Customs-duties, 53, 162, 170, 309, 520, 605, 606, n. 20, 609.

— — farmers of, 409, 609–10, 643, n. 83.

— officials, 609.

— stations, 609, 680, n. 62.

Cynic doctrine, 114, 116, 117, 395.

— ideal, 612, n. 27.

— kingship, 120, 586, n. 12.

— preaching (διατριβαί), 581, n. 25, 587, n. 19, 590, n. 33.

Cynics, 115, 117, 120, 126, 395, 586, nn. 11, 14, 16, 588, n. 26, 590, n. 33.

Cyprian, 432, 729, n. 61.

Cyprus, 396 (1).

Cyrenaean embassy, 558, n. 4.

Cyrenaica, 141, 308–10, 335, 338, 348, 362, 363, 680–1, n. 64, 699, n. 12.

Cyrene, 8, 141, 308–11, 338, 557–8, n. 4, 558–9, nn. 6, 8, 595, 680–1, n. 64.

— edicts from, 50, 308–10, 546, n. 12, 556, n. 1, 557, n. 4, 558, n. 6, 559, n. 8, 598, n. 7.

— ephebes of, 311, 681, n. 64.

— inscription of, 688, n. 99.

Cyzicus, 141, 596.

Factories, of soap, 164 (5).
— stamps used by, 575, n. 13, 611, n. 26.
— state, 278, 524.
— woollen, 175.
Fairs (*nundinae, ἐμπόρια*), 249, 251, 266, 325, 426, 427, 479, 648–9, nn. 93, 94, 657, n. 7, 685, n. 83, 724–5, n. 51.
Falcidii, 671 (III (15)).
Falcidius, 293, 671 (III (15)).
Falerienses, 685, n. 83.
Familia (household), 580, n. 23.
Famines, 101, 146, 149, 201, 202, 256 (3), 306, 387, 477, 599–600, 627, n. 11, 652, n. 101, 700, n. 21.
Fan, raffia, representation of, 289 (7).
Fannius, C., 585, n. 11.
— Synistor, P., 65, 552, n. 16.
Faras, 305, 678, n. 53.
Faraxen, 444, 474, 731, n. 12.
Farmers, 18, 31, 46, 107, 128, 214, 226, 228, 229, 237, 300 (1), 345, 369, 489, 561, n. 15, 564, 653, n. 2, 683, n. 74, 687, nn. 94–97; *see also* Peasants *and* Tenants.
— of customs-duties, 409, 609–10, n. 24, 643, n. 83.
— -general, 210, 327, 345, 366–8, 377, 389, 397, 398, 427, 485, 676, n. 50, 702, n. 30, 703, n. 34; *see also* Conductores.
— of pasture-lands, 643, n. 83.
— of salt-mines, 643, n. 83.
— of taxes, *see* Tax.
Farms, 31, 46, 63, 98, 99, 198, 204–6, 214, 217 (3), 219, 228, 229, 231, 262, 272, 313, 553, n. 27, 611, n. 26, 635, n. 48, 675, 692, n. 103.
— houses, 2, 564, 673; *see also* Villas.
— imperial, 673.
— model, 30, 61, 92.
— representation of, 20, 196 (1), 277 (2), 329.
Farnaces, *magister*, 160 (2).
Favellenianus, fundus, 628, n. 16.
Favourites of the emperors, 57, 99, 102, 103, 150, 293, 294, 394, 580, n. 25, 671 (IV).
Fayyûm, 103, 155, 280 (5), 281, 283, 289, 296, 406, 427, 481, 581–2, n. 29, 597, n. 5, 604, n. 19, 669, n. 45, 674–6, n. 49, 722.
Federal state, Italian, 24.
Federation of city-states, 131, 133–5, 138.
— of Etruscan cities, 11.
— of tribes, 238.
Fees to contractors, 342.
— to *beneficiarii*, 742, n. 27.
Fellahin, 194, 231, 280 (5), 345, 347, 348, 668, n. 41; *see also* Peasants.
Felt, 100 (2).
Ferae dentatae, 336 (2).

'Ferox' (horse), 168, 456 (2).
Ferries, owners of, 182.
Feudal system, 477.
Fezzan, 335, 338, 688, n. 98.
Fibulae, 603, n. 17, 613, n. 27; *see also* Pins.
Fides, 364 (k).
— *mutua Augustorum*, 440 (2 b).
Figs, 369, 547, n. 15, 673.
Finances, 54, 55, 79, 80, 82, 91, 110, 182, 373, 382, 388, 389, 391, 394, 411, 413, 422, 423, 430, 452–4, 515, 695–6, n. 6, 727, n. 59.
— of the cities, 186, 358, 362, 365, 391, 520, 598, n. 7.
— of Egypt, 286, 625, n. 53, 725, n. 53.
Fines, 296, 413, 625, n. 53.
Firemen, 40, 47, 81, 410, 462, 637, n. 57; see also *Centonarii*.
Firmus, usurper, 447, 737, n. 11.
Fiscus, 55, 182, 191, 198, 361 (2), 363, 373, 392, 406, 561–2, n. 16, 570, n. 2, 576, n. 18, 598, n. 7, 623, n. 49.
Fish, 36, 146, 154, 159, 261, 370, 700, n. 21.
— ponds, 329 (2), 609, n. 24.
— sauce (*garum*), 73, 566, n. 29, 579, n. 20, 690, n. 100.
Fisheries, 15, 16, 110, 245, 261, 273, 340, 688–9, n. 100.
Fishermen, 247, 274, 370, 689, 721, n. 45.
Flamines, 405, 662, n. 26, 711, n. 13.
Flavia Epimache, 676, n. 49.
— Prisca, 640, n. 69.
Flavii, 645, n. 89.
Flaviopolis, 134.
Flavius Damianus, T., 655, n. 5, 696, n. 6.
— Fronto, M., 640, n. 70.
— Longinus, 614, n. 31.
— Montanus, T., 602, n. 13.
— T. f. Quir. Macro, T., 686, n. 87.
— Vopiscus, *see* Vopiscus.
— Zeuxis, 613, n. 31.
Flax, 36, 213, 728, n. 60, 736, n. 39.
Fleet, 40, 155, 157, 226, 239, 244, 328 (3), 545, n. 7, 556, n. 2, 577, n. 18, 596, 605–6, n. 19, 677, n. 51; see also *Classis*.
— commanders of, 47, 671 (III (23)), 729, n. 61.
— commercial, *see* Commercial.
— corn, *see* Corn.
— *See also* Navy.
Flight, 374, 477, 479, 484, 485, 487, 488, 518, 582, n. 29, 738, n. 16; see also *Anachoresis*.
Flower-dealers, representation of, 92 (4).
Fodder, 381, 484, 565, n. 23; *see also* Chaff *and* Hay.
Food for agents of the state, 517.
— for the army, *see* Army.

Food for the cities, 145, 146, 162, 387, 453, 599, 700, n. 21.
— for the city of Rome, 159, 163, 165, 462, 463, 517, 547, n. 14, 686, n. 87, 701, n. 21, 735, n. 39, 740, n. 21.
— distribution of, 149.
— requisition of, 9, 424, 449.
— supply of, 700, n. 21.
Foodstuffs, 417, 519, 645, n. 87.
— commerce in, 36, 155, 158, 287, 462, 463, 700, n. 21.
— deliveries, *see* Compulsory.
— export, 155, 346.
— import, 145, 162, 163, 165, 249.
— requisition, 381, 412, 449.
— transportation, *see* Transportation.
Fora, 648, n. 93.
— imperial, 694, n. 3.
Forests, 110, 173, 210, 231, 233, 245, 327, 331, 340, 639, n. 64, 641, n. 75, 646–7, n. 90, 650, n. 97, 665, n. 34, 687, n. 97, 689–90, n. 100.
Forge, 230 (1).
Formianus, fundus, 92.
Fortifications, representation of, 248.
Fortified cities, 460, 462.
— — representation of, 196 (1), 236 (1).
— *emporia*, 648, n. 93.
— villages, 14, 461.
— — representation of, 248 (2).
— villas, *see* Villas.
Fortis, factory of, 70, 173.
Fortresses, 222, 239, 244–6, 249, 267, 301, 318, 403, 607, n. 20, 610, n. 26, 641, n. 73, 660, n. 18, 663, n. 28, 726, n. 54.
Forts, 221, 227, 232, 239, 246, 467, 642, n. 79, 662–3, n. 28, 725, n. 51, 735, n. 36.
Fortuna, 100 (2), 256 (1).
— *Redux*, 319.
Fortunes, large, 151, 153, 157, 167, 296, 331, 530, 562, n. 17, 581, n. 25, 661, n. 22, 675, 695, n. 6, 750, n. 7.
— private, of the Emperor, 55, 80, 122, 562, n. 17.
Forum, 31, 361, 709, n. 9.
— Boarium, 356 (2), 697, 709, n. 9.
— of Julius Caesar, 694, n. 3.
— Novum Severianum, 339.
— Pacis, 106.
— Traiani, 108 (1, 2), 248, 360 (1), 568, n. 36, 694, n. 3.
Foundations, 149–51, 182, 202, 325, 424, 453, 473, 687, n. 97, 732, n. 22; *see also* Benefactors *and* Gifts.
France, 175, 219, 594, 630, n. 24, 632, n. 34.
Franchise, city, *see* City franchise.
— Latin, *see* Latin rights.
— Roman, *see* Citizenship.

Franeker, 633, n. 38.
Franks, 443.
Freedmen, 562–3, n. 18, 565, n. 23, 580, n. 23, 583, nn. 32, 33.
— in the administration, 80, 104, 327.
— economic activity of, 54, 58, 92, 104, 152 (1), 186, 187, 190, 235, 379, 552 (31).
— imperial, 54, 82, 190, 583, n. 32, 638, n. 59.
— increase of, 63.
— social status, 40, 46, 47, 104, 187, 190, 198, 204, 370, 374, 525, 584, n. 33, 629, n. 22, 654, n. 4, 697.
— wealth, 58, 60, 150, 195, 293, 294, 579, n. 20, 581, n. 25, 671 (IV).
Fréjus, 690, n. 100.
Frisian cloths, 618, n. 40.
Frisii, 633, n. 38.
Frontiers of the Roman empire, 39, 40, 52, 127, 128, 221–3, 229, 247, 267, 353–5, 363, 365, 366, 421, 427, 429, 467, 511, 516, 724, n. 50, 725, n. 51, 737, n. 12; *see* also *Limes*.
Fronto, 589, n. 27, 693, n. 106, 709, n. 7.
Fruit, 9, 209, 217 (3), 314, 368, 369, 547, n. 15, 628, n. 12, 750, n. 6.
Frumentarii, 398, 402, 411–13, 454, 478, 513, 698, n. 11, 709, n. 7, 717, n. 31, 728, n. 61, 738, n. 17, 742, n. 26.
— *negotiatores*, 707, n. 48.
Frumentum emptum, 700, n. 21.
— *mancipale*, 209.
Fugitives, 729, n. 61.
Fulleries (*fullonicae*), 100, 230 (1), 578, 617–18, n. 40.
Fullers (*fullones, γναφεῖς*), 579, n. 20, 619, n. 43.
— — representation of, 96 (2), 220 (1).
Fundi, 63, 195, 219.
Furianum, pratum, 642, n. 81.
Furius Octavianus, C., 246, 642, n. 81.
Furniture, 168, 177.
Furs, 66, 154.

Gabinius, 555, n. 33.
— Quir. Datus, A., 686, n. 87.
Gadara, 94.
Gades, 211, 630, n. 25.
Gaetuli, *bellum Gaetulicum*, 338.
Gaius Caesar, grandson of Augustus, 53, 688, n. 99, 727, n. 57.
— emperor, *see* Caligula.
Galatia, 141, 247, 358, 556, n. 2, 596, 599–600, 627, n. 1, 645, n. 89, 653, n. 1, 657, n. 7.
Galatian peasants, 193.
— royal family, 695–6, n. 6.

Gems, engraved, *see* Stones.
Geneatae, 651, n. 97.
Geneva, lake of (*lacus Lemannus*), 616, n. 35.
Genii, 100 (2), 216, 312 (1), 416 (1), 440 (2 *e*), 569, n. 1.
Genius, of Rome, 160 (1).
Gentes, see Tribes.
Gentilicia, 311.
— imperial, 645, n. 89.
Γεωργοί, in Cyrene, 309, 310.
Gerasa (Jerash), 94, 141, 157, 271, 376, 575, nn. 14, 15, 592, n. 2, 596, 619, n. 43, 662, n. 28, 665, n. 33, 706, n. 47.
— ruins of, 136 (1, 2), 137.
German fortresses, 641, n. 73.
— invasions, 25, 129, 444, 446.
— markets, 94.
— native population, 635, n. 48.
— provinces, 128, 609.
— settlers, 225.
— soldiers, 444, 508.
— tribes, 41, 128, 222, 223, 353, 354, 373, 442, 446, 511.
— villas, *see* Villas.
Germanicus, 77, 292, 381, 600, 670 (II (9)).
— sons of, 670 (II (7)).
Germano-Celtic tribes, 222.
Germans, 87, 98, 129, 193, 227, 353–5, 371, 422, 429, 444, 447, 451, 467, 473, 511, 532, 540, 577, n. 19, 603, n. 17, 637, n. 57.
— representation of, 108 (2).
Germany, 119, 229, 231, 237, 375, 594, 636, n. 53, 641, n. 75.
— agriculture, 223, 344, 634, n. 42, 635, n. 49.
— army, 86, 427, 717, n. 30.
— cities, 141, 142.
— commerce, 21, 66, 69, 94, 97, 98, 153, 166, 167, 173, 199, 222, 228, 413, 566, n. 30, 575, n. 13, 576, n. 17, 577, n. 19, 603–4, n. 17, 616, n. 35, 631, n. 26, 634, nn. 41, 42.
— conquest, 221.
— economic conditions, 223.
— industry, 173, 228, 617, n. 38, 618, n. 40, 634, n. 42.
— Lower (*Germania inferior*), 221, 222.
— religion, 226, 227.
— revolts, 86, 708, n. 3.
— robbers, 411, 738, n. 17.
— social structure, 128, 221, 225, 272, 400, 428, 724, n. 50, 725, n. 52.
— Upper (*Germania superior*), 221, 222, 229, 231, 232, 427, 637, n. 57.
— urbanization, 111, 112.
— wars, 52, 373, 420, 421, 445, 451.
Gerousia, 645, n. 89, 654, n. 4, 657, n. 7, 698, n. 11.

Gessius, 647, n. 90.
Geta, emperor, 415, 710, n. 9, 727, n. 57.
Getae, 644, n. 84.
Gezireh, 305.
Ghirza, 324, 723, n. 48.
Gifts, to associations, 660, n. 15.
— to cities, 148–51, 186, 201, 325, 336 (2), 407, 453, 473, 590, n. 32, 599–601, nn. 9, 13, 631, n. 31, 650, n. 97, 687, n. 97, 694–5, n. 4, 707, n. 48, 732, n. 22.
— — by emperors, 339, 373, 623, n. 49.
— to citizens by emperors, 372 (*c*).
— to emperors, 335, 407, 714, n. 17.
— of land by rulers, 99, 281, 292, 376.
— to soldiers, 41, 80, 394, 399, 402, 493, 711, n. 12; *see also* Donatives.
— to the state, 695–6, n. 6.
— *See also* Compulsory, Distributions *and* Foundations.
Gigarteni de vico Sidoniorum, 662, n. 27.
Gigthis, 141, 322, 330, 335, 595, 687, n. 97.
Giraffes, representation of, 304 (2).
Girindi, 656, n. 7.
Gladiators, 129, 256 (3) ,392, 743, n. 42.
— barrack for, 565, n. 23.
Glass, 69–72, 74, 97, 98, 154, 157, 158, 169, 172, 173, 175, 566, n. 30, 567, n. 35, 576, n. 17, 610, n. 26, 614, n. 32, 616, n. 37, 618, n. 40, 728, n. 60.
— factories, 610, n. 26, 621, n. 44.
— industry, 175, 621, n. 44, 634, n. 42, 736, n. 39.
Glevum, 229.
Γνώμων ἰδίου λόγου, 625, n. 53, 667, n. 40, 668, n. 42, 676, n. 51, 698, n. 7.
Goats, 30, 61, 270, 329 (1), 360 (3), 712, n. 15, 721, n. 45.
— representation of, 20 (2–4), 92 (4), 196 (1), 313 (2), 456 (2), 528 (1).
Gold, 15, 66, 67, 70, 72, 97, 299, 301, 307, 338, 414, 610, n. 26, 680, n. 61, 694, n. 1.
— mines, 240 (2), 247, 302, 643, n. 83, 694, n. 1.
Golden Age, 53, 364 (*c*), 522.
Goldsmiths (*aurifices*), 578.
— representation of, 96 (3).
Golgotha, 384.
Gordians, 433, 435, 438.
Gordianus, M. Antonius (Gordian I), emperor, 439, 455, 457, 733, n. 29.
— — (Gordian III), emperor, 440 (2 *c*), 442, 451, 459, 478, 488, 497, 498, 706, n. 47, 727, n. 59, 730, n. 4, 733, n. 26, 737, n. 12.
Gorgippia, shipowners, 660, n. 15.
Gortyn, 308, 680, n. 63.
Gospels, 270, 348, 384.
Goths, 442, 443, 445–7, 473, 474, 478, 498, 603, n. 17, 737, n. 8.

II. INDEX OF CLASSICAL AUTHORS

Figures in brackets after the page-number refer to items in the descriptions of the Plates.

III. INDEX OF INSCRIPTIONS

IV b OSTRACA, PARCHMENTS, &c.

OTHER TITLES IN THIS HARDBACK REPRINT PROGRAMME FROM SANDPIPER BOOKS LTD (LONDON) AND POWELLS BOOKS (CHICAGO)

ISBN 0–19–	Author	Title
8143567	ALFÖLDI A.	The Conversion of Constantine and Pagan Rome
6286409	ANDERSON George K.	The Literature of the Anglo-Saxons
8228813	BARTLETT & MacKAY	Medieval Frontier Societies
8111010	BETHURUM Dorothy	Homilies of Wulfstan
8142765	BOLLING G. M.	External Evidence for Interpolation in Homer
8114222	BROOKS Kenneth R.	Andreas and the Fates of the Apostles
8203543	BULL Marcus	Knightly Piety & Lay Response to the First Crusade
8216785	BUTLER Alfred J.	Arab Conquest of Egypt
8148348	CAMPBELL J.B.	The Emperor and the Roman Army 31 BC to 235
826643X	CHADWICK Henry	Priscillian of Avila
826447X	CHADWICK Henry	Boethius
8219393	COWDREY H.E.J.	The Age of Abbot Desiderius
8148992	DAVIES M.	Sophocles: Trachiniae
825301X	DOWNER L.	Leges Henrici Primi
8154372	FAULKNER R.O.	The Ancient Egyptian Pyramid Texts
8221541	FLANAGAN Marie Therese	Irish Society, Anglo-Norman Settlers, Angevin Kingship
8143109	FRAENKEL Edward	Horace
8201540	GOLDBERG P.J.P.	Women, Work and Life Cycle in a Medieval Economy
8140215	GOTTSCHALK H.B.	Heraclides of Pontus
8266162	HANSON R.P.C.	Saint Patrick
8224354	HARRISS G.L.	King, Parliament and Public Finance in Medieval England to 1369
8581114	HEATH Sir Thomas	Aristarchus of Samos
8140444	HOLLIS A.S.	Callimachus: Hecale
8212968	HOLLISTER C. Warren	Anglo-Saxon Military Institutions
8223129	HURNARD Naomi	The King's Pardon for Homicide – before AD 1307
8140401	HUTCHINSON G.O.	Hellenistic Poetry
9240094	JONES A.H.M	Cities of the Eastern Roman Provinces
8142560	JONES A.H.M.	The Greek City
8218354	JONES Michael	Ducal Brittany 1364–1399
8271484	KNOX & PELCZYNSKI	Hegel's Political Writings
8225253	LE PATOUREL John	The Norman Empire
8212720	LENNARD Reginald	Rural England 1086–1135
8212321	LEVISON W.	England and the Continent in the 8th century
8148224	LIEBESCHUETZ J.H.W.G.	Continuity and Change in Roman Religion
8141378	LOBEL Edgar & PAGE Sir Denys	Poetarum Lesbiorum Fragmenta
8241445	LUKASIEWICZ, Jan	Aristotle's Syllogistic
8152442	MAAS P. & TRYPANIS C.A .	Sancti Romani Melodi Cantica
8148178	MATTHEWS John	Western Aristocracies and Imperial Court AD 364–425
8223447	McFARLANE K.B.	Lancastrian Kings and Lollard Knights
8226578	McFARLANE K.B.	The Nobility of Later Medieval England
8148100	MEIGGS Russell	Roman Ostia
8148402	MEIGGS Russell	Trees and Timber in the Ancient Mediterranean World
8142641	MILLER J. Innes	The Spice Trade of the Roman Empire
8147813	MOORHEAD John	Theodoric in Italy
8264259	MOORMAN John	A History of the Franciscan Order
8116020	OWEN A.L.	The Famous Druids
8131445	PALMER, L.R.	The Interpretation of Mycenaean Greek Texts
8143427	PFEIFFER R.	History of Classical Scholarship (vol 1)
8111649	PHEIFER J.D.	Old English Glosses in the Epinal-Erfurt Glossary
8142277	PICKARD–CAMBRIDGE A.W.	Dithyramb Tragedy and Comedy
8269765	PLATER & WHITE	Grammar of the Vulgate
8213891	PLUMMER Charles	Lives of Irish Saints (2 vols)
820695X	POWICKE Michael	Military Obligation in Medieval England
8269684	POWICKE Sir Maurice	Stephen Langton
821460X	POWICKE Sir Maurice	The Christian Life in the Middle Ages
8225369	PRAWER Joshua	Crusader Institutions
8225571	PRAWER Joshua	The History of The Jews in the Latin Kingdom of Jerusalem
8143249	RABY F.J.E.	A History of Christian Latin Poetry
8143257	RABY F.J.E.	A History of Secular Latin Poetry in the Middle Ages (2 vols)
8214316	RASHDALL & POWICKE	The Universities of Europe in the Middle Ages (3 vols)
8154488	REYMOND E.A.E & BARNS J.W.B.	Four Martyrdoms from the Pierpont Morgan Coptic Codices
8148380	RICKMAN Geoffrey	The Corn Supply of Ancient Rome
8141076	ROSS Sir David	Aristotle: Metaphysics (2 vols)
8141092	ROSS Sir David	Aristotle: Physics
8142307	ROSTOVTZEFF M.	Social and Economic History of the Hellenistic World, 3 vols.
8142315	ROSTOVTZEFF M.	Social and Economic History of the Roman Empire, 2 vols.
8264178	RUNCIMAN Sir Steven	The Eastern Schism
814833X	SALMON J.B.	Wealthy Corinth

8171587	SALZMAN L.F.	Building in England Down to 1540
8218362	SAYERS Jane E.	Papal Judges Delegate in the Province of Canterbury 1198–1254
8221657	SCHEIN Sylvia	Fideles Crucis
8148135	SHERWIN WHITE A.N.	The Roman Citizenship
8113927	SISAM, Kenneth	Studies in the History of Old English Literature
8642040	SOUTER Alexander	A Glossary of Later Latin to 600 AD
8222254	SOUTHERN R.W.	Eadmer: Life of St. Anselm
8251408	SQUIBB G.	The High Court of Chivalry
8212011	STEVENSON & WHITELOCK	Asser's Life of King Alfred
8212011	SWEET Henry	A Second Anglo-Saxon Reader—Archaic and Dialectical
8148259	SYME Sir Ronald	History in Ovid
8143273	SYME Sir Ronald	Tacitus (2 vols)
8200951	THOMPSON Sally	Women Religious
8201745	WALKER Simon	The Lancastrian Affinity 1361–1399
8161115	WELLESZ Egon	A History of Byzantine Music and Hymnography
8140185	WEST M.L.	Greek Metre
8141696	WEST M.L.	Hesiod: Theogony
8148542	WEST M.L.	The Orphic Poems
8140053	WEST M.L.	Hesiod: Works & Days
8152663	WEST M.L.	Iambi et Elegi Graeci
822799X	WHITBY M. & M.	The History of Theophylact Simocatta
8206186	WILLIAMSON, E.W.	Letters of Osbert of Clare
8114877	WOOLF Rosemary	The English Religious Lyric in the Middle Ages
8119224	WRIGHT Joseph	Grammar of the Gothic Language